AF678452

Competition and State Aid

International Competition Law Series

VOLUME 63

Editor

In its series editor, Alastair Sutton, Kluwer is fortunate to engage and benefit from the experience and expertise of one of the world's outstanding authorities on European Union and international economic law.

Introduction

In their efforts to regulate competition in an increasingly complex business environment, competition authorities face a daunting task. The European Commission and Courts, as well as national courts and legislatures, policymakers, and regulators, are constantly proposing, enacting, reviewing, and enforcing new legal measures, often addressing novel situations. Every industry and service is affected.

Contents/Subjects

With many titles currently available and new ones appearing regularly, the series' coverage includes detailed analyses of relevant legislation and case law in major global trading jurisdictions, defences used in cases involving the digital network economy, state aid cases, enforcement methodologies and a great deal more.

Objective & Readership

The purpose of Kluwer's International Competition Law Series is to follow the ever-changing contours of this dynamic area of the law, keeping the practice in sharp focus so that practising lawyers (including in-house counsel) and academics can be assured of the most up-to-date guidance and sources, in the widest possible range of applications.

The titles published in this series are listed at the end of this volume.

Competition and State Aid

An Analysis of the EU Practice

Third Edition

Edited by

Alberto Santa Maria

Wolters Kluwer

Published by:
Kluwer Law International B.V.
PO Box 316
2400 AH Alphen aan den Rijn
The Netherlands
E-mail: lrs-sales@wolterskluwer.com
Website: www.wolterskluwer.com/en/solutions/kluwerlawinternational

Sold and distributed by:
Wolters Kluwer Legal & Regulatory U.S.
920 Links Avenue
Landisville, PA 17538
United States of America
E-mail: customer.service@wolterskluwer.com

ISBN 978-94-035-2768-0

e-Book: ISBN 978-94-035-2778-9
web-PDF: ISBN 978-94-035-2788-8

© 2025 Alberto Santa Maria

All rights are reserved, including those for text and data mining, AI training, and similar technologies. No part of this publication may be reproduced, stored in a retrieval system, or transmitted in any form or by any means, electronic, mechanical, photocopying, recording, or otherwise, without written permission from the publisher. Permission to use this content must be obtained from the copyright owner.

Lector et auditor nostros probat, Aule, libellos,
sed quidam exactos esse poeta negat.
non nimium curo: nam cenae fercula nostrae
malim convivis quam placuisse cocis.
(M. Valeri Martialis, *Epigrammaton*
Liber de spectaculis, IX, LXXXI)

Editor

Alberto Santa Maria (editor and author), full Professor of International Law and European Union Law at the State University of Milan, is widely regarded as one of the most successful and estimated attorneys in Italy. He has been the founding partner, before, of Santa Maria, Studio Legale Associato and then of Greenberg Traurig Santa Maria (www.gtlaw.com), the Italian law firm, based in Milan, part of this prominent US Law Firm, active worldwide. The Italian team offers one of the most sophisticated international practices covering corporate and M&A transactions, joint ventures, privatizations, restructuring and financing, along with Competition and State aid cases before EU and national courts. Prof. Santa Maria is a highly respected author of important books and publications, particularly on International and European Economic Law.

Contributors

Martino Basilisco is an associate at Greenberg Traurig Santa Maria ('GTSM'). His practice is mainly focused on antitrust law, European Union law, and international trade law. He regularly supports clients on a broad range of Italian corporate law issues as well as on EU law-related matters.

Andrea Biondi was appointed as an Advocate General at the Court of Justice on 7 October 2024. He was Professor of European Union Law and, from 2001 to 2024, Director of the Centre of European Law at King's College, London. He has a distinguished academic record with visiting positions at leading universities, including Bocconi University, Georgetown University, the College of Europe, LUISS University and the University of Rome La Sapienza.

Bertone Biscaretti di Ruffia, LLM, Law of Internet Technologies, Bocconi University, Milan, is a senior associate at GTSM. His practice mainly focuses on tech matters and EU privacy law compliance. He is also experienced in the litigation field, having advised Italian and foreign companies both in arbitration proceedings and in disputes before national courts.

Claudio Biscaretti di Ruffia, formerly partner at Santa Maria Law Firm, is now Of Counsel at GTSM. He is Professor of European Union law at the State University of Milan-Bicocca. He specializes in EU law, Competition and State aid, Common Agricultural Policy and International Trade Law. He regularly advises major clients before EU and Italian courts and has appeared in numerous international litigation cases. He is also guest speaker at seminars and has authored a number of publications in his areas of practice.

Guendalina Catti de Gasperi obtained an LLM from King's College London and a PhD from Bocconi University. She has also been Energy Research Coordinator at the Centre of European Law of King's College, London. She has been an associate at Santa Maria Law Firm after having practised EU law in Brussels and Rome. At present, she is Senior

Counsel at Legance, where she practices EU and Italian competition law, as well as the State aid and Foreign Subsidies Regulation regimes.

Martino Ebner MSc in EU Competition Law, King's College, London, specializes in EU Competition, State aid, and Corporate Law and has extensive experience in domestic and international litigation. Having been formed at Santa Maria Law Firm where he spent many years, he regularly advises and represents Italian and international clients before the European courts in direct actions, appeals and references for preliminary rulings.

Edoardo Gambaro, LLM, European Law, College of Europe, Bruges, has been a partner in the EU and Competition Department of Santa Maria Law Firm and currently is a shareholder of GTSM. He has a broad range of experience in EU law and competition matters before the European Commission and Italian and European courts. He has been working on preliminary rulings as well as on State aid cases since the preliminary phase. He has lectured and widely published in these areas.

Filippo Ghersini a lawyer by training, has received law degrees from the University of Milan and from Columbia University and has worked for the EU and Competition Law departments of major Italian and international firms. In 2019, he left private practice to join the Italian foreign service: he has been working in Rome, lastly within a European affairs desk, and from mid-2024 he is posted at the Permanent Representation of Italy at the European Union in Brussels.

Ester Latorre, PhD in EU and Competition Law at the University of Milan is an associate at GTSM. She focuses on antitrust and State aid law, but regularly deals also with corporate law and works with companies operating in the energy sector.

Francesco Mazzocchi MA in EU Competition Law, King's College, London, has been a senior associate in the EU and Competition Department of Santa Maria Law Firm and currently is Counsel at Advant NCTM, Milan. He has worked on several State aid cases before the European Commission and the EU courts and regularly advises on matters relating to cartel, mergers and abuse of dominant position. He has a broad experience in Sports law and has published widely in his areas of practice.

Pietro Missanelli, LLM, European Law, College of Europe, Bruges, is a Senior Associate of GTSM. He focuses his practice on EU and competition law, covering litigation on State aid, antitrust, and merger control before the European Commission and the Italian Competition Authority. He also deals with unfair competition practices and commercial contracts, particularly in matters involving French-speaking parties.

Stefania Nardelli, after specializing in international and EU trade law, has worked for twenty years in European institutions. Thanks to her experience in DG Trade and at the European Parliament's Committee on International Trade she has gathered extensive experience in EU trade law, in particular with respect to the EU's economic security and the trade relations between the EU and the USA. Author of some articles published in Law Journals, her academic activity as a lecturer at the university focuses on the interaction between the EU trade policy and other EU policies (like the Green Deal). In 2023, she joined Milan's office of the Representation of the European Commission in Italy.

Antonio Papi Rossi specializes in administrative law and EU law, advising public and private clients on extrajudicial and judicial matters with regard to public work contracts, procurement, urban planning and real estate transactions. His experience covers State aid cases before European and Italian courts. He was partner of Santa Maria Law Firm until 2014 continuing his cooperation of counsel. At present, he is partner at Fivers. He has authored various publications in his areas of practice.

Giuseppe Pizzonia Adjunct Professor of Tax Law at the University of Reggio Calabria, is a prominent lawyer with a wide range of experience as advisor in tax matters as well as in tax litigations and in State aid issues relating to tax matters. In the light of his specialization, he is and has been skillfully cooperating with Santa Maria on several cases of State aid before the Supreme Court and the European Courts. He is the author of many publications on tax matters in academic journals.

Luigi Santa Maria LLM Fordham University, New York, N.Y., has been a partner at Santa Maria and, at present, is shareholder of Greenberg Traurig and co-managing partner at GTSM. He specializes in Corporate Law, Capital Markets, Banking and Finance, M&A, Competition and Sports Law. He is the referral of the Italian Desk of Greenberg Traurig in New York. Before joining the Italian law firm, he has been practising for almost ten years in New York, at Shea and Gould, then at Kramer Levin, assisting clients in major M&A deals and cross-border transactions. He is the author of publications and lectures regularly on corporate law matters.

Alberto Tedoldi Professor of Civil Procedure law at the University of Verona, specializes in civil litigation and arbitration, both domestic and international. His work encompasses all aspects of civil litigation, tort liability, commercial contract and insurance law. He has been practising at Santa Maria law firm working on a number of competition and State aid cases, before the European and national courts. At present, he is Of Counsel at GTSM.

Summary of Contents

Table of Contents

Introductory Note

Alberto Santa Maria

I A GENERAL OVERVIEW OF THE CHANGING WORLD

Since 2015, that is, since the second edition of this book was published, several events happened in the world with a strong impact on the international economy and with significant consequences also on that of the European Union.

Think, first of all, of the COVID-19 pandemic, whose dramatic effects (albeit with intensity and severity varying from one country to another and from one geographical area to another) have affected the world population for a couple of years and more.

The Russian aggression on Ukraine created a heavy burden having originated the war against the latter, which is still raging on Europe's borders and is the cause of substantial socio-economic negative effects on the EU: just consider the growing number of Ukrainian immigrants in the EU Member States (there is talk of over one and a half million refugees in neighbouring Poland alone), the increase in energy prices and the decisive impact on inflation in the EU, with all the consequences, including monetary ones, that this fact entails as well as the heavy expenditure that the EU has assumed, diverting it from different productive uses, to support Ukraine, which has formally requested, in addition to entry into NATO, to join EU membership receiving its consent for an accelerated procedure of accession.[1]

Finally, think of the current dramatic conflict in the Middle East, at the gates of Europe, considering that, beyond the growing risk of enlargement to total war, cannot fail to aggravate the problems caused, especially in the southern States of the EU, by consistent mass migrations.[2]

1. *See* the *European Council conclusions on Ukraine, the membership applications of Ukraine, the Republic of Moldova and Georgia, Western Balkans and external relations*, 23 Jun. 2022, following which the first intergovernmental conference marking the start of accession negotiations took place on 25 Jun. 2024.
2. On the phenomenon of mass migration, which has grown dramatically in the last decade, *see*: A. Santa Maria, *European Economic Law*, 4th ed., Wolters Kluwer, 2019, 8 et seq.

We then have a complete picture of the weight assumed by the succession of these exceptional and extraordinary events, if we only add the negative consequences of the economic and financial crises that preceded them towards the end of the first decade of the new century.[3]

And so, in today's highly interconnected world, on the sidelines and also as a consequence of the highly critical situations just mentioned, conflicts have grown between the main States, players in the international economy and trade, with macroeconomic interventions, but also with initiatives aimed at encouraging the foreign operations of their national companies, not only in the new technological business.

As a result, the current limitations of the European Treaties *ratione materiae* have become more evident. In order to keep up with the times and with their fast pace, and to counter the growing fear that in the not too distant future, the European Union (and with it each of its Member States) being relegated to a secondary role on the stage of world politics and world economy, a tendency is forming on the part of an important section of European public opinion in favour of taking away from the Member States the unitary management of broad sectors of socio-economic life, with their renunciation of new areas of sovereignty. These range from new technologies and artificial intelligence to issues of ecological transition and sustainable development, to areas which are less innovative, but certainly of not less importance for giving a meaningful direction to the Union's evolution, such as those attending financial and fiscal policy as well as international politics, going so far as to entrust the Union with a real common defence[4] for the primary purpose of giving effective security to the European people, and also to avoid the current disorderly overlaps in the relevant spending by the individual Member States that harm its efficiency and they result in substantial waste.[5]

It should be noted that, in the face of the dramatic events just mentioned of the war in Ukraine and the pandemic, the EU has not remained inactive. First, it has supported NATO, (of which organization several Member States are members, together with, among others, the United States and the United Kingdom),[6] directly contributing with economic efforts to the defence of Ukraine, in the context of being an active participant in the exercise (deliberately partial and contained) of the right of collective

3. For a comprehensive analysis of the crises that have developed in the international economy and finance, first, in the United States and, then, in the European Union, let me refer once again to my work, just cited, *passim* and particularly pp. 307 et seq. and 317 et seq.
4. It is proposed to go far beyond the current level of common defence integration, beyond the *Common Foreign and Security Policy* ('*CFSP*'), dusting off an attempt, that of the European Defence Community (EDC), rejected by French Prime Minister Pierre Mendés-Frances in the distant summer of 1954.
5. *See* the M. Draghi Report '*The Future of European Competitiveness*', 9 Sep. 2004, Part A, '*A competitiveness strategy for Europe*', *passim*, and Ch. 5, 61, where the author indicates that a minimum annual additional amount of EUR 750 to 800 billion in the annual budget of the Union is needed, corresponding to 4.4%-4.7% of EU GDP in 2023, to meet the objectives laid out in the same report.
6. The NATO currently has thirty-two members, including twenty-three of the twenty-seven members of the European Union, following the accession of Finland and Sweden in 2023 and 2024, respectively.

self-defence against the Russian aggressor, guaranteed by Article 51 of the Charter of the United Nations.

As per the COVID-19 pandemic, the EU reacted unitedly by signing agreements with major pharmaceutical companies for the development of vaccine research and then for the purchase and distribution of the tested product on behalf and in the interest of the twenty-seven Member States.[7]

In addition, on the basis of the principle of solidarity, which plays a fundamental role in the European Treaties, it has issued, in the common interest and taking into account the extent of economic damage suffered by individual Member States, the *Next Generation EU* (*'Recovery Fund'*), and has created, under the watchful control of the Commission, the *National Recovery and Resilience Plans* (*N.R.R.P.*) reached in 2021 with each of the twenty-seven Member States, in order to give them a material support, partly in *grants* and partly in *loans* with facilitated content, relating to the special economic situation of each Member State, with the aim of facilitating its economic recovery and promoting its overcoming of the critical phase through dedicated and declared structural investments.[8]

In the last period of the new century, we have also witnessed the consolidation of the euro as a 'single currency' (for twenty of the twenty-seven Member States, parts of the euro area), even though some of its initial shortcomings remain, to the detriment of the internal market[9] and this favourable result has also been facilitated by the withdrawal of the United Kingdom (with its pound-sterling) from the Community's scene.[10]

7. *See* the *Special Report on EU Covid-19 Vaccine Procurement*, European Court of Auditors, Audit Chamber I – Sustainable use of natural resources (2022).
8. *See NextGenerationEU*, European Commission, at: https://commission.europa.eu/strategy-and-policy/eu-budget/eu-borrower-investor-relations/nextgenerationeu_en.
9. The euro now enjoys wide credibility and has an increasingly wide international circulation. However, some fundamental defects have not been overcome and create imbalances that negatively affect the actual unity of the internal market. I am referring, in particular, to the persistent inability of a European institution to set and maintain the exchange rate of the euro with the main currencies of the world and to the perverse effects that the *spread* has in microeconomics, which daily differentiates the cost of the same currency unit for companies resident in nineteen of the twenty States of the euro area compared to the German benchmark. In particular, the higher interest spread applied to its national State, in differentiated terms from State to State depending on asserted market perceptions, may result in financing being granted at a consequently higher interest rate as compared to a competitor located in a Member State with less or even no spread on interest rates. In other words, even within the same euro area, the fact that bank financing keeps being issued at a domestic level results in a company located in a certain Member State facing – regardless of having similar assets and financial situation – greater difficulties to be granted a loan as compared to a company of a different Member State in its own domestic market. On these critical issues *see*: A. Santa Maria, *L'odierno diritto internazionale dell'economia*, Giappichelli, 2021, 77 et seq.
10. *See* below the following para. 3 of this note.

II THE IMPACT OF THE CURRENT SCENARIO ON THE STATE AIDS (COMPETITION LAW) AND ON THE ECONOMIC POLICY BY THE COMMISSION

In the complex and constantly evolving scenario described above, it is not surprising that State aid policy is becoming increasingly important on the Union's chessboard, managed within the framework of competition policy and the practical application of the rules relating to it, and essentially delegated to the Commission's exclusive competence, including in relation to the national authorities.

Having passed the transitional period of validity of the *Temporary Frameworks*[11] containing mitigating measures on State aid with the aim of supporting the European economy in difficulty during the pandemic, and net of any facilitation aimed at achieving a sustainable recovery, which has also been exhausted or is in the process of being exhausted,[12] the Commission resumes its usual commitment to avoid (and prevent) behaviour by Member States, which, by using any form of aid that is not permitted, lead to distortions of competition in the internal market.

At the same time, in relation to the international aspects of a similar phenomenon, the attention of the European institutions (and, *first and foremost*, of the Commission) is directed to strike at the distorting effects of the 'subsidies' granted by a third country to the national industry in breach of the GATT/WTO rules and/or the European Regulation on dumping and subsidies derived from such rules.[13]

In this framework of unbalances, granting wide discretional powers to the Commission in regulating the matter of State aid will have to address the need to reconcile – as it would be appropriate – efficiency and functionality of markets with the necessary safeguard of national interests, as well as with the protection of the rights – without limitation to the fundamental ones – of the undertakings involved.

The growing role played by the Commission, and what in fact amounts to a total devolution of powers from the Council to the Commission, comes from afar and is based on changes to the system aimed at controlling State measures meeting the conditions set forth by Article 107 TFEU. The reference is to the Treaty of Lisbon, which has introduced paragraph 4 within the wording of Article 108 TFEU: this update has promoted to a *primary source of legislation* the power of the Commission to adopt block exemption regulations, meant to set out the categories of aid and the conditions under which Member States can be exempted from prior notification under Article 108(3) TFEU.[14]

This amendment – in fact, the only substantial change brought about by the Treaty in the field of State aid since the original wording of the 1957 Treaty – has gone all but unnoticed, most likely as the Council Regulation (EC) No. 994/98 already

11. *See*: COM 2020/C91/I/01), as extended and supplemented several times.
12. *See* below Ch. 1 and 2 of this volume.
13. For an overview of the internal Regulation on dumping and subsidies, *see*: A. Santa Maria, *European Economic Law*, 4th ed., 229 et seq.
14. Article 108(4) TFEU states that: '*The Commission may adopt regulations relating to the categories of State aid that the Council has, pursuant to Article 109, determined may be exempted from the procedure provided for by paragraph 3 of this Article.*'

similarly entitled the Commission to declare certain categories of State aid as *ex ante* compatible with competition on the internal market.[15] The point is that the inclusion of this power within the Treaty had a strong *political* connotation officially sanctioning the wide discretion enjoyed by the Commission in the field of State aid.

Let aside the temporary framework disposals which, as said, have already exhausted or are going to exhaust their effects, the normal attitude of the Commission vis-à-vis the subject matter is further confirmed by Regulation (EU) No. 2015/1588,[16] which has consolidated the types of aid for which the Commission is able to adopt exemption regulations (i.e., the case, for instance, of the sectors of sports and of broadband infrastructure).

It is my opinion that these changes in legislation – which, it should be noted, are invariably proposed by the Commission to the Council or directly issued by the Commission itself – reveal two underlying confirmations.

On one hand, the Commission has taken on a policymaker role, supplemental as compared to that played by Member States and significantly exceeding the preventive control system targeted at addressing distortions of competition that had originally been envisioned in the European Treaties. It should be, to this effect, sufficient to pay closer attention to the substantially 'legislative' role played by the various Communications which the Commission has from time to time enacted on State aid to banks (lastly, the 2013 Banking Communication),[17] as well as the policies pursued with respect to energy and to renewable sources.[18]

However, the expansion of the derogations mandated by Article 107(3) TFEU as well as the 'green light' given by the Commission to State intervention decided in the stormy weather of the various crises have – in my opinion – put into question the ground assumption of the State aid control system – i.e., the general ban on the granting State aid, in fact setting it apart from assessments pertaining to competition law.

I believe that the main weakness of the system is, upstream, in the main assumptions under which the provisions of Article 107(1) TFEU are applied and, in particular, in the belief that State intervention *always* needs to be evaluated as though the State were a private investor – while we know that in many cases the State can be a 'patient' investor who acts – differently from a private undertaking – for reasons other

15. Including, in particular:
    (a) aid in favour of (i) SMEs; (ii) research and development; (iii) environmental protection; and (iv) employment and training;
    (b) regional aid;
    (c) the so-called *de minimis* aid (i.e., Aid *infra* a certain order of magnitude), modified by time to time, moreover in relation with the emergency situations occurred in the last decade).
16. Council Regulation (EU) 2015/1588 of 13 Jul. 2015 on the application of Arts 107 and 108 of the Treaty on the Functioning of the European Union to certain categories of horizontal State aid (codification), OJ L 248, 24/09/2015, 1-8.
17. Communication from the Commission on the application, from 1 Aug. 2013, of State aid rules to support measures in favour of banks in the context of the financial crisis, OJ C 216, 30.7.2013, 1-15. *See infra*, Ch. 13.
18. *See infra*, Ch. 15.

than immediate financial gain.[19] The current economic downturn experienced by the Union further highlights how such an assumption is at present inadequate to serve as the keystone of State aid regulation.

As to the rights of defence of undertakings involved in State aid proceedings, there is an urgent need for a balanced and fair management of the various procedural phases – a need in respect to which Regulation (EU) No. 1589/2015 (the 'Procedural Regulation')[20] seems to move backwards. To the same effect, there is a growing call for greater compliance with those fundamental principles of European law as legitimate expectation, right and equal treatment, and proportionality (with respect to recovery decisions), which are quintessential to a full realization of the freedom to conduct a business (Article 16 of the Charter of Fundamental Rights of the European Union).

III THE EU'S OUTLOOK AFTER BREXIT

Another important event that has affected the EU in the last decade cannot be overlooked, given its impact also on the subject matter of this book. Following the surprising result of the referendum in the United Kingdom on 23 June 2016 (which favoured the 'Leave' vote), the British government exercised the right of each Member State to withdraw from the European Union, which is expressly provided for in the Lisbon Treaty, in Article 50.1 TEU, an article which, in substance, reproduces Article I-60 of the Constitutional Treaty of the Union (which has never entered into force).

The agreement between the EU and the outgoing State, painstakingly reached on 30 December 2020 with the *Trade and Cooperation Agreement* ('TCA'), on the eve of the extended deadline, has entered into force on 1 January 2021 in order to govern Brexit in the transitional relationship and in the future.[21]

After the British reluctance to accept the versions that provided for a high degree of commercial cooperation between the EU and the UK and, in particular, the substantial retention for the UK of European competition rules, including those on State Aids, under the ultimate supervision of the EU Court of Justice,[22] the will of the UK, after some succession of British governments, to make a clean break out with the EU prevailed, with the declared aim of allowing the UK, mindful of its imperial past, to regain full freedom of action at international level.[23]

The result was a 'soft' discipline that essentially left open the weak point created by the hybrid position of Northern Ireland, which remains part of the single market (so

19. On the private investor principle *see* further, Ch. 1.
20. Council Regulation (EU) No. 2015/1589 of 13 Jul. 2015 laying down detailed rules for the application of Art. 108 of the Treaty on the Functioning of the European Union, OJ 2015 L 248/9. *See infra*, Ch. 3.
21. *See* P. Missanelli, M. Basilisco, *L'accordo commerciale tra UE e Regno Unito nel sistema WTO. Gli eventuali conflitti in tema di enforcement*, in *Diritto del Commercio Internazionale*, 737 et seq. (2021).
22. *See* European Commission, Draft Withdrawal Agreement on the Withdrawal of the United Kingdom of Great Britain and Northern Ireland from the European Union and the European Atomic Energy Community, Brussels, 28 Feb. 2018.
23. *See* E. Gambaro, M. Pizzonia, *Il controllo delle sovvenzioni/aiuti nei rapporti fra il Regno Unito e l'Unione Europea*, in *Diritto del Commercio Internazionale*, 269 et seq. (2021).

as not to create customs barriers with the Republic of Ireland), but at the same time remains an integral part of the UK, with the risk of reopening the wound of the civil war closed by the so-called Good Friday Agreement of 10 April 1998: it remains in force, but the new situations give rise to questions, still to be answered, particularly as regards its practical implications on the free movement of goods between the two islands and between them and the EU.

This means that, outside the EU's liberalization rules, the UK will continue to be subject to the rules of the WTO/GATT, the international organization to which, after Brexit, the UK automatically rejoined as a direct member.

On the side of the General Agreement, in relations concerning the trade in goods and services between the EU and the UK, the TCA gives disappointing results on the whole, both for its limited extension *ratione materiae* and for the tenuous *enforcement* measures it contains.

TCA is part of that group of treaties, bilateral or multilateral, concluded under Article XXIV of the GATT between Member States of the WTO, provided that customs unions and free trade areas of autonomous formation do not entail the imposition of tariffs or other restrictions on trade with other Member States of such an international organization.[24]

It is clear that the international discipline, based on treaties, whether multilateral or bilateral, exhausts its value in relations between States in respect of which the private enterprise concerned can only have the role of *amicus curiae*.

The growing number of preferential trade agreements between WTO Member States raises the issue of possible conflicts of application between the dispute settlement mechanisms present in each of them, and the general *Dispute Settlement Understanding* (DSU) of the GATT/WTO.[25] The concrete resolution of cases of conflict is entrusted to the so-called *fork-in-the-road* clauses in the various agreements, under which the State seeking satisfaction in respect of an alleged violation of the general agreement or of a specific trade agreement may choose between applying to the DSU or to the bodies provided for that purpose in the applicable sectoral agreement; however, once that route has been chosen, it is no longer possible to resort to the alternative solution unless the body before which the case is brought decides not to rule on the merits for lack of jurisdiction or for procedural reasons.[26]

24. The difficulties encountered in the Doha *Round* with regard to the process of adapting the General Agreement to current realities have led the contracting states to look for apparently less ambitious solutions, entrusting the regulation of sectors of international trade to agreements with more specific contents, whether bilateral or regional, the so-called free trade or partnership agreements. And so, compared to a few dozen treaties of this type concluded before 1994, at the end of 2020 the total number of international sectoral agreements notified to the WTO was 499, of which 305 were in force (*see* https://rtais.wto.org/UI/PublicMaintainRTAHome.aspx).
25. *See*: A. Santa Maria, *L'odierno diritto internazionale*, 64 et seq.
26. *See* Art. 12, *Annex Inst: Rules of Procedure of the Partnership Council and Committees*, of the TCA.

IV PRELIMINARY REMARKS ON THE THIRD EDITION

In presenting the third edition of the collective work originated on the far 2005 by the Santa Maria, Studio Legale Associato ('the Santa Marias'),[27] devoted to one of the principal objects of our shared daily work as lawyers and jurists, let me submit, as the team leader, a few preliminary observations somehow beyond the scope of the specific subject matter of this book. The idea to write down and publish our experiences in so stimulating and topical a field as 'State aids' originated from the fact that historically the Santa Marias have been called upon to defend many of the major cases purported by the Commission to be State aid that have been filed against Italy since the last decade of the nineteens and in the following ones. We have been assigned some cases by the Italian government itself, but our professional services have also been sought by private parties, whether through other law firms or individual lawyers on behalf of recipients of alleged State aid, both undertakings and trade or bank national associations, and sometime in the service of individual undertakings or trade associations claiming to have been harmed by domestic measures assumed to fall within the notion of State aid.

In the European internal market, which has long been a 'space without boundaries' where the four fundamental freedoms are (or ought to be) implemented in full, State intervention in the economy – though being legitimate in itself pursuant to Article 345 TFEU in relation to property ownership – turns especially dangerous for the harmonious functioning of such internal market when it is intended essentially to favour certain, usually domestic, undertakings or the production of certain goods or in the provision of certain services.

As the subject stands astride macro and microeconomics, it involves some of the issues that are crucial to the full accomplishment of the European Union's objectives.

As I will discuss further in the next sections of this introducing note, and as it will emerge clearly from other arguments set out in the chapters of this volume, the persisting all-embracing assessment of the unbecoming unbalance by the EU's Institutions (the Commission and the European courts alike) – deriving from a choice originally made in the Treaty of Rome (and remained unchanged despite several modifications over the years), whereby 'aid' granted by public bodies ('State aid', for simplification) is expressly linked to competition law – no longer appears suited to encompass the entire phenomenon.[28]

Indeed, as per 'aid schemes', let me anticipate that the gradual injection of such fundamental principles as legal certainty, legitimate expectations and proportionality into EU legal order is calling into question the widely discretionary approach the Commission takes to the field of State aid, over which, as said, it has exclusive

27. Now, Greenberg Traurig Santa Maria. *See* https://www.gtlaw.com/en/general/milan/santa-maria-studio-legale-associato-is-now-greenberg-traurig-santa-maria.
28. For the enlarged notion of 'public bodies' under the Commission's interpretation *see* Ch. 1 *infra*.

jurisdiction save for a quite specific instance.[29] Such exceptional instance is stigmatized as 'unlawful' aid, which, in the Union language, broadly means any 'public' aid measure - i.e., one granted by the State or by any other authority or body, whether central or local, or through *State resources* - which has not been notified and not yet made the object of a Commission decision, and over which limited to that transitional period, national courts have concurrent competence with the Commission's pursuant to the last sentence of Article 108(1) TFEU, in the sense explained below.[30]

In addition, the need to ensure compliance with the right of establishment and the principle of free movement of services - along with the necessary, now firmly established, requirement of the free movement of capital - throughout the internal market has resulted in the European courts being vested, upon appropriate reference by the Commission, with direct jurisdiction over cases heretofore summarily categorized as State aid.

Against such a complex background, our law firm's vast expertise in the field has not occurred by chance. Rather, it is the result of an accurate preparatory work on general issues of EU law, enriched by our day-to-day analytical work and ongoing professional commitment to advisory activities, even before litigation services, in the area of competition at large - which has made our firm a point of reference when State aid cases are to be dealt with. Hence, the considered choice to use our specialist expertise to popularize the results of our efforts in handling a number of different situations from many different points of view, on a case-by-case basis and depending on each client's specific position. Despite our being so deeply involved, we will not hesitate to criticize the workings of one or another of the devices applied within the complex system of State aid rules, in an attempt to help correct and improve it in the European Union's best interests.

This book provides a concrete legal analysis of individual elements of the State aid phenomenon and of the impact it has on free competition moreover from the standpoint of the involved undertakings. It is mainly addressed to those jurists and economists who concern themselves with State-aid issues for whatever reasons.

Thus, we have taken an entirely *practical* approach to the discussion offered here, combining the necessary knowledge of the basics of European Union law, which are closely related to the subject matter of this book, with the expertise we have built in our everyday practice, in an attempt to provide the reader with an intentionally simplified view - yet one as close to reality as possible - of the many specific profiles considered in our analysis.

As an obvious consequence of our direct involvement in several proceedings on the subject matters, we have been able, in dealing with the issues presented in the different chapters of this book, to rely not only on records still unpublished but also on documents that are by no means freely accessible, such as pleadings and replies lodged by each of the parties to, and the persons intervening in, any one case, the scripts of at

29. EU Courts have endorsed the wide discretionary power applied by the Commission in State aid's rules and regulations. *See* Ch. 6, *infra*.
30. *See* Ch. 7, *infra*.

least our own oral speeches at public hearings, and orders and notices from the Registries of the General Court and/or of the Court of Justice.

In revising the second edition of this book, we have necessarily taken into account the material changes that occurred in the economic world over the last decade, with particular reference to their impact in the EU, as recalled in the previous paragraphs.

It has therefore been decided to reorganize the whole work for the convenience of the reader, by making room for new contributions on topics that have recently come to the fore and that are treated in Chapters 9, 10 and 11, so concluding a first virtual general part of this volume, as well as by revising the subdivision of more specific topics placed in Chapter 12 *et seq*.

The resulting collective book is essentially due to substantial teamwork, gradually carried out by a group of lawyers who have grown up around me over more than three decades,[31] with the baton passed on to my brilliant pupil and partner Edoardo Gambaro, who has already defended so many cases before the Commission and also the European Courts. The volume is enriched by the contribution of the eminent jurist, Andrea Biondi, who has just been called to the prestigious position of Advocate General of the CJEU from his privileged London observatory, the Centre for European Studies at King's College. He is responsible for Chapter 11 on competition issues in the UK post-Brexit. I thank him warmly for the enlightening content and, above all, for his shared friendship.

Whether our purpose of upgrading the subject matter has successfully been accomplished, I leave my colleagues and friends – '*my table companions*', in the poet Martial's words[32] – to judge after they will have, as I hope, had at least a cursory glance at the result of our efforts.

V THE COMMISSION'S EXTENSIVE APPLICATION OF ARTICLE 107 TFEU, PARTICULARLY IN RELATION TO STATE AIDS SCHEMES: A CRITICISM

The European Commission's Directorate General for Competition has been applying the rules on State aid quite widely.

This basic approach is far removed from a somewhat subdued beginning, which dates back, if I am not mistaken, to the Commission's decision of 1994 to suspend aid granted in the *Ford Tractor Belgium* case.[33] Only thirteen 'negative' decisions then followed until 1980, while as many such decisions were taken in 1981 alone. But even more noteworthy has been the Commission's approach also to the most recent cases

31. By the way, the long partnership with Giuseppe Pizzonia was already well established in 1992, i.e. at the time of our common defence of *Ente Nazionale Risi*, before the ECJ, in the joined cases C-332/92, C- 333/92 and C-335/92, *Enrico Italia S.r.l., Viazzo S.r.l., F&P S.p.A.* v. *Ente Nazionale Risi*, concluded by the Court, called in preliminary ruling, with the judgment of March 3, 1994 (ECLI: EU:C:1994.79).
32. M. Valeri Martialis, *Epigrammaton (Liber de spectaculis)*, IX, 81, whose sentence is reported in full on the page following the title page of this volume.
33. *See Commission* Decision 64/651/EEC of 28 Oct. 1964.

(safe the parenthesis of the exemption due to the emergency situation, already closed or very close to termination,[34] in which it has sought to apply State aid legislation quite beyond the boundaries set by Article 107(1) TFEU.

While I am aware of going against the mainstream opinion, let me criticize the said trend and moreover call into question the very rationale underlying the current use by the Commission of the rules applicable to State aid, at least in respect of 'aid schemes', i.e., the ones granted by a domestic law. Indeed, these are usually legislative, especially tax-related, measures designed by a Member State to support not individual positions – which would entail 'individual' aid – but to grant benefits to *specific* categories of undertakings or to favour certain operations by only certain categories of undertakings.

For *general acts*, i.e., measures addressed to all the recipients involved in the same situation, do not fall, contrary to a widespread misunderstanding, within the category of State aid. They are, indeed, quite lawful in themselves or, in the words of the Treaty, 'compatible' with the internal market, precisely because of their general quality and in their being hardly apt to distort competition.

In principle, the EU rules applicable to whether *individual aid* or *aid schemes* provide a quite complex framework in many respects. First, because they apply to national measures that must necessarily fulfil a number of criteria, all of them essential: (i) the measure must have been issued by a public authority; (ii) it must have an impact on that public authority's budget; (iii) it must be *selective*; (iv) it must be capable to distort competition; and last but not least, (vi) it must affect trade between Member States.

Moreover, because State aid essentially falls within the scope of the EU rules on competition, its determination entails a *three-sided, inseparable relationship* between: (i) the *State* granting the aid; (ii) the *Commission*, which must ensure compliance with the applicable rules in order to assure fair competition in the relevant market; and (iii) the *undertakings*, whether or not they are in receipt of State aid.

Significantly, where the aid recipient is not an 'undertaking', the provisions of Articles 107 et seq. TFEU shall not apply,[35] as the Commission stated in its decision on the Italian banking foundations in relation to the so-called Ciampi Act.[36]

For the Commission's scrutiny to make sense in any one specific case, it must relate to the 'relevant market', as this notion is used in competition law in respect of both geographic and product markets.

Lastly, the EU rules applicable to State aid have brought about a complex system also because, in case a negative decision is taken on an aid being found to be

34. *See* Ch. 1 and 2.
35. *See* Commission Decision 2003/146/EC of 22 Aug. 2002 on the tax measures for banking foundations implemented by Italy, OJ 2003 L55/56.
36. The decision, based upon Arts 87 et seq. EU, then applicable (now Arts 107 et seq. TFEU), was confirmed in part by the judgment of the European Court of Justice (reference for a preliminary ruling from the Italian Supreme Court) in Case C-222/04 *Ministero dell'Economia e delle Finanze v. Cassa di Risparmio di Firenze SpA, Fondazione Cassa di Risparmio di San Miniato, Cassa di Risparmio di San Miniato SpA*, 10.1.2006, ECLI:EU:C:2006:8. On this issue, *see* furtherly Ch. 1 *infra*.

incompatible with the internal market, since Article 16 of Regulation No. 1589/2015 in general, the Commission will order that the Member State concerned must forthwith recover any sum already awarded to the beneficiary.

In theory, the *recovery obligation* is depicted not to be and should not be punitive in nature. Its sole function is to restore *ex tunc* the competitive situation that existed at the time the aid was granted and that the alleged State aid distorted.[37]

In practice, however, the *recovery order* issued in the Commission decision - which normally arrives with a consistent delay (of even several years) in respect of when the unlawful advantage has been granted by a State - can amount to a heavy burden and one that usually falls upon the aid recipient quite unexpectedly, notwithstanding an absolute presumption of the contrary pushed by the Commission and entered as a dogma in the EU's case law.

Further, recovery is not just a theoretical or merely potential occurrence, as the Commission's settled practice in taking negative decisions has consistently been to include a recovery injunction, both before and after Regulation No. 659/99 as lastly annulled and substituted by Regulation No. 1589/2015, and a negative decision without a recovery injunction - assessments left to the full discretion of the Commission - has only been an exception to the rule.[38]

Note, however, that originally this was not the case. Under primary EC law (specifically Articles 92 et seq., of the Treaty of 1957 establishing the European Economic Community), there was not (nor is there today, as those rules have been mainly left unchanged) any provision concerning the duty to recover aid unlawfully granted.

Only in 1973, in *Kohlengesetz (Commission v. Federal Republic of Germany)*,[39] did the ECJ establish the Commission's power, in order for a negative decision '*to be of practical effect*', to '*require repayment of aid granted in breach of the Treaty*' in addition to requiring the Member State concerned to abolish or modify any aid found to be incompatible with the common market.[40]

The Commission's power to order recovery has been confirmed, implicitly or explicitly, by several ECJ decisions.[41] In particular, in the *Alcan*[42] and *Siemens*[43] cases, respectively decided by the ECJ and the Court of First Instance (now General Court), a recovery injunction was held to be the necessary consequence of the Commission's finding that the aid was unlawful (i.e., that the relevant measure was not previously

37. This is a consolidated and crystal-clear principle. On the recovery obligation being necessarily limited to the restoration of the previous situation *see, inter alia,* the judgments in cases C-350/93, *Commission v. Italy,* 4.4.1995, ECLI:EU:C:1995:96, at para. 22, and C-75/97, *Belgium v. Commission,* 17.6.1999, ECLI:EU:C:1999:311, at paras 64-65.
38. In this sense *see* Commission Decision of 19 Dec. 2012, Case SA 20829.
39. *See* Case C-70/72, *Commission v. Germany,* 12.7.1973, ECLI:EU:C:1973:87.
40. *Ibid.*, para. 13.
41. *See, among others,* Case C-52/84, *Commission v. Belgium,* 15.1.1986, ECLI:EU:C:1986:3, and Case C-310/85, *Deufil GmbH & Co. KG v. Commission,* 24.2.1987, ECLI:EU:C:1987:96.
42. Case C-24/95, *Land Rheinland-Pfalz v. Alcan Deutschland GmbH,* 20.3.1997, ECLI:EU:C:1997:163.
43. *See* Case T-459/93, *Siemens SA v. Commission,* 8.6.1995, ECLI:EU:T:1995:100.

notified by the Member State's government and was, thus, taken without the Commission's prior authorization). The ECJ's decision of 21 March 1990 in the *Tubemeuse* case (*Belgium v. Commission*)[44] held likewise. Such case law ultimately found its way, as noted above, into the duty to recover expressly provided for in Regulation No. 659/1999 and reinstated in the Procedural Regulation.[45] In this context, therefore, it is understandable that undertakings (the ultimate addressees of the duty to recover aid) have been recognized a major role to play in the administrative proceedings before the Commission, in which they have full standing under the Procedural Regulation and also in judicially challenge the Commission's decision.

First, it is necessary to clear the field of a widespread misunderstanding. State aid is basically a technical subject and has nothing to do with a desire to ensure fairness. Suffice it to say that the Commission's practice in determining whether an aid distorts competition does not – as confirmed by consistent EU case law precedents – take into account either the potential disadvantages likely to arise from different structural rules among Member States or the differences still to be found, even to a great extent, among different tax systems generally applicable to undertakings in different Member States.[46] As general measures are never State aid, it is solely up to each Member State to modify the less favourable provisions under domestic law, provided that the other Treaty rules are complied with.

It should be further stressed that there is not, nor could likely there be, a general duty by the Commission to open a State aid case in similar and even contemporaneous situations. As a matter of fact, there is a lack of a system able to ensure that the Commission will intervene in any analogous case of individual aid or aid scheme any one Member State might introduce. This also affects the rights of defence of undertakings, substantially diminishing their amplitude. The Commission does not, in principle, take into any consideration the fact that similar situations – or at least situations putting competing undertakings at a distinct advantage – have not been the object of investigation proceedings.

European courts should pay the utmost attention to ensuring that the general principles of European law – namely, those of legal certainty, legitimate expectation and fair and equal treatment – be respected in regard to undertakings involved in State aid proceedings, so as to counterbalance the breadth of the discretionality enjoyed by the Commission when exercising its political powers – as outlined above.[47]

44. Case C-142/87, *Belgium v. Commission ('Tubemeuse')*, 21.3.1990, ECLI:EU:C:1990:125, para. 66.
45. Being part of a decision, binding *per se* its addressees *ex* Art. 288 TFEU, the recovery order – once duly implemented by the State – has a deterrent effect towards the aid recipient undertakings, depriving them of any previous scrutiny by a court on the legitimacy of the decision itself.
46. I wonder if – to date – this approach whereby the Commission does not generally interfere in the domestic legal orders of the Member States who have adopted the euro could be lawfully applied with respect to the microeconomic effects of monetary policy choices for the euro zone that primary EU legislation assigns to the exclusive competence of EU institutions. *See also* J. Lever, '*EU State Aid Law – Not a Pretty Sight*', in EStAL 2013, 1, 6 et seq.
47. I recall that, during the proceedings started by the Commission against Italy for the so-called *legge spalma debiti* applicable to football clubs (*see further* Ch. 16), it was expressly pointed out as defensive arguments that German football club Borussia Dortmund had been benefiting for

The demarcation between *lawful* aid, previously notified, and *unlawful* aid, not previously notified to the Commission, by a State or a State institution, is a distinction that basically would really have only procedural consequences. And the risk of a recovery injunction, which I briefly illustrated above, simply adds to the problem.

In a Communication issued in 1983, the Commission, faced with the spreading of unlawful aid measures, 'informed' the undertakings' potential beneficiaries of unlawful aid of the risks possibly arising from the fact that '*[A]ny recipient of an aid granted illegally, i.e. without the Commission having reached a final decision as to admissibility, may have to refund the aid.*'

In order to incentivize greater compliance with aid rules, the Commission has progressively introduced greater transparency requirements relating to aid measures: first, following the revision of the GBER in 2015 and later, with State aid modernization and subsequent legislative revisions, Member States are required to keep public registers of the beneficiaries and the measures granted.[48]

In fact, a realistic assumption is that Commission communications of this type are only directed to a select circle of experts and are quite unlikely to reach the undertakings, especially small or medium-sized enterprises – even more so today, with twenty-seven Member States in the European Union.

In addition, precisely because of the complex technical nature of the notion of 'aid' and of the Commission's wide discretionary powers (that include deciding whether to initiate a procedure, especially in cases of aid schemes or not notified legislative measures, and when to initiate a procedure – there are cases of proceedings commenced years after the contested fact), how could a recipient undertaking be expected not to apply the more favourable domestic law merely out of the fear that the relevant measure could be qualified in the future as 'incompatible aid'?

Yet, such absolute presumption is a *Leitmotiv*, among many in its favour, that the Commission has managed to have the EU courts recognize – with aberrant consequences in terms of substantive justice – not only against Member States but also and especially against the undertakings forced to repay the aid; then again, this can be the case when a considerable time has elapsed from the granting of the aid measures, thereby preventing recovery from having any actual impact on competition.

---

years, in the complete indifference of national supervisory Authorities and of the EC Commission, from tax and contribution privileges coming from an 'extensive' interpretation of a 1930 Statute, whose aim had been to protect 'group work during night' ... of labourers (maybe even of Ruhr coal miners!). I also recall the 'real-estate speculation' made by Spanish football team Real Madrid, which benefited from a convenient modification of land's destination after the low-price purchase of a property from Madrid's *Comunidad Autonoma* (a Spanish region). The former EU Competition Commissioner Mario Monti stated that he might not start a proceeding on such a case for lack of financial burden on the State (the *Comunidad Autonoma*, in that case). *See, in particular*, the two written questions addressed by Pere Esteve, respectively, on 2 Sep. 2002 (OJ 2003 C137/86), and on 22 Oct. 2002 (OJ C161/57), and the answers given by Commissioner Monti, respectively, on 26 Sep. 2002 (OJ C137/87) and on 29 Nov. 2002 (OJ C161/58).

48. *See* K. Lillerud, *The National Transparency Registers in Action*, 18 *European State Aid Law Quarterly*, 3, 239-248 (2019) https://doi.org/10.21552/estal/2019/3/4. For an analysis of the Italian case law *see* M.G. Reale, *The National State Aid Register – Italy's Experience*, 23 *European State Aid Law Quarterly*, 1, 15-21 (2024) https://doi.org/10.21552/estal/2024/1/4.

A first reflection is the confirmation that the State aid regulation itself, as it has evolved over time, depending on case law and secondary regulations, is substantially intended, whether or not prior notification has been given, to deal with two very different cases - individual aid as opposed to aid schemes - and that only in the former case does the Commission apply, or considers itself to be under a duty to apply, the rules of competition law.

In general, the Commission's preferred approach has been and still is to downplay the controversy about State aid granted by a domestic law as an issue of bilateral relationships between the Commission itself and the State granting purported aid schemes. This does, however, effectively deprive undertakings of any substantial jurisdictional protection of their interests.[49]

Also, it must be recalled the Commission's attempt - somehow supported by EU courts' decisions supposedly aiming to simplify State aid investigations- to review purported aid *without making any reference to a specific geographic and/or product market*.[50]

Consequently, a scrutiny which should be concrete in nature becomes only abstract and so remains under the full discretion of the Commission.

Lacking such a logical process, however, there could be no reliable benchmark against which to assess compliance with fair competition standards. As said, it also increases the discretionary power of the Commission in the subject matter.

In addition, neither the Commission's decision nor the EU Courts' judgment following the appeal against such a decision do in fact evaluate, in any specific case, whether the contested measure has a *real adverse impact on trade between Member States*. For the formal, unspecific reference the relevant decision makes to a prejudice to trade, oftentimes by plain repetitions of either primary norms or of articles of EC Regulation No. 1589/2015 is considered sufficient, without any reference being made to the actual elements that would demonstrate its real existence in the case at issue.

This is, however, in blatant contrast with basic principles of legal certainty and legitimate expectation. It is hardly justifiable to compromise on these principles on account of political choices taken by the Commission. Thus, the EU Courts appear to be satisfied that two of the essential criteria to establish a case of 'aid' are met, by relying rather on the Commission's use of standard phrases - than on a serious case-by-case preliminary investigation into the economics of the case, with a view to identifying

49. *See infra*, Ch. 6.
50. As a matter of fact, referring to the State aid matter, the Commission does apply a very different, formal, notion of 'relevant market' from the one defined and applied in all other areas of competition law. As expressly, stated in the *Communication from the Commission, Commission Notice on the definition of the relevant market for the purpose of Union Competition law* (C/2024/1645, n. 4: 'in general, market definition plays *less of a role* in the Commission's enforcement practice under Article 106 and 107 TFEU. In those cases, *the assessment focusses on the industry/sector concerned rather than identification of competitive constraints faced by the undertakings*. Nevertheless, when considerations of market power and accordingly of the relevant market are raised in particular cases pursued under Article 106 or Article 107 TFEU, the approach outlined in this Notice may be relevant for the assessment. In view of the more limited application of market definition in these two types of assessments, this Notice will not discuss their specific aspects further' [*Emphasis is mine*].

actual anti-competitive elements in the contested State measure or its real adverse impact on trade between Member States.[51]

The Commission's statement as to the substantive difference presumably existing in terms of competition between, on the one side, the rules about agreements, concerted practices, abuse of dominant position and merger control, and, on the other side, the rules governing State aid, merely because the State or any public bodies appear to play a crucial role only where State aid is at issue, seems to me to be inadequate in the latter case to exclude the logic process typical of any issue about competition from the process by which aid is assessed.

Quite beyond any considerations as to the homogeneity of such two sets of rules in the way each is structured – the general rule of prohibition (with exceptions) under Article 107 TFEU being so close, even at first sight, to the provisions of Article 101 – the key consideration is that the essential criteria to be met for a measure to be categorized as aid under Article 107 are the *effect on trade between Member States* and, most notably, the aptitude of that measure to *distort or threaten to distort competition* which are precisely the same criteria as are laid down in Article 101.

How could the Commission ever establish whether these criteria are met in any one specific case without applying the necessary benchmarks of the relevant market, albeit through a 'mitigated' assessment?

What can be said of the Commission's statement according to which a concrete analysis of the antitrust profiles of a non-notified legislative act would give an unfair advantage to illegal aid over a notified measure?

It is sufficient to mention the prospective test the Commission has to apply in scrutinizing a merger, both in case the merger has been carried through and in case it has not been completed.

One can hardly understand why the test to be applied when examining an instance of State aid, whether notified or not, must be substantially different. In either case, the assessment by the Commission must, in principle, apply the same hypothetical test on the effects the legislative act or the merger, as the case may be, might have on the relevant market.

Rather, the contrary is true. In the Commission's view, an unfair advantage is to be found in an aid not notified and already put into effect, i.e., one in relation to which, in addition to applying the standard hypothetical test, it is easier to point out anti-competitive elements already evident to the detriment of competitors.

51. Case law is not univocal on this point. On the subject, *see infra*, Ch. 6. In that chapter it is commented the ECJ decision on the Italian *Legge Ciampi*, in Case C-148/04, *Unicredito and others v. Agenzia delle Entrate* 15.12.2005, ECLI:EU:C:2005:774. I hereby point out also the irregularities of that case where the Court, in a proceeding *ex* Art. 234 EC (now Art. 267 TFEU), adhering to a preliminary objection, made by the intervened Commission, *in limine*, during the hearing of 3 Feb. 2005, and without even mentioning this request or its subsequent choice in the judgment, did not even take into account, thus violating the rule of due process, the defences based on Commission's lack of analysis on the law's impact on competition. Significantly, those defences were developed in *Unicredito*'s written observation and further recalled in the discussion. For the implications of the legitimate expectations principle in the *Legge Ciampi* case, *see* Ch. 4, to which I report also for further law cases.

But the approach the Commission also maintains in recent cases, likely due to the difficulties the same Commission faces when reviewing a State aid case resulting from a legislative act within the scope of competition law, creates a new issue, never examined in these terms heretofore, which is, in my view, the point of arrival of the very notion of *State aid scheme*.

From the Commission's approach, it clearly emerges that the illegality of an aid granted under a national legislative act is assumed to lie, in fact, in the resulting *discrimination* to the advantage of the undertakings in receipt of that aid operating in the State granting the aid and to the disadvantage of the undertakings operating in the same sector in another Member State. For in an *internal*, by now single, *market*, which is highly competitive by definition, it is the discrimination itself, in the Commission's view, that makes the aid unlawful, without the need for any further determination.

But this is the point. From a competitive perspective, not unless and until the potentially discriminatory effect of a national measure designed, in any form whatsoever, to favour a category of (assumedly domestic) undertakings is found to occur in the *same relevant (product and geographic) market*, could the competition- distorting criterion be deemed to have been met as a necessary requirement to be satisfied along with the other criteria specified in Article 107(1) TFEU. If, however, the discrimination between national and foreign undertakings, both based within the European Union, had its effect outside the relevant market, no distortion of competition could be found and as a consequence, there would be no State aid.

If the real issue were discrimination between nationals and EU foreigners, when the problem is looked at from a single Member State's point of view, then State aid legislation relating to competition law would not come into play.

The question would be, in fact, whether the Member State granting the aid has observed or, rather, has failed to observe, any of the four fundamental freedoms all of which are guaranteed by a set of EU provisions, whether primary or not, and especially by the provisions relating to the free movement of services or the freedom of establishment, as the case may be, both complemented by the freedom of capital movements.

VI AID BY ACT UNDER NATIONAL LEGAL ORDER IN THE US JURISDICTION: A DIFFERENT APPROACH TO THE QUESTION

The fact that State aid by an act of national law within a union of States can have little to do with the application of the rules on competition is consistent with the observation that the matter is not governed by the rules on competition in the US jurisdiction, which is the most important 'federal' system in the world and also the most sophisticated one, and the first that historically established a set of rules governing the fair competition.

Under the US federal laws, the issue of unlawful subsidies is primarily dealt with in connection with *subsidized exports*, which are penalized so long as, in their coming from non-US countries, they unduly favour imports into the US market from entities based in any such third country – thereby infringing the internal rules implementing the GATT 1994/WTO Agreements and, specifically, the Agreement on Subsidies and Countervailing Duties.[52]

Further, in the US legal system, the adoption of State measures aimed to support specific categories of businesses (in the form of subsidies, tax breaks, protective tariffs, etc.) is not a competition law issue and it is not subject to the jurisdiction of the Federal Trade Commission (and of the Department of Justice in some cases). The problem must, therefore, be considered in light of constitutional law, which falls within the direct and exclusive jurisdiction of the Federal Courts.

Although State protectionist measures are theoretically among the conducts forbidden by the Sherman Act and by the other antitrust laws, it is a well-established principle in federal case law that any measures taken by a State of the Union in the exercise of its sovereignty ('act of government by the State as sovereign') are not subject to antitrust laws, but have, instead, to comply with the provisions of the US Constitution (the Supreme Court's 'State action doctrine').

Therefore, under this profile, subsidies are dealt with in the light of the 'dormant' or 'negative commerce clause', which is a case law doctrine based on the *a contrario* interpretation of Article I, § 8, of the US Constitution, according to which the Congress has exclusive power to regulate interstate commerce. The *dormant commerce clause* bans a State from legislating with a view to granting monetary subsidies to its own businesses or levying such taxes or other similar burdens on companies based in other States as to generate the discriminatory effect of 'a visibly burdensome impact on out-of-state producers' or to have an adverse impact on interstate commerce.

A similar principle is applied under the EU law with respect to the golden share.[53] This issue is discussed here from the perspective of the constitutional law of the EU, having regard to the *non-discrimination obligation* intended to ensure compliance with certain fundamental freedoms.

With respect to subsidies to exports from third countries, the current US regulatory pattern is based on the same international framework (providing for an efficient two-tier jurisdictional system for the settlement of cross-border trade disputes within the WTO) as the one binding upon the EU, as well as all the one hundred sixty six countries to whom the WTO/GATT 1994 is applicable, under which the EU is treated as one single party separated from its Member States.

Conversely, beyond the international regulations governing macro-economic relationships, the European Union has – after the US approach – adjusted EU law to the requirements of the GATT 1994 to provide for a concurrent 'internal' system of EU regulations under which the active parties to judicial proceedings are deemed to include, as well as the Council, the Commission, the Member State concerned or other interested Member States, any undertakings variously interested therein because of their being either non-EU entities investigated for imports made into the European market by dumping or through the unfair advantage of subsidies, or EU-based

52. *See* A. Santa Maria, *European Economic Law*, 278 et seq. *See also* D. Wood, *State Aid Management in the United States*, EStAL, 1, 40 (2013) https://doi.org/10.21552/estal/2013/1/330.

53. *See* A. Santa Maria, *European Economic Law*, 111 et seq.

undertakings supposedly 'damaged' by the unlawful conduct of any such non-EU entity.

However, in compliance with the rules so provided at two different levels - one international and the other internal to the EU or the US - no one would ever blame a State member of either the European Union or the United States for having a less stringent legislation than other States on such matters as environmental protection of workplace safety, then one less burdensome for local undertakings. Nor would any one State challenge another State for legislating in favour of the latter's whole domestic manufacturing industry or any branch thereof, or for encouraging the settlement of out-of-state commercial firms in its territory through a simplified company legislation or an especially favourable tax regime.

In fact, where any such occurrence is viewed from the perspective of, and within, a union of States, the relevant arrangements clearly appear to foster competition between the Member States, the end result of which is bound to be an advantage for all consumers across the union's market.

Besides its international implications, a national legislative measure granting subsidies should not outright be construed as State aid in any event but should be viewed in either of two ways. In fact, it either will fall within legislation adopted by a non-EU country - e.g., the United States - in implementing the GATT1994/WTO agreements (as is the case for *dumping*), and will, as such, solely concern a system of *subsidies* granted, for example, to EU undertakings by their respective home countries for the ultimate purpose to unfairly favour their imports into the United States to the detriment of US undertakings, or be caught by a Member State's law favouring certain EU (own national) undertakings to the detriment of other European undertakings (i.e., incorporated under the law of a different Member State), in which case it must be prosecuted by the EU (national of any other Member State) for its being *discriminatory* on grounds of nationality, thus falling within the purview of Article 258 TFEU.

Observance of the four fundamental freedoms having been acknowledged to be the cornerstone of the European Union, I believe that the latter approach could be the right way to go with a view to penalizing any discrimination resulting from a legislative act of a Member State.

In conclusion, if the assessment as to the lawfulness of a State aid system were performed outside the competition context - which is entirely possible even today - the Commission could reach the desired outcome of having the Member State that adopted the contested statute as its only necessary counterparty in the procedure pursuant to Article 258 TFEU, thereby excluding the private parties, which would be left with no voice as a result.

With respect to safeguards, such exclusion would amply be offset by the different role the Commission has to play pursuant to Article 258 TFEU.

For the Commission, acting outside competition law and within its dictates applicable, for example, to golden shares' cases, would not have the authority to issue an immediately and directly effective decision. Still, after sending a letter of formal notice to the Member State concerned, the Commission is expected to issue a reasoned opinion (i.e., a non-binding act in itself) as to whether the applicable EU rules were infringed or not correctly applied, and to have the right to bring action before the Court of Justice against the non-complying Member State. It will be for the Court of Justice – in a role similar to that played by the US Federal Court pursuant to Article 1, § 8 of the US Constitution – to deliver a declaratory judgment as to whether the alleged infringement actually occurred.

Finally, it should be noted that in all the (frequent) instances in which a Member State does not voluntarily enforce a negative Commission decision on State aid – regardless of whether or not such decision has been appealed before the ECJ and/or the General Court – the Commission will be under a duty to bring action before the Court of Justice against the Member State that failed to comply with the obligation of terminating the effect of the measure declared incompatible and/or with the obligation to recover aid under the decision, which is self-executing in itself.

In summary, the solution suggested would further have the positive effect – in such a cumbersome jurisdictional system as is the European Union's today – of anticipating the ECJ's intervention, thus reducing the total length of the whole procedure.

VII THE SUBSTANTIAL DIVERSITY BETWEEN 'SUBSIDIES' TO EXPORT AND STATE 'AIDS'

In various passages of this introductory note, as in the development of several of the chapters that follow, we speak of State subsidy(ies) and/or State aid(s).

It should be pointed out, for the avoidance of doubt, that beyond the apparent equivalence, the two expressions are not at all interchangeable.
Indeed, both have in common the verification of the *public* advantage granted in some way to a specific undertaking or categories of undertakings.

Beyond this convergence, however, the first expression conceals a notion that is inextricably linked to the *increase in exports* by the beneficiary undertaking on the basis of which would be assessed the possible contrast of a State's act, omissive or commissive in nature, with the international rules put in place to protect free trade and equal treatment in trade in goods and services as developed (from the 1947 GATT to the 1994 agreements and the establishment of the WTO, and also to any specific provisions in bilateral trade or partnership agreements).[54]

The second, however, in European Union law, concerns the protection of free competition and aims to prevent its alterations in the internal market.

Such a difference in functions implies substantially different approaches to the assessments and the pertaining procedures in each single case.

From the standpoint of the EU, as is the case for the so-called *intra-Community dumping*, the recognized existence of an internal market, which is intended to be the 'unique' area without internal boundaries comprehensive as is of the territories of the

54. *See* above, in particular, para. 2 of this introductory note. For a list of the major commercial treaties of the last fifteen years of EU with third States, *see*: A. Santa Maria, *L'odierno diritto internazionale dell'economia*, 33.

twenty-seven Member States, excludes *in re ipsa* the possibility that the conduct of a Member State favouring the sales of goods or services by an undertaking or categories of undertakings to another State within the Union could be covered by the rules on the export of goods or services, and therefore such sales cannot even be assessed on the basis of the rules of international trade which prohibit State subsidies.

In fact, the only possible assessment of the lawfulness or unlawfulness of an advantage granted by a Member State to a particular undertaking or category of undertakings is left to a *decision* by the Commission under the competition rules on State aids. And it does not matter at all that the beneficiary company is part of a foreign group. What matters is that the anti-competitive effects occur in the EU market.[55] As the *Apple* case shows, once the anti-competitive liability of the (Irish) State for the ad hoc tax relief has been established, that State remains subject to the *recovery order* against the American group, as confirmed by CJEU.[56]

However, the scrutiny of the behaviour of a third country that has granted a subsidy to the beneficiary undertaking, thereby conferring an advantage on its exports to the EU, is taken away from the twenty-seven Member States and falls within the exclusive competence of the European Commission. As a result, it is either referred to the international procedure of the DSU[57] or becomes the subject of a procedure conducted by the Commission[58] which, if liability is established, ends with a regulation imposing *countervailing duties* on the beneficiaries of the illegitimate subsidies.[59]

55. In this respect, in its decision on State aids implemented by Ireland in favour of the Apple group in the form of tax relief, recently upheld by the ECJ in its judgment of 10 Sep. 2024, the Commission stated that Apples' Irish subsidiaries '*form part of a multinational corporate group, namely the Apple group, which is made up of numerous companies, all of which are ultimately controlled by Apple Inc. Separate legal entities may be considered to form one economic unit for the purpose of the application of State aid rules. That economic unit is then considered to be the relevant undertaking benefitting from the aid measure. As the Court of Justice has previously held, '[i]n competition law, the term "undertaking" must be understood as designating an economic unit [...] even if in law that economic unit consists of several persons, natural or legal*' (*see* Commission Decision (EU) 2017/1283 of 30 Aug. 2016 on State aid SA.38373 (2014/C) implemented by Ireland to Apple, point no. 416).
56. *See* Judgment of the Court in Case C-465/20 P, *Commission v. Ireland and Others*, 10.9.2024, ECLI:EU:C:2024:724.
57. *See* A. Santa Maria, *European Economic Law*, 229 et seq.
58. Pursuant to the Regulation (EU) 2022/2560 of the European Parliament and of the Council of 14 Dec. 2022 on foreign subsidies distorting the internal market, OJ L 330, 23.12.2022, and the Regulation (EU) 2016/1036 of the European Parliament and of the Council of 8 Jun. 2016 on protection against dumped imports from countries not members of the European Union, OJ L 176 30.6.2016. *See* A. Santa Maria, *European Economic Law*, 283 et seq.
59. However, this does not mean that the fact causing dumping or subsidization cannot have distorting effects not only on the EU's international trade but also on free competition in the internal market. As noted by Advocate General Verloren van Themaat in his Opinion in Joined Cases 239 and 275/82, *Allied Corporation and others v. Commission of the European Communities*, 10.1.1984, ECLI:EU:C:1984:1, para. 1.1: '[d]*dumping is a phenomenon by nature related to forms of distortion of competition which, under the system established by the EC Treaty, it is normally sought to counter by means of decisions. Dumping is, in particular, a form of cross-frontier price discrimination (made possible by the existence of customs and frontiers) which is by nature closely related to the discriminatory practices prohibited by Article 85(1) (d)* [now Article 101(1)(d)] *and Article 86(c)* [now, Article 102(c)] *of the Treaty*'. The Advocate General went on to state: '[m]*oreover, the effects of dumping are comparable to the effects*

Confirming the importance of words, I stress that it is no coincidence, and not surprising, that in the TCA between the EU and the UK the term 'State Aids' is absent, while the word 'subsidies' is used sixty-seven times. As a matter of fact, in the indications of anticompetitive business practices, State aid has no place in that international agreement.[60]

VIII IMPLEMENTING REGULATIONS OF ARTICLE 108 TFEU: FORM OVER SUBSTANCE?

Implementation of Article 108 TFEU takes place under Council Regulation (EU) No. 2015/1589 of 13 July 2015, so-called Procedural Regulation.

The reference to 'procedure', however, is somehow misleading, as this piece of legislation has a strong impact on the merit of the various cases, as well as on the substantial defence of the undertakings during the so-called administrative phase of the proceedings. The Regulation provides the Commission with a wide array of investigative powers, to the point of mandating fines against individual firms who fail to answer or are considered to answer inadequately to requests from the Commission.

In general, the system seems directed at strengthening the role of the two main players – the Commission and the Member State involved – at the expense of the private parties thereby increasing the 'asymmetry' of the proceeding.

It follows that, in a cost and benefit assessment of State aid regulation, unbalance is growing between the Commission seeking market efficiency and undertakings seeking respect of their individual rights. This is apparent as early as in the administrative phase of State aid proceedings, at which time decisions that acknowledge the existence of unlawful aid under Article 107 TFEU result in an obligation for the Member State to recover the aid measure from the undertaking at issue, following guidelines and directives contained in the decision itself.

After the decision has been issued, a private party seeking to defend itself before the Court faces a very challenging task, to the point of near impossibility without the support of the relevant Member State (which is difficult to obtain and often late).

---

produced by aid measures – which, according to Article 92 [now, Article 107], *are incompatible with the common market – and, in particular, by export aid measures which it is also sought to counter by means of decision*'.

60. Title XI of the TCA devotes two chapters to competition's subject, but their content does not go beyond a generic reference to the main principles of free competition and a shared recognition of the importance of safeguarding free and undistorted competition in their trade and investment relations. Even the undertaking to cooperate and coordinate in order to achieve such common objectives is expressed in soft wording, no more than an invitation addressed to both parties; they 'shall endeavor to *cooperate and coordinate, with respect to their enforcement activities concerning the same or related conduct or transactions,* where doing so is possible and appropriate' (roman font is mine). *See:* Art. 361(2) of the TCA. In other words, each party retains its own enforcement system to the content and extent it wishes, without any obligation of reciprocity. Art. 362 of the TCA excludes the application to the competition sector of the dispute settlement mechanism provided for in Title I, Part six. On the post-Brexit evolution of the British system from aids to subsidies, refer *infra* to Ch. 11 of this volume.

It should be borne in mind that the function of recovery must be only to restore the previous situation to the benefit of competition on the market, and that in no case should this be seen as a punitive measure for undertakings that are beneficiaries of aid. It follows that neither the Commission nor the State is allowed to exceed this specific limit, as they are both bound to respect fundamental rights of legitimate expectations, legal certainty, and proportionality –respect that needs to take place in practice and not to be limited to a perfunctory statement.

As for Member States in particular, I do not believe that they should be allowed to exceed – especially in the sense of greater or 'creative' harshness, applied to political situations that have much evolved from the times when the domestic aid measure was adopted – their obligation to enforce the decision of the Commission.[61] In the same way, the Commission should not claim to be unsatisfied with the enforcement of its decisions without mentioning specific reasons therefore.

Indeed, changes to the procedural framework of State aid law have an immediate substantive effect. A clear example is the criticisms already made with reference to State aid Modernization and the 2009 temporary framework, according to which the 'loosening' of the Commission's control would have benefited the Member States with higher financial capacities far more than those subject to more stringent financial limitations. This issue has dramatically re-emerged following the adoption of the Temporary Frameworks in the context of the pandemic crisis, first, and then the Russian-Ukrainian conflict and ecological transition as recently highlighted also in the report issued by Mario Draghi on the future of European competitiveness.[62]

IX RECOVERY INJUNCTION AND THE RIGHT TO DEFENCE

Aside from Council Regulation (EU) No. 2015/1589, displaying detailed (procedural) rules for the implementation of Article 108 TFEU, Commission Regulation No. 794/2004 remains applicable, laying down in the implementation of the Council Regulations of 1999 more stringent rules in the matter of recovery. The landscape resulting from the combined reading of this Commission Regulation with the Procedural Regulation raises serious concerns as to the lesser role attributed to private parties in cases under Article 107 TFEU.

I already noted that the availability of 'recovery orders' in the field of State aid, by now a natural consequence of any Commission decision whereby a State measure is found to be 'unlawful aid' – and a remedy that did not exist in primary legislation but was won by the Commission in case law – obviously requires that, in exchange, any undertaking in receipt of aid should have the standing to participate, not only in the

61. The reference is, in particular, to restitutory claims following decisions on aid implemented by fiscal legislative measures (*see* further Ch. 5 below).

62. *See* M. Draghi, *The Future of European Competitiveness*, *supra*, II, 4, 301, for instance, under the Temporary Crisis Framework and related Treaty provisions, over 50% of the volume of aid approved came from only one Member State (Germany), and over 80% came from three Member States (Germany, France, and Italy). The measures adopted under the Temporary Frameworks and their impact are analysed *infra* in Ch. 2.

administrative procedure but also in any subsequent jurisdictional stage, including through appeals against negative Commission decisions.

It is my view that, with respect to negative decisions in the matter of State aid, using the conventional literal interpretation of the 'individual concern' requirement, which the Commission has strongly affirmed in recent times, makes no sense. For this would ultimately deny *locus standi* to individual undertakings, thus depriving them of their rights of defence on the underlying issue of whether a State measure is aid in connection with aid schemes or aid by a legislative act.[63]

The Commission's power which ensues, in my view, can conflict with the 'formal' interpretation adopted by the EU Courts with respect to the principles of legitimate expectations, legal certainty and proportionality as the discriminating elements of recovery orders as adopted by the EU case law and today improved by the primary rules contained in Article 6 TEU to be applied as fundamental rights of the EU system.

Granting private entities the possibility to rely on any one of these principles is not enough if their applicability is actually restricted to extreme cases based on a case law assumption that seems to imply objective liability, whereby the private enterprise could not possibly ignore that a specific, non-notified statute contained the requirements of State aid.

Only two alternatives are allowed. Either the undertaking under investigation is enabled to actually be an active party in the proceedings, in which case its awareness at the time the procedure was officially opened may well be presumed *unless evidence to the contrary is given*, or, if it has no *locus standi* in the procedure, fair observance of the right of defence requires that such presumption of knowledge must be forgone, and it will be for the Commission to bear the *burden of proof* if and when it intends to incorporate a recovery order into its decision.

It will then be up to European Courts, as constitutional judge of the Union, to implement in practice the expectation of European people to have their undertakings rights safeguarded in actual reality, moving past a strictly literal interpretation of applicable provision in favour of a full application of the fundamental principles of EU law creating a balance between efficiency of the competition system and respect of individual rights.

In a modern system of law, living in the legacy of the century-old traditions of European democracies, the full achievement of such a balance appears to be, in my opinion and as I deem in that of the other co-authors, an unavoidable must.

63. I agree with Advocate General Jacobs' opinion in Case C-50/00 P, *Unión de Pequeños Agricultores v. Commission*, 21.3.2002, ECLI:EU:C:2002:197. That case dealt with a Council Regulation and, for this reason, the ECJ dismissed the appeal. This does not exclude that Advocate General Jacobs' arguments must necessarily recover validity when it is a Commission's *decision* that is under dispute. *See* Ch. 6.

CHAPTER 1
The Notion of State Aid

Martino Ebner & Edoardo Gambaro

§1.01 THE NOTION OF STATE AID

No definition of State aid is contained in the subsequent formulation of the European treaties. Lastly, Article 107(1) TFEU states that:

> any aid granted by a Member State or through State resources in any form whatsoever which distorts or threatens to distort competition by favouring certain undertakings or the production of certain goods shall, in so far as it affects trade between Member States, be deemed incompatible with the internal market.

This provision appears to be intentionally unspecific with a view to favouring the broadest possible application of the prohibition it contains. The phrase 'in any form whatsoever' accommodates a variety of different ways in which a Member State may grant aid pursuant to Article 107 TFEU.[1] Thus, the prohibition substantially differs from that of direct subsidies.[2] This is the approach the Court of Justice has taken since its earliest decisions, specifying that:

1. Several consecutive measures of State intervention must be regarded as a single intervention for the purposes of Art. 107(1) TFEU, in particular where consecutive interventions, having regard to their chronology, purpose and circumstances of the undertakings at the time of those interventions, are so closely linked that they are inseparable from one another. *See* case 72/79 *Commission v. Italy*, 24.4.1980, ECLI:EU:C:1980:109, para. 24; case C-486/15 *Commission v. France and Orange*, 30.11.2016, ECLI:EU:C:2016:912, para. 104. However, any extension of the duration of a given State measure may prove to be sufficient to establish a new aid regime, which is subject to notification to the Commission: *see* case C-590/14 P *Dimosia Epicheirisi Ilektrismou A.E. v. Alouminion tis Ellados A.E.*, 26.10.2016, ECLI:EU:C:2016:797.
2. The notion of State aid differs from that of 'subsidy' stemming from Art. XVI of the GATT 1994, recalled by Regulation (EC) No. 3284/94 of 22 Dec. 1994 on protection against subsidized imports from countries not members of the European Community, OJ 1994 L349/22. As clarified by the CFI in its judgment, Case T-55/99, *Confederación Espanola de Transporte de Mercancías ('CETM') v. Commission*, 29.9.2000, ECLI:EU:T:2000:223, para. 50: '[t]he reference to the concept of

> the concept of aid is [...] wider than that of a subsidy because it embraces not only positive benefits, such as subsidies themselves, but also interventions which, in various forms, mitigate the charges which are normally included in the budget of an undertaking and which, without, therefore, being subsidies in the strict meaning of the word, are similar in character and have the same effect.[3]

In fact, EU State aid rules pursue a different aim than the WTO framework on subsidies, given that they are intended to ensure a system of free competition, to allow the development and functioning of the internal market.[4]

By analogy with the prohibition prescribed by Article 101(1) TFEU, and Article 102 TFEU, both the Commission and EU Courts have held that, partly in connection with the prohibition contained in Article 107(1) TFEU, what matters in practice is rather the *effect* of the measure than its form or purpose or even the awareness of the State granting the aid or of the recipient of the aid.[5]

The effect criterion has been disputed by Member States on many occasions since it makes the scope for application of the prohibition in Article 107(1) TFEU also include measures intended to pursue general interests or even apt to offset any existing heavier charges borne by domestic undertakings than those levied on undertakings active in similar industries in other Member States.

In this respect, the Court of Justice has held that the fact that the measure involved falls within a policy for which a Member State alone is responsible, for example, in the areas of social welfare or social security, or that it has been introduced to attain a specific economic or social objective, is not enough for that measure to avoid being qualified as aid or being closely scrutinized under the applicable TFEU rules.[6]

---

subsidy within the meaning of the WTO Agreement on Subsidies and Countervailing Measures has [...] no relevance whatsoever to the classification of the measure in question as State aid within the meaning of Community law'. On this point, *see also* the introduction by Prof. Santa Maria.

3. Case C-30/59, *De Gezamenlijke Steenkolenmijnen in Limburg v. High Authority*, 23.2.1961, ECLI:EU:C:1961:2. Confirmed by the ECJ in Case C-387/92, *Banco Exterior de España SA v. Ayuntamiento de Valencia*, 15.3.1994, ECLI:EU:C:1994:100, para. 13. Statement confirmed in numerous judgments since, *see also* Case C-559/12 P, *France v. Commission*, 3.4.2014, ECLI: EU:C:2014:217, para. 94.
4. The fundamental purpose of the rules on competition of the Treaties, including those on State aid, is enshrined in is Art. 3(3) TEU, namely the establishment of an internal market, and in Protocol No. 27 on the internal market and competition, which forms an integral part of the Treaties in accordance with Art. 51 TEU, and states that the internal market includes a system ensuring that competition is not distorted. *See* Case T-25/04, *Gonzdlez y Díez v. Commission*, 12.9.2007, EU:C:2007:257, para. 55; Case C-496/09, *Commission v. Italy*, 17.11.2011, EU:C:2011:740, para. 60; case C-610/10, *Commission v. Spain*, 11 Dec. 2012, EU:C:2012:781, para. 131; case C-622/16 P to C-624/16 P, *Scuola Elementare Maria Montessori v. Commission*, 6.11.2018, EU:C:2018:873, para. 52; case T-47/19, *Dansk Erhverv*, 9.6.2021, EU:T:2021:331, para. 66.
5. *See* Case C-173/73, *Italy v. Commission*, 2.7.1974, ECLI:EU:C:1974:71, para. 13: 'Article 92 [now Article 107 TFEU] does not distinguish between the measures of state intervention concerned by reference to their causes or aims but defines them in relation to their effects.'
6. *See* Case C-61/79, *Amministrazione delle finanze dello Stato v. Denkavit italiana*, 27.3.1980, ECLI:EU:C:1980:100, para. 31; Case C-342/96, *Spain v. Commission*, 29.4.1999, ECLI: EU:C:1999:210, paras 21 et seq., and Case C-310/99, *Italy v. Commission*, 7.3.2002, ECLI: EU:C:2002:143, para. 51.

The same conclusions have been reached by the Court in relation to measures intended to offset heavier charges levied on domestic undertakings.[7]

In the context of State aid modernization, on 19 July 2016, the European Commission published the '*Commission Notice on the notion of State aid as referred to in Article 107(1) of the Treaty on the Functioning of the European Union*', providing further clarification on how the Commission understands, in line with the EU case law and the Treaty provisions, the key concepts relating to the notion of State aid.[8]

§1.02 THE REQUIREMENTS

Paragraph 1 of Article 107 TFEU contains a list of requirements that, according to consistent case law precedents, *must all be met* for 'State aid' to be deemed to have materialized:[9]

(1) it must be an intervention imputable to the State or carried out through State resources;
(2) it must give a gratuitous advantage to the recipient;
(3) it must be of a 'selective' character, i.e., intended to favour just certain undertakings or certain business sectors;
(4) it must have an impact on trade between Member States; and
(5) it must distort competition in the internal market.

Nevertheless, even if all the requirements indicated above have been met, if the stringent cumulative conditions contained in the *Altmark* judgment are met, an economic measure taken in favour of certain undertakings in compensation for services provided by the recipient undertakings in order to discharge public service obligations does not amount to State aid within the meaning of Article 107(1) TFEU.[10]

Moreover, Article 107 TFEU does not apply if the State acts 'by exercising public power'[11] or where public entities act 'in their capacity as public authorities'[12] as well as in cases where the aid measures do not involve an economic activity.[13]

7. *See* Case C-78/76, *Steinike & Weinlig v. Federal Republic of Germany*, 22.3.1977, ECLI: EU:C:1977:52, para. 24 where the Court stated: 'the effects of more than one distortion of competition on trade between Member States do not cancel one another out but accumulate and the damaging consequences to the internal market are increased'.
8. Commission Notice on the notion of State aid as referred to in Art. 107(1) of the Treaty on the Functioning of the European Union, C/2016/2946, OJ C 262, 19.7.2016, pp. 1-50.
9. Case C-142/87, *Belgium v. Commission ('Tubemeuse')*, 21.3.1990, ECLI:EU:C:1990:125, para. 25; Joined Cases C-278/92, C-279/92 and C-280/92, *Spain v. Commission*, 14.9.1994, ECLI: EU:C:1994:325, para. 20; Case C-482/99, *France v. Commission (' Stardust Marine ')*, 16.5.2002. ECLI:EU:C:2002:294, para. 68; Case C-280/00, *Altmark Trans GmbH and Regierungspräsidium Magdeburg v. Nahverkehrsgesellschaft Altmark GmbH*, 24.7.2003, ECLI:EU:C:2003:415, paras 74-75, and Case C-345/02, *Pearle BV and Others*, 11.3.2004, ECLI:EU:C:2004:145, para. 32.
10. Case C-280/00, *Altmark Trans*, paras 89-93. *See also infra* Ch. 2.
11. Case C-118/85, *Commission v. Italy*, 16.6.1987, ECLI:EU:C:1987:283, paras 7-8.
12. Case C-30/87, *Bodson v. Pompes funèbres des régions libérées*, 4.5.1988, ECLI:EU:C:1988:225, para. 18.
13. *See* section 1.02[B][2] infra.

With regard to the burden of proof, in the last decade, we have seen a high number of Commission decisions set aside by the EU Courts on the grounds that the Commission erroneously analysed the Article 107(1) requirements. Although in some cases the EU Courts annulled decisions due to errors of law (*Hungarian advertising tax,*[14] *Polish retail tax,*[15] *Dirk Andres*),[16] in many others the EU Courts upheld that the Commission failed to satisfy the required burden of proof in relation to a given condition (*Tercas,*[17] *Starbucks,*[18] *Futbol Club Barcelona,*[19] *Retegal*).[20] Generally, it seemed that the EU Courts required the Commission to take into account all the relevant factual elements and carry out a global assessment of all evidence. Contextually, the Courts tended to rule out the possibility for the Commission to rely on presumptions.

This said, following the surge of aid measures with the Temporary Frameworks (*see infra* Chapter 2), the Court seems to have shifted its focus more on the risk of under-deterrence, in several cases annulling Commission's authorization decisions.[21]

[A] State Intervention

For a measure to be caught by Article 107 TFEU as State aid, the advantage must have been granted by 'a Member State or through State resources and be attributable to the State'.[22]

[1] Imputability to the State and the Transfer of State Resources

EU Courts have given a quite broad interpretation to the notions of 'State' and 'State resources' within the meaning and for the purposes of Article 107 TFEU.[23] It does not only include aid granted directly by a central government but also measures issued by regional and local bodies[24] or even by private bodies designated or established by the

14. Case C-596/19 P, *Commission v. Hungary*, 16.3.2021, ECLI:EU:C:2021:202.
15. Case C-562/19 P, *Commission v. Poland*, 16.3.2021, ECLI:EU:C:2021:201.
16. Case C-203/16 P, *Dirk Andres v. Commission*, 28.6.2018, ECLI:EU:C:2018:505.
17. Case C-425/19 P, *Commission v. Italy and Others*, 2.3.2021, ECLI:EU:C:2021:154.
18. Case T-398/16, *Starbucks Corp. v. European Union Intellectual Property Office*, 16.1.2018.ECLI: EU:T:2018:4.
19. Case C-362/19 P, *Commission v. Football Club Barcelona*, 4.3.2021, ECLI:EU:C:2021:169.
20. C-70/16 P, *Comunidad Autónoma de Galicia, Redes de Telecomunicación Galegas Retegal SA (Retegal) v. European Commission*, 20.12.2017, ECLI:EU:C:2017:1002.
21. *See, e.g.*, Joined Cases T-34/21, *Ryanair v. Commission*, 10.5.2023, ECLI:EU:T:2023:248.
22. Para. C-385/18, *Arriva Italia and Others*, 19 Dec. 2019, EU:C:2019:1121, C-706/17, *Achema and Others*, 15.5.2019, EU:C:2019:407, para. 47; case C-434/19 and C-435/19, *Poste Italiane and Riscossione*, 3.3.2021, EU:C:2021:162, para. 39.
23. Therefore, those resources may take various forms and, which shall be identified and analysed carefully by the Commission. *See* case T-683/15, *Freistaat Bayern v. Commission*, 12 Dec. 2018, EU:T:2018:916, para. 65.
24. *See* Case C-248/84, *Germany v. Commission*, 14.10.1987, ECLI:EU:C:1987:437, para. 17. *See* Case C-248/84, *Germany v. Commission* [1987] ECR 4013 (para. 17). As for aid granted following a decision by a judicial authority, the Court stated that, although the national court may, where appropriate, deliver a judgment from which it follows that one of the parties must, in accordance

State.[25] As stated by the Court, in order to conclude that an advantage has been conferred through a 'designated body', 'it is not necessary for the sums corresponding to the measure in question to be permanently in the possession of the Treasury, the fact that they remain constantly under public control, and thus at the disposal of the competent national authorities, being sufficient for them to be classified as State resources'.[26]

The *imputability to the State* of an aid measure taken by a public undertaking may be inferred from a set of *indicators* arising from the circumstances of the case and the context in which that measure was taken.[27]

In that respect, the Court has determined the imputability to the State in cases in which the body in question could not take the contested decision without taking account of the requirements of the public authorities[28] or in which, apart from factors of an organic nature that linked the public undertakings to the State, those undertakings, through the intermediary of which aid had been granted, had to take account of directives issued by a public authority.[29]

An aid resulting from legislative measures is almost always imputable to the State, even if the designated (by law) public authority enjoys legal autonomy.[30] The

---

with national law, receive a sum corresponding to State aid, that does not mean that, in that case, it itself grants that aid. Indeed, the judgment only required the other party, generally the competent administrative authority, to pay that aid. In other words, legal proceedings seeking full entitlement to that right must be regarded as requests for payment of the portion of that State aid not received, and not as requests for the grant by the court of a separate State aid. *See* C-702/20 and C-17/21, *'DOBELES HES' SIA*, 12.1.2023, EU:C:2023:1, paras 75-79.

25. Joined Cases C-72/91 and C-73/91, *Sloman Neptun Schiffahrts AG v. See betriebsrat Bodo Ziesemer der Sloman Neptun Schiffahrts AG*, 17.3.1993, ECLI:EU:C:1993:97, para. 19; Case C-57/86, *Greece v. Commission*, 7.6.1988, ECLI:EU:C:1988:284, para. 12; Case C-379/98, *PreussenElektra AG v. Schleswag AG*, 13.3.2001. ECLI:EU:C:2001:160, para. 58, and Case C-345/02, *Pearle BV and others*, para. 34. Case C-78/76, *Steinike & Weinlig*, 22.3.1977, ECLI:EU:C:1977:52, para. 21; case C-262/12, *Association Vent De Colère! and Others*, 19.12.2013, ECLI: EU:C:2013:851, para. 20; case C-329/15, *ENEA*, 13.9.2017, ECLI:EU:C:2017:671, para. 23; case C-706/17, Achema, 15.5.2019, ECLI:EU:C:2019:407, para. 50.

26. Case C-405/16 P, *Germany v. Commission*, 28.3.2019, ECLI:EU:C:2019:268, para. 57; case C-706/17, *Achema and Others*, 15.5.2019, EU:C:2019:407, para. 53; case T-217/17, *FVE Holýšov I and Others v. Commission*, 20.9.2019, EU:T:2019:633, para. 106; case C-160/19 P, *Comune di Milano*, 10 Dec. 2020, EU:C:2020:1012, para. 30; case C-434/19 and C-435/19, *Poste Italiane and Riscossione*, 3.3.2021, EU:C:2021:162, para. 42; case C-596/19 P, *Commission v. Hungary*, 16.3.2021, EU:C:2021:202, §36.

27. If measures are adopted jointly by several Member States, they are imputable to all the Member States concerned. *See* Notice on the notion of State aid, para. 46.

28. Joined Cases 67/85, 68/85 and 70/85, *Kwekerij Gebroeders van der Kooy BV and Others. v. Commission*, 2.2.1988, ECLI:EU:C:1988:38, para. 37; Case C-290/83, *Commission v. France* (*'Crédit Agricole'*), 30.1.1985, ECLI:EU:C:1985:37, para. 15, and Case C-57/86, *Greece v. Commission*, para. 13.

29. Case C-482/99, *'Stardust Marine'*, para. 55; Case C-303/88, *Italy v. Commission*, 21.3.1991, ECLI:EU:C:1991:136, paras 11-12, and Case C-305/89, *Italy v. Commission*, ECLI:EU:C:1991:142, paras 13-14. According to Advocate General Jacobs in *Stardust Marine* (at para. 66), for the Commission it is 'sufficient to establish on the basis of an analysis of the facts and circumstances of the case that the undertaking in question could not take the decision in question without taking account of the requirements of the public authorities'. *See also* Advocate General Lenz's opinion of 22 Jun. 1994, Case C-44/93, *Namur-Les Assurances du Crédit v. Office national du ducroire and Belgian State*, 9.8.1984, ECLI:EU:C:1994:311, para. 44.

30. Case T-358/94, *Air France v. Commission*, 12.121996, ECLI:EU:T:1996:194, paras 59-62. In that

mere fact that a measure is taken by a public or publicly-owned undertaking is not per se sufficient to infer imputability.[31] However, it needs not be shown that the public authorities actually incited the public undertaking to adopt the aid measures at issue on foot of a specific instruction: (a) first of all, because the relationship between the State and public undertakings is close, there is a real risk that State aid may be granted through the intermediary of those undertakings in a non-transparent way; and (b) as a general rule, it will be very difficult for a third party to demonstrate in a particular case that aid measures taken by such an undertaking were in fact adopted on the instructions of the public authorities, precisely because of the privileged relations existing between the State and a public undertaking.[32]

For these reasons, the imputability may be inferred by the following (non-exhaustive) list of indicators arising from the circumstances of the case and the context in which the measure was taken:

(1) the body in question could not take the contested decision without taking account of the requirements of the public authorities;[33]

---

case, it was held that the conduct of the *Caisse des Dépôts et Consignations* was imputable to the French State although it enjoyed legal autonomy from the political authorities. According to the Court, that conclusion was not undermined by the arguments to the effect that the appointment of its Director-General was irrevocable, that the *Caisse* had a special statute in relation to the *Cour des Comptes*, and that it had a particular accounting and fiscal regime. The Court stated that EU law 'cannot permit the rules on State aid to be circumvented merely through the creation of autonomous institutions charged with allocating aid' (para. 62). *See also* Case T-251/11, *Austria v. Commission*, 11.12.2014, ECLI:EU:T:2014:1060, para. 87. Moreover, the mere fact that an entity under the control of the State carries out its activities in competition with private operators does not preclude the measures that the entity is likely to adopt from being imputed to the State. *See* Case T-507/12, *Slovenia v. Commission*, 28.1.2016, EU:T:2016:35, para. 92; Case T-901/16, *Elche Club de Fútbol v. Commission*, 12.3.2020, EU:T:2020:97, para. 62.

31. The concept of public undertakings can be defined by reference to Commission Directive 2006/111/EC, of 16 Nov. 2006, on the transparency of financial relations between Member States and public undertakings as well as on financial transparency within certain undertakings (OJ L 318, 17.11.2006, p. 17). Art. 2(b) of this Directive states that '"public undertakings" means any undertaking over which the public authorities may exercise directly or indirectly a dominant influence by virtue of their ownership of it, their financial participation therein, or the rules which govern it'.

32. Case C-482/99, '*Stardust Marine*', paras 53-54. *See also, inter alia,* Case T-387/11, *Nitrogénművek Vegyipari Zrt. v. Commission*, 27.2.2013, ECLI:EU:T:2013:98, paras 59-61. In practice, the 'origin' of the aid is often a key factor: for instance, in Case C-206/06, *Essent Netwerk Noord and Others v. Aluminium Delfzijl BV*, 17.7.2008, paras 65-75, the designated body was not entitled to use the proceeds from the charge for purposes other than those provided for by Dutch law. By contrast, in Case C-345/02, *Pearle BV and others*, paras 36-38, although the monies were collected by a professional body, the advertising campaign was organized by a private association of opticians, had a purely commercial purpose and had nothing to do with a policy determined by the authorities. In addition, the fact that the measure is granted by a private entity does not rule out imputability to the State; however, the Commission cannot confine itself to demonstrating, having regard to the circumstances of the case, that the lack of effective influence and control by the public authorities over that private entity is unlikely. The Commission is therefore required to prove that effective State control over the private entity is at least likely. *See* cases T-98/16, T-196/16 and T-198/16, *Italy v. Commission*, 19.3.2019, ECLI:EU:T:2019:167.

33. Notice on the notion of State Aid, para. 43(a).

(2) the fact that, besides factors of an organic nature which link the public undertaking to the State, the grantor undertaking had to take account of directives issued by governmental bodies;[34]
(3) the integration of the public undertaking into the structures of the public administration;[35]
(4) the nature of the undertaking's activities and their exercise on the market in normal conditions of competition with private operators;[36]
(5) the legal status of the undertaking (whether it is subject to public law or ordinary company law) and the way in which the undertaking was established. However, according to the Court, the fact that a public undertaking has been constituted in the form of a capital company under ordinary law cannot be regarded as sufficient to exclude the possibility of an aid measure taken by such a company being imputable to the State;[37]
(6) the intensity of supervision that the public authorities exercise over the management of the undertaking[38] (including the shareholding directly/indirectly held by the State,[39] the appointment by the State of members of the governing board and any control over the undertaking's budget);[40]
(7) how the measure is put forward by the public authorities;[41]
(8) any other indicator showing, in the particular case, an involvement by the public authorities in the adoption of a measure or the unlikelihood of their not being involved, having regard also to the compass of the measure, its content or the conditions which it contains.[42]

---

34. Notice on the notion of State Aid, para. 43(c). Case C-482/99, *'Stardust Marine'*, para. 55; Case T-384/08, *Elliniki Nafpigokataskevastiki AE Chartofylakeiou v. Commission*, 10.11.2011, ECLI:EU:T:2011:650, paras 57-58. *See* Decision to initiate Art. 108(2) procedure in Case C-14/10 (ex NN 25/10 and CP 175/06), *Italy – SEA Handling* [2011] OJ C 29, 29.1.2011, p. 10, where the Commission noted that certain evidence shows that the public authorities were 'involved' in the measures taken by SEA in respect of its subsidiary SEA Handling (paras 61-66). *See also* IP/12/1414 of 19 Dec. 2012 (negative decision with recovery not yet published on OJ).
35. Case C-482/99, *'Stardust Marine'*, para. 56.
36. Case C-482/99, *'Stardust Marine'*, para. 56. *See also, inter alia*, Case T-387/11, *Nitrogénművek Vegyipari Zrt. v. Commission* ECLI:EU:T:2013:98, 27.2.2005. para. 63.
37. Case C-482/99, *'Stardust Marine'* (para. 57) and Case C-305/89, *Italy v. Commission* (para. 13). *See, however*, Advocate General Slynn's opinion, Joined Cases 67/85, 68/85 and 70/85, *Van der Kooy BV and others v. Commission*, 2.4.1987, ECLI:EU:C:1987:177.
38. Joined Cases 67/85, 68/85 and 70/85, *Van der Kooy BV and others v. Commission*, 2.2.1988, ECLI:EU:C:1988:38, para. 36; Case C-482/99, *'Stardust Marine'*, para. 56; Case T-384/08, *Elliniki Nafpigokataskevastiki AE Chartofylakeiou v. Commission*, paras 64-65. *See* Decision to initiate Art. 108(2) procedure in Case C-14/10, *Italy – SEA Handling*, paras 67-70.
39. *See* Commission decision in Case N791/2006, *Business case Norrköping*, 10.7.2007.
40. Case C-160/19 P, *Comune di Milano v. Commission*, 10.12.2020, ECLI:EU:C:2020:1012; case T-525/20, *ITD and Danske Fragtmaend*, 13 Sep. 2023, EU:T:2023:542, para. 53.
41. Case C-290/83, *'Crédit Agricole'*, para. 15. According to Advocate General Jacobs' opinion in Case C-482/99, *'Stardust Marine'*, 13.12.2001, ECLI:EU:C:2001:685, para. 68, in particular cases circumstantial evidence (e.g., press reports) might be relied upon.
42. Case C-482/99, *'Stardust Marine'*, para. 56. *See also* Case C-242/13, *Commerz Nederland NV v. Havenbedrijf Rotterdam NV*, 23.10.2014, ECLI:EU:C:2014:2326, where the ECJ deemed relevant (though not decisive) that the sole director of the public undertaking providing guarantees acted

A measure is *not* imputable if the Member State is under an obligation to implement it under Union law without any discretion. In that case, the measure stems from an act of the Union legislature and is not imputable to the State.[43]

This rule does not, however, apply in situations where Union law simply allows for certain national measures and the Member State enjoys discretion: (i) on whether to adopt the measures in question; or (ii) in establishing the characteristics of the concrete measure which are relevant from a State aid perspective.[44] The requirement of *a transfer of State resources* is met where the aid has an impact on the State budget, i.e., whenever the State grants its resources *directly* or *indirectly* forgoes the recovery of sums due.[45] All resources of the public sector are considered State resources, including resources of intra-State entities (decentralized, federated, regional, etc.). Funds provided by the central bank of a Member State to specific credit institutions generally fall within the scope of State aid rules.[46]

There are a variety of manners in which State resources can be transferred, i.e., non-refundable subsidies, subsidies intended to offset operational losses or to meet new capital expenses, lower-rate loans, State guarantees for borrowings, subsidized export credit or special export credit insurance, extended terms of payment, conclusion of public supply contracts at higher-than-market prices, payment by the State of payroll or social security charges, publicly-owned real property sold below its value, tax relief

improperly, deliberately kept the provision of those guarantees secret (disregarding the undertaking's bylaws) and that the public authority would have opposed the provision of the guarantees, had it been informed of it.

43. *See* Case C-460/07, *Sandra Puffer v. Unabhängiger Finanzsenat, Außenstelle Linz,* 23.4.2009 ECLI:EU:C:2009:254, para. 70, on the right to tax deductions under the VAT system set up by the Union, and Case T-351/02, *Deutsche Bahn AG v. Commission,* 5.4.2006, ECLI:EU:T:2006:104, paras 99-106 on tax exemptions required by Union law. In the latter case, the Court held that there was no imputability to the State when a Directive, in spite of the wide wording, does not affect the unconditional nature of the obligation imposed to grant exemption.
44. Notice on the notion of State Aid, para. 45.
45. In Case C-279/08 P, *Commission v. Netherlands,* 8.9.2011, ECLI:EU:C:2011:551, paras 106-112, the ECJ held that the Dutch NOx emission trading scheme could entail an *additional burden* for the public authorities, as that the emission allowances were allocated *free of charge,* whereas they could have been sold or put up for auction. In addition, the Dutch State deprived itself of a revenue to which it was *potentially* entitled in the form of fines or pecuniary penalties imposed to undertakings for exceeding emission ceilings. According to the Court, such foregoing of resources could not be considered 'inherent' in any instrument designed to regulate emissions of atmospheric pollutants by an emission allowance trading scheme. Therefore, the ECJ found a '*sufficiently direct connection*' between the measure in question and the loss of revenue (that was not the case in *PreussenElektra*). In Case C-518/13, *Eventech Ltd. v. Parking Adjudicator,* 14.1.2014, ECLI:EU:C:2015:9, the ECJ distinguished the case from that in Case C-279/08 P, *European Commission v. Kingdom of the Netherlands*: the reason why Black Cabs can use bus lanes without being subject to fines is not that the public authorities have made a decision not to collect fines, but that taxis are permitted to use those bus lanes.
46. Notice on the notion of State Aid, para. 48. *See* Communication from the Commission on the application, from 1 Aug. 2013, of State aid rules to support measures in favour of banks in the context of the financial crisis ('Banking Communication') OJ C 216, 30.7.2013, p. 1. However, the Commission clarified that where a central bank reacts to a banking crisis not with selective measures in favour of individual banks, but with general measures open to all comparable market players in the market (e.g., lending to the whole market on equal terms), such general measures often fall outside the scope of State aid control.

or exemption or exceptional extensions of tax payment terms, para-fiscal levies[47] and other forms.

It is not necessary that a positive transfer of funds is performed, as the foregoing State revenue is sufficient. For instance, a transfer of State resources can occur by waiving revenue which would otherwise have been paid to the State,[48] through exemptions or reductions in taxes or social security contributions, exemptions from fines or other pecuniary penalties,[49] granting access to a public domain or natural resources or granting special or exclusive rights without adequate remuneration.[50]

However, a regulatory measure that generates a negative indirect effect on State revenues does not constitute a transfer of State resources where it is an inherent feature of the measure.[51]

According to case law, imposing a *potential burden* on State resources in the future, by a guarantee or by a contractual offer, is sufficient, provided that a sufficiently direct link is established between, on the one hand, the advantage given to the beneficiary and, on the other hand, a reduction of the State budget or a sufficiently concrete economic risks of burdens on that budget.[52] However, the ECJ added that the reduction in State resources does not have to be equivalent to the advantage.[53]

It emerges from the Court's case law that Article 107(1) TFEU covers all the financial means by which public authorities may actually support undertakings, irrespective of whether or not those means are permanent assets of the public sector.

In the latter case, the fact that the sums corresponding to a State aid measure constantly remain *available* to the competent national authorities is sufficient for them

47. Case C-78/76, *Steinike & Weinlig* and Case C-259/85, *France v. Commission*, 11.11.1987, ECLI:EU:C:1987:478. *See also* points 36-39 of the judgment in *Pearle BV and others*, where the Court held there was no transfer of State resources. On para-fiscal charges *see also infra*.
48. Case C-83/98 P, *France v. Ladbroke Racing Ltd and Commission*, 16.5.2000, ECLI: EU:C:2000:248, paras 48 to 51.
49. Case C-387/92, *Banco Exterior de España*, 15.3.1994, ECLI:EU:C:1994:100, para. 14 on tax exemptions.
50. Allowances granted by the national legislature to undertakings free of charge which because of their tradable character have an economic value and therefore could have been sold by the State entail an additional burden for the public authorities, thus involving a transfer of State resource. *See* Case C-279/08 P, *Commission v. Netherlands*, 8.9.2011, EU:C:2011:551, paras 106-111; Case T-47/19, *Dansk Erhverv*, 9.6.2021, EU:T:2021:331, para. 93 On SGEI and adequate remuneration, *see* Ch. 2.
51. Notice on the Notion of State aid, p. 56.
52. Joined Cases C-399/10 and C-401/10 P, *Bouygues SA and Bouygues Télécom SA v. Commission*, 19.3.2013, ECLI:EU:C:2013:175, para. 109; *see also* Case C-279/08 P, *Commission v. Netherlands*, para. 111. Earlier case law had already made clear that the grant of a guarantee by the State cannot avoid the State aid prohibition merely because that advantage was not conferred on the beneficiary by way of a direct and clear mobilization of State resources ('additional burden'): *see* Joined Cases T-204/97 and T-270/97, *EPAC v. Commission* 13.6.2000, ECLI:EU:T:2000:148, paras 80-81, and, more recently, Case T-384/08, *Elliniki Nafpigokataskevastiki AE Chartofylakeiou v. Commission*, paras 89 and 92.
53. Joined Cases C-399/10 and 401/10 P, *Bouygues and Bouygues Télécom v. Commission*, para. 110. In that case, the ECJ, unlike the GC in Case T-425/04, *France and Others v. Commission*, 21.10.2010, ECLI:EU:T:2010:216, held that apparently different (and consecutive) measures can be regarded as single measure if they are 'inseparable' from one another (para. 104 of the ruling).

to be categorized as State resources.[54] Therefore, the decisive criterion as far as concerns 'State resources' is '*public control*', and Article 107(1) TFEU encompasses all financial means, whether they result from mandatory contributions or not, which the public sector can actually use to support undertakings.[55]

Thus, subsidies financed through para-fiscal charges or other compulsory contributions imposed by the State and managed in accordance with the provisions of public rules imply a transfer of State resources, even if the fund is managed by entities separate from the public authorities and permanently in private hands.[56] Moreover, the mere fact that the subsidies are financed in part by voluntary private contributions is not sufficient to rule out the presence of State resources, since the relevant factor is the degree of intervention of the public authority within the definition of the measure and its method of financing.[57] However, it is irrelevant that the financing mechanism at issue does not, strictly speaking, fall within the category of fiscal levies under national law.[58]

Transfer of State resources can only be ruled out in specific circumstances. Notably, as in the *Pearle* and *Doux Élevage* cases – if resources from the members of a trade association are earmarked for a specific purpose in the interest of the members, decided on by a private organization and with a purely commercial purpose: in such cases, resources were deemed by the ECJ not to be constantly under public control.[59] In *Doux Élevage*, the Court added that private funds used by inter-trade organizations do not become 'State resources' simply because they are used alongside sums which may originate from that budget.[60]

54. Case C-482/99, *'Stardust Marine'*, para. 38, recalling Case C-83/98, *France v. Ladbroke Racing and Commission*, 16.5.2000, ECLI:EU:C:2000:248, para. 50. The same applies even if the resources do not become the property of the public authority: *see* Case T-358/94, *Air France v. Commission*, paras 65-67.
55. *See, inter alia,* Joined Cases T-267/08 and T-279/08, *Région Nord Pas-de-Calais v. Commission*, 12.5.2011, ECLI:EU:T:2011:209, para. 111. *See also* C-850/19 P, *FVE v. Commission*, 16.9.2021, ECLI:EU:C:2021:740: '*The fact of coming from a compulsory levy is, on the contrary, sufficient to identify State resources. On the other hand, it is irrelevant that the financing mechanism at issue does not, strictly speaking, fall within the category of fiscal levies under national law.*'
56. Case C-206/06, *Essent Netwerk Noord*, paras 66-70. Case C-206/06, *Essent Netwerk Noord* (paras 66-70). Case T-186/13, *Netherlands and Others v. Commission*, 30.6.2015, EU:T:2015:447, para. 66; C-405/16 P, *Germany v. Commission*, 28.3.2019, EU:C:2018:268, para. 53; C-706/17, *Achema and Others*, 15.5.2019, EU:C:2019:407, para. 54; T-217/17, *FVE Holýšov I and Others v. Commission*, 20.9.2019, EU:T:2019:633, para. 107; T-409/21, *Germany v. Commission*, 24.1.2024, EU:T:2024:34, para. 57.
57. Notice of the Notion of Aid, para. 58. Case T-139/09, *France v. Commission*, 27.9.2012, ECLI:EU:T:2012:496, paras 63-64). Assuming that the activities of undertakings benefiting from State aid were partially co-financed by other investors, including those operators themselves, that would in no way eliminate the State origin of the funds used by those undertakings. *See* Case T-8/18, *easyJet Airline v. Commission*, 13.5.2020, EU:T:2020:182, para. 104.
58. Case C-850/19 P, *FVE Holýšov I e.a. v. Commission*, 16.9.2021, EU:C:2021:740, para. 46.
59. *See* paras 36-39 of the judgment in *Pearle BV and others*, and Case C-677/11, *Doux Élevages SNC and Others* 30.5.2013, ECLI:EU:C:2013:348. In the latter case, the Court found that the State was simply acting as a 'vehicle' in order to make the contributions introduced by the trade organizations compulsory, for the purposes of pursuing the objectives established by those organizations (para. 40 of the ruling). *See also* Commission Decision in Case N 561/2008 – *Financement propre des organisations interprofessionnelles*, 17.5.2013, paras 25-33.
60. *See* para. 44 of the judgment in Case C-677/11, *Doux Élevages SNC and others*.

Moreover, in *EcoTLC*, the Court held that there was no use of State resources despite the contributions paid by companies under the so-called extended responsibility scheme had to be used in accordance with public interest objectives determined *ex ante* by public authorities, since the State: (i) did not have effective access to the funds and the entity in charge of the sums (i.e., the eco-body in charge of meeting waste treatment obligations demanded by law on behalf of producers of the products at issue) had no prerogatives of the public authority; and (ii) the funds were exclusively used for carrying out the tasks legally assigned to the eco-body, as determined by the national legislation (paragraph 41).[61]

In another case, where the French state had issued very favourable public statements in support of a certain company, the Court – overturning a Commission decision – has held that while the undertaking may have taken advantage of it, there was no reduction in the State budget or increase in the liabilities borne by the State.[62]

Article 107(1) TFEU does *not* cover in principle aid measures that lead to financial *redistribution* from one private entity to another without any further involvement of the State, if the money flows directly from one private entity to another, without passing through a public or private body designated by the State to administer the transfer.[63]

For example, an obligation imposed by a Member State on private electricity suppliers to purchase 'green' electricity at fixed minimum prices does not entail the direct or indirect transfer of State resources to undertakings which produce that type of electricity.[64] In this case, the undertakings concerned (i.e., the private electricity suppliers) are not appointed by the State to manage an aid scheme but are only bound

---

61. *See* case C-556/19, *Société Eco TLC v. Ministre de la Transition écologique et solidaire and Ministre de l'Économie et des Finances ('Eco TLC')*, 21.10.2020, ECLI:EU:C:2020:844. In particular, the Court stated that there is no transfer or use of State resources when the '*contributions remain private throughout their life cycle. The funds created by the payment of those contributions never pass through the State budget or that of another public entity, nor at any point do public authorities have access to them*' and '*the Member State in question has not relinquished any resources, in whatever form, such as taxes, duties, charges and so on, which, according to national legislation, should have been paid into the State budget*' (para. 33).
62. Joined Cases C-399/10 and 401/10 P, *Bouygues and Bouygues Télécom v. Commission*, paras 293 et seq. Judgment on appeal of T-425/04, *French Republic and Others v. Commission*, in turn in annulment of Commission Decision 2006/621, published in OJ 2006 L257, at p. 11.
63. Notice on the notion of State Aid, para. 61. *See* Case T-182/10, *AISCAT v. Commission*, 15.1.2013, ECLI:EU:T:2013:9, para. 105.
64. *See* Case C-379/98, *PreussenElektra* (paras 59-62): in the Court of Justice's view, the possible loss of tax revenues as a result of the application of a domestic measure, insofar as it is not the main purpose of the measure, but merely an 'inherent feature' thereof, does not amount to State aid. In the same vein, *see* the following Commission Decisions: Case NN 27/2000 *German Renewable Energy Law*, 22.5.2002; Case N 550/2000 *Green Electricity Certificates*, 25.7.2001; Case N 254/06 *Belgium Panneaux Photovoltaiques*, 24.10.2006, para. 10. *See also* Case T-182/10, *AISCAT v. Commission*, para. 105, where the sums corresponding to the result of the increase of the toll were paid directly to the beneficiary by private companies, without any public body thereby acquiring, if only transiently, possession or control. Similarly, in the latter case C 406/16 P, *European Medicines Agency v. Pari Pharma GmbH*, 18.10.2016, ECLI:EU:C:2016:775, the Court annulled the GC's ruling which had upheld the original Commission's decision qualifying the disputed scheme as State aid.

by an obligation to purchase a specific type of electricity with their own financial resources.[65]

A similar reasoning was applied by the Court in a case where national law placed an obligation on both private and public undertakings to purchase electricity produced by cogeneration, while national authorities could set the price of electricity produced by co-generation and the maximum electricity price for sales to end-users. The Court, in fact, stated that no transfer of State resources occurred as the electricity suppliers had to finance the purchase obligation imposed on them using their own financial resources, due to the circumstance that maximum electricity prices were fixed by law, while the collection of contributions from end-users to offset the additional costs was not required.[66]

In other cases, however, the Commission has deemed that green electricity purchase obligations do amount to 'State resources', where a part[67] or all the charges paid by private persons transit through a public or private entity designated by the State to channel them to the beneficiaries.[68] The same conclusion was reached by the Court in the *Achema* case, based on the following circumstances: (i) the contribution was compulsory for final consumers, self-producers of electricity and the network operators

65. *See* case C-329/15, *ENEA S.A.*
66. On the same line, in C 406/16 P, *European Medicines Agency,* the Court held that the national legislation: (a) did not implied transfer of State resources, as it did not impose a compulsory charge or a levy, since it did not require the operators concerned to pass on the costs to final consumers (*see* paras 65 to 71); (b) the State had no control or dominant influence over the disposal of the sums in questions, although the sums had been allocated exclusively to the financing of the scheme in question (*see* paras 74 to 76). *See also* Case T-745/18, *Covestro Deutschland AG v. Commission,* 6.10.2021, ECLI:EU:T:2021:644, where the General Court held that the exemption from electricity network surcharges was financed thought State resources, as the compensation mechanism established by the German scheme was a compulsory levy, as it was introduced by means of a regulatory measure and was binding on final customers, as the scheme obliged distribution system operators to pass on to those consumers the additional costs associated with the disputed surcharge. However, the Court did not find sufficient evidence to establish State control over the resources in question, which would have concerned '*the entire mechanism for levying the surcharge at issue and for allocating the revenue generated by that surcharge*'. The exclusive allocation of resources set ex ante by the law was thus '*tendered rather to show, in the absence of any other element to the contrary, that the State was precisely not in the position to dispose of those found, that is to say, to decide on an allocation other than that provided for in the legislative provisions in questions*'. Recently, the GC's judgment was upheld by the Court of Justice (joined Cases C-790/21 P and C-791/21 P, *Covestro Deutschland AG v. Commission* 26.9.2024, ECLI:EU:C:2024:792). *See also* Opinion of AG Op. Laila Medina in joined Cases C-790/21 P and C-791/21 P, *Covestro Deutschland AG v. Commission,* 9.11.2023, ECLI:EU:C:2023:849. *See also* case T-409/21, *Germany v. European Commission,* 24.1.2024, ECLI:EU:T:2024:34.
67. In Case C-262/12, *Association Vent De Colère! And Others v. Ministre de l'Économie, des Finances et de l'Industrie,* para. 27, the ECJ held that a mechanism for offsetting in full surcharges imposed by law on undertakings that is financed by final consumers may be considered an intervention through State resources, *even if not all the charges* transit through a public or private entity designated to channel them to the beneficiaries. In the same vein, *see* ECJ Order in Case C-275/13, *Elcogás v. Administración del Estado and Iberdrola SA,* 22.10.2014, ECLI:EU:C:2014:2314.
68. *See, inter alia,* Commission Decision in Cases NN 162/A/2003 and State aid N 317/A/2006 – *Austria (feed-in tariffs)*, 4.7.2006, paras 48-59; the decision was upheld in appeal by the General Court: Case T-251/11, *Austria v. Commission,* 11.12.2014, ECLI:EU:T:2014:1060.

collecting it, as the amount was set by the public body in charge of managing the contribution scheme; (ii) an entity directly controlled by the State managed the distribution of the funds.[69]

Resources coming from the Union (e.g., from structural funds) or international financial institutions, such as the IMF or the EBRD, should also be considered State resources if national authorities have discretion as to the use of those resources (in particular, the selection of beneficiaries).[70] By contrast, if such resources are awarded to the recipient directly by the Union[71] or the international financial institutions, with no discretion on the part of the national authorities, they do not constitute State resources.[72]

Still, in the Court of Justice's view, a negative indirect effect on State revenues (e.g., the possible loss of tax revenues) as a result of the application of a domestic measure, insofar as it is not the main purpose of the measure, but merely an 'inherent feature' thereof, does not amount to State aid.[73]

[2] From the Alternative Approach to the Cumulative Approach

The phrase 'by a Member State or through State resources' in paragraph 1 of Article 107 TFEU has been variously construed in EU case law over the years.

At first, the Commission and the Court interpreted this phrase in an *alternative sense*, i.e., more closely conforming to a literal construction of Article 107(1) TFEU. Thus, for a measure to qualify as aid, it was enough that it had been issued by a Member State even if in the absence of a consequent burden for that State's budget.[74]

Commencing in the early 1980s until the early 1990s, case law stood out for its lack of uniformity among judgments delivered on this matter. While some judgments

69. Judgment of the Court of 15.5.2019, *Achema*, C-706/17, ECLI:EU:C:2019:407. For a comprehensive review of this line of case law, *see*: BOUCHAGIAR A., *When Do Funds Become State Resources*, EStAL 1/2020, 19.
70. *See* Commission Decision in Case SA.32147, *Cable Car for London*, of 25.7.2012, para. 40: resources from the European Regional Development Fund – ERDF – which are transferred to the relevant national authority or body designated for that purpose by the Member State before being paid to the beneficiary are considered to be at the disposal of the national authorities and therefore amount to State resources.
71. Joined Cases 213-215/81, *Norddeutsches Vieh – und Fleischkontor*, 13.10.1982, ECLI:EU:C:1982:351, para. 22.
72. *See* Whereas No. 26 of Commission Regulation (EU) No. 651/2014. This is also the case for the Marco Polo programme: Regulation (EC) No. 1692/2006 (Marco Polo II), [2006] OJ L 328, p. 1.
73. Joined Cases C-72/91 and C-73/91, *Sloman Neptun*, para. 21; Case C-200/97, *Ecotrade S.r.l. v. AFS*, 1.12.1998, ECLI:EU:C:1998:579, para. 36 and Case C-379/98, *PreussenElektra*, para. 62.
74. *See* Case C-78/76, *Steinike & Weinlig* (para. 22) and Commission Decision 79/519/EEC, 18.5.1979 concerning the special financing scheme for investments to increase exporting firms' production capacity in France, OJ 1979 L138/30.

reiterated the alternative approach,[75] the Court ruled out some cases in which there was no direct or indirect burden for the State from the notion of aid.[76]

This phase of uncertainty came to an end in 1993, with the *Sloman Neptun* judgment, whereby the Court, in the face of the Commission's stance in favour of the alternative approach, referred to the *Van Tiggele* judgment to state clearly that:[77]

> only advantages which are granted directly or indirectly through State resources are to be regarded as State aid within the meaning of Article 92(1) of the EEC Treaty. The wording of this provision itself and the procedural rules laid down in Article 93 [now 108 TFEU] of the EEC Treaty show that advantages granted from resources other than those of the State do not fall within the scope of the provisions in question.

This approach was immediately restated in the *Kirsammer-Hack* judgment, where the Court further specified the following:[78]

> The distinction made [...] between aid granted 'by a Member State' and aid granted 'through State resources' does not signify that all advantages granted by a State, whether financed through State resources or not, constitute aid but is intended merely to bring within that definition both advantages which are granted directly by the State and those granted by a public or private body designated or established by the State.

The Commission tried again to call into question the Court's novel approach in the *PreussenElektra* case. In his final arguments in this proceeding, Advocate General Jacobs, while recognizing some value to the Commission's arguments in favour of a broader interpretation of the notion of aid, stated that financing through State resources remained a necessary element of the concept of State aid and recommended that the Court should conform to its own latest precedents.[79] And the Court complied.

The consecration of the *cumulative* approach is to be found in the *Stardust Marine* judgment, where the Court, in examining the two conditions of the imputability

75. Joined Cases 67/85, 68/85 and 70/85, *Van der Kooy BV and others v. Commission*, para. 35, and Case C-290/83, *'Crédit Agricole'*, para. 12: 'as is clear from the actual wording of Article 92 (1), aid need not necessarily be financed from state resources to be classified as state aid'.
76. Case C-82/77, *Ministère public of Kingdom of the Netherlands v. Jacobus Philippus van Tiggele*, 24.1.1978, ECLI:EU:C:1978:10, para. 25 and Joined Cases C-213/81 to C-215/81, *Norddeutsches Vieh – und Fleischkontor Herbert Will, Trawako, Transit – Warenhandels-Kontor GmbH & Co. and Gedelfi, Großeinkauf GmbH & Co. v. Bundesanstalt für landwirtschaftliche Marktordnung*, 13.10.1982, ECLI:EU:C:1982:351, paras 22-23.
77. Joined Cases C-72/91 and C-73/91, *Sloman Neptun*, para. 19.
78. *See* Case C-189/91, *Petra Kirsammer-Hack v. Nurhan Sidal*, 30.11.1993, ECLI:EU:C:1993:907, para. 16. In the same sense, *see* Joined Cases C-52/97 to C-54/97, *Viscido and others v. Ente Poste Italiane*, 7.5.1998, ECLI:EU:C:1998:209, para. 13; Case C-200/97, *Ecotrade S.r.l. v. AFS*, para. 35, and Case C-295/97, *Industrie Aeronautiche e Meccaniche Rinaldo Piaggio SpA v. International Factors Italia SpA (Ifitalia), Dornier Luftfahrt GmbH and Ministero della Difesa ('Piaggio')*, 17.6.1999, ECLI:EU:C:1999:313, para. 35; case C-677/11, *Doux Élevage and Coopérative agricole UKL-ARREE*, para. 26; case C-405/16 P, *Germany v. Commission*, 28.3.2019, ECLI: EU:C:2019:268, para. 57.
79. *See* Advocate General Jacobs' opinion of 26 Oct. 2000, paras 150-159, and the Court judgment in Case C-379/98, *PreussenElektra*, para. 58.

to the State and the transfer of State resources separately for the first time, expressly held that:

> for advantages to be capable of being categorized as aid within the meaning of Article 107(1) TFEU, they must, first, be granted directly or indirectly through State resources [...] and, second, be imputable to the State.[80]
>
> In particular, the Court held that the distinction between 'aid granted by a Member State' and aid granted 'through State resources' does not signify that all advantages granted by a State, whether financed through State resources or not, constitute aid, 'but is intended merely to bring within that definition both advantages which are granted directly by the State and those granted by a public or private body designated or established by the State'.[81]
>
> In summary, following the Court's interpretation, for a public measure to be classified as State aid, it must be both imputable to the State and involve a transfer of State resources. This includes not only direct funding from public budgets but also private funds under State control or financed through compulsory levies managed according to national legislation.[82]

[B] The Gratuitous Advantage

[1] The Aid Recipient: The Notion of 'Undertaking'

Within the meaning and for the purposes of Article 107 TFEU, the aid recipient must be an 'undertaking'. As the Treaty does not contain a definition of *undertaking*, EU case law has provided one, by stating that such classification applies to every entity engaged in an *economic activity*, regardless of its legal status and the way in which it is financed.[83]

80. Case C-482/99, *'Stardust Marine'*, para. 24.
81. Case C-379/98, *PreussenElektra*, 13.3.2001, EU:C:2001:160, para. 58; case C-222/07, *UTECA*, 5.3.2004, EU:C:2009:124, para. 34; case C-297/08 P, *Commission v. Netherlands*, 8.9.2011, EU:C:2011:551, para. 105; case C-677/11, *Doux Elevage and Others*, 30.5.2013, EU:C:2013:348, para. 26; T-468/08, *Tisza Erőmű v. Commission*, 30.4.2014, EU:T:2014:235, para. 167; C-405/16 P, *Germany v. Commission*, 28.3.2019, EU:C:2018:268, para. 53; C-179/20, *Fondul Proprietatea SA v. Guvernul României*, 27.1.2022, EU:C:2022:58, para. 91.
82. See more recently T-409/21, *Germany v European Commission*, 24.1.2024, ECLI:EU:T:2024:34
83. Case C-41/90, *Höfner and Elser v. Macroton*, 23.4.1991, ECLI:EU:C:1991:161, para. 21; Case C-35/95, *Commission v. Italy*, 9.7.1997, ECLI:EU:C:1997:344, para. 36, and Joined Cases C-264/01, C-306/01, C-354/01 and C-355/01, *AOK Bundesverband and Others v. Ichthyol-Gesellschaft Cordes and Others*, 16.3.2004, ECLI:EU:C:2004:150, para. 46; Case C-288/11 P, *Mitteldeutsche Flughafen and Flughafen Leipzig-Halle v. Commission*, 19.12.2012, ECLI: EU:C:2012:821, para. 50). The classification as an 'undertaking', within the meaning of Art. 107(1) TFEU, cannot be made conditional on the occurrence of uncertain circumstances subsequent to the granting of the advantage concerned, such as that consisting in the use of the good acquired for economic purposes, given the *ex ante* nature of State aid compatibility analysis. *See* C-325/22, *TS and HI v. Ministar na zemedelieto, hranite i gorite*, 19.10.2023, EU:C:2023:793, case 32.

Any activity consisting of supplying goods or services in a market is an *economic activity*.[84] As the ECJ clarified, whether or not an activity is economic in nature does not depend on the private or public status of the entity engaged in it or the profitability of that activity.[85]

Since the classification of a particular entity as an undertaking depends entirely on the nature of its activities, also members of liberal professions are, therefore, undertakings for the purposes of Article 107 TFEU, given that they carry on an economic activity, providing services against remuneration and assuming the financial risks related to the exercise of that activity.[86]

At the same time, as the Court of Justice held, neither the absence of profit-making purposes nor the fact that a social objective is pursued, or the presence of solidarity elements or of restrictions on, or control over, investments are sufficient to deprive the activities so engaged in of their quality as economic activities.[87]

Moreover, there is nothing to preclude an economic activity being carried out by a State body, irrespective of the position of that body in the organization of the State, whether it belongs to the central administration or whether it is a decentralized entity. In fact, nothing prevents the exercise of an economic activity from being integrated into the context of public administration organizations, and a public entity can be the recipient of State aid once the undertaking is active in the marketplace.[88]

On the contrary, levying a contribution does not, by itself, result in the application of competition regulations to the recipient undertaking if such a contribution is intended to fund an activity of general interest.[89]

In fact, the classification of an entity as an undertaking is always in relation to specific activities, so if an entity carries out both non-economic economic and

84. Case C-35/95, *Commission v. Italy*, para. 36 and Joined Cases C-180/98 to C-184/98, *Pavlov and Others v. Stichting Pensioenfonds Medische Specialisten*, 12.9.2000, ECLI:EU:C:2000:428, para. 75.
85. Case C-288/11 P, *Mitteldeutsche Flughafen AG*, para. 50.
86. Case C-309/99, *Wouters, Savelbergh and Price Waterhouse Belasting Belastingadviseurs BV v. Algemene Raad van de Nederlandse Orde van Advocaten*, 12.2.2002, ECLI:EU:C:2002:98, para. 38; Joined Cases C-180/98 to C-184/98 *Pavlov and Others*, para. 76; and Case C-1/12, *Ordem dos Técnicos Oficiais de Contas v. Autoridade da Concorrência*, 28.10.2013, ECLI:EU:C:2013:127 paras 37-38.
87. Joined Cases C-115/97, C-116/97 and C-117/97, *Brentjens 'Handelsonderneming BV v. Stichting Bedrijfspensioenfonds voor de Handel in Bouwmaterialen*, 21.9.1999, ECLI:EU:C:1999:434, paras 85-86; Case C-49/07, *Motosykletistiki Omospondia Ellados NPID (MOTOE) v. Elliniko Dimosio*, 1.7.2008, ECLI:EU:C:2008:376, paras 27-28; Case C-1/12 *Ordem dos Técnicos Oficiais de Contas*.
88. Case T-165/15, *Ryan Air and Airport Marketing Services v. Commission*, 13 Dec. 2018, EU:T:2018:953. In any case, The fact that a product or a service supplied by a public entity and connected to the exercise by it of public powers is provided in return for remuneration laid down by law and not determined, directly or indirectly, by that entity, is not alone sufficient for the activity carried out to be classified as an economic activity and the entity which carries it out as an undertaking. By contrast, services which, without forming part of the exercise of public powers, are carried out in the public interest and without a profit motive and are in competition with those offered by operators pursuing a profit motive have been classified as economic activities. *See* case T-138/15, *Aanbestedingskalender and Others v. Commission*, 28.9.2017, EU:T:2017:675, paras 36-37.
89. Case C-343/95, *Diego Calì & Figli S.r.l. v. Servizi ecologici porto di Genova S.p.A.*, 18.3.1997, ECLI:EU:C:1997:160.

economic activities it is considered an undertaking with regard to the latter. However, if the economic activity is purely ancillary to the non-economic operations those mixed activities fall outside the State aid rules.[90]

This was the case of the Italian banking foundations, which the Commission deemed to be not 'undertakings' within the meaning of Article 107(1) TFEU.[91] Yet, the Court of Justice has specified that:

> merely splitting an undertaking into two separate entities, one with the task of carrying on economic activities, the other with the task of controlling it by intervening in its management would be enough to deprive the EU rules on State aid of their practical effectiveness. This would allow the latter entity to benefit from subsidies or other advantages granted by the State or through State resources, and to use all or some of them for the former entity's benefit, in the interest of the economic entity made of both.[92]

The ECJ added that a banking foundation may well be categorized as an 'undertaking' within the meaning of Article 107(1) TFEU – and be subject, as such, to the EU provisions on State aid – if it is in a position, in taking direct actions in the areas of public interest and social utility, to supply goods or services in the market, in competition with other traders, for example, in such sectors as scientific research, education, the arts or healthcare.[93]

Moreover, in the presence of controlling share and other functional, economic and organic links, separate legal entities may be considered by the ECJ to form one economic unit that is the relevant undertaking for the purposes of the application of State aid rules.[94]

The Commission underlined that the question of whether a market exists for certain goods and services may depend on the way those services are organized in the Member State concerned and may thus vary from one Member State to another and also in the same Member State, in case of a change over time of the classification of a given activity.[95]

---

90. Notice on the notion of State Aid, para. 207. There is no precise threshold, expressed in percentage terms or in absolute terms, of non-economic activities carried out by an entity required to categorize it as entirely non-economic. *See* Case T-747/17 *Union des Ports de France v. Commission*, 30.4.2019, ECLI:EU:T:2019:271, para. 83; Case C-74/16 *Congregacion de Escuelas Pias Provincia Betania*, 27.7.2017, ECLI:EU:C:2017:496, paras 44-63.
91. Commission Decision 2003/146/EC of 22 Aug. 2002 on the tax measures for banking foundations implemented by Italy, OJ 2003 L55/56. The tax measures in favour of banking foundations were introduced by Art. 12, para. 2, of Legislative Decree No. 153/99.
92. Case C-222/04, *Ministero dell'Economia e delle Finanze v. Cassa di Risparmio di Firenze S.p.A. and others* 10.1.2006, ECLI:EU:C:2006:8, para. 114. The ECJ did not answer on the validity of Commission Decision 2003/146/EC and left the national judge to determine whether the foundation at issue (*i*) held controlling shareholdings in a banking company; and (*ii*) actually exercised that control by involving itself directly or indirectly in the management of the latter (para. 118).
93. *Ibid.*, paras 121-125.
94. Case C-480/09 P, *AceaElectrabel Produzione SpA v. Commission*, 16.12.2010, ECLI: EU:C:2010:787, paras 47-55; Case C-222/04, *Cassa di Risparmio di Firenze S.p.A. and others*, para. 112.
95. Notice on the notion of State Aid, para. 13.

In the Commission's view, the existence of a market cannot be ruled out by a decision of a public authority not to allow third parties to provide a certain service, since an economic activity can nevertheless exist if other operators would be willing and able to provide the service in the market concerned.[96]

[2] Economic Activities

In the absence of a definition of economic activity in the Treaties, there is no exhaustive list of activities that *a priori* would never be economic; nevertheless, in light of the ECJ case law and of the Commission's precedents, it is possible to draw the following conclusions.

[a] Exercise of Public Powers

Where the State acts 'by exercising public power'[97] or where public entities act 'in their capacity as public authorities',[98] Article 107 TFEU does not apply.

This is the case where the activities performed are part of the essential functions of the State and are connected with those functions by its nature, its aim and the rules to which it is subject, such as, among others, the army and the police,[99] the environmental protection,[100] air navigation and maritime traffic safety and control,[101] anti-pollution surveillance activities.[102]

In the Notice on the Notion of State aid, the Commission clarified that such activities are not of an economic nature unless the Member State concerned has decided to introduce market mechanisms.[103]

According to the ECJ case law, in so far as a public entity exercises an economic activity which can be separated from the exercise of its public powers, that entity, in relation to that activity, acts as an undertaking; on the contrary, if that economic activity cannot be separated from the exercise of its public powers, the activities

96. *Ibid.* (para. 14).
97. Case C-118/85, *Commission v. Italy*, paras 7-8; Case C-364/92 *SAT Fluggesellschaft v. Eurocontrol*, 19.1.1994, ECLI:EU:C:1994:7, para. 30; Case C-113/07 P, *SELEX Sistemi Integrati v. Commission and Eurocontrol*, 26.3.2009, ECLI:EU:C:2009:191, para. 70; Joined Cases T-231/06 and T-237/06, *Kingdom of the Netherlands and Nederlandse Omroep Stichting (NOS) v. Commission*, 16.12.2010, ECLI:EU:T:2010:525, para. 93.
98. Case C-30/87, *Bodson*, para. 18.
99. Commission Decision of 7 Dec. 2011, Case SA.32820 (2011/NN) – *United Kingdom – Aid to Forensic Science Services*, OJ C 29, 2.2.2012, p. 4 (para. 8).
100. Commission Decision of 30.5.2007, Case N 46/2007 – *Welsh Public Sector Network Scheme – UK*, OJ C 157, 10.7.2007.
101. Commission Decision of 16 Oct. 2002, Case N 438/02 – *Belgium – Aid to port authorities*, OJ C 284, 21.11.2002, p. 2.
102. Case C-343/95, *Calì & Figli*, para. 22. Other activities include: the organization, financing and enforcement of prison sentences; the development and revitalization of public land by public authorities; and the collection of data to be used for public purposes on the basis of a statutory obligation imposed on the undertakings concerned to disclose such data. *See* Notice on the notion of State aid, para. 17.
103. *Ibid.*, para. 17.

exercised by that entity as a whole remain activities connected with the exercise of those public powers.[104]

[b] *Social Security*

According to the ECJ case law, aid schemes in the area of social security do not involve an economic activity if they are supervised by the State[105] and based on the principle of solidarity, that is if those schemes pursue an exclusively social purpose, if the affiliation with them is compulsory and the benefits paid are statutory benefits, bearing no relation to the amount of the contributions or to the earnings insured persons.[106] If they combine features that are typical of economic activities (such as optional membership, the principle of capitalization, profit-making nature and provision of supplementary entitlements), the classification of the scheme depends on the analysis of the different elements and their respective importance.[107]

[c] *Health Care*

The existence of a market for health care services depends on national specificities, given that the systems differ significantly between Member States.

According to ECJ case law, organizations managing health funds do not act as undertakings when they are an integral part of a national health service almost entirely based on the principle of solidarity and they are directly funded from social contributions and other State resources and if provide their services free of charge on the basis of universal coverage.[108] In such systems also the activities of an economic nature, carried out merely for the purpose of providing non-economic services, do not constitute an economic activity.[109]

On the contrary, if health care providers offer their services for remuneration, there is competition between such providers and, therefore, even if health services are provided by a public hospital, the presence of a market for health care cannot be ruled

104. Case T-747/17 *Union des Ports de France v. Commission*, 30.4.2019, ECLI:EU:T:2019:271; Case C-138/11, *Compass – Datenbank GmbH v. Republik Österreich*, 12.7.2012, ECLI: EU:C:2012:449, para. 38, and Case C-113/07 P, *SELEX Sistemi Integrati v. Commission*, para. 72.
105. Joined Cases C-159/91 and C-160/91, *Poucet and Pistre v. AGF and Cancava*, 17.2.1993, ECLI:EU:C:1993:63, para. 14; Case C-218/00, *Cisal di Battistello Venanzio & C. Sas v. Istituto nazionale per l'assicurazione contro gli infortuni sul lavoro (INAIL)*, 21.1.2002, ECLI: EU:C:2002:36, paras 43-48; Joined Cases C-264/01, C-306/01, C-354/01 and C-355/01, *AOK Bundesverband and others*, paras 51-55); case C-687/17 P, *Aanbestedingskalender and Others v. Commission*, 7.11.2019, EU:C:2019:932, paras 15-17.
106. Joined Cases C-159/91 and C-160/91, *Poucet and Pistre*, paras 15-18; and Case C-218/00, *Cisal*, para. 40. Joined Cases C-264/01, C-306/01, C-354/01 and C-355/01, *AOK Bundesverband and others*, para. 47.
107. Notice on the notion of State aid, para. 21, 22. Case C-350/07, *Kattner Stahlbau*, 5.3.2009, ECLI:EU:C:2009:127, paras 33 et seq.
108. Joined Cases C-159/91 and C-160/91, *Poucet and Pistre*, paras 15 and 18; Case T-319/99, *Fenin v. Commission*, 4.3.2003, ECLI:EU:T:2003:50, paras 38-39; and Joined Cases C-264/01, C-306/01, C-354/01 and C-355/01, *AOK Bundesverband and others*, paras 47-51.
109. Case T- 319/99, *Fenin v. Commission*, para. 37.

out.[110] Similarly, health care services provided for remuneration by independent doctors, pharmacies and other private practitioners at their own risk are to be regarded as an economic activity.[111]

[d] Education and Research Activities

Public education organized within the national educational system funded and supervised by the State may be considered a non-economic activity, even where tuition and enrolment fees are requested to contribute to the operating expenses of the system. In such a system, in fact, Member States are not seeking to engage in a profitable activity but they are merely fulfilling their duties towards their community in the social, cultural and educational fields.[112]

By contrast, the ECJ has held that courses provided by establishments financed essentially by private funds, particularly by pupils and their parents, constitute services, the aim of such establishments being to offer a service for remuneration.[113]

In light of the ECJ case law, the Commission clarified that the primary activities of universities and research organizations[114] fall outside the ambit of the State aid rules, including knowledge transfer activities (licensing, creation of spin-off, etc.), where they are conducted by or jointly with the research organization or infrastructure (or jointly with, or on behalf of other such entities) and all income from those activities is reinvested in the primary activities of the research organizations or infrastructures concerned. Likewise, in a recent case, the digitalization of books by libraries has been held not to constitute an economic activity.[115]

---

110. Notice on the notion of State aid, para. 26. However, undue significance cannot be attributed to the fact that, within a national health system, health care providers or health insurance companies seek profit and face a certain degree of competition, if the system operates according to principles of solidarity and it is under State control. In such cases, EU Courts have nonetheless qualified the systems as 'non economic'. *See* Joined Cases C-262/18 P and C-272/18 P *Dovera v. Commission*, 11.6.2020, ECLI:EU:C:2020:450; Case T-223/18, *Casa Regina Apostolorum della Pia Società delle Figlie di San Paolo v. Commission*, 2.6.2021, ECLI:EU:T:2021:315. See also Commission Decision in Case SA.45844(2016/FC)-*Slovenie*, OJ C,C/2024/4421,11.7.2024.
111. Notice on the notion of State aid, para. 27.
112. *See* Case C-318/05, *Commission v. Germany*, 11.9.2007, ECLI:EU:C:2007:495, para. 68; Case C-109/92, *Stephan Max Wirth v. Landeshauptstadt Hannover*, 7.12.1993, ECLI:EU:C:1993:916, paras 15-16; and Case C-263/86, *Belgium v. René Humbel and Marie- Th érèse Edel*, 27.9.1988, ECLI:EU:C:1988:451, paras 17-18.
113. *See* Case C-318/05, *Commission v. Germany*, para. 69 and Case C-109/92. *Stephan Max Wirth v. Landeshauptstadt Hannover*, para. 17.
114. Such as: (a) education for more and better skilled human resources; (b) the conduct of independent research and development for more knowledge and better understanding, including collaborative research and development; and (c) the dissemination of research results. *See* para. 32 of the in the Draft Notice on the notion of State aid.
115. Commission Decision of 3 Jul. 2013, Case SA.35529 – *Libraries in the Czech Republic.*

[e] Infrastructure

In order to fall within the application of the State aid rules, public funding has to be directed to commercially exploited infrastructures.

In fact, where the infrastructures are used exclusively (or also almost exclusively)[116] for a non-economic activity (i.e.: general infrastructures, such as public roads, bridges or canals, which are made available for public use without any consideration) or for activities that the State normally performs in the exercise of its public powers (such as air traffic control-related infrastructure in airports, lighthouses and other equipment for the needs of general navigation, police and customs-related infrastructure) their public funding is in principle excluded from the application of the State aid rules.

If an infrastructure is used for both economic and non-economic activities, public funding falls under the State aid rules only to the extent that it covers the costs related to the economic activities. In such cases, Member States must ensure that public funding for non-economic activities is not used to cross-subsidize economic activities, e.g., by limiting public funding to the net cost (including the cost of capital) of the non-economic activities, to be determined on the basis of a clear separation of accounts.[117] In case of conversion of a non-economic infrastructure into an economic one, the costs incurred for the conversion of the infrastructure to economic use will be taken into account for the assessment under the State aid rules.[118]

It has to be highlighted that the approach to the public financing of infrastructures was different since it was considered a general measure of public policy and not an economic activity.[119] Such an approach was changed by the General Court in 2000 when it declared – in the *Aéroports de Paris* judgment[120] – that the operation of an airport constitutes an economic activity of which – as the General Court clarified in

116. Provided that the economic use remains purely ancillary that is when the activity is directly related to (and necessary for) the operation of the infrastructure, or intrinsically linked to its main non-economic use. On the contrary, if an infrastructure is used for both economic and non-economic activities, according to the Notice on the Notion of State Aid 'public funding will fall under the State aid rules only insofar as it covers the costs linked to the economic activities. When it is possible to separate the costs and revenues corresponding to the economic and non-economic activities, the State aid rules shall only apply with regard to the State support granted in excess of the amount covering the costs of the non-economic activities'. *See* para. 207 of the Notice on the notion of State aid.
117. *See* Notice on the notion of State aid, paras 206, 207.
118. *See* Notice on the notion of State aid para. 204 and Commission Decision in Case SA.23324 – *Tampere – Pirkkala Airport*, OJ L309, 13.11.2013, p. 27.
119. For example, in the Guidelines on the 'Application of Article 92 and 93 of the EC Treaty and Article 61 of the EEA Agreement to State aids in the aviation sector', OJ C 350, 10.12.1994, p. 5, (para. 12) the Commission stated that '[t]he construction [or] enlargement of infrastructure projects (such as airports, motorways, bridges, etc.) represents a general measure of economic policy which cannot be controlled by the Commission under the Treaty rules on State aids'.
120. Case T-128/98, *Aéroports de Paris v. Commission*, 12.12.2000, ECLI:EU:T:2000:290, para. 125, confirmed by the Court of Justice, Case C-82/01 P, *Aéroports de Paris v. Commission*, 24.10.2002, ECLI:EU:C:2002:617. The General Court confirmed this conclusion in Case T-196/04, *Ryanair v. Commission*, 17.12.2008, ECLI:EU:T:2008:585, para. 88.

2011 in the *Leipzig/Halle airport* judgment – the construction of airport infrastructure is an inseparable part.[121]

Against this background and in the light of the uncertainty that existed prior to the '*Aéroports de Paris*' judgment, the Commission clarified that financing measures granted before the '*Aéroports de Paris*' judgment will not be brought into question on the basis of State aid rules.[122]

In light of the above, the Notice thus provides an overview sector-by-sector of the general principles applicable to the assessment of aid to the developer/owner of an infrastructure.[123] For instance, funding of airports used for the provision of services to airlines against payment or non-aeronautical commercial services, is subject to State aid rules, while funding to activities that fall under the responsibility of the State in the exercise of its public powers does not fall under the State aid rules (e.g., air traffic control, aircraft rescue and firefighting, police, customs, etc.).[124]

[3] The Gratuitous Advantage Concept

Article 107(1) TFEU prohibits advantages that favour specific undertakings. The 'advantage' notion includes any economic benefits the recipient undertaking would not have obtained under normal market conditions,[125] in particular:

(1) interventions that mitigate the charges which are *normally* included in the budget of an undertaking, thereby preventing market forces from having their normal effect;[126] and
(2) measures simultaneously implying obligations and advantages for the recipient where there is a bias towards advantages.

121. Joined Cases T-443/08 and T-455/08, *Mitteldeutsche Flughafen AG and Flughafen Leipzig Halle GmbH v. Commission* ('*Leipzig-Halle airport*') [2011] ECR II-1311, in particular paras 93-94; confirmed by the Court of Justice in Case C-288/11 P, *Mitteldeutsche Flughafen AG*, 19.12.2012, ECLI:EU:C:2012:821.
122. *See* the Commission Guidelines on State aid to airports and airlines 2014 C 99/03 (para. 29) and Notice on the notion of State aid (para. 209). *See also* Decision C 38/2008 of 3 Oct. 2012 on Munich airport Terminal 2, OJ L 319, 29.11.2013, p. 8 (paras 74-81).
123. Notice on the notion of State aid, paras 213 et seq.
124. Notice on the notion of State aid, para. 214. Similar principles apply to port infrastructures (*ibid.*, para. 215). The Court specified that even if the port infrastructure was not developed in order to benefit a particular undertaking nor awarded to it, that finding does not rule out the possibility that the conditions under which that infrastructure is made available to that undertaking for commercial use may involve a grant of State aid to it. *See* case T-108/16 Naviera Armas, 15.3.2018, ECLI:EU:T:2018:145; *see also* C-518/13 *Eventech*.
125. Case C-39/94, *Syndicat français de l'Express international (SFEI) v. La Poste and Others*, 11.7.1996, ECLI:EU:C:1996:285, para. 60; and Case C-342/96, *Spain v. Commission*, para. 41; Case C-280/00, *Altmark Trans*, para. 84, Case C-279/08 P, *Commission v. Netherlands*, para. 87 and Case C-559/12 P, *France v. European Commission*, para. 94.
126. Case C-301/87, *France v. Commission*, 14.2.1990, ECLI:EU:C:1990:67, para. 41; and Case C-342/96, *Spain v. Commission*, para. 42.

Therefore, for the *gratuitousness* factor to be established, each case should be scrutinized separately, starting from the state of competition before the adoption of the State measure granting the benefit was issued.[127]

The 'advantage' consists of the preferential treatment accorded to the recipient over competitors in the same position in fact and in law that carry on similar activities, without: (a) the Member State in which they are established;[128] or (b) the fact that the advantage conferred would not place the beneficiaries in a position as favourable as that of their competitors from other Member States[129] having any relevance.[130]

Even in terms of gratuitous advantage, EU Courts have been constantly stressing the irrelevance: (i) of the form an intervention may take;[131] (ii) of its legal nature or cause;[132] (iii) of the objective it is intended to pursue as well as the irrelevance; and (iv) of the compulsory or voluntary nature of the measure.[133]

Compensation by the State of costs arising from regulatory obligations imposed on an undertaking confers an advantage, as they are deemed to relate to the inherent costs of the economic activity; however, an advantage is not present in the case of reimbursement of illegally levied taxes, compensation for damage caused by national authorities to certain undertakings or the payment of compensation for expropriation.[134]

The only relevant factor is therefore the result (the *effect*) of that intervention:[135] in case the effect is placing the recipient, by means of State resources, in a more favourable position than that of its competitors there is an advantage.[136]

The advantage may be granted also indirectly where the benefit is conferred on undertakings other than the direct recipient of the State resources;[137] also if the direct

127. Case C-173/73, *Italy v. Commission*, para. 17.
128. *See* opinion of Advocate General Cosmas in Case C-353/95 P, *Tiercé Ladbroke v. Commission*, 13.5.1997, ECLI:EU:C:1997:233, para. 25.
129. Case T-55/99, *CETM v. Commission*, 29.9.2000, ECLI:EU:T:2000:223, para. 85.
130. Notice on the notion of State aid, para. 72.
131. Case C-280/00, *Altmark Trans*, para. 84.
132. Case C-173/73, *Italy v. Commission*, para. 13.
133. Opinion of Advocate General Fennelly, Case C-251/97, *France v. Commission*, 26.11.1998, ECLI:EU:C:1998:572, para. 26; and Commission Decision 2004/339/EC of 15 Oct. 2003 on the measures implemented by Italy for RAI SpA, OJ 2004 L119, 23.4.2004, p. 1, recital 69.
134. Notice on the notion of State aid, para. 69, 71. For instance, the costs of complying with regulatory obligations for the protection of the environment, in particular that of wild fauna, and responsibility for the damage, which the latter may cause to an undertaking in the aquaculture sector, are part of the normal operating costs of such an undertaking. Therefore, the grant of compensation for damage caused to its undertaking by protected animals constitutes an economic advantage to which the undertaking concerned cannot in principle be entitled under normal market conditions. *See* case C-238/20, *'Satiņi-S' SIA*, 27.1.2022, EU:C:2022:57, para. 44.
135. Advocate General Ruiz-Jarabo Colomer's opinion, Case C-6/97, *Italy v. Commission*, 17.9.1998, of 17 Sep. 1998, ECLI:EU:C:1998:416, para. 22; Case C-173/73, *Italy v. Commission*, para. 13; and Case 30/59, *De Gezamenlijke Steenkolenmijnen in Limburg v. High Authority*, para. 19.
136. Case C-124/10 P, *Commission v. EDF*, 5.6.2012, ECLI:EU:C:2012:318, para. 90; Case C-387/92, *Banco Exterior de España*, para. 14; and Case C-6/97, *Italy v. Commission*, para. 16.
137. Case T-424/05, *Italy v. Commission*, 4.3.2009, ECLI:EU:T:2009:49, paras 136-146.

beneficiaries are not engaged in any economic activity (such as, for instance, consumers), the measure may nonetheless constitute indirect aid to economic operators.[138]

The Commission clarified that indirect advantages should be distinguished from mere secondary economic effects that are inherent in almost all State aid measures (as, for instance, through an increase in output). '*An indirect advantage is present if the measure is designed in such a way so as to channel its secondary effects towards identifiable undertakings or groups of undertakings. This is the case, for example, if the direct aid is, de facto or de jure, made conditional on the purchase of goods or services produced by certain undertakings only (e.g., only undertakings established in certain areas).*'[139] Likewise, for the purposes of that determination of the advantage, the Commission must not take into account any advantages that the beneficiaries may have indirectly derived from that aid, such as the alleged competitive advantage.[140]

[4] The Market Economy Operator Test

The key criterion to assess whether a gratuitous advantage exists – thus to establish whether a State measure indirectly amounts to State aid – is a hypothetical assessment of the behaviour of *private economic operators under normal market conditions.*[141]

If in a certain transaction, the State acts like a market economy operator no gratuitous advantage is granted, since the transaction would have been executed at similar conditions even without the intervention of the State and, therefore, State aid is ruled out.[142]

---

138. Case C-403/10 P, *Mediaset Spa v. Commission*, 28.6.2011, ECLI:EU:C:2011:533, para. 81. Case C-403/10 P, *Mediaset Spa v. Commission* [2011] ECR I-117 (para. 81). However, in the case of reductions in employees' contributions granted by a Member State to salaried employees, which are not borne by undertakings in their capacity as employers, but are payable by the employees (i.e., through a deduction of those contributions from the remunerations of the employees on each salary slip), the actual beneficiaries of those reductions are the employees. *See* case C-212/19, *Compagnie des pêches de Saint-Malo*, 17.9.2020, EU:C:2020:726, paras 42-51.
139. Notice on the notion of State aid, para. 117.
140. Case C-210/21 P, *Ryanair DAC v. Commission*, 23.11.2023, EU:C:2023:908, para. 99.
141. However, the applicability of the Market Economy Operator Test is excluded if there is no possibility of comparing the State conduct at issue in a particular case with that of a private operator. This can occur, for instance, when the conduct at issue is inextricably linked to the existence of an infrastructure which no private operator would ever have been able to create, or if the State is acting in its capacity as a public authority. *See* T-196/04, *Ryanair*, 17.12.2008, ECLI:EU:T:2008:585, para. 85; Case 234/84, *Meura*, 10.7.1986, ECLI:EU:C:1986:302; Case 40/85 *Boch II*, ECLI:EU:C:1986:305; Case T-156/04, *Electricitè de France v. Commission*, 15.12.2009, ECLI:EU:T:2009:505; Joined Cases C-278/92 to C-280/92, *Spain v. Commission*, 14.9.1994, ECLI:EU:C:1994:325; Joined cases C-331/20 P and C-343/20 P, *Volotea SA and Easy Jet Airline Co. Ltd. v. Commission*, 17.11.2019, ECLI:EU:C:2022:886, where the Court held that measures have to be examined disregarding the public interest objectives inherent in the State intervention and the benefits linked to the State position as a public authority which are likely to arise from implementing those objectives. Moreover, the MEOP cannot be applied in order to asses State's compensatory measures intended to prevent distortion of competition, following a previous Commission's decision; *see* case C-127/16 P, *SNCF v. Commission*.
142. The applicability of the test is not ruled out, instead, by the mere fact that the recipient undertaking has benefitted from aid in the past, as the new measure must be separated from the

On the contrary, if the beneficiary undertaking has received an economic advantage which it would not have obtained under normal market conditions,[143] placing it in a more favourable position to that of its competitors, an advantage under Article 107 TFEU exists.

In particular, the concept of 'normal market conditions' refers to the possibility for the undertaking to obtain on the market the same advantage as that which it derives from the aid, and not to the assessment of whether the market is functioning normally or whether it is in crisis.[144]

The criterion of a private economic operator's behaviour is nothing but a corollary of equal treatment of public and private ownership under Article 345 TFEU and it has been developed over the years by the Commission[145] and the Union Courts[146] to assess whether a transaction carried out by a public body involves State aid with regard to different economic transactions, to wit:

(1) the '*market economy investor principle*' ('MEOP'), to assess, in cases of public investment (in particular, capital injections), whether a private investor of a comparable size operating in normal conditions of a market economy could have been prompted to make the investment in question;
(2) the '*private creditor principle*', to assess, in cases where the State acts in a creditor's capacity, whether the debtor would have received the same treatment by a private-creditor; and

aid. *See* T-11/95, *BP Chemicals*, 15.9.1998, ECLI:EU:T:1998:199; C-224/12 P *Commission v. Netherlands and ING*, 3.4.2014, ECLI:EU:C:2014:213.

143. Case C-522/13, *Ministerio de Defensa and Navantia SA v. Concello de Ferrol*, 9.10.2014, ECLI:EU:C:2014:2262, para. 21, Case C-206/06, *Essent Netwerk Noord and Others*, para. 79; and Case C-451/03, *Servizi Ausiliari Dottori Commercialisti v. Giuseppe Calafiori*, 30.3.2006, ECLI:EU:C:2006:208, para. 59.

144. Case T-850/19, *Greece v. Commission*, 19.10.2022, EU:T:2022:638, paras 46, 47.

145. The criterion was first adopted in Commission Decision 81/2330/ECSC [1981] OJ L228/14. It was expanded in the Commission Communication to the Member States concerning public authorities' holdings in company capital, *Bulletin* EC 9-1984 and then further expanded in the Commission Communication to the Member States – Application of Arts 92 and 93 of the EEC Treaty and of Art. 5 of Commission Directive 80/723/EEC to public undertakings in the manufacturing sector, OJ 1993 C307/3.

146. Case C-39/94, *SFEI and others*, para. 60. The Court further clarified that 'normal market conditions', which are necessarily hypothetical, must be assessed by reference to the objective and verifiable elements which are available. *See* Case C-94/01 P, *Chronopost SA, La Poste and France v. Ufex, DHL International Federal Express International and CRIE*, 3.7.2003, ECLI:EU:C:2003:388, para. 38. In addition, the private investor principle must be applied strictly *ex ante*: according to the Court, 'it is necessary to place oneself in the context of the period during which the financial support measures were taken in order to assess the economic rationality of the State's conduct, and thus to refrain from any assessment based on a later situation'. *See* Case C-482/99, *'Stardust Marine'*, para. 71; and Case C-124/10 P, *Commission v. EDF*, para. 105. On the burden of proof in the MEOP test *see also* Case C-300/16 P, *Frucona Kosice II*, 20.9.2017, ECLI:EU:C:2017:706; case T-423/14, *Larko*, 1.2.2018, ECLI:EU:T:2018:57; case T-100/17, *BTP Holding Investments and Duferco Participations Holdings SA v. Commission*, 11.12.2019, ECLI:EU:T:2018:900.

(3) the *'private vendor principle'*, to assess, in cases of sales carried out by a public body, whether a private vendor, under normal market conditions, could have obtained the same or a better price.

More recently, the Court analysed the application of the MEOP test with reference to acquiring transactions, setting out the main criteria that should be taken into account when assessing whether the services or goods were acquired under normal market conditions: the rationality of such a transaction, its foreseeable prospects of profitability, the commercial and economic interests of the services to be provided for that purpose, the price to be paid for them and the legal and practical arrangements by which the contracts governing the provisions of those services and the payment of that price were concluded.[147]

As for the burden of proof, it is for the Commission to prove that the public authority has not acted in accordance with the MEOP.[148] In particular, the examination of the applicability of the private operator principle must be distinguished from the examination of the application of that principle. Where there are doubts as to the applicability of that principle, in particular, because of the use by the Member State concerned, at the time the measure at issue was adopted, of its powers of public authority, the Member State must establish unequivocally and on the basis of objective and verifiable evidence that the measure implemented falls to be ascribed to the State acting as a private operator. By contrast, when the private operator principle is applicable, it is one of the factors that the Commission is required to take into account for the purposes of establishing the existence of aid and the Commission therefore has the burden of proving whether or not the conditions for the application of the private operator principle have been satisfied. As a result, where it appears that the private creditor test might be applicable, it is for the Commission to ask the Member State concerned to provide it with all the relevant information enabling it to determine whether the conditions for applying that test are satisfied.[149]

147. Joined cases C-331/20 P and C-343/20 P, *Volotea SA and Easy Jet Airline Co. Ltd. v. Commission*, 17.11.2022, ECLI:EU:C:2022:886, para. 153.

148. *Ibid.*, para. 157. C-148/19 P, *BTP Holding Investments SA and Duferco Participations Holdings SA v. Commission.*

149. Case C-124/10 P, *Commission v. EDF*, 5.6.2012, EU:C:2012:318, paras 82-84; case C-244/18 P, *Larko v. Commission*, 26.3.2020, EU:C:2020:238, paras 62-69; case C-160/19 P, *Comune di Milano*, 10.12.2020, EU:C:2020:1012, paras 82-84. However, it is for the Member State or the public body concerned to communicate to the Commission objective and verifiable evidence showing that its decision is based on economic evaluations comparable to those which, in the circumstances, a rational private operator in a situation as close as possible to that of that State or of that body would have had carried out, before adopting the measure in question, in order to determine its future profitability. *See* case C-124/10 P, *Commission v. EDF*, 5.6.2012, EU:C:2012:318, §84, 105; case T-319/12 and T-321/12, *Spain and Others v. Commission*, 3.7.2014, EU:T:2014:604, para. 49; T-305/13, *SACE and SACE BT v. Commission*, 25.6.2015, EU:T:2015:435, para. 97; C-385/18, *Arriva Italia and Others*, 19.12.2019, EU:C:2019:1121, para. 48; T-561/18, *ITD and Danske Fragtmaend*, 5.5.2021, EU:T:2021:240, para. 357.

[a] The Assessment of the State Intervention

The assessment of whether a State intervention is in line with market conditions has to be made on an *ex ante* basis, having regard to the information available and to the foreseeable developments in the context of the period during which the financial support measures were taken, while no relevance is given to retrospective finding that the intervention was profitable.[150] Accordingly, factors arising after the measure at issue has been adopted cannot be taken into account for the purpose of applying the private operator principle.[151]

It has to be noted that even if a transaction is carried out at market prices, it may nevertheless be considered not in line with market conditions if from all the relevant circumstances it could be concluded that the State did not act in a manner similar to a private operator.[152]

At the same time, it is not relevant whether the intervention constitutes a rational means for the public authorities in order to pursue public policy considerations.[153]

One determining indicator for the Commission is the *recipient undertaking's financial position*. When resources are provided or guaranteed by the State to an undertaking *in financial difficulty*, the relevant financial contributions *may* contain State aid elements. In any event, case law has endorsed the Commission's practice, based on which the private-investor criterion should be applied to any undertakings, not just to the loss-making ones.[154] For the General Court has clarified, in principle, the profitability or unprofitability of the beneficiary is not, in itself, decisive in establishing whether such an advantage exists.[155]

---

150. Case C-124/10 P, *Commission v. EDF*, para. 85; and Case C-482/99, *'Stardust Marine'*, paras 71-72.
151. Case C-244/18 P, *Larko v. Commission*, 26.3.2020, EU:C:2020:238, paras 29-32.
152. For instance, in Case T-14/96 *BAI v. Commission*, 28.1.1999, ECLI:EU:T:1999:12, in particular para. 76, the General Court held that, in the light of specific circumstances of the case, since the purchase of travel vouchers by national authorities from P&O Ferries did not meet an actual need, the national authorities did not act as a private operator conferring an advantage on P&O Ferries; therefore, the sums paid in performance of the purchase agreement constituted State aid.
153. *See* Notice on the notion of State aid, para. 77. However, where the intervention was triggered by past actions of the State that were not commercially motivated, but was due to political reasons, the market operator test is deemed not applicable. *See* case T-98/00, *Linde v. Commission*, 17.10.2002, ECLI:EU:T:2002:248; T-384/08, *Hellenic Shipyard*, 10.11.2011, ECLI: EU:T:2011:650. The risks to which the State is exposed and which are the consequence of State aid that it has previously granted are linked to its actions as a public authority and are not among the factors that a private operator would, in normal market conditions, have taken into account in its economic calculations. However, such considerations may be taken into account in the assessment, under Art. 107(3) TFEU, of the compatibility of any subsequent aid measure with the internal market and may therefore lead the Commission to find, as in the present case, that the measure is compatible with the internal market. *See* case T-386/14 RENV, *FIH Holding and FIH v. Commission*, 19.9.2019, EU:T:2019:623, §§112-113.
154. Point 22 of Commission communication to the Member States, OJ 1993 C307/3.
155. Joined Cases T-228/99 and T-233/99, *Westdeutsche Landesbank Girozentrale and Land Nordrhein-Westfalen v. Commission*, 6.3.2003, ECLI:EU:T:2003:57, para. 208. *See also* Commission Decision 98/365/EC of 1 Oct. 1997 concerning alleged State aid granted by France to SFMI-Chronopost, OJ 1998 L164/37.

In assessing the expected *rate of return*, the Commission compares the return earned by the State through the transaction in dispute to the return a hypothetical private investor would have considered adequate for that transaction under as similar conditions as possible. Still, the General Court has pointed up that, in general, a private investor would not be content with the fact that an investment does not cause losses to him or only earns him limited profit. He will, rather, look for a reasonable maximization of the return on his investment, depending on the existing circumstances and on the satisfaction of his short-, medium- and long-term interests.[156] The EU Courts have made it clear that the behaviour of a private investor with which the intervention of the public investor must be compared – while not necessarily that of an ordinary investor placing his capital with a more or less short-term view of its profitability – must at least be that of a private holding or group of enterprises that pursue a structural, global or sectorial policy and that are guided by a longer-term view of profitability.[157]

As clarified by the Commission in the Notice on the notion of State aid, the compliance with market conditions of a transaction can be established: (a) empirically, by specific market data; or (b) in the absence of such data, on the basis of other available methods.

[i] Empirical Assessment

When the transaction: (1) is carried out *pari passu* by public entities and private operators; or (2) concerns the sale and purchase of assets, goods and services (or other comparable transactions) carried out through an open, transparent non-discriminatory and unconditional tender procedure, the compliance with market conditions can be empirically established:[158]

(1) *Pari passu.* If the State granting the aid can show that the public intervention occurred in parallel with a significant private intervention, then it can be inferred that the transaction is in line with market conditions, and the absence of an advantage – thus the inexistence of aid – can be presumed.[159]

156. Joined Cases T-228/99 and T-233/99, *Westdeutsche Landesbank Girozentrale v. Commission*, para. 314.
157. Case T-296/97, *Alitalia v. Commission*, 12.12.2000, ECLI:EU:T:2000:289, para. 96. The applicability of the MEOP test has however been excluded by the Court for those financial interests arising from previous State aid because of their legal nature as sovereign State act which private operators may not implement: *see* Case C-579/16 P, *Commission v. FIH*, 6.3.2018, ECLI:EU:C:2018:159.
158. Notice on the notion of State aid, para. 84.
159. Case T-358/94, *Air France v. Commission*, paras 148-149. However, the private investor involvement in a project can be disregarded in the MEOP assessment if it only commits to a marginal amount of the investment and it operates as a 'service provider' for the beneficiary. *See* cases T-319/12 and T-321/12, *Kingdom of Spain and Others v. European Commission ('Ciudad de la Luz')*, 3.7.2014, ECLI:EU:T:2014:604.

However, such private intervention must be: (*i*) under the same terms and conditions (and therefore with the same level of risk and rewards); (*ii*) significant;[160] (*iii*) actually comparable;[161] and (*iv*) concomitant.[162]

In the Notice on the notion of State aid, the Commission underlined that the '*pari passu*' condition may not apply in some cases where the public contribution is of such a nature or magnitude that it could not in practice be replicated by a market economy operator.[163]

(2) *Tender procedure.* In the Notice on the notion of State aid, the Commission clarified the characteristics a tender procedure should have in order for the compliance with market conditions of the transaction to be empirically established:

(a) the tender has to be *competitive*, allowing all interested and qualified bidders to participate in the process;[164]

(b) the procedure has to be *transparent*, providing for clear and accessible selection and award criteria and sufficient time for their assessment by any interested tenderer who should be equally and reasonably informed at each stage of the procedure;

(c) the tender has to be *sufficiently well-publicized* so that it can come to the notice of any interested tenderer; the degree of publicity needed to ensure sufficient publication depends on the characteristics of the assets, goods and services of the tender so that in some cases publicity should be made on Europewide or worldwide scale;

(d) the tender has to be of a *non-discriminatory* nature, providing for objective selection and award criteria specified in advance. Compliance with the procedures provided for in the Public Procurement Directives

---

160. For instance, in the Citynet Amsterdam case cited in footnote in the Notice on the notion of State aid, the Commission considered that two private operators taking up one-third of the total equity investments in a company (considering also the overall shareholding structure and that their shares are sufficient to form a blocking minority regarding any strategic decision of the company) could be considered economically significant (*see* Commission Decision 2008/729/EC of 11 Dec. 2007 on State aid C53/2006 Citynet Amsterdam, the Netherlands. OJ L 247, 16.9.2008, p. 27 recitals 96-100). By contrast, in case N429/2010 Agricultural Bank of Greece (ATE), OJ C 317, 29.10.2011, p. 5, the private participation reached only 10% of the investment, as opposed to 90% by the State, so that the Commission concluded that 'pari passu' conditions were not met, since the capital injected by the State was neither accompanied by a comparable participation of a private shareholder nor proportionate to the number of shares held by the State.
161. In the judgment T-296/97 *Alitalia v. Commission*, para. 84, the General Court held that the employees' actual participation in the applicant's capital does not itself show that IRI's contribution satisfies the private investor test. According to the Court, the employees' participation was motivated by the desire to keep their jobs and therefore, above all, by considerations pertaining to the applicant's viability and survival rather than by prospects of profitability.
162. In Case T-565/08, *Corsica Ferries France SAS v. Commission*, 11.9.2012, ECLI:EU:T:2012:415, para. 117, the General Court clarified however that 'The temporal aspect is naturally important, but simultaneity cannot be regarded, as a matter of principle, as being sufficient in itself.'
163. Notice on the notion of State aid, para. 88.
164. *Ibid.*, at para. 93.

should be sufficient to ensure fulfilment of the requirements above,[165] except if specific circumstances – such as the use of the negotiated procedure without publication of a contract notice – do not allow to establish a market price;[166] and

(e) the tender has to be *unconditional* so that any potential bidder is free to participate. If bidders have to assume special obligations – other than those arising from general domestic law or the decision of the planning authorities – for the benefit of the public authorities or in the general public interest, the tender cannot be considered unconditional. Indeed, any specific conditions should be non-discriminatory and closely and objectively related to the subject matter and to the specific economic objective of the contract, allowing for the selection of the more economically advantageous offer and leaving the successful bidder with a return not exceeding a normal value.[167]

[ii] Assessment Without Specific Market Data

In situations where it is not possible to establish that a transaction is in line with market conditions through specific market data, the Commission Notice on the notion of State aid clarifies that the assessment should be made through: (i) benchmarking, or (ii) other assessment methods:

(1) Terms and conditions under which comparable transactions were carried out by comparable private operators in comparable situations can constitute a benchmark to obtain a reference value for the assessment of the market conditions. Often benchmarking provides for a range of possible values: in such cases, normally the central tendency is identified as market value, such as the average or the median of the set of comparable transactions.[168]

165. *See*, for instance, case C-647/19 P, *Ja Zum Nurburgring*, 2.9.2021, ECLI:EU:C:2021:666, regarding preferential treatment given to the retained tenderer which has received only a non-bonding letter of intent from a financing partner.

166. Notice on the notion of State aid, para. 93. The Commission also specifies that if only one bid is submitted, the procedure would not normally be sufficient to ensure a market price, unless either: (i) there are particularly strong safeguards in the design of the procedure ensuring genuine and effective competition and it is not apparent that only one operator is realistically able to submit a credible bid; or (ii) the public authorities verify through additional means that the outcome corresponds to the market price.

167. Notice on the notion of aid, para. 96. Previously, in C-239/09, *Seydaland Vereinigite Agrarbeitriebe*, 16.12.2010, ECLI:EU:C:2010:778, para. 94, the Court held that 'in case of an open, transparent and unconditional tender procedure, it can be presumed that the market price corresponds to the highest offer, provided that it is established, fist, that that offer is bonding and credible, and second, that the considerations of economic factors other than the price is not justified'.

168. *Ibid.*, para. 100.

The Commission highlighted that it is necessary to pay particular attention to the kind of operator concerned,[169] the type of transaction at stake[170] and the markets concerned,[171] the timing of the transactions.[172]

(2) In situations where all the criteria examined before are not applicable, the assessment of the market conditions can be established for the Commission on the basis of a generally accepted, standard assessment methodology,[173] based on available objective, verifiable, reliable and detailed data.[174]

[iii] Objective Justifications

State interventions that appear to deviate from normal market practices can still conform with the market economy operator principle if, in the context of the relevant market, they are *objectively justified* on economic grounds.

This question was addressed by the Court for the first time in the *Van der Kooy* case. In that case, the Commission had held that a preferential tariff applied to horticulture in heated glasshouses in the Netherlands should be regarded as an aid incompatible with the internal market.[175] The Court clarified that the case could be deemed to fall outside the scope of application of Article 107 TFEU if it had been demonstrated that:

> the preferential tariff was, in the context of the market in question, objectively justified by economic reasons such as the need to resist competition on the same market from other sources of energy the price of which was competitive. In determining whether such competition is a real prospect account should be taken not only of the different price levels but also of the costs involved in conversion to a new source of energy, such as replacement and depreciation costs for heating equipment.[176]

However, the specific analysis of the situation led the Court to endorse the position taken by the Commission, which had found that the preferential tariff was lower than the costs necessarily incurred to shift to coal.[177]

---

169. As, for instance, a group holding, an operative company, a speculative fund, or a long-term investor seeking to secure profits in the longer run.
170. For example, equity participation or debt transaction.
171. For example, financial markets, fast-growing technology markets, utility or infrastructure markets.
172. Particularly relevant in Commission's view, in case significant economic developments have taken place.
173. Among which the Notice on the notion of State aid includes the internal rate of return (IRR) and the Net Present Value (NPV).
174. Notice on the notion of State aid, paras 101 ff.
175. Commission Decision 85/215/EEC of 13 Feb. 1985 on the preferential tariff charged to glasshouse growers for natural gas in the Netherlands, OJ 1985 L97/49.
176. Joined Cases 67/85, 68/85 and 70/85, *Kwekerij Gebroeders van der Kooy BV and others v. Commission*, para. 30.
177. *Ibid.*, at para. 55. For another case of dismissal of the 'objective justification' exception *see* Case C-169/84, *Société CdF Chimie azote et Fertilisants SA and Société Chimique de la Grande Paroisse SA (Cofaz) v. Commission*, 17.7.1990, ECLI:EU:C:1990:301, para. 51; and Commission

Still, there have also been cases in which the Commission and the Union Courts have reached the opposite conclusion, that prices below market average may well have a commercial justification.[178]

[b] The Private-Creditor Criterion

As indicated above, the notion of State aid also takes in interventions that, in various forms, mitigate the charges that are normally included in the budget of an undertaking. Any such State intervention may, therefore, also take the form of the forgoing of, or a delay in recovering, the whole or any portion of a loan issued to an undertaking, as well as by granting guarantees that would not have been conferred by market operators.

For instance, where a public body with responsibility for collecting social security contributions tolerates late payment of such contributions, its conduct undoubtedly gives the recipient undertaking a significant commercial advantage by mitigating, for that undertaking, the burden associated with the normal application of the social security system.[179]

As for guarantees, in most cases, aid is granted to the borrower, by enabling it to borrow at a more favourable rate than that it would have obtainable on the market without the guarantee (or to receive financing that would not otherwise be accessible without the guarantee). However, under specific circumstances, a public guarantee might also benefit the lender, for instance, where the guarantee is given *ex post* on an existing loan, where a complete passing on of the advantage to the borrower is not ensured or where a guaranteed loan is used to pay back a non-guaranteed one.[180]

In order to assess whether loans and guarantees amount to State aid within the meaning of Article 107 EC, EU case law has developed the *private-creditor criterion*, according to which it must be established if, having regard to the size of the economic advantage so conferred, the undertaking would have been unable to obtain comparable facilities from a private-creditor in the same situation vis-à-vis that undertaking as the collecting body.[181] The criterion under scrutiny is nothing, therefore, but the application of the private-investor principle to credit collection.

Decision of 6 Nov. 2013 on the measures implemented by Germany in favour of HoKaWe Eberswalde GmbH SA.34721 (2012/C) (ex 2012/NN), in OJ L/109/2014, p. 30.

178. Commission Decision of 29 Dec. 1992 regarding a preferential tariff system applied in the Netherlands for supplies of natural gas to Dutch nitrate fertilizer producers, OJ 1992 C344/4. Such decision has been upheld by the Court: Case C-56/93, *Belgium v. Commission*, 26.2.1996, ECLI:EU:C:1996:64, in particular, para. 10. *See also XXXth Report on Competition Policy* (2000), point 306, with regard to rebates granted to paper mills by Électricité de France (Case C-39/98 ex NN-52/98): the Commission considered that EDF's behaviour was justified on commercial grounds. *See also* Commission Decision of 15 Feb. 2012 on the State aid SA.19045 (ex CP 46/2005) – Germany in OJ C/196/2012.
179. In case C-256/97, *Démé nagements-Manutention Transport SA (DTM)*, 29.6.1999, ECLI: EU:C:1999:332, para. 19.
180. Notice on the notion of State aid, para. 109.
181. *Ibid.* (para. 30).

A special focus has been placed on whether the relevant public authority has or has not timely taken any possible legal actions to recover the sums of which it is a creditor.

The Commission clarifies that, lacking specific market information on a given debt transaction, compliance with market conditions may be established through benchmarking, by comparison with comparable market transactions. In any case, the Commission has developed proxies to determine the aid component of loans and guarantees.

For loans, a reference rate can be calculated according to the methodology set out in the Reference Rate Communication,[182] bearing in mind that if comparable transaction has taken place at a lower or higher rate, the latter should take precedence as a reference over the proxy value.[183]

For guarantees, the Notice on Guarantees[184] provides proxies and 'safe harbours' for guaranteed lending to SMEs. Therefore, aid is normally excluded when the borrower is not in financial difficulty, the guarantee is linked to a specific transaction, the lender bears part of the risk and the borrower pays a market-oriented price for the guarantee.[185]

[c] *The Private Vendor Criterion*

In the Commission Notice on the notion of State aid, the Commission expressed that a sale of assets goods, services or other comparable transactions can be presumed in line with market conditions if the transaction is carried out following an open, transparent, sufficiently well-publicized, non-discriminatory and unconditional tender procedure, in compliance with the principles of the Public procurement Directives[186] (even in cases where those Public procurement Directives are not as such applicable), it can be presumed that the transaction is in line with market conditions.

The Commission clarified that when public bodies sell assets, goods and services, the only relevant criterion for selecting the buyer should be the highest price, also taking into account the requested contractual arrangements (e.g., the vendor's sales guarantee or other post-sale commitments).

---

182. Communication from the Commission on the revision of the method for setting the reference and discount rates, OJ C 14, 19.1.2008, pp. 6-9.
183. Notice on the notion of State aid, para. 113.
184. Commission Notice on the application of Arts 87 and 88 of the EC Treaty to State aid in the form of guarantees, OJ C 155, 20.6.2008, pp. 10-22.
185. Notice on the notion of State aid, para. 114. Unlimited State-backed guarantees are generally deemed incompatible with EU law; however, for a case where such measure was considered compatible with EU law, *see* Case T-135/17, *Scor SE v. Commission*, 6.5.2019, ECLI: EU:T:2019:287.
186. Directive 2004/17/EC of the European Parliament and of the Council of 31 Mar. 2004 coordinating the procurement procedures of entities operating in the water, energy, transport and postal services sectors (OJ L 134, 30.4.2004, p. 1) and Directive 2004/18/EC of the European Parliament and of the Council of 31 Mar. 2004 on the coordination of procedures for the award of public works contracts, public supply contracts and public service contracts (OJ L 134, 30.4.2004, p. 114).

This statement follows the decision in *Land Burgenland and Austria v. Commission* where the Court created a presumption whereby when a public authority makes use of an open, transparent and unconditional tender procedure, the market price will correspond to the highest offer.[187]

It has to be highlighted that the Commission Notice on the notion of State aid repeals the Commission Communication on State aid elements in sales of land and buildings by public authorities.[188]

[C] The Selectivity Criterion

An equally necessary condition for State aid to occur is that it must favour *certain* undertakings or the production of certain goods, a condition that can be described as the 'selectivity criterion'.[189] Therefore, the so-called *general measures* intended to support not a specific industry or group of undertakings, but the development and equilibrium of the national economy as a whole, are not caught by the notion of State aid.[190]

The requirement as to selectivity under Article 107(1) TFEU must be clearly distinguished from the concomitant detection of an economic advantage. Where the Commission has identified an advantage, understood in a broad sense, as arising directly or indirectly from a particular measure, it is also required to establish that that advantage specifically benefits one or more undertakings.[191]

A specific definition of the 'general measure' concept can hardly be found in either the Commission's practice or EU case law.[192] Though the selectivity requirement has been assessed on a *case-by-case* basis, it has generally been deemed to encompass

187. Joined Cases T-268/08 and T-281/08, *Land Burgenland and Austria v. Commission*, 28.2.2008, ECLI:EU:T:2012:90, para. 87; confirmed by the Court of Justice in Joined Cases C-214/12 P, C-215/12 P and C-223/12 P, *Land Burgenland and Others v. Commission*, 24.10.2013, ECLI:EU:C:2013:682. It has to be noted that the EFTA Court took a similar approach in a case relating to the lease of an asset in Case E-1/13 *Míla ehf v. EFTA Surveillance Authority* of 27 Jan. 2014.

188. OJ 1997 C209/3. *See* Notice on the notion of State aid, para. 229.

189. On the selectivity criterion, *see* Cristina Romariz, *Revisiting Material Selectivity in EU State Aid Law – Or 'The Ghost of Yet-To-Come'*, in 13, *EStAL*, 1, 39-50 (2014); Phedon Nicolaides, Ioana Eleonora Rusu, *The Concept of Selectivity: An Ever Wider Scope*, in *EStAL* 4/2012, 791 https://doi.org/10.21552/estal/2012/4/314; Hugo López López, *General Thought on Selectivity and Consequences of a Broad Concept of State Aid in Tax Matters*, in 9, *EStAL*, 4, 807-819 (2010) https://doi.org/10.21552/estal/2010/4/203.

190. In its Notice on the application of the State aid rules to measures relating to direct business taxation, OJ 1998 C384/3, the Commission makes clear that 'tax measures which are open to all economic agents operating within a Member State are in principle general measures' (point 13).

191. Case C-15/14, *Commission v. MOL*, 4.6.2015, EU:C:2015:362, paras 59-60; C-270/15 P, *Belgium v. Commission*, 30.6.2016, EU:C:2016:489, para. 48; T-314/15, *Greece v. Commission*, 13.12.2017, EU:T:2017:903, para. 78. Case T-165/15, *RyanAir and Airport Marketing Services v. Commission*, 13.12.2018, EU:T:2018:953, §399.

192. In Case C-143/99, *Adria Wien Pipeline and Wietersdorfer & Peggauer Zementwerke v. Finanzlandesdirektion für Kärnten*, 8.11.2001, ECLI:EU:C:2001:598, para. 35, the ECJ implicitly qualified a general measure as 'a State measure which benefits all undertakings in national territory, without distinction'.

a far wider scope than the notion of *specificity* as defined within the context of the World Trade Organization (WTO). According to the WTO Agreement on Subsidies and Countervailing Measures, a subsidy shall not be deemed 'specific' when it is based on criteria or conditions 'which are neutral, which do not favour certain enterprises over others, and which are economic in nature and horizontal in application'.[193]

By contrast, with reference to 'apparently general' measures, the EU Courts have pointed up the fact that the aid is not aimed at one or more specific recipients defined in advance, but that it is subject to a series of objective criteria pursuant to which it may be granted to an indefinite number of beneficiaries who are not initially individually identified, cannot suffice to call in question the selective nature of the measure.[194] At the very most, that circumstance means that the measure in question is not an *individual* aid. It does not, however, preclude that public measure from having to be regarded as a *system of aid* constituting a selective, and therefore specific, measure if, owing to the criteria governing its application, it procures an advantage for certain undertakings or the production of certain goods, to the exclusion of others.[195]

To clarify the notion of 'selectivity', the Commission distinguishes between *material* and *geographical* selectivity.[196]

[1] Material Selectivity

The material selectivity of a measure implies that the measure applies only to certain (groups of) undertakings or certain sectors of the economy in a given Member State. Material selectivity can be established de jure or de facto.[197]

Even general measures discretionally applied by domestic public bodies or resulting in discriminatory outcomes may fall under the prohibition in Article 107(1) TFEU. In case law, when the public body granting financial advantages has discretional power allowing it to determine the recipients or the terms of the measure so granted, then such measure cannot be deemed to be of a general nature.[198] Likewise, if the

193. In particular, *see* footnote 2 to Art. 2.1(*b*) of the Agreement.
194. The EU Courts held that the fact that the scope of application of a measure is determined in an objective manner is not in itself sufficient to establish the general character of the measure and does not exclude selectivity: *see*, for instance, Case T-379/09, *Italy v. Commission*, 13.9.2012, ECLI:EU:T:2012:422, para. 47. The measure in question was a partial exemption from excise duty on the diesel used for the heating of greenhouses. The General Court indicated that the fact that the exemption could benefit all undertakings choosing greenhouse production was not sufficient to establish a general character of the measure. *See* however Cases C-106/09 and 107/09 P, *Commission v. Gibraltar*, 15.11.2011, ECLI:EU:C:2011:732, para. 83: according to the ECJ, the asymmetric effects of the national measure were 'merely the consequence of the random event that the undertaking in question is unprofitable or very profitable during the period of assessment'.
195. Case T-55/99, *CETM v. Commission*, para. 40); Case C-279/08 P, para. 50.
196. Notice on the notion of State Aid, paras 120 et seq. In recent Commission Decisions the selectivity criterion is often assessed at both a material and regional level: *see*, for instance, Decision of 16 Oct. 2013 – Case SA.34914 – *Gibraltar Corporate Tax Regime*.
197. Notice on the notion of State Aid, paras 121-123.
198. Case C-241/94, *France v. Commission*, 26.9.1996, ECLI:EU:C:1996:353, paras 23-24; Case C-256/97, *DM Transport*, 29.6.1999, ECLI:EU:C:1999:332, para. 27; and Case C-200/97,

national authorities have a broad discretion to determine the beneficiaries or the conditions under which the tax advantage is granted according to the characteristics of the investment project submitted to its assessment or on the basis of criteria unrelated to the tax system, such as maintaining employment, the exercise of that discretion must then be regarded as selective.[199]

Prior administrative authorization for granting tax relief does not automatically determine selectivity. For instance, it is excluded if the authorization is granted based on objective, non-discriminatory criteria which are known in advance, on the basis of a procedural system easily accessible and that ensures objectively and impartially evaluation within a reasonable time, as well as justiciability of the refusal of authorization.[200]

In complex cases (particularly, tax ones), according to the EU case law, the selectivity of the measures should normally be assessed by means of a *three-step analysis*.[201] First, the relevant system of reference must be identified. Second, it should be determined whether a given measure constitutes a derogation from that system insofar as it differentiates between economic operators who, in light of the objectives intrinsic to the system, are in a *comparable* factual and legal situation.[202] The third step

---

Ecotrade S.r.l. v. AFS, paras 39-41. Moreover, it is not necessary to determine whether the conduct of the national authority was actually arbitrary; it is enough to establish that the authority had a discretionary power: *see, inter alia*, Joined Cases T-227/01 to T-229/01, T-265/01, T-266/01 and T-270/01 *Territorio Histórico de Álava – Diputación Foral de Álava and Others v. Commission*, 9.9.2009, ECLI:EU:T:2009:315, para. 171.

199. Notice on the notion of State aid, para. 124. Case C-6/12 *P Oy.*, 18.8.2010, ECLI:EU:C:2013:525, para. 27.

200. Notice on the notion of State aid, para. 125.

201. Such case law is based on the judgment in Case C-143/99, *Adria Wien Pipeline and Wietersdorfer & Peggauer Zementwerke*, concerning a reduction on the tax on electricity granted in Austria to undertakings active predominantly in the manufacturing sector; for other precedents *see*, in particular, Case C-409/00, *Spain v. Commission*, 13.2.2003, ECLI: EU:C:2003:92, para. 47; Case C-88/03, *Portugal v. Commission*, 6.9.2006, ECLI:EU:C:2006:511, para. 54; Joined Cases C-428/06 to C-434/06, *Unión General de Trabajadores de La Rioja and Others v. Juntas Generales del Territorio Histórico de Vizcaya and Others*, 11.11.2008, ECLI: EU:C:2008:488, para. 46; and Case C-487/06 P, *British Aggregates v. Commission*, 22.12.2008, ECLI:EU:C:2008:757, para. 82. The Court of Justice and the General Court have had recourse to a similar methodology of analysis also in various areas beyond that of fiscal measures (*see*, for example, Case T-475/04, *Bouygues and Bouygues Télécom v. Commission*, 4.7.2007, ECLI: EU:T:2007:196; Case C-431/07 P, *Bouygues and Bouygues Télécom v. Commission*; and Case C-501/00, *Spain v. Commission*, 15.7.2004, ECLI:EU:C:2004:438. For a more recent application of the three-stage approach, *see* Case T-210/02 RENV, *British Aggregates v. Commission*, 7.3.2012, ECLI:EU:T:2006:253; Case C-522/13, *Ministerio de Defensa and Navantia*, paras 32-45; and Case T-399/11, *Santander SA and Santusa v. Commission*, 7.11.2014, ECLI: EU:T:2014:938, para. 37; Case C-347/17, *A-Brauerei*, 19.12.2018, ECLI:EU:C:2018:1024, where the Court did not follow AG Oe opinion, which argued in favour of returning to the earlier test of 'general availability' (Opinion of AG Sugmasgaard Oe in Case C-347/17, *A-Brauerei*, 19.9.2018, ECLI:EU:C:2018:741, para. 64).

202. Assessing whether a derogation exists allows a conclusion to be drawn as to whether the measure is prima facie selective. If the measure in question does not constitute a derogation from the reference system, then it is not selective. In Case T-399/11, *Santander SA and Santusa*, the GC held that the existence of a derogation was not enough to prove selectivity. More recently, the Gran Chamber of the Court of Justice held that it is not required for a prima facie discrimination that there is a clearly identifiable group of privileged undertakings, *see*

of the test consists in verifying whether the derogatory measure is *justified by the nature or the general scheme of the (reference) system.*[203]

The reference system constitutes the framework against which the selectivity of a measure is assessed.[204] In the case of taxes, the construction of the reference system is based on such elements as the tax base, the taxable persons, the taxable event and the tax rates applicable in the Member State concerned.[205] The three-step approach shall in all cases be based 'on an objective examination of the content and structure of the applicable rules under national law', while it is not required to take into account the objectives pursued by the legislature when adopting the measure under examination.[206] In addition, that reference framework must not itself be incompatible with EU law on State aid, which aims to ensure the proper functioning of the European Union's internal market by guaranteeing that measures taken by Member States in support of undertakings do not distort competition on that market.[207]

Once the reference system has been established, the second step is to examine whether, in the context of that framework, the measure derogates from the system and

---

Case C-53/19 P and C-65/19 P, *Banco Santander*. On this point, an opposite view was taken by AG Kokott in her Opinion in Case C-66/14 *Finanziamt Linz*, 16.4.2015, ECLI:EU:C:2015:242, para. 155.

203. In the case regarding progressive taxes, the Court states that if a tax is not hypothecated to an aid measure it is compatible with EU law. On the contrary, a tax whose revenues are allocated to an aid measure constitutes a breach of Art. 107 TFEU. *See* Cases C-75/18, *Vodafone Magyarorszag*, 3.3.2020, ECLI:EU:C:2020:139; Case C-323/18, *Tesco-Global Aruhazak*, 3.3.2020, ECLI:EU:C:2020:140; Case C321/04 to C-325/04, *Casino France and Others*, 27.10.2005, ECLI:EU:C:2005:657; Case C-333/07 *Regie Networks*. 22.12.2008, ECLI: EU:C:2008:764.

204. The examination of selectivity must be carried out within the context of 'a particular legal regime'. The examination therefore in principle requires the prior definition of the reference framework within which the measure concerned fits. This method is not limited solely to the examination of tax measures; however, the determination of the reference framework is of particular importance for those measures since the very existence of an advantage may be established only when compared with 'normal' taxation. *See* Case T-165/15, *Ryan Air and Airport Marketing Services v. Commission*, 13.12.2018, EU:T:2018:953, paras 407; T-673/17, *Port Autonome du Centre et de l'Ouest and Others v. Commission*, 20.9.2019, EU:T:2019:643, paras 138; C-53/19 P and C-65/19 P, *Banco Santander and Others v. Commission*, 6.10.2021, EU:C:2021:795, para. 60; case C-693/21 P and C-698/21 P, *EDP España SA and Naturgy Energy Group SA v. Commission*, 14.12.2023, ECLI:EU:C:2023:989, paras 70-72; case C-558/22, *ARERA v. Fallimento Esperia SpA*, 7.3.2024, EU:C:2024:209, para. 81.

205. T-308/00, *Saltzgitter I*, 22.10.2013, ECLI:EU:T:2004:199, paras 81 et seq.; Case C-53/19 P and C-65/19 P, *Banco Santander*, 6.10.2021, ECLI:EU:C:2021:795 paras 35, 61, 62, 65. On the application of the three-step test to progressive taxes, *see also* Case T-836/16, *Poland v. Commission*, 16.5.2019, ECLI:EU:T:2019:338; Case T-20/17, *Hungary v. Commission*, 27.5.2019, ECLI:EU:T:2019:448, where the General Court found that progressive tax structures, non-taxable amounts or other differentiation mechanism does not necessarily indicate the existence of selective advantages (paras 80 and 92, respectively).

206. Case C-53/19 P and C-65/19 P, *Banco Santander*, para. 65; Case C-347/17, *A-Braurerei*, para. 36. *See also* C-885/19 P and C-898/19 P, *Fiat Chrysler Finance Europe v. Commission*, 8.11.2022, EU:C:2022:859, para. 72; C-558/22, *ARERA v. Fallimento Esperia SpA*, 7.3.2024, EU:C:2024:209, para. 84.

207. C-579/16 P, *Commission v. FIH Holding and FIH Erhvervsbank*, 6.3.2018, EU:C:2018:159, para. 45; C-558/22, *ARERA v. Fallimento Esperia SpA*, 7.3.2024, EU:C:2024:209, para. 83.

therefore is prima facie selective.[208] Prima facie selective measures do not constitute State aid where the differentiation between undertakings introduced by State measures results from the nature or the overall structure of the system of which they form part.[209]

In particular, where the measure at issue is conceived as an aid scheme and not as individual aid, it is for the Commission to establish that that measure, although it provides for an advantage that is of general application, confers the benefit of that advantage exclusively on certain undertakings or certain sectors of activity.[210]

The application of the three-step test was refined by the Court in several judgments. Namely, it is not always necessary for a derogation from a common tax system to be present in order to establish that a tax measure is selective, the regulatory technique not being decisive in this respect.[211] Even a measure which is not formally a derogation and founded on criteria that are in themselves of a general nature may be selective if in practice discriminates between companies which are in a comparable situation in the light of the objective of the tax system concerned. In the latter case, it is also necessary to find a tax system selective that the criteria forming the basis of assessment under the tax system should be such to characterize the recipient undertakings, by virtue of properties which are specific to them, as a privileged category. However, in the case of a measure that derogates from an ordinary tax system, it is

208. In Case T-210/02 RENV, *British Aggregates v. Commission*, 7.3.2012, ECLI:EU:T:2012:110, para. 72, the General Court noted from the documents on the case-file emerged that the Commission showed 'at least a potential link in terms of competition or of substitutability between the various aggregates'. *See also* Case T-210/02, RENV, *British Aggregates v. Commission*, para. 47; Case C-403/10 P, *Mediaset*, 28.7.2011, ECLI:EU:C:2011:533, para. 36; Case C-518/13, *Eventech Ltd. v. Parking Adjudicator*, paras 54-61. In the latter case, the ECJ held that Black Cabs and minicabs are in distinct and not comparable factual and legal situations (therefore, the bus lane policy did not confer a selective economic advantage on Black Cabs). Interestingly, the Court acknowledged that there was a market segment in which the two categories are in direct competition, i.e., the pre-booking sector. According to the Commission (Notice on the notion of State Aid, paras 129-131), the three-step analysis cannot be applied in certain cases, e.g., whereas it is necessary to take into account the practical effects of the measures concerned. This means that in certain exceptional cases it is not sufficient to examine whether a given measure derogates from the rules of the reference system as defined by the Member State concerned, but it is also necessary to evaluate whether the boundaries of the system of reference have been designed in a consistent manner or, on the contrary, in a clearly arbitrary or biased way, so as to favour certain undertakings. *See* Cases C-106/09 and 107/09 P, *Commission and Spain v. Gibraltar and UK*, 15.11.2011, ECLI:EU:C:2011:732, paras 101-108: 'the fact that offshore companies are not taxed is [...] the inevitable consequence of the fact that the bases of assessment are specifically designed so that offshore companies [...] have no tax base under the bases of assessment adopted in the proposed tax reform' (para. 106). In the context of special purpose levies, *see also* Case C-53/00, *Ferring SA v. Agence centrale des organismes de sécurité sociale (ACOSS)*, 22.11.2001, ECLI:EU:C:2001:627, para. 20. On the correct system of reference *see* Case T-538/11, *Belgium v. Commission*, 25.3.2015, ECLI: EU:T:2015:188 (*see* the different positions taken by Belgium, Commission and Court).

209. Case C-558/22, *ARERA v. Fallimento Esperia SpA*, 7.3.2024, EU:C:2024:209, para. 91.

210. Case C-270/15 P, *Belgium v. Commission*, 30.6.2016; EU:C:2016:489, para. 49; C-596/19 P, *Commission v. Hungary*, 16.3.2021, EU:C:2021:202, para. 35. C-53/19 P and C-65/19 P, *Banco Santander and Others v. Commission*, 6.10.2021, EU:C:2021:795, para. 34.

211. Case C-106/09 P, *Commission and Spain v. Government of Gibraltar and United Kingdom*, paras 91-92; however, the fact that the legislator choses a specific technique could well confirm that two economic operators are treated differently, *see* Case C-53/19 P and C-65/19 P, *Banco Santander*, para. 95.

sufficient to demonstrate in order to establish its selectivity, that the measure benefits certain operators and not others, although all those operators are in an objectively comparable situation in the light of the objective pursued by the ordinary tax system.[212] Therefore, in the case of derogating measures, it is not required to identify certain specific features that are characteristic of and common to the undertakings that are recipients of the tax advantage, by which they can distinguished from those undertakings that are excluded from the advantage.[213] Finally, most recently the Court highlighted that selectivity can be established not only in the case of tax measures that make a distinction between undertakings in terms of their specific characteristics but also between undertakings which choose to carry out certain transactions and other undertakings which choose not to do so.[214]

Described below are the main applications of the selectivity criterion, over the years, in terms of Article 107 TFEU:

(1) In the presence of an *individual aid*, the selectivity criterion itself would be fulfilled. The Commission deemed a *transaction* between a Member State's tax authority and a specific undertaking to be also selective.[215]
(2) Likewise, if in a *tax ruling*, the tax authorities of a Member State accept that a tax base of a specific company is calculated in a more favourable way which does not correspond to market conditions, this would amount to a selective tax advantage.[216]
(3) The Commission has taken the view that the selectivity criterion should be deemed fulfilled if the aid is granted to certain *classes of undertakings*. This would be the case, for example, of aid granted to large undertakings,[217] SMEs,[218] manufacturing enterprises,[219] public undertakings, professional

212. In order to assess whether the measure is likely to confer an advantage, the various components of the tax regime must be assessed as a whole, as it is not sufficient to refer to the nominal tax rate, but it necessary to examine all the other components of the tax regime of the entity concerned. *See* Case T-865/16, *F.C. Barcelona v. Commission*, 26.2.2019, ECLI: EU:T:2019:113.
213. C-20/15 P, *Commission v. World Duty Free Group*, para. 78.
214. C-50/19 P, *Sigma Alimentos Exterior v. Commission*, 6.10.2021, ECLI:EU:C:2021:792, paras 44 et seq.
215. Invitation to submit comments pursuant to Art. 88(2) of the EC Treaty: Belgium – Aid C76/2003 ex NN69/2003 – Reduction of a VAT debt owed by Umicore SA (formerly Union Minière SA), OJ 2004 C280/10.
216. For a more detailed description of the Commission's practice on tax rulings and the related Court judgments *see infra*.
217. Case C-200/97, *Ecotrade S.r.l. v. AFS* and Joined Case T-127/99, T-129/99 & T-148/99, *Territorio Histórico de Álava – Diputación Foral de Álava and others v. Commission*. *See also* Commission Decision 2003/501/EC of 16 Oct. 2002 on the State aid scheme C 49/2001 (*ex* NN 46/2000) – Coordination Centres – implemented by Luxembourg, OJ 2003 L170/20.
218. Case T-55/99, *CETM v. Commission*. *See also* Case T-424/05, *Italy v. Commission*, 4.3.2009, ECLI:EU:T:2009:49, para. 147.
219. Case C-143/99, *Adria Wien Pipeline and Wietersdorfer & Peggauer Zementwerke*.

sports clubs,[220] coordination centres[221] or undertakings with significant financial resources.[222] A measure should be deemed selective if it favours certain undertakings, even if only de facto.[223]

(4) Even a *sectorial aid* is selective, irrespective of whether the relevant measure is applied to all the undertakings in that sector 'without differentiating'.[224]

(5) Similar considerations apply to *aid to export*. According to the Court, though these measures are potentially applicable to all domestic economic operators, they are aid prohibited under Article 107 TFEU, in that they favour exporting undertakings.[225]

---

220. *See* invitation to submit comments pursuant to Art. 88(2) of the EC Treaty: Italy – Aid C70/03 (*ex* NN 72/03) – Measure in favour of professional sports clubs – 'Decreto Salva Calcio', OJ 2003 C308/9, at points 17-18.

221. Commission Decision of 17 Feb. 2003 2003/755/EC on the aid scheme implemented by Belgium for coordination centres established in Belgium, OJ 2003 L282/25, annulled by the Court for breach of the legitimate expectations principle: Joined Cases C-182/03 and C-217/03, *Belgium and Forum 187 ASBL v. Commission*, 22.6.2006, ECLI:EU:C:2006:416.

222. *See, inter alia,* Cases T-227/01 to T-229/01, T-265/01, T-266/01 and T-270/01 *Territorio Histórico de Álava – Diputación Foral de Álava and Others v. Commission*, para. 162.

223. Commission Decision 80/932/EEC of 15 Sep. 1980 concerning the partial taking-over by the State of employers' contributions to sickness insurance schemes in Italy, OJ 1980 L264/28 and Case C-203/82, *Commission v. Italy* [1983] ECR 2525 (para. 4). In that occasion, the Italian Government provided for a greater reduction in employers' contributions to the sickness insurance scheme for female employees than for male employees. The Commission held that such a system favoured certain Italian industries employing large numbers of female employees, such as, in particular, those in the textile, clothing, footwear and leather-goods sector. *See also* Friederiszick, Röller, Verouden, *European State Aid Control: An Economic Framework*, in Buccirossi (ed.), *Handbook of Antitrust Economics*, Cambridge, 6 46 (2008): 'measures which are *de jure* not selective may *de facto* have a highly divergent economic impact on firms, sectors or regions'. In the same sense *see* para. 3.38. of the study *Public Subsidies*, published by the Office of Fair Trading (November 2004): 'a subsidy may be asymmetric in effect even if it is not selective in terms of its eligibility criteria'. *See, however,* Decision of 3 Jul. 2001, N232/01, OJ 2001 C268/5, where the Commission held that a reduction in employer's social security contributions in the event of the introduction of a thirty-eight-hour working week did not constitute an aid, but a general measure. Two examples of de facto selective measures can be found in Commission Decisions in Case SA.29064 – *Differentiated air travel tax rates implemented by Ireland* (25 Jul. 2012), paras 42-50 and in Case SA.32020 – *Germany – Tax reduction for flights to and from certain North Sea Islands* (19 Dec. 2012), para. 34. The former decision was quashed by the GC on other grounds: *see* Case T-473/12, *Aer Lingus Ltd v. Commission*, 5.2.2015, ECLI:EU:T:2015:78; and Case T-500/12, *Ryanair Ltd v. Commission*, 5.2.2015, ECLI:EU:T:2015:73.

224. Commission Decision 2002/581/EC of 11 Dec. 2001 on the tax measures for banks and banking foundations implemented by Italy, OJ 2002 L184/27; Case C-173/73, *Italy v. Commission;* Commission Notice on the application of the State aid rules to measures relating to direct business taxation, OJ 1998 C384/3, point 18. *See also* Case C-279/08 P, *Commission v. Netherlands*, para. 50. For a case of indirect sectorial aid, *see* Decision of 26 Apr. 2006 in Case N 142/2005, p. 7 (potential benefit for manufacturers producing environmentally friendly cars).

225. Joined Cases C-6/69 and C-11/69, *Commission v. France*, 10.12.1969, ECLI:EU:C:1969:68; Case C-57/86, *Greece v. Commission*, para. 8; Case C-501/00, *Spain v. Commission*, para. 120. *Contra*, Case T-399/11, *Santander SA and Santusa.* Interestingly, in the latter case the GC held that where a tax measure distinguishes between types of transactions (not identifying any class of undertakings or economic activity) the measure will not be selective unless it can be shown (it is up to the Commission to do so) that in practice it is available only to certain classes of undertakings.

(6) *Local or regional aid* is selective by nature since the relevant measures are limited in territorial scope. Where the geographic reference system is the whole of a Member State, aid to a specific region/area within that State may fall within the scope of Article 107(1) TFEU.[226] For the case of non-selective measures due to the fact that the relevant reference framework is itself a specific region, *see infra* section §1.02[C][2] of this chapter.
(7) The Commission has held the view that any measures only applying to companies formed *as from a certain date* to be selective as well since they discriminate against any companies formed theretofore.[227]

The selective nature of a measure can by no means be ruled out even if it is only designed to favour certain industries 'on an experimental basis'. That it is intended to be applied to every industry at a later time is irrelevant. In this case, the Commission was led 'to think that what is involved is a specific assistance measure designed to resolve not less cyclical economic problems'.[228]

It is not infrequent in practice that, in order to verify the selectivity criterion, the Commission, as well as EU Courts, have given relevance to *the intentions of the State granting the aid*, as inferred from the relevant report on the relevant statute, parliamentary debate or even statements given by ministers or other members of the government to the press.[229]

If a prima facie selective measure is justified 'by the nature or the general scheme of the system', it will not be considered selective and thus fall outside the scope of Article 107(1) TFEU. This principle was established in the 1970s by the Court of Justice[230] and has been subsequently confirmed by the case law.[231]

---

226. *See* Case C-248/84, *Germany v. Commission*; Case C-156/98, *Germany v. Commission*, 19.9.2000, ECLI:EU:C:2000:467, para. 23. In the latter case, the Court held that the fact that a tax concession favoured certain undertakings situated in the new Länder or West Berlin prevented its being a general measure of tax or economic policy. *See also* Case T-308/00, *Salzgitter v. Commission* [2004] ECR II-1933 (para. 38) and on appeal Case C-408/04 P, *Commission v. Salzgitter*, 22.4.2008, ECLI:EU:C:2008:236.
227. Commission Decision 2002/540/EC of 11 Jul. 2001 on the State aid scheme applied by Spain to certain newly established firms in Guipúzcoa (Spain), OJ 2002 L174/31. *See also* Commission Decision 2006/261/EC of 16 Mar. 2005 on aid scheme C 8/2004 (ex NN 164/2003) implemented by Italy in favour of newly listed companies, OJ 2006 L94/42. For a case of selective measure for a limited period *see* Case T-211/05 *Italy v. Commission*, 4.9.2009, ECLI:EU:T:2009:304, paras 120-121.
228. Commission Decision 97/811/EC of 9 Apr. 1997 concerning aid granted by France to the textile, clothing, leather and footwear industries, OJ 1997 L334/25, para. VII.
229. Case C-169/84, *CDF Chimie Azote and others v. Commission*, 12.7.1990, ECLI:EU:C:1990:301, para. 22; and Case C-148/04, *Unicredito Italiano v. Agenzia delle Entrate, Ufficio Genova 1*, 15.12.2005, ECLI:EU:C:2005:774.
230. Case C-173/73, *Italy v. Commission*.
231. Such a justification was deemed existing in the following cases: Joined Cases C-78/08, C-79/08 and C-80/08, *Ministero dell'Economia e delle Finanze, Agenzia delle Entrate v. Paint Graphos Soc. coop. arl*, 8.9.2011, ECLI:EU:C:2011:550, paras 71-76: tax exemptions for Italian '*società cooperative*'; Case C-308/01, *GIL Insurance v. Commissioners of Customs & Excise*, 29.4.2004, ECLI:EU:C:2004:252, paras 73-78: insurance premium tax scheme with differential rates; Case C-200/97, *Ecotrade S.r.l. v. AFS*, para. 36: special rules for SMEs; Case C-169/84, *CDF Chimie Azote and others v. Commission*, paras 22-23; Case C-61/79, *Amministrazione delle finanze*

A measure which creates an exception to the application of the general tax system may be justified only if it results directly from the basic or guiding principles of that tax system. Therefore, external policy objectives which are not inherent to the system cannot be relied upon.[232]

Member States should, however, introduce and apply appropriate control and monitoring procedures to ensure that derogatory measures are consistent with the logic and general scheme of the tax system.[233] The final condition is that the relevant derogation is consistent with the principle of proportionality and must not go beyond what is necessary to achieve the legitimate objective being pursued.[234]

[2] Regional Selectivity

In principle, only those measures whose scope encompasses the entire territory of the State escape the selectivity criterion laid down in Article 107(1) TFEU. However, as anticipated, the reference system need not necessarily be defined within the limits of the Member State concerned. A measure favouring undertakings active in a part of the national territory should therefore not automatically be considered selective.[235]

---

dello Stato v. Denkavit italiana, 27.3.1980, ECLI:EU:C:1980:100, para. 31; and Case T-471/93, *Tiercé Ladbroke v. Commission*, 18.9.1995, ECLI: ECLI:EU:T:1995:167, para. 62. *See also* Commission Decisions of 12 Sep. 2007 in Case N 184/2007 – *Cuneo fiscale* (tax wedge), at paras 31-37 and of 7 Feb. 2007 in Case N 820/2006 – Tax exemptions for certain energy intensive processes, at pp. 5-6. On the contrary, the argument was dismissed in Case C-351/98, *Spain v. Commission*, 26.9.2002, ECLI:EU:C:2002:530, para. 41; Case C-143/99, *Adria Wien Pipeline and Wietersdorfer & Peggauer Zementwerke*, paras 47-53; and Case T-55/99, *CETM v. Commission*, paras 52-54; Case C-487/06 P, *British Aggregates v. Commission*, followed by Case T-210/02, RENV *British Aggregates v. Commission*; Case C-279/08 P, *Commission v. Netherlands* (paras 74-78); *See also* Commission Decision 2002/778/EC of 9 Apr. 2002 on the aid schemes C 74/2001 (ex NN76/2001) implemented by Belgium and which Belgium is planning to implement for the diamond industry, OJ 2002 L272/25.

232. Cases C-78/08 and 80/08 *Paint Graphos*, paras 69-70; Case C-88/03, *Portugal v. Commission* (para. 81); Case C-279/08 P, *Commission v. Netherlands, supra*; Case C-487/06 P, *British Aggregates v. Commission* In Cases T-427/04 and T-17/05, *France and France Télécom v. Commission* [2009] ECR II-4315 (para. 230), the GC referred to the 'consistency of a tax measure with the internal logic of the tax system of which it forms part'. More recently, *see* C-233/16, *Anged v. Catalunya*, 26.4.2018, ECLI:EU:C:2018:280; Joined Cases C-105 to 113/18, *Unesa*, 7.11.2019, ECLI:EU:C:2019:935 which confirmed that Member States can pursue national interests, regardless of the attainment of goals of EU interest, if national measures are deployed consistently.
233. Cases C-78/08 and 80/08 *Paint Graphos* (paras 73-74); Case C-88/03, *Portugal v. Commission*, para. 81.
234. Cases C-78/08 and 80/08 *Paint Graphos*, para. 75. C-51/19 P and C-64/19 P, *World Duty Free Group v. Commission Judgement.*
235. This problem has been addressed in the context of taxation of devolved or autonomous regions: Case C-88/03, *Portugal v. Commission*, para. 57; Joined Cases C-428/06 to C-434/06 *UGTRioja*, para. 47; Joined Cases T-211/04 and T-215/04, *Gibraltar v. Commission*, 18.12.2008, ECLI: EU:T:2008:595, subsequently quashed on other grounds: Cases C-106/09 and 107/09 P, *Commission v. Gibraltar* The EU Courts held in such cases that 'the "normal" tax rate is the rate in force in the geographical area constituting the reference framework': *see* Case C-88/03, *Portugal v. Commission*, para. 56.

As established by the case law, measures with a regional or local scope of application may not be selective if certain requirements are fulfilled. In this regard, three scenarios concerning tax measures must be distinguished:[236]

(1) In the first scenario (central fiscal competence), which results in the regional selectivity of a measure, the central government of a Member State unilaterally decides to apply a lower level of taxation within a defined geographical area.
(2) The second situation is the so-called symmetrical devolution of tax powers, in which all the local authorities at the same level (regions, districts or others) have the autonomous power to decide, within the limit of the powers conferred on them, the tax rate applicable in the territory within their competence. In this case, it is impossible to determine a normal tax rate capable of constituting the reference framework.
(3) In the third scenario (asymmetrical devolution of tax powers), only certain regional or local authorities can adopt tax measures applicable within their territory. In this case, the assessment of the selective nature of the measure at stake depends on whether the authority concerned is *sufficiently autonomous* from the central government of the Member State.[237] The regional or local authority shall be deemed 'sufficiently autonomous' from the central government of the Member State if it plays a fundamental role in the definition of the political and economic environment in which the undertakings operate.[238] This is the case when three *cumulative* criteria of autonomy are fulfilled: *institutional, procedural and economic autonomy*.[239] If all of these criteria of autonomy are present when a regional or local authority decides to adopt a tax measure applicable only within its territory, then the region in question, not the Member State, constitutes the geographical reference framework:[240]

236. Case C-88/03, *Portugal v. Commission*, paras 63-66. *See also* Opinion of Advocate General Geelhoed in C-88/03, *Portugal v. Commission*, 20.10.2005, ECLI:EU:C:2005:618; and Notice on the notion of State Aid, para. 144.
237. Case C-88/03, *Portugal v. Commission*, paras 58, 62 and 65 et seq.
238. Joined Cases C-428/06 to C-434/06, *UGTRioja*, paras 51 and 55.
239. Case C-88/03, *Portugal v. Commission*, para. 67. A regional tax measure does not have to be completely separate from the general tax system for it not to be selective. In particular, it is not necessary that: (i) the tax system is fully devolved to the infra-State body; and (ii) the tax revenues are collected by the regional/local authorities (the key criterion to this purpose is that the collection costs are borne by the infra-State authority). *See* Draft Notice on the notion of State Aid, paras 155-156.
240. The three autonomy criteria were deemed by the GC to be fulfilled in the *Gibraltar* case: Joined Cases T-211/04 and T-215/04, *Gibraltar v. Commission*, paras 114-115, subsequently set aside by the ECJ for other grounds: Cases C-106/09 and 107/09 P, *Commission v. Gibraltar*. *See also* Commission Decision of 16 Oct. 2013 – Case SA.34914 – *Gibraltar Corporate Tax Regime*, paras 53-58. In the *Azores* case, the ECJ confirmed the Commission's view that economic autonomy was lacking due to budgetary transfers by the central government: Case C-88/03, *Portugal v. Commission*, paras 75-78. In Joined Cases C-428/06 to C-434/06, *UGTRioja*, the Court of Justice left to the national court to determine whether the Historical Territories and the Autonomous Community of the Basque Country have economic autonomy, paras 123-140.

(a) *Institutional autonomy* can be established when the regional or local authority '*has, from a constitutional point of view, a political and administrative status separate from that of the central government*'.[241] In the *Azores* case, the Court observed that the Portuguese Constitution recognized the Azores as an autonomous region with its own political and administrative status and self-governing institutions, which also have their own fiscal competence, and the power to adapt national fiscal provisions to regional specificities.[242]

(b) *Procedural autonomy* arises when a tax measure is adopted '*without the central government being able to directly intervene as regards its content*'.[243] The fact that a consultation or conciliation procedure exists between the central and regional authorities to avoid conflicts does not preclude establishing the procedural autonomy of an infra-State body, provided that this body, and not the central government, has the final word on the adoption of the measure at stake.[244]

(c) *Economic autonomy* exists where an infra-State body assumes responsibility for the political and financial consequences of a tax reduction measure.[245] This means that the financial consequences cannot be offset by aid or subsidies from other regions or the central government.[246] The mere fact that there are financial transfers between the central State and its infra-State bodies cannot, in itself, suffice to demonstrate that those bodies do not assume the financial consequences of the tax measures which they adopt, since such transfers may take place for reasons unconnected with the tax measures.[247]

[3] Specific Issues Concerning Tax Measures

The Notice on the notion of State aid addresses certain specific issues that may arise with reference to certain subjects, such as cooperative societies and undertakings for

241. Case C-88/03, *Portugal v. Commission*, para. 67.
242. *Ibid.*, para. 70.
243. *Ibid.*, para. 67.
244. Joined Cases C-428/06 to C-434/06, *UGTRioja*, paras 96-100. The Court added that the mere fact that the acts which the infra-State body adopts are subject to judicial review does not in itself mean that this body lacks procedural autonomy, since the existence of the latter is an inherent feature of the rule of law (*see* paras 80-83 of the ruling).
245. Case C-88/03, *Portugal v. Commission*, paras 67-68. This cannot be the case if the infra-State body is not responsible for managing a budget, i.e., when it does not have control of both revenue and expenditure.
246. According to the Commission, the existence of economic autonomy is not undermined by the fact that a shortfall in tax revenues as a result of the implementation of devolved tax powers (e.g., a lower tax rate) is offset by a parallel increase in the same revenues due to the arrival of new businesses attracted by the lower rates. *See* Notice on the notion of State Aid, para. 151.
247. Joined Cases C-428/06 to C-434/06, *UGTRioja*, para. 135. The Court deemed necessary to verify whether the formal laws may result in '*hidden compensations*' from the Spanish State to the Basque authorities, para. 137.

collective investment, as well as specific procedures such as amnesties, tax rulings and settlements.

First, cooperative societies are deemed as not being in a comparable factual and legal situation to commercial companies, given their specificity in terms of admission requirements, mutualistic character, limits to the distribution of profits, etc., therefore, preferential tax treatment for cooperative societies fall outside the scope of State aid rules, provided that the following conditions are met: (i) they act in the economic interest of their members; (ii) their relations with members are not purely commercial, but personal and individual; (iii) the members are actively involved in the running of the business; (iv) they are entitled to equitable distribution of the results of economic performance.[248]

Second, undertakings for collective investment can be subject to specific tax rules aimed at ensuring tax neutrality and avoiding double economic taxation on the target, the ultimate investors and the intermediate investment structure. A tax regime for undertakings for collective investment aimed at these purposes may be justified by the logic of the tax system in question, provided that these principles are inherent to the tax system in question. On the contrary, preferential tax treatment for specific investment vehicles to the detriment of other investment vehicles that are in a comparable legal and factual situation is considered selective.[249]

Moreover, in order to consider tax amnesties as general measures, the following conditions shall be met: they are open to any undertakings of any sector and size; they do not entail any de facto selectivity and are applied without any discretionary power by the national authorities. The limited temporary application, instead, is considered inherent in the concept of amnesties.[250]

Finally, the Commission states in the Notice that a selective advantage may be conferred to the undertakings in cases where national tax authorities provide prior administrative rulings on the fiscal treatment of specific transactions (tax rulings). This often occurs, for instance, in relation to the application of bilateral tax treaties or national fiscal provisions, or to the treatment of 'arm's-length profits' in related party transaction and transfer pricing arrangements. According to the Commission, selectivity may be found where the ruling misapplies national tax law, resulting in a lower amount of tax, or whether the ruling is not available to undertakings in a comparable situation, or when the tax authority applies a more 'favorable' treatment (e.g., a transfer pricing arrangement that is not arm's length).[251] For this assessment, the Commission applies the 'arm's-length' criteria, despite its actual presence in the Member State's legal system, taking into account the guidance of the 'OECD Transfer Pricing Guidelines for Multinational Enterprises and Tax Administrations'.[252]

Similarly, tax settlements in the context of disputes between a taxpayer and tax authorities may entail a selective advantage in case a more 'favourable' discretionary

248. Notice on the notion of State aid, paras 157 et seq.
249. *Ibid.*, paras 161 et seq.
250. *Ibid.*, paras 164 et seq.
251. *Ibid.*, paras 169 et seq.
252. *Ibid.*, paras 172-173.

tax treatment is granted compared to other taxpayers in a similar factual and legal situation or the settlement is contrary to the applicable tax provisions and has resulted in a lower amount of tax, outside a reasonable range.[253]

Indeed, since June 2013, the tax ruling practice of seven Member States (Cyprus, Ireland, Luxembourg, Malta, the Netherlands, Belgium and the UK) has fallen under the scrutiny of the Commission pursuant to State aid rules. Furthermore, the Commission requested information about intellectual property taxation regimes, so-called patent boxes, from the ten Member States with such a regime. On 11 June 2014, the Commission opened formal investigations in three cases, respectively: *Apple* in Ireland, *Starbucks* in the Netherlands and *Fiat Finance& Trade* in Luxembourg.[254] On 7 October 2014, the Commission opened another investigation regarding Amazon in Luxembourg.[255]

Commission's decisions on tax ruling were appealed before EU Courts: in certain cases, they were annulled by the General Court (*Starbucks, Amazon*) or later by the Court of Justice (*Fiat, Engie*), while in other cases the Commission's decisions were upheld by the Judges (*Apple*).

In the recent *Apple* ruling, the Court of Justice confirmed that the Commission can use the 'arm's length principle' to assess whether transactions between related companies take place at market conditions. Furthermore, the judgement states that advance tax rulings can be selective if granted only to groups of companies and that the tax base of such groups must be determined through a realistic allocation of assets and costs between parent and subsidiary companies.[256] In particular, the Court of Justice clarified, *inter alia*, the conditions for the identification of the reference system of taxation for the purpose of applying the three-step test for selectivity. In particular, the reference framework should be identified according to 'the content, the structure and the specific effects of the applicable rules under the national law of that State', meaning that the Commission shall respect the discretion of Member States.

Moreover, in the *Magnetrol* case,[257] the Court of Justice overturned the GC's ruling, finding that the concept of 'aid scheme' according to Article 1(d) of Regulation (EU) 2015/1589 also encompassed a consistent administrative practice of a Member

253. *Ibid.*, paras 175 et seq.
254. *See* Commission Decision (EU) 2017/1283 of 30 Aug. 2016 on State aid SA.38373 (2014/C) (ex 2014/NN) (ex 2014/CP) implemented by Ireland to Apple (notified under document C(2017) 5605) C/2016/5605, OJ L 187, 19.7.2017, pp. 1-110; Commission Decision (EU) 2017/502 of 21.10.2015 on State aid SA.38374 (2014/C ex 2014/NN) implemented by the Netherlands to Starbucks (notified under document C(2015) 7143), C/2015/7143, OJ L 83, 29.3.2017, pp. 38-115; and Commission Decision (EU) 2016/2326 of 21.10.2015 on State aid SA.38375 (2014/C ex 2014/NN) which Luxembourg granted to Fiat (notified under document C(2015) 7152) OJ L 351, 22.12.2016, pp. 1-67.
255. Commission Decision (EU) 2018/859 of 4.10.2017 on State aid SA.38944 (2014/C) (ex 2014/NN) implemented by Luxembourg to Amazon (notified under document C(2017) 6740) C/2017/6740, OJ L 153, 15.6.2018, pp. 1-142. *See* Press Release IP/14/2742 of 17 Dec. 2014 and Statement of European Commissioner for Competition Margrethe Vestager of 6 Nov. 2014 No. 14/1480.
256. C-465/20 P, *Commission v Ireland, Apple Sales International Ltd and Apple Operations International Ltd*, 10.09.2024, ECLI:EU:C:2024:724.
257. C-337/19 P, *Commission v. Belgium and Magnetrol*, 16.9.2021, ECLI:EU:C:2021:741.

State tax authority, so that the Commission may 'bundle' a large number of tax ruling as being an aid scheme.

[D] Distortion of Competition and Its Impact on Trade Between Member States: The Significance of Economic Analysis

Under Article 107(1) TFEU, a State measure in favour of an undertaking or of the provision of a good or service needs, in order to be categorized as State aid, to distort or threaten to distort competition and, at the same time, to affect trade between Member States.

In the wording of the Treaty, the conditions of distorted competition and affected trade are distinct. This notwithstanding, case law has been consistently holding these requirements to be *intrinsically* and *mutually linked* to each other.[258]

Case law has developed two requisites to be met to this effect: first, a financial aid granted by a Member State that strengthens a firm's position over other competing firms in intra-EU trade is considered to affect that trade;[259] second, the General Court has held that, in the presence of an aid actually affecting trade, the Commission is not required to prove that the aid in question has distorted or threatened to distort competition.[260]

The two requirements are only nominally similar to those provided for in Article 101 TFEU – at least under the approach taken by the Commission – as the different aims assumed to be pursued by Article 107 TFEU result in a different approach to their evaluation.[261]

Provisions governing State aid fall into the greater picture of competition law. Accordingly, they primarily address *undertakings* and, in particular, the undue advantages they may from time to time derive from legislative measures enacted by Member States – regardless of whether notified or not. The Commission is the *only entity having jurisdiction* over the matter, being able to deem a measure illegitimate or incompatible.

State aid issues are bound to involve distinct parties: a Member State, the Commission, and two different cohorts of private undertakings. The effect on the market – the '*distortion or threat to competition*' – needs to favour an economic operator (or a group thereof) at the expense of others. These damaged undertakings are, in turn, active parties to the case.

---

258. *See, inter alia*, Case T-298/97 *et al. Mauro Alzetta v. Commission*.
259. Case C-730/79, *Philip Morris Holland BV v. Commission*, 17.9.1980, ECLI:EU:C:1980:209, para. 11.
260. Case T-288/97, *Regione Autonoma Friuli Venezia Giulia v. Commissione*, 15.6.1999, ECLI: EU:T:1999:125, paras 49-50; Case T-298/97 *et al. Mauro Alzetta v. Commission* and the case law mentioned therein.
261. According to Art. 101 TFEU: '[t]he following shall be prohibited as incompatible with the internal market: all agreements between undertakings, decisions by associations of undertakings and concerted practices *which may affect trade between Member States* and which have as their object or effect the prevention, restriction or *distortion of competition* within the internal market [...]'.

The TFEU, in regulating these issues, adopts an approach of comparison between the substantive position of the undertakings receiving the assumed aid and those not benefiting from it. This comparison is carried out taking into account as a parameter the *relevant market or markets*, as it is in general the case in the application of EU competition law.

The following paragraphs will break down the definition provided above and take individually into account the various factors at issue.

[1] Methodology

It has been deemed useful to start with a methodological section outlining the procedure through which State aid cases are analysed. On this point, the Commission has recently published a widely awaited document setting out guidance for the methodology to be followed in State aid evaluation.[262] This document is declared a corollary of the modernization of State aid enforcement of 2012, which focused on larger aid schemes while streamlining the assessment of smaller cases.[263]

The Working Document envisages a central role of evaluation, whose objective is said to be '*to assess the relative positive and negative effects of a scheme, i.e. the public objective of the aid relative to its impact on competition and trade between member states*'.[264] The evaluation aims to gather information and empirical data on aid measures and their outcome, enabling the Commission and stakeholders to know more about aid schemes. State aid evaluation is to be carried out *alongside* the design of the aid scheme, and is to result in an evaluation plan. The evaluation is then to be approved by the Commission before implementation.[265]

Evaluation is not to be confused with *ex post* procedures which the Commission carries out to enforce State aid provisions - i.e., monitoring and reporting.[266] From a timeframe perspective, aid measures can be analysed by the Commission taking into account their *ex ante* or *ex post* characteristics. In any event, the effects of the aid measure on inter-State trade are evaluated with respect to the time in which the aid was granted - regardless of whether the State at issue has complied with the notification procedure.[267]

262. *Commission Staff Working Document on the Common methodology for State aid evaluation*, published on 28 May 2014, SWD(2014) 179.
263. *See* p. 4 of the Working Document. On the modernization, *see Communication from the Commission to the European Parliament, the Council, the European Economic and Social Committee and the Committee of the Regions, EU State Aid Modernisation (SAM)*, Document of 8 May 2012, COM(2012) 209.
264. Paragraph 2 at p. 4 of the Working Document.
265. *See* para. 3 at p. 6 of the Working Document.
266. *See* p. 4 of the Working Document.
267. C-351/98, *Spain v. Commission*, para. 66.

[2] Definition of the Relevant Market

Unlike in cases of abuse of dominant position or control over concentrations, the *definition of the relevant market* offered by the Commission in evaluating cases of State aid is not supported by any in-depth analysis of the market involved.

While the *relevant product market* has been defined according to the PRODCOM classification,[268] the *relevant geographic market* has almost automatically been identified with the European Economic Area. In practice, this has translated into the virtual absence of any assessment of the actual competitive position of recipients of aid. This attitude is reflected, *inter alia*, in the new 'Market definition notice', that states that:

> In general, market definition plays less of a role in the Commission's enforcement practice under Article 106 and 107 TFEU. In those cases, the assessment focuses on the industry/sector concerned rather than identification of competitive constraints faced by the undertaking.[269]

However, the Commission clarifies that when consideration of market power and therefore of the relevant market are raised in any particular State aid case, elements of the approach outlined in the Market Definition Notice might serve as a basis for the assessment.

EU Courts have generally endorsed this approach of the Commission.[270] However, the General Court has been acknowledging a greater role played by market definition in State aid cases, by setting aside a decision taken by the Commission on grounds that it failed to carry out the necessary investigations to identify the relevant market.[271]

268. Council Regulation (EEC) No. 3924/91 of 19 Dec. 1991 on the establishment of a Community survey of industrial production, OJ 1991 L374/1. *See also* Commission Regulation (EC) No. 317/2006 of 22 Dec. 2005 establishing for 2005 the PRODCOM list of industrial products provided for by Council Regulation (EEC) No. 3924/91, OJ 2006 L60/1.
269. *See* Commission Notice on the definition of the relevant market for the purposes of Union competition law, C/2023/6789, OJ C, C/2024/1645, para. 2., footnote 4. The same principle was already expressed in the previous version of the Market Definition Notice. *See* Commission Notice on the definition of relevant market for the purposes of Community competition law, OJ 1997 C372/5, footnote 1.
270. According to settled case law, it is sufficient for the Commission to explain how the aid in question distorted competition and affected trade between Member States. Therefore, it is not necessary to carry out an economic analysis of the actual situation on the relevant market, of the market share of the undertakings in receipt of the aid, of the position of competing undertakings and of trade flows in question between Member States. *See, inter alia*, T-52/12, *Greece v. Commission*, 16.7.2014, EU:T:2014:677, para. 111; T-253/12, *Hammar Nordic Plugg v. Commission*, 28.10.2015, EU:T:2015:811, para. 131; T-233/11 and T-262/11, *Greece and Ellinikos Chrysos v. Commission*, 9.12.2015, EU:T:2015:948, para. 169; T-160/16, *Groningen Seaports and Others v. Commission*, 31.5.2018, EU:T:2018:317, para. 91; C-654/17 P, *Bayerische Motoren Werke and Freistaat Sachsen v. Commission*, 29.7.2019, EU:C:2019:634, para. 91.
271. Case T-155/98, *SIDE v. Commission*, 28.2.2002, ECLI:EU:T:2002:53, para. 71.

[3] *Distortion of Competition*

Article 107 TFEU mandates that a measure is to distort competition between Member States in order to amount to (unlawful) State aid. This requirement has been interpreted widely by the Commission, whose assessment of the markets from time to time involved in State aid cases is generally far less pervasive than the one carried out in investigations pursuant to Article 101 TFEU.

In general, a distortion of competition for the purposes of State aid rules is found when a State measure improves the competitive position of the recipient compared to its competitors.[272] This would normally be found when the State grants a financial advantage to an undertaking operating in a liberalized sector.[273]

It is not necessary that the recipient expands and gains market share as a result of the support measure; it is sufficient that the aid enables the recipient to maintain a stronger competitive position than it would have had in the absence of the aid,[274] for example, by relieving it of expenses that it would otherwise have had to bear in the course of its day-to-day operations.[275]

In fact, the distortion of competition or effect on trade for the purpose of State aid rules does not need to be 'significant or material'. Therefore, a low amount of aid or the small size of the recipient undertaking will not in itself rule out the element in question, provided that the likelihood of such a distortion is not merely hypothetical.[276]

In most instances, the analysis of the Commission contented itself with establishing that competitors of the aid recipient in fact existed, without looking into the actual characteristics of the particular market. The paradoxical consequence ensues that the only case in which distortion of competition is deemed absent is where the aid recipient's product has no other products which are in competition with or substitutable for it.[277]

The practical implications of this approach are twofold: on the one hand, the threshold of influence on competition is low – it is only required that the measure be

272. Notice on the notion of State aid, para. 187.
273. Joined Cases T-298/97 et al., *Mauro Alzetta v. Commission*, paras 141 to 147; Case C-280/00, *Altmark Trans*. The Commission highlights that the assignment of a public service to an in-house provider can determine a distortion of competition, unless the following conditions are met: (i) a service is subject to a legal monopoly (in compliance with EU law), which excludes any possible competition for the service in question (not only *on* the market but also *for* the market); (ii) the service does not compete with other services; (iii) cross-subsidization to other services provided by the service provider on competitive markets is excluded (e.g., through separate accounts, allocation of costs and revenues, etc.) (*see* Notice on the notion of State aid, para. 189). *See also* Case C-385/18 P, *Arriva Italia Srl and others v. Ministero delle Infrastrutture e dei Trasporti*, 19.12.2018, ECLI:EU:C:2019:1121.
274. Notice on the notion of State aid, para. 189.
275. Case C-172/03, *Heiser*, 3.3.2005, ECLI:EU:C:2005:130, para. 55.
276. Notice on the notion of State aid, para. 189. Case T-55/99, *Confederación Espanola de Transporte de Mercancías v. Commission*, 29.9.2000, ECLI:EU:T:2000:223, para. 89; Case C-280/00, *Altmark Trans*, para. 79, 81.
277. Opinion of Advocate General Capotorti in Case C-730/79, *Philip Morris Holland BV v. Commission*, 18.6.1980, ECLI:EU:C:1980:160.

'capable' of affecting trade between Member States;[278] however – from a burden of proof standpoint – the distortion of competition requirement is *essentially presumed*, in that there is no need to prove actual effects on competition. EU Courts have endorsed the approach followed by the Commission in a number of cases.[279] For example, in its *Imepiel* decision, the Commission only observed that, since the market was more price than volume orientated, the financial assistance granted by the State was bound to have a significant negative effect on competition.[280]

The approach of the Commission on the point of the impact State aid has on competition has attracted criticism from many sources – *inter alia*, the UK Office of Fair Trading,[281] and the OECD.[282] To reflect this criticism, the Commission could change its approach broadening the scope of its assessment from the mere selective quality of an aid measure to include other factors such as: (*a*) the aid recipient's long-term market power;[283] or (*b*) the existence of a causation link between a selection bias and distortion of competition.[284]

These criticisms should not, however, lead to the conclusion that the Commission has no duty to provide grounds for the existence of an effect on competition. The Commission is required to undertake a minimal analysis to show that a measure is

278. In particular, there is no prescription mandating for the effect to be substantial or in any event meeting a relevance threshold. *See* Case T-298/97 *et al*, *Mauro Alzetta v. Commission*, para. 80; Case C-480/09, *AceaElectrabel v. Commission*, para. 102; Joined Cases C-71/09 et seq., *Comitato 'Venezia vuole vivere' et al. v. Commission*, 9.6.2011, ECLI:EU:C:2011:368, para. 134.
279. Case C-72/87, *Exécutif Régional Wallon v. Commission*, 8.3.1988, ECLI:EU:C:1988:132, paras 17-18; Case C-730/79, *Philip Morris Holland BV v. Commission*, paras 9-12; Case T-214/95, *Vlaams Gewest v. Commission*, 30.4.1998, ECLI:EU:T:1998:77, para. 67; Case T-55/99, *CETM v. Commission*, para. 102; and Joined Cases T-227/01 to T-229/01, T-265/01, T-266/01 and T-270/01 *Territorio Histórico de Álava and others v. Commission*; Case C-494/06 P, *Commission v. Italy and Wam*, 30.4.2009, ECLI:EU:C:2009:272, para. 50; T-211/05, *Italy v. Commission*, paras 77 et seq.
280. Commission Decision 92/318/EEC of 25 Mar. 1992 on aid granted by Spain to Industrias Mediterraneas de la Piel SA (*Imepiel*), OJ 1992 L172/76.
281. The OFT has pointed out how, in its opinion, 'the European state aid rules should be improved to take better account of the potential for competition distortions to arise. We support the current review insofar as this results in guidelines that have a more rigorous economic basis'. *See* the OFT document Public Subsidies, November 2004, p. 31, available on www.oft.gov.uk.
282. In the words of the OECD itself: 'The EU approach, because it does not focus directly on competition, may label as state aid some forms of benign assistance and may not label as state aid some forms of assistance, which are inefficient. For example, an exemption on petrol taxes for a producer in a country with high petrol taxes who competes in an international market may not have a distorting effect on competition, yet might be labelled a state aid [...]. Conversely low interest loans for capital investment which applies to all firms in a small economy may nevertheless distort competition in the market in which the firms operate (although the cost of such policies may make them rare in practice). In addition, the Commission cannot question whether the decision to grant aid is the best way of achieving the underlying public policy objective.' *See* the OECD document *Competition Policy in Subsidies and State Aid* of 12 Nov. 2001, p. 10, available on www.oecd.org.
283. For example, if a subsidy is granted to a recipient having significant market power, this could increase the risk of predatory behaviours. *See* the OECD document *Competition Policy in Subsidies and State Aid* of 12 Nov. 2001, p. 37.
284. Such causation link would restrict the definition of 'aid' thereby reducing the current inconsistencies of the system.

liable to distort competition;[285] it has to explicate its reasoning, connecting the circumstances of the case to the conclusion that the practice is liable to affect intra-State trade.[286] In general, an *unspecified reason* based on mere reference to case law principles or on the fact that an effect on trade or competition cannot be ruled out cannot be deemed to be sufficient grounds.[287] In a fairly recent case, the Court has held that the Commission had not examined all the consequences that the aid measure was likely to entail and accordingly annulled the decision at issue.[288]

We have seen how – as much as the threshold of distortion is comparatively low – the Commission is nonetheless expected to carry out an evaluation of the extent to which a certain aid measure is capable of affecting trade between Member States. The primary method to this effect is to assess the ability of the measure to strengthen the position of a certain undertaking in relation to its competitors.[289] In the Commission practice, this tends to be a test of the potential advantage an undertaking may attain as a result of the measure,[290] rather than a comparative analysis of competing entities – to the point that it is not held as necessary to establish the very existence of competing undertakings.[291] Also, the fact that an economic sector has been liberalized at the Union level is an element which may serve to determine whether the aid has a real or potential effect on competition and trade between Member States.[292]

The distortion of competition requirement is linked to the selectivity criterion, but the two concepts do not entirely overlap. Accordingly, the Commission in its

285. Case T-298/97 *et al. Mauro Alzetta v. Commission*, para. 83. *Contra see* para. 188 of the Notice on the notion of State Aid, according to which a distortion of competition is '*assumed*' as soon as the State grants a financial advantage to an undertaking in a liberalized sector.

286. Joined Cases C-296/82 and C-318/82, *Netherlands and Laeeuwarder Papierwarenfabriek v. Commission*, 13.3.1985, ECLI:EU:C:1985:113, para. 24; Case C-279/08 P, *Commission v. Netherlands*, para. 131.

287. Joined Cases T-304/04 and T-316/04, *Italy and Wam S.p.A. v. Commission*, 6.9.2006, ECLI: EU:T:2006:239, paras 66 and 73-76, confirmed on appeal by Case C-494/06 P, *Commission v. Italy and Wam*.

288. Case C-405/11 P, *Buczek Automotive v. Commission*, 21.3.2013, ECLI:EU:C:2013:186.

289. Case C-730/79, *Philip Morris Holland BV v. Commission*, para. 11; *see also* Joined Cases C-182/03 and C-217/03 *Belgium and Forum 187 v. Commission*, 22.6.2006, ECLI: EU:C:2006:416, para. 131.

290. Case T-14/96, *BAI v. Commission*, 28.1.1999, ECLI:EU:T:1999:12, para. 78.

291. *See* the opinion of Advocate General Darmon *in re* Joined Cases C-72/91 and 73/91, *Sloman Neptun*.

292. C-93/15 P, *Banco Privado Português and Massa Insolvente do Banco Privado Português*, 15.10.2015, EU:C:2015:703, para. 50; C-211/15 P, *Orange v. Commission*, 26.10.2016, EU:C:2016:798, para. 65; C-76/15, *Vervloet and Others*, 21 Dec. 2016, EU:C:2016:975, para. 105; C-150/16, *Fondul Proprietatea*, 18.5.2017, EU:C:2017:388, para. 34; C-706/17, *Achema and Others*, 15.5.2019, EU:C:2019:407, para. 94. Furthermore, if the market concerned is only partially open to competition, State aid can still be liable to affect trade between Member States and to distort or threaten to distort competition. To this end, it is sufficient that, at the time of the entry into force of an aid measure, there is a situation of effective competition on the relevant market. C-387/17, *Presidenza dei Consiglio dei Ministri v. Fallimento Traghetti del Mediterraneo SpA*, 23.1.2019, EU:C:2019:51, paras 39, 40; C-702/20 and C-17/21, *'DOBELES HES' SIA*, 12.1.2023, EU:C:2023:1, para. 51.

decisions is expected to make reference to specific facts to conclude that a distortion of competition in fact exists.[293]

[4] Trade Between Member States

The second condition in order for a measure to amount to unlawful State aid is that it needs to distort *trade between Member States*. This assessment is carried out on a case-by-case basis. What is certain is that the condition is met when the undertaking at stake carries out activity across Member State borders – whether or not the activity is directly involved by the aid measure.[294]

A different situation does not, however, necessarily imply otherwise: an activity carried out within the border of a Member State may this notwithstanding deemed to affect trade between States. The criterion, in general, is that markets are to be open to competition from other Member States, thereby allowing for undertakings located in another Member State to be affected by the aid measure.[295]

Over the years, the impact on trade requirement has been interpreted broadly by EU Courts – as we have seen is also the case for the distortion of competition criterion. The Court of Justice has, in particular, ruled that there is no specific threshold below which trade between Member States may be deemed to have not been affected.[296] The standard of proof is, then again, low: in a case the Court has deemed sufficient that competition with operators in other Member States was '*not inconceivable*'.[297] The ECJ held that whereas the effect of the aid on trade is '*less immediate and even less discernible*', this requires a '*greater effort to state reasons*' on the part of the Commission.[298]

In particular, it is not necessary to establish that the aid has a real effect on trade between the Member States and that competition is actually being distorted, but only to examine whether that aid is liable to affect such trade and distort competition.[299] Moreover, the assessment of the 'effect on trade' does not require a definition of the relevant market nor a detailed analysis of the impact of the measure on the position of the beneficiary and its competitors.[300] What is relevant is that when aid granted by a Member State strengthens the position of an undertaking compared to other undertakings competing in intra-Community trade, the latter must be regarded as affected by

293. Joined Cases C-15/98 and 105/99, *Italy and Sardegna Lines v. Commission*, 19.10.2000, ECLI:EU:C:2000:570, paras 66-67.
294. *See* the Commission decision of 5 Dec. 2012 in the case SA.33952, *Deutscher Alpenverein*.
295. Case C-403/10 P, *Mediaset*.
296. *See, inter alia*, Case C-280/00, *Altmark Trans*, para. 81.
297. Case C-659/17 *Azienda Napoletana Mobilità*, 29.7.2019, ECLI:EU:C:2019:633; Case C-172/03, *Wolfgang Heiser v. Finanzamt Innsbruck*, 3.3.2005, ECLI:EU:C:2005:130, paras 33 et seq. However, the case law does *not* seem to establish a *legal presumption* of an effect on trade.
298. Case T-578/17, *a&o hostel and hotel Berlin Gmbh*, 20.6.2019, ECLI:EU:T:2023:723. Case C-494/06, *Commission v. Italy and Wam*, para. 62.
299. Case C-518/13, *Eventech Ltd v. Parking Adjudicator*, para. 65.
300. Case 730/79, *Philip Morris*, 17.9.1980, ECLI:EU:C:1980:209; Case T-211/05, *Italy v. Commission*, 4.9.2009, ECLI:EU:T:2009:304, paras 157 to 160; Joined Cases T-298/97, T-312/97, *Alzetta*, para. 95.

that aid.[301] However, the effect cannot be merely hypothetical or presumed and shall be established based on the foreseeable effects of the measure.[302]

Case law shows how the individual tiny amount of aid, the comparatively small size of the recipient undertaking, or the local dimension of its activities cannot rule out *a priori* that trade between Members States might be affected.[303] For example, even a relatively small aid may affect trade between Member States when the sector in which the recipient undertaking operates is highly competitive,[304] or that sector is characterized by production overcapacity.[305] In the Court's view, when an industry stands out for a large number of small enterprises, an aid, even if individually small,[306] but potentially available to all or most of the enterprises in that industry may affect trade between Member States.[307] Export aid has also been held to be apt to affect intra-EU trade.[308]

The affected trade requirement has been found not met in some cases, all of which involved diminutive aid granted to undertakings: (i) operating in sectors that obviously did not participate in cross-border trade (e.g., essentially local activities such as swimming pools and other leisure or sport facilities to be used mainly by the local population,[309] local transport,[310] conference centres,[311] local hospitals,[312] museums or

301. Case C-518/13, *Eventech Ltd v. Parking Adjudicator*, para. 66.
302. Case T-728/17, *Marinvest and Porting v. Commission*, 14.3.2019, ECLI:EU:T:2019:325, paras 100-106; Case C-497/06 P, *Commission v. Italy and Wam*. 30.4.2009, ECLI:EU:C:2009:273; Joined Cases T-447/93, T-448/93 and T-449/93, *AITEC and others v. Commission*, 6.7.1995, ECLI:EU:T:1995:130, para. 141.
303. Case T-214/95, *Vlaams Gewest v. Commission*, paras 48-49, and the case law mentioned therein. According to the GC, the Commission must carry out also an examination of the *foreseeable effects* of the aid, at the time when it was granted, on competition and intra-Community trade: Case T-449/93, *AITEC and others v. Commission*, 6.7.1995, ECLI: EU:T:1995:130, paras 139-141.
304. Case C-409/00, *Spain v. Commission*, 13.2.2003, ECLI:EU:C:2003:92, para. 75; and Case C-148/04, *Unicredito Italiano*, para. 57. It is not necessary that the beneficiary undertaking itself be involved in intra-Community trade. Aid granted by a Member State to an undertaking may help to maintain or increase domestic activity, with the result that undertakings established in other Member States have less chance of penetrating the market of the Member State concerned. *See* Case C-148/04, *Unicredito Italiano*, para. 58, and Case C-310/99, *Italy v. Commission*, para. 84; *see also* Joined Cases C-197/11 and C-203/11, *Libert and Others v. Vlaamse Regering*, 8.5.2013, ECLI:EU:C:2013:288 para. 78.
305. Case C-142/87, *Belgium v. Commission ('Tubemeuse')*, 21.3.1990, ECLI:EU:C:1990:125, para. 37; Case C-303/88, *Italy v. Commission*, para. 27, and Case C-75/97, *Belgium v. Commission*, 17.7.1999, ECLI:EU:C:1999:311, paras 47-49; C-351/98 *Spain v. Commission*.
306. Case T-254/00, *Hotel Cipriani et al. v. Commission*, 28.11.2008, ECLI:EU:T:2008:537, para. 247.
307. Case C-71/04, *Administración del Estado v. Xunta de Galicia*, 21.7.2005, ECLI:EU:C:2005:493, para. 43.
308. In particular, *see* Case C-142/87, *'Tubemeuse'*, paras 32 and 38. In that case, the objective announced by Tubemeuse – whose exports represented 90% of its turnover – was to direct its efforts, with the help of the aid granted to it, to other markets. It was thus reasonably foreseeable that Tubemeuse would redirect its activities towards the internal EU market. *See also* Case C-102/87, *France v. Commission*, 13.7.1988, ECLI:EU:C:1988:391, para. 19.
309. *See* Commission Decision in case N258/2000, *Germany – Leisure pool Dorsten* and Press Release IP/00/1509 of 21 Dec. 2000 'On application by Germany, Commission decides that municipal aid for public swimming is not state aid' ('the Commission concluded that the amenity is used by the inhabitants of the town and the surrounding area. [...] the Commission took the view that there was practically no likelihood of intra-EU trade being affected, especially since the catchment area of the swimming pool did not extend to the nearby

other touristic infrastructure unlikely to attract cross-border visitors,[313] food catering, car repairs[314] or local press/theatre events);[315] or (ii) entirely foreign to the European Union.[316] According to the Commission, common features of such decisions are that:[317]

(1) the beneficiary supplied goods or services to a limited area within a Member State;

Netherlands'); Commission Decision of 9 Apr. 2002, cases N560/01 and NN17/02 - *United Kingdom - Brighton West Pier* (points 32-36); Commission Decision 2004/114/EC of 29 Oct. 2003 on measures in favour of non-profit harbours for recreational crafts in the Netherlands, points 54-59. *See also* the Commission decision of 5 Dec. 2012 in case SA.33952, *Deutscher Alpenverein*, point 62. In Case N376/01, *Regime di aiuti a favore degli impianti a fune*, concerning the financing of ski-lifts, the Commission clarified that the following factors should be taken into account to draw a distinction between installations liable to have a local catchment area and others: (a) the location of the installation (e.g., within cities or linking villages); (b) operating time; (c) predominantly local users (proportion of daily as opposed to weekly passes); (d) the total number and capacity of installations relative to the number of resident users; (e) other tourism-related facilities in the area (point 27 of the Decision of 27 Feb. 2002). *See also* Cases SA.33149 - *Germany - Städtische Projektgesellschaft 'Wirtschaftsbüro Gaarden - Kiel'*; SA.39403 - *The Netherlands - Investment Aid for Lauwersoog Port*; SA.37963 - *United Kingdom - Glenmore Lodge*; SA.38209 - *United Kingdom - Member-owned Glof Clubs*.

310. Commission Reply to Written Question E-3484/96 by Sérgio Ribeiro, OJ 1997 C186/96 (aid to local transport). *See* the Opinion of AG Jacobs in Case C-126/01, *Ministère de l'Économie, des Finances et de l'Industrie v. GEMO SA* [2003] ECR I-13769 (para. 145), referring to '*taxi services*' as an example of economic sector with little intra-Community trade. However, in Case SA.34056, *Cable Car for London*, the Commission did not exclude a potential effect on trade (points 42-46, applying the criteria of Case N 376/01, *Regime di aiuti a favore degli impianti a fune*). In the same vein, *see* para. 70 of the judgment of 14 Jan. 2015, Case C-518/13, *Eventech Ltd v. Parking Adjudicator*: according to the ECJ, 'it is conceivable that the effect of the bus lanes policy is to render less attractive the provision of minicab services in London, with the result that the opportunities for undertakings established in other Member States to penetrate that market are thereby reduced'.

311. *See* Commission decision in case N 486/2002 *Sweden - Congress hall in Visby*.

312. *See*, for instance, Commission decisions in cases N 543/2001 *Ireland - Capital allowances for hospitals* and SA.34576 *Portugal - Jean Piaget North-east Continuing Care Unit*. *See also* Cases SA.37432 - *Czech Republic - Hradec Králové Public Hospitals*; SA.37904 - *Germany - Medical Centre in Durmersheim* and SA.38035 - *Germany - Landgrafen Klinik*.

313. *See*, for instance, Commission decisions in cases N 610/2001, *Germany - Tourism infrastructure program Baden Württemberg*; N 630/2003 *Local Museums Sardinia*; N 377/2007, *The Netherlands - Reconstruction of a vessel from the 17th century* and SA.34466 *Cyprus - Center for Visual Arts and Research*. *See also*: Decision SA.35909 of the Commission of 26 Nov. 2013, *Infrastructure for Tourism in South-East Czech Republic* (paras 35 et seq.) and Decision SA.35281 of the Commission of 6 Nov. 2013, *Archaeological Museum of Messara (Greece)*, at para. 47.

314. *See* the Opinion of AG Jacobs in Case C-126/01, *GEMO*, 30.4.2002, ECLI:EU:C:2002:273, para. 145.

315. *See*, for instance, Commission decisions in cases N 257/2007 *Subsidies for theatre productions in the Basque country*; N 458/2004 *Editorial Andaluza Holding*; SA.33243 *Jornal de Madeira*. *See also* Commission Reply to Written Question E-2260/95 by Susanne Riess-Passer, OJ 1996 C161/2 (subsidies to Austrian local press).

316. Case T-34/02, *EURL Le Levant 2001 and Others v. Commission*, paras 115-117.

317. *See* para. 196 of the Notice on the notion of State Aid and p. 6 (footnote 27) of the Commission Notice on a simplified procedure for treatment of certain types of State aid. *See* Commission Press Release IP/15/4889 of 29 Apr. 2015, 'State Aid - Commission gives guidance on local public support measures that can be granted without prior Commission approval'.

(2) the aid was unlikely to attract customers from other Member States;[318]
(3) it could not be foreseen that the measure would have more than a marginal effect on the conditions of cross-border investments or establishment.[319]

As much as EU authorities agree on the capability of diminutive aid measures granted to smaller undertakings to distort competition, they do acknowledge a threshold under which aid is deemed as compatible with the internal market. This exemption is commonly referred to as the *de minimis* rule and is regulated by Commission Regulation (EU) 2023/2831,[320] superseding the previous *de minimis* regulation.[321]

Pursuant to this provision, aid – granted to a single undertaking' –[322] not exceeding a ceiling of EUR 300,000 over a period of three fiscal years does not affect trade between Member States and/or does not distort or threaten to distort competition and therefore does not fall under Article 107(1) TFEU.[323] Special provisions do, however, govern the *de minimis* rule with respect to services of general interest.[324]

In conclusion, it can be stated that, in the matter of State aid, trade is presumed to be affected unless:

(1) the aid is *de minimis*;
(2) the measure only affects domestic trade; or
(3) the situation is entirely outside the European Union.

The approach the Commission has taken to the impact of State aid on trade is subject to criticism, including from an economic perspective. For an aid is only deemed to generate an adverse impact on competition if the relevant geographic scope is not domestic,[325] or the market is not perfectly competitive.[326]

318. The 'attractiveness' of the activity shall determine a 'significant incentive effect' (*'un effect incitative important'). See* Case T-728/17, *Marinvest and Porting v. Commission*; Commission Decision SA.36581 (2013/NN) of 6.11.2013; Commission Decision N 337/2007 of 28.11.2007; Commission Decision SA.39403 (2014/N) of 29 Apr. 2015; Commission Decision SA.19864 (2014/C) of 5.7.2016.
319. Only when there is an exclusionary or deterrent effect as a result of the beneficiary's activity, this may lead to the conclusion that there is 'more than a marginal effect'.
320. Commission Regulation (EU) 2023/2831 of 13 Dec. 2023 on the application of Arts 107 and 108 of the Treaty on the Functioning of the European Union to *de minimis* aid, C/2023/9700, OJ L, 2023/2831, 15.12.2023. *De minimis* aid.
321. Commission Regulation (EU) No. 1407/2013, superseding Commission Regulation (EC) No. 1998/2006.
322. What is a 'single undertaking' is outlined in Art. 2(2) of the same Regulation No. 2831/2023.
323. Commission Regulation (EU) No. 1407/2013 of 18 Dec. 2013 on the application of Arts 107 and 108 of the TFEU to *de minimis* aid.
324. To this respect *see infra* Ch. 2.
325. This seldom happens given that, in the State aid field, the Commission as a rule identifies the geographical dimension with the European Economic Area.
326. In an imperfectly competitive market, the aid recipient can gain some rent or *supra* normal profits that only exist in such a context.

It is apparent that the EU's current practice is unsatisfactory in this respect. An improved approach could be to demand that the Commission's economic analysis be strengthened, especially with respect to the relevant market definition.

CHAPTER 2

Derogations: Mandatory and Discretionary Exemptions – GBER – State Aids in Times of Crisis – The Temporary Frameworks

Edoardo Gambaro

§2.01 THE DEROGATIONS TO THE GENERAL INCOMPATIBILITY PRINCIPLE UNDER ARTICLE 107(2) AND (3) TFEU

Pursuant to Article 107(1) TFEU, save as otherwise provided in the Treaty, State aid is incompatible with the internal market if it distorts or threatens to distort competition because of its selective character.

However, this prohibition is neither absolute nor unconditional. In fact, an aid scheme or an individual aid that may appear as incompatible with the internal market under the above-mentioned Article 107(1) TFEU *may* (or, in some cases, *shall*) be considered compatible with it. In particular, the last two paragraphs of Article 107 TFEU provide for the applicable exemptions: State aid deemed compatible *ipso jure* in paragraph 2 and State aid that *may* be deemed compatible in paragraph 3.

The assessment of the compatibility of a measure which is a 'State aid' within the meaning of Article 107(1) TFEU under Article 107(2) and/or (3) TFEU[1] is a task conferred to the European Commission by the Treaty itself (Article 108 TFEU).[2] While carrying out this assessment, the European Commission must bear in mind that any

1. *See* EGC, Case T-388/20, *Ryanair v. Commission*, 14 Apr. 2021, EU:T:2021:195, §34, in which the General Court acknowledged that 'the FEU Treaty does not preclude a concurrent application of Article 107(2)(b) and Article 107(3)(b) TFEU, provided that the conditions of those two provisions are met. That applies in particular where the facts and circumstances giving rise to a serious disturbance in the economy are result of an exceptional occurrence', such as in the case of the COVID-19 pandemic. *See also infra*, §2.03 for further remarks on State aid and the COVID-19 pandemic.
2. *See* Ch. 3 for a description of the procedure before the Commission.

derogation to the general incompatibility principle laid down in Article 107(1) TFEU – as well as any term used in an exemption decision – must be interpreted as narrowly as possible,[3] since the European Commission cannot authorize Member States to derogate from provisions of EU Law that are not strictly related to the application of Article 107(1) TFEU.[4] However, such interpretation must also be consistent with the actual purposes of the derogations, in order not to deprive the latter of its intended effects.[5]

[A] Mandatory Exceptions in Article 107(2) TFEU

According to Article 107(2) TFEU, the following aids are considered *a priori* not apt to generate distorting effects on competition (and, therefore, are exempted from the overall prohibition laid down in Article 107(1) TFEU):

(a) aid having a social character, granted to individual consumers, provided that such aid is granted without discrimination related to the origin of the products concerned;[6]
(b) aid to make good the damage caused by natural disasters or other exceptional occurrences; and
(c) aid granted to the economy of certain areas of the Federal Republic of Germany affected by the division of Germany, in so far as such aid is required in order to compensate for the economic disadvantages caused by that division.

Before any measure deemed to fall in any one of the classes of aid listed above can be granted by the Member State concerned, it must be notified by the Member State to the Commission.[7] The Commission will carry out a mere legality control, in the context of which the Commission has significantly less room for scrutiny than the one it has under Article 107(3) TFEU. Indeed, the Commission will limit itself to assessing the proposed measures for compliance with the formal and technical requirements provided for by the TFEU, without being permitted to exercise any discretion in the matter.

3. *See* EGC, Case T-8/18, *easyJet Airline v. Commission*, 13 May 2020, EU:T:2020:182, §242.
4. *See* CJEU, joined cases C-134/91 and C-135/91, *Kerafina and Vioktimatiki*, 12 Nov. 1992, EU:C:1992:434, §20.
5. *See* CJEU, Case C-320/21 P, *Ryanair v. Commission*, 23.9.2023, EU:C:2023:712, §§51-52.
6. *See* Commission Regulation (EU) No. 651/2014 of 17 Jun. 2014 (GBER, on which *see infra* section §2.02 of the present chapter); in particular, Art. 51 on social aid for transport for residents of remote regions.
7. In particular, with reference to the need to notify aids falling within the scope of the exceptions laid down in Art. 107(2) TFEU to the European Commission, while there is no clear case law in relation to Art. 107(2)(a) TFEU aids (accordingly, one might argue that aid to individual consumers could be excluded from the scope of the prohibition and thus be excluded from the obligation of prior notification), aids covered by Art. 107(2)(b) and (c) are subject to notification requirements.

[1] *Article 107(2)(a): Aid Having a Social Character Granted to Individual Consumers*

First of all, under Article 107(2)(a) TFEU, individual aids or aid schemes must be deemed compatible with the internal market if: (i) they have a social character; (ii) they are granted to individual consumers;[8] and (iii) they are granted without discrimination related to the origin of the products concerned. Accordingly, as long as the aid benefits individual consumers, the actual way in which the latter is granted (e.g., vouchers, rebates financed by state resources, etc.) is entirely irrelevant.

Moreover, in order to be deemed compatible with Article 107(2)(a) TFEU, the aid must be granted to certain categories of consumers whose situation justifies social intervention, such as, for example, individuals travelling to remote islands or territories, high-risk public employees taking out health or accident insurance policies, low-income citizens buying television equipment. However, it is not necessary that each individual beneficiary actually needs the aid. Indeed, aids may be granted to certain sub-sets of the general population, which reasonably need social assistance.[9]

Finally, the exemption provided for under Article 107(2) TFEU may only be invoked if the aid measure is granted to individual consumers and does not result in an indirect benefit or advantage for the undertakings providing the goods or services in question.

Indeed, the mere fact that an aid measure has social purposes and is granted to individual consumers is not enough to prevent the measure from coming within the scope of Article 107(1) TFEU.[10] Social aids granted to consumers may in fact conceal, for instance, indirect forms of aid to economic operators.[11]

Thus, determining the actual existence of a discrimination related to the origin of the product concerned by the aid becomes crucial in the assessment of the potential applicability of the exemption referred to in Article 107(2)(a) TFEU. To do so, the Commission must ascertain whether consumers would benefit from a given aid

---

8. *See* EGC, case T-445/05, *Associazione Italiana del Risparmio Gestito and Fineco Asset Management v. Commission*, 4 Mar. 2009, EU:T:2009:50, in which the General Court found that 'although it is common ground that the aid was granted without discrimination relating to the origin of the investment vehicles concerned, it is aimed at all categories of investors, whose taxes or charges are reduced. Accordingly, the measure at issue has no social character'.
9. For instance, a scheme aimed at supporting the purchase of public transport tickets by children, students and apprentices in the Rhineland-Palatinate Land of Germany was deemed compatible with the internal market based on Arts 107(2)(a) TFEU (and 93 TFEU), based on its social character, since the aid was 'reserved for a particular category of passengers whose situation justifies the payment of aid for social reasons. Pupils, students and trainees are passengers who are dependent on regular transport to their schools, universities and training places and who usually have no significant income. As explained above, the measure aims at an open access to education by providing cheap public transport tickets for pupils, students and trainees to their schools, universities and training places. Furthermore, the scheme pursues specific social aims by financially disburdening families with children'. EC, Case SA.34155 (2013/N) (ex 2011/PN) – Germany – Regional law on the compensation of school bus transport in the Land Rhineland-Palatinate, 22 Jan. 2014.
10. *See* CJEU, Case T-93/02, *Confédération national du Crédit mutuel v. Commission*, 18 Jan. 2005, EU:T:2005:11.
11. *See* CJEU, Case C-403/10, *Mediaset v. Commission*, 28 Jul. 2011, EU:C:2011:533, §81.

measure regardless of who the economic operator that provides the product or the service suitable to pursue the social goal invoked actually is. In the lack of any evidence showing that final consumers could equally benefit from the aid by recurring to products or services offered by other companies suitable to fulfil the social goal of the measure, the Commission should opt for the existence of a discrimination determined by the origin of such products or services,

In the lack of evidence proving that final consumers could equally benefit from the disputed aid by using the services of other companies suitable to achieve the social objective pursued by the competent authority, the European Commission is entitled to conclude that an aid has not been granted to individual consumers without discrimination determined by the origin of the products. In this event, the conditions set by Article 107(2)(a) TFEU would not be met.[12]

[2] Article 107(2)(b): Aid to Make Good the Damage Caused by Natural Disasters or Other Exceptional Occurrences

Article 107(2)(b) states that an individual aid or an aid scheme must be deemed compatible with the internal market whenever such aid measure is granted 'to make good the damage caused by natural disasters or exceptional occurrences'.

An aid granted pursuant to Article 107(2)(b) must therefore meet the following criteria.

First, it must be due to an exceptional occurrence, this meaning an unforeseen/unpredictable event that is clearly out of the norm and that is suitable to have a significant impact over the potential beneficiaries of the aid.[13]

As pointed out by the case law of the CJEU, Article 107(2)(b) TFEU cannot be invoked to compensate damages that occurred due to phenomena that are the physiological expression of the interaction of market forces that are normally faced by

12. *See* EGC, joined Cases T-116/01 and T-118/01, *P&O European Ferries (Vizcaya) and Diputación Foral de Vizcaya v. Commission*, 5 Aug. 2003, EU:T:2003:217, 162-163 and 167. In this case, the European Courts have been asked to rule on several agreements between a shipping company and Bilbao's local authority for a ferry service. Under such agreements, end users would have benefitted from a special system of vouchers purchased, on their behalf, by the authorities of Bilbao. First, the Commission adopted a negative decision (EC, Case SA.4748 – Aide en faveur de la societé Ferries Golfo de Vizcaya S.A., 29 Nov. 2000), considering that they did not in fact reflect the actual needs of individual users. Ruling over the appeal brought against such decision, the EGC rejected the applicants' arguments that Art. 107(2)(a) TFEU was applicable to the aid scheme in question. Indeed, the EGC accepted the Commission's arguments that the provision could not apply if only one undertaking benefited from the aid at issue and it was not proven that the social objectives pursued by the aid could only be achieved by purchasing travel vouchers from that undertaking. Please consider that the aforementioned ruling of the EGC has been upheld by the CJEU (*see* CJEU, Case C-442/03 P and C-471/03 P, *P&O European Ferries (Vizcaya) and Diputación Foral de Vizcaya v. Commission*, June 2006, EU:C:2006:356). Indeed, the CJEU stated that the agreement had not been concluded to meet the real needs of individual consumers, but had been concluded in order to give the shipping company an advantage it would not have obtained under normal market conditions.
13. *See* Phedon Nicolaides, *Application of Article 107(2)(b) TFEU to Covid-19 Measures: State Aid to Make Good the Damage Occurred by an Exceptional Occurrence*, 11, JECLAP 5-6 (2020), pp. 238-243 https://doi.org/10.1093/jeclap/lpaa026.

any business (such as high-interest aids), or to weather conditions the specific severity of which has not been accurately demonstrated by the State.[14]

However, while Article 50 of the Commission Regulation (EU) No. 651/2014 of 17 June 2014 (the so-called General Block Exemption Regulation, also known as GBER), in referring to Article 107(2)(b) TFEU, gives some (non-exhaustive) examples of natural disasters,[15] it is more complex to define which events may fall within the group of 'other exceptional events'.

This can be considered an open category in which, over the years, the Commission has included events such as wars, terrorist attacks, strikes, nuclear, naval or industrial accidents, fires and epidemics. This definition, in essence, covers all those circumstances in which companies are victims of situations for which they cannot be held responsible.

Anyway, since, as already noted *supra* subsection [1], all the provisions that introduce an 'automatic' derogation to the general principle of incompatibility of state aids with the internal market must be construed narrowly, even Article 107(2)(b) must be interpreted in the most literal way possible.[16] Accordingly, the European Commission has generally maintained a restrictive interpretation of the notion of exceptional circumstances and natural disasters.

Up to 2020, Member States have thus made recourse to the exemption under Article 107(2)(a) TFEU as a legal basis for aid measures in various circumstances, such as Italy did in the cases of the earthquake in Abruzzo of 2009,[17] which were overall all in line with the idea of 'natural disaster' and/or 'exceptional occurrence' described above.

However, as further observed *infra*, §2.03, this approach has not prevented the European Commission from considering the COVID-19 pandemic as an 'exceptional occurrence' within the meaning of Article 107(2)(b) TFEU; thus, authorizing a number of aid measures granted under the 2020 Temporary Framework for State aid measures to support the economy of the Member States amid the pandemic.

Indeed, in a decision on a Danish compensation scheme following the cancellation of numerous events, the Commission officially acknowledged the COVID-19 pandemic as an 'exceptional occurrence' within the meaning of Article 107(2)(b) TFEU.[18] With this ruling, an important precedent was set, and Member States have

14. *See* joined cases C-346/03 and C-529/03, *Atzeni and Others*, 23 Feb. 2006, EU:C:2006:130, §§80-81.
15. Such as 'earthquakes, avalanches, landslides, floods, tornadoes, hurricanes, volcanic eruptions and wild fires of natural origin'. *See* Commission Regulation (EU) No. 651/2014 of 17 Jun. 2014 (GBER, on which *see infra*, §2.02 of the present chapter); in particular, Art. 50 on aid schemes to make good the damage caused by certain natural disasters.
16. *See* CJEU, Cases C-278/00, *Greece v. Commission*, 29 Apr. 2004, EU:C:2004:289, §§81-82, C-73/03, *Spain v. Commission*, 11 Nov. 2004, EU:C:2004:711, §§36-37 and joined cases C-346/03 and C-529/03, *Atzeni and Others*, §79.
17. *See* EC, Case SA.29112, Aid scheme for compensation for damage caused by the earthquake in Abruzzo of 6 Apr. 2009 (outside the field of Annex I of the Treaty), 16 Oct. 2009.
18. *See* EC, decision on SA.56685, DK – *Compensation scheme for cancellation of events related to COVID-19*, 12 Mar. 2020.

been indeed relieved from having to prove, in subsequent notifications, that the pandemic was an exceptional event.[19]

Second, there must be a clear, direct causal link between the damage suffered by the potential beneficiary due to an exceptional occurrence or natural disaster and the aid measure. Such link must be assessed with diligence by the Commission, considering, if needed, the potential consequences that the aid measure might have on the specific industry.[20]

In this relation, please consider that:

- the definition of exceptional occurrence applicable under Article 107(2)(b) is controversial;[21]
- for the aid measure to be deemed compatible with the internal market under Article 107(2)(b) TFEU, the potential beneficiaries of the aid must have already suffered a quantifiable damage due to such exceptional circumstances;
- a causal link between the damage suffered and the aid measure pursuant to Article 107(2)(b) TFEU cannot be said to exist if, despite being intended to make good the damages suffered because of an exceptional occurrence, the aid measure is ultimately motivated by considerations that are arbitrary or extraneous to the mentioned objective. This might occur, for instance, when an aid is granted with the sole goal of favouring one undertaking over another one.[22]

19. Please consider that the criteria for the application of Art. 107(2)(b) TFEU in the context of COVID-19 have been further detailed in the Commission Communication Temporary Framework for State aid measures to support the economy in the current COVID-19 emergency (*see infra*, §2.03).
20. *See* EGC, Case T-132/96 and T-143/96, *Freistaat Sachsen and Volkswagen v. Commission*, 15 Dec. 1999, EU:T:1999:326, §280.
21. Indeed, on the one hand, the terrorist attacks of 11 Sep. 2001 and their consequences for air traffic have been defined as such, while, on the other hand, situations generated by the normal strategic decisions of one or more undertakings have been excluded from this category. For example, in 1998, following the decision of the British cruise company P&O to stop transporting livestock by sea from Ireland to France, the Commission declared an Irish plan to promote domestic sea transport services, drawn up with a view to protecting the island's livestock exporters, incompatible with the internal market. In this decision, the Commission reiterated that normal entrepreneurial risk cannot be considered an 'exceptional occurrence' and that the inability to conduct business with diligence excludes a right to aid.
22. *See* CJEU, Case C-320/21 P, *Ryanair DAC v. Commission*, 28 Sep. 2023, EU:C:2023:712, §28. However, please consider that 'the objective pursued by Article 107(2)(b) TFEU, which is to compensate for the disadvantages caused directly by an exceptional occurrence, does not mean that a Member State cannot, without that being dictated by a desire to favour one undertaking over its competitors, choose, for objective reasons, to grant only a single undertaking the benefit of a measure adopted under that provision. Moreover, a contrary interpretation of Article 107(2)(b) TFEU would deprive that provision of much of its effectiveness. If that provision only allowed a Member State the option of granting aid to all the victims of an exceptional occurrence without being able to reserve that aid to a limited number of undertakings, or even just one, Member States would often be deterred from making use of that option because of the costs involved in the grant, in such circumstances, of significant aid to all undertakings that suffered damage coming under its authority'. *Ibid.*, §§24-25.

Finally, the amount of aid granted must be proportionate to the damages suffered, meaning that it cannot exceed the actual total cost of such damage. Indeed, as pointed out by the Court of Justice of the EU, aid measures that improve the financial situations of their recipients exceeding what is strictly necessary cannot be considered compatible with the internal market.[23]

If the European Commission finds that the aid scheme or individual measure meets all the criteria set about, it has to declare the compatibility of such aid with the internal market. Indeed, Article 107(2)(b) leaves no room for discretion to the European Commission in establishing whether to authorize the aid or not. This, of course, besides the aids that fall within the scope of the General Block Exemption Regulation (*see infra*, §2.02).

Article 107(2)(b) is, therefore, a purely *ex post* tool. This makes Article 107(2)(b) less suitable to tackle circumstances in which losses are due to short-time events and are still ongoing (such as, in the event of economic aftershocks due to a pandemic, or a terroristic attack), or in which a State may desire to act in a pre-emptive manner, to avoid a further deterioration in the financial situation of the aid's beneficiaries.[24]

[3] Article 107(2)(c): Aid Granted to the Economy of Certain Areas of the Federal Republic of Germany Affected by the Division of Germany

Finally, the last circumstance in which an individual aid or an aid scheme should be considered indisputably not suitable to distort competition on the internal market pursuant to Article 107(2) TFEU is when such measures are granted to the economy of certain areas of the Federal Republic of Germany affected by the division of Germany, but only if such aid is required to compensate the economic advantage of such division.[25]

In line with what has already been said in relation to the derogations provided for under letters (a) and (b) of Article 107(2) TFEU, even the one laid down in letter (c) must be construed narrowly. Accordingly, as pointed out by the case law of the European Courts, 'the phrase "division of Germany" refers historically to the establishment of the dividing line between the two occupied zones in 1948',[26] and 'the "economic disadvantages caused by that division" can only mean the economic

23. *See* CJEU, Case C-320/21 P, *Ryanair DAC v. Commission*, §30.
24. *See* Jakub Kociubiński, *The New Normal? The European Union's Temporary Frameworks for State Aid*, 14 Wroc. Review Law, Adm. Econ. (2024) https://doi.org/10.2478/wrlae-2024-0001, available at the following link: https://sciendo.com/article/10.2478/wrlae-2024-0001?tab=articles-in-this-issue. *See also* Nicolaides, *supra* n. 13, p. 238.
25. At first, aid measures or schemes granted after the unification of Germany in 1990, but related to economic advantages accrued before that date, were approved by the Commission (subject to certain conditions) under Art. 107(2)(c) TFEU. However, given the large amounts of aid granted by Germany in such period (over 30% of the total aid granted in the then European Community in the mid-1990s), the Commission, in order to maintain greater control over such aid, generally assessed the post-German unification aid under Art. 107(3) TFEU.
26. *See* CJEU, Case C-334/99, *Germany v. Commission*, 28 Jan. 2003, EU:C:2003:55, §120.

disadvantages caused in certain areas of Germany by the isolation which the establishment of that physical frontier entailed, such as the breaking of communication links or the loss of markets as a result of the breaking off of commercial relations between the two parts of German territory'.[27]

Article 107(2)(c) TFEU states that five years after the entry into force of the Treaty of Lisbon (i.e., after 1 December 2014), the Council, acting on a proposal of the Commission, could have adopted a decision to repeal this point of Article 107(2) TFEU. However, as of today, no decision has been taken in this relation. Therefore, Article 107(2)(c) technically still represents a primary legal basis on which State aid measures might be authorized under EU law.

[B] Discretionary Exceptions in Article 107(3) TFEU

Having established that a measure would be suitable to constitute a State aid pursuant to Article 107(1) TFEU, the Commission may consider such aid to be compatible with the internal market under Article 107(3) TFEU if it meets any of the following criteria:

(a) aims at promoting the economic development of certain regions; in particular, regions in which the standard of living is abnormally low or in which there is serious underemployment, as well as the regions identified under Article 349 TFEU,[28] in view of their structural, economic and social situation;
(b) promotes the execution of an important project of common European interest, or remedies to a serious disturbance in the economy of a Member State;[29]
(c) facilitates the development of certain economic activities or of certain economic areas, where such aid does not adversely affect trading conditions to an extent contrary to the common interest; or
(d) promotes culture and heritage conservation where such aid does not affect trading conditions and competition in the Union to an extent that is contrary to the common interest.[30]

---

27. *See* CJEU, Case C-277/00, *Germany v. Commission*, 29 Apr. 2004, EU:C:2004:238, §50.
28. In particular, Art. 349 TFEU specific mentions Guadeloupe, French Guiana, Martinique, Réunion, Saint-Barthélemy, Saint-Martin, the Azores, Madeira and the Canary Islands.
29. On the notion of 'project of common European interest' *see* the Communication from the Commission – Criteria for the analysis of the compatibility with the internal market of State aid to promote the execution of important projects of common European interest 2021/C 582/02, published in OJ C 528 of 30 Dec. 2021.
30. This derogation was introduced in 1993 by the EU Treaty and has been generally used to authorize among others aid measures regarding films and audiovisual works, theatre, music, dance and festival production. *See* Communication from the Commission on State aid for films and other audiovisual works, 2013/C 332/01, published in OJ C 332, 15.11.2013. *See also* with regard to aid in the broadcasting sector the Communication from the Commission on the application of State aid rules to public service broadcasting, 2009/C 257/01, published in OJ C 257, 27.10.2009. In addition, *see* Commission Regulation (EU) No. 651/2014 of 17 Jun. 2014 (GBER, on which *see infra* §2.02 of the present chapter); in particular, Arts 53 and 54, respectively, on aid for culture and heritage conservation and aid schemes for audiovisual works.

Such list is open to expansion: indeed, according to Article 107(3)(e) TFEU, the Council, acting on a proposal of the Commission, might decide to increase the categories of aids that may be deemed to be compatible with the internal market under Article 107(3) TFEU.[31]

Contrary to what has been said in relation to the exemption provided for by Article 107(2) TFEU, under Article 107(3) the Commission is not automatically bound to declare an aid compatible with the internal market. Indeed, even the wording of Article 107(3) itself makes clear that under Article 107(3) aids *may* be considered compatible with the internal market by the EC, while under Article 107(2) aids *shall* have been considered compatible.[32]

This implies that in applying Article 107(3) TFEU the Commission enjoys a wide discretion, the exercise of which involves assessments of complex economic and social nature that must be made within an EU context rather than a merely national one.[33]

In particular, as pointed out by the case law of the European Courts, the European Commission may refuse the grant of an aid if the latter:

- does not induce the beneficiaries to adopt conducts that are likely to assist attainment of the objectives mentioned above;[34]
- is not necessary for the attainment of the objectives recalled in Article 107(3), (a)-(d), meaning that, without the intervention of the aid measure, market forces alone would not succeed in getting the undertakings to adopt conducts likely to assist the attainment of the aforementioned goals;[35]
- does not reconcile the aims of the derogation with those of free competition on the internal market.[36]

31. In this relation, please consider that recently the European Commission has reduced the number of individual assessment cases under Art. 107(3) TFEU. Indeed, the Commission is adopting a number of sectorial block exemption regulations, which allow to automatically establish whether an aid measure is compatible with the internal market or not. Moreover, if an aid measure does not fall under a block exemption, the Commission may still apply the criteria set out in the guidelines that might be applicable to the given sector to exempt the measure concerned. Finally, and only if an aid measure does not even fall within the scope of one of the Guidelines, the Commission will then directly apply Art. 107(3) TFEU in order to verify whether the aid can be considered compatible with the internal market.
32. *See* EGC, Case T-457/09, *Westfälisch-Lippischer Sparkassen- und Giroverband v. Commission*, 17 Jul. 2014, EU:T:2014:683, §182.
33. *See* CJEU, Case C-730/79, *Philip Morris v. Commission*, 17 Sep. 1980, EU:C:1980:209, §24, Case C-301/87, *France v. Commission (Boussac)*, 14 Feb. 1990, EU:C:1990:67, §49 and Case C-303/88, *Italy v. Commission*, 21 Mar. 1991, EU:C:1991:136, §34. More recently, *see* EGC, Case T-463/13 and T-464/13, *Comunidad Autónoma de Galicia and Retegal v. Commission*, 26 Nov. 2015, EU:T:2015:901, §119 and Case T-298/97, *etc.*, *Alzetta and Others v. Commission*, 15 Jun. 2000, ECLI:EU:T:2000:151, §129.
34. *See* EGC, Case T-417/16, *Achemos Grupé and Achema v. Commission*, 12 Sep. 2019, EU:T:2019:597, §68.
35. *See* EGC, Case T-388/20, *Ryanair v. Commission (Finnair I, COVID-19)*, 14 Apr. 2021, EU:T:2021:196, §33 and the case law mentioned therein.
36. *See*, among the others, EGC, Case T-671/14, *Bayerische Motoren Werke v. Commission*, 12 Sep. 2017, EU:T:2017:599, §110 and Case T-162/06, *Kronopoly v. Commission*, 14 Jan. 2009, EU:T:2009:2, §66.

It can be clearly inferred from the above that the discretion power of the EC under Article 107(3) TFEU is far wider than that conferred on the Commission in furtherance of the exemption provided for by Article 107(2) TFEU, based on which it may only verify the fulfilment of certain formal conditions.

Despite this wide discretion, in its assessment of the potential compatibility of State aid measures under Article 107(3) TFEU, the European Commission must always bear in mind that, as pointed out by the European Courts:

- the European Commission cannot approve an aid measure that is in conflict with one of the other provisions of the Treaty;[37]
- moreover, the mere fact that a plan for new aid measures is aimed at meeting the goals laid down in a provision of a Treaty other than Article 107(3) TFEU does not in itself mean that the plan satisfies the conditions for that exemption to apply.[38]

Finally, in its compatibility assessment under Article 107(3) TFEU, the European Commission must always carry out, on a case-by-case basis, the so-called balancing test, namely it must always balance the negative effects on trade and competition in the internal market of an aid with its positive effects in terms of a contribution to the achievement of well-defined objectives of common interest.

In practice, this implies that the Commission must always verify the below:

(1) Is the aid measure aimed at a well-defined objective of common interest?
(2) Is the aid well designed to deliver the objective of common interest, i.e., does the proposed aid address the market failure or other objectives?
(3) Is the aid in question really necessary, i.e., couldn't the situation be resolved by market dynamics?
(4) Is the aid an appropriate policy instrument to address the policy objective concerned, i.e., could the same objectives also be achieved by other forms of intervention, different in nature or amount, which are less distortive of competition?
(5) Is there an actual incentive effect on its beneficiaries, i.e., does the aid change the behaviour of the aid recipient?
(6) Is the aid measure proportionate to the problem tackled, i.e., could the same change in behaviour not be obtained with less aid?
(7) Are the distortions of competition and effect on trade limited, so that the overall balance is positive, i.e., does the aid have no negative effects on competition and trade between Member States?
(8) Is the aid granted in a transparent manner, i.e., such that the institutions and operators have access to all relevant documents and information?

37. Indeed, regardless of whether an aid measure could be exempted from the prohibition of State aid, it cannot be approved if, for example, it conflicts with freedom of establishment or the right of free movement of goods. *See*, for instance, EGC, Case T-388/20, *Ryanair v. Commission (Finnair I, COVID-19)*, §77.
38. *See* CJEU, joined cases C-261/01 and C-262/01, *Van Calster*, 21 Oct. 2003, EU:C:2003:571, §47.

[1] *Article 107(3)(a): Aids Granted to Areas Where the Standard of Living Is Abnormally Low or Where There Is Serious Underemployment*

As mentioned above, according to Article 107(3)(a) TFEU, aids 'to promote the economic development of areas where the standard of living is abnormally low or where there is serious underemployment' could be considered compatible with the internal market.

Article 107(3)(a) allows the European Commission to authorize aid that is aimed at promoting the economic development of areas that, with an abnormally low standard of living or serious underemployment, have an extremely disadvantaged economic situation if compared to the European Union as a whole.[39]

The comparison with the EU level is what makes such a rule different from Article 107(3)(c) (yet another rule that allows for the granting of regional aids). Indeed, the fact that Article 107(3)(c) allows for the granting of aids addressed to the development of areas of a given Member State that are more disadvantaged than the average of such specific Member State implies that regions covered by Article 107(3)(a) TFEU are usually less developed than those covered by Article 107(3)(c) TFEU.

However, such a severe situation of economic underdevelopment of a geographical region if compared to the rest of the EU does not imply that any aid project that might be carried out for such reason is automatically considered necessary to the development of such an area. Albeit essential to the authorization of an aid under Article 107(3)(a) TFEU, the underdevelopment of a region is not sufficient, in itself, to define an aid scheme as indispensable to its development.[40] Indeed, the Commission will still have to verify not only that the measures actually contribute to the economic development of the regions concerned but also assess the impact of the aid on trade between Member States and, in particular, the sectoral repercussions at the EU level.[41]

In this relation, please consider that, in the past, the European Commission has considered that the conditions of Article 107(3)(a) of the Treaty are fulfilled in:

(1) NUTS 2 regions[42] with a gross domestic product (GDP) per capita below or equal to 75% of the Union's average.[43]

39. *See* EGC, Case T-60/06 RENV II and T-62/06 RENV II, *Italy and Eurallumina v. Commission*, 22 Apr. 2016, EU:T:2016:233, §143 and CJEU, Case C-310/99, *Italy v. Commission*, 7 Mar. 2002, EU:C:2002:143, §77.
40. *See* CJEU, Case C-630/11 P to C-633/11 P, *HGA and Others v. Commission*, 13 Jun. 2013, EU:C:2013:387, §§111-112.
41. *See* CJEU, Case C-113/00, *Spain v. Commission*, 19 Sep. 2002, EU:C:2002:507, §67.
42. *See* Commission Guidelines on Regional State aid for 2022 to 2027, 2021/C 153/01, §158. Reference is made to Regulation (EC) No. 1059/2003 of the European Parliament and of the Council on the establishment of a common classification of territorial units for statistics (NUTS) (OJ L 154, 21.6.2003) as amended by Commission Delegated Regulation (EU) 2019/1755 (OJ L 270, 24.10.2019).
43. Please consider that the 'average' based on the average of the last three years for which Eurostat data are available.

(2) Outermost regions.[44]

[2] Article 107(3)(c): Aids Aimed at the Development of Certain Economic Areas

Article 107(3)(c) TFEU considers compatible with the internal market an aid aimed at 'facilitat[ing] the development of certain economic activities or of certain economic areas, where such aid does not adversely affect trading conditions to an extent contrary to the common interest'.

The role played by Article 107(3)(c) TFEU in State aid assessment is crucial. As pointed out by the doctrine, such a rule represents the legal basis for most of the State aid cases assessed by the European Commission, as well as for most of the provisions laid down in the GBER.[45]

In fact, as confirmed by the case law of the CJEU,[46] for an aid to be declared compatible with the internal market under Article 107(3)(c) TFEU only two conditions must be met.

Under the first condition, the aid scheme or measure must be aimed at facilitating the development of certain economic activities or economic areas. In this relation, the wording of Article 107(3)(c) TFEU, using the conjunction 'or' (which, by its nature, implies the existence of alternatives), makes clear that an aid may be regarded as compatible with the internal market even when it is exclusively aimed at helping the development of a given region.[47]

Indeed, according to the Court of Justice, '[t]he exemption in Article (107)(3)(c) [...] permits the development of certain areas without being restricted by the economic conditions laid down in Article (107)(3)(a), provided such aid "does not adversely affect trading conditions to an extent contrary to the common interest"'. That provision gives the Commission power to authorize aid intended to further the economic development of areas of a Member State which are disadvantaged in relation to the national average (so-called c areas).[48]

Please consider that, as illustrated by the European Commission, there are two main categories of 'c areas':

44. For example, Canary Islands in Spain and the Madeira Region in Portugal. *See* Annex I of the Guidelines on regional State aid for 2014-2020 providing for Regional aid coverage by Member States for 2014-2020.
45. Phedon Nicolaides, *Shedding Light into the 'Black Box' of State Aid: The Impact of Hinkley Point C on the Assessment of the Compatibility of State Aid*, 20, *EStAL*, 4 (2020) https://doi.org/10.21552/estal/2021/1/3.
46. *See*, in particular, CJEU, Case C-594/18 P, *Austria v. Commission*, 22 Sep. 2020, EU:C:2020:742.
47. *See* EGC, Case T-110/97, *Kneissl Dachstein v. Commission*, 6 Oct. 1999, EU:T:1990:244, §61.
48. *See* Cases C-248/84 *Germany v. Commission*, §19 and C-113/00, *Spain v. Commission*, §65. *See also* EC, Commission Guidelines on Regional State aid for 2022 to 2027, §161.

(1) the so-called predefined c-areas, i.e., areas that fulfil certain pre-established conditions and that a Member State may therefore designate as 'c' areas without any further justification; and
(2) areas that a Member State may, at its own discretion, designate as 'c' areas provided that the Member State demonstrates that such areas fulfil certain socioeconomic criteria ('non-predefined "c" areas').[49]

Moreover, according to the second condition laid down in Article 107(3)(c) TFEU, the aid must not adversely affect trading conditions to an extent contrary to the 'common interest'. This means that, as pointed out by the CJEU in the well-known *Hinkley Point* case, in its assessment, the European Commission must balance the positive effects of the proposed aid on the development of the targeted activities and the potential negative effects it might have on the internal market (and, in particular, on competition and trade between Member States), without taking into account the potential negative effects a measure might have on other principles.[50]

[a] Regional Aid

State aids - even ad hoc ones[51] - that fall under Article 107(1), but that might be deemed compatible with the internal market pursuant to Article 107(3)(a) and/or Article 107(3)(c) TFEU are generally known as 'Regional Aids'.[52]

In particular:

- under Article 107(3)(a) TFEU, may be declared compatible with the internal market an 'aid to promote the economic development of areas where the standard of living is abnormally low or where there is serious underemployment, and of the regions referred to in Article 349, in view of their structural, economic and social situation';
- under Article 107(3)(c) TFEU, instead, may be declared compatible with the internal market an 'aid to facilitate the development of certain economic activities or of certain economic areas, where such aid does not adversely affect trading conditions to an extent contrary to the common interest'.

---

49. *See* EC, Commission Guidelines on Regional State aid for 2022 to 2027, §§163 and ff.
50. *See* CJEU, Case C-594/18 P, *Austria v. Commission*, §§101-102. Indeed, the CJEU notes that 'the General Court did not err in law in holding that, when identifying the negative effects of the measures at issue, the Commission did not have to take into account the extent to which those measures are detrimental to the implementation of the principle of protection of the environment, the precautionary principle, the "polluter pays" principle and the principle of sustainability relied on by the Republic of Austria'. *See also*, Phedon Nicolaides, *Demystifying the Balancing of the Positive and Negative Effects of State Aid*, 23, *EStAL*, 2 (2024) https://doi.org/10.21552/estal/2024/2/6.
51. *See* CJEU, Cases C-278/92 to C-280/92, *Spain v. Commission (Hytasa)*, 14 Sep. 1994, EU:C:1994:325, §49 and EGC, Case T-127/99, etc., *Territorio Histórico de Álava and Others v. Commission*, 6 Mar. 2002, EU:T:2002:59, §267.
52. *See*, CJEU, Case 248/84, *Germany v. Commission*, 14 Oct. 1987, EU:C:1987:437, §19 and Case C-113/00, *Spain v. Commission*, 19 Sep. 2002, EU:C:2002:507, §64.

As highlighted by the case law of the EGC, Article 107(3)(a) and Article 107(3)(c) TFEU introduce two derogations that are based on the fundamental objective of Union solidarity. Therefore, in assessing the compatibility of an aid with the internal market under such derogations, the European Commission must take into account that the aim of Union solidarity (the influence of which varies depending on the circumstances having more of an influence to the detriment of competition in the crisis situations described in paragraph 3(a) than in the cases provided for in paragraph 3(c)) and that of free competition should be reconciled while complying with the principle of proportionality.[53]

In particular:

- the wording of Article 107(3)(a) TFEU suggests that such exemption concerns only areas in which the economic situation is extremely unfavourable in relation to the EU as a whole;
- the wording of Article 107(3)(c) TFEU, however, has a wider scope, since it makes no reference to the economic conditions recalled in Article 107(3)(a) TFEU. Indeed, under such latter exemptions, the only limitation to the granting of the measure is that it 'does not adversely affect trading conditions to an extent contrary to the common interest', thus granting the Commission the power to authorize aid schemes and measures even to the benefit of areas of a Member States that are disadvantaged in relation to the national average.[54]

Regional aid both under Article 107(3)(a) and under Article 107(3)(c) is regulated extensively in the aforementioned GBER,[55] which entered into force on 1 July 2014.

53. In this context, the Commission is under a duty to evaluate the sectoral effects of the planned regional aid, even where regions likely to fall within para. 3(a) are concerned, in order to avoid a situation in which, as a result of an aid measure, a sectoral problem is created at Union level which is more serious than the initial regional problem. However, so as not to deprive para. 3(a) of its utility, the Commission has a broader discretion in balancing those objectives in the case of an aid project intended to promote the development of a region coming under para. 3(a) than it has in the case of identical aid to a region covered by para. 3(c). *See* EGC, Case T-380/94, *AIUFFASS and AKT v. Commission*, 12 Dec. 1996, EU:T:1996:195, §§54-55, Case T-126/96 and T-127/96, *BFM and EFIM v. Commission*, 15 Sep. 1998, EU:T:1998:207, §101 and Case T-132/96 and T-143/96, *Freistaat Sachsen and Volkswagen v. Commission*, 15 Dec. 1999, EU:T:1999:326, §187.
54. *See* CJEU, Case 248/84, *Germany v. Commission*, §19, Case C-113/00, *Spain v. Commission*, §§65-66 and Case C-169/95, *Spain v. Commission (Pyrsa)*, 14 Jan. 1997, EU:C:1997:10, §§15-16. Please consider that the aforementioned difference in wording between Art. 107(3)(a) and Art. 107(3)(c) TFEU does not mean that, in the application of Art. 107(3)(a) TFEU, the Commission should take no account of the Union's, and must confine itself to verifying the regional specificity of the measures involved without assessing their impact on the relevant market or markets in the Union as a whole. Indeed, as highlighted by the Court of Justice in its case law, in such cases, the EC has not only to verify that the measures are such as to contribute effectively to the economic development of the regions concerned but also to evaluate the impact of the aid on trade between Member States, and in particular to assess the sectorial repercussions they may have at Union level. *See* CJEU, Case C-169/95, *Spain v. Commission (Pyrsa)*, §§7, 17, Case C-113/00, *Spain v. Commission*, §67, and EGC, and Cases EGC T-126/96 and C-127/96, *BFM and EFIM v. Commission*, 15 Sep. 1998, EU:T:1998:207. §101.
55. *See* Commission Regulation (EU) No. 651/2014 of 17 Jun. 2014, Arts 13-16.

Accordingly, most regional aid is now exempted, without the need for notification to and approval by the Commission.

For regional aid that is not exempted, the Commission will apply the Guidelines on Regional State Aid for 2022 to 2027,[56] which illustrate how Member States can grant investment aid to companies to support the development of disadvantaged regions in Europe between 2022 and 2027. These guidelines, which entered into force on 1 January 2022, replace the previous Guidelines on Regional State Aid (for 2014 to 2020), which also entered into force on 1 July 2014.[57]

[b] *Sectorial and Horizontal Aid*

The Commission may consider compatible – again under Article 107(3)(c) TFEU – also '*aid to facilitate the development of certain economic activities [...] where such aid does not adversely affect trading conditions to an extent contrary to the common interest*'. Such provision represents the most often used legal basis for authorizing *sectorial aids* and *horizontal aid*.

The Commission has adopted over the years (a) sectorial and (b) horizontal rules setting out its policies on individual categories of aid, to wit.

(1) *Sector-specific rules:*
- agriculture;[58]
- audiovisual production;[59]
- broadband;[60]
- broadcasting;[61]
- electricity;[62]

56. *See*, EC, Commission Guidelines on Regional State aid for 2022 to 2027, §1.
57. *See*, EC, Commission Guidelines on Regional State aid for 2014 to 2020, 2013/C 209/01.
58. The new agricultural *de minimis* Regulation (Commission Regulation (EU) No. 1408/2013 of 18 Dec. 2013, OJ L 352, 24.12.2013, p. 9) is in place since 1 Jan. 2014. The new Agricultural Block Exemption Regulation (ABER) and the Guidelines for State aid in the agriculture and forestry sector apply as from 1 Jan. 2023: *see*, respectively, Commission Regulation (EU) No. 2472/2022 of 14 Dec. 2022 declaring certain categories of aid in the agricultural and forestry sectors and in rural areas compatible with the internal market in application of Arts 107 and 108 of the Treaty on the Functioning of the European Union, OJ L 327, 22.12.2022, p. 1 and the Communication from the Commission Guidelines for State aid in the agricultural and forestry sectors and in rural areas, OJ C 485, 22.12.2022, p. 1. For a detailed analysis on State aid rules in the agriculture sector *see* Ch. 12 *infra*.
59. *See* Communication from the Commission on State aid for films and other audiovisual works, OJ C 332, 15.11.2013, p. 1.
60. *See* Communication from the Commission Guidelines on State aid for Broadband networks, OJ C 36, 31.1.2023, p. 1. *See also* Commission Regulation (EU) No. 651/2014 of 17 Jun. 2014 (GBER, on which *see infra* §2.02 of the present chapter); in particular, Art. 52 on aid for broadband infrastructures.
61. *See* the Communication from the Commission on the application of State aid rules to public service broadcasting, OJ C 257 of 27.10.2009, p. 1.
62. *See* Commission Communication relating to the methodology for analysing State aid linked to stranded costs of 26 Jul. 2001.

- financial sector;[63]
- fishery and aquaculture;[64]
- postal services;[65]
- shipbuilding;[66]
- steel;[67]
- transport.[68]

(2) *Horizontal rules:*

- Training and Employment Aid.[69]
- Aid for Research and Development and Innovation.[70]

---

63. For a detailed analysis on State aid rules to measures taken in the context of the global financial crisis *see* Ch. 13 *infra*.
64. *See* Commission Regulation (EU) No. 2473/2022 of 14 Dec. 2022 declaring certain categories of aid to undertakings active in the production, processing and marketing of fishery and aquaculture products compatible with the internal market, OJ L 327, 21.12.2022, p. 82. *See also* Commission Regulation (EU) No. 717/2014 of 27 Jun. 2014 on the application of Arts 107 and 108 TFEU to *de minimis* aid in the fishery and aquaculture sector, OJ L 190, 28.6.2014, p. 45.
65. *See* the Notice from the Commission on the application of the competition rules to the postal sector and on the assessment of certain State measures relating to postal services, OJ C 39, 6.2.1998, p. 2.
66. *See* the Framework on State aid for shipbuilding of 7 Dec. 2011, OJ C 364, 14.12.2011, p. 9.
67. *See* the Communication from the Commission, Rescue and restructuring aid and closure aid for the steel sector, OJ C 70, 19.3.2002, p. 21.
68. For a detailed analysis on State aid rules applicable to the transport sector *see* Ch. 17 *infra*. Inland transport (i.e., transports taking place by rail, road, or inland waterways) is subject to the provisions of Art. 93 TFEU, as supplemented, *inter alia*, by Regulation (EC) No. 1370/2007 of the European Parliament and of the Council of 23 Oct. 2007 on public passenger transport services by rail and by road and repealing Council Regulations (EEC) Nos 1191/69 and 1107/70, OJ L 315, 3.12.2007, p. 1. Air and maritime transport, conversely, are governed by no specific disciplines, let alone some partial exceptions provided respectively by Regulation (EU) No. 1008/2008 of 24 Sep. 2008 on common rules for the operation of air services in the Community (Recast), OJ L 293, 31.10.2008, p. 3 and Regulation (EEC) No. 3577/92 of 7 Dec. 1992 applying the principle of freedom to provide services to maritime transport within Member States (maritime cabotage), OJ L 364, 12.12.1992, p. 7. The Commission has supplemented the provisions set out hereinbefore with sets of Guidelines: in particular, this is the case of the Maritime Guidelines (Commission Communication, Community guidelines on State aid to maritime transport, OJ C 13, 17.1.2004, p. 3); of the Rail Guidelines (Communication from the Commission, Community guidelines on State aid for railway undertakings, OJ C 184, 22.7.2008, p. 13); and of the Air Transport Guidelines (Communication from the Commission, Guidelines on State aid to airports and airlines, OJ C 99, 4.4.2014, p. 3).
69. Communication from the Commission, Criteria for the analysis of the compatibility of State aid for training subject to individual notification, OJ C 414, 28.10.2022, p. 1, and Communication from the Commission, Criteria for the analysis of the compatibility of State aid for the employment of disadvantaged and disabled workers subject to individual notification', OJ C 188, 11.8.2009, p. 6. *See also* Commission Regulation (EU) No. 651/2014 of 17 Jun. 2014 (GBER, on which *see infra* §2.02 of the present chapter); in particular, sections 5 and 6 of the same GBER, respectively, on training aid and aid for disadvantaged workers and for workers with disabilities.
70. Communication from the Commission, Framework for State aid for research and development and innovation, OJ C 198, 27.6.2014, p. 1. *See also* Commission Regulation (EU) No. 651/2014 of 17 Jun. 2014 (GBER, on which *see infra* §2.03 of the present chapter); in particular, section 4 of the same GBER on aid for research and development and innovation.

- Environmental Aid.[71]
- Rescue and Restructuring Aid.[72]
- Risk Capital and Risk Finance.[73]
- Aid to SMEs.[74]

[3] *Article 107(3)(b): Aids Granted in Support of Projects of Common European Interest or to Remedy a Serious Disturbance in the Economy of a Member State*

Under Article 107(3)(b) TFEU, the first type of aid that can be exempted pursuant to Article 107(3)(b) are those relating to the execution of an 'Important Project of Common European Interest'.

In order to benefit from the aforementioned exemption, the aid measure must meet a number of requisites and cumulative following criteria, which are laid down by the European Commission in a dedicated Communication.[75] In sum:

- The aid must relate to a single project that must be clearly defined in its objectives and implementation terms. However, 'integrated' projects (namely, a group of individual projects within a common structure or programme, with the same objective and a coherent systemic approach), may be authorized.
- The project must contribute significantly to one or more of the EU's objectives (e.g., the European Green Deal, the Digital Strategy and the Digital Decade, the

71. For a detailed analysis on State aid rules applicable to the energy sector *see* Ch. 15 *infra*. *See also* Commission Regulation (EU) No. 651/2014 of 17 Jun. 2014 (GBER, on which *see infra* §2.02 of the present chapter); in particular, section 7 of the same GBER on aid for environmental protection.
72. Communication from the Commission, Guidelines on State aid for rescuing and restructuring non-financial undertakings in difficulty, OJ C 249, 31.7.2014, p. 1.
73. Communication from the Commission Guidelines on risk finance aid for 2014-2020, OJ C 19, 22.1.2014, p. 4.
74. The category of micro, small and medium-sized enterprises (SMEs) is made up of enterprises which employ fewer than 250 persons and which have an annual turnover not exceeding EUR 50 million and/or an annual balance sheet total not exceeding EUR 43 million as determined by Commission Recommendation 2003/361/EC, OJ L 124, 20.5.2003, p. 36 The same definition is contained in Annex I of Regulation (EU) 651/2014 of 17 Jun. 2014 (GBER, on which *see infra*, §2.02 of the present chapter); in particular, ss 2 and 3 on aid to SMEs and on aid for access to finance for SMEs. The Commission has repeatedly highlighted the importance of SMEs, considered the backbone of Europe's economy: in fact, there are more than 23 million SMEs in the EU, representing 99% of European undertakings and employing more than 100 million employees. To facilitate the development of the economic activities of SMEs, the Commission has thus introduced over the years several measures to create a favourable environment for their development that may be hampered by market failures. In fact, SMEs often have difficulties in obtaining capital or loans, given the risk-averse nature of certain financial markets and the limited collateral that they may be able to offer. Their limited resources may also restrict their access to information, notably regarding new technology and potential markets.
75. Communication from the Commission, Criteria for the analysis of the compatibility with the internal market of State aid to promote the execution of important projects of Common European interest, C(2021) 8481 final, 25.11.2021.

New Industrial Strategy for Europe, etc.) and must have a significant impact on EU competitiveness, sustainable growth and value creation.
- The project must demonstrate that it is designed to overcome important market or systemic failures.
- The project must cover more than one Member State (at least four) and its benefits must extend to a large part of the EU. Purely national initiatives are therefore not enough.
- The benefits of the project must not be limited to the companies or sectors concerned but must have a wider relevance and application for the European economy and society.
- The project must provide for a co-financing share from the beneficiary.
- The project must be important from a quantitative and qualitative point of view (e.g., large scope or size, high technological or financial risk). The Commission will, however, assess the necessity and proportionality of the aid and its appropriateness as a policy instrument, as well as its effects on trade and competition.

See, as an example, the 'IPCEI ME/CT' project, supporting research and innovation and the first industrial deployment of microelectronics and communication technologies, approved by the Commission on 8 June 2023.[76] It includes sixty-eight projects from fifty-six companies; Jointly designed and notified by fourteen Member States: Austria, Czech, Finland, France, Germany, Greece, Ireland, Italy, Malta, the Netherlands, Poland, Romania, Slovakia and Spain; up to EUR 8.1 billion in public funding.

[4] Article 107(3)(b): Serious Disturbance of the Economy of a Member State

On top of the above, Article 107(3)(b) allows for the possible declaration of compatibility with the internal market of the EU of aid measures that are addressed at remedying 'a serious disturbance in the economy of a Member State'.

Until 2008, the European Commission and the Courts of the EU have interpreted such provision in a restrictive manner, applying it only in exceptional circumstances. In particular, the exemption was traditionally applied to economic disturbances affecting the national economy of the Member State as a whole, and not the economy of a single region or area of a Member State, or that of a single sector, or even a single economic operator.[77]

76. https://ec.europa.eu/commission/presscorner/detail/en/IP_23_3087.
77. The exemption had therefore been excluded in the case of aid for the restructuring of credit institutions (*see*, for instance, Commission Decision 98/490/EC of 20 May 1998, *Credit Lyonnais* and Commission Decision NN 70/2007 of 5 Dec. 2007 on SA.24126, *Northern Rock*) or the economic consequences in some Länder following the reunification of Germany (CJEU, Case C-301/96, *Germany v. Commission*, 30.9.1996, ECLI:EU:C:2003:509).

However, the financial crisis of 2008 led the European Commission to reconsider its approach to the application of this potential exemption. The new approach has been described, at first, through the Financial Crisis Temporary Framework of 2008,[78] and has been further developed in the COVID-19 Temporary Framework.[79] According to such a new approach, Article 107(3)(b) can now be invoked in the event that the crisis of individual banks or the banking system could have an immediate impact on the economy of a Member State as a whole. The Commission's new approach was developed in the Financial Crisis Temporary Framework and later in the COVID-19 Temporary Framework, which will be discussed later.

[5] Article 107(3)(d): Aids Aimed at the Promotion of Culture and Heritage Conservation

This further exemption aims at extending to aid to support the cultural content of audiovisual programmes. However, the actual relevance of this exemption is reduced by the fact that most aid for culture and artistic heritage is exempted under the GBER, which also contains specific exemptions for audiovisual works or for sport and recreational infrastructure.

§2.02 THE GENERAL BLOCK EXEMPTION REGULATION

State funding meeting the criteria in Article 107(1) TFEU constitutes State aid and requires notification to the Commission by virtue of Article 108(3) TFEU.[80]

However, according to Article 109 TFEU, the Council may determine categories of aid that are exempted from this notification requirement. In accordance with Article 108(4) TFEU, the Commission may adopt regulations relating to those categories of State aid.

In 1998 the Council adopted Regulation (EC) No. 994/98 on the application of Articles 107 and 108 TFEU to certain categories of horizontal aid empowering the Commission to adopt legislative instruments defining general compatibility criteria.

Pursuant to Regulation (EC) No. 994/98 in the early 2000s Commission adopted several Block exemption regulations ('BER') providing that state aid measures fulfilling certain substantive and procedural conditions set out in the BERs are deemed compatible with Article 107(3) TFEU and are exempted from the notification requirements of Article 108(3) TFEU.

In 2005 in the 'State Aid Action Plan' the Commission announced a simplification and consolidation of the existing BERs through the adoption of a single block exemption Regulation.

---

78. Communication from the Commission, *Temporary Community framework for State aid measures to support access to finance in the current financial and economic crisis*, OJ C 83, 7.4.2009, pp. 1-15.
79. Communication from the Commission, *Temporary Framework for State aid measures to support the economy in the current COVID-19 outbreak*, OJ C 91I, 20.3.2020, pp. 1-9, and ff. aa.
80. *See* Ch. 3 for a detailed analysis of the procedure before the Commission.

'GBER' was then adopted in July 2008, replacing the previous BERs adopted by the Commission with a single block exemption covering not only the previously exempted categories of aid but also a number of further categories of aid not previously exempted by the existing BERs (namely aid for female entrepreneurship, aid for environmental protection, aid for research and development and innovation, aid in the form of risk capital, aid for disadvantaged and disabled workers).

In 2012 'EU State Aid Modernisation', the Commission announced a revision and extension of the GBER and in 2013 Regulation No. 994/98 was amended by Council Regulation No. 733/2013 empowering the Commission to extend the block exemption to new categories of aid.[81]

[A] Commission Regulation (EU) No. 651/2014: The 2014 General Block Exemption Regulation

Finally, on 17 May 2014, the Commission adopted a revised GBER ('GBER') that entered into force on 1 July 2014 and repealed Regulation No. 800/2008. As of today, will be applicable until 31 December 2026.[82]

The scope of the previous GBER has been extensively widened, covering almost all categories of exception in Article 107(2) and (3).

The maximum allowable aid intensity for several types of aid has been raised and many thresholds for notification of individual amounts of aid have also been raised.

The GBER is divided into four parts:

(1) Chapter I containing common provisions and definitions which apply to all types of aid covered by the GBER.

81. This has been done, for instance, in 2017, when GBER's scope has been extended also to ports and airports (*see* Regulation (EU) n. 1084/2017 of the Commission amending Regulation (EU) No. 651/2014 as regards aid for port and airport infrastructure, notification thresholds for aid for culture and heritage conservation and for aid for sport and multifunctional recreational infrastructures, and regional operating aid schemes for outermost regions and amending Regulation (EU) No. 702/2014 as regards the calculation of eligible costs, OJ L 156, 20.6.2017, p. 1), or in 2023, with the so-called Green Deal GBER amendment, which has been aimed at simplifying and speeding up the support for EU's green and digital transition (*see* Regulation (EU) No. 1315 of 2023 of the Commission amending Regulation (EU) No. 651/2014 declaring certain categories of aid compatible with the internal market in application of Arts 107 and 108 of the Treaty and Regulation (EU) 2022/2473 declaring certain categories of aid to undertakings active in the production, processing and marketing of fishery and aquaculture products compatible with the internal market in application of Arts 107 and 108 of the Treaty, OJ L 167, 30.6.2023, p. 1.

82. Initially, GBER was supposed to be applicable until 31 Dec. 2020. However, after a first amendment that extended its applicability until 31 Dec. 2023, in June 2023 the applicability of 2014 GBER has been further extended to 31 Dec. 2026 (*see* Regulation (EU) No. 2023/1315 of 23 Jun. 2023 amending Regulation (EU) No. 651/2014 declaring certain categories of aid compatible with the internal market in application of Arts 107 and 108 of the Treaty and Regulation (EU) 2022/2473 declaring certain categories of aid to undertakings active in the production, processing and marketing of fishery and aquaculture products compatible with the internal market in application of Arts 107 and 108 of the Treaty, OJ L 167 of 30.6.2023, pp. 1-90).

(2) Chapter II containing requirements regarding the reporting by the Member States of aid measures and rules concerning the records that Member States should keep regarding the aid exempted.
(3) Chapter III containing specific provisions for different categories of aid.
(4) Chapter IV which contains transitional provisions on the interaction between GBER and the previous general block exemption regulation.

[1] Common Provisions: The Scope of the GBER

Starting from 2014, the categories of aid to which GBER is deemed applicable have increased. As of today, GBER shall apply to the following categories of aid:[83]

(1) regional aid;
(2) aid to small and medium-sized enterprises ('SME') in the form of investment aid, operating aid and SMEs' access to finance;
(3) aid for environmental protection;
(4) aid for research and development and innovation;
(5) training aid;
(6) recruitment and employment aid for disadvantaged workers and workers with disabilities;
(7) aid to make good the damage caused by certain natural disasters;
(8) social aid for transport for residents of remote regions;
(9) aid for broadband infrastructures;
(10) aid for culture and heritage conservation;
(11) aid for sport and multifunctional recreational infrastructures;
(12) aid for local infrastructures;
(13) aid for regional airports;
(14) aid for ports;
(15) aid for European Territorial Cooperation projects; and
(16) aid involved in financial products supported by the InvestEU Fund.

Article 1 2014 GBER outlines also a number of aid measures that are excluded from the application of the GBER.[84]

[2] Conditions for Exemptions

Aid schemes, individual aid granted under aid schemes and ad hoc aid shall be compatible with the internal market within the meaning of Article 107(2) or (3) TFEU and shall be exempted from the notification requirement of Article 108(3) TFEU provided that such aid fulfils all the conditions laid down in Chapter I of the GBER, as

83. *See* Art. 1(1) of Commission Regulation (EU) No. 651/2014.
84. *See* Art. 1(2), (3), (4) and (5) GBER.

well as the specific conditions for the relevant category of aid laid down in Chapter III of the GBER.[85]

The common conditions are described under Chapter I of the GBER, and could be summarized as follows:[86]

(1) Aid measures shall not meet the thresholds set out under Article 4 of the 2014 GBER.[87]
(2) Aid measures shall be transparent; i.e., it should be possible to calculate precisely the gross grant equivalent of the aid *ex ante* without any need to undertake a risk assessment.[88]
(3) Aid measures shall have an incentive effect.[89]

In order to ensure that the aid is necessary and acts as an incentive to further develop activities or projects, GBER should not apply to aid for activities in which the beneficiary would in any case engage even in the absence of the aid.

In general, an aid is considered to have an incentive effect if the beneficiary has submitted a written application for the aid to the Member State concerned before work on the project or activity starts.

GBER provides for further conditions for an aid to have an incentive effect with regard to ad hoc aid granted to large enterprises and measures in the form of tax advantages,[90] and also a list of categories of aid that are not required to have or shall be deemed to have an incentive effect if the specific conditions set out for those categories of Chapter III of the GBER are fulfilled.[91]

[3] Aid Intensity and Eligible Costs

With a view to ensuring that aid is proportionate and limited to the amount necessary, maximum aid amounts should, whenever possible, be defined in terms of aid intensities in relation to a set of eligible costs, where 'aid intensity' means the gross aid amount expressed as a percentage of the eligible costs, before any deduction of tax or other charge.

In this regard, Article 7 GBER contains the principle to be used in order to ensure that the maximal allowable aid intensities provided for in Chapter III of the GBER are respected.

85. *See* Art. 3 GBER.
86. *See* Ch. I GBER.
87. Article 4(2) GBER provides that such thresholds shall not be circumvented by artificially splitting up the aid schemes or aid projects.
88. *See* Art. 5 GBER. Article 5(2) contains a list of categories of aid considered transparent.
89. *See* Art. 6 GBER.
90. *See* Art. 6(3) GBER.
91. *See* Art. 6(4) GBER.

[4] Cumulation

Under Article 8, GBER specifies the circumstances under which different categories of aid may be cumulated.[92]

Aid exempted by the GBER and any other compatible aid exempted under other Regulation or approved by the Commission may be cumulated as long as those measures concern different identifiable eligible costs; such aids can also be cumulated in case of the same eligible costs as long as such cumulation does not exceed the highest intensity or aid amount applicable to such aid under the 2014 GBER.

The 2014 GBER also set out rules for cumulation of aid measures with and without identifiable eligible costs,[93] for cumulation with *de minimis* aid and for cumulation with aid in favour of workers with disabilities.[94]

The 2014 GBER clarifies that Union funding centrally managed by the institutions, agencies, joint undertakings or other bodies of the Union, that is not directly or indirectly under the control of Member States, does not constitute State aid.[95] Where such Union funding is combined with State aid, only the latter should be considered for determining whether notification thresholds and maximum aid intensities are respected, provided the total amount of public funding granted in relation to the same eligible costs does not exceed the most favourable funding rate laid down in the applicable rules of Union law.[96]

[5] Publication Reporting and Monitoring

To increase the quality of controls and public awareness over aid granted, the 2014 GBER provides for specific obligations with regard to transparency, such as:

(1) Member States shall publish, after the granting decision, key information in the Commission's transparency award module, or on a comprehensive State aid website at national or regional level, of all the information laid down in Article 9(1), (a), (b) and (c) GBER.[97]

(2) Under Article 11 GBER, Member States shall transmit to the Commission within twenty working days following its entry into force the summary information about each aid measure exempted under the 2014 GBER, as

92. *See* Art. 7 GBER.
93. *See* Art. 8(3) and (4) GBER.
94. *See* Art. 8(5) and (6) GBER. Please consider that, under (7), 'in determining whether the ceilings for regional operating aid in outermost regions, as set out in Article 15(4), are respected, only regional operating aid in outermost regions implemented under this Regulation shall be taken into account'.
95. Whereas No. 26 of GBER.
96. *See* Art. 8(2) GBER. Please consider that, by way of derogation, total public funding for projects that are supported by the European Defence Fund) might be up to the total eligible cost of the project, as long as the notification thresholds, and the aid intensity/amount laid down under this Regulation are met.
97. For further details on Member States' publication duties under GBER, *see* Art. 9 GBER.

well as an annual report, in electronic form, on the application of this Regulation.[98]

(3) Finally, in relation to their monitoring duties under Article 12 GBER. Member States shall maintain for ten years detailed records with the information and supporting documentation necessary to establish that all the conditions laid down in the GBER are fulfilled.[99]

The Commission will publish on its website the links to national State aid websites and the summary information provided by the Member States.[100]

In the Commission's view, the introduction of these transparency requirements will facilitate enforcement for national authorities and will lead to better control of aid granted, eventually reducing the need for reporting, thereby contributing to further reduction of the administrative burden.[101]

[6] Withdrawal of the Benefit of the Block Exemption

To reinforce the effectiveness of compatibility conditions set out in GBER, a deterrent sanction was introduced with regard to the failure to comply with the conditions set out in the Regulation: the withdrawal of the benefit of the block exemption.

In fact, in case a Member State grants aid allegedly exempted from the notification requirement without fulfilling the conditions set out in GBER the Commission may, after having provided the Member State concerned with the possibility to make its views known, adopt a decision stating that all or some of the future aid measures adopted by the Member State concerned which would otherwise fulfil the requirements of this Regulation, are to be notified to the Commission in accordance with Article 108(3) of the Treaty.[102]

The Commission may also restrict the withdrawal of the benefit of the block exemption to certain types of aid, certain beneficiaries or aid measures adopted by certain authorities, where non-compliance with this Regulation affects only a limited group of measures or certain authorities.[103]

§2.03 THE TEMPORARY FRAMEWORKS

[A] Temporary Framework for State Aid Measures to Support the Economy in the COVID-19 Outbreak

Soon after the outbreak of the COVID-19 pandemic, on 19 March 2020, the European Commission adopted a Communication on a Temporary Framework for State aid

98. For further details on Member States' reporting duties under GBER, *see* Art. 11 GBER.
99. For further details on Member States' monitoring duties under GBER, *see* Art. 12 GBER.
100. *See* Art. 9(5) GBER.
101. *See* Commission Draft GBER – EXPLANATORY MEMORANDUM. http://ec.europa.eu/competition/consultations/2013_gber/gber_explanatory_memo_en.pdf.
102. *See* Art. 9(5) GBER.
103. *See* Whereas No. 29 and Art. 10 GBER.

measures to support the economy in the current COVID-19 outbreak (the 'COVID-19 TF').[104]

Please consider that, before this experience, the European Commission had adopted just one Temporary Framework for State aid, namely the 2008 *Temporary Community Framework for State aid measures to support access to finance in the current financial and economic crisis*,[105] which was aimed at tackling the consequence of the worldwide 2008 financial crisis on the real economy within the internal market.

The COVID-19 TF is based on Article 107(3)(b), according to which, as already illustrated *supra*, may be considered compatible with the internal market aid measures or schemes aimed at 'remedy[ing] a serious disturbance in the economy of a Member State'. This is because, as pointed out in the literature, the structure of Article 107(3)(b) seemed more suitable to tackle the issues that might arise in a situation such as the one of the COVID-19 pandemic, since allows aid measures and schemes to be granted both not only *ex post* (as in the case, for instance, of Article 107(2)(b), *see supra*) but also *ex ante*, i.e., to prevent the aggravation of the already existing 'serious disturbance'.[106]

The COVID-19 TF also provided Member States with the possibility to mitigate the socio-economic impact of the coronavirus pandemic with other tools from the EU's State Aid 'toolbox', such as Article 107(2)(b), which, as better illustrated *supra*, advocates for the compatibility with the internal market of aid measures and schemes 'to make good the damage caused by natural disasters or exceptional occurrences' (exception under which, as confirmed by the data made available by the European Commission,[107] has been approved a significant number of COVID-19-related State aid measures), and Article 107(3)(c).

Measures granted by Member States under the COVID-19 TF still needed to be notified and authorized by the Commission, and the authorization was generally issued a few days after the notification (whereas, in ordinary circumstances, it takes longer for the EC to authorize State aid).

However, the faster approval process did not exempt Member States from demonstrating that the aid measures/schemes were necessary, appropriate and proportionate to remedy a serious disturbance in the economy, and that all the conditions outlined by the EC in the relevant communications were fully respected.

The COVID-19 TF was amended and prorogated several times throughout 2020 and 2021, in order to expand its scope. It has been effective (with the sole exception of investment and solvency support measures, which will be effective as of 31 December 2023) as of 30 June 2022.

---

104. Communication from the Commission, *Temporary Framework for State aid measures to support the economy in the current COVID-19 outbreak*, C/2020/1863, OJ C 91 I, 20.3.2020.
105. Communication from the Commission, *Temporary Community framework for State aid measures to support access to finance in the current financial and economic crisis*, OJ C 83, 7.4.2009.
106. *See* Nicolaides, *supra* n. 13.
107. *See* the 'List of Member State Measures approved under Articles 107(2)(b), 107(3)(b) and 107(3)(c) TFEU and under the State Aid Temporary Framework' available at the following link (last updated on 10 Jul. 2024): https://competition-policy.ec.europa.eu/document/download/fd113a0a-9c99-4405-aa4c-4ed52134f657_en?filename=State_aid_decisions_TF_and_107_2b_107_3b_107_3c.pdf.

[B] The Temporary Crisis Framework for State Aid Measures to Support the Economy Following the Aggression Against Ukraine by Russia

Shortly after the upheaval caused by the COVID-19 outbreak, the EU internal market had to deal with another crisis, this time caused by the outbreak of the Russian-Ukrainian conflict in February 2022.

Once again, the European Commission saw fit to react to this new crisis scenario by adopting a temporary ad hoc state aid scheme. Indeed, on 23 March 2022, the European Commission decided to adopt a new Temporary Framework to support the economy of the Member States and the EU itself, the *Temporary Crisis Framework for State Aid measures to support the economy following the aggression against Ukraine by Russia* ('Ukraine TF').[108]

Similarly to the COVID-19 TF, even the Ukraine TF was based on Article 107(3)(b), complementing the possibility under Article 107(2)(b) TFEU to mitigate direct damages of the Russian invasion and of the following economic sanctions, as well as existing instruments of EU State aid law (e.g., *de minimis* regulation, GBER), and the measures notified under the Ukraine TF were assessed means of an accelerated procedure upon receiving clear and complete notifications. Moreover, aid measures granted under the Ukraine TF could have been expressly combined with those already approved under the COVID-19 TF, provided the respective conditions are met.

The Ukraine TF, which applied retroactively from 1 February 2022, has been then complemented and replaced by the new 'Temporary Crisis and Transition Framework', which will be discussed below.

[C] The Temporary Crisis and Transition Framework for State Aid Measures to Support the Economy Following the Aggression Against Ukraine by Russia

On 9 March 2023, the Commission adopted a new Temporary Framework, the *Temporary Crisis and Transition Framework for State Aid measures to support the economy following the aggression against Ukraine by Russia* ('TCTF TF'),[109] which was also based on Article 107(3)(b) TFEU.

The TCTF TF, which complements and replaces the Ukraine TF, supports state aid schemes or measures that pursue two main goals, namely the competitiveness of the EY from an energy point of view and the transition to a net-zero emission economy, in compliance with the Green Deal Industrial Plan.

In particular, the temporary State aid measures covered by the TCTF are described below:

---

108. Communication from the Commission, *Temporary Crisis Framework for State Aid measures to support the economy following the aggression against Ukraine by Russia*, OJ C 131I, 24.3.2022.
109. Communication from the Commission, *Temporary Crisis and Transition Framework for State Aid measures to support the economy following the aggression against Ukraine by Russia*, OJ C 101, 17.3.2023.

- aids providing liquidity support in the form of State guarantees and subsidized loans, as well as any other measure aimed at supporting electricity demand reduction, which has already phased out on 31 December 2023;
- aids providing compensation for high energy prices, which have phased out on 30 June 2024;[110]
- limited amounts of aid aimed at ensuring that Member States might mitigate the impact of the Russian-Ukrainian conflict. Please consider that such aids have already been phased out as of 30 June 2024 for all industries and sectors, with the sole exception of agricultural primary production, fisheries and aquaculture (which will be phased out by 31 December 2024);[111]
- aids aimed at ensuring the promotion of the transition towards a net-zero emissions economy, which will be granted up to 31 December 2025, for the purposes of accelerating the roll-out of renewable energy, storage and renewable heat, decarbonizing the industrial production processes and fostering investments in the manufacture of equipment and components that are crucial for the transition towards a net-zero emissions economy (e.g., solar panels, batteries, wind turbines, recycling of critical raw materials, electrolysers, etc.).

[D] The Experience of Temporary Frameworks: Some General Remarks

Based on the above, it appears clear that, in general, Temporary Frameworks could now be considered *ex se* as a new 'tool' available to the European Union to tackle a situation of economic turmoil and crisis of the whole internal market due to an exceptional, unpredictable occurrence, such as a global financial crisis, a pandemic or a conflict on European soil.

However, the 'full flexibility' that is usually recognized by the Temporary Frameworks, and the exceptional circumstances in which they are usually adopted should not allow us to forget that State aid measures and schemes are always suitable to create a potential distortion of the internal market.

Indeed, while the 'full flexibility' recognized by the Temporary Frameworks theoretically applies to all Member States, experience has shown that it has mostly benefitted the deeper-pocketed Member States, i.e., the ones with the means and the budget to spend the greatest resources.[112]

110. Communication from the Commission, *Amendment to the Temporary Crisis and Transition Framework for State Aid measures to support the economy following the aggression against Ukraine by Russia*, OJ C, C/2023/1188, 21.11.2023.
111. Communication from the Commission, *Second amendment to the Temporary Crisis and Transition Framework for State Aid measures to support the economy following the aggression against Ukraine by Russia*, OJ C, C/2024/3113, 2.5.2024.
112. For instance, as pointed out by the European Commission in its 2023 State aid Scoreboard (p. 27, https://competition-policy.ec.europa.eu/document/download/0b2037c5-c43f-4917-b654-f48f74444015_en?filename=state_aid_scoreboard_note_2023.pdf), 'Concerning the COVID-19 State aid measures […] Germany is the Member State that has granted the most with 31.5% of the total aid paid out under COVID19 measures (EUR 24.16 billion), followed by France with EUR 18.64 billion (24.3%), Italy (EUR 14.68 billion, 19.2%) […]. Focusing on TCF-related State

This occurred because the compatibility of an aid measure or scheme under one Temporary Framework is assessed (only) against the backdrop of the EU's strategic goals; while the key point should remain the risk of a potential distortion of competition on the internal market as a whole. Thus, the EC should pay more attention to the negative effects of an aid scheme or measure on competition within the internal market, requiring the existence of actual, proportionate, countervailing positive effects (not only politically).

Otherwise, as pointed out by reputable literature, one might begin to wonder: '[i]f State aid control is regarded as inappropriate precisely when it is needed the most, then one may start wondering what is the point of keeping it in place at every other time'?

It is no surprise that the same issue was also the subject of particular scrutiny in Mario Draghi's recent report on the relaunch of EU competitiveness,[113] which highlighted the risk of the adverse impact on the Single Market when the largest Member States with the most fiscal capacity can provide greater support than others and emphasized that:

> The application of State aid control in times of crisis, like those triggered first by the COVID-19 pandemic and later by the energy crisis, has entailed expanded ability for Member States to support companies, thus effectively easing the pain of EU citizens and businesses but it also fragmented the common market, distorted competition, deteriorated public finances and triggered inefficient subsidy races.[114]

Therefore, the quick phasing out of such temporary measures when no longer necessary should be overall welcomed, Indeed, despite the temporary nature of such derogations, the effects that they might have on the internal market will certainly be long-lasting.

This said, awareness of this side-effect of 'full flexibility' has led to the adoption of a number of important policy initiatives, all aimed at trying to reduce asymmetries and distortions. These are, in particular:

- the European instrument for temporary support to mitigate Unemployment Risks in an Emergency (SURE);[115] and

aid measures (light blue bar), Germany has granted 61.5% of the total aid paid out under TCF-related measures (EUR 24.18 billion), followed by Spain with EUR 7.29 billion (18.5%), Italy (EUR 3.83 billion, 9.7%), France (EUR 1.38 billion, 3.5%) and Poland (EUR 666.8 million, 1.7%).'

Over 50% of the volume of aid approved so far under the Ukraine TF and related Treaty provisions came from only one Member State (Germany), and that over 80% came from three Member States (Germany, France, and Italy). Similar figures have also been recorder with reference to aids granted under the COVID-19 TF.

113. M. Draghi, *The future of European competitiveness*, 9 Sep. 2024, 12; available at: https://commission.europa.eu/topics/strengthening-european-competitiveness/eu-competitiveness-looking-ahead_en (14 Oct. 2024).

114. *Ibid.*, 301.

115. For further information, *see* https://economy-finance.ec.europa.eu/eu-financial-assistance/sure_en.

- the Next Generation EU stimulus package.[116]

However, the inherently 'sectorial' nature of these instruments makes them not suitable to counterbalance the distortions caused by the aid measures adopted under a relaxed State aid regime.

For the reasons above, the recent Draghi report also highlighted that a policy for the support of industrial development and the revival of the EU economy cannot be based neither on temporary derogations from State aid rules nor on sectoral and temporary common funding instruments such as the programs described above but must broaden its horizon and develop joint funding policies for investments for productivity, also through the issuance of common safe assets.[117]

116. Discussed *infra* in Ch. 9. For further information, *see* https://commission.europa.eu/strategy-and-policy/recovery-plan-europe_en.
117. Mario Draghi, *The future of European competitiveness*, 290.

CHAPTER 3

The Procedures Before the Commission

Francesco Mazzocchi

§3.01 INTRODUCTION

Article 108 of the TFEU provides a rough outline of the procedural rules for the constant review and monitoring of State aid by the Commission.[1]

1. Article 108 TFEU provides that:

> 1. The Commission shall, in cooperation with Member States, keep under constant review all systems of aid existing in those States. It shall propose to the latter any appropriate measures required by the progressive development or by the functioning of the internal market.
> 2. If, after giving notice to the parties concerned to submit their comments, the Commission finds that aid granted by a State or through State resources is not compatible with the internal market having regard to Article 107, or that such aid is being misused, it shall decide that the State concerned shall abolish or alter such aid within a period of time to be determined by the Commission.If the State concerned does not comply with this decision within the prescribed time, the Commission or any other interested State may, in derogation from the provisions of Articles 258 and 259, refer the matter to the Court of Justice of the European Union direct.On application by a Member State, the Council may, acting unanimously, decide that aid which that State is granting or intends to grant shall be considered to be compatible with the internal market, in derogation from the provisions of Article 107 or from the regulations provided for in Article 109, if such a decision is justified by exceptional circumstances. If, as regards the aid in question, the Commission has already initiated the procedure provided for in the first subparagraph of this paragraph, the fact that the State concerned has made its application to the Council shall have the effect of suspending that procedure until the Council has made its attitude known. If, however, the Council has not made its attitude known within three months of the said application being made, the Commission shall give its decision on the case.
> 3. The Commission shall be informed, in sufficient time to enable it to submit its comments, of any plans to grant or alter aid. If it considers that any such plan is not compatible with the internal market having regard to Article 107, it shall without delay initiate the procedure provided for in paragraph 2. The Member State concerned shall not put its proposed measures into effect until this procedure has resulted in a final decision.

Incumbent upon the Commission is a 'specific duty of supervision' of State aid,[2] which is exercised in the context of an administrative procedure that is part of the Commission's wider role as 'guardian of the Treaties' pursuant to Article 17 TEU. In exercising this task, the Commission adopts decisions addressed to Member States who plan or execute aid, which are subject to review by the General Court in the first instance and by the Court of Justice in appeal.

Against the background of a single procedural rule, State aid control has developed empirically for decades, mainly through the exchange of correspondence and 'negotiations' between the Commission and the Member State granting the aid, and through the case law of the Community judicature, which has contributed over the years to the definition of the scope of application of Article 108 TFEU.[3]

Although the Treaty contained an appropriate legal basis for laying down rules for the application of Article 108 TFEU from the outset,[4] it was only in 1999 that a

---

> 4. The Commission may adopt regulations relating to the categories of State aid that the Council has, pursuant to Article 109, determined may be exempted from the procedure provided for by paragraph 3 of this Article.

The first three paragraphs of the provision have remained substantially unchanged since the entry into force of the Treaty of Rome in 1957, while the Treaty of Lisbon in 2009 added a fourth paragraph to Art. 108 TFEU, relating to the Commission's power (previously provided in Regulation (EC) No. 994/98) to adopt regulations relating to the categories of State aid that the Council has determined may be exempted from notification.

2. *See* Case C-171/83 R, *Commission of the European Communities v. French Republic,* 20.9.1983, ECLI:EU:C:1983:230, para. 10; Case C-143/99, *Adria-Wien Pipeline GmbH and Wietersdorfer & Peggauer Zementwerke GmbH v. Finanzlandesdirektion für Kärnten,* 8.11.2001, ECLI: EU:C:2001:598, para. 23; and Case T-538/11, *Kingdom of Belgium v. European Commission,* 25.3.2015, ECLI:EU:T:2015:188, para. 63.
3. To this end, it must be recalled that State aid legislation constitutes a *unique experiment* for the European law and there were no 'precedents' to refer to. State aid control was conceived as a necessary complement of the rules on the freedom of circulation (goods, services, persons and capital) and aimed, in particular, at ensuring an optimum allocation of economic activities. This rationale is also illustrated by the jurisprudence of the Court of Justice: *'[...]. The provisions relating to the free movement of goods, the repeal of discriminatory tax provisions and aid have a common objective, namely to ensure the free movement of goods between Member States under normal conditions of competition.' See* Case C-188/84, *Commission of the European Communities v. French Republic,* 28.1.1986, ECLI:EU:C:1986:43, para. 13; and Case C-518/16, *ZPT AD v. Narodno sabranie na Republika Bulgaria and Others.* 28.2.2018, ECLI:EU:C:2018:126, para. 34. However, over the years the State aid policy has also placed increasing value on general interest, with growing focus on the social dimension of Europe. The severe economic crisis suffered by Europe since 2008 and the COVID-19 outbreak in 2020-2022 led to an entirely new phase for Europe, raising significant challenges for EU State aid law. *See* Ch. 9.
4. Namely Art. 94 (EC), now 109 TFEU, pursuant to which: 'The Council, on a proposal from the Commission and after consulting the European Parliament, may make any appropriate regulations for the application of Arts 107 and 108 and may in particular determine the conditions in which Art. 108(3) shall apply and the categories of aid exempted from this procedure.' Some early reform proposals by the Commission were not successful: *see*, respectively, *Proposition d'un Reglement du Conseil,* COM (66) 95 Final (March 1966), modified by *Modifications a la Proposition d'un Reglement du Conseil,* COM (66) 457 (November 1966) (withdrawn in 1975) and the *Proposition d'un Reglement du Conseil,* COM (72) 1523 Final (December 1972) (withdrawn in 1976).

detailed body of procedural provisions came into force, with the approval of Council Regulation (EC) No. 659/99.[5]

On the one hand, Regulation (EC) No. 659/99 codified a large part of Commission practice and of EU case law, with the aim of increasing transparency and legal certainty and, on the other, it introduced new elements to the procedure, providing a systematic reorganization of the categories of aid present in Article 108 TFEU and outlining four distinct types of procedure, regarding, respectively, *notified* aid, *unlawful* aid, *misused* aid and *existing* aid schemes.

Regulation (EC) No. 659/99 was complemented by the Commission Regulation (EC) No. 794/2004, which provides, *inter alia*, detailed rules on the form and content of the notification of State aid measures to the Commission, as well as on calculation of time limits and of interest rate for recovery on unlawful aid.[6]

In 2009, as part of the State Aid Action Plan ('SAAP'),[7] the Commission adopted a set of 'soft law' measures aimed at accelerating the adoption of State aid decisions and creating greater transparency for Commission activity (the 'Simplification package'). This included the Commission Notice on a Simplified Procedure for the treatment of certain types of State aid[8] and the Best Practices Code on the conduct of State aid control proceedings,[9] updated in 2018, a sort of 'vademecum' of State aid control carried out by the Commission.

Regulation (EC) No. 659/99 was amended in several respects in 2013 by Council Regulation (EU) No. 734/2013,[10] and then repealed by Council Regulation (EU) No. 1589/2015 (the Procedural Regulation),[11] with these amendments especially intended to ensure more effective gathering of information from the market and improve the efficiency of the treatment of complaints. The Procedural Regulation did not put on a statutory basis rules already established by the EU Courts or the Commission practice but inserted innovative provisions, which appear to derive from the antitrust experience.

§3.02 MAIN FEATURES OF STATE AID CONTROL

Before examining the different procedural rules on State aid, this section will attempt to describe the main principles governing this area of law.

5. Council Regulation (EC) No. 659 of 22 Mar. 1999, laying down detailed rules for the application of Art. 93 of the EC Treaty, OJ 1999 L 83/1. Pursuant to Art. 30, Council Regulation (EC) No. 659/99 entered into force on 16 Apr. 1999 until it was repealed by Council Regulation (EU) No. 1589/2015 (art. 35).
6. Commission Regulation (EC) No. 794/2004 of 21 Apr. 2004, implementing Council Regulation (EC) No. 659/99, OJ 2004 L140/3.
7. State Aid Action Plan: Less and better targeted aid: a roadmap for State aid reform 2005-2009, COM (2005) 107 final.
8. OJ 2009 C136/3.
9. OJ 2009 C136/13.
10. Council Regulation (EU) No. 734/2013 amending Regulation (EC) No. 659/99 laying down detailed rules for the application of Art. 93 (now 108 TFEU) of the EC Treaty OJ 2013 L204/15.
11. Council Regulation (EU) No. 2015/1589 of 13 Jul. 2015 laying down detailed rules for the application of Art. 108 of the Treaty on the Functioning of the European Union, OJ 2015 L 248/9.

The aid monitoring system is essentially based on *ex ante* verification of aid projects: pursuant to Article 108(3) TFEU, the Member State must promptly notify the Commission of any new aid plan. The Commission can also investigate an aid measure upon receipt of a complaint or upon its own initiative.

The Commission holds a central role in the aid monitoring procedure.[12] It has exclusive jurisdiction over decisions on whether aid is *compatible* with the internal market, except for exceptional circumstances where the Council may intervene.[13]

The national courts have a separate and complementary role to the Commission:[14] while the latter is responsible for assessing the compatibility of aid measures, the national courts have an important role in preserving, until the final decision by the Commission, the rights of private parties against any violation, by the State in question, of the prohibition set out by Article 108(3) TFEU (the so-called *standstill clause*), i.e., the clause that obliges the Member State concerned not to put its proposed measure into effect until the Commission has reached a final decision.[15]

---

12. On the central role of the Commission in the system for monitoring aid, *see also* Case C-110/02, *Commission of the European Communities v. Council of the European Union*, 11.12.2003, ECLI:EU:C:2003:667, paras 29 et seq.; Case C-354/90, *Fédération national du commerce extérieur des produits alimentaires et Syndicat national des négociants et transformateurs de saumon v. French Republic*, 21.11.1991, ECLI:EU:C:1991:440, paras 9 and 14. The Commission's prominent role in the aid monitoring system had already been stated in the so-called Spaak Report of 1956 – the Report on the common market prepared by the Intergovernmental Committee on European Integration – which led to the signing, on 25 Mar. 1957, of the Treaties of Rome establishing a European Economic Community and the European Atomic Energy Community.
13. Article 108(2) TFEU third and fourth subparagraphs outline the power of the Council, on application by a Member State, to decide, upon unanimous vote, that an aid should be considered compatible with the internal market, in derogation from the provisions of Art. 107 TFEU or from the regulations provided for in Art. 109 TFEU, if such a decision is justified by exceptional circumstances. If, as regards the aid in question, the Commission has already initiated the formal examination of the measure, the fact that the State concerned has made its application to the Council shall have the effect of suspending that procedure until the Council has made its attitude known. If, however, the Council has not made its attitude known within three months of said application being made, the Commission shall give its decision on the case. As for the exceptional power wielded by the Council under Art. 108(2) TFEU, *see* Case C-110/02, *Commission v. Council, supra* (paras 29-33 and 45). Furthermore, the Council, pursuant to Art. 107 TFEU, third paragraph, letter e), has the power to determine, upon proposal by the Commission, further categories of aid compatible with the common market compared to those listed in the same Art. 107 TFEU. This residual power has predominantly been used to set a specific regime for the granting of aid in the shipbuilding and coal industry sectors. These powers of the Council are similar to those provided under Art. 42(2) TFEU which, in the agricultural and fisheries sector, grant the Council, upon proposal by the Commission, the power to authorize the granting of aid for the protection of enterprises negatively affected by structural or natural conditions; or within the framework of economic development programmes.
14. *See* Case C-150/16, *Fondul Proprietatea SA v. Complexul Energetic Oltenia SA*, 18.5.2017, ECLI:EU:C:2017:388, para. 41; Case C-69/13, *Mediaset S.p.A. v. Ministero dello Sviluppo economico*, 13.2.2014, ECLI:EU:C:2014:71, para. 19, Case C-284/12, *Deutsche Lufthansa v. Flughafen Frankfurt-Hahn*, 21.11.2013, ECLI:EU:C:2013:755, para. 27; Case C-354/90, *Fédération nationale du commerce extérieur des produits alimentaires et Syndicat national des négociants et transformateurs de saumon v. France*, para. 8 and Case C-39/94, *Syndicat français de l'Express international (SFEI) v. La Poste and Others*, 11.7.1996, ECLI:EU:C:1996:285, para. 41.
15. The Court of Justice declared that Art. 108(3) TFEU applies not only to notified aid implemented upon a decision from the Commission but also to aid that had not been notified; individuals

Another distinctive feature of the procedure is that the Commission review of a State aid measure may entail two steps: (i) a preliminary examination; and (ii) a formal investigation procedure. The second phase is optional, in the sense that it is only necessary where the Commission experiences serious difficulties with the assessment. The preliminary examination pursuant to Article 108(3) TFEU is intended to allow the Commission to form a prima facie opinion as to the legal qualification of the measure at issue. If doubts remain as to the nature of the measure and/or its compatibility at the end of this preliminary analysis, a formal investigation procedure *must be* initiated by the Commission according to Article 108(2) TFEU. The formal investigation has a twofold purpose: it is designed to safeguard the right of potentially interested parties to submit their views and to allow the Commission to be fully informed of all the facts of the case before making a final decision on the measure at issue.[16]

Finally, as a general remark, it must be observed that the administrative procedure develops mostly through a 'bilateral dialogue' between the Commission and the Member State(s) since the procedure for reviewing a State aid is a procedure initiated against the Member State responsible for granting the aid. Private 'interested parties' as defined in Article 1 h) of the Procedural Regulation or, to use the wording of Article 108(2) TFEU, 'parties concerned' – such as aid recipients, competitors of beneficiaries and trade associations[17] – are primarily viewed as *sources of information* for the Commission and enjoy limited procedural rights.[18]

(usually, competitors of the aid recipients) can rely on that provision before national courts, asking for the suspension and recovery of the aid before the outcome of the Commission's compatibility assessment. Case C-120/73, *Gebrüder Lorenz GmbH v. Federal Republic of Germany and Land Rheinland-Pfalz,* 11.12.1973, ECLI:EU:C:1973:152.

16. *See,* among others, Case T-188/95, *Waterleiding Maatschappij 'Noord -West Brabant' NV v. Commission of the European Communities,* 16.9.1998, ECLI:EU:T:1998:217, para. 52; Case C-198/91, *Cook v. Commission of the European Communities,* 19.5.1993, ECLI:EU:C:1993:239, para. 22; Case C-225/91, *Matra SA v. Commission of the European Communities,* 15.6.1993, ECLI:EU:C:1993:239, para. 16; Case C-78/03, *Commission of the European Communities v. Aktionsgemeinschaft Recht und Eigentum eV,* 13.12.2005, ECLI:EU:C:2005:761, para. 34; Case C-174/19 P, *Scandlines Danmark et Scandlines Deutschland v. Commission of the European Communities,* 6.10.2021, ECLI:EU:C:2021:801, footnote 22; Case C-594/19 P, *Deutsche Lufthansa AG v. of the European Communities,* 20.1.2022, ECLI:EU:C:2022:40, para. 33; Case C-466/21 P, *Land Rheinland-Pfalz v. Deutsche Lufthansa* 14.9.2023, ECLI:EU:C:2023:666, para. 29.
17. '*Interested party*' according to Art. 1 h) of the Procedural Regulation 'means any Member State and any person, undertaking or association of undertakings whose interests might be affected by the granting of aid, in particular the beneficiary of the aid, competing undertakings and trade associations'.
18. A confirmation of this approach may be found in the judgment of the Court, in Case C-139/07 P, *Commission of the European Communities v. Technische Glaswerke Ilmenau GmbH,* 29.6.2010, ECLI:EU:C:2010:376, paras 57-58, according to which the procedure for reviewing State aid is, in view of its general scheme, a procedure initiated in respect of the Member State responsible for granting the aid and private parties do not have a right under the procedure for reviewing State aid to consult the documents on the Commission's administrative file. *See infra* §3.06[B]. The amendments to the procedure brought by Regulation No. 734/13 – which introduced the possibility for the Commission to request information directly from undertakings and association of undertakings and to impose sanctions on them should they submit incomplete or incorrect information – confirms, if not exacerbates, this approach.

§3.03 OVERVIEW OF COMMISSION PROCEDURE

[A] Different Types (and Procedures) of State Aid

As anticipated, the Procedural Regulation includes four separate chapters with four different types of procedure, dependent on the type of aid in question: the procedure regarding *notified (new) aid*, the *unlawful aid* procedure, the *misused aid* and the *existing aid* procedure.[19] Below is a summary of the different types of aid and the relevant procedures, which will be analysed in the subsequent paragraphs.

The 'archetype' of the aid procedure is represented by the body of rules regarding *notified aid* (i.e., to say every plan to grant new aid). New aid – which can be either *individual* aid or *aid schemes*[20] – must be notified to the Commission prior to its implementation, and may not be put into effect until the Commission has made a decision. The Commission may either approve the measure on the basis of the simplified procedure for certain kinds of aid or apply the normal preliminary review procedure (pursuant to Article 108(3) TFEU). If doubts arise as to the compatibility of the aid with the internal market, the Commission will open a formal investigation procedure (Article 108(2) TFEU procedure) before reaching a decision.

The notion of *unlawful aid* comprises three situations: aid that has not been notified, and thus put into effect without authorization from the Commission; aid that has been notified but put into effect before authorization; and aid that has been awarded in breach of authorization terms. Unlawful aid is often brought to the attention of the Commission by private parties (often undertakings that are competitors of the beneficiary). Unlawful aid does not mean incompatible aid. In fact, the Commission is obliged to examine on the merit whether or not the illegally granted aid is compatible with the common market. The simplified procedure does not apply in relation to unlawful aid and the aid must be assessed under the normal preliminary examination procedure and, should it be necessary, the formal investigation procedure.

Misused aid is an aid used by the beneficiary in violation of a decision made by the Commission that authorized the aid. In case of misused aid, the Commission must

19. On State aid procedure *see* Bacon, *European Union Law of State Aid*[3] (Oxford, 2017); Peretz QC, Mackersie, *State Aids, in Bellamy & Child* (edited by Bailey & John), *European Union Law of Competition*[8] (Oxford, 2019); Hancher, Ottervanger, Slot, *EU State Aids*[6] (London, 2021); *Grespan, EU Competition Law, in Tosato Bellodi, Procedure Antitrust- Merger- State Aid, Volume 1* (Deventer- Leuven, 2014); *Mederer, Pesaresi, Van Hoof, EU Competition Law – State Aid (Volume IV)* (Leuven, 2008); *Rossi, Procedura in tema di aiuti in Disciplina della concorrenza nella UE* (ed. Frignani, Bariatti) (Milan, 2012).

20. Under Art. 1, clause d) of the Procedural Regulation, aid scheme means: (i) any act on the basis of which, without further implementing measures being required, individual aid awards may be made to undertakings defined within the act in a general and abstract manner; and (ii) any act on the basis of which aid which is not linked to a specific project may be awarded to one or several undertakings for an indefinite period of time and/or for an indefinite amount. Individual aid shall mean aid that is not awarded on the basis of an aid scheme and notifiable awards of aid on the basis of an aid scheme (Art. 1, clause e) of the Procedural Regulation).

open a formal investigation procedure pursuant to Article 108(2) TFEU. The powers of the Commission are similar to those provided for unlawful aid.

Existing aid shall mean, according to Article 1(1)(b) of the Procedural Regulation:

(1) Aid which existed prior to the entry into force of the Treaty in the respective Member States (subject to certain conditions for the Member States that joined the EU from 1995 onwards).
(2) Authorized aid, that is to say, aid schemes and individual aid that have been authorized by the Commission or by the Council.
(3) Aid that is deemed to have been authorized.
(4) Aid for which the ten-year limitation period has expired.
(5) Aid that is deemed to be an existing aid because it can be established that at the time it was put into effect, it did not constitute an aid, and subsequently became an aid due to the evolution of the internal market and without having been altered by the Member State. Where certain measures become aid following the liberalization of an activity by Community law, such measures are not to be considered existing aid after the date fixed for liberalization.

Existing aid does not have to be notified, but is subject to constant review by the Commission. If the aid is subsequently deemed incompatible with the internal market, the Commission may propose appropriate measures to the Member State and, if those measures are not accepted, open a formal investigation procedure.

[B] Sector Inquires

Article 20 a) of the Procedural Regulation provides that, where the Commission has reasonable suspicion that State aid measures in a particular sector or based on a particular aid instrument may materially restrict or distort competition within the internal market in several Member States, or that existing aid measures in a particular sector in several Member States are not, or no longer, compatible with the internal market, the Commission may conduct an *enquiry across various Member States* into the sector of the economy or the use of the aid instrument concerned.

The Commission will collect horizontal information by sending requests for information to the Member States and to any relevant market players. At the end of its enquiry, the Commission shall publish a report on the results of its enquiry and the information obtained may be used in the framework of procedures under the Regulation.

This tool, which should help the Commission to focus on the most distortive cases for the functioning of the internal market,[21] was borrowed from the Commission's antitrust experience and, namely, from Article 17 of Regulation 1/2003.[22]

To date, however, there has only been one sector enquiry case initiated by the Commission, in the energy sector.[23] Such tool, also because of the crises that have affected Europe in sequence (from the 2009 financial and economic crisis to the COVID-19 pandemic and the Russian-Ukrainian energy crisis) with massive use of public resources authorized by the Commission to cope with such emergencies, has so far remained basically unused.

§3.04 NOTIFICATION OF NEW AID

[A] Obligation to Notify

Article 108(3) TFEU and Article 2 of the Procedural Regulation impose on Member States to timely notify the Commission of any plan to grant new aid or modify existing aid.[24] All aid that falls within the conditions set out in Article 107(1) must be notified and approved before implementation.

Even the extension of previously notified and approved aid constitutes new aid and must be notified.[25] Likewise, transitional rules intended to maintain the effects of a new aid scheme which has not been notified and has been declared incompatible by the Commission, constitute a new State aid scheme that must be notified, without prejudice to the compatibility of those transitional rules.[26]

21. *See* the Explanatory Memorandum of the European Commission – Proposal for a Council Regulation amending Regulation (EC) No. 659/1999 of 5 Dec. 2012 COM (2012) 725 Final, p. 10.
22. *See* Regulation (EC) No. 1/2003 of 16 Dec. 2002 on the implementation of the rules on competition laid down in Arts 81 and 82 of the Treaty OJ 2003 L1/25.
23. On 29 Apr. 2015, the Commission launched a state aid sector enquiry into Member States' measures to ensure sufficient electricity supplies (so-called capacity mechanisms). The sector enquiry examined in particular whether capacity mechanisms ensure sufficient electricity supply without distorting competition or trade in the EU's Single Market.
24. Article 4(1) of the implementing Regulation (EU) 794/2004 defines an alteration of an existing aid as any change other than modifications of a purely formal or administrative nature which cannot affect the evaluation of the compatibility of the aid measure with the internal market. Any substantive change in a system of aid will therefore normally constitute an alteration to the aid. However, an increase inferior to 20% of the original provision of an aid scheme is not considered a modification to existing aid.
25. Case C-70/72, *Commission of the European Communities v. Federal Republic of Germany*, 12.7.1973, ECLI:EU:C:1973:87, para. 11 and Case C-197/99 P, *Kingdom of Belgium v. Commission of the European Communities*, 11.9.2003, ECLI:EU:C:2003:444, para. 109; Case C-590/14 P, *Dimosia Epicheirisi Ilektrismou AE (DEI) and European Commission v. Alouminion tis Ellados VEA*, 26.10.2016, ECLI:EU:C:2016:797, para. 45-46.
26. *See* Case C-297/01, *Sicilcassa S.p.A. v. IRA Costruzioni S.p.A. and Francesco Gaetano Restivo Graci and Others and Francesco Gaetano Restivo Graci and Others v. IRA Costruzioni S.p.A., Amministrazione straordinaria della Holding personale Graci Gaetano and Sicilcassa S.p.A.*, 24.7.2003, ECLI:EU:C:2003:416, para. 45.

The obligation to notify is subject to relevant exceptions. Firstly, measures that meet the conditions of the General Block Exemption Regulation (GBER),[27] as well as the conditions provided for by the block exemptions relating to the agriculture and fisheries sector[28] do not need to be notified.

Similarly, public compensation for the operation of services of general economic interests falling within Article 106(2) TFEU are exempt from the obligation to notify. To this end, the Commission, following the landmark judgment of the ECJ *Altmark*[29] issued a decision based on Article 106(3) TFEU, which clarifies the conditions under which State aid for the provision of public services is compatible with State aid rules and does not have to be notified in advance to the Commission.[30]

Furthermore, it should be recalled that even *de minimis aid* is not subject to notification, since they are measures that do not meet all the conditions provided by Article 107(1) TFEU (lacking the requirement on the impact on competition and trade in the internal market).[31]

In terms of timing, aid measures must be notified to the Commission while they are still at the *draft* stage, that is to say, before they are implemented and while they can still be adjusted in the light of any observations the Commission may have.[32] As a consequence, the Court of Justice has declared, for example, that a Member State fails to fulfil its obligation under Article 108(3) TFEU when it notifies measures entailing an aid scheme after their adoption as laws.[33] The guiding principle provided by the

27. Commission Regulation (EU) No. 651/2014 of 17 Jun. 2014 declaring certain categories of aid compatible with the internal market in application of Arts 107 and 108 of the Treaty (GBER). In those cases, the Member State concerned is nevertheless required to forward to the Commission a summary of the aid measure within the time periods specified in those block exemptions for publication in the Official Journal. On the General Block Exemption Regulation *see* Ch. 1.
28. Aid granted in the fishery and aquaculture sector are covered by Regulation (EU) No. 1379/2013 of the European Parliament and of the Council of 11 Dec. 2013 on the common organization of the markets in fishery and aquaculture products, as amended by Regulation (EU) 2020/560.
29. *See* Case C-280/00, *Altmark Trans GmbH and Regierungpräsidium Magdeburg v. Nahverkehrsgesellschaft Altmark GmbH*, 24.7.2003, ECLI:EU:C:2003:415.
30. Commission Decision of 20 Dec. 2011 on the application of Art. 106(2) of the TFEU to State aid in the form of public service compensation granted to certain undertakings entrusted with the operation of services of general economic interest, in OJ 2012 L7, p. 3/10. On public service compensation *see also* the Communication from the Commission – European Union framework for State aid in the form of public service compensation, in OJ 2012 C8, p. 15/22. *See also* the Communication from the Commission on the application of the European Union State aid rules to compensation granted for the provision of services of general economic interest; in OJ 2012 L7, p. 4/14 and the Commission Regulation (EU) 2023/2832 on the application of Arts 107 and 108 of the TFEU to *de minimis* aid granted to undertakings providing services of general economic interest (SGEI).
31. *See* Commission Regulation (EU) 2023/2831, replacing Regulation (EU) No. 1407/2013 of 18 Dec. 2013 on the application of Arts 107 and 108 of the TFEU to *de minimis* aid regulation, which exempts aid amounts of up to EUR 300,000 per undertaking over a three-year period.
32. Case T-62/08, *ThyssenKrupp Acciai Speciali Terni S.p.A. v. European Commission*, 1.7.2010, ECLI:EU:T:2010:268, para. 235; and Case T-188/95, *Waterleiding Maatschappij v. Commission*, *supra* (para. 118). *See also* Case T-109/01, *Fleuren Compost BV v. Commission of the European Communities*, 14.1.2004, ECLI:EU:T:2004:4 para. 74; and the letter from the Commission to the Member States SG (89) D/5521 of 27 Apr. 1989.
33. *See* Case C-169/82, *Commission of the European Communities v. Italian Republic*, 26.10.1983 ECR 1603, para. 11.

Regulation requires the measure to be notified 'in sufficient time' for the Commission to reach its decision prior to implementation of the measure.

In many cases, a Member State will engage in informal discussions before State aid notification is submitted. Pre-notification discussion is compulsory if the Member States wishes an aid measure to be assessed under the simplified procedure and encouraged in other cases, in particular for cases raising novel issues.[34] The pre-notification phase offers an opportunity for discussion and for the Commission to provide guidance to Member States concerned about the scope of information to be submitted with the notification form to ensure its completeness from the date of notification.[35]

Pursuant to Article 4(5) of the Procedural Regulation, the Commission has a period of two months to conclude the preliminary examination phase, which only commences upon receipt of a *complete* notification.[36]

A notification is deemed complete when the Commission requests no further information within two months from the reception of the notification or of any supplementary information requested.[37] To this regard, the Court of Justice recalled that the preliminary stage of the procedure for reviewing aid is intended merely to allow the Commission a sufficient period of time for reflection and examination, in order to form a prima facie opinion of whether the notified aid plans are in partial or complete conformity with the Treaty.[38] Consequently, for the purpose of the preliminary phase, the notification can be regarded as complete, which will trigger the beginning of the two-month period, if it contains the information that will enable the Commission to form *a* prima facie opinion as to the compatibility of the aid,[39] either immediately or once the Member States has replied to further questions raised by the Commission.[40]

34. *See* s. 3 of the Best Practices Code on the conduct of State Aid control proceedings.
35. It is worth noting that, even if the Commission has started its investigation on the basis of a third-party complaint, the Member State should make a formal notification in order to protect itself from the consequences of a decision declaring the aid unlawful. *See* Joined Cases T-116/01 and T-118/01, *P&O European Ferries (Vizcaya) v. Commission of the European Communities*, 5.8.2003, ECLI:EU:T:2003:217 and on appeal Case C-442/03 P, *P&O European Ferries (Vizcaya)SA and Diputación Foral de Vizcaya v. Commission of the European Communities*, 1.6.2006, ECR I-4845.
36. Article 4, para. 5, of Regulation (EU) No. 659/99.
37. Pursuant to the mentioned Art. 4, para. 5, this term can be extended with the consent of the Member State concerned. Moreover, the Commission, can apply a reduced instalment period if appropriate.
38. *See* Case C-95/81, *Commission of the European Communities v. Italian Republic*, 9.6.1984, ECLI:EU:C:1982:216, para. 11. Case C-367/95 P, *Commission of the European Communities v. Chambre syndicale nationale des entreprises de transport de fonds et valeurs (Sytraval) and Brink's France Sarl*, 2.4.1998, ECLI:EU:C:1998:154, para. 38; Case C-204/97, *Portuguese Republic v. Commission of the European Communities*, 3.5.2001, ECLI:EU:C:2001:233, para. 32.
39. *See* Case T-520/09, *Télévision française 1 (TF1) and Others v. European Commission*, 10.7.2012, ECLI:EU:T:2012:352, paras 61-62; and Case T-79/10, *Colt Télécommunications France v. European Commission*, 16.9.2013, ECLI:EU:T:2013:463, para. 46.
40. The Court has held that the Commission may not artificially extend the two-month period by making a trivial request for further information close to the deadline. *See* in this regard Case C-99/98, *Republic of Austria v. Commission of European Communities*, 15.2.2001, ECLI: EU:C:2001:94, paras 52-56. In that case the Court annulled a decision to open the Art. 108(2)

The ECJ clarified that the obligation to notify is of a procedural nature and does not create a definitive situation in itself. Therefore, whether aid is compatible must be assessed in light of the provisions in force when the Commission makes its decision and not those in force at the moment of notification.[41]

Detailed provisions on the notification procedure are outlined by Regulation No. 794/2004. The notification forms are now all available from the Commission's State Aid Notification Interactive (SANI) web application and all notifications must now be made electronically via that system. The SANI application incorporates the standard notification form required by Regulation 794/2004 (including supplementary information sheets for specific types of aid), a form for pre-notification of a State aid, a simplified notification form for certain alterations to existing aid and a form for the summary reporting of measures covered by one of the block exemptions. All correspondence in connection with a notification should also be sent electronically via the Commission's secure email system. Other means of communication may only be used by prior agreement with the Commission.[42]

In 2020, the Commission adopted a Temporary Framework,[43] prolonged until 2022, in order to address the COVID-19 outbreak and, later on, similar rules to support the EU economies following the aggression against Ukraine.[44] (the 'Temporary Frameworks'). These rules have not introduced ad hoc procedural rules, although notifications were often dealt with informally and quickly.[45] The Temporary Frameworks also

decision procedure taken long after the two-month period had expired since a letter containing a single question on a subsidiary aspect of the plan, and representing less than 2% of the total investment, was held not necessary to enable the Commission to form a prima facie opinion on the compatibility of the aid. The Court held that, in reality, the purpose of the letter was not to obtain clarification of the facts but to gain extra time in which to consider the proposed aid. That, according to the Court, amounted to 'an artificial extension of the preliminary review phase'. *See also* the Opinion of the Advocate General Medina, Case C-758/21 *P, Ryanair DAC, Airport Marketing Services Ltd v. European Commission*, 23.11.2023, ECLI:EU:C:2023:917, para. 79.

41. *See* Case C-167/11 P, *Cantiere navale De Poli S.p.A. v. European Commission*, 22.3.2012, ECLI:EU:C:2012:164, para. 51; and Case C-334/07 P, *European Commission v. Freistaat Sachsen*, 11.12.2008, ECLI:EU:C:2008:709, paras 52 and 53; *see* Opinion of Advocate General Wathelet, *Case C-303/13 P, European Commission v. Jørgen Andersen*, 6.10.2015, ECLI:EU:C:2015:647, paras 42-43.
42. Should a State intend to make modifications to the aid plan following notification, there is no need to notify the plan again. It is sufficient that the State communicates this intention to the Commission following the initial notification. *See* Joined Cases C-91/83 and C-127/83 *Heineken Brouwerijen Bv v. Inspecteurs Der Vennootschapsbelasting, Amsterdam and Utrecht*, 9.10.1984, ECLI:EU:C:1984:307, para. 17.
43. Temporary Framework for State aid measures to support the economy in the current COVID-19 outbreak, adopted by the Commission on 20 Mar. 2020 as further amended.
44. Temporary Crisis Framework for State Aid measures to support the economy following the aggression against Ukraine by Russia, adopted by the Commission on 24 Mar. 2022 as further amended.
45. Commission decisions on aid measures within the Temporary Framework were generally taken swiftly and sometimes generated critics and concerns by competitors of the beneficiaries. *See* in this regard Case T-238/20, *Ryanair DAC v. European Commission* 17.2.2021, ECLI:EU:T:2021:9; Case T-379/20, *Ryanair v. Commission (SAS, Suède; Covid-19)* 14.4.2021, ECLI:EU:T:2021:195; Case T-378/20, *Ryanair DAC v. European Commission (SAS, Denmark; Covid-19)* 14.4.2021, ECLI:EU:T:2021:194, where Ryanair alleged the infringement of the procedural rights under Art. 108(2) TFEU as Commission failed to initiate a formal investigation procedure despite the alleged existence of serious doubts. The General Court rejected the plea in all the above decision

included an invitation to Member States to inform the Commission of their intentions and to notify drafts of such measures as early and as fully as possible, and the Commission's duty to provide guidance and assistance to Member States at all stages of the procedure.

[B] Standstill Obligation

A logical corollary of the obligation to notify is the standstill clause provided by Article 108(3) TFEU and Article 3 of the Procedural Regulation, according to which the Member State *cannot* implement the aid until a positive decision has been reached by the Commission.[46]

This prohibition is intended to guarantee that an individual aid or an aid scheme is not put into effect before the Commission has had sufficient time to examine the plan and begin, where necessary, the procedure outlined in the second paragraph of Article 108 TFEU.[47]

The standstill obligation remains in force during the preliminary examination and throughout the formal investigation procedure until the Commission adopts a decision. Obviously, if the Commission states by decision that the aid measure is *compatible* with the internal market (so-called positive decision) or that it *does not* constitute aid ('no aid' decision) the standstill clause will lapse. If the Commission, at the end of the formal investigation procedure, adopts a 'negative decision', that is to say, a decision declaring the measure *incompatible* with the internal market,[48] the standstill clause will also cease to be applicable, although it will be replaced by the prohibition contained in the final decision.[49]

The standstill clause is primarily enforced by national judges,[50] but can also be enforced by the Commission itself which, under Article 13 of the Procedural Regulation, has the power to order the State to suspend the delivery of aid granted and can also order it to provisionally recover the aid, until it has reached its decision regarding the compatibility of said aid.[51]

---

and the rejection was then confirmed by the Court of Justice (*see* Case C-209/21 P, *Ryanair DAC v. European Commission* 23.11.2023, ECLI:EU:C:2023:905; Case C-320/21 P, *Ryanair DAC v. European Commission.* 28.9.2023, ECLI:EU:C:2023:712; Case C-321/21 P, *Ryanair v. Commission* 28.9.2023, ECLI:EU:C:2023:713.

46. Article 3 of the Procedural Regulation equates this hypothesis to the case in which the Commission *'is deemed to have taken'* a decision authorizing the aid. *See* in this regard §3.05[A].
47. *See* Case C-301/87, *French Republic v. Commission of the European Communities,* 14.2.1990, ECLI:EU:C:1990:67.
48. *See infra* §3.05[B].
49. If the Commission's decision is annulled, the consequences of the annulment on the standstill obligation will depend on the reasons underlying the judgment and on the type of decision annulled by the EU case law. *See* Case T-301/01, *Alitalia- Linee Aeree Italiane S.p.A. v. European Commission,* 9.7.2008, ECLI:EU:T:2008:262, para. 98; Case C-587/12 P, *Italian Republic v. European Commission* 7.11.2013, para. 12.
50. On this topic *see* Ch. 7.
51. These powers are attributed to the Commission not only in the hypothesis of aid that has not been notified or of aid that has been notified but implemented by the Member State before a decision by the Commission as to the compatibility of said aid but also those implemented

§3.05 THE PRELIMINARY REVIEW PROCEDURE

[A] Standard Preliminary Review

The Commission must examine the notification as soon as it is received. Following a (complete) notification, the Commission has a period of *two months* to terminate the preliminary review.[52] The purpose of this time limit - which does not apply to unlawful aid[53] - is to provide *legal certainty* by quickly informing the Member State as to the compatibility of a particular aid with the Treaty.

It has been mentioned that where the Commission considers the information provided by the Member State to be incomplete, it must request additional information.[54] The Code of Best Practice specifies that the Commission will endeavour to group requests for information at this stage into one comprehensive request for information, normally sent within four weeks after the date of notification.[55] If the Member State concerned does not provide such information within the period requested or provides incomplete information, the Commission must send a *reminder* and allow the State a further appropriate period to respond. If the Member State does not provide the information requested, the notification may be deemed to be *withdrawn*.[56]

Where the Commission, upon receiving a complete notification, does not take a decision concluding the preliminary examination within the two-month period referred to above - which may only be extended by consent of both the Commission and the Member State concerned - the aid will be *deemed to be authorized*. However, before implementing the measures in question, the Member State concerned must give the Commission *prior notice* thereof, and grant to the Commission a further fifteen working days period for adopting a decision on the case. This form of 'silent consent' procedure, which is intended to protect the State's interest in being rapidly informed by the Commission as to the possibility of granting aid, was introduced by the ECJ in *Lorenz*[57] and then codified into Article 4, paragraph 6, of the Procedural Regulation.[58]

---

unlawfully (misused aid). It must be clarified however that these latter can be the object of an injunction to suspend but not an injunction for recovery. *See*. Art. 20 of the Procedural Regulation.

52. Article 4(5) of the Procedural Regulation.
53. Nevertheless, despite not being bound to a specific deadline, the Commission cannot prolong the preliminary review of State measures that have not been notified *ad infinitum*. *See* in this regard §3.07[B].
54. Article 5(1) of the Procedural Regulation.
55. Section 5.1. of the Best Practices Code on the conduct of State aid control proceedings.
56. Unless before the expiry of that period, the period has either been extended with the consent of both the Commission and the Member State concerned, or the Member State informs the Commission that it considers the notification to be complete because the additional information requested is not available or has already been provided.
57. *See* Case C-120/73, *Gebrüder Lorenz GmbH v Federal Republic of Germany and Land Rheinland-Pfalz., supra*.
58. Under Art. 1 b) iii), the aid implemented by the State, after silent assent by the Commission, becomes *existing aid* and, as such, is subject to the relevant monitoring process by the Commission under Arts 21-23 of the Procedural Regulation. *See infra* §3.09. In order to be clear on the date from which the aid becomes existing aid, the Commission is required to notify through the publication of a notice in the Official Journal of the European Union.

It has already been stated that the purpose of the preliminary review phase is to allow the Commission to form a prima facie opinion as to whether the notified plan is compatible with the Treaty. With regard to aid schemes, the Commission may simply examine the general characteristics of the scheme without necessarily examining the individual situation in which it is liable to apply.[59]

The preliminary review is conducted by exchange of letters between the State providing the aid and the Commission. The Commission may not initiate the formal investigation procedure in respect of a measure without discussing its concerns with the Member States involved.[60] Interested parties (including complainants) do not play a formal role in it and do not enjoy the same rights as Member States, since the procedure is only initiated in respect of the Member State responsible for granting the aid.[61] Although the Commission is under no obligation at the preliminary stage to consult with the Member States or any other interested parties, it must examine all the facts and points of law brought to its attention by persons, undertakings or associations whose interests may have been affected by the granting of the aid.[62]

[B] Concluding the Preliminary Review

There are three ways in which the Commission may conclude the preliminary review:

(1) a decision pursuant to Article 4(2) of the Procedural Regulation that the notified measure *does not constitute aid*, since the requirements outlined in Article 107(1) TFEU were not all met ('no aid' decision);
(2) a 'positive' decision provided for in Article 4(3) of the Procedural Regulation, which implies that a notified measure *constitutes aid but can be exempted* under one of the exemptions provided by the Treaty;[63]

59. *See, inter alia,* Joined Cases C-71/09, C-73/09 and C-76/09 P, *Comitato 'Venezia vuole vivere' and Others v. European Commission,* 9.6.2011, ECLI:EU:C:2011:368, para. 63. *See also* Court of Justice of 4 Mar. 2021, Case C-362/19 P – *Commission v. Fútbol Club Barcelona* where the ECJ confirmed that in state aid regimes the Commission is not bound to consider the situation of the individual beneficiaries of the regimes and the relevant situation '*must be examined on an ex-ante basis, having regard to the information available at the time the intervention was decided upon*'.
60. In Case C-400/99 *Italian Republic v. European Commission,* 9.10.2001, ECLI:EU:C:2001:528 (the *Tirrenia* case) the Court partially annulled the Commission's decision to open the Art. 108(2) TFEU procedure on grounds that certain measures were included in that decision that had not ever been discussed with the Italian authorities.
61. On the position of interested parties in the formal investigation *see infra* §3.06[B]. With specific regard to complainants *see* §3.07[A].
62. Case C-204/97, *Portugal v. Commission,* paras 34-35.
63. Where it is decided not to raise objections, the Commission does not have the power to impose conditions, unlike the provisions of Art. 9, para. 4, Regulation (EU) No. 1589/2015 regarding the decisions issued at the end of the formal review. Nevertheless, in practice, and not infrequently, over the course of meetings with the State concerned, the latter 'spontaneously' modifies its original plan or consents to certain commitments in order to placate the Commission's doubts.

(3) a decision to *initiate the formal investigation procedure* pursuant to Article 4(4) of the Procedural Regulation and Article 108(2) TFEU. The Commission is under obligation to initiate the 'phase 2' procedure where it has *doubts* as to the compatibility of the notified aid with the internal market.

Whichever decision is adopted at the end of the preliminary review, it must be addressed to the Member State concerned and notified to that State without delay. 'No aid' decisions and decisions not to raise objections are published in a summary form in the Official Journal, with the full text of the decisions appearing on the Commission's website. The decision to initiate the formal investigation procedure must be published in full in the Official Journal in the authentic language version accompanied (where necessary) by a summary in the language of the Official Journal.[64]

It should be noted that the Commission has the power *to revoke* the decision by which it has declared that a measure does not constitute aid or compatible aid under Article 4, paragraphs 2 and 3 of Regulation No. 659/99, respectively.[65] This can only occur in cases where the decision was based on *imprecise information* provided by the Member State in question for assessment by the Commission. Before moving to revoke its previous decision, the Commission is obliged to give the State concerned the opportunity to present its observations. Furthermore, before revoking a decision and adopting another, the Commission must also start proceedings for a formal investigation.[66]

[C] The Simplified Procedure

In 2009, the Commission issued a Notice that introduced a simplified procedure, in an effort to streamline the notification process.[67] The procedure is aimed at reviewing within an accelerated timeframe certain types of State support measures that only require the Commission to verify that the measure abides by existing regulations and practice without exercising any discretionary powers.

Where the conditions set forth in this Notice are met, the Commission shall try to the best of its endeavours to make a short-form, no aid or no objections decision within twenty working days from the date of notification.

This special procedure can be used for three categories of aid:

64. *See* Art. 32(1) and (2) of the Procedural Regulation. The Commission will endeavour to publish the decision within two months of the date of the adoption, where the Member State concerned does not request the removal of confidential information. *See* Code of Best Practice, para. 48. In case of controversy surrounding confidentiality issues, however, publication times are longer in practice.
65. Article 11 of the Procedural Regulation.
66. *Ibid.* Aid provided as part of a decision that is then revoked is treated as unlawful aid and, therefore, during review of the decision, the Commission has the power to suspend the aid. Furthermore, once the review process is finished, the aid declared incompatible with the internal market will be subject to a recovery procedure. *See* §3.07[B] *infra*.
67. Notice from the Commission on a simplified procedure for treatment of certain types of aid OJ 2009 C136/3.

Category 1: aid measures that meet the conditions of the 'standard assessment' sections of existing frameworks or guidelines.[68]
Category 2: aid measures corresponding to well-established Commission practice, that is, measures approved in at least three precedents ten years prior to the date of pre-notification ('precedent decisions').[69]
Category 3: prolongation or extension of existing schemes. Namely: (a) increases in the budget of an authorized aid scheme exceeding 20%; (b) prolongation of an existing authorized scheme by up to six years; and (c) the tightening of the criteria for an authorized aid scheme, a reduction in its intensity or a reduction of eligible expenses.

Member States wishing to apply the simplified procedure shall contact the Commission prior to notification. In this context, the Member State is invited to submit a draft notification form with the necessary accompanying information, including the relevant precedent decisions if appropriate, via the Commission SANI application. Contacts with the Commission usually follow, via email or conference calls. Within five working days from the last pre-notification contact, the Commission shall communicate to the Member State concerned their decision on whether or not the case qualifies prima facie for treatment under the simplified procedure, which information is still to be provided for the measure to qualify for this procedure, or whether the case shall remain subject to the normal procedure.

The Member State shall notify the aid measure concerned no later than two months after it receives the communication from the Commission services about the prima facie eligibility of the measure. The submission of the notification triggers the start of the twenty working days period mentioned above for the adoption of the Commission decision.

A summary of the notification is published on the Commission website and interested parties have ten working days to submit observations. Where substantiated competition concerns are raised by interested parties with respect to the notified measure, the Commission will revert to the normal procedure.[70]

If the Commission is satisfied that the notified aid fulfils the criteria for the simplified procedure it will issue a short-form decision of 'no aid' or 'positive decision' pursuant to Article 4(2) or 4(3) of the Procedural Regulation.

68. Reference can be made to certain types of risk capital measures, environmental investment aid, aid for young innovative enterprises and innovation clusters, ad hoc regional aid, rescue aid in the manufacturing and services sector, some form of rescue and restructuring aid for small and medium enterprise, export credits in the shipbuilding sector and audiovisual support schemes falling under the Cinema Communication. This list is only illustrative and the Commission may update it from time to time.
69. The types of measures for which the Commission is ready to consider applying the simplified procedure are: aid measures for the preservation of national cultural heritage, aid schemes for theatre, dance and musical activities, aid schemes for the promotion of minority languages, aid measures in favour of the publishing industry, aid in favour of broadband connectivity in rural areas, etc. As per category No. 1 the list is only illustrative.
70. The Member State concerned will be informed of any substantiated concerns and be given the opportunity to comment thereon.

§3.06 THE FORMAL INVESTIGATION PROCEDURE

[A] Aims and Scope of the Formal Investigation

Where the Commission has *doubts* about the compatibility of a certain measure, it is obliged to adopt the decision to launch the formal investigation pursuant to Article 4(4) of Council Regulation (EU) No. 1589/2015. In that decision, published in the Official Journal,[71] the Commission must give notice to interested parties to submit their comments, as provided for by Article 108(2) TFEU and Article 6(1) of the Procedural Regulation.[72]

The decision to launch a formal investigation expresses a preliminary assessment of the measure in question aimed at determining whether it qualifies as aid and whether the doubts with regard to its compatibility with the internal market are pertinent.[73]

According to EU law, the notion of *serious difficulties* that justify the launch of a formal investigation is *objective* and is the exclusive criteria for starting a formal investigation.[74] The EU Courts review on this point goes *beyond* simple consideration of whether or not there has been a *manifest error* in the Commission's assessment.[75] In

71. The decision is published in the authentic language (that of the Member State submitting the notification) and a summary of it is translated into all languages of the Union.
72. It has been mentioned that 'Interested party' according to Art. 1 h) of the Procedural Regulation '*shall mean any Member State and any person, undertaking or association of undertakings whose interest might be affected by the granting of aid, in particular the beneficiary of the aid, competing undertakings and trade associations*'. This definition covers an indeterminate group of persons; questions have arisen however, as to the interpretation of the word 'in particular' and the possibility of extending the opportunity for intervention to undertakings falling outside the categories expressly mentioned by the law. The criterion applied by the Court examines whether the aid is likely to have a specific effect on the undertakings' situation. For example, the Court clarified that undertakings that are not direct competitors of the aid beneficiary, but which are active in the upstream or downstream market where their competitive position may be affected by the aid can also be interested parties – Case C-83/09 P, *European Commission v. Kronoply GmbH & Co. KG and Kronotex GmbH & Co. KG,* 24.5.2011, ECLI:EU:C:2011:341, paras 63-64; *see also ex multis*, Case T-69/18, *Verband Deutscher Alten- und Behindertenhilfe, Landesverband Niedersachsen/Bremen und Hamburg/Schleswig-Holstein eV and CarePool Hannover GmbH v. European Commission* 29.6.2022, ECLI:EU:T:2021:189, para. 70; Case T-777/19, *Coopérative des artisans pêcheurs associés (CAPA) and Others v. European Commission* 15.9.2021, ECLI: EU:T:2021:588, paras 63-64. However, the Court clarified that it is not sufficient for an undertaking to claim to be a 'competing undertaking' where the aid scheme defines the potential beneficiaries only in a general and abstract manner, in such that the undertaking is only 'indirectly and potentially' affected by the aid – Case T-398/94, *Kahn Scheepvaart v. European Commission,* 5.6.1996, ECLI:EU:T:1996:73, paras 49-50. The question of whether an undertaking may be regarded as an 'interested party' is also relevant to the issue of submitting complaints (*See infra* §3.07[A]) as well as of standing to bring proceedings before the European Courts (*See* Ch. 6).
73. *See* Arts 4(4) & 6(1) of Council Regulation (EU) No. 1589/2015.
74. *See* Case T-137/10, *Coordination bruxelloise d'institutions sociales et de santé (CBI) v. European Commission* 7.11.2012, ECLI:EU:T:2012:584 (para. 74); Case T-49/93, *Société internationale de diffusion et d'édition (SIDE) v. European Commission* 18.9.1995, ECLI:EU:T:1996:99, para. 60.
75. *See* Case T-30/03, RENV *3F v. European Commission* 27.9.2011, ECLI:EU:T:2011:534, para. 55; *ex multis*, Case T-57/11, *Castelnou Energía SL v. European Commission* 3.12.2014, ECLI: EU:T:2014:1021, para. 53, Case T-108/16, *Naviera Armas SA v. European Commission*

accordance with such an approach, the ECJ held that the existence of serious difficulties leading to the need to launch a formal investigation procedure may justify the annulment of a decision of the Commission to close the preliminary investigation even if the Commission's assessments as to substance are not wrong in fact or in law.[76]

Whether or not such difficulties exist requires an investigation of both the circumstances under which the decision was adopted and its content, comparing the grounds of the decision with the information available to the Commission when it took the said decision.[77] The ECJ clarified that the Commission's duty of diligence and impartiality cannot go so far as to hold that it is incumbent on it to seek, on its own initiative, all the information that might be connected with the case before it, even if such information is in the public domain. In other words, the ECJ, annulling the General Court's judgment on that point,[78] stated that, in order to demonstrate the 'serious doubts' justifying the opening of a formal procedure, it is not sufficient for the applicant to rely on any relevant information that was available or could have been available to the Commission on the date when the Commission adopted the challenged decision. To put it another way, the Commission would not be under an obligation to seek, examine and take into consideration 'all the relevant information', including information not brought to the attention of the Commission and information of which the Commission was unaware as regards its existence or its relevance to the examination of the notified measure. In the Court's view, an obligation of such scope would greatly exceed the Commission's duty of diligence.

However, the EU Courts have on more than one occasion established that the *duration* of the preliminary procedure is indicative of the presence of serious doubts.[79] A period that is significantly longer than the time allowed for initial review under Article 108(3) TFEU, can, in fact, alongside other elements, lead to admission that the Commission had great difficulty with its assessment, which required the launch of the procedure under Article 108(2) TFEU.

The position assumed in the opening decision is *provisional* in the sense that the Commission may modify its assessment in its final decision, in light of the evolution of

---

15.3.2018, ECLI:EU:T:2018:145, para. 49; Case T-68/15, *HH Ferries and Others v. European Commission* 19.9.2018, ECLI:EU:T:2018:563, para. 61; Case T-561/18, *ITD and ITD, Brancheorganisation for den danske vejgodstransport A/S and Danske Fragtmænd A/S v. European Commission* 5.5.2021, ECLI:EU:T:2021:240, para. 49; Case T-112/22, *Svenska Bankföreningen e Länsförsäkringar Bank v. European Commission* 17.4.2024, ECLI:EU:T:2024:250, para. 26.

76. *See* Case C-209/21 P, *Ryanair v. Commission, supra*, para. 112.

77. *See* Case C-431/07 P, *Bouygues and Bouygues Télécom SA v. European Commission*, 2.4.2009, ECLI:EU:C:2009:223 (para. 63), Case T-49/93, *SIDE v. Commission*, para. 60; *ex multis*, Case C-148/09 P, *Kingdom of Belgium v. Deutsche Post and DHL International* 22.9.2011, ECLI:EU:C:2011:603, para. 79; Case C-209/21 P, *Ryanair v. Commission*, para. 112; Case C-210/21 P, *Ryanair v. European Commission*, 23.11.2023, ECLI:EU:C:2023:908, para. 123; Case C-320/21 P, *Ryanair v. Commission, supra* (para. 147); Case C-321/21 P, *Ryanair v. Commission*, para. 135; Case C-440/22 P, *Wizz Air Hungary v. European Commission* 11.1.2024, ECLI:EU:C:2024:26, para. 98.

78. *See* Case C-57/19 P, *Commission v. Tempus Energy and Tempus Energy Technology*, 2.9.2021, ECLI:EU:C:2021:663 (paras 49-52), which refers, in this respect, Case C-847/19 P, *Achemos Grupé and Achema v. European Commission*, 29.4.2021, ECLI:EU:C:2021:343, paras 49 and 50.

79. *See* Case T-73/98, *Société chimique Prayon-Rupel SA v. Commission of the European Communities*, 15.3.2001, ECLI:EU:T:2001:94, para. 93.

the investigation and, in particular, in light of comments submitted by interested parties (such as beneficiaries of the aid and competing undertakings) in the course of the proceedings.[80]

For instance, in this regard, the General Court underlined that the Commission enjoys a certain degree of discretion in the opening decision with respect to the classification of aid and is entitled to treat a measure as being individual aid without being obliged to verify beforehand whether that measure may have been derived from such a scheme.[81]

By virtue of Article 9(6) of the Procedural Regulation, the Commission will endeavour to adopt a final decision within a period of *eighteen months* from the opening of the procedure. This time limit may be extended by a common agreement between the Commission and the Member State concerned.[82] In its Best Practices the Commission declares that, in order to ensure effective implementation of this deadline, it will endeavour to adopt the final decision no later than six months after the submission of the last piece of information by the Member State, or fruitless expiry of the last deadline.

Although the eighteen-month deadline – which applies to notified aid but not unlawful aid[83] – is indicative and therefore not binding, the EU Courts have reiterated on several occasions that the Commission is in any case obliged, on the basis of the principle of *good administration*, to act within a *reasonable time* in adopting decisions following administrative proceedings relating to competition policy.[84] Whether or not the duration of an administrative procedure is reasonable must be determined in relation to the particular circumstances of each case, and especially its context, the various procedural stages to be followed by the Commission, the complexity of the case and its importance for the various parties involved.[85]

80. However, the Commission may not adopt a final decision on the aid measure entirely outside the scope of an opening decision, since the parties concerned must be able to participate effectively in the formal investigation procedure, by understanding the reasoning that led to the provisional conclusion that the measure might be incompatible with the internal market. *See infra* §3.06[B].
81. *See* Case T-648/19, *Nike European Operations Netherlands and Converse Netherlands v. Commission*, 14.7.2021, ECLI:EU:T:2021:428 (para. 153); *see* however, the judgment in Case C-167/19, *Commission v. Freistaat Bayern* 10.3.2022, ECLI:EU:C:2022:176, para. 99, where the Court annulled an opening decision of the Commission that did not clarify how a given measure was to be financed, thus preventing interested parties from taking a clear and informed position on the issue.
82. *See* para. 64 of the Code of Best Practices.
83. *See* Art. 15, para. 2, of Council Regulation (EU) No. 1589/2015.
84. *See* Case T-303/10, *Wam Industriale* S.p.A. *v. European Commission* 27.9.2012, ECLI:EU:T:2012:505, para. 196; Case T-190/00, *Regione siciliana v. European Commission* 27.11.2003, ECLI:EU:T:2003:316, para. 136. *See also* Case C-282/95 P, *Guérin automobiles v. European Commission* 18.3.1997, ECLI:EU:C:1997:159 para. 38.
85. *See* Joined Cases T-394/08, T-408/08, T-453/08 and T-454/08, *Regione autonoma Sardegna and Others v. European Commission*, 20.10.2011, ECLI:EU:T:2011:493. In Case C-223/85, *Rijn-Schelde-Verolme (RSV) Machinefabrieken en Scheepswerven NV v. European Commission*, 24.11.1987, ECLI:EU:C:1987:502, paras 12-17, the Court found a twenty-six month period of examination of a notified aid to be excessive. In that case, according to the Court the Commission's delay had established a legitimate expectation on the part of the State so as to prevent the Commission from requiring the latter to order the refund of the aid. Conversely, the Court held that a period of twenty-two months could not be considered unreasonable merely

It must be noted that, if the Commission has not taken a decision on the notified aid by the deadline of eighteen months, should the Member State concerned so request, the Commission must adopt a decision on the basis of the information available to it within two months.[86]

[B] Rights of Member State and the Position of Interested Parties

In the decision opening the formal investigation interested parties are invited to submit comments within a period which normally cannot exceed one month.[87] The *dies a quo* of said period is the publication of the decision in the Official Journal.

Article 6(2) of the Procedural Regulation requires that the comments received by interested parties shall be communicated to the Member State, which may reply to the comments submitted and shall do so within one month.[88] Upon request of an interested party, on grounds of potential damage, its identity shall be withheld from the Member State concerned.

The forwarding of third parties to the Member State concerned is intended to protect its rights of defence. According to EU case law, in view of its general scheme, the procedure for reviewing State aid is an adversary procedure initiated in respect of the Member State responsible for granting the aid and the Commission cannot, without infringing the rights of the defence, use in its final decision information on which that Member State was not afforded an opportunity to comment.[89]

---

because it exceeded the period of eighteen months. *See* Case T-190/00, *Regione siciliana v. Commission*, para. 139; and Case T-176/01, *Ferriere Nord S.p.A. v. European Commission* 18.11.2004, ECLI:EU:T:2004:336, para. 69, confirmed in appeal Case C-49/05 P, *Ferriere Nord S.p.A. v. European Commission* 8.5.2008, ECLI:EU:C:2008:259, para. 51.

86. Article 9, para. 6, of Council Regulation (EU) No. 1589/2015. If appropriate, where the information provided is not sufficient to establish compatibility, the Commission shall take a *negative decision* (declaring the incompatibility of the measure with the internal market).
87. *See* Art. 24(1) of the Council Regulation (EU) No. 1589/2015. The Commission may extend the prescribed period in exceptional and duly justified cases. *See* Code of Best Practices (para. 50).
88. In the Best Practice Code (2018 version), the Commission strengthened its intention to strictly enforced the deadline para. 54 provides that: 'If a Member State does not submit comments on the opening decision or on third-party comments within 1 month, the Commission services may extend the deadline by another month, if the request from the Member State is justified, stating that, except in exceptional circumstances, no further extension will be granted. If the Member State does not send a sufficient and meaningful reply, the Commission may take a decision on the basis of the information available to it.'
89. *See* Case C-139/07 P, *Commission v. Technishe Glaswerke Ilmenau*, para. 57; Joined Cases T-231/06 and T-237/06, *Kingdom of the Netherlands and Nederlandse Omroep Stichting (NOS) v. European Commission*, 16.12.2010, ECLI:EU:T:2010:525, para. 35, Joined Cases C-74/00 P and C-75/00 P, *Falck and Acciaierie di Bolzano S.p.A. v. European Commission*, 24.9.2002, ECLI:EU:C:2002:524, para. 81. *See* also Case C-56/18, *Commission v. Gmina Miasto Gdynia and Port Lotniczy Gdynia Kosakowo*, 11.3.2020, ECLI:EU:C:2020:192, para. 73. Equally, failure by the Member State to challenge comments of interested parties sent to it in the course of the Commission's investigation may preclude it from challenging the same comments in an appeal against the decision. Case T-139/09, *French Republic v. European Commission*, 27.9.2012, ECLI:EU:T:2012:496 paras 54-55.

With a view to protecting the rights of defence, EU case law has consistently held that the Member State's right to be heard constitutes an *essential* procedural requirement.[90] It follows that, if this requirement is not met, the Commission's decision ordering the abolishment or modification of aid must be annulled. However, the EU Courts have demonstrated a considerable degree of flexibility in assessing cases where the Member State concerned was not allowed to express its views on certain documents produced during the proceeding,[91] and specified that this irregularity would only result in the annulment of the Commission's decision if it is established that, had it not been for that irregularity, the outcome of the procedure might have been different.[92]

It must be emphasized that in accordance with consistent case law, a Member State which has granted or seeks permission to grant aid under one of the exceptions provided for in the Treaty rules has *a duty to cooperate* with the Commission and must, in particular, provide the relevant information.[93] As with the preliminary review procedure, in a formal investigation, the Commission can request *additional information* from the Member State.

Moreover, before adopting a decision closing the formal investigation, the Commission shall give the Member State concerned the opportunity to make known its views on the information provided to the Commission by an undertaking, an association of undertakings or another Member State.[94]

Interested parties do not enjoy the same rights as the Member State. The opening decision is normally *not* notified to them (including the beneficiary of the aid),[95] they do *not* receive copies of the observations or information submitted by the Member State (and by other parties) and *cannot* claim the right to debate the issues with the

90. *See* Case T-211/05, *Italian Republic v. European Commission*, 4.9.2009, ECLI:EU:T:2009:304 (para. 53), the decision was then confirmed by the ECJ in the Case C-458/09, *Italian Republic v. European Commission* 34.11.2011, ECLI:EU:C:2011:769.
91. *See* Joined Cases T-228/99 and T-233/98, *Westdeutsche Landesbank Girozentrale and Land Nordrhein-Westfalen v. Commission*, 6.3.2003, ECLI:EU:T:2003:57, paras 153-159; Case C-288/96, *Federal Republic of Germany v. European Commission*, 5.10.2000, ECLI: EU:C:2000:537, para. 94 and Case T-198/01, *Tecnishe Glaswerke Ilmenau* GmbH *v. European Commission*, 8.7.2004, ECLI:EU:T:2004:222.
92. *See* Case T-53/08, *Italian Republic v. European Commission*, 1.7.2010, ECLI:EU:T:2010:267 (para. 115) and Case C-301/87, *France v. Commission*, para. 31. *See also* Joined Cases C-106/09 P and C-107/09 P, *Commission v. Government of Gibilter* 14.11.2011, ECLI:EU:C:2011:732, para. 181.
93. *See* Case C-364/90, *Italian Republic v. European Commission* 28.4.1993, ECLI:EU:C:1993:43, para. 20; Joined Cases T-132/96 and T-143/96, *Freistaat Sachsen and Others v. European Commission* 15.12.1999, ECLI:EU:T:1999:326, para. 140; and Case T-25/07, *Iride S.p.A. and Iride Energia S,p.A. v. European Commission*, 11.2.2009, ECLI:EU:T:2009:33, para. 100; joined Cases C-106/09 P and C-107/09 P, *Commission v. Government of Gibilter*, para. 147; Case T-527/13, *Italian Republic v. European Commission*, 24.6.2015, ECLI:EU:T:2015:429, para. 17; Case T-79/14, *Secop GbmH v. European Commission* 1.3.2016, ECLI:EU:T:2016:118, para. 74.
94. Article 9(8) of the Procedural Regulation. *See infra* §3.06[C].
95. The only exception to this is where the Commission decides to send the decision to 'identified third parties', including trade or business associations and invite them to comment on specific aspects of the case. In that case, in order to respect equal treatment between third parties, the Commission will send the same invitation to comment to the aid beneficiary. *See* Case T-198/01, *Technishe Glaswerke Ilmenau v. Commission* and Best Practice Code (para. 51). *See also* Case T-62/08, *ThyssenKrupp Acciai Speciali Terni v. Commission*, para. 163.

Commission in the same way as the Member State can.[96] Moreover, where comments on the measure have been submitted, the Commission is not required to hear the views of interested parties on the Commission's legal assessment of the measure in question or to inform the recipient of the aid of its position before adopting its final decision.[97] The provisions on the procedure for reviewing State aid do not reserve a special role, among the interested parties, for the recipient of aid and the EU Courts have endorsed the position of the Commission, whereby the procedure for reviewing State aid is not a procedure initiated 'against' the recipient of the aid. As a consequence, the procedure does not entail rights as extensive as the rights of the defence on which beneficiaries may rely.[98]

However, although interested parties cannot rely on the rights of defence, they do have the right *to be associated with it in an adequate manner*, taking into account the circumstances of the case at issue.[99] The practical implications of this principle – which is aimed at safeguarding the procedural rights of interested parties – are limited: this entails, for example, requirement on the part of the Commission to sufficiently define the framework of its investigation in the decision pursuant to Article 108(2) TFEU so as not to render *meaningless* the right of interested parties to put forward their comments,[100] to clearly describe in the opening decision the method of financing of the aid measure at issue,[101] to check the effect of overcompensation in favour of an undertaking liable to result from the cumulation of aids[102] or the impossibility for the

96. *See* Case T-62/08, *ThyssenKrupp v. Commission*, para. 162.
97. *See* Case T-198/01, *Technische Glaswerke Ilmenau v. Commission*, para. 198; Case T-53/08, *Italy v. Commission, supra*; Case T-103/14, *Frucona Košice v. European Commission* 16.3.2016, ECLI:EU:T:2016:152, para. 70.
98. *See* Case T- 62/08, *ThyssenKrupp v. Commission*, para. 162; Joined Cases C-74/00 P and C- 75/00 P, *Falck and Acciaierie di Bolzano v. Commission*, para. 83; and Case T-198/01, *Technische Glaswerke Ilmenau v. Commission*, para. 193. Case C-56/18 P, *Commission v. Gmina Miasto Gdynia and Port Lotniczy Gdynia Kosakowo, supra* (para. 75); *See also* Case C-758/21 P, *Ryanair DAC and Airport Marketing Services* 23.11.2023, ECLI:EU:C:2023:917, para. 95-97, Case T-356/15, *Austria v. European Commission* 12.7.2018, ECLI:EU:T:2018:439, para. 702; Case T-220/14, *Saremar v. European Commission* 6.4.2017, ECLI:EU:T:2017:267, para. 83; Case T-219/14, *Regione autonoma della Sardegna v. European Commission* 6.4.2017, ECLI: EU:T:2017:266, para. 86; Case T-242/12, *SNCF v. European Commission* 17.12.2015, ECLI: EU:T:2015:1003, para. 361.
99. *See* Case C-167/19, *European Commission v. Freistaat Bayern* 10.3.2022, ECLI:EU:C:2022:176 (para. 52); Case C-56/18 P, *Commission v. Gmina Miasto Gdynia and Port Lotniczy Gdynia Kosakowo*, para. 71.
100. *See* Case T-354/99, *Kuwait Petroleum BV v. European Commission* 31.5.2006, ECLI: EU:T:2006:137 (para. 85). *See also* in this regard Case T-291/06, *Operator ARP sp. z.o.o. v. European Commission*, 1.7.2009, ECLI:EU:T:2009:235, para. 38; Case T-778/17, *Autostrada Wielkopolska SA v. European Commission* 24.10.2019, ECLI:EU:T:2019:756, para. 56.
101. *See* in this regard also Case C-167/19, *European Commission v. Freistaat Bayern* 10.3.2022, ECLI:EU:C:2022:176. By such judgment, the ECJ annulled the Commission's decision for not having identified in the opening decision the method of financing the aid measure at issue, which is one of the conditions under Art. 107(1) TFEU (State resources), thus providing an incomplete and over-simplified description of the measure, unsuitable to enable the interested third parties to usefully submit their comments on the grounds that led the Commission to initiate the formal investigation procedure and, consequently, to ensure the effectiveness of Art. 108(2) TFEU.
102. *See* Case T-626/20, *Landwärme v. European Commission*, 21.12.2022, ECLI:EU:T:2022:853, para. 80. According to the General Court, if the analysis carried out by the Commission during

Commission to base its final decision on *new principles*, absent in the opening decision, without inviting them to submit their comments.[103] In any case, the ECJ specified that the beneficiary and any other interested party *do not*, in principle, have the *right of access* to documents in the Commission's administrative file.[104]

It can be argued, therefore, that the role of interested parties is essentially to act as a *source of information* for the Commission.[105] This view has been confirmed and even reinforced by the amendments brought to the Procedural Regulation by Council Regulation (EU) 734/2013, which in order to improve efficiency introduced the possibility of *consulting the market* in State aid cases, granting the Commission new powers to request information from undertakings and associations of undertakings modelled on those set out for antitrust and merger proceedings, combined with the

the preliminary examination procedure as regards the overcompensation which is liable to result from the cumulation at issue is insufficient or incomplete, this is an indication of the existence of serious difficulties. [...] Accordingly, the fact that the Commission analysed the absence of overcompensation in an insufficient and incomplete manner, in that it did not take account of the cumulation at issue, may suffice to establish the existence of serious difficulties.

103. *See* Case T-176/01, *Ferriere Nord v. Commission*, para. 75; confirmed on appeal by Case C-49/05 P, *Ferriere Nord v. Commission*, para. 71. Case C-334/07 P, *Commission v. Freistaat Sachsen*, para. 56. *See* more recently in this regard also Case C-56/18 P, *Commission v. Gmina Miasto Gdynia and Port Lotniczy Gdynia Kosakowo*, para. 79. Despite referring to said principle, the Court 'saved' the Commission's decision on the basis of the principle, mentioned above, whereby a procedural irregularity will entail the annulment of a decision in whole or in part only if it is shown that in the absence of such irregularity the decision being challenged might have been substantively different.

104. *See* Case C-139/07, *Commission v. Technische Glaswerke Ilmenau*, paras 56-58. The Court of Justice overturned the General Court judgment which held the Commission's pure and simple refusal of access to the documents by the recipient of the aid relating to the procedure to be unlawful. In that judgment the General Court stated that the obligation of the Commission to apply the Regulation 1049/01 regarding public access to European Parliament, Council and Commission documents extended also to procedures relating to State aid matters and imposed an obligation on the Commission to undertake a *concrete, individual examination* of the documents covered by the applicant's application for access. Conversely, the ECJ held that Council Regulation (EC) No. 659/1999, and, in particular, Art. 20 thereof, does not lay down any right of access to documents in the Commission's administrative file for interested parties and the Commission could refuse access to the file on the basis of the *general presumption* provided for Art. 4(2) of Regulation No. 1049/2001 which allows the EU Institutions to refuse access to a document where disclosure would undermine protection of the objectives of investigation activities. However, that general presumption does not exclude the right of those interested parties to demonstrate that a given document, the disclosure of which has been requested, is not covered by that presumption, or that there are a higher public interest justifying the disclosure of the document concerned according to Art. 4(2) of Regulation No. 1049/2001. The inexistence of a right to access to the file in the context of the review procedure opened in accordance with Art. 108(2) TFEU – whether that be on the basis of the Procedural Regulation or, in principle, in the context of Regulation (EC) No. 1049/2001 has been recently confirmed by the ECJ in Case C-758/21 P, *Ryanair and Airport Marketing Services*, para. 55; Case T-165/15, *Ryanair DAC and Airport Marketing Services v. European Commission* 13.12.2018, ECLI:EU:T:2018:953 para. 57.

105. Case T-362/10, *Vtesse Networks Ltd v. Commission*, 5.11.2014, ECLI:EU:T:2014:928, para. 95; Case T- 62/08, *ThyssenKrupp v. Commission*, para. 162; Case T-266/94, *Skibsværftsforeningen and Others v. European Commission*, 22.101996, ECLI:EU:T:1996:153, para. 256; and Joined Cases T-371/94 and T-394/94, *British Airways plc and Others v. European Commission*, 25.6.1998, ECLI:EU:T:1998:140, para. 59.

power to issue fines and periodic penalty payments in case of incorrect, incomplete or misleading information (*see* paragraph below).

[C] Market Investigation Tools

Article 7 of the Procedural Regulation sets out the possibility of requesting the information necessary to enable the Commission to complete its assessment *directly from any undertaking, association of undertaking or (other) Member States*. Such a request for information 'made to other sources' can be addressed only after the opening of the formal investigation and with respect to 'technical complex cases'.

Moreover, the Commission may request information only: (a) if it is limited to formal investigation procedures that have been identified by the Commission *as being ineffective to date;*[106] (b) in so far as aid *beneficiaries* are concerned, if the *Member State* concerned *agrees* to request.[107]

Recital 11 of Council Regulation (EU) 1589/2015 provides that when the Commission requests information from the aid beneficiary, the information submitted cannot constitute the basis for bilateral negotiation between the Commission and the aid beneficiary.[108]

Whilst Member States shall provide information upon request by the Commission and within a time limit which should not exceed one month, there are two possible ways for the Commission to request information from undertakings and associations of undertakings: (i) by *simple request;*[109] and (ii) by *decision*.[110] In both cases, the Commission must specify the purpose of the request, what information is required and prescribe a proportionate time limit for the reply as well as the possibility of imposing *fines* and *periodic penalty payments* in case of failure to provide information (*see* below).

In addition, Article 7(7) of the Procedural Regulation provides that the undertakings or association of undertakings concerned must be informed about the possibility of *challenging* the *decision* on request of information before the Court of Justice.[111]

Article 7, paragraph 8, provides that the Commission shall simultaneously provide the Member State concerned with a copy of the request for information sent to 'other sources', while according to Article 7, paragraph 3, replies from undertakings must be submitted *simultaneously* to the Commission and the Member State concerned

106. It can be reasonably argued that the formal investigation can be considered ineffective after the expiry of the deadline for submitting comments set pursuant to Art. 6(1) of Council Regulation (EU) 1589/2015.
107. Moreover, Art. 6(1) provides that the use of the power to request information is subject to 'the principle of proportionality, in particular for small and medium sized enterprise'.
108. This is a paradigmatic expression of the view of private parties (including aid recipients) as mere sources of information.
109. Article 7(6), The provision mirrors that contained in Art. 18(2) of Regulation No. 1/2003.
110. Article 7(7), mirroring Art. 18(3) of Regulation No. 1/2003.
111. On the possibility of challenging decisions addressed to private parties *see* Ch. 6.

(unless the undertaking concerned deems that the reply includes information that is confidential vis-à-vis the Member State).[112]

As per the type of information sought, Recital 12 of Council Regulation (EU) 1589/2015 clarifies that it should consist, specifically, of factual company and market data and fact-based analysis of the functioning of the market.

As mentioned above, in order to render the powers of the Commission more effective, fines and periodic penalty payments may be imposed on *undertakings and associations and undertakings*. Conversely, when the request for information is addressed to another Member State, *no sanction* is applicable and the Commission will only send a reminder.[113]

To examine this in further detail, where requesting information by *simple request*, the Commission may impose fines of up to 1 % of their turnover on undertakings and associations for supplying *incorrect* or *misleading* information. Where the information is requested *by decision*, the Commission may also impose fines up to 1 % for supplying *incomplete* information or for not supplying it within a prescribed time limit[114] as well as *periodic penalty payments* where an undertaking or association of undertakings fails to supply complete and correct information. The periodic penalty payments shall not exceed 5 % of average daily turnover until the undertaking or association of undertakings provides the information.[115]

Before adopting any decision imposing fines or periodic penalty payments, the Commission shall set a final deadline of two weeks in which to receive the missing information and also give the undertaking or association of undertakings concerned the opportunity to make their views known. Decisions imposing fines or periodic penalty payments shall be published in the Official Journal. The Court of Justice shall have unlimited jurisdiction as per Article 261 TFEU to review fines or periodic penalty payments and it may cancel, reduce or increase such sanctions.[116]

It can be argued that the recognition of the right of private parties to challenge decisions requesting information and imposing penalties addressed to them constitutes a significant development of the traditional principle governing State aid law, according to which all Commission decisions are to be addressed to the Member State concerned.[117] Also, the Commission's obligation to hear private parties before adopting

112. Article 7 para. 3, second sentence, provides that the Commission shall steer and monitor the information transmission between the Member States, undertakings and associations of undertakings concerned and verify the purported confidentiality of the information transmitted.
113. Recital 16 of Council Regulation (EU) 1589/2015 stress the fact that Member States are under a duty to cooperate sincerely with the Commission in accordance with Art. 4 of TUE.
114. Fines may be triggered where the incorrect, mislead or incomplete information is given intentionally or through gross negligence.
115. The periodic penalty payment can be reduced or waived altogether once the undertaking has replied, therefore fulfilling the obligation that the penalty was intended to enforce.
116. *See* Art. 7 paras 5 and 6. The Commission's power to impose sanction and periodic penalty payments is subject to a three-year limitation period (Art. 18(1)), while the Commission's power to enforce those fines and periodic penalty payments is subject to a five-year limitation period (Art. 19(1)). Arts 18 and 19 regulate when the limitation periods start to run, their interruption and their suspension.
117. *See* Art. 31(1) of the Procedural Regulation.

a sanction thereby respecting its rights of defence in the (sub)-procedure concerning the provision of information seems to be (indirect) confirmation of the ontological 'hybrid' nature of State aid proceeding, although the Commission remarked that undertakings remain 'third parties' in the context of the procedure and nothing in the Procedural Regulation grants them anywhere near as extensive participation in the State aid investigation as the Member State.[118]

[D] Closing the Formal Investigation Procedure

Pursuant to Article 9 of Council Regulation (EU) No. 1589/2015, the formal investigation procedure may be closed in one of four ways, as follows:

(1) Where the Commission finds that, where appropriate following modification by the Member State concerned, the notified measure *does not constitute aid*, it shall record that finding by way of a decision (Article 9(2)).
(2) Where the Commission finds that – where appropriate following modification by the Member State concerned and after considering all relevant issues and any previous decisions – *doubts* as to the compatibility of the notified measure with the common market *have been removed*, it shall decide that the aid is compatible with the common market, in which case a *positive decision* occurs, which, pursuant to Article 9(3) of Council Regulation (EU) No. 1589/2015, must specify which exception under the Treaty has been applied.
(3) At times, certain conditions may be attached to a positive decision, and certain obligations may be laid down therein to enable compliance therewith, in which case the decision is referred to as a *conditional decision* (Article 9(4)).
(4) Where the Commission finds that the notified aid is not compatible with the common market, it shall take a *negative decision* whereby it decides that the aid shall not be put into effect (Article 9(5)).

Each of these possible decisions must be adequately grounded,[119] notified to the Member State concerned,[120] and published in the Official Journal of the European

118. *See* the Proposal for a Council Regulation amending Regulation (EC) No. 659/1999 laying down detailed rules for the application of Art. 93 of the EC Treaty, COM (2012) 725 FINAL – Explanatory Memorandum.
119. *See, inter alia*, Case C-367/95 P, *Commission v. Sytraval and Brink's France*, *supra* (paras 63 and 67); Case C-150/09 P, *Iride S.p.A. and Iride Energia S.p.A. v. European Commission* 21.1.2010, ECLI:EU:C:2010:34, para. 21. According to this jurisprudence: '*it is settled case-law that the statement of reasons required by Art. 296 TFEU must be appropriate to the act at issue and must disclose in a clear and unequivocal fashion the reasoning followed by the institution which adopted the measure in question in such a way as to enable the persons concerned to ascertain the reasons for the measure and to enable the competent Union court to exercise its power of review. The requirements to be satisfied by the statement of reasons depend on the*

Union.[121] Moreover, pursuant to Article 24 of the Procedural Regulation, any interested party that has submitted comments pursuant to Article 6, any beneficiary of individual aid and any complainant shall be sent a copy of the decision taken by the Commission.

The formal investigation procedure may also be terminated *without a decision*, where continuing the procedure serves no useful purpose. This is the case, for instance, where the measure concerned has been discontinued or withdrawn.[122]

When it comes to *conditional decisions* specifically, a common condition attached to a positive decision is based on the so-called *Deggendorf* principle, whereby the Commission may require the Member State to recover from an undertaking aid previously declared to be unlawful, before new aid is paid to the same undertaking. This approach has been endorsed by the ECJ, which clarified that the Commission does not exceed the limits of its discretion when, a Member State proposing to grant aid to an undertaking, takes a decision declaring that aid to be compatible, but subject to the condition of prior repayment by the undertaking of unlawful aid received earlier, by reason of the cumulative effect of the aid in question which might distort competition within the internal market to a considerable extent.[123] The ECJ clarified that this principle applies equally to (unlawful) individual aid and aid part of an aid scheme and that it may also extend to the undertaking controlling an aid beneficiary, where there

circumstances of each case, in particular the content of the measure in question, the nature of the reasons given and the interest which the addressees of the measure, or other parties to whom it is of direct and individual concern, may have in obtaining explanations' and that '*the statement of reasons meets the requirements of 296 TFEU of the Treaty must be assessed with regard not only to its wording but also to its context and to all the legal rules governing the matter in question*'. *See* in this regard also Case C-758/21 P, *Ryanair and Airport Marketing Services*, paras 95-97; After having recalled that State aid proceedings are commenced against Member States and the 'interested parties cannot themselves seek to engage in an adversarial debate with the Commission in the same way as is offered to that Member State the ECJ concluded that the General Court was fully entitled to hold that the decision at issue contained sufficient reasoning as regards the application of the limitation period laid down in Article 17(1) of Regulation 2015/1589. In particular, it was not necessary for the Commission, in order to fulfil its obligation to state reasons for the decision at issue in that regard, to address the appellants' arguments since, in accordance with the case-law and principles above the recipient of the aid cannot seek to engage in an adversarial debate with the Commission in the same way as is offered to the Member State concerned and since it was apparent, at least implicitly, from that decision that the Commission considered that the arguments advanced before it by the appellants could not be accepted'; *see also* Case T-333/21, *Ryanair DAC v. European Commission (Alitalia II; COVID-19)* 18.10.2023, ECLI:EU:T:2023:646, paras 162-164; Case T-225/21, *Ryanair DAC v. European Commission (Alitalia I; COVID-19)* 18.10.2023, ECLI:EU:T:2023:644, paras 139-141,; Case T-737/20, *Ryanair DAC v. European Commission (airBaltic; COVID-19)* 17.11.2023, ECLI:EU:T:2023:641, paras 284-286; Case T-718/20, *Wizz Air Hungary v. European Commission (TAROM; aide au sauvetage)*, 24.6.2022, ECLI:EU:T:2022:276, paras 118-120.

120. *See* Art. 31(2) of Council Regulation (EU) No. 1589/2015.
121. *Ibid.*, Art. 32(3).
122. *See* Decision 2006/743/EC, *AZ and AZ Vastgoed* (2006) OJ L 307/194.
123. *See* Case C-355/95 P, *Textilwerke Deggendorf GmbH (TWD) v. European Commission* 15.5.1997, ECLI:EU:C:1997:241, paras 25-27; Case T-527/13, *Italy v. Commission*, para. 61. On cumulation of aid from two Member States *see* Case *See* Case T-626/20, *Landwärme v. Commission*,.

are sufficient 'organic and functional links' between the companies part of the same economic entity.[124]

Any failure to comply with a conditional decision will make the aid unlawful or misused aid (depending on whether such failure is due to a fault of the Member State concerned or of the aid recipient, as the case may be). It follows that the aid cannot be released without a new Commission decision granting a formal derogation from the condition in question.[125] Accordingly, the Commission is obliged to re-open the formal investigation procedure, except in the event of relatively minor deviations from the initial condition, which leaves it with no doubt as to whether the aid at issue is still compatible with the internal market.

In any event, where the Member State to which a conditional decision is addressed does not fulfil the stated conditions, the Commission will be entitled to bring infringement proceedings directly before the Court pursuant to Article 108(2) TFEU and Article 28 of the Procedural Regulation. The same power of the Commission is provided for negative decisions, in particular in the event of non-compliance with the recovery obligation set out in Article 16 of the Council Regulation (EU) No. 1589/2015.

Pursuant to Article 11 of the Procedural Regulation, the Commission may, after having given the Member State concerned the opportunity to submit its comments, *revoke* a positive or conditional decision or a 'no aid' decision, where it was based on incorrect information provided during the procedure that was a determining factor for the decision. In this case, the Commission is under duty to re-open the formal investigation and give the Member State concerned the opportunity to submit its comments, in order to safeguard its rights of defence and to take a fresh decision

124. *See* in this regard Case C-480/09 P, *Acea Electrabel Produzione S.p.A. v. European Commission* 16.12.2010, ECLI:EU:C:2010:787, paras 46-63 and para. 96; Case T-146/22, *Ryanair DAC v. European Commission (KLM II; COVID-19)*, 15.3.2024, ECLI:EU:T:2024:68, paras 55 and 66-67, Case T-494/21, *Ryanair and Malta Air v. European Commission (Air France; COVID-19)* 20.12.2023, ECLI:EU:T:2023:831, paras 61 and 73-74; Case T-216/21 *Ryanair DAC and Malta Air v. Commission (Air France; COVID-19)* 20.12.2023, ECLI:EU:T:2023:822, paras 61 and 71-72; Case T-643/20, *Ryanair DAC v. European Commission (KLM; Covid-19)* 19.5.2021, ECLI:EU:T:2021:286, para. 47, in which the General Court summarized the factors taken into account by the case law in order to determine the presence or absence of an economic unit in the field of State aid, namely '*the undertaking concerned being part of a group of companies which is directly or indirectly controlled by one of those companies, the pursuit of identical or parallel economic activities, and the companies concerned having no economic autonomy (see, to that effect, judgment of 14 October 2004, Pollmeier Malchow v. Commission, T-137/02, EU:T:2004:304, paragraphs 68 to 70); the formation of a single group controlled by one entity, despite the constitution of new companies each having a separate legal personality (see, to that effect, judgment of 14 November 1984, Intermills v. Commission, 323/82, EU:C:1984:345, paragraph 11); the possibility, for an entity having a controlling shareholding in another company, to exercise functions relating to control, direction and financial support in relation to that company which go beyond the simple placing of capital by an investor, and the existence of organic, functional and economic links between that entity and that company (see, to that effect, judgments of 16 December 2010, AceaElectrabel Produzione v. Commission, C-480/09 P, EU:C:2010:787, paragraph 51, and of 19 May 2021, Ryanair v. Commission (KLM; Covid-19), T-643/20, EU:T:2021:286, paragraph 47); the existence of relevant contractual clauses (see, to that effect, judgment of 16 December 2010, AceaElectrabel Produzione v. Commission, C-480/09 P, EU:C:2010:787, paragraph 57)*'.

125. *See* Case T-140/95, *Ryanair Limited v. European Commission*, 15.9.1998, ECLI:EU:T:1998:201, paras 86-88.

formally revoking that decision. Article 11 does not deal with the revocation of a negative decision or of a decision to take no further action on a complaint regarding unlawful aid.[126] However, the EU Courts clarified that the possibility to revoke a decision is not restricted to the situations referred to in that provision. Rather, Article 11 is only a specific expression of the general principle of law according to which the retrospective withdrawal of an unlawful administrative act which has created subjective rights is permissible, provided that the institution takes into account the legitimate expectation of beneficiaries of the act who have been entitled to rely on its lawfulness.[127]

§3.07 UNLAWFUL AID

[A] Review of Complaints

Aid is unlawful where it is implemented without notification to and approval by the Commission under Article 108(3) TFEU.

The procedure for reviewing unlawful aid[128] is modelled on the procedure for notified aid. Therefore, in general, the rules described above also apply to unlawful aid. There are however some differences. The first obvious difference is that aid is investigated following a complaint or on the Commission's own initiative, and not notification from the Member State.

Article 12 of the Procedural Regulation provides that the Commission may, on its own initiative, examine information regarding alleged unlawful aid *from whatever source*. In practice, most such investigations will be triggered by a *complaint* from a competitor of the beneficiary of the aid. If a complaint is received, the Commission is under a duty to conduct a *diligent and impartial* examination of the matter, which may include considering issues not raised by the complainant.[129]

Regulation (EU) No. 734/2013 has significantly amended the procedure for the handling of complaints that was provided in Article 10 of the Council Regulation (EC) 659/1999 (now Article 12 of Council Regulation (EU) 1589/2015). The previous rules in this area gave rise to divergent views between the Commission and the EU Courts,

126. *See infra* §3.07[A].
127. *See* Case T-421/07 RENV, *Deutsche Post AG v. European Commission*, 18.9.2015, ECLI:EU:T:2015:654, para. 4; Case T-25/04, *Gonzáles y Díez SA v. European Commission*, 12.9.2007, ECLI:EU:T:2007:257, paras 94-97.
128. For a definition of unlawful aid *see supra* §3.03[A].
129. *See* Case T-95/96, *Gestevision Telecinco SA v. European Commission*, 15.9.1998, ECLI:EU:T:1998:206, paras 53 and 72; Case T-167/04, *Asklepios Kliniken GbmH v. European Commission* 11.7.2007, ECLI:EU:T:2007:21, para. 81; Case T-394/08, *Regione autonoma della Sardegna v. European Commission*, 14,10,2011, ECLI:EU:T:2011:493, para. 99. *See also* Case T-108/16, *Naviera Armas v. European Commission*, 15.3.2018, EU:T:2018:145, paras 101-102. *See also* in this regard, Case C-367/95 P, *European Commission v. Sytraval and Brink's France*, 2.4.1998, ECLI:EU:C:1998:154, para. 62; Case C-290/07 P, *European Commission v. Scott*, 2.9.2010, ECLI:EU:C:2010:480, para. 90; Case T-89/09, *Pollmeier Massivholz v. European Commission*, 17.3.2015, ECLI:EU:T:2015:153, (para. 106); Case T-626/20, *Landwärme v. Commission*, para. 80.

which resulted in a number of judgments concluding that the Commission did not handle complaints in compliance with the procedural rules on State aid.[130]

It is important therefore to take a step back and fully understand which provisions (before Council Regulation (EU) No. 734/2013 came into force) gave rise to these divergent approaches and how the Council, upon proposal of the Commission, attempted to resolve this *impasse* in the Procedural Regulation:

(1) Article 10(1) of Council Regulation (EC) No. 659/99 provided that the Commission was under obligation to examine ('*shall examine*') information regarding alleged unlawful aid received from whatever source *without delay*.
(2) Article 20(2) of Council Regulation (EC) No. 659/99 provided: 'Any interested party may inform the Commission of any alleged unlawful aid and any alleged misuse of aid. Where the Commission considers that on the basis of the information in its possession there are insufficient grounds for taking a view on the case, it shall inform the interested party thereof.'
(3) Article 13 of Council Regulation (EC) No. 659/99 provided that the examination of possible unlawful aid *shall result* in a decision pursuant to Article 4(2), (3) or (4) of the same Regulation and namely that (a) the measure does not constitute aid, or (b) the aid is compatible or (c) it is necessary to launch an 'in-depth' investigation according to Article 108(2) TFEU.[131]

The Court of Justice in *Athinaïki Techniki* stated that Article 10(1) and the first sentence of Article 20(2) of Regulation No. 659/99 grant a complainant the *right to set in motion the preliminary examination* stage provided for in Article 108(3) TFEU, by sending information regarding any allegedly unlawful aid to the Commission, which is then obliged to examine, without delay, the possible existence of aid and its compatibility with the internal market.[132]

Moreover, the Court held that, where the Commission informs the complainant, in accordance with Article 20(2) of the Council (EC) Regulation No. 659/99, that there are insufficient grounds for taking a view on the case, it is required to allow the complainant to submit *additional comments* within a reasonable period.[133] Furthermore, the ECJ made it clear that once those comments had been lodged, or a

130. *See* in this regard Grespan, *EU Competition Law*, in Tosato Bellodi, *Procedure Antitrust – Merger – State Aid*, Volume 1, Deventer- Leuven, 2014, pp. 463 et seq.
131. *See supra* §3.05[B].
132. *See* Case C-521/06 P, *Athinaïki Techniki AE v. European Commission* 17.7.2009, ECLI: EU:C:2008:422 para. 38. *See also* Case C-322/09 P, *NDSHT Nya Destination Stockholm Hotell & Teaterpaket AB v. European Commission*, 18.11.2010, ECLI:EU:C:2010:701, para. 49; Case C-615/11 P, *European Commission v. Ryanair Ltd*, 16.5.2013, ECLI:EU:C:2013:310, para. 28; Case T-626/20, *Landwärme v. Commission*, para. 79.
133. *Ibid.*, paras 38-39. Interestingly, the Court based this conclusion on the fact that complainants in the preliminary examination *have the right to be associated with the procedure in an adequate manner*, taking into account the circumstances of the case. In the previous case law, the need to associate private parties to the procedure were stated by the Court of Justice where dealing

'reasonable period' has expired, Article 13(1) of Council Regulation (EC) No. 659/99 *obliges* the Commission *to close the preliminary examination stage by adopting a decision* pursuant to Article 4(2), (3) or (4).[134] This jurisprudence had a significant impact on the Commission's procedure for handling complaints. First, by recognizing the complainant's right 'to set in motion' the procedure, the Court seemed to rule out the existence of a margin of discretion for the Commission to decide whether or not to launch the preliminary investigation following a complaint, which seems to imply that the Commission may not legitimately decline to pursue a complaint on the basis of 'lack of EU interest' as is the case for antitrust investigations.[135]

Second, this case law suggests that when dealing with a complaint the only option available to the Commission is to conclude its assessment by a decision '*on the merit of the aid*' pursuant to Article 4(2), (3) or (4) of the Council Regulation (EC) No. 659/1999.

The unconditional nature of the abovementioned provisions, as interpreted by the Court of Justice, caused many practical difficulties for the Commission, which receives hundreds of complaints each year and has a limited administrative capacity. Furthermore, until 2013, no formal or substantive requirements were imposed in connection with complaints and, therefore, the Commission's task of conducting a

with the involvement of interested parties (namely, the beneficiary) during the *formal procedure* – please refer to §3.06[B]. *supra* and to Case C-49/05 P, *Ferriere Nord v. Commission*, para. 69. *See also* in this regard Case T-702/21, *Ekobulkos v. European Commission*, 21.12.2022, ECLI:EU:T:2022:842, para. 29.

134. *See* Case C-521/06, *Athinaïki Techniki*, para. 40. The ECJ added that the Commission can take one of the aforementioned decisions provided for in Art. 4, without, however, describing it as a decision pursuant to Art. 4. *Ibid.*, para. 41. From the *substance* of the letter sent to the complainant by the Commission and from the *intention* of the latter, the Court stated that the latter decided to bring to an end the preliminary examination procedure and 'classified' its letter as a decision within the meaning of Art. 4(2) of Council Regulation (EC) No. 659/99. And such a decision, according to the ECJ, *constituted a challengeable act*. To this aim, the fact that (i) the Commission did not describe its position as a decision pursuant to Art. 4, (ii) the interested party could still have provided the Commission with additional information which might have led the Commission to review its position on the measure at issue, (iii) the act was not notified to the Member State concerned by the Commission, in violation of Art. 25 of Regulation No. 659/99, (iv) the act in question did not satisfy certain formal requirements, was deemed to be *irrelevant*. For a throughout comment on this judgment *see* Gambaro, Mazzocchi, Cases C-521/06 P, *Athinaiki Techniki v. Commission, Judgment of the Court of Justice (Fourth Chamber) of 17 July 2008*, ECR I-5829; Case C-322/09 P, *NDSHT v. Commission;* Case C-362/09 P, *Athinaiki Techniki v. Commission, Judgment of the Court of Justice (Third Chamber) of 18 December 2010*, in 48 *Common Market Law Review*, 2011, 2083-2106. *See also* Nehl, *Judicial Protection of Complainants in EC State Aid Law: A Silent Revolution?*, in *European State Aid Law Quarterly*, 2009, 401.

135. Case T-24/90, *Automec S.r.l. v. European Commission*, 18.9.1992, ECLI:EU:T:1992:97. In such a decision, dealing with complainant's rights in the context of antitrust proceedings, the ECJ observed that the task entrusted to the Commission by the Treaty in the field of competition law does *not* mean that the Commission is *bound to commence proceedings* seeking to establish the existence of any infringement of Community law and added that the relevant regulations *do not include a right to obtain a decision* as regards the existence or otherwise of the alleged infringement.

diligent and impartial examination of the case was made even more difficult by the presence of submission lacking essential information or being overly concise.[136]

Against this background, Council Regulation (EU) No. 734/2013 essentially introduced a 'filter system' prescribing certain *subjective* and *objective* conditions that must be fulfilled in order for the Commission to be in full possession of information regarding alleged unlawful aid and set in motion the preliminary examination.[137]

First, the complaint must demonstrate its status as an 'interested party' as intended by Article 108(2) of the TFEU and Article 1(h) of the Procedural Regulation. Second, the complaint must provide some obligatory information and meet certain formal requirements: submissions not meeting those conditions will be treated as general market information.

Accordingly, Article 24(2) of the Procedural Regulation, sets out that:

> Any interested party may submit a complaint to inform the Commission of any alleged unlawful aid or any alleged misuse of aid. To that effect, the interested party shall duly complete a form that has been defined in an implementing provision referred to in Article 33 and shall provide the mandatory information requested therein.

This provision complements Article 12(1) of the Procedural Regulation which states that the Commission is *only* obliged to examine – without *undue* delay – complaints submitted by an *interested party in due form*.

The procedure for dismissing complaints, introduced for the first time by the Council Regulation (EU) No. 734/2013, is provided for by Article 24(2) second paragraph of the Procedural Regulation, reading as follows:

---

136. In Case T-442/07, *Ryanair Ltd v. Commission*, 29.9.2011, ECLI:EU:T:2011:547 (summary publication), the General Court underlined that, unlike the clear rules for lodging a complaint under Arts 101 and 102 TFEU, there are no formal requirements to be satisfied in order to file a State aid complaint before the Commission. *See also* appeal Case C-615/11 P, *Commission v. Ryanair*, *supra*, in which the Court, with regard to a letter sent by a complainant argued: '*Notwithstanding its brevity, such a letter, by the nature and the wording of the information transmitted, must be regarded as enabling the Commission to identify, with sufficient precision, inter alia, the presumed beneficiary of the alleged unlawful aid, the nature of the advantage at issue and the mechanism by means of which that advantage has been granted. That being the case, such a letter cannot be regarded as failing to satisfy the requirements laid down in Art. 10(1) and 20(2) of Council Regulation (EC) No. 659/1999, given that those provisions cannot be construed as making the Commission's duty to act conditional on the inclusion of a greater level of detail in the complaint or information sent to the Commission*' (paras 36 and 37). *See also* Case T-182/10 *Associazione Italiana delle Società Concessionarie per la costruzione e l'esercizio di Autostrade e trafori stradali (Aiscat) v. Commission*, 15.1.2013, ECLI:EU:T:2013:9, in which the General Court stated that 'the poor quality of information submitted in support of a complaint [...] cannot relieve the obligation to open the preliminary examination stage or to close that examination by a way of decision under Article 4 of Regulation 659/1999'. *See*, conversely, Case T-245/17 *ViaSat, Inc. v. European Commission*, 10.3.2021, ECLI: EU:T:2021:128, para. 38, in which the General Court stated that 'Whilst there is no particular requirement as to form, the notice must be sufficiently clear and precise to enable the Commission to ascertain in specific terms the nature of the decision which it is being asked to adopt and must make clear that its purpose is to compel the Commission to state its position.'
137. *See* Recital 14 of Council Regulation (EU) No. 734/2013.

> Where the Commission considers that the interested party does not comply with the compulsory complaint form, or that the facts and points of law put forward by the interested party do not provide sufficient grounds to show, on the basis of a prima facie examination, the existence of unlawful aid or misuse of aid, it shall inform the interested party thereof and call upon it to submit comments within a prescribed period which shall not normally exceed one month. If the interested party fails to make known its views within the prescribed period, the complaint shall be deemed to have been withdrawn. The Commission shall inform the Member State concerned when a complaint has been deemed to have been withdrawn.

The discipline for handling complaints still raises a not insignificant number of interpretative doubts. In particular, the procedure put forward in Article 24 second paragraph provides a form of 'automatic withdrawal' in case the complainant fails to submit their comments within the prescribed period fixed by the Commission which is hardly reconcilable with Article 15(1) of the Procedural Regulation, which has not been modified by the Council Regulation (EU) No. 734/2013 ('*the examination of possible unlawful aid shall result in a decision[...]*') which has not been modified by the Council Regulation (EU) No. 734/2013.[138] It has already been stated that, according to the Court of Justice, Article 15(1) obliges the Commission to *close* the preliminary examination stage by *adopting a decision* pursuant to Article 4(2), (3) or (4) (i.e., to say a decision of 'no aid' raising no objections or initiating the formal investigation procedure).

Moreover, Article 24(2) of the Procedural Regulation does not mention what happens if the complainant *does* submit comments within the prescribed period given by the Commission. At least in this case, it would seem that the principle established in *Athinaiki Techiniki* remains valid: once those comments have been lodged, Article 13(1) still obliges the Commission to close the preliminary examination by adopting a decision pursuant to Article 4.[139] This has been expressly confirmed by the EU Courts, which defined this obligation as '*the corollary of recognition of the right enjoyed by a complainant in a State aid matter to set in motion, by submitting a complaint or information regarding any allegedly unlawful aid, the preliminary examination stage, which the Commission is obliged to close by means of a decision pursuant to Article 4 of Regulation 2015/1589*'.[140] The EU Courts clarified that the obligation to adopt a decision applies *mutatis mutandis* to a complaint introduced by an interested party which alleges that the conditions of a block exemption regulation, such as Regulation No 651/2014, providing a basis on which to consider that an aid measure is exempted

138. For a critical analysis of the new provisions *see* Nehl, *2013 Reform of EU State Aid Procedures: How to Exacerbate the Imbalance Between Efficiency and Individual Protection*, in *European State Aid Quarterly* February 2014, pp. 235 et seq.; Jaeger, *The Inquisition Retakes Brussels (Via the New Procedural Regulation)*,in *EStAL* Mar. 2013, p. 441; Dilkova, *The New Procedural Regulation in State Aid: Whether 'Modernisation' Is in the Right Direction?*, in *European Competition Law Review*, February 2014, p. 88.
139. And this decision should, in principle, be open to challenge by the private party. *See* Case C-521/06 P, *Athinaiki Techiniki*, para. 40.
140. *See* Case T-745/17, *Kerkosand spol. S r.o. v. Commission* 9.9.2020, ECLI:EU:T:2020:400 (paras 35-37), not appealed before the ECJ. *See also* in this regard Case C-228/16 P, *Dimosia Epicheirisi Ilektrismou AE DEI v. European Commission* 31.5.2017, ECLI:EU:C:2017:409, para. 29.

from the notification obligation under Article 108(3) TFEU, are inapplicable or have been incorrectly applied.[141]

[B] Further Peculiar Features of the Review of Unlawful Aid

As for the notified aid procedure, the investigation of unlawful aid may entail two successive phases. However, when investigating unlawful (or misused) aid the Commission is not bound by the timetables provided for the preliminary and formal examination of notified aid (respectively, two and eighteen months).[142]

However, should the Commission fail to adopt a decision within a *reasonable period*, a declaration for failure to act pursuant to Article 265 TFEU may be sought by the complainant before the EU courts.[143] However, the EU Courts stressed that the mere adoption of a decision after the expiry of a reasonable period is not per se sufficient to render unlawful that decision at the conclusion of an initial examination conducted under Article 108(3) TFEU.[144]

If the examination of unlawful aid leads to the adoption of a *negative* decision, the Commission must decide that the Member State must take all necessary measures to *recover* the aid from the beneficiary, unless recovery would be contrary to a general principle of EU law or the limitation period of ten years provided for by Article 17 of the Procedural Regulation has lapsed without the Commission taking any action vis-à-vis

141. *See* Case T-745/17, *Kerkosand v. Commission, supra* (para. 38): According to the General Court by adopting such block exemption regulations, the Commission does not delegate to the national authorities its supervisory and decision-making powers concerning State aid, including in relation to the handling of complaints, but fully retains its power of oversight under Art. 108 TFEU and Art. 12(1) of Regulation 2015/1589, as regards, *inter alia*, those authorities' observance of the fundamental obligation to notify aid measures and of the prohibition on their implementation under Art. 108(3) TFEU. *See also* in this regard the Court of Justice, judgment of 29 Jul. 2019, *Bayerische Motoren Werke and Freistaat Sachsen v. Commission*, C-654/17 P, EU:C:2019:634, paras 132 to 135 and 140 to 144.
142. There is one exception to this rule: Art. 13(2), second paragraph of the Procedural Regulation provides that after the aid has been effectively recovered following a recovery injunction (*see infra* in this section), the Commission shall take a decision within the time limit applicable to notified aid.
143. As mentioned *supra*, whether a certain period for the examination of the measure must be considered unreasonable chiefly depends on the circumstances of the cases. Time periods exceeding, respectively, thirty-three, thirty-one or twenty-six months have been held by the General Court to be too long for preliminary investigation. *See* Case T-46/97, *SIC – Sociedade Independente de Comunicação SA v. European Commission* 10.5.2000, ECLI:EU:T:2000:123, para. 106; Case T-17/96, *Télévision française 1 SATF1 v. European Commission*, 3.6.1999, ECLI:EU:T:1999:119, paras 76 et seq.; Case T-95/96, *Gestevisión Telecinco v. Commission*, paras 80 et seq. However, in Case T-303/10, *Wam Industriale v. Commission, supra* (para. 196), the General Court found not excessive a forty-two month period for the conclusion of the preliminary investigation, since the delay was deemed to be imputable to the inaction of the Member State concerned in providing the required information.
144. *See* Case T-378/02 R, *Technishe Glaswerke Ilmenau* GbmH *v. European Commission*, 1.8.2003, ECLI:EU:T:2003:216, para. 65. In Case T-579/08, *Eridania Sadam S.p.A. v. European Commission*, 20.10.2011, ECLI:EU:2011:332, para. 80, the General Court stressed that the excessive length of the procedure could be grounds for annulment only if it caused a violation of rights of defence; *see also*, Case T-668/21, *Sicilia Regionale Marittima S.p.A – Siremar v. Commission*, 9.12.2022. ECLI:EU:T:2022:677, para. 109.

the aid in question. Recovery is a distinctive feature of unlawful aid and will be examined in Chapter 4.

Finally, it must be observed that, in the matter of unlawful aid, the Procedural Regulation has expressly vested the Commission with the power to issue injunctions. Specifically, three types of injunction have been provided for, as follows: (i) information injunctions; (ii) suspension injunctions; and (iii) recovery injunctions.

Information injunctions are interlocutory decisions, as they are intended to obtain more information where the Member State concerned has failed, despite a reminder, to respond to the Commission's request for complete information.[145] By such a decision, the Commission must specify what information is required and prescribe an appropriate period within which it is to be supplied.[146]

It should be noted that the adoption of an information injunction is a necessary step the Commission is required to take before adopting a decision merely on the basis of the information available. Should the Commission fail to comply, it cannot rely, in justification of its decision, on the fragmentary nature of the information sent to it by the Member State concerned.[147]

The purpose of *suspension injunctions* is to require the Member State to suspend any unlawful aid until the Commission has taken a decision on the compatibility of the aid with the internal market. The Commission may adopt it only after giving the Member State concerned the opportunity to submit its comments.[148] This type of injunction proves quite effective where an aid has not yet been completely paid or the relevant State measure provides for aid to be paid in instalments on a regular basis. In fact, if the aid has already been paid, such injunctions are fruitless. The Commission has rarely made use of this power.[149]

Lastly, in the case of a *recovery injunction*, the Commission may, after giving the Member State concerned the opportunity to submit its comments, require that the State provisionally recover any unlawful aid until the Commission has taken a decision on the compatibility of the aid with the common market.[150] Such power of injunction may only be exercised if the following criteria are fulfilled:

145. *See* Art. 12(3) of Procedural Regulation.
146. *Ibid.*, Art. 13(1) of Procedural Regulation. Pursuant to Art. 24(3) of the Procedural Regulation, any interested party may obtain a copy of such decision on request. If a Member State fails to comply with an information injunction, that decision will be taken on the basis of the information available.
147. *See* Case C-342/90, *Germany and Pleuger Worthington GmbH v. European Commission*, 13.4.1994, ECLI:EU:C:1994:129, para. 29 and Case T-323/99, *Industrie Navali Meccaniche Affini SpA (INMA) and Italia Investimenti SpA (Itainvest) v. European Commission*, 26.2.2002, ECLI:EU:C:2001:280, para. 91. *See also* Case GmbH, *Commission of the European Communities v. MTU Friedrichshafen*, 17.9.2009, ECLI:EU:C:2009:557, para. 41.
148. *See* Art. 13(1) of Procedural Regulation.
149. For cases of suspension injunction simultaneously issued with the decision to open the formal investigation. *See* Commission Decision in Case 41/07, *A tax exempt reserve fund to certain companies in Greece* OJ 2006 C20/16 and in Case C41/2007, *Privatisation of Tracturol – Romania* OJ 2007 C249/21.
150. *See* Art. 13(2) of Procedural Regulation.

(1) according to an established practice, there are no doubts about the aid character of the measure concerned;
(2) there is an urgency to act; and
(3) there is a serious risk of substantial and irreparable damage to a competitor.

The recovery injunction almost invariably specifies the amount to be recovered, unless it cannot be accurately determined, in which case the amount will be specified by the Member State concerned at a later time, in accordance with the national recovery procedure. The aid to be so recovered will include interest at an appropriate rate fixed according to Regulation No. 794/2004, payable from the date on which the unlawful aid was at the disposal of the beneficiary until the date of its recovery.[151]

If the Member State fails to comply with a suspension injunction or a recovery injunction, the Commission will be entitled, while carrying out an examination into the matter on the basis of the information available, to refer the matter to the Court of Justice directly and apply for a declaration that the failure to comply constitutes an infringement of the Treaty.[152]

§3.08 MISUSED AID

The procedure for controlling misused aid is modelled on the procedure applicable to unlawful aid. Aid is misused when it is used by the beneficiary in contravention of the decision authorizing the aid. Article 20 of the Procedural Regulation[153] deals with misused aid and provides that the Commission may open the formal procedure pursuant to Article 108(2) TFEU. However, the Commission may not adopt a recovery injunction but can only order the recovery of the misused aid at the end of the formal investigation. When the Member State concerned does not reply to the information injunction issued by the Commission requiring it to provide information as to the actual use of to which the aid has been put, the Commission can conclude on the basis of the available information that the aid has been misused.

The procedure concerning misused aid is not subject to the time limits applicable to lawful aid.[154]

151. Article 16(2) of Procedural Regulation. For further reference *see* Ch. 4 on recovery of State aid.
152. *Ibid.*, Art. 14. *See also* Case C-301/87, *France v. Commission*, para. 23, where the Court affirmed that this means is 'a variant of the action for a declaration of failure to fulfil Treaty obligations, specifically adapted to the special problems which State aid poses for competition within the common market'. In this sense, *see also* Opinion of Advocate General, Case C-456/18 P, *Hungary v. European Commission*, 16.1.2020, ECLI:EU:C:2020:8, para. 56.
153. Article 20 of Procedural Regulation provides that 'Without prejudice to Article 28, the Commission may, in cases of misuse of aid, initiate the formal investigation procedure pursuant to Article 4(4). Articles 6 to 9, 11 and 12, Article 13(1) and Articles 14 to 17 shall apply mutatis mutandis.'
154. *See* Joined Cases T-394/08, T-408/08, T-453/08 and T-454/08, *Regione autonoma Sardegna and Others v. Commission*, para. 101.

§3.09 REVIEW OF EXISTING AID

Chapter VI of the Council Regulation (EU) No. 1589/2015 lays down the procedural rules for reviewing existing aid schemes.

Before examining the procedure regarding existing aid, a few considerations on the different categories of existing aid provided for Article 1(b) of Procedural Regulation will be provided.[155]

The first category of existing aid is aid which existed prior to the entry into force of the Treaty in the respective Member States and is *still applicable* after the entry into force of the Treaty.[156] In *AEM*, the applicant, relying on the ECJ judgment *Namur-Les Assurances*, argued that certain tax exemptions introduced by Italy in favour of municipal undertakings should qualify as existing measures under this provision. The General Court, however, stated that such measures were *substantially different* from those existing prior to the entry into force of the Treaty of Rome and dismissed the argument relying on Article 1(c) of the Procedural Regulation, pursuant to which any existing aid that is *altered* is to be regarded as new aid.[157] In particular, where the alteration affects the *actual substance* of the original scheme, the latter is transformed into a new aid scheme; and there can be no question of such a substantive alteration where the new element is *clearly severable* from the original scheme.[158]

The second category of aid is *authorized aid*, that is to say, aid schemes and individual aid that have been authorized by the Commission following the preliminary or the formal investigation or by the Council under the rather unusual procedure of Article 108(2) TFEU, third paragraph.[159] According to the Court's case law prolonging the period for application of a previously authorized aid scheme, whether or not combined with an increase in the budget allocated to that scheme, gives rise to new aid,

155. *See supra* §3.03[A].
156. In particular, Art. 1(b)(i) provides that 'without prejudice to Articles 144 and 172 of the Act of Accession of Austria, Finland and Sweden, to point 3 and the Appendix of Annex IV to the Act of Accession of the Czech Republic, Estonia, Cyprus, Latvia, Lithuania, Hungary, Malta, Poland, Slovenia and Slovakia, to points 2 and 3(b) and the Appendix of Annex V to the Act of Accession of Bulgaria and Romania, and to points 2 and 3(b) and the Appendix of Annex IV to the Act of Accession of Croatia, all aid which existed prior to the entry into force of the TFEU in the respective Member States, that is to say, aid schemes and individual aid which were put into effect before, and are still applicable after, the entry into force of the TFEU in the respective Member States'.
157. *See* Case T- 301/02, *AEM S.p.A. v. European Commission*, 11.6.2009, ECLI:EU:T:2009:191, paras 117 et seq., confirmed in appeal Case C-320/09 P, *A2A S.p.A. (formerly AEM S.p.A.) v. European Commission*, 21.12.2011, ECLI:EU:C:2011:858. *See also* Case T-189/03, *ASM Brescia S.p.A. v. European Commission*, 11.6.2009, ECLI:EU:T:2009:193, paras 99 et seq., confirmed in appeal Case C-318/09 P, *A2A S.p.A. (formerly ASM Brescia S.p.A.) v. European Commission*, 21.12.2011, ECLI:EU:C:2011:856.
158. *See* Joined Cases T-195/01 and T-207/01, *Government of Gibraltar v. European Commission*, 30.4.2002, ECLI:EU:T:2002:111, paras 109-111; *ex multis, Case C-510/16,* Opinion of Advocate General of 30 Nov. 2017, *Carrefour Hypermarchés SAS, Fnac Paris, Fnac Direct, Relais Fnac, Codirep, Fnac Périphérie v. Ministre des finances et des comptes publics*, 20.9.2018, ECLI: EU:C:2018:751, paras 51-56.
159. *See supra* §3.02.

distinct from the authorized aid scheme, which, in principle, shall be notified (*see* below).[160]

The third category of existing aid provided for by Article 1(b) of Procedural Regulation is aid that is *deemed to have been authorized*, in accordance with the procedure set out in Article 4(6) of the Council Regulation (EU) No. 1589/2015.[161]

The fourth category is aid for which the *ten-year limitation period* has expired. This provision is the only one exception to the rule that unlawful aid may not be considered to be existing aid. For Article 1(1)(b)(iv) permits such aid to be classified as existing aid in case the ten-year limitation period from the day on which the unlawful aid was awarded has expired. The date of expiry of such period is the latest day on or prior to which the Commission is allowed to order the recovery of the aid, pursuant to Article 17 of Regulation No. 659/1999. According to Article 17, after an (uninterrupted) period of ten years has elapsed without the Commission having ordered the recovery of an aid put into effect without prior notification, such aid must be deemed to be existing aid – with the added consequence that the Commission will be barred from ordering the recovery of the amount paid by the Member State concerned.

The fifth category is aid that is deemed to be an existing aid because it can be established that at the time it was put into effect, it did not constitute an aid, and subsequently *became an aid* due to the *evolution of the common market* and without having been altered by the Member State. This category reflects the view of State aid policy as a *dynamic process*, strictly linked to the evolution of the internal market. The underlying idea is that a State measure, which at the time that it was enacted did not have an anti-competitive effect because the relevant market was not liberalized or only partially opened up to competition may subsequently take on the character of State aid. In that case, such a measure is deemed to be *existing aid*. However, the second sentence of Article 1(1)(b)(v) restricts the scope of application of this principle, specifying that if the evolution of the market is due to EU law or following the *liberalization* of an activity *by EU law*, the measure is considered to be new aid after the date fixed for the liberalization of the market.

In the *Alzetta* case, the General Court made a distinction between the two relevant markets affected by the State measure at stake. In the market of international road haulage, operators from other Member States could already compete with Italian transporters where the aid scheme in question was established; conversely, the market for cabotage (national good transport) was reserved for Italian operators. In that situation, the General Court concluded that the aid scheme had to be classified as new for undertakings operating in the international road haulage sector and as existing aid, from the date of the opening of the cabotage market to international competition, for undertakings which exclusively carried out this type of service. This approach, if

160. *See* to that effect, Case C-128/19, *Azienda Provinciale di Catania*, 20.5.2021, ECLI: EU:C:2021:401, para. 37. *See also* C-138/09, *Todaro Nunziatina & C.*,20.5.2010, EU:C:2010:291, paras 46 and 47; C-111/10; *Commission v. Council*, 4.12.2013, EU:C:2013:785, paras 58; C-121/10, *Commission v. Council*, 4.12.2013, EU:C:2013:784, paras 59; and C-590/14 P, *DEI and Commission v. Alouminion tis Ellados*, 26.12.2016, EU:C:2016:797, paras 50, 58 and 59.

161. *See supra* §3.05[A].

applied rigorously, requires an assessment of the situation of each undertaking (and each relevant market) to which the measure is applied. In other cases, however, the EU Courts adopted a rather 'cursory' approach on the matter and held that certain measures could not be regarded as existing aid since at the time they were introduced, 'there was a degree of competition' in the sector involved and the markets were open to competition 'albeit almost certainly to differing degrees'.[162]

As per the relevant procedure, unlike new aid, existing aid does *not* have to be *notified*, but is subject to constant review by the Commission.

In particular, pursuant to Article 21 of Procedural Regulation, the Commission shall obtain from the Member State concerned all necessary information for the review, in cooperation with the Member State, of existing aid schemes pursuant to Article 108(1) TFEU.

Where the Commission considers that an existing aid scheme is not, or is no longer, compatible with the internal market, it shall inform the Member State concerned of its preliminary view and give the Member State concerned the opportunity to submit its comments within a period of one month. In duly justified cases, the Commission may extend this period.

Article 22 provides that where the Commission, in the light of the information submitted by the Member State pursuant to Article 21, concludes that the existing aid scheme is not, or is no longer, compatible with the internal market, it shall issue a recommendation. The recommendation may propose a substantive amendment to the aid scheme or the introduction of procedural requirements or the abolition of the aid scheme.

If, according to Article 23(1) of Council Regulation (EU) No. 1589/2015, the Member State accepts the proposal, it shall inform the Commission. The latter shall confirm such acceptance whereupon the Member State concerned shall be bound by its acceptance to implement the appropriate measure. The terms of the recommendation and the fact of its acceptance by the Member State must then be published in the Official Journal.[163] Where the Member State does not accept the proposal and the Commission still considers that those measures are necessary, it is required to initiate the formal investigation procedure. The procedure then follows the same course as with the formal investigation of newly notified aid and all the relevant procedural rules apply (except for the standstill clause). It follows that, as with notified aid, the Commission may *not* order *recovery* or *suspension* of the aid.

The Court of Justice clarified that when the Commission deals with a specific grant of aid alleged to have been made in pursuance of a previously authorized scheme, it cannot at the outset examine it directly in relation to the Treaty. Prior to the initiation of any procedure, it must first examine whether the aid is covered by the general scheme and satisfies the conditions laid down in the decision approving it. If it did not do so, the Commission could, whenever it examined an individual aid measure, go back on its decision to approve the aid scheme, which had already involved an

162. *See* Case T-301/02, *AEM v. Commission*, paras 129-130.
163. *See* Case T-354/05, *Télévision française 1 SA – TF1 v. European Commission*, 11.3.2009, ECLI:EU:T:2009:66, para. 46.

examination in the light of Article 107 TFEU. This would jeopardize the principles of the protection of legitimate expectations and legal certainty.[164]

§3.10 ANNUAL REPORTS AND ON-SITE MONITORING

Article 26 of the Procedural Regulation obliges the Member State to submit annual reports on all existing aid schemes. According to Article 26(2), the Commission may commence the procedure for existing aid if the Member States fail, despite a reminder, to submit the report. The annual report must be submitted to the Commission in compliance with a standard form not later than 30 June of the year following the year to which the report relates. The Commission is required to publish a summary of the information transmitted by the Member States.

Article 27 of the Procedural Regulation provides that the Commission may, after giving the Member State concerned the opportunity to submit its comments, undertake on-site monitoring visits where it has serious doubts as to whether any of its decisions in the field of State aid is being complied with by that Member State.

In order to verify actual compliance with any such decision, the officials authorized by the Commission[165] are empowered:

(1) to enter any premises and land of the undertaking concerned;
(2) to ask for oral explanations on the spot; and
(3) to examine books and other business records and take, or demand, copies.

The Commission shall inform the Member State concerned, in good time and in writing, of the on-site monitoring visit and of the identities of the authorized officials and experts. If the Member State has duly justified objections to the Commission's choice of experts, the experts must be appointed in common agreement with the Member State. Where an undertaking opposes a monitoring visit ordered by a Commission decision, Article 27(6) requires the Member State concerned to afford the necessary assistance to the officials and experts authorized by the Commission to enable them to carry out the monitoring visit.

Before starting the visit, the officials of the Commission and the experts authorized to carry out the on-site monitoring shall produce authorization in writing specifying the subject matter and purpose of the visit. Following the visit, the Commission shall provide the Member State with a copy of any report produced as a result of monitoring activities.

---

164. *See* Case C-321/99 P, *Associação dos Refinadores de Açúcar Portugueses (ARAP) and Others v. Commission*, 16.5.2002, ECLI:EU:C:2002:292, para. 83.
165. The Commission may be assisted, if necessary, by independent experts.

CHAPTER 4

Recovery of Unlawful and Incompatible Aid

Antonio Papi Rossi & Pietro Missanelli

§4.01 THE RECOVERY DECISION

[A] The Rationale Behind Recovery Decisions

As indicated above, Article 108(3) TFEU requires that the Commission must be notified, in sufficient time to enable it to provide its comments, of any plans to grant or alter aid. Pursuant to Article 108(2) TFEU, if the Commission finds that an aid is not compatible with the common market, then the Member State concerned is required not to implement the national legal provisions instituting aid.

A distinction must be made though. When the Community Commission has to assess the impact on the common market of an aid *not yet granted*, the declaration whereby the aid measure in question is found incompatible blocks at the very onset any effect that measure might have. The problem arises, however, when the Commission considers an aid to be incompatible though it was put into effect before or irrespective of any Community authorization. If this is the case, then the aid incompatibility declaration may only prevent additional advantages from being further awarded (however they materialize) but is hardly apt to affect those already awarded. Hence, the need to order *recovery*.

The European Court of Justice (ECJ) first stated this principle in 1973, but it only did so in terms of an 'option' to issue a recovery order and by relating it to the 'practical effect' principle.[1] Point 13 of the relevant judgment reads: 'to be of practical effect, this abolition or modification [of the aid found incompatible, Ed.] may include an obligation to require repayment of aid granted in breach of the Treaty'.

1. Case C-70/72, *Commission v. Germany*, 12.7.1973, ECLI:EU:C:1973:87.

Yet, the Commission failed to use this option at that early stage, but it waited for years before issuing systematic orders for the recovery of aid declared incompatible. The reversal of the trend was announced in a letter dated 13 July 1980 to the Member States,[2] whereby the Commission responded to the increase in unlawful aid cases by warning that it was going to use 'all measures at its disposal to ensure that Member States' obligations under Article 93(3) (now 108(3) TFEU) are respected'. Subsequently, the Commission sent its Communication dated 24 November 1983 to the Member States,[3] whereby it expressly laid down the principle that a State that had granted an aid later found to be incompatible with the common market was under an obligation to ask for refund thereof.

Recovery is then the logical consequence of the declaration of incompatibility of an aid already awarded, which implies also that the Commission is not obliged to state reasons for it in its decisions.[4] The rationale behind the requirement to refund is to restore the *status quo ante*, thus to endeavour to remedy the competition-distorting effect of granting an unlawful aid.[5]

Obviously, an aid is by no means refunded spontaneously. The ECJ has recognized the Commission's power to order a Member State to recover an aid unlawfully granted and declared incompatible. This power is of case law origin, and it has been firmly established by the ECJ in two separate judgments in early 1990.

By the first of such judgments,[6] the Court of Justice determined that, if the planned contribution has been granted in contravention to the provisions of Article 108(3) of the TFEU, the Commission's decision may be taken in the form of an order for the national authorities to order repayment. In the second judgment,[7] the ECJ stated that the abolition of an unlawful aid by *recovery* is a natural consequence of determining that the aid is unlawful.

The ECJ's case law has become firmly established along these lines, by consistently holding that the duty to recover is the necessary consequence of the practical effect of the EU rules prohibiting unlawful State aid awards.[8] In the presence of unlawful aid, the rule is, therefore, that the Member State concerned must claim repayment from the recipient undertakings for the purpose of re-establishing the

2. OJ 1980 C252.
3. OJ 1983 C318/3.
4. Merola, M. *Rimedi per violazione delle norme sugli aiuti di Stato: misure repressive o di ripristino* 31 (Giappichelli 2018); Case C-148/04, *Unicredito Italiano*, 15.12.2005, ECLI:EU:C:2005:774.
5. At the same time, the situation of the aid recipient cannot be made worse following the recovery order than it was before the aid was granted. The argument has sometimes been used by the parties in court. Joined Cases C-91/17 P and C-92/17 P, *Cellnex Telecom SA and Telecom Castilla-La Mancha, SA v. European Commission*, 26.4.2018, ECLI:EU:C:2018:284; Case T-850/19, *Greece v. Commission*, 19.10.2022, ECLI:EU:T:2022:638 (paras 159-161).
6. Case C-301/87, *France v. Commission ('Boussac')*, 14.2.1990, ECLI:EU:C:1990:67.
7. Case C-142/87, *Belgium v. Commission ('Tubemeuse')*, 21.3.1990, ECLI:EU:C:1990:125 (para. 66).
8. Joined Cases C-278/92, C-279/92 and C-280/92, *Spain v. Commission*, 14.9.1994, ECLI:EU:C:1994:325.

situation existing before the grant of such aid distorted competition or affected intra-Community trade.[9]

The 'restoring' character of an order to recover aid affects both the Member State concerned – to which recovery has been ordered – and the recipient undertakings, which had already attracted the Commission's special attention in the 1983 Communication referred to above. The Commission had, in that document, clearly warned the potential recipients of State aid against the insecure status of any aid unlawfully granted to them, specifying that:

> any recipient of an aid granted unlawfully, i.e., without the Commission having reached a final decision, may be required to repay the aid. Whenever the Commission learns that a Member State has implemented aid measures without fulfilling it the requirements under Article 93(3) (now Article 108(3) TFEU) it will issue a specific notice in the Official Journal warning potential aid recipients of the risk involved.

Following that Communication, the Commission began to supplement each notice initiating the procedure pursuant to Article 108(2) TFEU with a specific warning addressed to the relevant beneficiary.

In particular, in the second half of the 1980s and in the 1990s, the Commission repeatedly ordered the recovery of incompatible aid. In 1999, Council Regulation (EC) No. 659/1999 (which has then been replaced by Council Regulation (EU) 2015/1589, hereinafter also the 'Procedural Regulation'),[10] introduced specific rules on recovery while more detailed provisions were laid down in the s.c. Implementing Regulation (Commission Regulation (EC) No. 794/2004).[11]

Article 13 of the Procedural Regulation now states that the Commission may, after allowing the Member State concerned to submit its comments, adopt a decision instructing the Member State to suspend any unlawful aid until the Commission has determined the aid's compatibility with the internal market (by mean of a 'suspension injunction'). After giving the Member State concerned the opportunity to submit its comments, the Commission may adopt a decision requiring the Member State to provisionally recover any unlawful aid until the Commission has made its determination on the compatibility of the aid with the internal market ('recovery injunction').

However, the Commission may do so only if all the following criteria are fulfilled:[12]

---

9. *See, ex multis,* Case C-350/93, *Commission v. Italy,* 4.4.1995, ECLI:EU:C:1995:96 (para. 21) and Case C-75/97, *Belgium v. Commission,* 17.6.1999, ECLI:EU:C:1999:311 (para. 64). More recently, *see* joined cases C-164/15 P and C-165/15 P, *Commission v. Aer Lingus,* 21.12.206. ECLI: EU:C:2016:990 (para. 89).
10. Council Regulation (EU) 2015/1589 of 13 Jul. 2015 laying down detailed rules for the application of Art. 108 of the Treaty on the Functioning of the European Union (codification), OJ L 248, 24.9.2015.
11. Commission Regulation (EC) No. 794/2004 of 21 Apr. 2004 implementing Council Regulation (EC) No. 659/1999 laying down detailed rules for the application of Art. 93 of the EC Treaty OJ L 140, 30.4.2004.
12. Article 13(2) of the Procedural Regulation.

(a) according to an established practice, there are no doubts about the aid character of the measure concerned;
(b) there is an urgency to act;
(c) there is a serious risk of substantial and irreparable damage to a competitor.

After the aid has been effectively recovered, the Commission shall take a decision within the time limits applicable to notified aid. Moreover, the Commission may authorize the Member State to couple the refunding of the aid with the payment of rescue aid to the firm concerned.

Subsequently, a (first) notice from the Commission, which was aimed at explaining its policy and practice on the recovery of unlawful and incompatible State aid, was issued and then replaced in 2019 by a second one ('Recovery Notice').[13]

The Recovery Notice recalls that the Commission has the discretion to issue a recovery injunction already during its investigation of the aid measures in question – i.e., before reaching a final decision on the compatibility of the aid measures with the internal market – provided a series of cumulative criteria are fulfilled. The Recovery Notice also restates the principle that:

> [...] where adopting a decision finding that aid is incompatible with the internal market ('negative decision'), the Commission has no discretion and must order the recovery of the aid (29) unless that would be contrary to a general principle of European Union law. For this reason, once the Commission has established that an aid measure is unlawful and incompatible with the internal market, it is not required to state additional reasons to order its recovery.

And, more importantly, that:

> Irrespective of the source of the recovery obligation, be that a recovery injunction or a recovery decision, the Member State concerned must implement recovery effectively and immediately, in accordance with Article 16(2) and Article 16(3) of the Procedural Regulation. The measures taken by the Member State cannot only aim at an immediate and effective execution of the recovery decision but must actually attain it.[14]

[B] Contents of the Order to Recover: Interest

As for its contents, the object of each recovery order is to determine the sum the Member State concerned awarded to an undertaking or to a class of undertakings. This is a direct consequence of the restoring nature of the order to recover, which tends to re-establish the situation (in terms of market and competition) that existed prior to the time when the unlawful aid was granted. Restoration of the *status quo ante* cannot, however, be accomplished in full, in the sense that repaying an unlawful and

13. Communication from the Commission – Commission Notice on the recovery of unlawful and incompatible State aid C/2019/5396, OJ C 247, 23.7.2019.
14. Recovery Notice (paras 28-29).

incompatible aid may not be suitable to restoring the previous market situation. Only think of a recipient undertaking that, though required to repay any sums received as aid to the State authorities, has benefited from them to the disadvantage of its competitors throughout the period of time from the grant of the aid and its repayment, which period may last for years in actual practice.

Should the decision of the Commission quantify the amount of the aid, the relevant Member State is bound to implement such a decision. However, neither case law nor any provisions of EU law require the Commission to determine the sum to be reimbursed when it demands repayment of aid declared incompatible with the common market.[15] It is for the Member State concerned to discharge the task of calculating the amount of aid to be recovered, and such task should be viewed as part of the wider obligation of genuine cooperation between the Commission and the Member States in the implementation of the Treaty provisions relating to State aid.[16] This especially applies to cases in which such calculation depends on information not previously disclosed by the Member State concerned to the Commission.[17]

In the judgment *Mediaset*,[18] the ECJ reiterated that no provision of European Union law obliges the Commission to determine the exact amount of the aid to be repaid and that it is sufficient for the Commission's decision to provide sufficient information that allows the recipient to work out himself, without undue difficulty, that amount.[19]

In particular, the ECJ clarified that the Commission, when it is faced with an *aid scheme*, is generally not in a position to identify exactly the amount of aid received by individual recipients and that, accordingly, the specific circumstances of one of the recipients of an aid scheme can be assessed only at the stage of recovery of the aid by the national authorities of the Member State concerned. In this regard, the ECJ made two important clarifications. First, any letter, guidance or statement of position made by the Commission *following* its decision (in the context of implementing of the latter) as regards the quantification of the amount of aid to be recovered cannot be regarded as being binding on the national court.[20] Second, the national court may fix an amount of aid equal to zero to the extent that that determination follows directly from the

15. Case T-67/94, *Ladbroke Racing Ltd. v. Commission*, 27.1.1998, ECLI:EU:T:1998:7 (para. 187). *See also* Case C-102/87, *France v. Commission*, 8.3.1988, ECLI:EU:C:1988:391 (paras 32-33), Case C-480/98, *Spain v. Commission*, 12.10.2000, ECLI:EU:C:2000:559 (para. 25).
16. Case T-67/94, *Ladbroke Racing Ltd. v. Commission* (para. 187).
17. *See* Case C-382/99, *Netherlands v. Commission*, 2002, ECLI:EU:C:2002:363 (para. 91): the case concerned a State aid granted to a high number of gasoline distributors.
18. Case C-69/13, *Mediaset v. Ministero dello Sviluppo economico*, 13.2.2014, ECLI:EU:C:2014:71 (para. 21). *See also* Case C-480/98, *Spain v. Commission* (para. 25); Case C-403/10 P, *Mediaset v. Commission*, 28.7.2011, ECLI:EU:C:2011:533 (para. 126); and Case C-81/10 P, *France Télécom v. Commission*, 8.12.2011, ECLI:EU:C:2011:811 (para. 102); Case C-441/06, *Commission v. France*, 18.10.2007, ECLI:EU:C:2007:616 (para. 41); Case T-642/19, *JCDecaux Street Furniture Belgium*, 7.9.2022. ECLI:EU:T:2022:503 (para. 96).
19. See also Aalbers, M., & Adriaanse, P. C. *Recovery of Unlawful Aid* in *EU State Aids*, (London, Sweet & Maxwell 2021), retrieved from https://hdl.handle.net/1887/3278513.
20. Although 'under the principle of cooperation in good faith laid down in Article 4(3) TEU, the national court must take the statements of position into account as a factor in the assessment of the dispute before it', in Case C-69/13, *Mediaset v. Ministero dello Sviluppo economico* (para. 32).

quantification of the sums to be recovered (provided that the validity and effectiveness of the Commission's decision are not called into question).[21]

Yet, the fact that the recipient undertaking has been able to enjoy the unlawful aid for some time has led the Commission to order recovery of interest on the amount issued as well as recovery of principal. It has done so in order to dispose of any competitive advantage the recipient undertaking has obtained. This provision is now contained in Procedural Regulation, Article 16(2) of which reads as follows:

> The aid to be recovered under a recovery decision shall include interest calculated at an appropriate rate set by the Commission. Interest will accrue from the date on which the unlawful aid was made available to the beneficiary until the date of its recovery.

Initially, the Commission's applicative practice had undergone a first stage (1984-1988) during which its decisions contained no express reference to the recipient's duty to pay interest on the amounts received. In 1989, the Commission, however, introduced this requirement in its recovery decisions, though showing some uncertainty as to the date on which interest should begin to accrue.[22] Thus, Article 14 of Regulation No. 659/1999 (then replaced by Article 16 of Regulation No. 1589/2015) has aptly clarified that: (i) interest must be paid on any aid amounts already received; and (ii) interest shall accrue not from the time the relevant recovery decision was issued, but from the far earlier time when the aid was awarded (rather, made available to the recipient).[23]

This provision appears to be consistent with the *compensatory* nature of interest. Such interest is not payable on account of late payment (as a result of the delay in discharging the refund obligation) but as the equivalent of the financial advantage arising from the recipient being able to rely on capital made available at no cost for some time. Consequently, the applicable interest rate will not be the *legal* rate ruling in the Member State concerned, but the market rate, as the Commission officially clarified in a *letter* to the Member States some years before Regulation No. 659/1999 was issued.[24] This is because, if the recipient undertaking had applied for a loan from a bank (instead of receiving an unlawful State aid), the applicable rate would not have been the legal rate, but the one charged by the bank (the *market rate*), which is usually higher than the legal interest rate. Thus, if interest were to be paid based on the legal rate, a further financial advantage would clearly be allowed to the recipient

21. Case C-69/13, *Mediaset v. Ministero dello Sviluppo economico* (para. 39).
22. According to some decisions (*see, ex multis*, Commission Decision (EEC) 1992/11 of 31 Jul. 1991 concerning aid provided by the Derbyshire County Council to Toyota Motor Corporation, OJ L 6, 11.1.1992) interests had to pass from the date of the recovery decision; according to other decisions OJ L 6, 11.1.1992 (*see* Commission Decision (EEC) 1991/390 of 26 Mar. 1991 on aid granted by the French Government to the undertaking Saint-Gobain (Eurofloat) at Salaise-sur-Sanne, OJ L 215, 2.8.1991, and Commission Decision (EEC) 1992/318 of 25 Mar. 1992 on aid granted by Spain to Industrias Mediterraneas de la Piel SA, OJ L 172, 27.6.1992) interests pass from the date of granting of the unlawful State aid.
23. According to the traditional interpretation, the relevant criterion is the legally binding act by which the competent national authorities undertake to grant aid.
24. European Commission, 'Commission letter to Member States SG(95) D/1983 of 22 Feb. 1995 concerning interest rates to be applied when aid granted unlawfully is being recovered.'

undertaking. For recovery decisions notified *after* the date of entry into force of Regulation No. 794/2004, the methodology for fixing and applying interest for the recovery of unlawful aid is set out in Articles 9 and 11 of such Regulation. In particular, according to Article 11(2), the interest rate shall be applied on a *compound* basis until the date of the recovery of the aid.[25] The Recovery Notice specifies that although 'is the task of the Member State concerned to quantify the exact amount of interest to be recovered'. However, in order to facilitate that task, the Commission has made available to Member States a tool to calculate interest according to the rules established by the Implementing Regulation.[26]

Also with regard to interest, the ECJ stated that national courts, in case of violation of Article 108(3) TFEU, shall order the aid recipient to pay interest in respect of the period of unlawfulness, even if the investigation of the Commission ends with a positive decision.[27]

It is exclusively for the relevant national authorities, however, to determine and take into account the incidence of tax on the sums the recipient undertaking has actually had at its disposal.[28] This is because national authorities alone are in a position to determine the precise extent of any tax levied on undertakings receiving State aid. It would be patently unfair to expect a firm to refund the *gross* amount of a sum it received in the past, while it has been able to rely only on the *pre-tax* amount.

---

25. In Case C-89/14, *A2A and Agenzia delle entrate*, 3.9.2015 ECLI:EU:C:2015:537, the Court of Justice was asked to take position on the possibility for a Member State to apply Arts 9 and 11 of Regulation No. 794/2004 (and to apply interest on a compound basis) for a recovery decision notified by the Commission *before* the entrance into force of such Regulation. This preliminary reference case involved not only the interpretation of Art. 14 of Regulation No. 659/1999 and of Regulation No. 794/2004 but also the EU principles of legitimate expectations, legal certainty and equal treatment. The Court pointed out that EU law does not preclude national legislation providing for the application of compound interest to the recovery of State aid, even though the decision declaring that aid incompatible with the common market and ordering its recovery was adopted and notified to the Member State concerned before that regulation entered into force. In fact, this finding from the Court has been interpreted as granting, before the entry into force of Regulation 794/2004, national jurisdictions the power to decide on these aspects. On this point *see* Merola, *supra* n. 4 at 34. However, in order not to jeopardize the enforcement of State aid rules, the calculation of interests has then been harmonized. On the application of compound interest to recovery decisions *see also* Case C-295/07 P, *Commission v. Département du Loiret e Scott SA*, 11.12.2008, ECLI:EU:C:2008:707.
26. Footnote 125 of the Recovery Notice now specifies that access to that tool is granted following a registration process at both national and European Union level, which ensures that only the authorized officials of the authorities of the Member State concerned and of the Commission's services can access the tool.
27. *See* Case C-199/06, *Centre d'exportation du livre français (CELF) and Ministre de la Culture et de la Communication v. Société internationale de diffusion et d'édition (SIDE)*, 12.2. 2008, ECLI:EU:C:2008:79 (para. 51). *See also* Case C-445/19, *TV2 v. Danmark A/S*, 24.11.2020, ECLI:EU:C:2020:952, where it was pointed out that Art. 108(3) TFEU must be interpreted as meaning that the obligation which is incumbent on national courts to order the recipient of State aid implemented in breach of that provision to pay illegality interest in respect of that aid applies: (i) where, by its final decision, the European Commission finds that that aid is compatible with the internal market pursuant to Art. 106(2) TFEU; and also (ii) to aid which that recipient has transferred to affiliated undertakings and to aid received by it from a publicly controlled undertaking.
28. Case T-459/93, *Siemens SA v. Commission*, 8.6.1995, ECLI:EU:T:1995:100 (para. 82).

A decision of the Regional Administrative Tribunal of Lazio has then pointed out, following an extensive statement of reasons, that a recipient of unlawful aid is not under an obligation to pay currency revaluation on the sums so received in addition to principal and interest.[29]

There is no justification for a greater amount to be charged as a result of currency revaluation (according to ISTAT indicators), both because it is not so required under Community rules ... and because the repeal of the measure whereby an aid deemed by the Community to be unlawful was granted has resulted not in an *inadempimento* (failure to pay a sum as and when due) but in an *indebito oggettivo* (the right to claim restitution for money transferred under an unlawful contract), in respect of which, pursuant to Article 2033 of the Civil Code, only accrued interest must be repaid together with principal.[30]

[C] Limitation Period for an Order to Recover Aid

Before Regulation No. 659/1999 was issued, the Commission's actions in respect of non-notified State aid were not liable to any statute of limitations.[31]

Then, Article 15(1) of Regulation No. 659/1999 (then replaced by Article 17(1) of Regulation No. 1589/2015) introduced a time limit for decisions ordering recovery, by requiring that '[t]he powers of the Commission to recover aid shall be subject to a limitation period of ten years'. Much as this requirement had not been contemplated by the Commission in its original draft, it was later introduced following the comments the Economic and Social Committee had submitted in its opinion of 1 July 1998:

> In the interests of legal certainty, the Committee also recommends that aid which was paid unlawfully more than ten years previously should be treated as de facto aid. After this period, neither notification nor recovery would be necessary. Such a provision is justifiable because after ten years there is no danger of competition being distorted or competitors suffering directly.[32]

The ten-year limitation period begins on the day on which the unlawful aid is awarded to the beneficiary.[33]

---

29. Administrative Regional Court ('TAR') of Lazio – Roma, sect. II *ter*, of 11 Jan. 2005, No. 167, in https://dejure.it; Cfr. Cassazione civile sez. I, 26.9.2019, n. 24040 in https://dejure.it.
30. TAR Lazio No. 167 of 2005, *supra*.
31. *See* Joined Cases T-126/96 and T-127/96, *Breda Fucine Meridionali and Others v. Commission*, 15.9.1998, ECLI:EU:T:1998:207 (para. 67).
32. OJ 1998 C284/10, at point 4.10.2.
33. *See* Joined Cases T-427/04 and T-17/05, *French Republic and France Télécom SA v. Commission of the European Communities*, 30.11.2009, ECLI:EU:T:2009:474. The Italian Supreme Court has clarified that the ten-year limitation period established by Art. 15(1) of Regulation (EC) No. 659/1999 only applies vis à vis the Commission and the Member States. As such, it is different from the limitation period established by Art. 2946 of Italy's Civil Code. The latter period governs the action to recover the aid that the Member State is obliged to bring following the Commission's decision.

    See Italian Supreme Court, Tax Section, 12 Sep. 2012, Judgment No. 15207, in *Online Database DeJure*. The courts have also determined that the limitation period begins when the Commission notifies its decision to the Member State, as it is only at that point that the aid in

The limitation period is subject to either interruption or suspension. As for the reasons for *interruption*, Article 17(2) of Regulation No. 1589/2015 provides that any 'action taken by the Commission or by a Member State, acting at the request of the Commission, with regard to the unlawful aid shall interrupt the limitation period'. The General Court has clarified that even a *letter of request for information* the Commission has sent to the Member State concerned before initiating the relevant administrative procedure amounts to a measure interrupting the ten-year limitation period, much as the beneficiary was unaware of such a letter at that time.[34] Each interruption shall reset the time limit, starting it anew.

Regarding *suspension*, the limitation period is paused for the duration of any proceeding before the Community Courts concerning the Commission's decision.

The final paragraph of Article 17 clarifies that any aid with for which the limitation period has expired will be regarded as existing aid. This means that, after ten years have elapsed, the aid is legally allowed to continue while it is under the Commission's constant review, and recovery cannot be ordered even if the Commission is inclined to regard the aid as incompatible with the common market.

This said, it should be noted that ECJ has recently ruled that such a limitation period does not bind national courts.; In fact, the ECJ recalled that national courts may be required to uphold compensation claims for damage caused by the unlawful State aid to competitors of the beneficiary. In these damage actions, national courts, in exercising their functions of protecting the rights of individuals, maintain a degree of independence from Commission intervention.[35]

The Court has confirmed this principle by stating that Article 17(1) of Regulation 2015/1589, which provides for a limitation period of ten years, refers only to the powers of the Commission to recover aid.[36] Therefore, that limitation period does not extend to the procedure applicable to the recovery of unlawful aid by the competent national authorities.[37] As established by the Court's case law, it is now clear that the Procedural Regulation does not address the powers and obligations of the national courts, which continue to be governed by the provisions of the Treaty as interpreted by the Court.[38]

---

question becomes unlawful. *See* Italian Supreme Court, Employment Section, 3 May 2012, Judgment No. 6671 in *Online Database DeJure*; and, similarly, Italian Constitutional Court, 30 Apr. 2009, Judgment No. 125, *Medcenter Container Terminal and others v. Pres. Cons.*

34. *See* Case T-366/00, *Scott SA v. Commission*, 10.4.2003, ECLI:EU:T:2003:113 (para. 60). This judgment has been appealed before the ECJ (Case C-276/03 P) who dismissed the appeal on 11 Oct. 2005.
35. Case C-387/17, *Fallimento Traghetti del Mediterraneo*, 23.1.2019, ECLI:EU:C:2019:51. (paras 56 et seq.). *See* Alessandra Franchi, *The Never Ending 'Saga' of the Fallimento Traghetti del Mediterraneo*, 18(3) European State Aid Law Quarterly 391-397 (2019) https://doi.org/10.21552/estal/2019/3/19.
36. Case C-387/17, Fallimento Traghetti del Mediterraneo (para. 52).
37. *See*, to that effect, Case C-349/17, *Eesti Pagar*, 5.3.2019, ECLI:EU:C:2019:172 (paras 108 and 109).
38. Case C-349/17, *Eesti Pagar* (para. 110).

§4.02 IMPLEMENTING THE COMMISSION'S DECISION

[A] The Recovery Decision and Its Direct Effect

It must be found out whether the Commission's decision ordering recovery – which is addressed to the relevant Member State alone – is also enforceable against the aid recipient. In other words, the question should be raised whether the Member State concerned, which has become a creditor of the aid recipient following the decision, should revoke the legal measure whereby the aid was granted, and issue a recovery order against the beneficiary, or the decision has a direct, immediate binding effect on the latter as well.

The ECJ has held that any EU act must be deemed directly applicable so long as it is 'unconditional and sufficiently clear and precise', its implementation is not subject to the adoption of any further act and leaves the addressee with no scope for discretion.[39] Now, any decision as to aid seems to satisfy case law requirements. Although a negative decision taken by the Commission is addressed to the Member State concerned, it must be deemed binding upon the aid recipient as well, without the need for the State aid measure involved to have previously been repealed. Obviously, this is the case so long as the amount to be recovered can be determined easily and univocally as to both principal and interest.

[B] The Addressees of an Order for Recovery

The Commission is required to identify the entity from which aid is to be recovered. This is usually the *aid beneficiary*.[40]

In any event, it is for the Member State concerned, possibly following consultation with the Commission, to submit its proposals as to the way in which recovery can be made. Even the entities from which aid can be recovered must have a voice.[41]

Advocate General Van Gerven observed that the repayment of aid granted illegally is not a sanction but a civil law liability arising out of the unlawful and thus undue payment of aid, which liability is therefore *transferable*. As a consequence, while it is a general rule that the aid must be recovered from the beneficiary, it cannot be excluded that recovery of aid may also be demanded of the party that has taken over liability for repayment from the beneficiary.[42]

An especially complex issue is how the entities required to refund illegal State aid can be identified in the case of a transfer of the aid recipient's shares or other units of equity (a 'share deal') or of its assets (an 'asset deal').

39. Case C-9/70, *Franz Grad v. Finanzamt Traunstein*, 6.10.1970, ECLI:EU:C:1970:78. (paras 3-9).
40. *See* the opinion of AG Van Gerven in Case C-303/88, *Italy v. Commission*, 11.10.1990, ECLI:EU:C:1990:352 (para. 23).
41. Case C-303/88, *Italy v. Commission* (para. 58).
42. *See* the opinion of AG Van Gerven in Case C-305/89, *Italy v. Commission*, 10.1.1991, ECLI:EU:C:1991:4 (paras 22-23).

EU case law on State aid should preliminarily be reviewed in respect of share deals, in order to identify which of the entities involved are under an obligation to refund the unlawful aid – whether the *seller*, the *recipient undertaking* or the *purchaser*.

In this connection, a first indication comes from the *ENI-Lanerossi* judgment, which seems to imply that the aid granted to four subsidiaries wholly owned by Lanerossi (itself a subsidiary of ENI) should be recovered from those subsidiaries even after Lanerossi had sold them to private investors, regardless of whether or not the liability arising from the recovery of the aid had been taken into consideration in the conditions of sale.[43] Yet, this decision seems to be belied by the ECJ's own holding in the action the Commission later brought on grounds of failed recovery of aid unlawfully granted (*ENI-Lanerossi II* judgment).[44] By this second judgment, the Court essentially conceded that the aid might be returned by the former owner of the four recipient undertakings (the seller, that is), without demanding that recovery be made from them or, even less, from the private investors who had purchased them.

In the subsequent *Banks* judgment, the ECJ had to deal with the issue of how aid should be recovered following the privatization of the recipient undertakings.[45] By that judgment, the Court excluded, in particular, that the purchasers could be required to repay the aid in question, specifying that:

> The fact that the State-owned companies that succeeded British Coal [*i.e. the recipient undertakings*] were later acquired through an open and competitive tendering process under market conditions indicates that the of aid previously received by British Coal and those State companies does not apply to the private companies that won tenders [...]. Since those undertakings purchased the assets under non-discriminatory competitive conditions and, by definition, at the market price, that is to say at the highest price which a private investor acting under normal competitive conditions was ready to pay for those companies in the situation they were in, in particular after having enjoyed State aid, the aid element was assessed at the market price and included in the purchase price. In such circumstances, the undertakings to which the tenders were granted cannot be considered to have received an advantage over other market operators.[46]

The undertaking to which such tenders had been awarded could not therefore be asked to repay such State aid.

The Court further stated that, in principle, where a company that has received aid has been sold at the market price, the purchase price reflects the impact of the previous aid, and it is the seller of that company who retains the benefit of the aid. In that case, the previous situation is to be restored primarily through repayment of the aid *by the seller*.[47]

43. Case C-303/88, *Italy v. Commission* (paras 56-60).
44. Case C-350/93, *Commission v. Italy*, 4.4.1995, ECLI:EU:C:1995:96.
45. Case C-390/98, *Banks v. Coal Authority*, 20.9.2001, ECLI:EU:C:2001:456.
46. *Ibid.*, at para. 77.
47. *Ibid.* (para. 78). *See also* Joined Cases C-74/00 P and C- 75/00 P, *Falck and Acciaierie di Bolzano v. Commission*, 24.9.2002, ECLI:EU:C:2002:524 (paras 180-181). AG Tizzano, in his opinion in Case C-277/00, *Germany v. Commission*, 19.6.2003, ECLI:EU:C:2003:354, at para. 79, stated: 'that solution might not apply, however, where the selling price was determined taking into

Nor did the Court take a definite stance as to recovery of unlawful aid in connection with a *share deal* in its *Multimedia decision*.[48] On the one hand, by holding that 'it is correct that the sale of shares in a company which is the beneficiary of unlawful aid by a shareholder to a third party does not affect the requirement for recovery', the ECJ showed it endorsed the argument that recovery should invariably be sought from the undertaking that received the aid.[49] On the other hand, it apparently belied this interpretation in the following paragraph, where it referred to the *Banks* judgment essentially to state that the seller, when selling the beneficiary company's shares to a third party at the market price, could be assumed to have retained the benefit of the aid.[50]

As the brief review of precedents offered above shows, the ECJ's attitude dangles between two positions on the issue of the recovery of aid in case the recipient undertaking's shares are sold: (a) the position that aid must be repaid by the beneficiary company in any event; and (b) the position that, if the shares are sold at a price reflecting that company's fair value after aid was granted, the aid must be repaid by the seller.

Advocate General Tizzano thought the Court's position under (a) to be certainly preferred over its position under (b), in its being more in line with the principles governing the recovery of unlawful aid. In fact, if the recipient company is not dissolved and remains active in the market, then the distortion of competition caused by the aid can only be eliminated (or, at least, attenuated) if the obligation to refund the aid is placed upon the recipient company. Only in this case:

> does it actually forfeit the advantage which it had enjoyed over its competitors on the market, and the situation prior to payment of the aid is restored.[51]

Furthermore, the position that recovery must be sought from the beneficiary company in any event also appears to be preferred, since it allows undertakings greater certainty. The contrary position, that aid should be recovered from the seller under certain circumstances, creates considerable uncertainty since it is often difficult to

---

account the possibility that the beneficiary company might have to repay (at least in part) the aid received since, in that case, the value of the aid might not be entirely included in the selling price'.

48. *Ibid.* (para. 81).
49. *See* Case C-399/00, *SIM 2 Multimedia v. Commission*, 2003, ECLI:EU:C:2003:252 (para. 83).
50. *Ibid.* (para. 83).
51. Opinion of AG Tizzano in case C-277/00, *Germany v. Commission* (para. 83). Advocate General Tizzano continued stating that: 'although it is true that any person selling the shares of the beneficiary company at a price which reflects their market value after the grant of aid gains an advantage from the revaluation of the company, it is nonetheless clear that any such advantage does not remove that which the beneficiary company secures over its competitors. And indeed, it is this latter *advantage which causes distortions of competition* and which therefore needs to be removed by recovery of the aid, whilst the *financial advantage* obtained from sale of the shares may even not have an effect on the competitive operation of the markets, since the person selling the shares will not necessarily be an economic operator'. *See also* Case C-348/93, *Commission v. Italy*, 4.4.1995, ECLI:EU:C:1995:95 (para. 27), Case C-480/98, *Spain v. Commission*, (para. 35), Joined Cases C-622/16 P to C-624/16 P, *Scuola Elementare Maria Montessori v. Commission*, 6.11.2018, ECLI:EU:C:2018:873 (para. 77) – Case C-627/18, *Nelson Antunes da Cunha*, 30.4.2020, ECLI:EU:C:2020:321.

determine whether the sales price fully reflects the beneficiary's market value after the grant of aid, and it by no means discounts the risk for the beneficiary of having to repay the aid at least in part. Moreover, if the latter approach is taken, it may create great confusion and substantial difficulties in practice in case the aid recipient undertaking is a large, listed company, whose shares are traded in a high number of transactions on a daily basis. And each such transaction may, in fact, result in a financial advantage for the seller and place on him the corresponding obligation to refund the aid.[52]

Yet, in 2000, when faced with a typical instance of a share deal, the Commission held in its decision that the aid must be repaid by the undertaking that had purchased the beneficiary's shares, though it had not made any assessment as to the sales price.[53] The ECJ fully endorsed the conclusions submitted by Advocate General Tizzano and annulled the Commission's decision, specifying that it was the undertaking to which unlawful State aid was granted that had to repay the aid, insofar as it retained its legal personality and continued to carry out its activities in the market, and the buyer could not, therefore, be asked to repay such aid.[54]

In fact, it has been noticed that the case law of the ECJ seems to distinguish between two cases: (i) if the transaction price was calculated at arm's length (i.e., a price that included the aid and thus the advantages resulting from the aid), the Seller should be responsible for the recovery of the aid; while (ii) in the opposite case, the Buyer shall be in charge of the restitution.[55]

In order to provide guidance on this matter, the Recovery Notice of 2019 now clarifies that the sale to a third party of shares in a beneficiary of incompatible aid does not affect the obligation of the beneficiary to reimburse such aid. Where the shares of the undertaking to which unlawful State aid was granted are sold, but the undertaking retains its legal personality and continues to carry out the activities subsidized by the State aid, the Member State must recover the aid from it as it is that undertaking which maintains an advantage over its competitors.[56]

Specific guidance is provided for cases related to mergers and other reorganizations, about which the Commission reinstates the principle that, in order to find the entity in charge of the restitution of the aid attention the Member State has to identify the legal successor of the beneficiary of the aid and recover the aid from the surviving entity.[57]

The same or even increased difficulties for the identification of the entity in charge of the restitution of the aid apply in case of 'asset deals', i.e., when the beneficiary undertaking has transferred its assets to another undertaking.[58] In *System*

52. *Ibid.* (para. 85).
53. *See* Commission Decision (EC) 2000/567 of 11 Apr. 2000 on the State aid implemented by the Federal Republic of Germany for System Microelectronic Innovation GmbH, Frankfurt/Oder (Brandenburg), OJ 2000 L238/50.
54. Case C-277/00, *Germany v. Commission*, *supra* (para. 81).
55. Merola, *supra*, n. 4, at 200-202.
56. *See* Case -357/14 P, *Electrabel and Dunamenti Erőmű v. Commission*, C-357/14 P, 1.10.15, ECLI:EU:C:2015:642, para. 113.
57. Recovery Notice 2019 (para. 95).
58. *See XXX Report on Competition Policy* (2000), points 420 and 421.

Microelectronic Innovation GmbH (SMI)[59] and *CDA Compact Disc Albrechts GmbH (CDA)*,[60] the Commission ordered the German Government to recover the aid from the *transferee* as the real beneficiary, in that it was using the assets of the company in liquidation whose situation had improved through the aid (the 'spill-over effect'). In any event, in order to prevent Germany from evading the consequences of the recovery decision, the Commission resolved to extend such decision to aid measures granted to *any other firm* that carried on the original undertaking's activities by using the latter's assets and/or infrastructure.

Yet, the EU Courts have reversed this view as well, finding that the Commission had failed to show the existence of any form of evasion that could find an obligation for any undertakings other than the beneficiaries, or for any other undertakings to which the relevant assets and/or infrastructure had been transferred, to repay unlawful aid.[61]

Conversely, on other occasions, the ECJ did ascertain the beneficiary or Member State's intent to frustrate the Commission's decision.[62] In *Commission v. Spain*, for example, the Court of Justice stated that recovery obligation may apply to the *new entity* even if it acquired the assets at market price, where the intention was to *evade the recovery order* of the Commission.[63]

Similarly in the *Olympic Airways* case, a legislative measure had resulted in the transfer of the most profitable assets free of all of the company's debts, to a new company of the same group. The deal had been structured in such a way as to make it impossible, based on the national legislation, to recover the former company's debts from the new firm. Thus, the ECJ implicitly confirmed the legal principle expressed by the Advocate General as follows:

> [i]n order to prevent the effectiveness of the decision from being frustrated and competition from continuing to be distorted, the Commission may be compelled to require that the recovery is not restricted to the original firm but is extended to the firm which continues the activity of the original firm, using the transferred means of production, in cases where certain elements of the transfer point to economic continuity between the two firms.[64]

The General Court has been exploring the subject of economic continuity between two undertakings in greater detail, following on from the asset deals. It has reaffirmed the principle that where aid was granted to a company that transferred some of its assets to another company, the latter may be considered the real beneficiary of the aid only where there is 'economic continuity' between the undertakings. Economic continuity must be assessed in the light of a number of factors whose importance varies depending on the circumstances of the case. These factors include the purpose of the

59. *See* Commission Decision (EC) 2000/56, mentioned *supra*.
60. *See* Commission Decision (EC) 2000/796 of 21 Jun. 2000 on State aid granted by Germany to CDA Compact Disc Albrechts GmbH, Thuringia, OJ 2000 L318/62.
61. Case C-277/00, *Germany v. Commission* (paras 84-100); Case T-318/00, *Freistaat Thüringen v. Commission*, 19.10.2005, ECLI:EU:C:2004:238 (paras 307-346) and Case T-324/00, *CDA Datenträger Albrechts GmbH v. Commission*, 19.10.2005, ECLI:EU:T:2005:364 (paras 76-114).
62. Case C-415/03, *Olympic Airways*, 12.5.2005, ECLI:EU:C:2005:287.
63. *See* Case C-529/09, *Commission v. Spain*, 24.1. 2013, ECLI:EU:C:2013:31 (paras 78-81).
64. *See* the opinion of AG Geelhoed, Case C-415/03, '*Olympic Airways*' (para. 33).

transfer (such as assets and liabilities, maintenance of the workforce, grouped assets), the transfer price, the identity of the shareholders, the time at which the transfer takes place (after the start of the investigation, the initiation of the procedure or the final decision) and lastly the economic rationale behind the transaction. The Court also clarified that the Commission is not required to examine *all* of the above factors.[65]

The Recovery Notice of 2019 has reinforced the case law of the ECJ, emphasizing that in an asset deal scenario, the Commission must assess the economic continuity between undertakings on a case-by-case basis, considering the following criteria:[66] (i) the scope of the transfer (assets and liabilities, maintenance of the workforce and/or management);[67] (ii) the price of the transfer;[68] (iii) the identity of the shareholders or the owners of the seller and of the buyer; (iv) the time at which the transfer takes place (during the preliminary investigation pursuant to Article 4 of the Procedural Regulation or the formal investigation pursuant to Article 6 of the Regulation, or after adoption of the recovery decision); (v) the economic logic of the operation.[69]

---

65. Case T-123/09, *Ryanair v. Commission*, 28.3.2012, ECLI:EU:T:2012:164. In that judgment the Court deemed that the Commission had explained the reasons why it considered that there was no economic continuity between Alitalia and CAI, concluding that 'no undue advantage could be transferred to the buyer of Alitalia Group assets, having regard to the fact that all measures were taken to ensure that the transfer took place at a price not lower than the market price'. In a similar case, the Commission is investigating under Art. 108(2) TFEU the *economic continuity* between the companies of the *Tirrenia* group, formerly owned by the Italian State, and their acquirers Compagnia Italiana di Navigazione (*CIN*). *See* Case SA.32014 (2011/C), SA.32015 (2011/C), SA.32016 (2011/C) – *Italia State aid to the companies of the former Tirrenia Group and their acquirers*.
66. Footnote 106 of the Recovery Notice refers to Judgment of the General Court in Case T-123/09, *Ryanair v. Commission*, ECLI:EU:T:2012:164 (paras 155 and 156), specifying that he Commission is not required to take into account all of the criteria.
67. Footnote 107 of the Recovery Notice specifies that the larger the share of the original business that is transferred to a new entity, the higher the likelihood that the economic activity related to the assets sold continues to benefit from the incompatible aid, referring to Commission Decision (EU) 2015/1826 of 15 Oct. 2014 on the State aid SA.33797 – (2013/C) (ex 2013/NN) (ex 2011/CP) implemented by Slovakia for NCHZ OJ L 269 15.10.2015, and, with regard to the economic continuity, to Commission Decision of 17 Sep. 2008, State aid N 321/08, N 322/08 and N 323/08 – Greece – *Vente de certains actifs d'Olympic Airlines v. Olympic Airways Services*; as well as to the Commission Decisions of 12 Nov. 2008 State aid N 510/2008 – Italy – Sale of assets of Alitalia and of 4 Apr. 2012 SA.34547 – France – *Reprise des actifs du groupe SERNAM dans le cadre de son redressement judiciaire.*
68. Footnote 108 of the Notice specifies that where the assets are sold through an open, transparent, non-discriminatory and non-conditional tender to the highest bidder, the price paid is generally presumed to be the market price. This principle was followed by the Commission in Commission Decision of 1.10.2014 on the State aid SA.31550 (2012/C) (ex 2012/NN) implemented by Germany for Nürburgring; Commission Decision of 27.3.2014 on the State aid SA.34572 (13/C) (ex 13/NN) implemented by Greece for Larco General Mining & Metallurgical Company S.A.; Commission Decision of 7.5.2015 on the State aid SA.35546 (2013/C) (ex 2012/NN) implemented by Portugal for Estaleiros Navais de Viana do Castelo S.A.
69. Footnote 109 of the Notice highlights that the Commission found economic continuity in cases where there would be no change in the way the business was run, in the scope of the activity or in production, referring to Commission Decision (EU) 2015/1826 of 15 Oct. 2014 on the State aid SA.33797 – (2013/C) (ex 2013/NN) (ex 2011/CP) implemented by Slovakia for NCHZ, OJ L 269, 15.10.2015. Conversely, in cases where significant changes in the activity or the business strategy were demonstrated, the Commission took the view that there was no economic continuity, as it was the case in Commission Decision (EU) 2016/151 of 1 Oct. 2014 on the State aid SA.31550 (2012/C) (ex 2012/NN) implemented by Germany for Nürburgring, OJ L 34,

[C] Failure to Comply with Recovery Decisions

The second sentence of Article 108(2) TFEU requires that, if the Member State concerned does not comply with a decision relating to State aid, the Commission may, in derogation from the provisions of Article 258 TFEU refer the matter to the Court of Justice *directly*.[70] This means that the Commission may bring the matter before the ECJ forthwith, without being required to deliver a reasoned opinion.[71] According to the EU Courts' case law, this is a 'variant' of the action for non-compliance specifically adjusted to the particular problems State aid creates in terms of competition within the common market.[72]

Regulation No. 659/1999 recognized that the Commission may refer the matter to the Court of Justice directly in case of non-compliance of a Member State with: (i) final (conditional or negative) decisions, in particular in cases of recovery (Article 23(1), now Article 28(1) of Regulation (UE) 2015/1589); or (ii) with injunction decisions (for suspension or recovery, pursuant to Article 12, now Article 14 of Regulation (UE) 2015/1589).[73]

Since 1999, the Commission has brought a number of actions pursuant to Article 108(2)(2) TFEU before the Court of Justice to pursue Member States' failure to adopt the necessary measures to recover illegal or incompatible aid from the beneficiaries within the prescribed period.[74]

The system of judicial remedies laid down in the Treaty provides a distinction between actions for non-fulfilment, intended to establish that a Member State has not fulfilled its obligation, and actions brought pursuant to Article 263 TFEU and Article 265 TFEU, intended to have it ascertained whether any of the Community institutions' acts or omissions were lawful. These judicial remedies pursue different aims and are

10.2.2016; Commission Decision (EU) 2016/152 of 1 Oct. 2014 on State aid SA 27339 (12/C) (ex 11/NN) implemented by Germany for Zweibrücken airport and airlines using the airport, OJ L 34, 10.2.2016. Finally, the Notice stresses that 'In any event, economic logic alone has not been considered a conclusive element when looking for economic continuity between two undertakings.'

70. Similarly, under Art. 108 TFEU, a Member State can directly resort to the ECJ without dealing with Commission, in exception to Art. 259 TFEU.
71. The reason for this simplified procedure consists in the following: the Commission, during the procedure provided by Art. 108(2) (subpara. 1), EC can *already* allow the defaulting State to submit its observations, establishing an adversary process comparable to the one set forth in Art. 258 TFEU.
72. Case C-301/87, *'Boussac'* (para. 23). It is settled case law that the Commission has a discretion in deciding whether to bring proceedings before the Court of Justice for failure to fulfil Treaty obligations. That discretion is not in any way conditional on the submission by an individual of a request that the Commission should take specific action, whether under Art. 258 TFEU or under the second subparagraph of Art. 108(2) TFEU. *See* Case T-277/94, *Associazione Italiana Tecnico Economica del Cemento AITEC v. Commission*, 22.5.1996, ECLI:EU:T:1996:66 (para. 67).
73. Such possibility, with regard to provisional decisions, had been already admitted by the ECJ in the supra mentioned *Boussac* case, at para. 23. *See also* Art. 23(2) of Regulation No. 659/1999, which provides that if the Commission considers that the Member State concerned has not complied with a judgment of the ECJ, the Commission may pursue the matter in accordance with Art. 228 of the Treaty (now Art. 260 of the TFEU).
74. *See* Table 'Active pending recovery cases' on European on Statistics, studies and report – State aid Recovery performed by European Commission update 30 Jun. 2014.

applied in different ways. Therefore, a Member State, failing a provision expressly authorizing it to do so under the Treaty, *may not raise objections as to the lawfulness of a decision* addressed to it as a defence in an action for non-fulfilment of obligations grounded on its failure to execute that decision. A different course might only be taken if the act at issue were so serious and clearly flawed as to be regarded as non-existent.[75]

It is worth noting that the number of recovery decisions adopted by the Commission has *significantly increased* since the entry into effect of Regulation 659/1999. Fifty-six out of sixty-four negative decisions delivered by the Commission in the six years from 2008 to 2014 contained an order for recovery.[76]

Yet, the Commission pointed out, at the same time, that recovery decisions were all too often not implemented by Member States. For the number of 'pending recovery cases', i.e., recovery decisions requiring implementation at a national level, was still on the increase. Faced with this issue, the DG Competition set up a unit (DG Competition H4) specifically responsible for ensuring the implementation and monitoring of State aid decision.

Furthermore, in accordance with the case law of the ECJ, notably with the *Deggendorf* ruling, when assessing the compatibility of new aid, the Commission also takes into account the fact that the beneficiaries may not have complied with earlier Commission decisions requiring the reimbursement of previous illegal and incompatible aid.[77] In such cases, the Commission must evaluate the impact on the beneficiaries of combining the new aid with the old incompatible aid that has not yet been reimbursed.[78]

Recovery of incompatible State aid is a lengthy process, if one only considers that fifteen of the decisions pending at the end of June 2014 had been adopted before the year 2004.

The number of pending recovery cases began to decrease in the last few years. Only three recovery decisions were adopted in 2023, compared to seven in 2018 and nineteen in 2015. The geographical distribution of pending recovery cases remains relatively stable: Italy accounts for the largest number of recovery decisions (seven cases in the period 2018-2023) followed by Romania (four cases in the period 2018-2023), and France (three).

The statistics made available by the Commission also provide information about the total amount of aid to be recovered. Of the over EUR 15 billion of aid to industry and

75. *See* Case C-207/05, *Commission v. Italy*, 2006, ECLI:EU:C:2006:366 (paras 42-43).
76. *See* Statistics, studies and report – State aid Recovery performed by European Commission, available on the Commission website. The data does not include negative decision on notified aid not put into effect.
77. Case C-355/95 P, *Textilwerke Deggendorf GmbG (TWD) v. Commission*, 15.5.1997, ECLI:EU:C:1997:241. *See* Commission Press Release IP/06/1544 of 10 Nov. 2006: '*Commission orders Italy to suspend payment of aid to AEM Torino until it pays back previous illegal aid.*'
78. In Case C-480/09 P, *Acea Electrabel v. Commission*, 16.12.2010, ECLI:EU:C:2010:787 the ECJ stated that the effects of the *Deggendorf* principle may extend also to undertaking controlling an aid beneficiary, where there are sufficient 'organic and functional links' between the companies that the controlling company forms part of the same economic entity as the aid beneficiary.

service to be recovered under 325 decisions adopted since 1 January 2000, the aid repaid amounted to EUR 11.7 billion, while aid for about EUR 3.8 billion was lost.[79]

§4.03 LIMITS TO THE EXECUTION OF ORDERS FOR RECOVERY OF AID

Pursuant to Article 16(3) of Regulation No. 1589/2015:

> recovery shall be effected without delay and in accordance with the procedures under the national law of the Member State concerned, provided that they allow the immediate and effective execution of the Commission's decision.

Therefore, under this provision, Member States' autonomy in their recovery activities is limited by the requirement that aid must be recovered immediately and effectively. In other words, any measures of national law that may come to the fore in the fulfilment of a recovery obligation must not be such as to obstruct the effectiveness of EU law.[80] If the domestic law conflicts with the principle of effectiveness, the court will be obliged to disapply the domestic law.[81]

One consequence of the *principle of effectiveness* is the prohibition for the Member States to claim provisions, practices or situations of their own national laws to avoid fulfilment of their obligations under EU law,[82] and the obligation upon Member States to take all suitable measures to ensure implementation of Commission decisions on the recovery of aid.[83]

An interesting potential application of the effectiveness principle is to be found in the proceedings the Commission has brought pursuant to the second paragraph Article 108(2) TFEU, for the failure by France to comply with the Commission Decision (EC) 2002/14, whereby the Commission ordered recovery of aid granted to Scott Paper SA/Kimberly-Clark.[84] Advocate General Ruiz-Jarabo Colomer submitted that the Court

79. *See* State Aid Recovery Statistics, 1 Mar. 2024, available on Commission's website at the following link: https://competition-policy.ec.europa.eu/state-aid/procedures/recovery-unlawful-aid_en on recovery of unlawful aid in Statistics, studies and reports.
80. On the effectiveness principle in EC law *see* Joined Cases C-205/82 to 215/82, *Deutsche Milchkontor GmbH and Others v. Germany,* 21.9.1983, ECLI:EU:C:1983:233 and Case C-142/87, '*Tubemeuse*' (para. 61).
81. *See, inter alia,* Italian Supreme Court, Tax Section, 20 Dec. 2010, Judgment No. 26286, in *Online Database DeJure.*
82. Cfr. Case C-404/97, *Commission v. Portugal,* 27.6.2000, ECLI:EU:C:2000:345 (para. 55). *See also,* for an application of the effectiveness principle to a national law concerning the burden of proof, Case C-526/04, *Laboratoires Boiron SA v. URSAFF,* 7.9.2006, ECLI:EU:C:2006:528.
83. *See* Case C-304/09, *Italy v. Commission,* 22.12.2010, ECLI:EU:C:2010:812 (para. 42). The Court of Justice held in that judgment where legislative steps intended to ensure the implementation by national courts of a Commission decision requiring a Member State to recover unlawful aid are taken too late or prove ineffective, they do not meet the requirements under EU law. *See also* Case C-305/09, *Commission v. Italy,* 2011, ECLI:EU:C:2011:274 and Case C-613/11, *Commission v. Italy,* 21.3. 2013, ECLI:EU:C:2013:192; C-24/95, *Alcan Deutschland,* 20.3.1997, ECLI: EU:C:1997:163 (paras 34-38); C-627/18, *Nelson Antunes da Cunha,* 30.4.2020, ECLI: EU:C:2020:321 (paras 57-59).
84. Commission Decision (EC)2002/14 of 12 Jul. 2000 on the state aid granted by France to Scott Paper SA Kimberly-Clark (Text with EEA relevance) (notified under document number C(2000) 2183) OJ L 12, 15.1.2002.

of Justice should declare the French State's non-fulfilment of obligations, in that the application of a national provision contained in the French Local Authorities General Code – whereby the enforceability of liquidation notices is automatically suspended – would be contrary to the principle of effectiveness since it gave rise to 'interim protection which is disproportionate'.[85]

Furthermore, Member States are expected to comply with the principle of *non-discrimination*, which means that the application of provisions of national law must not be discriminatory against similar cases solely governed by national legislation.[86]

[A] The Principle of the Protection of Legitimate Expectations

The protection of legitimate expectations is a general principle of EU law, which has gradually been recognized in case law. EU Courts' precedents have described it as 'a superior rule of law', 'one of the fundamental principles of the Community' or 'a general superior rule of Community law for the protection of individuals'.[87] Its inobservance can well jeopardize the validity of the act involved.

The principle of the protection of legitimate expectations is the *corollary of the principle of legal certainty*, which demands that legal rules be clear and precise. Its purpose is to ensure that situations and legal relationships governed by EU law remain foreseeable.[88]

It is by no means easy to provide an exhaustive definition of the principle of the protection of legitimate expectations, because of its *subjective* purport. Still, based on its practical application by EU case law, a fair statement is that it may be invoked against EU rules only to the extent the following conditions (all of them equally necessary) are fulfilled:

85. *See* the opinion of AG Ruiz-Jarabo Colomer in Case C-232/05, *Commission v. France,* 2006, 18.5.2006 ECLI:EU:C:2006:337 (paras 80-81). The opinion was confirmed by the ECJ on 5 Oct. 2006.
86. *See* Joined Cases C-205/82 to 215/82, *Deutsche Milchkontor GmbH* (paras 18-25); Case C-94/87, *Commission v. Germany,* 2.2.1989, ECLI:EU:C:1989:46 (para. 12); Case T-459/93, *Siemens SA v. Commission* (paras 82 et seq.). *See also* Case C-480/98, *Spain v. Commission* (paras 36-37), where the Court of Justice has considered not discriminatory the Spanish law by which the debts of the enterprises declared insolvent do not produce interests from the date of the insolvency declaration. *See* Case C-17/03, *Vereniging voor Energie, Milieu en Water (VEMW) v. Directeur van the Dienst uitvoering en toezicht energie,* 7.6.2005, ECLI:EU:C:2005:362 (para. 73).
87. *See* Case C-74/74, *CNTA v. Commission,* 15.6.1976, ECLI:EU:C:1975:59 (para. 44); Case-104/97 P, *Atlanta AG and others v. Commission and Council,* 14.10.1999, ECLI:EU:C:1997:348 (para. 52); Joined Cases C-37/02 and C-38/02, *Di Lenardo and Dilexport v. Ministero del Commercio con l'Estero,* 15,7.2004, ECLI:EU:C:2004:443 (para. 70); Case C-17/03, *Vereniging voor Energie, Milieu en Water (VEMW) v. Directeur van the Dienst uitvoering en toezicht energie,* 7.6.2005, ECLI:EU:C:2005:362 (para. 73).
88. Case C-63/93, *Fintan Duff and Others v. Minister for Agriculture and Food and Attorney General,* 15.2.1996, ECLI:EU:C:1996:51 (para. 20); Case C-107/97, *Criminal proceedings against Rombi and Arkopharma,* 18.5.2000, ECLI:EU:C:2000:253 (para. 66).

- an EU act or conduct has previously created a situation which can give rise to a legitimate expectation (so-called legal basis of legitimate expectations).[89] In particular, such expectations must be based on specific statements (or assurances) by an EU institution or conduct by that institution such as to give rise to confusion in the mind of a party acting in good faith;[90]
- a prudent and discriminating trader could not have foreseen the adoption of an EU measure likely to affect his interests (so-called legitimacy of expectations);[91] and
- legitimate expectations as to the legality of a favourable administrative act may only be countered by a public-policy interest which overrides the beneficiary's interest in the maintenance of a situation which he was entitled to regard as stable.[92]

In addition, due to the mandatory nature of the supervision of State aid by the Commission pursuant to Article 108 TFEU, undertakings to which aid has been granted may not, in principle, entertain a legitimate expectation that the aid is lawful unless it has been granted in compliance with the procedure laid down in that article, and furthermore, an economic operator exercising due care should normally be able to determine whether that procedure has been followed.[93]

Moreover, where aid is implemented without prior notification to the Commission, with the result that it is unlawful under Article 108(3) TFEU, the recipient of the aid cannot have at that time a legitimate expectation that its grant is lawful.[94]

The significance of this principle for the matter at hand has been reinforced by Article 14 of Regulation No. 659/1999, now Article 16 of the Council Regulation (EU) 2015/1589, according to which:

> [t]he Commission shall not require recovery of the aid if this would be contrary to a general principle of Community law.

89. *See* Case C-289/81, *Mavridis v. Parliament,* 19.5.1983, ECLI:EU:C:1983:142 (para. 21); Case C-177/90, *Kuehn v. Landwirtschaftskammer Weser-Ems,* 10.1.1992, ECLI:EU:C:1992:2 (para. 14); Case C-107/97, *Rombi and Arkopharma* (para. 67); *Weidacher,* 2002, ECLI:EU:C:2000:253 (para. 31); Case C-459/02, *Gerekens and Procola v. Luxembourg,* 15.7.2004, ECLI:EU:C:2004:454 (para. 29).
90. This is not the case for general public declarations made by a Member of the Commission nor for repeated contacts between the interested party and the Commission. *See* the ECJ Order in Case C-44/00 P, *Société de distribution mécanique et d'automobiles (Sodima) v. Commission,* 13.12.2000, ECLI:EU:C:2000:686 (para. 50); Case C-195/91 P, *Bayer v. Commission,* 15.12.1994, ECLI:EU:C:1994:412 (para. 26); Case C-285/93, *Dominikanerinnen-Kloster Altenhohenau,* 23.11.1995, ECLI:EU:C:1995:398 (para. 27); Case C-82/98 P, *Kögler v. Court of Justice,* 25.5.2000, ECLI:EU:C:2000:282 (para. 33).
91. *See* Case C-265/85, *Van den Bergh en Jurgens v. Commission,* 11.3.1987, ECLI:EU:C:1987:121 (para. 44); Case C-22/94, *Irish Farmers Association and others v. Minister for Agriculture, Food and Forestry, Ireland e Attorney General,* 15.4.1997, ECLI:EU:C:1997:187 (para. 25); Joined Cases C-37/02 and C-38/02, *Di Lenardo and Dilexport, supra* (para. 70); Case C-17/03, *VEMW and others* (para. 74).
92. Case C-90/95 P, *De Compte v. European Parliament,* 17.4.1997, ECLI:EU:C:1997:198 (para. 39).
93. C-349/17, *Eesti Pagar* (para. 98).
94. *Ibid.* (para. 98). Cfr. C-148/04, *Unicredito Italiano* (para. 104), and C-672/13, *OTP Bank,* 19.3.2015, EU:C:2015:185 (para. 77).

In practice, there are decisions in which the Commission has, specifically in order to ensure the protection of legitimate expectations, waived its right to demand recovery of an illegal aid it had considered to be incompatible with the internal market.

Among these decisions there are the following:

- Commission Decision 92/329/EEC of 25 July 1990 on aid granted by the Italian Government to a manufacturer of ophthalmic products (Industrie Ottiche Riunite - IOR).[95]
- Commission Decision 93/625/EEC of 22 September 1993 concerning aid granted by the French Government to the Pari mutuel urbain (PMU) and to the racecourse undertakings:[96] the Commission ordered recovery only as from the time when the initiation of proceedings was notified to the French authorities, namely on 11 January 1991.
- Commission Decision 95/195/EC of 14 February 1995 concerning aid granted by the Region of Sardinia (Italy) in the fisheries sector (temporary withdrawal of vessels).[97] In that case, the Commission decided not to demand recovery of the aid owing to the time elapsed since the scheme was brought to the attention of the Commission until the publication of the decision.
- Commission Decision 96/617/ECSC of 17 July 1996 concerning aid granted by the Autonomous Province of Bolzano (Italy) to Acciaierie di Bolzano.[98] The Commission deemed it fair not to demand recovery of the aid paid prior to 1 January 1986, for only as of such date was the obligation to give prior notification of any aid granted to the steel industry deemed to be certainly known.
- Commission Decision 2001/212/EC of 16 May 2000 concerning the aid scheme implemented by Italy to assist large firms in difficulty.[99] In this case, though the application of derogations had been excluded and the aid was considered to be illegal, the Commission declined to impose recovery, in that it deemed this to be contrary to the principle of the protection of legitimate expectations. On the other hand, the Commission had erroneously raised a legitimate expectation by qualifying aid under the Prodi Act as existing aid, in addition to having protracted investigations for over twenty years. As it happens, the

95. OJ 1992 L183/30, para. VIII, where the Commission 'has decided that ... repayment of the aid should not be demanded. This decision is based on the time which has passed between the date the aid became known to the Commission and the date this Decision was taken. This long interval would be difficult to justify with respect to the case-law of the Court of justice concerning procedural time limits'.
96. OJ 1993 L300/15. This decision was later reversed by the Court of First Instance, in this as in other respects, by its judgment of 27 Jan. 1998 in Case T-67/94, *Ladbroke Racing v. Commission* and this judgment was confirmed in a judgment delivered by the Court of Justice on 16 May 2000, in Case C-83/98 P, *France v. Ladbroke Racing Ltd and Commission*, 16.5.2000, ECLI: EU:C:2000:248.
97. OJ 1995 L126/32, para. VI.
98. OJ 1996 L274/30, confirmed by Case T-158/96, *Acciaierie di Bolzano S.p.A. v. Commission*, 16.12.1999, ECLI:EU:T:1999:335 (paras 84 et seq.) and substantially also by Joined Cases C-74/00 P and C- 75/00 P, *Falck and Acciaierie di Bolzano v. Commission*.
99. OJ 2001 L79/29.

peculiarity of this decision is that the Commission recognized that its conduct might have fostered a legitimate expectation both on the part of the recipient undertakings and on the part of the authority which granted the aid.

- Commission Decision C(2004)3060 of 2 August 2004 concerning the State aid implemented by France for France Télécom, points 257-264, where the Commission decided ex officio to refrain from demanding recovery because of the respect due to the legitimate expectations of the recipients. The Commission itself recognized, in fact, 'that this is the first time it has had to examine whether this type of conduct constitutes aid'.[100]
- Commission Decision 2003/757/EC of 17 February 2003 concerning the aid scheme implemented by Belgium for coordination centres established in Belgium.[101] In that case, not only did the Commission refrain from demanding recovery of aid – nor could it do otherwise, in that it was existing aid – but it also allowed centres authorized prior to 31 December 2000 to continue to benefit from the scheme until the expiry of the authorization in force as at the date on which notification was given and, otherwise, not later than 31 December 2010.[102] The ECJ then endorsed the observations of Advocate General Léger, who had proposed that the Court should annul the Commission Decision in so far as 'it prohibits the Kingdom of Belgium from renewing, even temporarily, approvals that were in force on the date of notification of the decision and which expire before 31 December 2010'.[103]
- Commission Decision 2003/515/EC of 17 February 2003 referred to State aid performed by The Netherlands in favour of international financial activities.
- Commission Decision 2005/565/EC of 9 March 2004 on an aid scheme implemented by Austria for a refund from the energy taxes on natural gas and electricity in 2002 and 2003.
- Commission Decision 2006/323/EC of 7 December 2005 concerning the exemption from excise duty on mineral oils used as fuel for the production of alumina in the Gardanne region, the Shannon region and Sardinia.
- Commission Decision 2006/940/EC of 19 July 2006 on aid scheme C 3/2006 implemented by Luxembourg for 1929 holding companies and billionaire holding companies.
- Commission Decision 2011/282/EU of 12 January 2011 on the tax amortization of financial goodwill for foreign shareholding acquisitions (case of partial acceptance).

Clearly enough, the expectations of the type relevant to the aid recovery procedure are those of undertakings that have benefited from *illegal aid*. It seems then appropriate to distinguish the case in which (i) non-compliance with EU provisions

100. *See* Commission Press Release IP/04/981 of 20 Jul. 2004.
101. OJ 2003 L282/25.
102. *See*, in particular, para. VI.4. of the Decision (Recitals 117-120).
103. *See* para. 447 of the opinion of AG Léger in Joined Cases C-182/03 and C-217/03, *Belgium and Forum 187 ASBL v. Commission*, 9.2.2006, ECLI:EU:C:2005:266 and in Case C-399/03, *Commission v. Council*, 22.6.2006, ECLI:EU:C:2006:417.

only depends on the conduct of the State that granted the aid, from the case in which (ii) legitimate expectations arose from the Commission's conduct.

In fact, the EU Courts have substantially thwarted the principle of the protection of legitimate expectation, by denying it in practical application. The reason is that in view of the mandatory nature of the review of State aid by the Commission under Article 108 of the TFEU, undertakings to which aid has been granted may not, in principle, entertain a legitimate expectation that the aid is lawful unless it has been granted in compliance with the procedure laid down in that article. According to case law precedents, a diligent businessman should *normally* be able to determine whether that procedure has been followed. Thus, where aid is paid without prior notification to the Commission so that it is *unlawful* under Article 108(3) of the TFEU, the recipient of the aid cannot have at that time a legitimate expectation that its grant is lawful.[104]

These determinations by the EU Courts make the above distinction almost ineffectual in practice. In other words, no legitimate expectation can be pleaded in respect of the conduct of the State that has granted the aid. Only the Commission's conduct is deemed to generate legitimate expectations, though within the limits mentioned above, of which more below.

Therefore, the difficulties the undertakings that receive unlawful aid are bound to encounter in practice when trying to plead legitimate expectations *before a Community Court* can easily be foreseen.

In this respect, one should consider the paradoxical issue the Court of Justice decided in Case C-169/95.[105] In that case, the Commission had authorized an aid scheme by a decision of 26 May 1987. A competitor of the recipient undertaking had then brought action for the annulment of such a decision, of which it had become aware in 1991. The ECJ had annulled the original decision by its judgment of 19 May 1993 – *six years after the relevant authorization*, in fact. In execution of that judgment, the Commission re-opened the procedure and adopted its decision of 29 March 1995, by which it declared the aid in question to be unlawful and incompatible with the common market and therefore ordered the relevant sums to be repaid.

The Member State concerned applied to the Court of Justice once more. The latter then held that not even the fact that the Commission had initially decided *not to raise any objections* to the aid at issue could be regarded as capable of having caused the

104. *See* Joined Cases C-346/03 and C-529/03, *Atzeni and others v. Regione Autonoma della Sardegna* 23.2.2006 ECLI:EU:C:2006:130 (paras 64-65); Joined Cases C-183/02 P and C-187/02 P *Demesa and Territorio Histórico de Álava v. Commission*, 11.11.2004, ECLI:EU:C:2004:701 (paras 44-45); Case C-24/95, *Land Rheinland-Pfalz v. Alcan Deutschland GmbH*, 20.3.1997, ECLI:EU:C:1997:163 (paras 25 and 30-31); Case C-169/95, *Spain v. Commission*, 14.1.1997, ECLI:EU:C:1997:10 (para. 51); Case C-5/89, *Commission v. Germany*, 20.9.1990, ECLI: EU:C:1990:320 (para. 14). In Case C-148/04, *Unicredito Italiano v. Agenzia delle Entrate, Ufficio Genova 1*, the ECJ stated that '[n]either the Member State in question nor the operator involved can plead the principle of legal certainty either, in order to prevent recovery of the aid, since the risk of national proceedings ... was foreseeable from the moment that the aid was implemented' (para. 104 of the judgment). Most recently, *see*, *inter alia*, Case C-519/07 P, *Commission v. Koninllijke Friesland Campina*, 17.9.2009, ECLI:EU:C:2009:556 (para. 84), and Case C-537/08, *Kahla Thüringen Porzellan v. Commission*, 16.12.2010, ECLI:EU:C:2010:769 (para. 63).

105. *See* Case C-169/95, *Spain v. Commission*.

recipient undertaking to entertain any legitimate expectation if that decision had been challenged by the undertaking's competitor in due time before the Court, *which had subsequently annulled it.*

According to the ECJ, however regrettable it may be, the Commission's error cannot erase the consequences of the unlawful conduct of the Member State that has granted the aid.[106] As a consequence, not even a decision of the Commission granting authorization is enough to cause the aid recipient to entertain legitimate expectations as to the lawfulness of the aid. So long as the period allowed to any third parties (the recipient undertaking's competitors, that is) to bring an action against that decision has not expired or, in case such an action is brought, it has not been decided, the recipient cannot be certain as to the lawfulness of the proposed aid.[107] Because of the double-instance approach to Community judicial proceedings, a final decision may be delayed for years, during which the aid recipient would be prevented from legally using the aid (lest it should ultimately be required to make a refund if it does so).

According to the EU judicature, endorsing the censure of the recipients' legitimate expectations would be tantamount to depriving of all practical effects the judges' scrutiny as to the legality of a positive decision of the Commission on State aid. For the recipient's competitors, or any third parties adversely affected by such a decision, *would no longer have any interest* in challenging the flawed act. This is because the potential annulment of a positive decision of the Commission in the field of State aid might end up a Pyrrhic victory since the harmful effects of the decision might be never removed.[108]

More recently, the European courts have found that the beneficiary of aid could rely upon a legitimate expectation only where there has been sufficiently precise reassurance, resulting from active intervention of the Commission that a measure is not State aid.[109]

---

106. *Ibid.* (para. 53).
107. *See*, in this sense, Case T-126/99, *Graphischer Maschinenbau v. Commission*, 14.5.2002, ECLI:EU:T:2002:116 (para. 42) and Case C-91/01, *Italy v. Commission* 29.4.2004 (para. 66).
108. *See* Joined Cases T-116/01 and T-118/01, *P&O European Ferries (Vizcaya) SA and Diputación Foral de Vizcaya v. Commission*, 5.8.2003, ECLI:EU:T:2003:217 (paras 206 et seq.), confirmed by AG Tizzano's opinion of 9.2.2006 (paras 154-157) and by the ECJ in case C-442/03 P – *P&O European Ferries (Vizcaya) v. Commission*, 1.6.2006. ECLI:EU:C:2006:356. *See also XXXII Report on Competition Policy* (2003), at point 605. *See also* Advocate General Mazák's opinion of 24 May 2007, in Case C-1/09, *Centre d' exportation du livre français – Ministre de la Culture et de la Communication v. Société internationale de diffusion et d'édition CELF and Ministre de la Culture et de la Communication v. SIDE*, 11.3.2010, ECLI:EU:C:2010:136 (paras 38 et seq.).
109. *See* Joined Cases T-427/04 and T-17/05, *France v. Commission* (paras 259 et seq.), upheld by in Case C-81/10 P (paras 58 et seq.). According to the ECJ, the beneficiary of the aid can rely upon the principle of legitimate expectations provided that the recipient has sufficiently *precise assurances*, arising from a positive action taken by the Commission, which leads him to believe that a measure does not constitute State aid for the purposes of Art. 107(1) TFEU. If the Commission does not give an express opinion on a measure which has been notified to it, however, its *silence* cannot, on the basis of the principle of the protection of the legitimate expectations of the recipient undertaking, preclude recovery of that aid. See to that effect, Joined Cases C-183/02 P and C-187/02 P, *Demesa and Territorio Histórico de Álava v. Commission* 11.11.2004 EU:C:2004:701 (para. 44).

In balancing interests between the legitimate expectations and the position of the party adversely affected by the aid (i.e., the beneficiary's competitor), the ECJ evidently thought the latter deserved protection more than the former. It is fair to surmise that the EU judicature intended to protect the case - objectively not frequently - of a competitor contesting the relevant decision. Yet, while this seems to support the principle of actual judicial protection of third parties' interests, it appears to squeeze the beneficiaries to a disproportionate extent.

Against this background, it is clear that where the national authorities incur the 'original sin' of failing to dutifully observe the notification procedure,[110] whatever action the Commission may take is bound to remain inconsequential.[111]

In a decision, the ECJ found that no legitimate expectation about aid arises even where there have been three positive decisions by the Commission, each subsequently annulled by the Court of Justice. On the contrary, far from giving rise to a legitimate expectation, according to the Court, it would rather appear likely to increase the recipient's doubts as to the compatibility of the disputed aid.[112] One single case of application by the Community Courts of the principle of the protection of legitimate expectation occurred in a proceeding in which the Commission had waited twenty-six months from notification before adopting its final decision ordering recovery.[113] In that case, the Court of Justice held that the Commission's decision was illegal in that it violated that principle.

After having so reviewed the principle of the protection of legitimate expectations in terms of EU law, the focus must be shifted to a Member State's domestic legal

110. Actually, this is inherent in the concept of unlawful State aid and, therefore, in the concept of recovery.
111. Moreover, the Commission's final decision does not have the effect of regularizing *ex post facto* the implementing measures which were invalid because they had been taken in breach of the prohibition laid down by the last sentence of Art. 108(3) of the TFEU. *See* Case C-354/90, *Fédération nationale du commerce extérieur des produits alimentaires et Syndicat national des négociants et transformateurs de saumon v. France*, 21.11.1991, ECLI:EU:C:1991:440 (paras 14 et seq., in particular, para. 16).
112. *See* Case C-1/09, *CELF and Ministre de la Culture et de la Communication v. SIDE, supra* (para. 51).
113. Case C-223/85, *RSV v. Commission*, 24.11.1987, ECLI:EU:C:1987:502 (paras 12 et seq.). An opposite outcome can be found in Joined Cases C-346/03 and C-529/03, *Atzeni and others v. Regione Autonoma della Sardegna*, where the applicant's claim concerning the alleged lengthy Commission procedure (nine years had passed between the institution of the aid scheme and the adoption of the recovery decision) was dismissed by the ECJ who stated that 'some of the delay may be attributed to the Italian Government' (paras 58 et seq.). In that case, in fact, a Regional Law of 1988 had not been notified to the Commission: only in 1992 did the Commission receive a communication about a modification of that law. Moreover, the Italian Government, on several occasions, was slow in responding to the Commission's requests, sometimes taking several months to do so. In Case C-372/97, *Italy v. Commission*, 29.4.2004, ECLI:EU:C:2004:234 (paras 116-118) the Court seemed to confirm the link between excessive delay of procedure and the protection of legitimate expectations. However, the Court stated that such a delay may be imputed to the Commission only from the time when it learnt of the existence of the aid incompatible with the internal market and that a delay of twenty-two months from the moment the Commission had knowledge of the aid to the closure of the formal investigation was not excessive (para. 119).

system, to see whether this principle can successfully be pleaded *before the national courts* as well.

It is the ECJ's settled case law that EU law does not preclude national legislation from considering the protection of legitimate expectations, when excluding the recovery of unduly paid aid, as long as the conditions applied are consistent with those for recovering purely national financial benefits and the interests of the Community are taken fully into account.[114]

Yet, two factors make measures of national legislation for the protection of legitimate expectations hardly applicable in practice:

(1) it is appropriate to observe that the Commission, in initiating the formal investigation procedure pursuant to Article 108(2) TFEU, invariably gives the beneficiaries warning of the 'insecure' status of, and the consequent risk attaching to, any aid granted illegally.[115] Such warning, which is duly published in the Official Journal, is designed, *inter alia*, to involve the beneficiaries in the investigation procedure. It is just obvious that such a caveat undermines one of the requirements indicated above for the application of the Community principle of the protection of legitimate expectations – its very legitimacy, in fact;[116]

(2) as observed earlier, EU case-law has placed on individual traders the burden of using their best endeavours to establish whether the EU procedure has been complied with.[117] In the words of Advocate General Darmon:

> Traders in receipt of State aids are professionals who have a duty to take care [...]. The obligation under which they are placed to verify that prior notification of the aid granted to them has been given to the Commission does not appear to me to be either excessive or particularly difficult to fulfil.[118]

This having been said, it should be acknowledged that there may be cases in which the fundamental rights of an undertaking, *although it has not verified whether the aid had been notified*, should still be granted the protection of legitimate

114. *See* Joined Cases C-205/82 to 215/82, *Deutsche Milchkontor GmbH* (para. 33) and Case C-5/89, *Commission v. Germany* (paras 13-16).

115. As a rule, after having requested the Member State authorities 'to forward a copy of this letter to the potential recipient of the aid immediately', the Commission reminds them that Art. 108(3) TFEU has suspensory effect and draws their attention to Art. 14 of Council Regulation (EC) No. 659/1999, 'which provides that all unlawful aid may be recovered from the recipient'.

116. *See* Case C-5/89, *Commission v. Germany* (para. 15).

117. *Ibid.*, para. 14. Such a formalistic approach is justified by the need to avoid a Member State whose authorities have granted aid contrary to the procedural rules laid down in Art. 108 relying upon the legitimate expectations of recipients to justify a failure to comply with the obligation to take the steps necessary to implement a Commission recovery decision. *See* Case C-5/89, *Commission v. Germany*,(para. 17). *See*, similarly, Regional Administrative Court of Cagliari, First Section, 19 Jan. 2011, Judgment No. 41.

118. *See* the opinion of AG Darmon in Case C-5/89, *Commission v. Germany*, 8.5.1990 EU:C:1990:187 (para. 25).

expectations.[119] Just think of the doubts with which some undertakings may be assailed, when faced with 'atypical' forms of aid, as to whether notification is necessary.[120]

Settled case law has thus conceded that the recipients of State aid illegally granted may, when requested to refund that aid, invoke *exceptional circumstances* on which they relied in legitimately assuming the aid was lawful.[121]

It is for the national court alone to assess the *actual* conduct of the recipient undertaking, if necessary, after obtaining from the Court of Justice a preliminary ruling on interpretation pursuant to Article 267 TFEU and to establish whether such exceptional circumstances did exist in that specific case.[122]

Further hints for thought in the matter of legitimate expectations might have derived from a question the Court of Justice has been faced with following a reference order for a preliminary ruling submitted by the Provincial Tax Commission of Pordenone (Italy).[123] The issue the Court originating the order had been called upon to decide was the validity of a decision of 11 December 2001, whereby the Commission had declared certain provisions of the Ciampi Act to be incompatible with the internal market, much as, in the complainants' view, such provisions duplicated tax advantages already provided for by the previous Amato Act, which had already been scrutinized by the Commission in two previous investigation proceedings relating to State aid – though in different respects – and considered compatible in those respects at that time.

In answering the ECJ's specific question about the resumption of the C-336/04 proceedings, that had been stayed pending the conclusion of the 'parallel' cases C-66/02 and C-148/04 (relating to the same issues of law and dismissed by the Court in its judgment of 15 December 2005), the Provincial Tax Commission of Pordenone had insisted in maintaining its order for reference. By an order issued on 26 March 2006, it submitted the following questions to the ECJ:

> Assuming the substantial coincidence of the object and the addressees between the Amato Act and the Ciampi Act, and based on this assumption in case this Tax

119. *Ibid.* (para. 26).
120. *Ibid.* (para. 26). *See also* the opinion of Advocate General Jacobs delivered on 14.12. 1995 in Case C-39/94, *Syndacat Français de l'Express International (SFEI) v. La Poste and Others*, 1996, ECLI:EU:C:1996:285 (para. 76). An application of the same principle can be found in Commission Decision C(2004)3060 of 2.8.2004 concerning the State aid implemented by France for France Télécom (para. 63).
121. *See* Case C-5/89, *Commission v. Germany* (para. 16); Case C-183/91, *Commission v. Greece*, 1993, ECLI:EU:C:1993:233 (para. 18). *See also* Case T-459/93, *Siemens SA v. Commission*, *supra* (para. 104); Case T-486/93, *Textilwerke Deggendorf GmbG (TWD) v. Commission* 13.9.1995 ECLI:EU:T:1995:160 (para. 69); Case T-67/94, *Ladbroke Racing v. Commission* (para. 182); Case T-55/99, *Confederación Española de Transporte de Mercancías (CETM) v. Commission*, 29.9.2000, ECLI:EU:T:2000:223 (para. 122). More recently, *see also* the judgment of the General Court of, *Deutsche Telekom v. Commission*, T-207/10, 15.11.2018, ECLI: EU:T:2018:786 (para. 42).
122. *See* Case C-5/89, *Commission v. Germany*, *supra* (para. 16). In the same sense, *see* Case T-486/93, *TWD v. Commission*,(para. 69) and Case T-55/99, *CETM v. Commission* (para. 122).
123. *See* Case C-336/04 *Banca Popolare FriulAdria S.p.A. v. Agenzia delle Entrate, Ufficio di Pordenone*, 14.9.2006, ECLI:EU:C:2006:567.

Commission has established it to be so, may the Court of Justice rule that there is a legitimate expectation in the case in issue (Banca FriulAdria) or *should it refer the case to the national courts for actual assessment?* Based on the same assumption, does not the Court deem the Commission Decision of 11 December 2001 to be flawed because of the Commission's failure to provide grounds for changing its previous conclusions on the legislation in question?

The actual, novel departure from the *Unicredito* judgment of the Court of Justice[124] was the way in which rules of national legislation (the Amato Act and the Ciampi Act) were interpreted by the Provincial Tax Commission of Pordenone. In its view, it was for the national court, not for the ECJ, *to assess the material case*, specifically as to what extent two Italian set of rules matched each other in relation to the facts at issue. By holding this to be the case, as clearly emerges from the order for reference, the national court seemed to claim precedence in establishing the actual occurrence of legitimate expectations – something the EU judicature has consistently affirmed.

Yet, the Court of Justice missed this particular opportunity. In a mere order, it referred to its own *Unicredito* judgment without picking up on the novelty indicated above.[125]

In conclusion, the protection of legitimate expectations is, in fact, apt to cripple the aid recovery procedure only if the national court called upon to settle the issue, recognizes the existence of such exceptional circumstances surrounding a recipient of illegal aid as to warrant protection, though invariably in compliance with the compelling requirements of EU law. Moreover, it has been the EU Court's constant view that the occurrence of legitimate expectations is subject to a stringent burden of proof placed upon the complaining undertaking and cannot be demonstrated on the basis of mere presumption.[126]

The EU judicature has failed – intentionally, perhaps – to provide a precise definition of 'exceptional circumstances'.[127] For example, the Court of First Instance

124. Case C-148/04, *Unicredito Italiano v. Agenzia delle Entrate, Ufficio Genova 1*.
125. *See* the ECJ Order of 14 Sep. 2006 *ex* Art. 104(3) of the ECJ Rules of Procedure. The Provincial Tax Commission of Pordenone delivered its final judgment on the merits on 27 Feb.-27 Mar. 2007. The Pordenone Commission recognized that the ECJ had failed: (i) to answer the question of who was to assess legitimate expectations in that case; and (ii) to rule on the interpretation the Tax Commission gave of the rules of national law under scrutiny (Amato Act and Ciampi Act). On these assumptions the national judge could well have expressed its independent judgment as to legitimate expectations and, therefore, could have granted the refund of the sum unduly paid by Banca Popolare FriulAdria. Notwithstanding, the Pordenone Commission rejected the appeal complying with the ECJ decision 'in accordance with the principle that Community law and the laws of Member States are integrated into one body of laws, subject to the prevalence of the rules of Community law over the national laws of Member States'.
126. *See* the opinion of AG Darmon in Case C-5/89, *Commission v. Germany* (para. 26).
127. There are cases in which the conduct of the Commission could originate a legitimate expectation: for example, the interpretative difficulties that can rise from a Commission Notice or from the qualification as a new State aid of an existing State aid or vice versa. Then, there are some situations in which the qualification of the measure as 'State aid' or as 'new State aid' is objectively doubtful. A complex hypothesis can be represented by aids granted to an indeterminate number of recipients or by 'diffuse' State aids set forth in general measures.

ruled, in *CETM*, that neither the SMEs' purported unawareness of the rules applicable to State aid nor the complexity of the State aid notion could be pleaded as exceptional circumstances suitable to justify legitimate expectations as to the lawfulness of the aid granted. Nor may aid recipients be relieved, based on considerations as to their size, from the duty to keep abreast with any provisions of EU law, lest the material effects of the Community law system should be jeopardized.[128]

The EU Courts have clarified that, in proceedings *before national courts*, it is not for the Member State concerned, but for the recipient undertaking, to plead such exceptional circumstances.[129]

The Recovery Notice consolidates the principles settled by the case law of the ECJ and provides an overview of the situations that do not create legitimate expectations,[130] i.e.:

- the silence of the Commission on an aid measure notified to it;
- any apparent failure of the Commission to react to an aid measure which was not notified;
- the adoption of a decision opening a formal investigation pursuant to Article 6 of the Procedural Regulation, in which the Commission merely carries out a provisional assessment of the aid measures at issue, since an aid beneficiary cannot base legitimate expectations on a provisional decision;
- absence of action by the Commission for a relatively long period;
- an earlier decision from the Commission;
- the adoption of several successive Commission decisions authorizing the grant of aid, subsequently annulled by the Luxembourgish Courts;
- a proposal for a decision from the Commission submitted to the Council.

[B] Other Principles of EU Law

Attempts to invoke other principles of EU law with a view to having the Commission's recovery decisions annulled have equally gone unheard by the EU Courts.[131]

128. *See* Case T-55/99, *CETM v. Commission* (para. 126); Case T-486/93, *TWD v. Commission* (para. 73) and Case C-83/98 P, *France v. Ladbroke Racing and Commission* (paras 59-61).
129. *See* Case T-459/93, *Siemens SA v. Commission* (para. 104) and Case T-67/94, *Ladbroke Racing v. Commission* (para. 183). *See also* the opinion of AG Darmon in Case C-5/89, *Commission v. Germany* (para. 26) and the opinion of AG Tesauro in Case C-169/95, *Spain v. Commission* (para. 14). In that opinion Advocate General Tesauro stated that 'the Court has drawn an important distinction between the situation of the undertaking in receipt of the aid and that of the Member State which has paid it'. Furthermore, according to Advocate General Tizzano, it is appropriate to distinguish between the reference to the legitimate expectations of the public authorities which granted the aid and those of the recipient of the aid: *see* the opinion of 9 Feb. 2006 in Case C-442/03 P, *P&O European Ferries (Vizcaya) SA and Diputación Foral de Vizcaya v. Commission.*
130. Recovery Notice 2019, p. 42.
131. For a case in which the principle of equal treatment was recognized, *see* Joined Cases C-182/03 and C-217/03, *Belgium and Forum 187 ASBL v. Commission* (paras 170-175) and the opinion of Advocate General Léger (paras 455-464). In that case, the ECJ – following on this matter the

In Case C-142/87, the Belgian government argued that the obligation to recover an aid imposed in a negative decision of the Commission ordering recovery of the aid was disproportionate to the objectives laid down in Articles 107 e 108 TFEU, inasmuch as the declaration of the debt by the Belgian State in the composition procedure would have led the beneficiary to bankruptcy, thereby causing serious damage to other creditors.[132] The ECJ turned down this argument, by ruling that recovery of unlawful aid is the logical consequence of the finding that it is unlawful.[133]

Consequently, the recovery of State aid unlawfully granted – which is intended, as observed above, to restore the previously existing situation – cannot in principle be regarded as disproportionate to the objectives of the Treaty in regard to State aid.[134] The same principle was asserted by the Court in regard to the charging of interest in respect of the period between the payment of the aid and its actual repayment.[135]

The Hellenic government argued, with respect to aid unlawfully granted in the form of a *tax exemption*, which would, as such, violate the general principles of EU law, that recovery must necessarily take the form of a *retroactive tax*.[136] On the basis of the precedent referred to above, the ECJ rejected such a censure, by stating that the authorities of the Member State granting the aid merely have to take measures ordering the undertakings that have received the aid to pay sums corresponding to the amount of the tax exemption unlawfully granted to them.

In *Saltzgitter*, the General Court stated for the first time that the Commission had infringed the principle of *legal certainty*. The General Court found that the legal

---

Advocate General – 'derived' the violation of such principle from the violation of the legitimate expectation principle. The infringement of the principle of equal treatment made by the Commission consisted in not holding that all centres of coordination could benefit of the authorization until 31 Dec. 2010.

132. Case C-142/87, *'Tubemeuse'* (para. 65).

133. *Ibid.*, at para. 66. *See also* Case C-310/85, *Deufil GmbH & Co. KG v. Commission*, 24.2.1987, ECLI:EU:C:1987:96; Joined Cases C-278/92, C-279/92 and C-280/92, *Spain v. Commission* (para. 75); Case C-404/97, *Commission v. Portugal*,; Case C-298/00 P, *Italy v. Commission*, 29.4.2004, ECLI:EU:C:2004:240 (paras 103 and 104); Case C-148/04, *Unicredito Italiano* (paras 113-121); Case T-298/97, *Alzetta and Others v. Commission*, 15.6.2000, ECLI:EU:T:2000:151 (para. 169); Case T-288/97, *Regione Autonoma Friuli Venezia Giulia v. Commission*, 4.4.2001, ECLI:EU:T:2001:115 (para. 105); C-164/15 P and C-165/15 P, Aer Lingus and Ryanair, 21.12.2016, ECLI:EU:C:2016:990 (paras 89-90); C-349/17, *Eesti Pagar*, 5.3.2019, ECLI: EU:C:2019:172 (para. 31); T-121/15, *Fortischem and Others v. Commission*, 24 Sep. 24.9.2019, ECLI:EU: T:2019:684 (para. 205); C-627/18. Nelson Antunes da Cunha, 30.4.2020, ECLI: EU:C:2020:321 (para. 42).

134. However, in Case C-148/04, *Unicredito Italiano*, the ECJ acknowledged that 'reestablishing the *status quo ante* ... enables account to be taken, at the stage of recovery of the aid by the national authorities, of tax treatment which may be more favourable than the ordinary treatment which, in the absence of unlawful aid and in accordance with domestic rules which are compatible with Community law, would have been granted on the basis of the operation actually carried out' (para. 119 of the judgment). Therefore, compliance with the principle of proportionality and with the rationale behind a recovery order (restoring the *status quo ante* and not making worse the recipient's condition) would imply a comparative analysis of the tax advantage granted by the aid measure and of the *ordinary treatment* which would have been granted in the absence of such aid. In the same sense *see* the reasoning of the Genoa Tax Provincial Commission order.

135. *See* Case C-169/95, *Spain v. Commission* (para. 47).

136. *See* Case C-183/91, *Commission v. Greece* (para. 17).

situation concerning the need to notify a certain measure was characterized by uncertainty and lack of clarity, which was imputable to the Commission. Therefore, in the specific circumstances of the case, the Commission could not order the recovery of the aid without infringing the fundamental principle of legal certainty. However, the ECJ annulled the judgment of the General Court stating that the General Court did not examine whether the Commission had manifestly failed to act and clearly breached its duty of diligence in the exercise of its supervisory power. The ECJ stressed that this is the sole ground which, in exceptional cases can render illegal a Commission decision ordering recovery.[137]

Finally, it is worth noting that the Commission partially renounced order recovery in the *Alcoa* decision by evoking the *principle of good administration.* The Commission had written a letter to the Italian authorities that might have created the impression that the aid could have been considered compatible.[138]

[C] National Statutes of Limitations

As noted above, once the Commission has issued a recovery decision, all necessary steps to effect recovery must be taken under the national law of the Member State concerned (Article 14(3) of Regulation 659/1999). The relevant measures provided for in individual national legal systems may, however, be found in conflict with EU law.

National authorities have frequently claimed domestic provisions attributing a special value to the passing of time – i.e., statutes of limitations with a view to protecting legitimate expectation and legal certainty – to justify non-compliance with an order for recovery issued under a decision of the Commission. As a rule, the recovery measures directly affecting aid recipients are administrative acts of *revocation* setting aside measures formerly introduced to grant aid.

In Cases 94/87 and C-5/89, the German Government contended before the Court of Justice that a provision of its domestic legal system (paragraph 48 of the *Verwaltungsverfahrensgesetz*, the law on administrative procedure) prohibited the revocation of an administrative measure granting a benefit if more than one year had passed since the administrative authority became aware of the circumstances that justified the revocation.[139] According to the German Government, it was absolutely impossible for

137. *See* Case T-308/00, *Salzgitter v. Commission*, 22.1.2013, ECLI:EU:T:2013:30 and Case C-408/04, *Commission v. Salzgitter*, 22.4.2008, ECLI:EU:C:2008:236. Following the ECJ judgment, the General Court adopted a fresh decision finding that the Commission did not commit a manifest violation of its duty of diligence.
138. Commission Decision of 19 Nov. 2009 on State measures C38/A/04 (ex NN 58/04) and C 36/B/06 (ex NN 38/06) implemented by Italy for Alcoa Trasformazione.
139. *See* Case C-94/87, *Commission v. Germany*, 2.2.1989, ECLI:EU:C:1989:46 (para. 6); Case C-5/89, *Commission v. Germany*, 20.9.1990, ECLI:EU:C:1990:320 (paras 9-11). In its Defence in Case C-5/89, the German Government first stated that the one-year period had in any event already expired when the Commission adopted its decision in that case, because it had started to run when the competent authority of the Land of Baden-Württemberg granted the aid in question in 1985. In its Rejoinder, instead, the German Government suggested that the one-year period should be made to run from the date on which the Commission became aware of the aid.

a public administration, under that provision and pursuant to the German constitutional principles, to revoke an illegal administrative measure that had created any rights, without first weighing the different interests at stake. Thus, the relevant national authority was required to prioritize the protection of the legitimate expectations of the undertaking that received the aid over the Community's public interest in recovering the aid.

The ECJ, on the basis of the effectiveness principle mentioned above, turned down this contention and stated that a provision laying down a time limit for the revocation of an administrative act of entitlement must, like all the relevant provisions of national law, be applied in such a way that the recovery required by EU law is not rendered practically impossible.[140]

The situation is quite different in Italy. True, an administrative measure whereby recovery of aid is ordered qualifies as an act for the *revocation* of the previous administrative measure under which aid was granted. But no administrative act may be set aside subject to an express time limit, so that any such act may be revoked by a public authority even after considerable time has elapsed from the effective date of the act to be so revoked. In general, the revocation of a previous administrative act may be ordered if this is justified on grounds of public interest. Settled Italian case law requires that such grounds be adequately reasoned, including in terms of their prevalence over the protection of any expectations as the execution of the act to be so set aside might have created among the intended recipients of the aid. Such prevalence criterion must also be met where the administrative measure involved might have originally violated an existing requirement of law, in that the mere restoration of legality is not deemed to provide, *alone, sufficient grounds* for revocation.

Italian legal doctrine and case law qualify the power to revoke administrative acts as independent of the one attributed by the provision of law based on which the act to be revoked was issued in the first place. Specifically, such power has been deemed to be a general power under the *principle of administrative self-protection*, itself an expression of the principle of *proper and fair operation of public affairs* laid down in Article 97 of the Italian Constitution.[141] In general, the revocation of an administrative act presupposes adequate weighing of an actual public interest in revocation against the sacrifice of private interest. Though the time span between the act formerly issued and its revocation is relevant to the obligation to provide reasoned grounds, which is more stringent the longer the time elapsed, it is not *in itself* a time limit to revocation.

In relation to powers of revocation, Article 21*quinquies* (*Revocation of a decision*) of Law 241/1990 requires that:

140. *See* Case C-5/89, *Commission v. Germany* (para. 19); Joined Cases C-205/82 to 215/82, *Deutsche Milchkontor GmbH* (paras 18-25); Case C-94/87, *Commission v. Germany* (para. 12); Case T-486/93, *TWD v. Commission* (paras 66 et seq.) and Case T-459/93, *Siemens SA v. Commission* (paras 82 et seq.).

141. *Consiglio di Stato*, section V, 18 Jun. 2002, No. 6389, *Foro amm.*, 2002, 2910; *Consiglio di Stato*, section V, 19 May 1998, No. 633, *Appalti urbanistica edilizia*, 1999, No. 87; *Consiglio di Stato*, section IV, 23 Jan. 1988, No. 20, *Foro amm.*, 1988, 40; *TAR Lazio*, 8 Jan. 1993, No. 15, *I T.A.R.* 1993, No. 367.

> For intervening reasons of public interest or in case a change has occurred in the situation in fact, or the original public interest has been newly assessed, the administrative act with lasting effects may be revoked by the authority which first issued it or by any other body provided for by law. Revocation will cause the act so revoked to be incapable to generate any further effects [...].

In connection with the matter here under scrutiny, it appears easy to qualify a recovery decision issued by the Commission as an 'intervening reason of public interest' or a 'new assessment of the original public interest' in its being a decision of a Community authority every Member State is required to comply with.

In terms of contents, a recovery decision does not appear to be an order intended merely to restore legality, since recovery of aid has a clear financial purport consisting – as discussed above – of the repayment of sums paid in the past. This fact becomes materially important when public interest is weighed against private interest, in that it is settled case law that the recovery of any sums unlawfully paid (whether as State aid or otherwise) by public authorities is regarded *in itself* as an issue of public interest in itself, which overrides any other interests at stake.

Based on the foregoing considerations, an order for recovery issued by the competent national authority is not, under the Italian legal system, subject to either a term of expiration or a term of limitation (except for the 'general' ten-year limitation period imposed on the Commission).

Conversely, since the order for the recovery of illegal aid ultimately resulted from the unlawful conduct of the Italian State, which issued aid without giving prior notification to the Commission, it appears interesting to highlight a *compensatory* provision contained in the reform of the Italian legislation on revocation. The second part of Article 21*quinquies* of Act 241/1990 referred to above requires, in general, that:

> if revocation is prejudicial to the persons directly concerned, then the administrative authority is under an obligation to pay damages to them. Any disputes as to the determination and payment of damages shall be referred to the exclusive jurisdiction of the administrative court.

It will be interesting to see whether this provision may, when actually applied in court, be claimed by an undertaking that has been granted unlawful State aid and is, therefore, expected to repay the relevant sums. Yet, a serious obstacle may hamper compensation, since, as indicated above, any undertaking eligible for a grant of State aid is liable to the specific obligation to verify the *lawfulness* of the aid about to be awarded to it, and so its claim to be paid damages should be deemed admissible less because of a prejudice it suffered from the *repayment in itself* than because of other behaviours – assumedly prejudicial and 'fringe' ones, in fact – of the Italian State.

As for the date on which the applicable period should be made to run, Advocate General Darmon considered that the adoption by the Commission of a final decision on the incompatibility of the aid with the common market constitutes the starting point for the time within which the measure granting the aid that has been unlawfully maintained is to be withdrawn.[142] This approach was shared by the ECJ in a later judgment it delivered following a reference for a preliminary ruling, whereby it held that the recipient of unlawfully granted aid ceases to be in a state of uncertainty once the Commission has adopted a decision finding the aid incompatible with the common market and requiring recovery. This is because the principle of legal certainty cannot preclude repayment of the aid on the ground that the national authorities *were late* in complying with the decision requiring such repayment. If it could, recovery of unduly paid sums would be rendered practically impossible and the EU provisions concerning State aid deprived of effectiveness.[143]

[D] Absolute Impossibility to Recover Aid

The only defence available to a Member State in validly opposing an application by the Commission under Article 108(2) of the TFEU for a declaration that it has failed to fulfil its Treaty obligations is to plead that it was absolutely impossible for it to implement the decision properly.[144] According to the EU judicature, the national authorities' failure to recover sums paid under an unlawful aid system may only be justified if they have encountered such *unforeseen or unforeseeable difficulties* as to make implementation of the decision absolutely impossible.[145]

In such a case, the Member State concerned must, pursuant to Article 4 TEU,[146] discharge its duty of genuine cooperation with the Commission, by giving it prompt notice of such difficulties, while fully observing the Treaty provisions, and in particular the provisions on aid.[147] However, the condition of an absolute impossibility of implementation is by no means fulfilled if the government concerned has merely submitted the difficulties it has encountered in implementing the decision to the

142. *See* the opinion of AG Darmon in Case C-5/89, *Commission v. Germany* (para. 31). *See also* the judgment of the Administrative Court of Appeal of Nordrhein-Westfalen Region, 9 Jan. 1992, in the *Deufil* case (Commission Decision of 10 Jul. 1985, OJ 1985 L278/26) and the ruling of the *Cour Administrative d'Appel de Paris*, 5 Oct. 2004, *Ministre de la Culture, CELF et SIDE* (*see*, in particular, the conclusions of M. Pascal Trouilly, *Commissaire du Gouvernement*), that invites the Court not to take into account the principle set forth in the previous judgment of the *Conseil d'Etat*, 26 Oct. 2001, *Ternon*. In the latter ruling, the *Conseil d'Etat* had stated that administrative (even illegal) acts generating rights could be revoked *only within four months* from their adoption.

143. Case C-24/95, *Land Rheinland-Pfalz v. Alcan Deutschland* (paras 36-37).

144. Case C-348/93, *Commission v. Italy* (para. 16) and Case C-404/97, *Commission v. Portugal* (para. 39).

145. This principle has been affirmed by the ECJ since 1986 in the *Boch* case: Case C-85/85, *Commission v. Belgium*, 18.3.1986, ECLI:EU:C:1986:129 (para. 16). It has been reiterated in several judgments: Case C-5/86, *Commission v. Belgium*, 9.4.91987, ECLI:EU:C:1987:198 (paras 8 et seq.); Case C-94/87, *Commission v. Germany* (para. 9); Case C-348/93, *Commission v. Italy*, 4.4.1995, ECLI:EU:C:1995:95; Case C-348/93, *Commission v. Italy* (para. 17); Case C-404/97, *Commission v. Portugal* (para. 40).

146. The Art. 10 of the Treaty has been replaced in the substance by the Art. 4, para. 3 of the (EU) Treaty.

147. Case C-404/97, *Commission v. Portugal* (para. 41); Case C-404/00, *Commission v. Spain*, 26.6.2003, ECLI:EU:C:2003:373 (para. 46); Case C-99/02, *Commission v. Italy*, 1.4.2004, ECLI:EU:C:2004:207 (para. 17).

Commission, without taking any effective steps with the recipient's undertakings to recover the aid and without making any proposals whatever to the Commission for the adoption of other suitable measures to overcome such difficulties.[148]

The ECJ has not only failed to provide a general definition of 'absolute impossibility to implement the decision' but also to concede the existence of any grounds for such absolute impossibility.[149] On many an occasion, it has, however, specified in which cases adequate reasons for the existence of such impossibility cannot be pleaded. According to the ECJ, absolute impossibility cannot be claimed by merely alleging any serious consequences[150] or legal, political or practical difficulties[151] that may arise from implementing a recovery decision.

In the case of tax credit granted to haulers, the Italian Republic had claimed, first, that any demand for the payment of the sums in question would cause social conflict from which the State could only emerge as the loser, and second, that the technical operations necessary to recover those sums would raise problems that might reasonably be considered to be insuperable, given the huge number of persons concerned and the need to break down the tax credit as between various taxes and rates of tax. The Court simply noted that, since the Italian Government *had made no attempt* to recover the tax credit in question, implementation of the decision to effect recovery could not be shown to be impossible.[152]

An interesting case of application of the *legal impossibility* to implement a recovery decision is provided by a decision delivered by the *Consiglio di Stato* in an action pending between Lucchini Siderurgica S.p.A. and the Ministry for Industry, Commerce and Craft Trades.[153] The relevant facts can be summarized as follows: in 1985, Lucchini had received a State aid from the *Cassa per il Mezzogiorno* (Fund for the

148. *See* Case C-94/87, *Commission v. Germany* (para. 10); Case C-404/97, *Commission v. Portugal* (para. 52); Case C-404/00, *Commission v. Spain* (para. 47); Case C-99/02, *Commission v. Italy* (para. 18); Case C-207/05, *Commission v. Italy* (para. 48).
149. However, a Member State which, in giving effect to a Commission decision on State aid, encounters unforeseen and unforeseeable difficulties or becomes aware of consequences overlooked by the Commission, is not prevented from submitting those problems to the Commission for consideration, together with proposals for suitable amendments to the decision in question. In such cases, the Commission and the Member State must, by virtue of the rule imposing on the Member States and the Community institutions a duty of genuine cooperation which underlies, in particular, Art. 10 EC, work together in good faith with a view to overcoming the difficulties while fully observing the Treaty provisions and, in particular, the provisions on aid. *See* Case C-378/98, *Commission v. Belgium*, 3.7.2001, ECLI:EU:C:2001:370 (para. 31).
150. *See* Case C-457/98, *Commission v. Greece*, 14.12.2000, ECLI:EU:C:2000:692. *See also* Case C-404/97, *Commission v. Portugal* (para. 53).
151. *See* Case C-94/87, *Commission v. Germany* (para. 10); Case C-183/91, *Commission v. Greece* (para. 20); Case C-280/95, *Commission v. Italy*, 29.1.1998, ECLI:EU:C:1998:28 (para. 14).
152. *See* Case C-6/97, *Italy v. Commission*, 19.5.1999, ECLI:EU:C:1999:251 (paras 32-34). In the Case C-348/93, *Commission v. Italy*, the Italian Government merely referred, in very general terms, to difficulties connected with the winding up of EFIM and claimed that the non-recovery of the aid in question was accounted for by the procedure for considering new aid envisaged as part of the restructuring programme (para. 15 of the judgment). *See also* Case C-280/95, *Commission v. Italy* (para. 15) and Case C-378/98, *Commission v. Belgium* (para. 32).
153. *See Consiglio di Stato*, section VI, Decision and order of referral to the ECJ, 22 Oct. 2004-16 Feb. 2005, in www.giustizia-amministrativa.it.

Development of the South) in the form of a planned scheme of public grants. The *Cassa per il Mezzogiorno* was shortly replaced with *Agensud* (the Southern Development Agency), which failed, however, to award the planned grants because, in the meanwhile, the Commission had, by Notice No. 497 of 13 January 1989, determined that aid to be contrary to ECSC Decision No. 484/1985. Lucchini sued *Agensud* before the Tribunal of Rome seeking an order against *Agensud* for the payment of the planned amount. The Tribunal of Rome upheld this request and its decision was subsequently confirmed by the Appellate Court of Rome in Judgment No. 2238 of 6 May 1994. On 29 December 1995, after this judgment had conclusively been entered as res judicata, Lucchini notified the Ministry for Industry (by then the successor to *Agensud*) of an injunction whereby the Ministry was ordered to pay the relevant sum. Thereupon, in order to avoid forced execution, the Ministry paid Lucchini such sum, though expressly requiring recovery thereof.

In a notice dated 15 July 1996, the Commission pointed out that both judgments delivered by the Tribunal of Rome and the Appellate Court patently clashed with ECSC Decision No. 484/1985, and, in its subsequent Notice No. 5259 of 16 September 1996, the Commission ordered the Italian Government to recover the aid. The Ministry then adopted a Decree of the Director General for Manufacturing dated 20 September 1996, whereby it revoked the grant and ordered Lucchini S.p.A. to repay the amount it had been awarded.

Lucchini impugned the ministerial decree for revocation before the *TAR* (Regional Administrative Tribunal) of Lazio, alleging that the res judicata under the Rome Appellate Court's judgment had made its right to receive the grant indisputable. By Judgment No. 1831/1999, the Third Chamber of the *TAR* of Lazio upheld Lucchini's claim. The Ministry impugned the judgment before the State Council and the case was litigated in the Sixth Section. By the decision here under scrutiny, the State Council found the issue of law so raised to be relevant and material, in that it brought out an objective conflict between (i) a civil court's final judgment, which forced compliance upon an administrative body, pursuant to Article 4(2) of Act No. 2248 of 20 March 1865, a time-honoured provision still in force, and (ii) a Community decision of the opposite sign. Therefore, by its order of reference dated 22 October 2004-16 February 2005, the Sixth Chamber of the State Council requested the ECJ to give a preliminary ruling pursuant to Article 234 EC (now Article 267 TFEU) in relation to a judicial decision that had become res judicata, pursuant to Article 2909 of Italy's Civil Code, on one hand, and a contrasting Commission decision.[154]

---

154. The question submitted to the EU judge, translated unofficially from the Italian version, was:

> (1) In light of the principle of the primacy of immediately applicable Community law, in the form in this case of general ECSC Decision No. 3484 of 1985, the Commission decision of 20 Jun. 1990, notified on 20 Jul. 1990, and Commission Decision No. 5259 of 16 Sep. 1996, requiring the recovery of aid–which all formed the basis for the recovery measure challenged in the present proceedings (namely Decree No. 20357 of 20 Sep. 1996 overturning Decrees Nos 17975 of 8 Mar. 1996 and 18337 of 3 Apr. 1996) – is it legally possible and compulsory for the national administrative authority to recover aid from a private recipient even though a final civil judgment has been delivered confirming the unconditional obligation to pay the aid in question?

In its judgment, the Court of Justice held that EU law precluded the application of a provision of national law, such as Article 2909 of the Italian Civil Code (which seeks to lay down the principle of res judicata) in so far as the application of that provision prevented the recovery of State aid that was granted in breach of Community law and which had been found to be incompatible with the common market in a decision of the Commission which had become final.[155]

An interesting set of facts in which *Lucchini* was not applied was addressed in the infringing procedure brought by the Commission against the *Slovak Republic* for failure to comply with a recovery decision.[156] In that ruling, the ECJ distinguished the case from Lucchini on the basis that the internal decision possessed of the force of res judicata relied upon by the Slovak Republic (a judgment approving the agreement in the arrangement with creditors) had preceded the decision whereby the Commission required the recovery of the aid at issue. As a result, the Court of Justice found that the *Lucchini* precedent was not of direct relevance to the case.

The Court emphasized the importance, both in the European Union legal order and in the national legal orders, of the principle of res judicata. In order to ensure stability of the law and legal relations, as well as the sound administration of justice, it is important that judicial decisions which have become definitive after all rights of appeal have been exhausted or after the expiry of the time limits provided to exercise those rights can no longer be called into question.[157] Accordingly, the ECJ clarified that EU law does not in all circumstances require a national court to disapply domestic rules of procedure conferring the force of res judicata on a judgment, even if to do so would make it possible to remedy an infringement of European Union law by the judgment in question.

Likely the Court was concerned to reassert the importance of res judicata as a principle, perhaps because of the risks that its decision in that case carried. Having restated the importance of such principle, in the final analysis, the Court of Justice did effectively disapply the national judgment, finding that the Slovak Republic failed to show that it had taken all the measures necessary to recover the aid from the beneficiary. In any case, the principle established in *Lucchini* has become consolidated

---

(2) Or, in view of the generally accepted principle that decisions on the recovery of aid are governed by Community law but the implementation thereof and the associated recovery procedure, in the absence of Community provisions on the matter, is governed by national law (regarding which principle *see* the judgment of the Court of Justice in Joined Cases C-205/82 to 215/82, *Deutsche Milchkontor GmbH*), is the recovery procedure rendered legally impossible by virtue of a specific judicial decision that has become res judicata (Art. 2909 of the Civil Code), thereby being conclusive as between the private individual and the administration, and requires the administration to comply with it?

155. *See* Case C-119/05 *Ministry of Industry v. Lucchini S.p.A.*, 18.7.2007, ECLI:EU:C:2007:434 (para. 63). In the opinion he delivered on 14 Sep. 2006, Advocate General Geelhoed considered that the Court should decide preliminary issues first, such that a judgment by a national court that is res judicata cannot impinge upon the Commission's powers under Arts 87 and 88 EC.
156. Case C-508/08, *Commission v. Slovak Republic*, 6.10.2011, ECLI:EU:C:2010:643.
157. *Ibid.* (para. 59).

case law and has been even by national jurisdictions.[158] With specific regard to unlawful aid, while the rules implementing the principle of res judicata are a matter for the legal system of each Member State in accordance with the principle of procedural autonomy, they cannot render any final decision by a national court an obstacle, nor can they have the consequence of making it impossible for the national courts or authorities to draw the necessary consequences from the breach of the standstill obligation.[159]

Another standard sometimes relied upon by Member States in support of allegations as to the absolute impossibility of recovering aid is – quite understandably – the recipient undertakings' *difficult financial position*, whether in existence or likely to result from implementing the decision properly. Yet, in the ECJ's case law, not even the difficult financial position of an undertaking receiving aid *in the form of capital injection may* be pleaded in alleging the impossibility of implementing the decision. This is because the objective to abolish the aid can well be attained by proceedings for winding up the company, which the Member State's authorities could institute in their capacity as shareholders or creditors.[160]

158. *See* the judgment of the Italian Supreme Court of Cassation 23418/2010: In terms of recovery of State aid, the national legislation on limitation must be disapplied for conflict with the principle of effectiveness of Community law, if such legislation prevents the recovery of State aid declared incompatible with a decision of the European Commission which has become final. Interestingly, in that judgment the Italian Supreme Court of Cassation held that it would not make sense, in this regard, to appeal to the so-called counterlimits theory developed by some internal constitutional courts as a defence of state sovereignty in the event that it was threatened by community primacy in some values considered indispensable by the internal system. On the one hand, it is difficult to ascribe the prescription pursuant to art. 2946 c.c. within the scope of the 'indispensable values of the legal system', on the other hand, the same theory of counter limits, if it found reasonable justifications in the 70-80s of the last century, when the integration process was in its initial phases, today seems to be in clear contradiction with the very concept of integration as it has developed today, both in light of the evolution of the jurisprudence of the Court of Justice – which has provided sufficient evidence of protection of fundamental rights – and for the incorporation or reference to the Charter of Fundamental Rights of the European Union, also having binding value towards the European institutions. To the point that the conflict between community and state law no longer seems conceivable in a truly integrated European legal space.
159. *See* Recovery Notice 2019, p. 46, and related footnote 56, which quotes the judgment of the Court of Justice of 11 Nov. 2015, Klausner Holz Niedersachsen, C-505/14, ECLI:EU:C:2015:742 (para. 40); *see also* Judgment of the Court of Justice of 5 Mar. 2019, Eesti Pagar, C-349/17, ECLI:EU:C:2019:172 (paras 138 et seq). Notably, in the latter judgment the ECJ clarifies that 'A national rule that would prevent a national judge or a national authority from taking action to respond to the consequences of an infringement of the third sentence of Article 108(3) TFEU must be regarded as being incompatible with the principle of effectiveness [...] In this case, it is clear from that case-law that, while unlawful aid must be recovered in accordance with the rules of the applicable national law, the fact remains that Article 108(3) TFEU requires those rules to ensure full recovery of the unlawful aid and that, therefore, the beneficiary of that aid must be ordered to pay, inter alia, interest for the whole of the period over which it benefited from that aid and at a rate equivalent to that which would have been applied if the beneficiary had had to borrow the amount of the aid at issue on the market within that period.'
160. *See* Case C-52/84, *Commission v. Belgium*, 15.1.1986, ECLI:EU:C:1986:3 (para. 14). With the same meaning, *see* Case C-5/86, *Commission v. Belgium*, *supra* (paras 6 et seq.), in which the Belgian Government implemented the winding up of the company after the term prescribed by the Commission.

Further, in *Tubemeuse*, the ECJ was requested to assess the Belgian Government's claim that the Commission had disregarded the fact that Tubemeuse was undergoing judicial composition proceedings when the contested decision was adopted and, therefore, such a decision could not be implemented.[161] In this respect, the Belgian government had submitted that:

- the contested decision was without purpose, and thus not liable to implementation, since the undertaking had ceased to exist in economic terms;
- the state of composition in bankruptcy made immediate implementation impossible; and
- because of pending judicial composition proceedings, the obligation to recover the aid was disproportionate.

First, the Court found the Belgian Government's submission that the contested decision was without purpose to be unacceptable. For it was common ground that Tubemeuse continued its production activities, albeit at a reduced rate, throughout the composition proceedings and that it was ultimately sold to another undertaking.[162] Second, the Court found that the fact that the recipient undertaking was subject to composition proceeding was not, in itself, sufficient ground to argue for the absolute impossibility of implementing the decision. For the Member State could fulfil its obligations in regard to the recovery of the aid by having its debt registered as one of Tubemeuse's unsecured liabilities.[163]

Moreover, the Court referred its own *Deufil* precedent, according to which recovery of unlawful aid is the logical consequence of the finding that it is unlawful. Consequently, the recovery of State aid unlawfully granted for the purpose of re-establishing the previously existing situation cannot in principle be regarded as disproportionate to the objectives of the Treaty in regard to State aids.[164]

In case T-52/12 R, the President of the General Court *temporarily suspended* a Commission decision ordering recovery of illegal aid that Greece granted to farmers who suffered damage from natural causes. The reason for granting interim relief from recovery was the *financial situation of the beneficiaries* and social situation in Greece: the Court held that due to the *exceptional circumstances* that Greece is facing priority should be given to preserving the economic and social peace.[165] The General Court, however, did not confirm this position on the *merit* and rejected the request for annulment of the recovery decision brought by Greece.[166]

161. *See* Case C-142/87, '*Tubemeuse*'.
162. *Ibid.* (para. 51).
163. *Ibid.*, at paras 60-63.
164. *See* Case C-142/87, '*Tubemeuse*', *supra* (para. 66 that mentions the ECJ judgment in Case C-310/85, *Deufil v. Commission, supra*); T-298/97, etc., *Alzetta and Others v. Commission*, 15.6.2000, ECLI:EU:T:2000:151 (para. 170); T-288/97, Regione Friuli-Venezia Giulia/Commission, 4 Apr. 2001, EU: T:2001:115 (para. 106).
165. Order of the President of the General Court in Case T-52/12 R, *Greece v. Commission* (Order of 19 Sep. 2012), published in the electronic Reports of Cases.
166. *Ibid.*

Finally, in *ICI*, dealing with certain tax exemptions granted to the Italian State to real estate used by non-commercial entities (e.g., involved in religious activities) the Commission accepted the Member State's claim that recovery was *absolutely impossible* because, due to the lack of data in the Italian cadastre relating to the period preceding the decision, the beneficiaries of the aid could not be identified and the aid could not be calculated objectively.[167]

Subsequently, the Courts of Luxembourg clarified the interpretation of the impossibility of recovery in a case concerning certain tax exemptions granted to the Italian State to real estate used by non-commercial entities (e.g., those involved in religious activities).[168]

The ECJ acknowledged the principle that 'no one is obliged to do the impossible' as being among the general principles of EU law while highlighting that the related case law does not address the issue of whether such impossibility may already be established at the stage of the formal investigation procedure.[169]

In particular, the ECJ established that the recovery of unlawful aid may be considered objectively and absolutely impossible only upon the finding of two conditions by the Commission: (i) the difficulties encountered by the Member State genuinely exist; and (ii) no alternative methods of recovery are available. Hence, the Member State cannot be discharged from its duty to recover incompatible aid unless it has first suggested alternative methods to recover it, if only in part.[170]

In the specific case, the Commission's decision only ascertained the absolute impossibility of recovery based on the fact that it was impossible for the Italian authorities to obtain sufficient information for the recovery from the Italian lad register and tax databases while omitting to consider alternative methods for, at least partial, retrieval of the relevant amounts.

Indeed, the Italian authorities were deemed liable by the Court for the failure to keep appropriate records, as the inadequacy of the Italian land registry and tax database was regarded as '*caused by internal difficulties attributable to the national authorities' own acts or omissions*'.[171] The Court finding thus implies that Member

167. Decision of 19 Dec. 2012 on a scheme concerning the municipal real estate tax exemption granted to real estate used by non-commercial entities for specific purposes implemented by Italy OJ L 2013 166/24.

168. *See*, *ex multis*, Alain Ronzano, *Exoneration: The Court of Justice of the European Union annuls the decision of the General Court as the European Commission denounced the recuperation of unlawful aid in the form of exemption from the municipal tax on buildings, because of the lack of proof of the absolute impossibility of recovery (Scuola Elementare Marie Montessori v. Commission)*, Concurrences (6 Nov. 2018) https://www-concurrences-com.coleurope.idm.oclc.org/en/review/issues/no-1-2019/alertes/unlawful-state-aid-the-court-of-justice-of-the-european-union-annuls-the.

169. Joined Cases C-622/16 P and C-624/16 P, *Scuola Elementare Maria Montessori v. Commission*, 6.11. 2018, ECLI:EU:C:2018:873 (paras 79-80).

170. *Ibid.* (para. 92).

171. *Ibid.* (para. 95).

States cannot avoid their duty to recover aid by simply failing to accurately register their contributions.[172]

The Commission subsequently consolidated the principles of the Court's case law described above in the Recovery Notice.[173]

In summary, the Recovery Notice states that Member States must demonstrate the existence of reasons justifying the total or partial impossibility of recovery, in accordance with the type of evidence that is relevant to the specific circumstances of the case.[174]

First, the absolute impossibility cannot be found upon the mere allegation of legal, political, practical or internal difficulties, such as limitation periods, the absence of a right under national law to impose recovery, a legal vacuum or risks of social unrest. A legal justification, if compliant with EU law, can apply only in very specific cases. Recovery measures shall be adopted without delay by the Member State, including by the adoption or repeal of legal acts and regulations, and attempts to recover shall be exhaustive and duly substantiated with evidence.[175]

Second, the economic situation of the beneficiary, including financial difficulties and insolvency, does not constitute sufficient ground for the impossibility of recovery, unless the undertaking has been liquidated and no assets are available or when the beneficiary no longer exists and no legal or economic successor is present.[176]

Lastly, possible losses by the Member State in its quality of shareholder or creditor of the beneficiary are not an adequate justification for the failure to retrieve the amounts due.

In any case, the Commission states that it is possible to establish the absolute impossibility of recovery already during the formal investigation phase, pursuant to Article 6 of the Procedural Regulation.

§4.04 IMPLEMENTATION OF RECOVERY DECISIONS IN ITALY

Recently, Law No. 234 of 24 December 2012 has introduced in Italy ad hoc provisions for recovery of State aid.

The Law attempts to address the long-standing absence of rules in Italy specifically governing the procedure by which public administrators are required to implement a recovery decision and the identification of 'Authorities' or 'Departments' specifically responsible for implementing any such decision as is the case in other Member States.[177]

172. Pheidon Nicolaides, *The Recovery of Incompatible Aid Cannot be Absolutely Impossible Unless it is first Attempted*, Lexxion (4 Dec. 2018), https://www.lexxion.eu/en/stateaidpost/the-recovery-of-incompatible-aid-cannot-be-absolutely-impossible-unless-it-is-first-attempted/.
173. Recovery Notice.
174. *Ibid.* (para. 49).
175. *Ibid.* (paras 50-52).
176. *Ibid.* (para. 53).
177. It is the case, for example, of the *Ministère de l'Economie et des Finances in France* and the Federal Minister of Economy in Germany.

Traditionally, recovery fell under the jurisdiction of the same authority that has granted the aid in the first place, following merely 'diplomatic' steps taken before the Permanent Representation of Italy to the European Union, which receives the recovery decision and forwards it to the Italian authorities.

Moreover, the Italian authorities enjoyed some discretion in choosing the measures by which an aid previously granted should actually be recovered. In general, these measures depended on how the aid was first awarded, in accordance with the *contrarius* actus principle.

The provisions contained in Articles 48 and 49 of Law No. 234/2012 have brought significant innovations in internal recovery procedures that may be summarized as follows.

First, following a negative decision of the Commission, the appropriate Minister, within two months from the notification of the said decision, must issue an executive decree identifying the persons obliged to return funds, the amounts, and the payment terms. (Article 48(2)).

Second, the collection of the sums due is to be carried out by the entity in charge of recovering taxes, contributions and sanctions on behalf of the State, Equitalia S.p.A.;[178] *irrespective* of the *form* of the aid (Article 48(1)).

Third, where the aid has regarded entities other than the State (such as regional or other local authorities) the executive decree mentioned above must be issued by the authority concerned and collection is carried out by the agency that collects for the relevant entity (Article 48(3)).

Moreover, in case of several administrations that would be competent, the President of the Council of Ministry may appoint, via a decree, an extraordinary Commissioner which would deal with the identification of the entities from which the aid must be recovered as well as with the conditions and timing of the recovery.[179]

Finally, the disputes regarding the acts and measures taken pursuant to a recovery decision are under the *sole jurisdiction of the administrative courts*.[180] Indeed, said jurisdiction, as set out in Article 49 of Law No. 234/2012, is *very broad*. In fact, the disputes falling within the jurisdiction of the administrative courts are *not only* those relating to the acts and measures taken pursuant to a recovery decision – irrespective of the form of the aid and the entity by which it was granted – but *also* those relating to the internal measures granted in violation of the standstill obligation pursuant to Article 108(3) TFEU.[181]

---

178. Where the aid has regarded entities other than the State (such as regional or other local authorities), collection is carried out by the agency that collects for the relevant entity (*see* Art. 48, third paragraph, Law No. 234/2012).
179. Law of 7 Jul. 2016 No. 122.
180. *See* Art. 49, second paragraph, Law No. 234/2012, which amended the Administrative Procedural Code. *See* Fiorentino, Gottuso, *La riforma della l. 234/2012 con riferimento agli aiuti di Stato*, in Pace (ed.), *Dizionario sistematico del diritto della concorrenza*, Naples, 2013, pp 715 et seq.
181. On this topic *see* further Ch. 7. *See also* Fiorentino, Gottuso, *La riforma della l. 234/2012 con riferimento agli aiuti di Stato*, in Pace (ed.), *Dizionario sistematico del diritto della concorrenza*, Naples, 2013, pp 715 et seq.

§4.05 CONCLUDING REMARKS

Some interesting observations in relation to the procedure for the recovery of unlawful State aid are to be found in the opinion of Advocate General Ruiz-Jarabo Colomer, delivered in Case C-232/05.[182]

The Advocate General did not share the optimism exhibited by certain academic writers with regard to the removal of the risk of an unsatisfactory and inconsistent application of the rules governing the repayment of State aid, owing to the gradual delimitation of the principle of the procedural autonomy of Member States arising from actions for failure to fulfil obligations, actions for annulment and references for preliminary rulings.[183]

Ruiz-Jarabo Colomer went on to observe that:

> the unfortunate reality of the situation and the paltry sums recovered must serve as grounds for a detailed review of the causes.

First, attention must be drawn to the ambiguous position of Member States which grant State aid without reservations, probably with laudable reasons but in contravention of Community law. When those States are subsequently asked to provide the necessary cooperation to recover illegally granted aid, the most extraordinary arguments are put forward as a defence in the proceedings for failure to fulfil obligations which the Commission is required to bring because another action has repeatedly failed to yield satisfactory results. [...]

Second, the Commission might oversee more effectively the requirement for repayment in this field, since it has a wide discretion but has not been provided with the most suitable mechanisms for preventing obstacles to the recovery of State aid and, moreover, has fluctuated between an attitude which on occasions is too flexible and on others is too Utopian and obstinate and has been correctly labelled 'external rigour'.

Frequently, the last resort of the Commission is to bring an action before the Court for a declaration that the defaulting Member State concerned has failed to fulfil its obligations. However, the meagre results obtained led me to two conclusions.

First, the judgments handed down in proceedings brought under Article 226 EC or, as in the case of the present action, under the second paragraph of Article 88(2) EC do not compensate for the absence of enforcement proceedings under Community law and, as a result, their effectiveness is reduced considerably. It is almost childish to claim that those decisions lay the foundations for a subsequent fine under Article 228 EC because it plays into the hands of those whose sole aim is to delay the repayment of State aid. In that situation, it might be appropriate to suggest a more selective use of proceedings for failure to fulfil obligations by assessing which cases are actually

182. *See* paras 100-111 of the opinion delivered by Advocate General Ruiz-Jarabo Colomer on 18 May 2006 in Case C-232/05, *Commission v. France, supra*; C-331/09, *Commission v. Poland*, 14.4.2011, ECLI:EU:C:2011:250 (para. 56).
183. On this topic, *see* Lenaerts, 'L'articulation entre ordres juridiques à l'oeuvre: le régime de récupération des aides d'Etat versées en violation du droit communautaire', in *Problèmes d'interprétation à la mémoire de Constantinos N. Kakouris*, Brussels, 2004, 282.

capable of serving as an example and which reveal the poor level of cooperation by Member States. The Commission is well aware of the criteria for establishing the most urgent cases.

Second, the range of procedures available for addressing this type of dispute is excessive and does not bear any relation to the low rewards obtained by way of repayments. There is nothing to preclude a decision concerning the recovery of State aid from being contested before the Court of First Instance or a subsequent appeal on a point of law. The methods of enforcing Community measures in a Member State may also be open to challenge, with frequent attendant difficulties [...]. It is also possible for a national court to refer for a preliminary ruling a question concerning the validity of the Community decision giving rise to the national administrative action or concerning the compatibility of national measures implementing that decision. Moreover, the Commission freely resorts to proceedings for failure to fulfil obligations when repayment is not forthcoming.

The use of that arsenal of measures takes many years and does not overcome the stubborn delay which infiltrates these situations because there are few examples of Member States with a structure designed for repayment and a policy of abolishing State aid which bears even the slightest resemblance to those of the Community.

Finally, regard must be had to the requirement that competition must be restored retroactively to the time when the aid was paid. In the present dispute, to invoke that fundamental reason behind the legislation on State aid borders on the absurd, because the distortion of the market began nearly twenty years ago. The undertakings which demanded the restoration of the previous situation will surely no longer exist or will have attempted to secure similar advantages for themselves. It is clear that the Utopian goal does not adequately reflect the real needs which prevail in this field.[184]

As can be seen, the authoritative analysis such a favoured observer has provided - in an almost fatalist vein at that - not only reveals a gap between the objectives of the rules in force and the actual application of such rules, which is a condition somewhat physiological in any system of laws, but it also seems to expose the relevant implementation tools as intrinsically inadequate, in the face of the purport of some of the Commission's official statements.

184. *See* the opinion of AG Ruiz-Jarabo Colomer in Case C-232/05, *Commission v. France* (paras 103-110).

CHAPTER 5

Recovery in the Case of Aid Schemes in Tax Matters

Giuseppe Pizzonia

§5.01 THE APPLICATION OF ARTICLE 107(1) TFEU IN TAX MATTERS

The granting by States of aid in the form of tax advantages gives rise to prohibited state aid,[1] irrespective of the legislative source from which they may arise (be that primary or secondary legislation, or as a result of administrative measures). In this regard, the Commission has dealt with the topic of tax aid in its Communication on the concept of State aid,[2] has issued a Communication on fiscal aid relating to direct tax,[3] and has released a Working Paper on the topic of tax rulings.[4]

Aid in the form of tax benefits may be provided in a number of different ways, including tax exemptions; reduced tax rates; reductions in the taxable base; payment rescheduling; tax rulings for determining taxes in particular sectors; and tax credits. Postponement and unusual renegotiations of tax liabilities may also be considered to constitute tax aid.[5]

1. Under Art. 107(1) TFEU, aid granted 'in any form' is generally prohibited, and the fiscal nature of a scheme is thus irrelevant.
2. *See*, Commission Notice on the notion of State aid as referred to in Art. 107(1) of the Treaty on the Functioning of the European Union (C/2016/2946), OJ C 262, para. 5.4.
3. *See* Commission Notice on the application of the State aid rules to measures relating to direct business taxation (98/C 384/03), OJ C 384, 3-9.
4. *See* DG Competition Working Paper on State Aid and Tax Rulings, Internal working paper - Background to the High Level Forum on State Aid, 3.12.2016.
5. *See* Commission Notice on the application of the State aid rules to measures relating to direct business taxation (98/C 384/03), OJ C 384, *supra* para. 9.

There is also no shortage in practice of more sophisticated forms of aid, such as special and/or temporary measures related to corporate finance transactions, (contributions in tax suspension, realignment of tax and accounting, relegation to tax exemption of assets).[6]

Over time both the Commission and the European courts have had occasion to consider a number of different arrangements of this sort. Their analyses have resulted in a variety of findings, but more often than not, they have concluded that the prohibition under Article 107 TFEU applied.[7]

There are no specific rules governing when and how tax measures may constitute prohibited aid. As the TFEU requires, however, they must be measures financed out of State resources,[8] which in this case means smaller tax contributions (or postponements); and they must be selective in nature, such that they distort, or threaten to distort, competition.

More specifically, it has been observed, 'Tax measures must accord extraordinary tax treatment, reducing the tax burden that would normally apply for certain beneficiaries, which confers a selective benefit that distorts competition.'[9]

The key concepts are thus the aid's *impact upon competition*, and *trade* between Member States; and its *selective nature*.[10] There is an effect upon trade where the undertaking that receives the aid carries on an economic activity that gives rise to trade between Member States, but this requirement has been interpreted rather broadly. Undertakings that do not make any exports (or that export only to countries outside the European Union) may be considered recipients of unlawful aid, as merely *potential* prejudice is considered sufficient. Moreover, the size of the undertaking, and the amount of the aid, are irrelevant.[11]

A measure qualifies as selective where it does not apply generally.[12] It is thus not sufficient that there is an exception to the application of the tax system, that is, a

---

6. *See* Case C-66/02, *Italian Republic v. Commission of the European Communities*, 15.12.2005 ECLI:EU:C:2005:768 and Case C-148/04, *Unicredito Italiano SpA v. Agenzia delle Entrate, Ufficio Genova 1*, 15.12.2005, ECLI:EU:C:2005:774 related to certain measures for the restructuring of the Italian banking system. For a general discussion of tax aid, *see* Alexander Rust, Claire Micheau, *State Aid and Tax Law* (2013).
7. *See* Alberto Santa Maria, *European Economic Law* 470 et seq. (2014).
8. The consumption of State resources (fiscal expenditure) arises out of the loss of tax revenues. This test applies also to aid granted to regional and local authorities (Commission Notice on the application of the State aid rules to measures relating to direct business taxation (98/C 384/03), para. 10). On aid from regional authorities, *see* Giuseppe Graziano, *La selettività e gli aiuti regionali* (Livia Salvini, *Aiuti di Stato in materia fiscale* (2007)) 221 et seq.
9. *See* Pierpaolo Rossi-Maccanico, *Aiuti di stato: divieti a maglie larghe specialmente in materia fiscale*, Fiscalità internazionale 3 (2010).
10. *See*, more generally, Ch. 1.
11. Commission Notice on the application of the State aid rules to measures relating to direct business taxation (98/C 384/03), para. 11, with the obvious exception of *de minimis* aid.
12. *See* Giuseppe Tesauro, *Diritto comunitario* 815 et seq. (2008); Philipp Werner, Vincent Verouden, *Eu State Aid Control. Law and Economics* 119 et seq. (2016); Caputi, *La selettività in generale* 191 et seq. (Manlio Ingrosso & Giuseppe Tesauro, *Agevolazioni fiscali e aiuti di stato* (2009); *See* Case C-885/19, *Fiat Chrysler Finance Europe and Ireland v. European Commission*, 8.11.2022, ECLI:EU:C:2022:859.

derogation from general tax rules – that exception must also be such as to favour, exclusively, certain identified or identifiable beneficiaries.

The Court of Justice has made some interesting observations on this when discussing the tax treatment of cooperative firms in Italy.[13] It is necessary, the Court found, to begin by identifying the common or 'normal' regime that would apply in the Member State concerned; and then to assess whether any advantage granted by the tax measure 'differentiates between economic operators who, in light of the objective assigned to the tax system of the Member State concerned, are in a comparable factual and legal situation' (paragraph 49). In the particular case, the Court reached the conclusion that the requirement that the tax measure be selective was not met, precisely because of the cooperative societies' special status and legal nature, recognised also under EU law.[14]

The Court's analysis was based on the features that in the abstract are typical of cooperative societies, concluding that the tax treatment did not satisfy the requirement that it be selective, because such firms operate in situations that are, in fact and in law, different from those of commercial firms.[15] More particularly, it found that such firms *'act in the economic interest of their members and their relations with members are not purely commercial but personal and individual, the members being actively involved in the running of the business and entitled to equitable distribution of the results of economic performance'* (paragraph 61).

The Court did not rule out the possibility that *in practice* there could be situations in which cooperative societies would be in situations analogous to those of commercial firms. It would however be a matter for the national court to assess whether that was true in any particular case.[16]

13. *See* Joint Cases C-78-79-80/08, *Ministero dell'Economia e delle Finanze, Agenzia delle Entrate v. Paint Graphos Soc. coop. arl* (C-78/08), *Adige Carni Soc. coop. arl, in liquidation, v. Agenzia delle Entrate, Ministero dell'Economia e delle Finanze* (C-79/08), and *Ministero delle Finanze v. Michele Franchetto* (C-80/08), 8.9.2011, ECLI:EU:C:2011:550. Further commentary in Giuseppe Pizzonia, *Agevolazioni fiscali per le cooperative, aiuti di stato, ruolo dei giudici nazionali*, 71 Riv. Dir. Fin. Sc. Fin. 2, 37 et seq. (2012).
14. The court's reasoning is based in large part on European-derived principles drawn from sources of soft law (on the role of flexible legal instruments in increasing the consistency of national tax systems *see* Silvia Cipollina, *I confini giuridici nel tempo presente* 122 et seq. (2003)). In particular, in addition to the reference to Regulation No. 1435/2003 (on the Statute for a European Cooperative Society (SCE)), consideration was also given to the Communication from the Commission to the Council and the European Parliament, the European Economic and Social Committee and the Committee of Regions on the promotion of co-operative societies in Europe (23.2.2004, COM/2004/18).
15. This is consistent with the approach set forth in the conclusions by the Advocate General N. Jääskinen, which stated, 'the tax regime for producers' and workers' cooperative societies, as provided for in particular by Article 11 of [Presidential Decree] No. 601/1973, cannot be regarded as selective'. The European Commission (which appeared in this case) had reached similar conclusions.
16. It is nonetheless possible, also in such cases – as the judgment in Case C-88/03, *Portuguese Republic v. Commission of the European Communities*, 6.9.2006, ECLI:EU:C:2006:511 suggests – that a measure may be justified anyway, if it is consistent with the basic or guiding principles of the tax system (*see also* Case C-106/09 P, *European Commission (C-106/09 P) and Kingdom of Spain (C-107/09 P) v. Government of Gibraltar and United Kingdom of Great Britain and*

A second, consequent, factor that would mean that the measure was not selective was also considered. This regarded – in the light of the effects of the measure – the mechanisms inherent in the tax system (paragraphs 64 to 72), which qualify the nature and structure of the tax in question.[17]

The Court distinguished between the objectives sought by the tax system, extrinsic thereto, and the mechanisms inherent in the system itself, which are necessary for the achievement of those objectives, ruling that 'tax exemptions which are the result of an objective that is unrelated to the tax system of which they form part cannot circumvent the requirements' arising out of the prohibition of State aid (paragraph 70). On the other hand, the need for the system to be internally consistent, including the need to treat different situations differently may mean that measures that would in theory be selective, because of their highly specific nature, may overcome the prohibition on State aid.[18]

In this regard, it is the Member State that must 'show that that measure results directly from the basic or guiding principles of its tax system',[19] in particular with reference to 'mechanisms inherent in the tax system itself, which are necessary for the achievement of such objectives'.[20]

We should at this point highlight a feature peculiar to – and, in many cases, typical of –tax aid. Ordinarily, tax aid is not directed to a particular individual or entity,[21] but takes the form of an aid scheme. In other words, these are measures that theoretically regard a fairly broad range of beneficiaries, *selectively* identified or identifiable.

Northern Ireland, 15.11.2011, ECLI:EU:C:2011:732 and Case C-452/10 P, *BNP Paribas and Banca Nazionale del Lavoro SpA (BNL) v. European Commission*, 21.6.2012, ECLI:EU:C:2012:366, paras 101-120).

17. *See also* Commission Notice on the application of the State aid rules to measures relating to direct business taxation (98/C 384/03), paras 23 et seq.
18. It has been observed in this regard that the justification – or not – of the requirement of selectivity could result from the national court's different preference for the theory which treats taxes on companies as an advance of taxes payable by shareholders, as opposed to that which considers them collective entities taxable on the basis of their own capacity to pay tax (*see* Stefania Gianoncelli, *Sulla compatibilità con il divieto di aiuti di Stato del regime agevolato delle società cooperative di produzione e lavoro*, 70 Riv. Dir. Fin. Sc. Fin. 2, 89-106 (2011).
19. The Court's view, and the State's, was that the assessment regarding the presence of grounds connected with the features of the tax system may be made also by a national court (*see* Manilo Ingrosso, *La pronuncia pregiudiziale della corte di giustizia sulle agevolazioni fiscali alle cooperative italiane*, 2 Rass. Trib, 529-551 (2012)). The author maintains that the question of inherence to the tax system (as a means of establishing there is no selectivity) serves to resolve borderline cases of market failure, which however introduces assessments that go beyond fiscal matters, and as such not inherent in the tax system.
20. *See* Case C-6/12, *P Oy*, 18.7.2013, ECLI:EU:C:2013:525, para. 22. Similarly, Case C-88/03, *Portuguese Republic v. Commission of the European Communities*, 6.9.2006, ECLI: EU:C:2006:511, para. 80, and Case C-148/04, *Unicredito Italiano SpA v. Agenzia delle Entrate, Ufficio Genova 1*, para. 51.
21. Individual tax measures could easily conflict with constitutional principles of equal treatment and non-discrimination, irrespective of whether they breach the prohibition of State aid. However, it should be noted that this can occur in the case of aid provided through tax rulings (*see*, Report on tax rulings and other measures similar in nature or effect, 5.11.2015, 2025/2066(INI)).

That this is an aid scheme, rather than aid towards one or more particular beneficiaries, has consequences for the manner of the Commission's review – indeed, as a rule the practice is that it is *not* possible to identify all the undertakings that received illegal or incompatible aid in a decision. For the same reason, the Commission may not be able to identify the amount of aid that should be recovered.[22] It has been observed that 'in the case of an aid scheme, the Commission may confine itself to examining the general characteristics of the scheme in question without being required to examine each particular case in which it applies in order to establish whether the scheme involves elements of aid'.[23] Under this approach – which, while somewhat questionable,[24] has prevailed – there is no need to carry out a detailed analysis of the relevant market and the beneficiary undertakings, because 'it is only at the stage of recovery of the aid that it is necessary to look at the individual situation of each undertaking concerned'.

Given the rule that recovery is mandatory,[25] it is not sufficient for the European Commission to identify measures amounting to prohibited aid. There is in fact the risk that since the European Commission's review is limited to an examination of general matters, it cannot thereby expect to pick out the special features that are peculiar to individual sets of facts, especially when the range of potential beneficiaries is wide.

That is reflected in recovery activities, since, as we explore in more detail below, where there is an aid scheme, it is inevitable, indeed necessary, that 'the Member State ... verify the individual situation of each undertaking concerned by such a recovery operation'.[26]

---

22. *See* Notice from the Commission towards an effective implementation of Commission decisions ordering Member States to recover unlawful and incompatible State aid (2007/C 272/05) OJ C 272, paras 35, 39 and 49.
23. *See* Joint Cases C-71-73-76/09, *Comitato 'Venezia vuole vivere' (C-71/09 P), Hotel Cipriani S.r.l. (C-73/09 P) and Società Italiana per il gas S.p.A. (Italgas) (C-76/09 P) v. European Commission*, 9.6.2011, ECLI:EU:C:2011:368, para. 130. *See* Case C-278/00, *Greece v. Commission*, 29.4.2004, ECLI:EU:C:2004:239, para. 24; and Case C-148/04, *Unicredito Italiano SpA v. Agenzia delle Entrate, Ufficio Genova 1*, para. 67. *See also* Joint Cases C-622-623-624/2016 P, *Scuola Elementare Maria Montessori Srl v. European Commission, European Commission v. Scuola Elementare Maria Montessori Srl and European Commission v. Pietro Ferracci*, 6.11.2018, ECLI: EU:C:2018:873, the Commission's Negative Decision was annulled insofar as it did not order the recovery of aid deemed illegal granted by the Italian state to church entities.
24. *See* Alberto Santa Maria, *European Economic Law* 470 et seq. (2014).
25. *See* Antonio Afonso, *Recovery of fiscal State aid* (Alexander Rust & Claire Micheau, *State aid and tax law* (2013)); Vittorio Di Bucci, *Gli atti di recupero di aiuti illegali e il contenzioso davanti ai giudici nazionali* (Adriano Pietro & Andrea Mondini, *Aiuti di Stato fiscali e giurisdizioni nazionali: problemi attuali* (2015)); Maurizio Orlandi, *Le discriminazioni fiscali e gli aiuti di Stato nel diritto dell'Unione Europea* (2018).
26. *See* Joint Cases C-71-73-76/09, *Comitato 'Venezia vuole vivere'* (C-71/09 P), *Hotel Cipriani S.r.l.* (C-73/09 P) and *Società Italiana per il gas S.p.A. (Italgas)* (C-76/09 P) *v. European Commission*, para. 64. The issues that may flow from such an approach, in relation to the fundamental rights of those who benefited from the aid scheme to a defence, are described in Alberto Santa Maria, *European Economic Law* 481 (2014).

§5.02 THE COMMISSION'S NEGATIVE DECISIONS IN STATE AID SCHEMES

The concept of a negative decision was contained in Council Regulation (EC) [No. 659/1999] of the Council of 22 March 1999, which laid down 'detailed rules for the application of Article 108 of the treaty on the functioning of the European Union'.[27]

A decision may be *negative* either where it relates to a finding that notified aid is *incompatible*,[28] or where it establishes that aid was *illegal*.[29]

The recovery rules in Reg. No. 659 were not only referred to unlawful aid but also extended to further cases of recovery.[30] Principles on this issue drawn from ECJ case law were contained in Commission Communication 2007/C 272/05[31] and in the Commission Regulation (EC) No. 794/2004.[32]

Reg. No. 659 was later replaced by Reg. No. 2025/1589,[33] according to which '*Where the Commission finds that the notified aid is not compatible with the internal*

27. For the consolidated version of Regulation No. 659/1999.
28. *See* Art. 7(5) of Regulation No. 659/1999, 'Where the Commission finds that the notified aid is not compatible with the common market, it shall decide that the aid shall not be put into effect (hereinafter referred to as a "negative decision").'
29. *See* Art. 14(1) of Regulation No. 659/1999: '1. Where negative decisions are taken in cases of unlawful aid, the Commission shall decide that the Member State concerned shall take all necessary measures to recover the aid from the beneficiary (hereinafter referred to as a "recovery decision"). The Commission shall not require recovery of the aid if this would be contrary to a general principle of Community law.

   2. The aid to be recovered pursuant to a recovery decision shall include interest at an appropriate rate fixed by the Commission. Interest shall be payable from the date on which the unlawful aid was at the disposal of the beneficiary until the date of its recovery.

   3. Without prejudice to any order of the Court of Justice of the European Communities pursuant to Article 185 of the Treaty, recovery shall be effected without delay and in accordance with the procedures under the national law of the Member State concerned, provided that they allow the immediate and effective execution of the Commission's decision. To this effect and in the event of a procedure before national courts, the Member States concerned shall take all necessary steps which are available in their respective legal systems, including provisional measures, without prejudice to Community law'.

   Recognition of aid's unlawfulness does not release the European Commission from its obligation to decide upon its compatibility (*see* Commission Decision of 29 May 1996 concerning certain measures granted by Italy in favour of Breda Fucine Meridionali SpA 96/614/EC). *See* Case C-301/87, *French Republic v. Commission of the European Communities*, 14.2.1990, ECLI: EU:C:1990:67; Case C-142/87, *Kingdom of Belgium v. Commission of the European Communities*, 21.3.1990, ECLI:EU:C:1990:125.
30. *See* Art. 9 of Regulation No. 659/1999 on revocation of a decision; Art. 11(2) of Regulation No. 659/1999 on interim recovery; Art. 16 of Regulation No. 659/1999 on misused aid.
31. Notice from the Commission towards an effective implementation of Commission decisions ordering Member States to recover unlawful and incompatible State aid (2007/C 272/05).
32. On the limited significance of that Communication vis-à-vis third parties, *see* Ch. 4.
33. *See* Regulation (EU) No. 2015/1589 of 13 Jul. 2015 laying down detailed rules for the application of Art. 108 of the Treaty on the Functioning of the European Union. *See also* the Commission Notice on the recovery of unlawful and incompatible State aid (C/2019/5396), OJ C 247. The purpose of this Notice is to explain the European Union rules and procedures governing the recovery of State aid, and how the Commission works with Member States to ensure compliance with their obligations under European Union law. It is addressed to the authorities of the Member States in charge of implementing a decision by which the Commission has ordered the

market, it shall decide that the aid shall not be put into effect ("negative decision")' (Article 9, paragraph 5, Reg. No. 2025/1589). Similarly, in the case of unlawful aid, after the opening of the formal investigation procedure, it takes a decision pursuant to the aforementioned Article 9, pronouncing either a positive, a conditional, or a negative decision, as the case may be. The ECJ has repeatedly ruled on the effectiveness of negative decisions on matters of State aid, ever since the *Kohlegesetz* judgment,[34] to the effect that where there is a formal decision by the Commission, a Member State is obliged to comply with it, taking all such statutory measures as are necessary.[35] The recovery must be effective and immediate.[36]

Additionally, the ECJ has found, that Article 288(4) TFEU (ex Article 249 EC) must be interpreted in the light of the principle of the pre-eminence of European law, specifically meaning here that a decision addressed to a Member State must be considered binding on all the organs of that State, including all its courts.[37] That is moreover consistent with how the Commission has defined itself and its work in this area, acting as the '*administrative authority responsible for the implementation and development of competition policy in the Community's public interest*'.[38] It is also in line with Article 288(4) TFEU, under which a decision by the Commission not only constitutes a secondary or derivative European legislative act (a source of European Union law) but is also binding upon any persons to whom it is addressed.

---

recovery of State aid (a 'recovery decision'). Jan Blockx, *The EU Commission publishes a new State aid recovery notice*, e-Competitions Art. N° 91349 (22 Jul. 2019), https://www.concurrences.com/en/bulletin/news-issues/july-2019/the-eu-commission-publishes-a-new-state-aid-recovery-notice.

34. *See* Case C-70/72, *Commission of the European Communities v. The Federal Republic of Germany*, 12.7.1973, ECLI:EU:C:1973:87, 813, para. 13.
35. *See* among others, Case C-130/83, *Commission of the European Communities v. Italian Republic*, 11.7.1984, ECLI:EU:C:1984:263; and Case C-94/87, *Commission of the European Communities v. Federal Republic of Germany*, 2.2.1989, ECLI:EU:C:1989:46.
36. *See* Art. 14(3) of Regulation No. 659/1999. Notice from the Commission towards an effective implementation of Commission decisions ordering Member States to recover unlawful and incompatible State aid (2007/C 272/05), para. 3, does however point out that 'there is practically not a single case in which recovery was completed within the deadline set out in the recovery decision'.
37. *See* Case C-249/85, *Albako Magarinefabrik Maria von der Linde GmbH & Co. KG v. Bundesanstalt für landwirtschaftliche Marktordnung*, 21.3.1987, ECLI:EU:C:1987:245; the ECJ's stance goes well beyond the principle of compliance with the Commission's decisions, to the point that it considers that as early as the standstill stage, citizens (and thus not just the State and its organs) is obliged not to apply domestic rules that constitute aid *'if and to the extent that the citizen is called in some way by the law to apply it autonomously'*. If that does not happen, one might suggest the ECJ considers a recipient of undue aid might be liable for damages (Case C-39/94, *Syndacat Français de l'Express International – SFEI v. La Poste and Others*, 11.7.1996, ECLI:EU:C:1996:285).
38. *See* Commission Notice on the enforcement of State aid law by national courts (2009/C 85/01) OJ C 85, 1-22, para. 20, which states, 'the Commission's main role is to examine the compatibility of proposed aid measures with the common market, based on the criteria laid down in Article 87(2) and (3) of the Treaty. This compatibility assessment is the exclusive responsibility of the Commission, subject to review by the Community courts'. *See*, Rossi, *Riflessi fiscali dell'applicazione a livello nazionale delle norme comunitarie sugli aiuti di stato*, Fiscalità internazionale, 210 (2009).

The question of the Commission's decisions on aid taking direct effect has been examined in great detail by the Italian Supreme Court, in particular in a well-known judgment that regarded tax matters.[39]

The national court's reasoning was based on an analysis of two competing sets of principles that the ECJ and Italy's Constitutional Court had in parallel developed in their case law, worked out in detail over an extended period, but which now look rather dated.[40]

Both the European Court's single-tier and the Constitutional Court's dual-tier approach recognised the primacy of European law and its consequent direct effects. These underlying principles formed the basis of the ECJ's single-tier approach, which held that every provision of European law stands higher in the hierarchy than the domestic law of Member States, and thus must prevail over any contrary provision of domestic law, irrespective of its kind or nature, legislated before or after.

Consequently, in the view of the European Court of Justice, European law (whether primary or derivative), provided it has certain characteristics,[41] must be treated by national courts the same way as domestic law (that is, immediately giving rise to subjective legal situations that may be enforced in the domestic courts).

That obligation arises quite independently of whether there is or is not domestic implementing legislation and is without prejudice to the obligation upon each individual State to enact such legislation. Such an approach thus amounts to considering European law and the Member States' law in an integrated way, as expressions of what is really a single corpus.[42]

---

39. Italian Supreme Court of Cassation, No. 17564/2012. This was the first judgment to explore in detail the question of the effectiveness of the Commission's decisions, aside from one earlier judgment of the Council of State (24.12.1989, No. 30) which had adopted a rather formalistic position, finding that where the Commission had reached a negative decision on aid that had been legislated, its implementation would only be possible following a change in the law that in its effects was equivalent to that which had instituted the aid.
40. For an account of the ECJ's single-tier approach, *see* Case C-106/77, *Amministrazione delle Finanze Dello Stato (Italian Finance Administration) v. Simmenthal S.p.A.*, 9.3.1978, ECLI: EU:C:1978:49, and more recently, Case C-258/98, *Carra and Others*, 8.6.2000, ECLI: EU:C:2000:30. On the dual-tier approach adopted by the Italian Supreme Court of Cassation, No. 183/1973 (*Frontini, Parte prima: giurisprudenza costituzionale e civile*, Il Foro 1, 97 (1974), 314); Italian Supreme Court of Cassation, 8.6.1984, No. 170, *Granital*, Il Foro it., 1984, I, 2062. *See also* on this Alberto Santa Maria, *European Economic Law* 4 et seq. (2014), including the footnotes.
41. The characteristics required for European legislation to have direct effect are well-known, and specifically regard:

    - the existence of an obligation that is sufficiently clear and precise (in terms of, for example, both its scope and its content);
    - the existence of an unconditional provision (that is, not subject to terms and conditions for its implementation); and
    - the absence of any discretionary power on the part of the Member State or States to which it is addressed for implementation (as discretion on the part of an individual State being obviously incompatible with the notion of direct effect).

42. *See* Gianpaolo Provaggi, *La Suprema corte sancisce l'efficacia immediata e diretta delle decisioni della commissione europea nell'ordinamento interno*, Rivista di giurisprudenza tributaria, 451 (2003).

The alternative, dual-tier, view (alternative at least from a formal, logical, standpoint, but not so much in substance), may be identified in the case law of the Italian Constitutional Court. Specifically, with regard to the primacy of European law, the Constitutional Court recognised that position, but nonetheless took the position that European and domestic law constituted *'separate, autonomous, albeit coordinated, systems'*.[43] On this basis, in the view of the domestic court, the basis of EU law's primacy, and its direct effect, lies in the limitations upon sovereignty admitted under Article 11 of the Italian Constitution, the basis for the country's interrelationship with the European Union.[44] Consequently, direct effect would not be the consequence of a pre-eminent position in the legal hierarchy, but rather in the fact that the EU's institutions operate in accordance with the allocation of powers and jurisdictions laid down in the Treaty (ex Article 5 of the TEC). That principle of prevalence would, said the court, operate always subject to limits, namely its consistency with: (i) *'the fundamental principles of constitutional law'*; and (ii) *'inalienable human rights'*.[45] On this basis, under the dual-tier scheme articulated by the Constitutional Court (and which the Supreme Court had followed in its own rulings, but which it has more recently deprecated),[46] European law's direct effect in Italian law is seen in terms of *'prevalence'* over domestic law (including constitutional law),[47] provided that it regards matters that are exclusively within the jurisdiction of the European institutions, does not conflict with fundamental principles of constitutional law, and does not breach inalienable human rights. It is in these (limited) terms, and in situations where there is a conflict between domestic and European law, that an Italian court is entitled

43. Among many others, Italian Constitutional Court, Nos 183/1973, 170/1984, 126/1996, 93/1997.
44. Italian Constitutional Court, No. 337/2001.
45. This is known as the theory of 'counter-limits'. *See* Italian Constitutional Court, Nos 98/1965, 1146/1988, 232/1989, and 168/1991. The Court of Justice's different position should be mentioned – that the validity of acts by the Community's institutions must be assessed only on the basis of European law, such that a violation of constitutional principles under Member States' legal systems cannot be considered to affect the validity or effectiveness of a Community act (*see* Case C-11/70, *Internationale Handelsgesellschaft mbH v. Einfuhr- und Vorratsstelle ffr Getreide und Futtermittel*, 17.12.1970, ECLI:EU:C:1970:114; and Case C-234/85, *Staatsanwalt (Public Prosecutor) Freiburg v. Franz Keller*, 8.10.1986, ECLI:EU:C:1986:377).
46. *See* Italian Supreme Court of Cassation, No. 7663/2012 and Italian Supreme Court of Cassation, No. 8817/2012, which found that the theory of counter-limits no longer applied, given the developments in the process of European integration, and the confirmation in the European Union's statutes and case law of the principles that safeguard fundamental human rights and values. Among the academic authorities, *see* Andrea Caligiuri, *Modelli costituzionali a confronto: la specificità della tutela dei diritti fondamentali nel processo di adattamento al diritto dell'Unione europea* 51-73 (Andrea Caligiuri, Giuseppe Cataldi, Nicola Napoletano, *La tutela dei diritti umani in Europea: tra sovranità nazionale e ordinamenti sovranazionali* (2010)). It should be noted in any event that even in a situation in which integration of European legal systems has evolved, there may yet be areas in which counter-limits would be relevant, for example, where a principle or a right has greater protection under a domestic legal system than afforded by European Union law, or where a principle or right does not have a counterpart in European Union law, or the domestic concept of a principle or right does not correspond exactly to a similar European concept.
47. *See* Italian Constitutional Court, No. 117/1994.

to examine whether such a conflict exists (applying the criteria indicated above), and to disapply the incompatible domestic law.[48]

More recently, the Italian Constitutional Court reaffirmed these principles, at the same time ordering a preliminary reference before the EU Court of Justice on a case of non-application of a *norma penale nazionale in materia di prescrizione*.[49] The Court of Justice in preliminary rulings has recognised that the principle of legality has a fundamental character in the constitutional traditions of the Member States and is therefore endowed with staying power. Specifically, the pursuit of the Union's financial interests cannot undermine the certainty of the national criminal rule, with the consequence that the national court may – if the conditions are met – rely on the legality test and will not be obliged to disapply the national rule.[50]

The Italian Supreme Court, in the aforementioned judgment No. 17564, established the effect of decisions on aid, and established, as a preliminary matter, that one requirement would definitely not apply – there would be no need for a decision to be res judicata. Even if the Commission's decision remains potentially subject to review by the courts, it is nonetheless mandatory with respect to the persons to whom it is addressed. As for a decision's content, it has been observed that in a similar way to other European legislative acts, a decision must contain an obligation that is '*sufficiently clear and precise*', that is not subject to conditions, and that does not presuppose the exercise of discretionary powers by the State. Where those requirements are satisfied, a decision is, in the view of Italy's Supreme Court, capable of producing direct effects in domestic law, essentially of a vertical nature (that is, related to relationships between public authorities, and private individuals and entities).[51] These principles are now well-established in the case law of Italy's Supreme Court, and it applies them with some strictness.[52]

---

48. It is worth mentioning in passing that the relationship between legal systems is complicated further by the reforms to Title V of the Italian Constitution, in that they established that 'legislative power is exercised by the State and by the Regions in accordance with the Constitution, and the restrictions deriving from the European legal system and international obligations' (Art. 117 of the Italian Constitution). A quite different sensitivity to questions of the relationship between European law and national constitutional principles may be found in the case law of the *Bundesverfassungsgericht*, which has been resolute in asserting its right to review whether European rules were in practice consistent with the principles of the *Grundgesetz* (*see* BverfGE 30.6.2009 'the Federal Constitutional Court reviews whether the inviolable core content of the constitutional identity of the Basic Law [...] is respected'. *See also BverfGE*, 12.9.2012).
49. *See* Italian Constitutional Court, No. 24/2016.
50. *See* Case C-42/17, *Criminal proceedings against M.A.S. and M.B.*, 5.12.2017, ECLI: EU:C:2017:936.
51. Taking the principles articulated in that judgment as a starting point, Francesco Tesauro, *Processo tributario e aiuti di stato*, 30 Corr. Trib. 45, 3665 et seq. (2007), distinguishes between self-executing decisions, and decisions that require an implementation process. The Commission decision of 28 May 1991 concerning aid granted to enterprises in the Friuli-Venezia Giulia region (91/500/EEC), falls into the former category. It decided that certain measures in favour of the region of Friuli Venezia Giulia (Italian Law No. 26/1986) constituted prohibited aid, but allowed their application for a limited period. Tesauro considers that decisions that anticipate a domestic recovery work may be categorised as requiring an implementation process.
52. Among others, *see* Italian Supreme Court of Cassation Nos 23418/2010, 26286/2010, 8817/2012, 6544/2012, 8108/2012 and 7663/2012.

§5.03 THE EXECUTION OF THE COMMISSION'S DECISIONS BY NATIONAL AUTHORITIES: RECOVERY OF THE TAX, OR RECOVERY OF THE AID?

The recovery of unlawful (and similarly incompatible) aid now has its legal basis in Article 16 EU Reg. No. 1589/2015,[53] according to which it is up to the Member State to take the necessary measures to recover the aid.

One problem that has arisen regards the nature of the work on recovering aid that has been supplied through tax measures. That work may be considered fiscal in nature – that is to say, it may be considered to be a matter of recovering taxes that were not paid as a result of the prohibited measures; or alternatively, it may be seen as the implementation of a decision by the Commission, the purpose of which is restore the pre-existing situation,[54] in which case the recovery has a character all its own, and cannot be considered strictly fiscal.

The importance of this issue, with respect to national legal systems, is reflected in the rules, procedures and consequences of recovery, including those relating to administrative powers, statutory disqualifications, and judicial protection. If taxes are to be recovered, the appropriate procedures are tax procedures. Not surprisingly, the Commission has pointed out that '*the Member State concerned must calculate the correct tax amount that an undertaking should have paid without the unlawful aid measure*'.[55] Verifications that should be carried out according to national tax rules, with the corresponding guarantees and safeguards; and with the expressly provided

53. Regulation No. 1589/2015, recovery of aid '1. Where negative decisions are taken in cases of unlawful aid, the Commission shall decide that the Member State concerned shall take all necessary measures to recover the aid from the beneficiary ("recovery decision"). The Commission shall not require recovery of the aid if this would be contrary to a general principle of Union law.

    2. The aid to be recovered pursuant to a recovery decision shall include interest at an appropriate rate fixed by the Commission. Interest shall be payable from the date on which the unlawful aid was at the disposal of the beneficiary until the date of its recovery.

    3. Without prejudice to any order of the Court of Justice of the European Union pursuant to Article 278 TFEU, recovery shall be effected without delay and in accordance with the procedures under the national law of the Member State concerned, provided that they allow the immediate and effective execution of the Commission's decision. To this effect and in the event of a procedure before national courts, the Member States concerned shall take all necessary steps which are available in their respective legal systems, including provisional measures, without prejudice to Union law.' The Commission has issued instructions on the recovery of aid; those in force are contained in the Commission Notice on the recovery of unlawful and incompatible State aid (2019/C 247/01), OJ C 247.
54. This aim for a recovery decision, of restoring the situation, rather than imposing penalties upon recipients, has been stated repeatedly by the ECJ. Among many others, *see* Case C-310/85, *Deufil GmbH & Co. KG v. Commission of the European Communities*, 24.2.1987, ECLI:EU:C:1987:96; and Case C-277/00, *Federal Republic of Germany v. Commission of the European Communities*, 29.4.2004, ECLI:EU:C:2004:238.
55. *See* Commission Notice on the recovery of unlawful and incompatible State aid (2019/C 247/01), paras 105 et seq.

possibility of recognising other deductions established by national law, if automatically applicable.[56]

Otherwise, there will have to be rules established specially, in the absence of which one would have to rely upon the usual rules for recovering undue payments.

In the Italian context, it has been suggested that the recovery of fiscal aid implies the non-application of the more favourable domestic rule and the application of that which would ordinarily apply. That is an activity that by nature must be governed by fiscal rules and procedures.[57]

Others maintained that, while recovery is closely related to tax matters, the fiscal rules merely constitute a yardstick used to establish the quantum of the aid to be returned,[58] and the consequent effect of the recovery, to restore the pre-existing situation.

Dealing with the undertakings obliged to return tax aid was under the Italian law, for a particular period of time, a matter for the tax courts.[59] Some have taken this as confirmation of the tax nature of such recovery,[60] while others have seen it as deserving censure.[61]

---

56. *See* Commission Notice on the recovery of unlawful and incompatible State aid (2019/C 247/01) *supra* para. 106. It has also been emphasised in the case law of the ECJ that, in the case of negative decisions that do not identify beneficiaries, the situation of each individual must be taken into account (Case C-69/13, *Mediaset SpA v. Ministero dello Sviluppo economico*, 13.2.2014, ECLI:EU:C:2014:71, para. 22), 'The Commission, when it is faced with an aid scheme, is generally not in a position to identify exactly the amount of aid received by individual recipients. Accordingly, the specific circumstances of one of the recipients of an aid scheme can be assessed only at the stage of recovery of the aid (*see*, to that effect, Case C-310/99 *Italy v. Commission* [2002] ECR I-2289, paragraphs 89 to 91).'
57. *See* Francesco Tesauro, *Processo tributario e aiuti di stato*, 30 Corr. Trib. 45, 3665 et seq. (2007), in particular with reference to the issuance of deeds bearing a tax claim (so-called *atti impositivi*); Pasquale Russo, *Le agevolazioni e le esenzioni fiscali alla luce de principî comunitari in materia di aiuti di Stato*, Rivista Italiana di diritto pubblico comunitario 1 (2024), among documentation for the conference, Franco Gallo, *L'applicazione del diritto comunitario nella giurisprudenza della Sezione Tributaria della Corte di Cassazione*, Rass. Trib. 1, 330 (2003).
58. *See* Cesare Glendi, *Recupero di aiuti di stato nella legislazione anti-crisi*, 32 Corr. Trib. 17, 997 et seq. (2009); *see also*, Cesare Glendi, *Processo tributario e recupero di aiuti di Stato*, Corr. Trib. 21, 1670 (2008).
59. In Italy, all tax disputes, of any kind, are for the jurisdiction of the Tax Courts (so-called *Corti di giustizia tributarie*), as specialised courts (*see* Art. 2 of Italian Legislative Decree No. 546/1992). Under the terms of Art. 47-*bis* of Italian Legislative Decree 546/1992, which was introduced by Art. 2(1) of Italian Law Decree No. 59/2008, converted into law as Italian Law No. 101/2008), the Tax Courts have been expressly granted jurisdiction over the national procedures for the recovery of tax aid, following particular procedural rules that depart from the ordinary procedures. In particular, there are restrictions upon the ability to obtain interim suspension of recovery actions, and speedier procedural rules, with the terms for appeals (other than the period in which an appeal may be sought) halved, and the reading of the judgment publicly at the hearing *See* Annalisa Pace, *Recupero aiuti di stato e tutela cautelare*, Riv. dir. trib. 10, 867 et seq. (2008). *See also* Lorenzo Del Federico, *La Corte di giustizia chiamata a pronunciarsi sulle agevolazioni per i redditi delle fondazioni bancarie*, Riv. Dir. Trib. 10, passim (2004).
60. *See* Francesco Tesauro, *Processo tributario e aiuti di stato*, 30 Corr. Trib. 45, 3665 et seq. (2007). *See also* Pietro Boria, *Diritto tributario europeo* 232 et seq. (2010).
61. *See* Cesare Glendi, *Recupero di aiuti di stato nella legislazione anti-crisi*, 32 Corr. Trib. 17, 997 et seq. (2009). Under the Italian constitutional system, specialised courts only have jurisdiction other particular areas, including tax matters (*see* Francesco Tesauro, *Manuale del processo*

Both positions - which conflict more in their form than in their substance - have taken what are obviously key issues as their cornerstones. Restoration of the pre-existing order, with which recovery is connected, does indeed take the form of the application of taxes, and in particular in subjecting to taxation a capacity to pay which - as a result of the prohibited aid - had remained exempt.[62] Consider, for example, aid related to taxes that constitute the Union's *own resources*. The consequent recovery clearly should not deprive the Union of the resources which it is due, by way of confirmation that what is being recovered is ultimately, in the case of tax aid, a *tax*.[63]

The truth however is that this would be a very unusual form of tax recovery, subject to special rules and procedures.[64] For example, looking at a number of past examples, there may be no scope for sanctions to be imposed; the interest may be calculated under the European system; defence in the proceedings may be subject to restrictions, as a result of the special nature of the dispute; and specific procedural rules may apply.[65]

The regulatory framework, again in relation to the Italian situation, was, however, radically changed with the approval of Law No. 234 of 24 December 2012 (Articles 48 and 49), containing general provisions on aid and recovery.[66]

---

tributario 4 et seq. (2020)). If one argues that recovery action is not fiscal in its purpose, the assignment of such disputes to the Tax Commissions (as specialised courts) may be considered to conflict with the Constitution.

62. In the well-known *Unicredito Italiano* case, the Court pointed out that the purpose of recovery is to restore the 'situation that would have occurred if the transactions under consideration had taken place without the tax reduction' (*see* Court of Justice, Case C-148/04, *Unicredito Italiano SpA v. Agenzia delle Entrate, Ufficio Genova 1*, para. 120). This implies the need to calculate the taxes due *as* if the prohibited measure had not been there. The restorative (and non-innovative) nature of recovery measures has also been confirmed by the Italian Constitutional Court (*see* Italian Constitutional Court, Order No. 36/2009).
63. The view appears to be confirmed by Case C-705/20, *Fossil (Gibraltar) Limited v. Commissioner of Income Tax*, 15.9.2022, ECLI:EU:C:2022:680, according to which credit is allowed in recovery for taxes paid abroad against taxes initially considered exempt under domestic law.
64. *See* Augusto Fantozzi, *Problemi di adeguamento dell'ordinamento fiscale nazionale alle sentenze della Corte Europea di Giustizia e alle decisioni della Commissione CE,* Atti del Convegno Aiuti di Stato nel diritto comunitario e misure fiscali Rass. Trib., 2266 et seq. (2003); Franco Gallo, *L'inosservanza delle norme comunitarie sugli aiuti di Stato e sue conseguenze nell'ordinamento fiscale interno,* Atti del Convegno Aiuti di Stato nel diritto comunitario e misure fiscali, Rass.Trib., 2281 (2003); Alessandro De Stefano, *Le controversie sul recupero degli aiuti illegali e incompatibili dinanzi al giudice tributario prima della riforma della legge n. 234/2012* 764 et seq. (Lorenzo F. Pace, *Dizionario sistematico del diritto della concorrenza* (2013)).
65. *See* Italian Legislative Decree No. 153/1999; Italian Law Decree No. 282/2002, on recovery of aid measures in favour of Italian banks; Art. 27 of Italian Law No. 62/2005, later amended by Art. 1, para. 132 of Italian Law No. 266/2005; Art. 1 of Italian Law Decree No. 10/2007; Art. 24 of Italian Law Decree No. 185/2008. The interpretation within the case law was that it did not matter whether the tax liability was no longer open either because too much time had passed, or for any other reason (such as its inclusion in a tax amnesty or res iudicata). *See* Italian Supreme Court of Cassation Nos 7663/2012 and 8108/2012; and in relation to time-barring, it has been ruled that the limitation period indicated by Art. 15 of Regulation No. 659/1999 applies only to dealings between the European Commission and a Member State, and in relation to the recovery of aid from recipients, one must have reference to the decision's notification (Italian Supreme Court of Cassation Nos 7940/2014 and 15207/2012).
66. *See* Armando Lamberti, *Il giudice nazionale e le decisioni della Commissione Europea. Gli atti di accertamento* (Andrea Mondini & Adriano Di Pietro, *Aiuti di Stato fiscali e giurisdizioni nazionali: problemi attuali* (2015)).

The articles are dealt with in more detail in Chapter 4, but in summary, they introduced the following rules:

- the jurisdiction lies with the appropriate Minister, and following a negative decision, within two months of its notification he or she must issue an executive decree identifying the persons obliged to return funds, the amounts, and the payment terms.[67,68] By Law No. 122/2016, it was specified that in the case of several competent administrations being affected, an extraordinary Commissioner is appointed by decree of the President of the Council of Ministers;
- the collection of the sums due is to be carried out by the public entity in charge of recovering taxes, contributions and sanctions on behalf of the State and public entities (Agenzia delle entrate Riscossione, former Equitalia S.p.A.);[69] and
- the disputes regarding the acts and measures taken pursuant to a recovery decision are under the sole jurisdiction of the administrative courts, irrespective of the form of the aid, and the entity by which it was granted.[70]

The terms of this legislation seem to exceed the thesis set out above, that for tax aid, the recovery is fiscal in nature, albeit with some peculiarities. That the administrative courts are awarded exclusive jurisdiction is symptomatic of a desire to introduce 'an organic regulatory treatment of the subject', under a 'declination of the principle of a unified nature of a notion of State aid, irrespective of the form of its grant'. That was intended to 'systematise and proceduralise the activities for the enforcement of recovery decisions', meeting a need that was 'particularly felt in relation to aid granted

67. Where the aid has regarded entities other than the State (such as regional or other local authorities), it is that entity that must implement the recovery (*see* Art. 48, third paragraph, of Italian Law No. 234/2012).
68. The institution of a single, unified set of rules based upon administrative recovery procedures is consistent with the approach stated by the Commission in its Notice from the Commission towards an effective implementation of Commission decisions ordering Member States to recover unlawful and incompatible State aid (2007/C 272/05), para. 51, which stated: 'administrative procedures, on the whole, tend to be much more efficient than civil procedures, because administrative recovery orders are or can be made immediately enforceable'.
69. Where the aid has regarded entities other than the State (such as regional or other local authorities), collection is carried out by the agency that collects for the relevant entity (*see* Art. 48, third paragraph, of Italian Law No. 234/2012).
70. *See* Art. 49, second paragraph, of Italian Law No. 234/2012, which amended the Administrative Procedural Code, inserting into the *corpus* of Art. 133, on matters of exclusive administrative jurisdiction, the letter *z-sexies*. The administrative courts' jurisdiction is also extended to the disputes over acts and measures that grant State aid in breach of the obligations under Art. 108(3) TFEU. *See* Fiorentino & Gottuso, *La riforma della l. 234/2012 con riferimento agli aiuti di Stato* 715 et seq. (Lorenzo F. Pace, *Dizionario sistematico del diritto della concorrenza* (2013); Rosanna De Nictolis, *Codice del processo amministrativo Commentato,* Commento all'Art. 133 (2017)). The attribution to an administrative judge is also reflected in the aforementioned Commission Notice on the recovery of unlawful and incompatible State aid (2019/C 247/01), para. 141, which states 'In the experience of the Commission, proceedings before administrative courts, where available, tend to guarantee a faster enforcement of recovery orders than proceedings before civil courts.'

in the form of a scheme, where recovery presupposes the "individualisation" of the Commission's recovery decision'.

It has been observed, in fact, that 'enforcement of a decision that declares a system of subsidies unlawful assumes subsequent confirmation, on a case-by-case basis, of the satisfaction by individual beneficiaries of all the essential requirements of the State aid, including the fact that the aid produces an actual or potential prejudice to competition and trade between member States'.[71]

While such legislation has the advantage of producing general effects and better system-wide coordination, there are nonetheless aspects that present issues,[72] when one considers the special nature of the subject matter, and of tax disputes.

It is no accident that under Italian law, jurisdiction over tax disputes is attributed to special courts, separate from the administrative courts, considered to have particular expertise in the area.[73] In fact, the Tax Commissions, which operated until 15 September 2022, were formed with the contribution, in addition to magistrates, of experts from the academic world and the professions as well as former officials of the tax administration.

Subsequently, with the establishment of the Courts of Tax Justice, replacing the Tax Commissions, the creation of a role of tax magistrates, selected by means of a special competition, was provided for, although on a transitional basis, and pending the recruitment of new tax magistrates, the Courts continue to operate with the composition of the former Tax Commissions. The special nature of tax courts may be seen also at Italy's Supreme Court, where a dedicated section (V civil section) has been instituted to deal with tax disputes.

Bringing all matters regarding recovery to the administrative courts, including those regarding tax aid, could deprive the courts of essential expertise useful for identifying the persons who benefited from the aid measure, and the satisfaction of the requirements for the prohibited aid, but also in quantifying the taxes to be returned, in accordance with national tax rules. That requires a detailed and confident knowledge of the applicable tax rules and principles, not only by the administrative authorities in charge of the recovery activity (the Revenue Agency) but also by the courts that must reach the decision on the appeals by the companies against whom the recovery is made. Nor would the above-mentioned Commission Communication (paragraph 141) be an obstacle to the recognition of the jurisdiction of tax courts, since in Italian law the

71. *See* Fiorentino & Gottuso, *La riforma della l. 234/2012 con riferimento agli aiuti di Stato* 716-717 (Lorenzo F. Pace, *Dizionario sistematico del diritto della concorrenza* (2013)).
72. *See* Altieri, *Prime impressioni sulla giurisdizione del giudice amministrativo in materia di aiuti di stato,* Riv. Dir. Trib., 197 (2013).
73. It is worth noting that the question of exactly what the tax courts are qualified to consider has been a matter of debate for some time in Italy, and under recent legislation the government has been mandated by parliament to pursue reform of the tax process (*see* Art. 10 of Italian Law No. 23/2014), with a view to strengthening the safeguards for taxpayers and ensuring the independence of the courts. The article also calls for a strengthening in the professional qualifications of the members of tax commissions, in order to ensure that they have 'appropriate specialist instruction' (part (b)(8)). In any event, the necessity of tax commissions has never been questioned, and indeed the reforming measures will tend to boost their specialisation and specificity.

tax court is also traditionally considered an administrative (as well as a special) jurisdiction.[74]

In fact, it appears reductive to consider that, since recovery must be effected against anyone who has benefited from the prohibited measure, the specific examination of individual positions would be irrelevant.

In fact, a distinction must be made between prohibited measures (unlawful or incompatible) tout court, to be recovered as such, and measures whose recovery requires targeted checks on the existence – or otherwise – of the conditions for entitlement to the benefit. As is moreover clear from the aforementioned Communication on the recovery of prohibited aid, which in providing specific indications on fiscal measures expressly requires the following to be calculated *the correct tax amount that an undertaking should have paid without the unlawful aid.*[75] The subject of recovery is therefore a tax (*tax amount*).

Statements of this kind have led some authors to consider that tax jurisdiction still exists with regard to acts of recovery of tax measures.[76]

However, the jurisdiction of the administrative courts must be considered to cover both disputes concerning aid granted by specific acts or measures and disputes concerning acts or measures for the recovery of State aid, without exception, even if justified by the peculiarities relating to fiscal measures. This does not mean that, independent of any other assessment regarding the choices of the Italian legislator whether it was desirable to award jurisdiction to the administrative courts, rather than a specialist court, the fiscal nature of recovery actions cannot be overlooked.

Above all, in terms of the administrative process for enforcing the negative decision, the jurisdiction lies with the Minister responsible for the particular area (which in the case of tax aid, is the Minister of Finance). It should be quite apparent that the decision's implementation will regard qualitative and quantitative assessments of fiscal questions and will proceed along procedural rules that are fiscal in nature, such as those governing access, inspections and reviews, the submission of questionnaires, the issue of summons to appear, hearings, the safeguards in place for taxpayers, and so forth. All of these are governed by tax law,[77] given the constitutional principle that taxation requires legislation,[78] and in light also of the related questions regarding fundamental rights, such as the inviolability of domicile.

This also applies with respect to the *substance* of the claim intended to restore a pre-existing situation, which will ordinarily imply – in accordance with the Commission's statements - determining the taxes that would have been due in the absence of the prohibited aid, and its implementation will require analysis of the tax legislation

---

74. *See* Enrico Allorio, *Diritto processuale tributario* passim (1969); Francesco Tesauro, *Manuale del processo tributario* 4 et seq. (2020); Massimo Basilavecchia, *La giurisdizione* 75 et seq. (Claudio Consolo, Giuseppe Melis, Angelina-Maria Perrino, *Il giudizio tributario* (2022)).
75. *See* Commission Notice on the recovery of unlawful and incompatible State aid (2019/C 247/01), para. 106.
76. *See* Altieri, *Prime impressioni sulla giurisdizione del giudice amministrativo in materia di aiuti di stato,* Riv. Dir. Trib., 197 (2013).
77. *See* Arts 32 et seq. of Italian Presidential Decree No. 600/1973 and Italian Law No. 212/2000.
78. *See* Art. 23 of the Italian Constitution.

that would have applied to the particular set of circumstances, in any case without delay as determined by the Commission. There is nothing to prevent the Ministerial Decree regarding the recovery from delegating the conduct of these complex activities to the Revenues Agency,[79] as the body that holds the professional expertise on tax assessments.[80]

Ultimately, it is reasonable to assume, and highly likely, that enforcement of negative decisions will continue, in its administrative stages, to follow procedural models that are fiscal in nature.

There will however be differences in any of the procedures that apply in any court process, given the switch from the smoother workings of the Tax Courts, to the more cumbersome machinery of the Administrative Courts.

A different case is where recovery results directly from an act of the tax administration that does not implement a Commission Recovery Decision.[81]

This could occur in the case of undue (abusive) use of compatible or otherwise non-prohibited State aid, in the case of exceeding the *de minimis* limit,[82] or in the case of illegally used aid.

The exclusive jurisdiction of the administrative courts is in fact provided for, not only in the case of appeals against acts granting aid but also in the case of recoveries implemented in execution of a negative Commission Decision. In the absence of such a decision, and where the recovery takes place on the initiative of the financial administration on the basis of the typical taxation procedures (e.g., with notices of assessment or recovery or revocation of aid), tax jurisdiction can still be considered to maintain, according to the rules of the tax process.[83]

In any event, irrespective of these issues of jurisdiction, and given the European law's indifference as to which national rules of process apply, provided there is always compliance with principles of effectiveness, equivalence and non-discrimination,[84] there are some observations that may be made, based on national and European case law, regarding the role that national courts play in recovery procedures. The next

79. or the Customs Agency, where the matter is within its remit.
80. The Italian Constitutional Court itself, albeit with reference to a recovery activity that predates Italian Law No. 234/2012, has pointed out that 'recovery involves the taxation of income that [...] was already taxable' (*see* Italian Constitutional Court Order No. 36/2009).
81. or, the case where it is the national tax court that disapplies the domestic favourable rule if it is found to be contrary to the EU framework.
82. *See* Italian Supreme Court of Cassation No. 15006/2024.
83. *See* Italian Legislative Decree No. 546/1992, where there is a specific provision (Art. 47-bis), previously introduced, regarding the 'suspension of acts aimed at the recovery of state aid and the settlement of related disputes', which provides a more expeditious procedure for these particular disputes (*see* Massimo Montanari, *Art. 47-bis Sospensione di atti volti al recupero di aiuti di Stato e definizione delle relative controversie* 648 (Claudio Consolo & Cesare Glendi, *Commentario breve alle leggi del Processo tributario* (2023)). However, the cited Art. 47-*bis* presupposes the implementation of a negative Recovery Decision. Therefore, it does not seem that it can be applied in cases where this is lacking; what leads one to consider its tacit repeal due to the provision on the exclusive jurisdiction of the administrative judge.
84. *See* Case C-35/05, *Reemtsma Cigarettenfabriken GmbH v. Ministero delle Finanze*, 15.3.2007, ECLI:EU:C:2007:167.

section discusses these, after a brief discussion of the Italian experience of some recovery cases.

§5.04 THE RELEVANCE OF INTERNAL TAX PROCEDURES

As mentioned above, the reference *regula iuris* is now contained in the aforementioned Article 16 EU Reg. No. 1589/2015: it is up to the Member State to adopt the *necessary measures to recover the aid.*[85]

If that does not occur, the Commission may take action against the Member State before the ECJ.[86]

In practice, identifying the national legal instruments to be used in recovery has often been fraught with problems, as may be observed from the experience in Italy.

There has been quite a variety of favoured solutions over time. In a case on tax relief for innovative investment deemed incompatible State aid to firms in the motor vehicle, shipbuilding and synthetic fibre industries and to steel firms,[87] recovery was ordered to occur through the application of ordinary tax procedures, without any specific rules being instituted. Administrative instructions governing the conduct of tax assessments, the application of interest, and the non-application of fines, were all set out in a circular.[88]

Another relevant example regarded tax aid to banks made under Legislative Decree No. 153 of 1999 (Decision of 11 December 2001, 2002/581/EC).[89] Here the domestic reaction had more structure.

85. Previously, the provisions of Art. 14 of Council Regulation (EC) No. 659/1999 of 22 Mar. 1999 laying down detailed rules for the application of Art. 93 of the EC Treaty, OJ L 83, laying down the detailed rules for the implementation of the Treaty rules on state aid, according to which 'in the event of negative decisions on cases of unlawful aid, the Commission shall adopt a decision requiring the Member State concerned to take all necessary measures to recover the aid from the beneficiary'; and again, 'recovery shall be effected without delay in accordance with the procedures provided for in the law of the Member State concerned provided that they allow the immediate and effective execution of the Commission's decision'.

86. *See* Art. 108(2) TFEU, third sub-paragraph. This has indeed occurred on occasion, as with, for example, the aid to publicly-owned former municipal utilities (*see* Case C-207/05, *Italian Republic v. Commission of the European Communities*, 1.6.2006, ECLI:EU:C:2006:366).

87. Tax relief that was the subject of the Commission Decision of 13 May 1998 on State aid granted by Italy by way of tax relief under Law No. 549/95 to firms in the motor vehicle, shipbuilding and synthetic fibres industries and to steel firms covered by the ECSC Treaty (notified under document number C(1998) 1434) OJ L 47, final.

88. *See* Circular 15 Sep. 1998, No. 218/E/138725, which stated there should be partial assessments (that is, limited to the particular set of facts, and without prejudice to any other fiscal reviews), and interest should be calculated on the basis of the reference rate determined by the European Commission. In terms of penalties, the principle applied was that 'a person who commits a breach shall not be punished where the breach resulted from objective conditions of uncertainty as to the extent and scope of application of the measures in question, or by vagueness in the requests for information and forms for making a declaration or payment' (*see* Art. 6, second paragraph, of Italian Legislative Decree No. 472/1997). In particular, consideration has been given to the fact that although the law established reliefs, the instructions governing preparation of tax declarations contained no references to the European regulation of the individual sectors affected by the Commission's decision.

89. *See* Commission decision of 11 Dec. 2001 on the tax measures for banks and banking foundations implemented by Italy (notified under document number C(2001) 3955) OJ L 184.

Initially, the relief granted was frozen;[90] subsequently,[91] recovery of the aid was ordered, under a special procedure, that was materially different from the ordinary fiscal procedure, and which allowed for sanctions to be imposed in the event of non-compliance.

Another decision - again involving certain fiscal measures for the restructuring of the banking sector - is of particular interest.[92] Measures had already been enacted for the revaluation of shareholdings by undertakings generally; these provisions brought forward in time those measures' application within the banking sector. The European Court allowed recovery to proceed on the basis of the difference between the favourable treatment initially contemplated for the banks (deemed prohibited aid), and the favourable treatment that subsequently applied generally, in similar circumstances, to undertakings generally.[93]

Yet other solutions were applied in relation to aid in the form of temporary exemption from income taxation, to undertakings belonging to local authorities that converted into joint-stock companies. Subsequent legislative solutions were all *built* upon tax recovery models, albeit with some tweaks.[94] Typically, recovery was of *aid equivalent to unpaid taxes*,[95] applying the *principles and ordinary procedures for the*

---

90. *See* Art. 5 of Italian Law Decree No. 63/2002, converted with amendments into Italian Law No. 112/2002. This was not a straightforward suspension - that had already taken place, out of the normal course of matters, following the Commission opening its procedure. Rather, it anticipated that the periods for taking advantage of the reliefs would restart once the case before the European courts contesting the negative decision had reached a favourable conclusion.
91. *See* Art. 1 of Italian Law Decree No. 282/2002, converted into Italian Law No. 27/2003.
92. *See* Commission Decision of 11 Mar. 2008 on State aid C 15/07 (ex NN 20/07) implemented by Italy on the tax incentives in favour of certain restructured banks (notified under document number C(2008) 869) OJ L 237.
93. *See* Case T-335/08, *BNP Paribas and Banca Nazionale del Lavoro SpA (BNL) v. European Commission*, 1.7.2010, ECLI:EU:T:2010:271, which upheld the negative decision, but established that recovery would occur under a later, favourable, set of rules. *See* Marco Greggi, *Regime fiscale delle ristrutturazioni bancarie e aiuti di Stato: il caso BNP Paribas-BNL sotto la lente del Tribunale UE*, Rass. Trib. 4, 1082 (2011). *See* Notice from the Commission towards an effective implementation of Commission decisions ordering Member States to recover unlawful and incompatible State aid (2007/C 272/05), para. 50.
94. The recovery would take place over as much as three stages, which resulted in a lot of litigation, first in the tax commissions and latter, in the Italian Supreme Court of Cassation, some of which is still ongoing in relation to certain aspects of the quantum of interest. Initially, legislation (in the form of Art. 27 of Italian Law No. 62/2005) anticipated that pending the court's ruling on the negative Commission Decision 2003/193/EC, the affected companies would voluntarily declare the amount of aid they had enjoyed. That procedure proved unsuccessful, and, under pressure from the European Commission (culminating in an action for breach before the ECJ which ended in defeat for Italy, Case C-207/05, *Italian Republic v. Commission of the European Communities*, 1.6.2006, ECLI:EU:C:2006:366 (Summary publication)), measures were introduced for compulsory recovery (in Italian Law Decree No. 10/2007, converted as Italian Law No. 46/2007) based on self-certification by the affected company. Subsequently, under Art. 24 of Italian Law Decree No. 185/2008, converted as Italian Law No. 2/2009, measures were introduced for further recoveries, stating the methods by which the aid would be assessed and quantified; then Art. 19 of Italian Law Decree No. 135/2009 (converted with amendments into Italian Law No. 166/2009) provided for stricter rules for determining the amount to be recovered.
95. This form of words is contained in Italian Law Decree No. 185/2008, superseding the previous legislation's references to recovery of taxes, or of aid equivalent to the unpaid taxes, thereby overcoming the arguments over whether recovery is a matter that is fiscal in nature or not.

assessment and collection of income taxes, with sanctions not to be applied. Unlike less unusual fiscal procedures, there was no way of suspending a decision or delaying payment, and interest was determined under the European rules. Additionally, where the sums due went unpaid, a coercive collection procedure could be begun within thirty days and would proceed to a faster timetable than was usual. Additionally, participation in a tax amnesty under Law No. 289 of 27 December 2002, as amended, could not be good grounds for seeking to have the obligation to return taxes extinguished.[96]

As previously discussed in paragraph 3, this procedural diversity should no longer apply under the rules of Law No. 234/2012. Nonetheless, the peculiar character of tax matters, including tax aid, does mean that even under the new structure it is quite likely that recovery of tax aid will be modelled upon the schemes that are typical of tax assessments, subject to appropriate adaptations to ensure recovery is swift and effective.

§5.05 THE ROLE OF THE NATIONAL COURT IN THE RECOVERY PHASE

As mentioned earlier, recovery following a negative decision must be implemented in accordance with principles of immediacy, effectiveness and equivalence, and all national authorities are obliged to comply with those principles, including the national courts.[97] The national courts' role, like that of the European Commission, is also subject to a principle of sincere cooperation.[98] The Commission may upon request be

96. The issue over the relevance of a tax amnesty is closely bound up with the nature of recovery. If recovery is strictly fiscal in nature, then participation in a tax amnesty should be relevant as a grounds for extinguishing the liability, impeding recovery of the tax aid enjoyed in tax periods covered by the amnesty. Indeed, the direct effect of a decision is one thing, and whether recovery can be effected, another, requiring as it does an assessment under domestic rules, including those that determine whether tax periods are open or closed. The same should be true also in relation to other grounds by which tax obligations become definitive, as where the passage of time means it is no longer possible to make assessments of taxes. The very fact that the legislation expressly mentioned, and excluded, tax amnesties is indicative of how persuasive this argument is, in principle. It should be emphasised in any event that the Italian Supreme Court of Cassation's case law (discussed in more detail in the next section) was always very clear that such factors had no bearing, relying upon the direct effect and the principle of effectiveness.

97. For a systematic account of actions for the recovery of prohibited aid, and how it compares to actions for the rebate of incompatible taxes, both subject to principles of effectiveness and equivalence, *see* Francesco Tesauro, *Processo tributario e diritto comunitario* (Massimo Basilavecchia & Giuliano Tabet, *La giurisdizione tributaria nell'ordinamento* giurisdizionale (2009)); Lorenzo Del Federico, *Tutela del contribuente ed integrazione giuridica europea* 210 et seq. (2010); *see also* Lorenzo Del Federico, *I principi di equivalenza ed effettività nelle procedure di recupero degli aiuti di Stato fiscali* (Manlio Ingrosso, & Giuseppe Tesauro, *Agevolazioni fiscali e aiuti di Stato*, 353-361 (2009)).

98. *See* Art. 29 of Council Regulation (EU) 2015/1589 of 13 Jul. 2015 laying down detailed rules for the application of Art. 108 of the Treaty on the Functioning of the European Union (codification), OJ L 248, *supra*; Commission Notice on the recovery of unlawful and incompatible State aid (2019/C 247/01) *supra* para. 2.2.

called to assist the national courts, by providing information and advice on the application of relevant provisions.[99]

These principles are of crucial importance for negative decisions regarding aid schemes. In such cases, the aid beneficiaries may not be specifically identified, and the extent of the aid may not be determined in the decision. It follows that the analysis of each individual case of aid is a matter for the authorities of the Member State carrying out the recovery.

The issue arose in a case concerning the recovery of tax and social security measures in favour of the areas affected by the earthquake in Abruzzo, which was the subject of Decision C(2015) 5549. The national recovery measure,[100] with the appointment of a Commissioner *ad acta* also provided for the carrying out of a rapid preliminary investigation to determine the amounts to be recovered from each identified beneficiary.

It follows that implementing recovery requires particular care, as it consists of much more than simple execution - not only must the beneficiaries be identified but also one must determine whether, and to what extent, the aid was such as to distort competition, as well as quantifying the extent of recovery.[101] In cases of this kind, it is for the national courts to establish whether the recovery is consistent with the principles implicit in the Decision. Clearly, they are not entitled to examine the legitimacy of the Decision, as that is a matter reserved to the European courts.

As to the role of the national courts in the implementation of negative decisions on aid, and the recovery of prohibited aid, the Italian experience[102] has been one of a certain inconsistency between the principles that may be deduced from the rules and from the European case law, and the positions often taken by the national courts (as well as the tax authorities).

---

99. *See* Chiara Fontana, *Gli aiuti di stato di natura fiscale* 405 et seq. (2012). Such cooperation is not simply the possibility of addressing to the Commission. It has been found that a person prejudiced by the application of an aid measure that is as yet unauthorised may apply to the court for it to disapply a measure considered to conflict with European law, as early as the standstill stage.
100. *See* Italian Decree of the President of the Council of Ministers 14 Nov. 2017 published in the Italian Official Journal on 9 Mar. 2018.
101. *See* Case C-320/09, *A2A SpA, formerly AEM SpA v. European Commission*, 21.12.2001, ECLI:EU:C:2011:858 (Summary publication), para. 162. The national courts do not have any discretion regarding the recovery of aid declared unlawful and incompatible (para. 160), except with respect to the manner in which the decision is implemented (para. 161). Nonetheless, the national courts may, 'like the Commission, interpret the concept of State aid' (Case C-78/76, *Steinike & Weinlig v. Federal Republic of Germany*, [1977] 22.3.1977, ECLI:EU:C:1977:52 para. 14; Case C-39/94, *Syndicat français de l'Express international (SFEI) and others v. La Poste and others*, 11.7.1996, ECLI:EU:C:1996:285, para. 49; Case C-368/04, *Transalpine Ölleitung in Österreich GmbH and Others v. Finanzlandesdirektion für Tirol and Others*, 5.10.2006, ECLI: EU:C:2006:644, para. 39).
102. *See* Francesco Tundo, *Il microsistema procedimentale e processuale della disciplina di recupero degli aiuti fiscali [Nota a sentenza: Comm. trib. reg. Lombardia, Sez. XLVI, 30 giugno 2010, n. 82]*, Giurisprudenza tributaria 18, 723 (2011).

Generally, it has been observed, 'National courts also play an important role in the enforcement of recovery decisions.'[103] More particularly, 'In the case of an unlawful and incompatible aid scheme, the Member State will be required to carry out a detailed analysis of each individual aid granted on the basis of the scheme in question.'[104]

The European Court of Justice's position now reflects that articulated by the Commission: *'It is only at the stage of recovery of the aid that it is necessary to look at the individual situation of each undertaking concerned.'* Consequently, *'where the Commission rules in a general and abstract way on a scheme of State aids, which it declares incompatible with the common market ordering recovery of the amounts received under that scheme, it is for the Member State to verify the individual situation of each undertaking concerned by such a recovery operation'*.[105]

Even more plainly, it has been emphasised that 'it is a matter for the national authorities to determine in each individual case the precise amount of the aid to be recovered, in accordance with its own procedures, and under the supervision of the national courts'.[106] Moreover, 'before proceeding to the recovery of an advantage, the national authorities were necessarily required to verify, in each individual case, whether the advantage granted was, in the hands of its beneficiary, capable of distorting competition and affecting intra-Community trade, as otherwise that additional verification, essential to the classification of individual advantages received as State aid, could not be made'.[107]

---

103. *See* Commission notice on the enforcement of State aid law by national courts (2009/C 85/01), OJ C 85 para. 21(b).
104. *See* European Commission, Communication 2007/C 272/05, para. 49. This applies also in determining the amount of the aid to be recovered. On the recovery of State aid, *see* Francesco Tesauro, *Processo tributario e aiuti di stato*, 30 Corr. Trib. 45, 3665 et seq. (2007), in which the role of the domestic court is emphasised, as the court of European law; Fabrizio Amatucci, *Il ruolo del giudice nazionale in materia di aiuti fiscali*, Rass. Trib. 5, 1282 (2008), which is critical of the limitations upon the safeguards the court can provide in relation to the recovery of State aid; Chiara Fontana, *Gli aiuti di stato di natura fiscale* 273 et seq. (2012); and Clemente Ciampolillo, *Incompatibilità e recupero* 351 et seq. (Livia Salvini, *Aiuti di Stato in materia fiscale* (2007)).
105. *See* Joint Cases C-71-73-76/09, *Comitato 'Venezia vuole vivere'* (C-71/09 P), *Hotel Cipriani S.r.l.* (C-73/09 P) and *Società Italiana per il gas S.p.A. (Italgas)* (C-76/09 P) *v. European Commission*, para. 64.
106. *See* Case C-320/09, *A2A SpA, formerly AEM SpA v. European Commission*, para. 162. *See* Fabrizio Amatucci, *Il ruolo del giudice nazionale in materia di aiuti fiscali*, Rass. Trib. 5, 1282 (2008), at para. 4 points out how the European case law (Court of Justice, Case C-428/06, *Unión General de Trabajadores de La Rioja (UGT-Rioja) and Others v. Juntas Generales del Territorio Histórico de Vizcaya and Others*, 11.9.2008, ECLI:EU:C:2008:488 and Case C-434/06, Comunidad Autónoma de Castilla y León, 11.9.2008, ECLI:EU:C:2006:757) emphasises the importance of the domestic courts, which are responsible for interpreting and applying the domestic law, and how such courts are well-placed to make a proper assessment of the facts. *See also* Lorenzo Bianchi, *Gli incerti confini dell'onere della prova nella procedura di recupero degli aiuti di Stato illegittimi*, Giurisprudenza tributaria 907 (2009).
107. *See* Joint Cases C-71-73-76/09, *Comitato 'Venezia vuole vivere'* (C-71/09 P), *Hotel Cipriani S.r.l.* (C-73/09 P) and *Società Italiana per il gas S.p.A. (Italgas)* (C-76/09 P) *v. European Commission*, para. 115, which criticised a judgment that had found no need for the national authorities to review individual positions.

That approach is consistent with the longstanding position, that 'in the case of an aid scheme, the Commission may confine itself to examining the characteristics of the scheme in question in order to determine, in the grounds of its decision, whether, by reason of the terms of that scheme, it is likely to benefit in particular undertakings engaged in trade between Member States (Case C310/99 Italy v. Commission[2002] ECR I 2289)'.[108]

Since 'it is also evident from the case-law that there is no need for a negative decision concerning an aid scheme to provide an analysis of the aid granted in individual cases under the scheme', it follows that 'it is only at the stage of recovery of the aid that it is necessary to look at the individual situation of each undertaking concerned (*Italy v. Commission*, paragraph 89 above, paragraph 91)'.[109]

If this were not the case, recovery would merely be a matter at the discretion of the national administrative authorities, which would carry the risk of errors, or even abuse.[110]

Where, in relation to a recovery, the necessary analyses and enquiries by the competent administration of the State are absent (or fall short of the required standards, or are contested), in particular those regarding the quantum of aid, properly one may conclude that these essential activities may, indeed, be a matter for the national court, at a hearing. Whether a recovery order made in connection with an aid scheme should apply to any particular case - a matter for the national authorities - is thus subject to oversight by the courts.[111]

That oversight does not encroach upon the jurisdiction of the European courts, or the scrutiny of the law by the General Court or the Court of Justice, and neither does it conflict with the decisions that order recovery. Rather, it represents a means of properly enforcing the decision, to establish who it affects and to what extent - a role that is often necessary, especially with regard to aid schemes.

If one reviews the rulings that the national courts have made, they do not seem always consistent with the Court of Justice's approach. Indeed, they appear to have undergone a degree of role reversal, with the European courts acknowledging the role of the domestic courts, and the domestic courts (in particular, the Supreme Court) touched by a Draconian sense of loyalty to Europe.

108. *See* Case T-301/02, *AEM SpA v. Commission of the European Communities*, 11.6.2009, ECLI:EU:T:2009:191, para. 89.
109. *See* Case T-301/02, *AEM SpA v. Commission of the European Communities*, para. 161.
110. One should not overlook the potential (and inevitable) conflict of interest faced in reality by the administration responsible for recovering the aid (*see also* below), and the possible pressure that the European Commission may seek to bring to bear for a strict and comprehensive recovery.
111. *See* Case C-320/09, *A2A SpA, formerly AEM SpA v. European Commission*, para. 162. The importance of oversight by the national courts is importance in one particular respect, peculiar to the recovery of tax aid. It is obviously rather strange that a Member State is obliged to recover tax aid. On the one hand, it has the duty to defend the domestic legal system, and the economic policy underlying the tax regime considered inappropriate. On the other, it has the opportunity, through the recovery imposed by the European Commission to obtain additional, possibly unexpected, revenues, which gives rise to an unusual conflict of interest (*see* European Commission Report, State Aid Scoreboard, COM/2004/256).

The national courts have indeed found that, after a measure has been identified by the Commission as State aid, and that decision upheld by the European courts, the consequences in law are for 'the compulsory nature of the recovery of the State aid ... that does not permit the national court to reach any assessment, in that scrutiny of the compatibility of a national measure of State aid is a matter within the exclusive jurisdiction of the Commission of the European Communities'.[112]

This statement is in its own terms correct, but the fact is that it is not the question of the aid's compatibility that is usually brought before the national court, rather, it is the quite different question of the recoverability of the aid in the particular case, with regard to the particular conditions affecting the undertaking in question. This is not a matter beyond the jurisdiction of the national courts, not just as a function of the European case law referred to earlier, but also in light of the approach articulated by the European Commission itself.

It has been observed that 'the national courts must verify the compatibility of domestic law with the European rules, also of their own motion'.[113]

The Commission has emphasised that 'a decision on aid schemes is without prejudice to the possibility that individual aid may be deemed, wholly or partially, compatible with the common market on its own merits'.[114]

According to Italy's Supreme Court,[115] by contrast, 'There is no way that the Revenue Agency is obliged to carry out any investigation ... regarding whether the taxpayer was entitled to the benefit on another basis', although it admitted that 'in the substantive claim, the existence of any other basis would have to be argued'.

The case law of the Supreme Court in this area is based upon a strict interpretation of the principles by which the European decision is obligatory, effective and immediate, and the work of the national courts considered *'merely in service of the recovery'*,[116] making no consideration of the peculiar nature of the decisions related to aid schemes.

---

112. In similar vein, with regard to the recovery of aid given to public utilities, *see* Italian Supreme Court of Cassation, No. 6546/2012.
113. *See* Francesco Tesauro, *Processo tributario e aiuti di stato*, 30 Corr. Trib. 45, 3665 et seq. (2007); Italian Supreme Court of Cassation, No. 7909/2000.
114. Commission Decision of 5 Jun. 2002 on State aid granted by Italy in the form of tax exemptions and subsidised loans to public utilities with a majority public capital holding (notified under document number C(2002) 2006) (2003/193/CE) para. 126. A specific case in which the assessment could only be a matter for the national authorities and the national courts, who would be acting in such a case as courts of European law.
115. Italian Supreme Court of Cassation No. 23414/2010. The Italian Supreme Court of Cassation (Italian Supreme Court of Cassation No. 7659/2012) has said in that regard that the legislative provision could not have 'enabled the national legislature to evaluate individual hypotheses for compatibility, and thus to exclude individual grants of aid from the recovery'. This, however, is what in part happened with Art. 19 of Italian Law Decree No. 135/2009, converted as Italian Law No. 166/2009, which expressly stated (until the provision was abolished, likely following pressure from the European Commission) that in relation to the recovery of State aid enjoyed by publicly-owned former municipal utilities, 'capital gains derived from the extraordinary transactions carried out are to be disregarded'.
116. Italian Supreme Court of Cassation, Nos 6546/2012, 7660/2012. Under this logic, the identification of one person who in fact gained from the incompatible aid is sufficient. In its Judgments (Italian Supreme Court of Cassation, Nos 7659/2012 and 7660/2012), the Italian Supreme

Unlike decisions on individual State aid, such decisions require work that is necessarily national, in the assessment of particular cases.

That need derives from European case law and practice. It has been observed how every time that a particular set of facts must be examined in light of various aspects of competition, an economic analysis of the relevant market must be carried out, based upon a comparison between an ideal model and a real-world context.[117] An analysis must also be made regarding the actual anti-competitive impact upon European trade of the measure in question.

Nonetheless, there is a prevailing attitude that when considering an aid scheme, the European Commission 'may confine itself to examining the general characteristics of the scheme in question without been required to examine each particular case in which it applies in order to determine whether that scheme comprises aid elements'.[118]

The European Commission also 'is required not to establish that the aid has a real effect on trade between Member States and that competition is actually being distorted, but only to examine whether that aid is liable to affect such trade and distort competition'.[119]

The European Court has found, similarly that 'in the case of an aid scheme, the Commission may confine itself to examining the characteristics of the scheme in question in order to determine, in the grounds of its decision, whether, by reason of the terms of that scheme, it is likely to benefit in particular undertakings engaged in trade between Member States'.[120]

The European case law clearly recognises that the national authorities, including the courts, have an important role to play that goes beyond mere mechanical implementation. The limited and general duties the Commission has, when examining an aid scheme, have their counterpart in the necessary national activity of evaluating the particular set of facts. If this were not the case, the right of a domestic undertaking

Court of Cassation criticised the theory of the counter-limits (*see* Italian Constitutional Court, No. 288/2010), which it considered to have been superseded, as there was now 'sufficient proof of the safeguarding of fundamental rights' in European statute and case law (*see also* Italian Supreme Court of Cassation, No. 23418/2010). There was no consideration however of the terms of Art. 4 of the Lisbon Treaty, in which there is explicit recognition of the national identities inherent in the fundamental political and constitutional structure of the individual members of the Union. Although this may be considered a weakening of the counter-limits theory, one cannot but observe how the Lisbon Treaty, in recognising fundamental national principles, in part adds the protection offered by the European courts to that offered by national courts. On the broader issue of the relationship between European and national law, with particular reference to tax matters, *see* Claudio Sacchetto, *Principi di diritto tributario europeo e internazionale* (2011); Claudio Sacchetto, *Il diritto comunitario e l'ordinamento tributario italiano*, 1 Dir. Prat. Trib. Int. 1, 13 (2001); and Christian Califano, *Ordinamento tributario e ordinamento comunitario. Profili costituzionali*, Corso Perfezionamento Dir. Trib. Berliri, 6 (2002).

117. *See* Alberto Santa Maria, *European Economic Law* 453 et seq. (2014).
118. *See* Case C-148/04, *Unicredito Italiano SpA v. Agenzia delle Entrate, Ufficio Genova 1*, para. 67.
119. *See* Case C-148/04, *Unicredito Italiano SpA v. Agenzia delle Entrate, Ufficio Genova 1*, para. 54. *See*, similarly, Case T-301/02, *AEM SpA v. Commission of the European Communities*, paras 88 and 83, which stated that 'the Commission was not bound to conduct an examination by sector in order to evaluate the effects' of the measure.
120. *See* Case T-301/02, *AEM SpA v. Commission of the European Communities*, para. 89.

to defend itself against an allegation that it had gained unduly from an aid measure, or against a recovery procedure, would be undermined.

The prevailing position in the national case law does not seem to respond particularly well to this fundamental need, even leaving aside the special considerations that may apply at this particular point in time. That said, some recent decisions by the Supreme Court deserve mention. These examined a particular kind of tax aid (which conferred benefits where employees were taken on), and whether in the particular case, this amounted to prohibited State aid or not. The Supreme Court concluded that it did not, in that the rules applied to undertakings generally. In relation to another measure, which was restricted in its geographical scope, the court found that this did constitute State aid, but it was not prohibited on the basis that it was below the *de minimis* threshold. It did so via an (albeit succinct) analysis of the various requirements established by the European legislation, including that related to the distortion of competition, and the obligation to give prior notice.[121]

While one cannot deny that these judgments carry the risk of intruding upon areas for which the European Commission has exclusive jurisdiction, it does indicate the emergence of an approach that is consistent with European case law and practice, one that places greater emphasis on the role of the domestic courts and ensures businesses are able to exercise the legal redress to which they should be entitled.

121. *See* Italian Supreme Court of Cassation, Nos 8138/2012 and 8139/2012, relating to tax credits made available where new employees were taken on pursuant to Art. 63 of Italian Law No. 289/2002, intended as a means of boosting employment. The Italian Supreme Court of Cassation held that the measure provided for in Art. 63, first paragraph, of Italian Law No. 289/2002 did not constitute State aid because of its general nature, while the additional measure in the same subsection, related to the geographical areas indicated in Art. 7 of Italian Law No. 388/2000 (the central and southern regions), could theoretically constitute *selective* State aid, but this in practice had not happened, as the amount was within the *de minimis* threshold. This same factor has led the Italian Supreme Court of Cassation to hold that prior notification to the European Commission was not required under Art. 108(3) TFEU, based upon the principle contained in Art. 2(1) of Regulation No. 1998/2006 (*see also* Regulation No. 994/1998; and Art. 109 TFEU, under which it is possible, in circumstances identified through in Commission Regulations, to exempt certain categories of aid from the notification requirement).

CHAPTER 6

The Judicial Phase

Edoardo Gambaro

§6.01 JUDICIAL CONTROL OVER DECISIONS RELATING TO STATE AID

Decisions of the Commission – or of the Council – are in general presumed to be valid and effective, and decisions taken in the field of State aid are no exception.[1]

Traditionally, State aid litigation corresponds, together with competition and intellectual property litigation, to the largest volume of activity of the Court of Justice of the European Union:[2] between 2009 and 2013, 245 such cases were filed with the General Court.[3] *New* actions brought before the General Court had spiked around the turn of the century (100 actions brought in 1999 and 80 in 2000), then experiencing a decline in number in the following decades (25 actions brought in 2003, 28 in 2006)[4] and apparently stabilized in the last years, with new cases roughly averaging around 40 per year in 2018-2022.[5] In 2023, only 10 new cases were registered in the field of State aid, touching all time low since 1993, when jurisdiction was conferred on the General Court to hear actions brought by individuals in the field of State aid.

1. The Court first stated this principle in Case C-15/85, *Consorzio cooperative d'Abruzzo v. Commission*, 26.2.1987, ECLI:EU:C:1987:111 para. 10. The CFI restated it, in the State aid field, in Case T-123/97, *Salomon SA v. Commission*, 6.10.1999, ECLI:EU:T:1999:245 para. 46.
2. For the avoidance of doubt, the official definition of 'Court of Justice of the European Union' is employed here, thereby encompassing the Court of Justice proper, the General Court (formerly Court of First Instance), and – albeit not relevant in the case at stake – the Civil Service Tribunal; *see* Art. 19 TEU.
3. Statistics concerning the judicial activity of the General Court, available on <www.curia.europa.eu>, p. 8 (statistics 2023).
4. Statistics concerning the judicial activity of the Court of First Instance, available on <www.curia.europa.eu>, p. 204 (statistics 2004) and p. 231 (statistics 2005).
5. Specifically, new State aid cases brought before the General Court were 134 in 2019, 42 in 2020, 46 in 2021, 68 in 2022, 10 in 2023. Data taken from the 2023 Statistics concerning the judicial activity of the General Court (*see supra*).

The numbers concerning State aid actions that have been *completed* by the General Court appear to largely mirror those set forth above regarding filed actions, with an average of sixty cases decided per year between 2018 and 2023.[6]

State aid proceedings before the General Court remain the longest, after competition proceedings, with an average duration of more than twenty months.[7]

In recent years, the General Court's State aid decisions have been one of the most frequently challenged before the Court of Justice (around 50% of cases; second only to appeals concerning competition law, between 2019 and 2023).[8]

Chapter 6 will discuss the nature of the main judicial proceedings that can be brought against a decision of the Commission (or the Council) in matters of State aid, whether through an action for annulment, or for failure to act, or for a preliminary ruling.

§6.02 ARTICLE 263 TFEU: ACTIONS FOR ANNULMENT

Actions for annulment are likely to be the judicial tool most frequently used in European legal practice: the following paragraphs will outline their subject matter, object, as well as possible grounds. The procedural features of actions for annulment will then be examined in the remainder of this section.

Actions for annulment are heard on first instance before the General Court and on appeal before the Court of Justice.[9]

Actions for annulment are quintessentially an item of review jurisdiction, in that their sole purpose is to decide on the legality of 'acts' issued by EU institutions.[10] In the words of the TFEU, the subject matter of actions for annulment is to '*review the legality*' of those acts, enacted by EU bodies, that are '*intended to produce legal effects vis-à-vis third parties*'.[11] In particular, the acts subject to annulment are: legislative acts, acts of the Council, acts of the Commission and of the European Central Bank, other than recommendations and opinions, and acts of the European Parliament and of the European Council intended to produce legal effects vis-à-vis third parties, and acts of bodies, offices or agencies of the Union that are likewise intended to produce legal effects vis-à-vis third parties.

In the field of State aid, actions for annulment are brought against decisions of the Commission or of the Council – the two bodies who deal with State aid cases firsthand.

Actions for annulment can be brought exclusively on grounds of *lack of competence*; of *infringement of an essential procedural requirement*; of *infringement of the*

6. *Ibid.*, 75; specifically, new State aid cases completed by the General Court were 75 in 2019, 28 in 2020, 65 in 2021, 48 in 2022, 127 in 2023.
7. Statistics concerning the judicial activity of the General Court, available on <www.curia.europa.eu>, p. 13 (statistics 2023).
8. *Ibid.*, p. 23.
9. Article 256(1) TFEU.
10. To this respect, drafters of the Treaty have ostensibly drawn their inspiration from the models of administrative redress of continental Europe.
11. Article 263(1) TFEU.

Treaty or of any rule of law relating to its application, or of *misuse of powers*.[12] The two former grounds – relating to the so-called external standing – may be claimed ex officio, while the two latter grounds – relating to the so-called internal standing – may only be claimed by concerned parties.

Restrictions to standing are one of the major features of actions for annulment.[13] The provision draws a clear distinction between two categories of applicants: privileged and non-privileged. Privileged applicants – i.e., Member States, the European Parliament, the Commission and the Council – can institute proceedings against a certain act on grounds of general interest, without the need to demonstrate a specific interest thereon.[14] In fact, Member States do happen to institute proceedings against the alleged granting of State aid in *other* Member States.[15]

Non-privileged applicants – i.e., natural or legal persons – may, however, only institute proceedings against a decision in three cases:[16] (i) if the decision is addressed to the applicant her- or himself;[17] (ii) if the decision, albeit in the form of a regulation or a decision addressed to another person, is of *direct and individual concern* to the applicant – which concern the applicant will need to show; or (iii) if they are directly concerned by a 'regulatory act' – i.e., an act of general application not being a legislative act – not entailing implementing measures.[18]

The proceedings provided for in Article 263 TFEU must be instituted within *two* months of the *publication of the measure*, or of its *notification to the plaintiff*, or, in the absence thereof, of *the day on which it came to the knowledge of the latter*, as the case may be;[19] the applicable time-limits are regulated, depending on the relevant Court, by Articles 80 through 82 of the Rules of Procedure of the ECJ and by Articles 101 through 103 of the Rules of Procedure of the GC. The relevant time-limits are extended *on account of distance* by a single period of ten days.[20]

The Court of Justice has constantly applied these time-limits very strictly.[21] According to the ECJ, the application of EU rules on procedural time-limits can only be

12. Article 263(2) TFEU.
13. *See* §6.02[B] of the present Chapter for an analysis of *locus standi* towards a Commission decision in the field of State aid.
14. *See, inter alia*, Joined Cases C-463/10 and C-475/10, *Deutsche Post and Germany v. Commission*, 13.10.2011, ECLI:EU:C:2011:656, paras 36 et seq.
15. A case to this effect is Case C-84/82 *Germany v. Commission* (*'State Aid to the Belgian textile industry'*), 20.3.1984, ECLI:EU:C:1984:117.
16. Article 263(4) TFEU.
17. Which however does not seem to be an applicable case, considering that decisions concerning State aid invariably have Member States as their addressees. *See* Art. 25 of Regulation No. 659/99.
18. The two former cases were already envisioned in the TEC, while the last case has been introduced by the Treaty of Lisbon: accordingly, actions on these grounds have been subject to be brought only effective from 1 Dec. 2009.
19. Article 263(6) TFEU.
20. Article 81(2) of the Rules of Procedure of the ECJ and Art. 102(2) of the Rules of Procedure of the GC.
21. Case C-276/85, *Cladakis v. Commission*, 4.3.1987, ECLI:EU:C:1987:57; Case T-126/00, *Confindustria and Others v. Commission*, 19.1.2001, ECLI:EU:T:2001:17, para. 21.

derogated in exceptional cases of either unforeseeable circumstances or force majeure.[22] Such a strict position taken by the Court explains in light of reasons of legal certainty, on the one hand, and of the necessity of avoiding discrimination or unequal or arbitrary treatment in the administration of justice on the other hand: accordingly, the Court of Justice considers timing as a matter of *ordre publique*.[23]

Settled case law has clarified how the period of eligibility for instituting proceedings runs from the publication or notification of the measure or, subsidiarily, from the day on which a measure came to the knowledge of the relevant applicant. This creates a distinction between cases wherein the applicant is the Member State concerned – to which, alone, the decision is formally notified –and cases wherein the applicant is not the addressee of the measure. In the former case, time starts running from the date of notification of the measure, which is prior in time to its publication; in the latter case, time starts running from the date on which the decision is published in the *Official Journal of the European Union* (hereinafter the 'OJ'), regardless of whether the applicant had in fact become aware of the decision before that time.[24] This includes cases where an applicant other than a Member State – such as a beneficiary of State aid or a complainant – is communicated, but not formally notified, of the decision by the Commission.[25]

In the field of State aid, the problem arises in connection with the decisions provided for in Article 4(2) and (3) of Regulation No. 659/1999.[26] Pursuant to Article 26 thereof, the Commission is required to publish in the OJ only a summary notice of any such decision. Being however the full text of each decision available on the website of the Commission's Secretariat General,[27] the date of publication in the OJ is nonetheless the starting point of the period prescribed for bringing the action.[28]

According to the case law of the Court, lacking either publication or notification, it is up to the party who has knowledge of a decision of its own concern to request the whole text thereof within a reasonable period.[29] Subject thereto, the ECJ has ruled that the period for bringing an action does not start to run until the third party concerned acquires *precise knowledge* of the content of the decision in question and of the reasons

22. Article 45 of the Statute of the Court of Justice.
23. Case C-500/07 P, *Territorio Energia Ambiente S.p.A. (TEA) v. Commission* 25.11.2008, ECLI:EU:C:2008:651, summary publication (para. 20); *see* Case C-33/72, *Gunnella v. Commission*, 8.5.1973, ECLI:EU:C:1973:49, para. 4.
24. *See, ex plurimis*, Case C-122/95, *Germany v. Commission*, 10.3.1998, ECLI:EU:C:1998:94, para. 35 and Case T-123/97, *Salomon SA v. Commission*, para. 42.
25. Joined Cases T-273/06 and T-297/06, *ISD Polska and Others v. Commission*, 1.7.2009, ECLI:EU:T:2009:233, para. 58; Case T-354/05, *Télévision Française 1 S.A. (TF1) v. Commission*, 11.3.2009, ECLI:EU:T:2009:66, para. 31.
26. Published in OJ L 83/1 of 7 Mar. 1999.
27. *See* <ec.europa.eu/community_law/eulaw/index_en.htm#aides>.
28. Case T-388/02, *Kronoply GmbH and Kronotex GmbH v. Commission*, 10.12.2008, para. 34; Case T-321/04, *Air Bourbon v. Commission*, 19.9.2005, ECLI:EU:T:2005:328, para. 34.
29. Case C-102/92, *Ferriere Acciaierie Sarde v. Commission*, 5.3.1993, ECLI:EU:C:1993:86, para. 18; Case C-236/86, *Dillinger H ü ttenwerke v. Commission*, 6.7.1988, ECLI:EU:C:1988:367, para. 14 and Case C-180/88, *Wirtschaftsvereinigung Eisen – und Stahlindustrie v. Commission*, 6.12.1990, ECLI:EU:C:1990:441, paras 22-24.

on which it is based, in such a way as to enable it to exercise its right of defence and to bring action accordingly.[30]

It is not relevant, to the end of enabling a party to challenge a decision, whether such decision produces immediate effects or not. As much as the effects of an act may not take place until a later date set forth in the act itself, individuals are still able to initiate proceedings for annulment of said act right away, prior to that date.[31]

[A] Actions for Annulment: Challengeable Measures

The ECJ has held that actions for annulment be available with respect to all measures adopted by EU institutions, whatever their nature or form, which are intended to have *legal effects*.[32] These legal effects are, according to the consistent case law of the Court, those capable of affecting the interests of the applicant by bringing about a distinct change in his legal position;[33] it should be noted that the notion of 'act open to challenge' has then been extended by case law, with particular respect to the right of actions of complainants.[34] In order to determine whether an act or a decision produces such legal effects, it is necessary to look first at its *substance*, and then at the intention of those who have drafted it.[35]

Where a measure against which an action for annulment has been brought comprises *essentially distinct parts*, only those parts of that measure which produce binding legal effects capable of bringing about a significant change in the applicant's

30. Case C-236/86, *Dillinger H ü ttenwerke v. Commission*, para. 14. *See also* Case T-468/93, *Frio Naval e Industrial SA (Frinil) v. Commission*, 10.02,1994, ECLI:EU:T:1994:18, para. 32; *contra, see* Joined Cases T-485/93, T-491/93 and T-494/93 and T-61/98, *Dreyfus and Others v. Commission*, 8.11.2000, ECLI:EU:T:2000:255, paras 50-52.
31. Case T-40/04, *Bonino and Others v. Parliament and Council*, 11.7.2005, ECLI:EU:T:2005:279, paras 46 et seq.
32. *See*, lastly, Case T-517/12, *Alro SA v. Commission*, 16.10.2014, ECLI:EU:T:2014:890, para. 22. *See also* Case C-22/70, *Commission v. Council ('AETR/ERTA')*, 31.3.1971, ECLI:EU:C:1971:32, para. 42; Case C-316/91, *Parliament v. Council*, 2.3.1994, ECLI:EU:C:1994:76, para. 8. With more specific respect to the matter of State aid *see* Case C-400/99, *Italy v. Commission ('Tirrenia I I')*, 10.5.2005, ECLI:EU:C:2005:275, para. 49.
33. Case C-60/81, *IBM v. Commission*, 11.11.1981, ECLI:EU:C:1981:264, para. 9; Case T-63/89, *Automec v. Commission*, 10.7.1990, ECLI:EU:T:1990:42, para. 42; Case T-3/93, *Air France v. Commission*, 24.3.1994, ECLI:EU:T:1994:36, para. 43; Case T-154/94, *Comité des Salines de France v. Commission*, 22.10.1996, ECLI:EU:T:1996:152, para. 37; Case T-117/95, *Corman v. Commission*, 30.1.1997, ECLI:EU:T:1997:9; Case T-178/94, *ATM v. Commission*, 18.12.1997, ECLI:EU:T:1997:210, para. 53; Case T-81/97, *Regione Toscana v. Commission*, 16.7.1998, ECLI:EU:T:1998:180, para. 21; Case T-112/99, *M6 and others v. Commission*, 18.9.2001, ECLI:EU:T:2001:215, para. 35.
34. *See* Case C-521/06 P, *Athinaïki Techniki v. Commission ('Athinaïki Techniki I')*, 17.7.2008, ECLI:EU:C:2008:422, para. 47; Case C-362/09 *Athinaïki Techniki v. Commission ('Athinaïki Techniki II')*, 16.12.2010, ECLI:EU:C:2010:783.
35. *See* Case C-322/09 P, *Nya Destination Stockholm Hotell & Teaterpaket AB (NDSHT) v. Commission*, 18.11.2010, ECLI:EU:C:2010:701, paras 46 et seq.; Case C-249/02, *Portugal v. Commission*, ECLI:EU:C:2004:704, para. 35; Case C-50/90, *SunZest v. Commission*, 13.7.1991, ECLI: EU:C:1991:253, para. 12. *See also* Joined Cases C-68/94 and C-30/95, *France and Others v. Commission*, 31.3.1998, ECLI:EU:C:1998:148, para. 63 and Joined Cases T-125/97 and T-127/97, *Coca-Cola v. Commission*, 22.3.2000, ECLI:EU:T:2000:84, para. 78.

legal situation can be challenged.[36] This reasoning disqualifies from being challenged, *inter alia*, the assessments made to base the decision: the reasoning included therein is subject to judicial review only inasmuch as it constitutes the basis for the operative part of the decision.[37]

Having regard to Regulation No. 659/1999, the following measures are deemed *challengeable* under Article 263 TFEU: decisions whereby the Commission either: (a) finds that *the measure does not constitute aid;* or (b) *decides not to raise objections*, and – subject to certain conditions – *decisions to initiate the formal investigation procedure under Article 4(4)* of Regulation No. 659/1999.

With respect to the former decisions,[38] it is settled case law that the decision *refusing* to initiate the formal investigation procedure provided for by Article 108(2) of the Treaty can, as a rule, be challenged, in that it is definitive and therefore cannot be characterized as a mere preparatory measure.[39]

With respect to the latter decisions,[40] they are subject to challenge having taken into account the following conditions: (a) the decision regards a measure in the course of implementation; (b) the Commission has an affirmative consideration of the measure – i.e., it considers it as new aid; and (c) the relevant Member State objects to such classification. In these circumstances, the act is subject to challenge, with limitation to the part that is not merely provisional; that is, the prima facie assessment of the measure, and whether the Commission has made a manifest error thereupon.[41]

In particular, in the *Tirrenia I* case, notably, the Court of Justice held that the decision whereby the Commission initiated the procedure under Article 108(2) TFEU in relation to a measure in the course of implementation and classified as *new aid* could well be challenged, *notwithstanding the absence of a suspension injunction*. According to the Court, even such a decision necessarily alters the legal position of the measure under consideration and that of the undertakings that are its beneficiaries, particularly as regards the pursuit of its implementation.[42]

In another case the Court has taken into consideration the application to annul a decision to initiate formal proceedings against a measure which was no longer in the

36. Case C-184/97, *BP Chemicals v. Commission*, 22.9.2000, ECLI:EU:T:2000:217, para. 34.
37. Case C-367/95 P, *Commission v. Sytraval and Brink's France*, para. 45; Case T-46/97, *SIC – Sociedade Independente de Comunicação SA v. Commission*, 10.3.2000, ECLI:EU:T:2000:123, para. 45. *See also* Case C-521/06 P, *Athinaïki Techniki I*, para. 47.
38. Paragraphs 2 and 3, respectively, of Art. 4 of Regulation No. 659/1999.
39. Case C-313/90, *Comité international de la rayonne et des fibres synthétiques (CIRFS) and Others v. Commission*, 24.3.1993, ECLI:EU:C:1993:111, paras 26-27; Case T-82/96, *ARAP and others v. Commission*, 17.7.1999, ECLI:EU:T:1999:127, para. 36; Case T-114/00, *Aktionsgemeinschaft Recht und Eigentum eV v. Commission*, 5.12.2002, ECLI:EU:T:2002:298. *See also* Case C-198/91, *Cook plc v. Commission*, 19.3.1993, ECLI:EU:C:1993:197; C-225/91, *Matra v. Commission*, 15.7.1993, ECLI:EU:C:1993:239, and Case T-188/95, *Waterleiding Maatschappij 'Noord -West Brabant' NV v. Commission* 16.9.1998, ECLI:EU:T:1998:217.
40. *See* Art. 108(2) TFEU.
41. Case T-421/07 *Deutsche Post v. Commission*, 18.9.2015, ECLI:EU:T:2011:720, para. 50.
42. Case C-400/99, *Tirrenia I*, 9.10.2001, ECLI:EU:C:2001:528, paras 59, 62 et seq.; Case C-400/99, *'Tirrenia II'* (paras 15 et seq., 35 et seq.). *Contra*, with limitation to the non-challengeability of the mere assessment of the provision of a service constituting a public facility, *see* Case T-87/09, *Andersen v. Commission*, 25.11.2009, ECLI:EU:T:2009:468.

course of implementation at the time the action was brought: the outcome has been negative, as such acts have been deemed not challengeable.[43]

As far as State aid is concerned, also provisional measures having *legal effects unrelated* to the eventual final decision they were preparatory to are subject to be challenged.[44] While this may appear as an exception to the principle of non-challengeability of provisional measures, it needs to be taken into account that an affirmative decision thereon creates a standstill obligation requiring the Member State concerned to – until the Commission reaches a final decision – suspend the grant of aid, or to recover any unlawful aid already paid.[45] In *Italgrani*, the ECJ held that the effects of the decision initiating the formal investigation procedure differ depending on whether the aid in question is new aid or existing aid. In the former case, the State is prevented from implementing the aid proposal submitted to the Commission; that prohibition does not, however, apply where the aid is existing aid.[46]

An action for annulment must also be available in the case of:

- the Commission's *failure to take a decision* within two months of receiving a complete notification from the Member State concerned;[47,48]
- the Commission's *decisions closing the formal investigation procedure*.[49] These are decisions whereby the Commission: (i) finds that the notified measure does not constitute aid (Article 7(2)); (ii) decides that the aid is compatible with the common market (a 'positive decision', Article 7(3)); (iii) attaches conditions to a positive decision (a 'conditional decision', Article 7(4)); or (iv) finds that the aid is not compatible with the common market (a 'negative decision', Article 7(5));
- a *decision revoking a prior decision*;[50]
- a *decision requiring the Member State to suspend any unlawful aid until the Commission has taken a decision on the compatibility of the aid*;[51]
- a *decision requiring the Member State provisionally to recover unlawful aid* (Article 11(2) of Regulation No. 659/1999);

43. Case T-517/12, *Alro SA v. Commission*paras 34 et seq.
44. Case C-47/91, *Italgrani*, 9.7.1992, ECLI:EU:C:1992:255 paras 22-30; Case C-400/99, *Tirrenia I*, para. 57; Joined Cases T-195/01 and T-207/01, *Gibraltar v. Commission*, 30.4.2002, ECLI: EU:T:2002:111, para. 82.
45. Articles 3, 11(1) and 11(2), Regulation No. 659/1999.
46. Case C-47/91, *Italgrani*, para. 25; Case C-400/99, *Tirrenia I*, para. 56. *See also* Case C-312/90, *Spain v. Commission*, 30.7.1992, ECLI:EU:C:1992:282, para. 17.
47. Article 4(5) and 4(6) of Regulation No. 659/1999.
48. If one adheres to the thesis that such a failure amounts in substance to a 'positive' decision. *See* Soltész, Bielesz, *Judicial review of State Aid Decisions – Recent Developments*, in *ECLR*, 2004, p. 133 (at p. 134). *Contra*, Blasi, Munari, *sub Art. 88 CE*, in Tizzano, *Trattati dell'Unione europea e della Comunità europea*, Milan, 2004, p. 622, according to whom one can instead bring an action for failure to act *ex* Art. 232 EC.
49. Article 7 of Regulation No. 659/1999.
50. Article 9 of Regulation No. 659/1999.
51. Article 11(1) of Regulation No. 659/1999.

- a *negative decision whereby the Commission does not require recovery of unlawful aid* (e.g., where this would be contrary to a general principle of EU law, *see* Article 14 of Regulation No. 659/1999);
- a decision whereby the Commission *extends* the validity of the framework for State aid at the EU level in an economic sector beyond its expiry date;[52]
- an *information injunction* under Article 10 of Regulation No. 659/1999, as it constitutes a formal decision in the meaning set forth by Article 288 TFEU[53] – a request for information in the framework of the Commission's monitoring activity is conversely not subject to judicial review;[54]
- a *letter/decision pursuant to Article 20(2)* of Regulation No. 659/99 whereby the Commission informs the complainant that there are insufficient grounds in the complaint for identifying the existence of a State aid:[55] according to the Court of Justice, such a letter, in which the Commission '*adopts a clear and definitive position*', is of a substantially decision-making nature, in that it contains a decision within the meaning of Article 4(2) of Regulation No. 659/1999.[56] It needs also be considered that only by bringing an action against such a decision can a party ensure that its procedural guarantees under Article 6(2) of Regulation No. 659/1999 be respected. The new wording of Articles 10 and 20(2) of the Procedural Regulation does,[57] however, cast a shadow over the ability of the *Athinaïki Techniki* case law to endure in the future:[58] the Regulation confirms the Commission's earlier practice requiring a number of

52. Case C-135/93, *Spain v. Commission*, 29.7.1995, ECLI:EU:C:1995:201, paras 20-30.
53. Joined Cases C-463/10 and C-475/10, *Deutsche Post and Germany v. Commission*.
54. Case T-22/07, *IS Steel Košice v. Commission*, 14.5.2009, ECLI:EU:T:2009:158.
55. Article 20(2) of Regulation No. 659/1999. In the past, in practice, the Commission usually sent a letter to the complainant informing him that there were insufficient grounds for taking a view on the case; more than once, the Commission added that the assessment was not to be considered definitive in compliance with the second sentence of the former version of Art. 20(2) of Regulation No. 659/99.
56. Case C-322/09 P, *NDSHT v. Commission*, paras 58 et seq.; *see* Case C-521/06 P, *Athinaïki Techniki I*, para. 62. This case law was confirmed among others by Case T-182/10, *Associazione italiana delle società concessionarie per la costruzione e l'esercizio di autostrade e trafori stradali (Aiscat) v. Commission*, 15.1.2013, ECLI:EU:T:2013:9. Before *Athinaïki Techniki I*, the case law was far from consistent: for example, in the *Sytraval* case (and in Case T-182/98, *UPS v. Commission*, 30.9.1999, ECLI:EU:T:1999:243) the EU Courts regarded the letter to the complainant as an informal and therefore not a challengeable communication, The consequence that the only applicable form of redress was that of an action for failure to act under Art. 265 TFEU. Conversely, in the *Deutsche Bahn* case, the EU Courts had already suggested a substantive approach, according to which if the Commission takes a clear and reasoned position on the aid, it can be acting only in accordance with Art. 4(2) of Regulation No. 659/99: Case T-351/02, *Deutsche Bahn AG v. Commission*, 5.4.2006, ECLI:EU:T:2006:104, paras 34-63.
57. As amended by EU Regulation 743/2013.
58. On the *Athinaïki Techniki* and *NDSHT* cases, *see* Edoardo Gambaro, Francesco Mazzocchi, 'Case C-521/06 P *Athinaïki Techniki v. Commission*, 17.7.2008, ECLI:EU:C:2008:422; Case C-322/09 *NDSHT v. Commission* of 18 November 2010, nyr and C-362/09 P *Athinaïki Techniki v. Commission* of 16 December 2010, nyr', 48 *Common Market Law Review* 2083 (2011). *See also* Hanns Peter Nehl, *Judicial Protection of Complainants in EC State Aid Law: A Silent Revolution?*, European State Aid Law Quarterly 401 (2009); Küllike Jürimäe, *Standing in State Aid Cases: What's the State of Play?*, European State Aid Law Quarterly 303 (2010) https://doi.org/10.21552/estal/2010/2/188.

procedural steps to be taken.[59] It should be borne in mind, all the same, that a communication under Article 20(2) may be challenged independently of whether the Commission decides that the measure constitutes existing or new aid: the choice of one position over the other implies the choice of initiating the proceedings pursuant to Article 108(1) rather than 108(2) TFEU[60]

- *potential decisions of the Council under* the third subparagraph of Article 108(2) TFEU;[61]
- the Commission's 'record' under Article 19 of Regulation No. 659/99 of the Member State's acceptance of its proposal if appropriate measures in case of existing aid;[62]
- the decision by which the Commission requests information from private parties (the so-called market information tool).[63]

As it has been apparent from the list above, a decision, to be subject to judicial review, has that it is to bring about a change in the legal situation of the applicant: a corollary of this principle is the inability of two categories of acts to be challenged: *confirmatory acts*, and *intermediate measures*. The former acts are those which purely confirm an earlier decision which has already become final.[64] The latter acts are measures taken merely in preparation of a final decision, which is not challengeable inasmuch as the illegality contained therein can be also relied upon in the action to be brought against the relevant final decision.[65]

Coming to a more specific enumeration of measures not subject to judicial review, the following acts are *not challengeable*:

- in respect of existing aid, *recommendations* under Article 18 of Regulation No. 659/1999, whereby the Commission proposes appropriate measures to the

59. In particular, it is required: (a) to fill out a complaint form and to provide the mandatory information; (b) to dispatch a letter to the complainant requiring comments within one month of receipt in case the complaint be incomplete or unfounded; and (c) the automatic withdrawal of complaints in case of failure of the complainant to make its views known within the prescribed timeframe. On this point, *see* Hanns Peter Nehl, *2013 Reform of EU State Aid Procedures: How to Exacerbate the Imbalance Between Efficiency and Individual Protection*, European State Aid Law Quarterly 235 (2014).
60. Case C-313/90, *CIRFS v. Commission*, paras 25-27; Case C-321/99, *ARAP and Others v. Commission*, paras 61 et seq.
61. Case C-122/94, *Commission v. Council*, 29.2.1996, ECLI:EU:C:1996:68; Case C-309/95, *Commission v. Council ('Exceptional aid to producers of table wine in France')*, 19.2.1998, ECLI: EU:C:1998:66.
62. Case T-354/05, *Télevision Francaise 1 SA v. Commission*, 11.3.2009, ECLI:EU:T:2009:66.
63. Article 6a (7) of Regulation No. 659/99, as introduced by Regulation No. 734/2013.
64. Reasons for this exclusion can be traced in the necessity of not reopening for challenge an act which has already gained stability – ultimately, an issue of legal certainty. *See* Joined Cases T-529/08 and T-531/08, *Territorio Histórico de Álava – Diputación Foral de Álava and Others v. Commission*, 13.4.2010, ECLI:EU:T:2010:139, paras 28 et seq.; *see* Case C-480/93 P, *Zunis Holding SA and Others v. Commission*, 11.1.1996, ECLI:EU:C:1996:1, para. 14. *See* Case T-330/09, *RapidEye v. Commission*, 17.2.2011, ECLI:EU:T:2011:48, para. 28.
65. Should this not be the case, intermediate measures are also subject to legal review. *See* on the point Joined Cases C-463 and C-475/10, *Deutsche Post and Germany v. Commission*, paras 49 et seq.; *see* C-60/81, *IBM v. Commission*, paras 9-10, 12; Case T-63/89, *Automec v. Commission*, para. 42.

Member State concerned, or the *Commission's refusal to issue any such recommendation*;[66]

- a Commission *decision to initiate a procedure pursuant to Article 108(2) TFEU in respect of existing aid*;[67]
- a Commission decision to initiate the formal investigation procedure in respect of a measure which is no longer in the course of implementation;[68]
- *confirmatory acts*, as seen above. This also applies to cases where the communication from the Commission contains an 'interpretation' of the earlier decision;[69]
- a *decision whereby the Commission requests the Member State concerned to provide information* (Article 10(3) of Regulation No. 659/1999);
- *information measures*;[70]
- *the Commission's failure* to adopt a decision following a complaint, in which case the complainant may take action for failure to act pursuant to Article 265 TFEU;[71]
- *mere correspondence* from the Commission to complainants;[72]
- a *letter* from the Commission informing the beneficiary of an EU aid of the *suspension of the contribution* and of the recovery of the amount already paid.[73]

In any case, for an action for annulment to be deemed admissible, the challengeable nature of the act in question does not suffice, as the applicant also needs to be qualified to file the relevant claim – i.e., to have standing to bring action.

[B] Actions for Annulment: Standing to Bring Action

[1] Privileged and Non-privileged Applicants

Pursuant to Article 263(2) TFEU, actions for annulment may be brought by *Member States*, the *Council*, the *Commission* or the *European Parliament*.

A *typical case* in the field of State aid is when a Member State that has granted aid challenges a negative or conditional decision of the Commission. At the same time, any

66. Case T-330/94, *Salt Union v. Commission*, 22.10.1996, ECLI:EU:T:1996:154, para. 36. By analogy *see* Joined Cases C-97/86, C-193/86, C-99/86 and C-215/86, *Asteris v. Commission*, ECLI:EU:C:1988:199, para. 17.
67. *See* the CFI Order in Case T-276/02, *Forum 187 ASBL v. Commission*, 2.6.2006, ECLI:EU:T:2003:151, paras 42-52.
68. Case T-517/12, *Alro SA v. Commission* and Case T-129/13, *Alpiq RomIndustries*, 16.10.2014, ECLI:EU:T:2014:895.
69. Case T-330/09, *RapidEye v. Commission*, paras 44 and 46-47.
70. *See* the CFI Order in Case T-130/02, *Kronoply v. Commission*, 5.11.2003, ECLI:EU:T:2003:293, paras 45-55. In the same sense, Case T-17/96, *Télévision Française 1 SA (TF1) v. Commission*, 3.6.1999, ECLI:EU:T:1999:119, para. 105.
71. Case T-95/96, *Gestevisión Telecinco SA v. Commission*, 15.9.1998, ECLI:EU:T:1998:206 and Case T-17/96, *TF1 v. Commission*.
72. Case T-154/94, *CSF and CSME v. Commission*, 22.10.1996, ECLI:EU:T:1996:152 paras 37-54.
73. *See* the CFI Order in Case T-274/97, *Cà Pasta v. Commission*, 25.5.2000, ECLI:EU:C:2000:286.

Member State may contest a positive decision authorizing a State aid granted by another Member State.

The Commission may bring action against a decision wherein the Council has, pursuant to Article 108(2) TFEU, declared that an aid must be regarded as compatible with the common market in derogation from the provisions of Article 107 TFEU or from the regulations provided for in Article 109 TFEU. In any such case, the Commission might claim that the decision is not justified by '*exceptional circumstances*' under Article 108(2) TFEU.[74]

In the wording of Article 263(4) of the consolidated version of the Treaty:

> [a]ny natural or legal person may, under the same conditions, institute proceedings against a decision addressed to that person or against a decision which, although in the form of a regulation or a decision addressed to another person, is of direct and individual concern to the former.

Thus, a clear distinction is drawn under this provision between *'privileged' applicants*, i.e., Member States and EU institutions, and *'non-privileged' applicants*, i.e., the beneficiaries of the aid and their competitors.

The general principle is that privileged applicants are entitled to bring an action for annulment without the need to demonstrate an interest thereto,[75] while non-privileged applicants need to show an interest in bringing the proceedings.[76] The characteristics and the limits of this interest have been the object of much discussion in legal scholarship as well as in Court practice: the following paragraph will attempt to provide an outline in that respect.

While the distinction between privileged and non-privileged applicants may prima facie appear clear-cut, there is a grey area where the two cohorts are likely to overlap: the foremost case to this effect is perhaps that of local and regional authorities. In *DEFI v. Commission*, the European Court of Justice (ECJ) dismissed an action brought against a negative decision of the Commission by the national authority responsible for apportioning an aid - an entity established by ministerial decree and directly funded by the French government.[77] On that occasion, the ECJ found that the applicant did not meet the requirements prescribed in Article 263(4) TFEU since it had failed to show in what way the interests that it had described as peculiar to itself were distinct from the French State's interest in bringing proceedings - the French State itself having brought an action for annulment.[78] Private applicants do, as a matter of fact, also need to show an *interest distinct* from that of the Member State granting the aid.[79]

74. Case C-110/02, *Commission v. Council*, 29.6.2004, ECLI:EU:C:2004:395.
75. Case C-45/86, *Commission v. Council* (*'Tariff preferences'*), 26.3.1987, ECLI:EU:C:1987:163, para. 3; Joined Cases T-415/05, T-416/05 and T-423/05, *Greece, Olympiakes Aerogrammes AE and Olympiaki Aeroporia Ypiresies AE v. Commission*, 13.9.2010, ECLI:EU:T:2010:386, para. 57.
76. Article 263(4) TFEU, *see supra*.
77. DEFI stands for *Comité de développement et de promotion du textile et de l'habillement* – Committee for the development and promotion of the textile and garment [industry]. The DEFI has been established by Decree of the French Ministry for Economics No. 84-388 of 22 May 1984.
78. Case C-282/85, *Comité de Développement et de Promotion du Textile et de l'habillement (DEFI) v. Commission*, 10.7.1986, ECLI:EU:C:1986:316 paras 16-20.
79. *See infra* at §6.02[B][1].

Quite the opposite conclusion was reached by the - then - Court of First Instance in *Regione Autonoma Friuli-Venezia Giulia*, where the applicant - a regional authority autonomous from the Italian State - was found to possess rights and interests of its own. According to the CFI, the aid considered in the contested decision constituted a set of measures taken in the exercise of legislative and financial autonomy vested in that regional authority directly under Articles 115 and 116 of the Italian Constitution.[80]

All the same, it remains understood that:

> it is apparent from the general scheme of the Treaties that the term Member State [...] refers only to government authorities of the Member States of the European Communities and cannot include the governments of regions or autonomous communities, irrespective of the powers they may have.[81]

Some have advocated that regional authorities be included in the number of so-called semi-privileged applicants under Article 263(3) TFEU, seeing their being equated with private applicants as in contrast with the decentralization policies in force in many Member States and supported by the EU itself.[82] As of now, the privileged status remains the prerogative of Member States - i.e., signatories of the Treaty - and not of their subdivisions.[83]

[a] Privileged Applicants

Privileged applicants - as has been anticipated above - are considered to have a general interest in the annulment of decisions: accordingly, they do not need to show a particular degree of interest therein in order to challenge them. In other words, they enjoy unrestricted *locus standi* in actions for annulment of acts issued by EU institutions.

In addition to privileged applicants, there is another - intermediate - category, contemplated under Article 263(3) TFEU, that of *semi-privileged* applicants: these are the Court of Auditors, the European Central Bank and the Committee of the Regions, which may bring actions only in order to '*protect their prerogatives*'.[84]

80. Case T-288/97, *Regione Autonoma Friuli-Venezia Giulia v. Commission*, 15.6.1999, ECLI:EU:T:1999:125, para. 34.
81. Case T-214/95, *Vlaams Gewest v. Commission*, 30.4.1998, ECLI:EU:T:1998:77, para. 28. *See also* the CFI Order Case T-238/97, *Comunidad Autónoma de Cantabria v. Council*, 16.6.1998, ECLI:EU:T:1998:126.
82. *See, inter alia*, Türk, *Judicial Review in EU Law*, Cheltenham, 2011, p. 323.
83. *See* the ECJ Orders: Case C-95/97, *Région Wallonne v. Commission*, 21.3.1997, ECLI:EU:C:1997:184; Case C-180/97, *Regione Toscana v. Commission*, 1.10.1997, ECLI:EU:C:1997:451.
84. This provision was, in fact, a codification of earlier case law of the Court, which had been set out in Case C-70/88, *Parliament v. Council* ('*Chernobyl*'), 22.5.1990, ECLI:EU:C:1990:217.

[b] *Non-privileged Applicants*

Decisions relating to State aid are addressed to the Member State concerned *alone*. What this entails in practice had previously been established in case law and has ultimately been formally established in Article 25 of Regulation No. 659/1999.[85] As a result of this evolution, private parties are entitled to bring proceedings only where a decision can be shown to be of '*direct and individual concern*' to them and when they can show an *interest in bringing action*.[86] This interest will also need to be distinct from that of the Member State concerned.[87]

The lack of an effective legal remedy at the national level neither warrants, per se, a modification in the system of legal remedies and procedures laid down in the Treaty, nor can lead EU courts to exceed, in their activity, the scope of Article 263(4) TFEU.[88] This principle was re-affirmed in the *UPA* case, where the Court of Justice dismissed, as inadmissible, the appellant's argument by which:

> a direct action for annulment before the Community Court will be available where it can be shown, following an examination by that Court of the particular national procedural rules, that those rules do not allow the individual to bring proceedings to contest the validity of the Community measure at issue.[89]

---

85. In the *Sytraval* case, the Court clearly stated that: 'decisions adopted by the Commission in the field of State aid must be held to be addressed to the Member States concerned'. Case C-367/95 P, *Commission v. Sytraval and Brink's France*, para. 45.
86. For an overview of *locus standi* in the State aid field, *see* Edoardo Gambaro, *Locus Standi of Natural and Legal Persons before the European Courts in State Aid Cases*, in *Litigation and Arbitration in EU Competition* (Marquis & Cisotta ed., Edward Elgar Publishing, 2015) 201; Kelyn Bacon, *Enforcement in the European Court* in *European Union Law of State Aid* (Kelyn Bacon ed., Oxford, 2013) 489; Cristina Schepisi, *Aiuti di Stato e Tutela Giurisdizionale*, Giappichelli, 2012; James Flynn and Tom Ottervanger, *Judicial Protection*, in *EU State Aids* (Leigh Hancher, Tom Ottervanger & Pieter J. Slot eds, Sweet and Maxwell, 2012), 1022; Stephan Balthasar, *Locus Standi Rules for Challenges to Regulatory Acts by Private Applicants: The New Article 263(4) TFEU*, European Law Review, 4, 542 (2010); Henrik Peytz, Thomas Mygind, *Direct actions in State Aid Cases – Tightropes and Legal Protection?*, European State Aid Quarterly, 2, 331 (2010) https://doi.org/10.21552/estal/2010/2/178; B. Jankovec, V. Kronenberger, *Third parties in State aid litigation: locus standi and procedural guarantees*, in *The EC State Aid Regime* (Sanchez Rydelski ed., London, 2007) 705; Leo Flynn, *Remedies in the European Courts*, in *The Law of State aid in the EU* (Andrea Biondi and others eds, Oxford University Press, 2004).
87. This applies also with respect to the not frequent occurrence that the Council issue a decision in the field of State aid.
88. Case T-212/00, *Nuove Industrie Molisane S.r.l. v. Commission*, 30.1.2002, ECLI:EU:T:2002:21, para. 48; Case T-69/96, *Hamburger Hafen und Lagerhaus AG v. Commission*, 21.3.2001, ECLI:EU:T:2001:100, para. 51; Case T-138/98, *ACAV and others v. Council*, 22.2.2000, ECLI:EU:T:2000:45, para. 68; Case T-86/96, *Arbeitsgemeinschaft Deutscher Luftfahrt-Unternehmen v. Commission*, 11.2.1999, ECLI:EU:T:1999:25, para. 52; Case T-95/96, *Gestevisión Telecinco SA v. Commission*, 15.9.1998, ECLI:EU:T:1998:206 para. 68; Case T-398/94, *Kahn Scheppvart BV v. Commission*, 5.6.1996, ECLI:EU:T:1996:73; the ECJ Order in Case C-300/00, *Federación de Cofradías de Pescadores de Guipúzcoa and Others v. Council and Commission*, 12.10.2000, ECLI:EU:C:2000:567, para. 37. Partially *contra*, Case C-321/95 P, *Greenpeace v. Commission*, 2.4.1998, ECLI:EU:C:1998:153, paras 32-33.
89. Case C-50/00 P, *Unión de Pequeños Agricultores v. Commission*, 25.7.2002, ECLI:EU:C:2002:462, para. 43. The ECJ further specified that: 'Such an interpretation would require the Community

If an action for annulment is brought by *multiple applicants*, it is sufficient that one of them fulfils the requirements for standing, as the Court would then have to examine the merits of the case regardless of the number of applicants.[90]

[2] Direct Concern

As noted above, pursuant to Article 263(4) EC, a *natural or legal person* may institute proceedings against a decision addressed to another person only if such decision is of *direct and individual* concern to the former: this paragraph will deal with the former requirement – i.e., that an applicant needs to show that he or she is directly concerned by the decision at issue.[91]

Direct concern is held in case law to mean that contested EU measures must directly affect the legal situation of the interested individual and that its implementation – insofar as applicable – is purely automatic and results from EU rules alone, without the application of other intermediate rules.[92] The same applies where the possibility for addressees not to give effect to the EU measure is purely theoretical and their intention to act in conformity with it is not in doubt.[93]

Negative and positive decisions do – obviously – affect individuals in a different way: the respective approach to judicial review will accordingly differ in the two cases. In the former case, the beneficiary of an aid in respect of which the Commission has issued a *negative* decision or a recovery decision shall be regarded as directly concerned by that decision.[94]

A different line of reasoning applies to *positive decisions*. On the one hand, a competitor of the beneficiary might be considered directly concerned in a positive decision issued after the measure in question has been granted. For a Commission decision that considered the aid to be compatible with the Treaty would leave intact all the effects of the contested measure as already *implemented*.[95] On the other hand, a positive decision on a measure *previously notified* by the Member State granting the aid

---

Court, in each individual case, to examine and interpret national procedural law. That would go beyond its jurisdiction when reviewing the legality of Community measures.'

90. *See*, lastly, Joined Cases C-71/09, C-73/09 and C-76/09 P, *Comitato 'Venezia vuole vivere' and Others v. Commission*, 17.1.2024, ECLI:EU:T:2024:13, paras 37-38. *See also* Case T-452/08, *DHL Aviation S.A./N.V. and DHL Hub Leipzig GmbH v. Commission*, 7.10.2010, ECLI:EU:T:2010:427, paras 26 et seq.; Joined Cases T-127/99, T-129/99 and T-148/99, *Territorio Histórico de Álava – Diputación Foral de Álava and Others v. Commission*, 7.3.2002, ECLI:EU:T:2002:59, para. 52.
91. Case T-375/04, *Scheucher-Fleisch v. Commission*, 18.11.2009, ECLI:EU:T:2009:445, paras 35-39.
92. *See* Joined Cases C-463 and C-475/10, *Deutsche Post and Germany v. Commission*, paras 49 et seq.; Case C-386/96, *Dreyfus v. Commission*, 5.5.1998, ECLI:EU:C:1998:193, para. 43; Case T-9/98, *Mitteldeutsche Erdöl-Raffinerie GmbH v. Commission*, 22.11.2001, ECLI:EU:T:2001:271, para. 47; Case T-69/99, *DSTV v. Commission*, 13.12.2000, ECLI:EU:T:2000:302, para. 24.
93. Case T-289/03, *British United Provident Association (BUPA) Ltd and Others v. Commission*, 12.2.2008, ECLI:EU:T:2008:29, para. 81; *see* Case C-11/82, *Piraiki-Patraiki and Others v. Commission*, 17.1.1985, ECLI:EU:C:1985:18, paras 8-10; and Case C-386/96, *Dreyfus v. Commission*, para. 44.
94. *See, ex plurimis*, Joined Cases C-15/98 and C-105/99, *Italy and Sardegna Lines v. Commission*, 19.10.2000, ECLI:EU:C:2000:570, para. 36.
95. Case C-169/84, *Société CdF Chimie azote et Fertilisants SA and Société Chimique de la Grande Paroisse SA (Cofaz) v. Commission*, 12.7.1990, ECLI:EU:C:1990:301 (para. 30); Joined Cases

is not, as a rule, deemed to be of direct concern to the beneficiary's competitor. In such a case, the Commission's decision would have no direct effect on the interested individual's legal position, since it is usually necessary for the national authorities to take additional steps to implement the measure.

If, however, there is no doubt over national authorities being willing to grant the aid – the alternate option being merely theoretical – the requirement for the contested decision to be of direct concern to the applicant/complainant must be deemed satisfied.[96] Likewise, an undertaking that has lodged a complaint against an aid incompatible with the common market must be considered – in proceedings for failure to act pursuant to Article 265 TFEU – to be directly affected by the Commission's failure to take a decision on that complaint if there is no doubt that the national authorities intend to implement their plan to grant aid or have already granted such aid.[97]

[3] Individual Concern

The second requirement – as seen above – is that of the individuality of the concern. To this respect, case law holds that persons other than those to whom a decision is addressed may only claim to be individually concerned if that decision affects them by reason of certain attributes that are peculiar to them and, by virtue of these attributes, distinguishes them individually just as in the case of the persons addressed.[98]

This individual distinction of the potential applicant as compared to the generality of subjects is evaluated taking into account the market position of the aid beneficiary,[99] as well as the effect the Commission decision at stake has had thereon.[100]

This may – if not necessarily – apply also to cases wherein *the applicant is a competitor of the aid beneficiary*: in such cases, the individual concern will need to be assessed with respect to the effects the granting of State aid – as acknowledged and clearance by the Commission in the positive decision object of the challenge – has on the situation of the applicant. The burden of proof thereon will then lay on the applicant itself.[101]

T-447/93, T-448/93, T-449/93, *AITEC v. Commission*, 28.11.1996, ECLI:EU:T:1996:174, para. 41; Case T-149/95, *Etablissements J. Richard Ducros v. Commission*, 5.11.1997, ECLI:EU:T:1997:165, para. 32.

96. Case T-435/93, *Association of Sorbitol Producers Within the EC (ASPEC) and Others v. Commission*, 27.4.1995, ECLI:EU:T:1995:79, para. 60; Case T-442/93, *Association des Amidonneries de Céréales de la CEE (AAC) and Others v. Commission* [1995] ECR II-1329, para. 45; Case T-9/98, *Mitteldeutsche Erdöl-Raffinerie v. Commission*, 22.11.2001, ECLI:EU:T:2001:271, para. 48.
97. Case T-95/97, *Gestevisión Telecinco SA v. Commission*, para. 61; and Case T-17/96, *TF1 v. Commission*, para. 30.
98. Case C-25/62, *Plaumann v. Commission*, 15.7.1963, ECLI:EU:C:1963:17; Case C-106/98 P, *Comité d'entreprise de la Société française de production and Others v. Commission*, 23.5.2000, ECLI:EU:C:2000:277, para. 39; Case T-435/93, *ASPEC v. Commission*, para. 60; Case T-88/01, *Sniace SA v. Commission*, 14.4.2005, ECLI:EU:T:2005:128, para. 55. *See also* Case C-78/03 P, *Commission v. Aktionsgemeinschaft Recht und Eigentum e.V. (ARE)*, 13.12.2005, ECLI:EU:C:2005:761, paras 33 et seq.
99. Case C-169/84, *Cofaz v. Commission*, paras 22-25.
100. Case C-298/00 P, *Italy v. Commission*, 29.4.2004, ECLI:EU:C:2004:240, para. 39.
101. Case C-525/04 P, *Spain v. Commission*, 22.11.2007, ECLI:EU:C:2007:698, para. 35.

Over time, there has been much debate over the exact interpretation of this requirement and, relatedly, to the threshold of proof the applicant has to fulfil in order to successfully base a claim.

In the *Lenzing* case, the Court has stated that merely demonstrating the existence of a competitive relationship between the aid beneficiary and the applicant is not sufficient to that effect: the latter also needs to show how the granting of aid has damaged his or her economic situation.[102]

The same applies to applicants who have taken part in the administrative proceedings that have led to the decision object of the challenge: as much as the part they have played may have been active and relevant, it does not suffice - alone - to demonstrate there being individual concern and, thus, to determine the admissibility of the claim.[103]

In particular, the Court differentiates between appeals against decisions under Article 108(3) TFEU and those under Article 108(2) TFEU.

For the former, an action for annulment is admissible against a decision not to open a formal investigation procedure under Article 263(4) TFEU where the applicant seeks, through the bringing of the action, to safeguard his procedural rights.[104] Given the very broad definition of 'interested party' of Article 1(h) of the Rules of Procedure, in such cases, competitors do not have to demonstrate an individual concern under the *Plaumann* criteria.[105]

On the contrary, where an action concerns the merits of a decision taken on the basis of Article 108(3) TFEU or at the end of the formal investigation, qualifying as a competitor is not sufficient to confer standing, but the applicant will have to demonstrate a particular status, based on information concerning the market structure and the competitive position of the different parties, in order to demonstrate a substantial negative effect of the measure at issue.[106]

Another situation in which the same line of reasoning is followed is that of sectoral aid. In the *Federmineraria* case, certain ore mining and processing undertakings had brought an action for annulment against the Commission's Decision of 18 September 1991, whereby Italy was required to discontinue the system of support

---

102. Case C-525/04 P, *Spain v. Commission*, paras 37-39 and 41.
103. Case C-260/05 P, *Sniace v. Commission*, 22.11.2007, ECLI:EU:C:2007:700. Case C-169/84, *Cofaz v. Commission*, para. 24. *See* Case C-78/03 P, *Commission v. Aktionsgemeinschaft Recht und Eigentum e.V. (ARE)*, para. 56.
104. Case C-198/91, *Cook v. Commission*, para. 23; C-225/91, *Mantra v. Commission*, para. 17; C-83/09 P, *Commission v. Kronoply and Kronotex*, para. 48; T-693/14 *Hamr – Sport v. Commission*, 12.5.2016, ECLI:EU:T:2016:292.
105. This principle was applied in numerous cases in relation to State aid measures to support the economy during the COVID-19 pandemic, including, *inter alia*: T-643/20, *Ryanair v. Commission*, 19.5.2021, ECLI:EU:T:2021:286, paras 27-32; T-465/20, *Ryanair v. Commission*, 19.5.2021, ECLI:EU:T:2021:284 paras 20-29; T-665/20, *Ryanair v. Commission*, 9.6.2021, ECLI:EU:T:2021:344 paras 25-33.
106. Case C-33/14 P, *Mory and others v. Commission*, 17.9.2015, ECLI:EU:C:2015:609, para. 94 ff. The participation of the applicant in the procedure or the fact that it had brought action in front of national courts were not considered sufficient to prove an individual concern. *See also* case C-453/19 P, *Deutsche Lufthansa AG v. Commission*, 15.7.2021, ECLI:EU:C:2021:608, para. 57; case C-647/19 P, *Ja zum Nurburgring eV*, 2.9.2021, ECLI:EU:C:2021:666.

tariffs granted by state-owned *Ferrovie dello Stato* (state railways) for the shipment of ore and goods from the islands of Sicily and Sardinia.[107] In their application for annulment, the companies involved - and their professional association - submitted that they belonged to a known and limited category of persons - i.e., the undertakings involved in the mining of ore in the two islands - to whom the contested decision was of concern and that this category was or could have been identified by the Commission at the time the decision was adopted. The Court of Justice did, however, not accept such an argument.[108]

In a later case, the ECJ held that an undertaking cannot, in principle, contest a Commission decision prohibiting a *sectoral aid scheme* if it is concerned by that decision solely by virtue of its belonging to the sector in question and by being a potential beneficiary of the scheme. Such a decision is, vis-à-vis an undertaking seeking to contest it, *a measure of general application* and entails legal effects for a class of persons envisaged in a general and abstract manner.[109]

Sectoral aid also poses problems with respect to actions for annulment of negative decisions taken by the Commission - i.e., decisions that find the granting of aid incompatible with the common market. Private parties may decide to address the Court to pronounce such a decision annulled, thereby restoring the granting of aid. It should be noted that the Court of Justice has been upholding a comprehensive position on what constitutes an implementing measure, including both those taken at the EU level and at the national level.[110]

It should be borne in mind that applicants are entitled to bring action against implementing act issued by EU institution under Article 263 TFEU, but that in that context they may also plead in support of that action claiming the illegality of the basic act at issue, pursuant to Article 277 TFEU.[111] If, conversely, the implementation is up to the relevant Member States, applicants can claim invalidity of the basic act at issue before their national courts - which will then in turn request, under Article 267 TFEU, a preliminary ruling from the Court of Justice.[112]

107. Case C-6/92, *Federazione Sindacale dell'Industria Estrattiva (Federmineraria) and Others v. Commission*, 7.12.1993, ECLI:EU:C:1993:913.
108. *Ibid.*, at paras 14-15. In particular, the Court stated that: 'The Decision does not affect the interests of the applicant companies alone. It also affects the interests of the railways, whose competitive position compared to other modes of transport is favoured by the reduced tariff. It is also of interest to the carriers to whom the applicants may entrust the consignment of their goods and which can, themselves, make use of the railway services. Finally, it concerns their customers, who, depending on the terms of the sales contracts, may be induced to bear some or all of the transport costs. In these circumstances, the Decision cannot be considered to affect operators whose number or identity was fixed and ascertainable at the time of its adoption.'
109. Joined Cases C-15/98 and C-105/99, *Italy and Sardegna Lines v. Commission*, para. 33.
110. In another case, the Court of Justice has extended the concept to include implementing measures at the national level - in the case at stake, with respect to aid granted through fiscal reductions. *See* Case C-274/12 P, *Telefónica SA v. Commission ('Telefónica I')*, 19.12.2013, ECLI:EU:C:2013:852; *see also* the conclusions thereof of Advocate General Kokott, C-274/12 P, *Telefónica SA v. Commission (' Telefónica I')*, 21.3.2013, ECLI:EU:C:2013:204, in particular at paras 51-52.
111. Case C-274/12 P, *Telefónica I*, para. 29.
112. *See* Case C-583/11 P, *Inuit Tapiriit Kanatami and Others v. Parliament and Council*, 3.10.2013, ECLI:EU:C:2013:625, para. 93.

Subsequent rulings from the Court of Justice have, however, seemed to herald a cautious opening on the point of actions for annulment against positive decisions under Article 1(h) of Regulation 659/1999 taken without opening formal investigative proceedings – in cases wherein the Commission deems the measure not amounting to State aid, or that there be no doubts over its compatibility with the common market.[113] This – and the considerations set forth below – apply both to individual State aid and to sectoral aid.[114]

In this preliminary phase of proceedings, there is no obligation on the Commission to exchange information with complainants on the merits of the case.[115] The Commission fulfils its transparency and public information obligations by publishing a summary of the decision in the Official Journal.[116]

In the case at issue – that where the Commission decides not to take the matter at a further stage – the complainant suffers a compromise to its right to exploit its powers of intervention in the proceedings: it follows that the decision has produced effects in the meaning of Article 263(1) TFEU and that, accordingly, it is subject to judicial review for annulment.[117] While the principle is undisputed, its actual implementation proves more troublesome: proving individual concern is, in such cases, a demanding endeavour for applicants: they have no knowledge of the elements taken into account by the Commission in issuing its decision – preliminary proceedings are not public nor published – yet they have to explain to a certain degree of accuracy which issues they deem affect the decision itself.

This conundrum has been solved by case law by stating that – in light of the action for annulment being the only remedy for unsuccessful complainants – applicants need to prove their concerned status but also which serious difficulties would have allegedly justified the commencement of formal proceedings. To the end of this proof, the applicant can cite any reason apt to demonstrate that the evaluation of the information available to the Commission at the time of preliminary proceedings should have given rise to doubts as to the compatibility of the aid at stake with the common market.[118] It is however necessary that these reasons – as diverse as they may be – be cited, in failure whereof the Court is unable to establish *sua sponte* which the alleged grounds for bringing proceedings should be.[119]

All in all, the Court has been maintaining a very high threshold on the point. Such a stance has attracted criticism by many: the so-called *Plaumann* test, in particular, has been described as particularly hard for individuals to meet. The new wording of Article 263(4), introduced in the framework of the Treaty of Lisbon, was seen as a potential turning point to this effect: for a more comprehensive outlook on the relationship between the provisions of Article 263(4) and the field of State aid *see* hereinafter

113. *See* Art. 6(1) Regulation 659/1999, Arts 107, 108(2) TFEU.
114. Case T-289/03, *BUPA v. Commission*.
115. Case C-367/95 P, *Commission v. Sytraval and Brink's France*, para. 59.
116. Article 26(1) Regulation 659/1999.
117. Case C-322/09 P, *NDSHT v. Commission*, paras 50-51 and 55.
118. Case T-388/02, *Kronoply and Kronotex v. Commission*, paras 48, 56, and 59; Case T-304/08, *Smurfit Kappa Group plc v. Commission*, 10.7.2012, ECLI:EU:T:2012:351, paras 50-52 and 65.
119. Case T-304/08, *Smurfit Kappa Group plc v. Commission*, paras 50-52 and 65.

§6.03[D].[120] For now suffice it to say that, in spite of the hopes that had greeted the amendments therein, to date the accessibility to courts for annulment of decisions does not seem to have significantly increased.

[4] Interest in Bringing Action

In addition to the direct concern and individual concern requirements illustrated above, there is another, more general, requirement to be met by a private person upon claiming the right to bring an action for annulment. It is settled case law that an action for annulment brought by a natural or legal person is admissible only insofar as that person has an *interest* in the contested measure being annulled.[121] Such interest must be a vested and present interest,[122] and it must be assessed as such as on the day on which the application is made.[123]

If the interest that an applicant claims in his action concerns a *future* legal situation, he must demonstrate that the prejudice to that situation is already certain as of that date. As a consequence, an applicant may not rely only upon future and uncertain situations to justify his interest in applying for annulment of the contested act.[124] All the same, a beneficiary of aid cannot claim to have interest in annulling a positive decision with respect to that aid;[125] this has a partial exception with respect to decisions which are only partially favourable to the extent of not adequately protecting the legal situation of the applicant.[126]

In the *Mitteldeutsche Erdöl-Raffinerie* case, the Commission had pleaded that the applicant had no interest in having the Commission decision annulled because: (i) the German Government had fully complied with the contested decision; and (ii) it had stated it did not intend to reintroduce the aid scheme in question even if the decision were annulled. This notwithstanding, the CFI deemed the action to be not admissible, because it could not be excluded that the applicant might be able to put forward certain

120. *See* below.
121. Case T-483/93, *Antillean Rice Mills and others v. Commission*, 14.9.1995, ECLI:EU:T:1995:162, para. 59; Case T-102/96, *Gencor v. Commission*, 25.3.1999, ECLI:EU:T:1999:65, para. 40; Case T-141/03, *Sniace SA v. Commission*, para. 25. *See also* the CFI Orders: Case T-167/01, *Schmitz-Gotha Fahrzeugwerke v. Commission*, 30.4.2003, ECLI:EU:T:2003:121, para. 47; Case T-228/00, *Gruppo Ormeggiatori del Porto di Venezia Soc. Coop. a r.l. and others v. Commission*, 10.3.2005, ECLI:EU:T:2005:90, para. 23. For a case in which an appeal brought by a Member State has been dismissed for lack of interest, *see* Case C-242/00, *Germany v. Commission*, 18.7.2002, ECLI:EU:C:2002:380.
122. Case T-138/89, *NBV and NVB v. Commission*, 17.9.1992, ECLI:EU:T:1992:95, para. 33.
123. Case C-14/63, *Forges de Clabecq v. High Authority*, 16.12.1963, ECLI:EU:C:1963:60, para. 732; Case T-16/96, *Cityflyer Express v. Commission*, 30.3.1998, ECLI:EU:T:1998:78, para. 30; Case T-22/97, *Kesko v. Commission*, 15.12.1999, ECLI:EU:T:1999:327, para. 55; Case T-159/98, *Torre and others v. Commission*, 24.3.2001, ECLI:EU:T:2001:121, para. 28.
124. Case T-138/89, *NBV and NVB v. Commission*, para. 33.
125. *See*, for instance, Case T-212/00, *Nuove Industrie Molisane v. Commission*.
126. Case C-254/10 P, *Centre de coordination Carrefour v. Commission*, 3.3.2011, ECLI:EU:C:2011:120, in confirmation on appeal of Case T-94/08, *Centre de coordination Carrefour v. Commission*, 18.3.2010, ECLI:EU:T:2010:98; of the latter *see* at paras 48 et seq.

claims before the German authorities if the contested decision were found by EU Courts to be unlawful.[127]

In the *Sniace* case, the Court of First Instance has held that the beneficiary of an aid found *compatible with the common market* failed to prove its vested and present interest in instituting proceedings.[128] For the beneficiary had not demonstrated that it had, on the day it brought its action, an actual interest in seeing the contested decision annulled, since that decision approved, unconditionally and without limit of time, the measure in question.

Again, in the case of a reduction in social security charges for the benefit of undertakings in the areas of Venice and Chioggia, the applicant undertakings failed to prove their present interest in bringing proceedings against the contested decision. When questioned by the – then – Court of First Instance on this point, the Italian State declared, partly on the basis of the Commission's own indications, that it did not intend to recover the aid in question from the applicant undertakings.[129] It was the CFI's view that, in such a context in fact and in right, the applicants – in order to show their interest in bringing action – only pleaded *future and uncertain circumstances*, in particular, the assumption that the Commission would reach a different conclusion from the Italian Republic's and order that the aid should be recovered from the applicant undertakings: future and uncertain circumstances are consistently considered in case law as insufficient to establish a legitimate interest in annulment of an act.[130]

The underlying line of reasoning – which is apparent throughout the cases considered above – is ultimately that the annulment of the decision has to procure a benefit for the applicant.[131]

[C] Review by EU Courts

[1] Manifest Error of Assessment: Potential Case Law Developments

The assessments and evaluations carried out by the Commission when deciding on a State aid case are often times of a complex technical character, entailing judgments of

127. Case T-9/98, *Mitteldeutsche Erdöl-Raffinerie v. Commission*, para. 34. *See also* the CFI Order, Case T-111/01 R, *Saxonia Edelmetalle GnbH v. Commission*, 11.5.2005, ECLI:EU:T:2005:166, para. 17.
128. Case T-141/03, *Sniace SA v. Commission*.
129. Case T-228/00, *Gruppo Ormeggiatori del Porto di Venezia v. Commission*, paras 7 and 24-25.
130. *See* Joined Cases T-443/08 and T-455/08, *Freistaat Sachsen und Land Sachsen-Anhalt and Mitteldeutsche Flughafen AG and Flughafen Leipzig-Halle GmbH v. Commission*, 24.3.2011, ECLI:EU:T:2011:117, paras 58 and 63.
131. *See* Case T-1/08, *Buczek Automotive sp. z o.o. v. Commission*, 18.5.2011, ECLI:EU:T:2011:216; Case T-189/08, *Forum 187 ASBL v. Commission*, 18.3.2010, ECLI:EU:T:2010:99; *see* Case C-254/10 P, *Centre de coordination Carrefour v. Commission*, in confirmation on appeal of Case T-94/08, *Centre de coordination Carrefour v. Commission*,; of the latter *see* at para. 49. *See* to the same effect Case T-309/04, *TV 2/Danmark A/S v. Commission*, 22.10.1998, ECLI:EU:T:2008:457, para. 68; Case T-301/01, *Alitalia – Linee aeree italiane SpA v. Commission ('Alitalia II')*, 9.7.2008, ECLI:EU:T:2008:262, para. 36.

a social and economic character;[132] what is more, the Commission enjoys a particular degree of discretion in evaluating the compatibility of State aids with the provisions of Article 107(3) TFEU.[133]

These features concur in limiting the scope of the judicial review carried out by the Court of Justice which, in evaluating the existence as well as the compatibility of aid measures,[134] is not to substitute its own assessment of the facts – in particular with respect to the field of economics – for that of the Commission.[135] In particular, it appears that the Court should limit its review to the following points: (a) the observance of rules of procedure; (b) the material exactness of the facts that base the contested decision; (c) the absence of manifest errors in the appraisal of said facts; and (d) the absence of any misuse of powers.[136] From a statistical standpoint, the limited scope of review by EU Courts is likely to be the main cause of dismissal of actions for annulment brought against Commission decisions concerning State aid.

These '*manifest errors*' need to be proved by the party – whether a Member State or a private applicant – who alleges them.[137] The extent of these errors, and when exactly are they to be considered 'manifest', have been lately the object of debate.

In 2005, Advocate General Jacobs took a position on the proper scope of *review by the Court of Justice in the field of State aid.*[138] The Advocate General preliminarily remarked that, in many cases, where a Commission decision involves a complex

132. *See* Case T-274/01, *Valmont Nederland v. Commission*, 16.9.2004, ECLI:EU:T:2004:266, para. 37; *see also* Case T-98/00, *Linde AG v. Commission*, 17.10.2002, ECLI:EU:T:2002:248, para. 40.
133. Joined Cases T-228/99 and T-233/99, *Westdeutsche Landesbank Girozentrale (WestLB) and Others v. Commission*, 6.3.2003, ECLI:EU:T:2003:57, para. 282.
134. *See, inter alia*, on the point of the existence of aid: Joined Cases T-126/96 and T-127/96, *Breda Fucine Meridionali and Others v. Commission*, 15.9.1998, ECLI:EU:T:1998:207, para. 81; Case C-56/93, *Belgium v. Commission*, 29.2.1996, ECLI:EU:C:1996:64, para. 11. On the point of compatibility of aid *see*: Case C-409/00, *Spain v. Commission*, 13.2.2003, ECLI:EU:C:2003:92, para. 93; Case T-152/99, *Hijos de Andrés Molina SA (HAMSA) v. Commission*, 11.7.2002, ECLI:EU:T:2002:188, para. 48; Case T-110/97, *Kneissl Dachstein Sportartikel v. Commission*, 16.10.1999, ECLI:EU:T:1999:244, para. 46; Joined Cases T-371/94 and T-394/94, *British Airways and Others v. Commission*, 25.6.1998, ECLI:EU:T:1998:140, paras 79 et seq.; Case T-266/94, *Foreningen af Jernskibs – og Maskinbyggerier i Danmark, Skibsværftsforeningen and Others v. Commission*, 22.10.1996, ECLI:EU:T:1996:153, para. 170.
135. *See* Case T-152/99, *HAMSA v. Commission*, para. 38; Case T-110/97, *Kneissl Dachstein v. Commission*, para. 46; Joined Cases T-126/96 and T-127/96, *Breda Fucine Meridionali and Others v. Commission*, para. 81; Joined Cases T-371/94 and T-394/94, *British Airways and Others v. Commission*, para. 78; Case T-266/94, *Foreningen af Jernskibs – og Maskinbyggerier i Danmark*, para. 168; C-225/91, *Matra v. Commission*, para. 23.
136. The limits set forth here are inspired by the proposal of Keppenne, J.-P. *State Aid Litigation before the Community Courts*, in L. *EC Competition Procedure* 2 (Ortiz Blanco, ed., Oxford University Press, 2006) 924-925.
137. Case C-56/93, *Belgium v. Commission*, para. 35; Case C-288/96, *Germany v. Commission*, 5.10.2000, ECLI:EU:C:2000:537, para. 26. In Case T-234/95, *DSG v. Commission*, 29.6.2000, ECLI:EU:T:2000:174, para. 198, the CFI did not accept the applicant's argument by which the Commission should have used an *outside expert's report* in order to determine what the conduct of a private investor would have been.
138. Opinion of AGJacobs in Case C-222/04, *Ministero dell'Economia e delle Finanze v. Cassa di Risparmio di Firenze S.p.A. and others*, 27.10.2005, ECLI:EU:C:2005:655, paras 109-112.

economic appraisal, case law has generally allowed for a *limited review*, barring EU Courts from substituting their own economic assessment for that of the Commission.[139]

Yet, according to Jacobs, since State aid is a legal concept that must be interpreted on the basis of objective factors, the Court is to '*carry out a comprehensive review as to whether a measure falls within the scope of Article 87(1) of the Treaty* [i.e., art. 107(1) TFEU]', and in doing so '*having regard both to the specific features of the case before them and to the technical or complex nature of the Commission's assessments*'.[140] On the basis of such a line of reasoning, Jacobs concluded that '*Community Courts may, where appropriate, substitute their own economic assessment for that of the Commission, however complex the latter may be.*'[141]

Notwithstanding this authoritative opinion, the Court of Justice seems, as of today, inclined to maintain a restrictive approach as to the scope of its review: it has confirmed that it is not up to itself to decide on the compatibility with the common market of a specific measure,[142] and in general that it is not entitled to substitute its own assessment for that of the Commission.[143] The above does not apply to the Court reviewing the correctness and the accuracy of the facts and data whereon the economic analyses carried out by the Commission are based.[144]

[2] The Duty to State Reasons

The Treaty mandates a general obligation of EU institutions to state the reasons for their decisions.[145] Conversely, an absence of or inadequate statement of reasons

139. Case C-169/95, *Spain v. Commission*, 14.1.1997, ECLI:EU:C:1997:10, para. 34; Case C-288/96, *Germany v. Commission*, para. 26; Joined Cases T-371/94 and T-394/94, *British Airways and others* et *British Midland Airways v. Commission*, 25.6.1998, ECLI:EU:T:1998:140, para. 79; Joined Cases T-127/99, T-129/99 and T-148/99, *Territorio Histórico de Álava – Diputación Foral de Álava and others v. Commission*, 6.3.2002, ECLI:EU:T:2002:59, para. 273. *See also* Case C-730/79, *Philip Morris BV v. Commission*, 17.9.1980, ECLI:EU:C:1980:209, para. 24; Case C-142/87, *Belgium v. Commission ('Tubemeuse')*, 21.3.1990, ECLI:EU:C:1990:125, para. 56; Case C-303/88, *Italy v. Commission*, 21.3.1991, ECLI:EU:C:1991:136, para. 34.
140. Case C-83/98 P, *France v. Ladbroke Racing and Commission*, 16.5.2000, ECLI:EU:C:2000:248, para. 25. *See also* Case T-98/00, *Linde v. Commission*, para. 40; Case T-126/99, *Graphischer Maschinenbau GmbH v. Commission*, 14.5.2002, ECLI:EU:T:2002:116, paras 32 et seq.; Case T-134/00, *Kvaerner Warnow Werft GmbH v. Commission*, 28.2.2002, ECLI:EU:T:2002:54, paras 91 et seq.; Case T-9/98, *Mitteldeutsche Erdöl-Raffinerie v. Commission*, paras 113 et seq.; Case T-296/97, *Alitalia v. Commission*, 12.12.2000, ECLI:EU:T:2000:289, paras 95 and 138.
141. Opinion of Advocate General Jacobs in Case C-222/04, *Cassa di Risparmio di Firenze and others*, paras 109-112.
142. Case T-3/09, *Italy v. Commission*, 3.2.2011, ECLI:EU:T:2011:27, para. 76.
143. *See*, lastly, Joined Cases T-29/10 and T-33/10, *Netherlands and ING v. Commission*, 2.3.2012, ECLI:EU:T:2012:98, para. 103.
144. Joined Cases T-267/08 and T-279/08, *Région Nord-Pas-de-Calais and Communauté d'agglomération du Douaisis v. Commission*, 12.5.2011, ECLI:EU:T:2011:209, para. 132; *see* Joined Cases C-75/05 and C-80/05 P, *Kronofrance SA v. Germany*, 11.9.2008, ECLI: EU:C:2008:482, para. 59.
145. Article 296 TFEU states: 'Where the Treaties do not specify the type of act to be adopted, the institutions shall select it on a case-by-case basis, in compliance with the applicable procedures and with the principle of proportionality. Legal acts shall state the reasons on which they are based and shall refer to any proposals, initiatives, recommendations, requests or opinions

constitutes an infringement of an essential procedural requirement for the purposes of Article 263 TFEU.[146]

It is settled case law that the statement of reasons required by Article 296 TFEU must be appropriate to the act at issue and must disclose, in a clear and unequivocal fashion, the reasoning followed by the institution that adopted the measure in question, in such a way as to enable the persons concerned to ascertain the reasons for the measure and to enable the competent court to exercise its power of review.[147]

The necessity of a statement of reasons must be appraised in relation, *inter alia*, to the circumstances surrounding the case, and in particular '*the interest which the addressees or other persons concerned may have in obtaining an explanation*'.[148]

While the Commission is not required to discuss, in its statement of reasons, all the issues of fact and law raised by the applicants in administrative proceedings,[149] it must take into account all the circumstances and elements relevant to the case to enable the Court to review its lawfulness and make clear to the Member State and the persons concerned the criteria whereby it has applied the Treaty.[150]

In regard to the Commission's individual decisions concerning State aid, the EU case law has, over time, developed the following guidelines:

- As regards a Commission decision finding that *no State aid as alleged by a complainant exists*, the Commission must at least provide the complainant with an adequate explanation of the reasons for which the facts and points of law put forward in the complaint have failed to demonstrate the existence of State aid. The Commission is not required, however, to define its position on matters that are manifestly irrelevant or insignificant or plainly of secondary importance.[151]

required by the Treaties. When considering draft legislative acts, the European Parliament and the Council shall refrain from adopting acts not provided for by the relevant legislative procedure in the area in question.' According to the ECJ, the operative part of an act is inextricably linked to the statement of reasons for it, so that, when it has to be interpreted, account must be taken of the reasons which led to its adoption. *See* Case C-355/95P, *Textilwerke Deggendorf GmbG (TWD) v. Commission*, 15.5.1997, ECLI:EU:C:1997:241, para. 21.

146. *See* Case C-367/95 P, *Commission v. Sytraval and Brink's France*, para. 45.
147. *See* Case C-89/08 P, *Commission v. Ireland and Others* ('*Eurallumina*'), 2.12.2009, ECLI:EU:C:2009:742, para. 77. *See also* Joined Cases C-57/00 P and C-61/00 P, *Freistaat Sachsen v. Commission*, 30.9.2003, ECLI:EU:C:2003:510, para. 76; Case C-17/99, *France v. Commission*, 9.8.1994, ECLI:EU:C:1994:305, para. 35; Joined Cases C-296/82 and C-318/92, *The Netherlands and Leeuwarder Papierwarenfabriek v. Commission*, 13.3.1985, ECLI:EU:C:1985:113, para. 19; Case C-367/95 P, *Commission v. Sytraval*, para. 63; Case T-349/03, *Corsica Ferries France SAS v. Commission*, 15.6.2005, ECLI:EU:T:2005:221, para. 2.
148. Joined Cases C-57/00 P and C-61/00 P, *Freistaat Sachsen v. Commission*, para. 76; Case T-243/94, *British Steel v. Commission*, 24.10.1997, ECLI:EU:T:1997:159, para. 160.
149. Case T-66/89, *Publishers Association v. Commission*, 9.7.1992, ECLI:EU:T:1992:84, para. 39.
150. Joined Cases C-329/93, C-62/95 and C-63/95, *Germany v. Commission ('Bremer Vulkan Verbund')*, 24.10.1996, ECLI:EU:C:1996:394, para. 32; Case T-66/89, *Publishers Association v. Commission*, para. 39. *See also* Joined Cases T-371/94 and T-394/94, *British Airways and others v. Commission*, para. 94.
151. Case C-367/95 P, *Commission v. Sytraval*, para. 63.

- The General Court's approach, according to which the Commission is not even required to make express mention of all the requirements inhering in the concept of State aid, seems to be exceedingly in favour of the Commission. For it would be sufficient for the decision to reveal clearly and unequivocally that the Commission took those requirements into consideration when making its review pursuant to Article 107 TFEU.[152]
- If the Commission decides that an aid *is liable to affect trade between Member States and to distort or threaten to distort competition*, then it must, at least, set out, in the statement of reasons, the specific circumstances based on which it reached such decision in relation to either requirement under Article 107 TFEU.[153] The Commission is required to do nothing more and nothing less than this in the field of State aid.

Yet, in some cases, the General Court has taken the view that the Commission is not required to carry out an economic analysis of the actual situation in the relevant market, of the market share of the undertakings in receipt of the aid, of the position of competing undertakings and of trade flows of the services in question between Member States.[154] The fact that an economic sector has been *liberalized at the EU level* is sufficient, in itself, to show the real or potential effect of the aid on competition and its effect on trade between Member States.[155]

In the case of State aid granted to Italian banks (under the Ciampi Act),[156] the Court of Justice considered the statement of grounds supporting the relevant Commission decision to be adequate,[157] thereby entirely disregarding Unicredito's argument – as also submitted at the oral hearing of 3 February 2005 – according to which the Commission ought to have examined all the different geographic and product markets

152. Case T-55/99, *Confederación Española de Transporte de Mercancías (CETM) v. Commission*, 29.9.2000, ECLI:EU:T:2000:22, para. 60.
153. Case C-409/00, *Spain v. Commission*, 13.2.2003, ECLI:EU:C:2003:92, para. 74; Joined Cases C-15/98 and C-105/99, *Italy & Sardegna Lines v. Commission*, 19.10.2000, ECLI: EU:C:2000:570, para. 66; Joined Cases C-329/93, C-62/95 and C-63/95, *Bremer Vulkan*, para. 52; Joined Cases C-296/82 and C-318/92, *The Netherlands and Leeuwarder Papierwarenfabriek v. Commission*, para. 24.
154. Case T-55/99, *CETM v. Commission*, para. 102. *See also* Case C-730/79, *Philip Morris v. Commission*, paras 9-12; Case T-214/95, *Vlaams Gewest v. Commission*, para. 67.
155. Case C-409/00, *Spain v. Commission*, para. 75 and Case C-148/04, *Unicredito Italiano v. Agenzia delle Entrate, Ufficio Genova 1*, 15.12.2005, ECLI:EU:C:2005:774, para. 57. It is not necessary that the beneficiary undertaking itself be involved in intra-Community trade. Aid granted by a Member State to an undertaking may help to maintain or increase domestic activity, with the result that undertakings established in other Member States have less chance of penetrating the market of the Member State concerned – *See*, to that effect, in particular, Case C-148/04, *Unicredito v. Agenzia delle Entrate*, para. 58 and Case C-310/99, *Italy v. Commission*, 7.3.2002, ECLI:EU:C:2002:143, para. 84. Furthermore, the strengthening of an undertaking which, until then, was not involved in intra-EU trade may place that undertaking in a position which enables it to penetrate the market of another Member State.
156. Italian Law No. 461 of 23 Dec. 1998.
157. Case C-148/04, *Unicredito v. Agenzia delle Entrate*, para. 60. The Court stated that: 'financial services sector has been involved in an important liberalization process at Community level, enhancing the competition that may already have resulted from the free movement of capital provided for in the EC Treaty'.

possibly relevant to the case in issue, depending on the different types of banking operations.[158]

Conversely, in *Sardegna Lines*, the Court of Justice found that the Commission had not provided the least information concerning competition between the Sardinian shipping companies and those established in Member States other than Italy. The Court also established that the Commission had failed to take into account, in that respect, the fact that, until 1 January 1999, island cabotage in the Mediterranean *was excluded from the liberalization* of maritime transport services within the Member States.[159]

As it happens, EU Courts have ruled on many occasions that, in the case of aid granted illegally, the Commission is not required to demonstrate the *actual effect* that that aid has had on competition and on trade between Member States. It is so because, if the Commission were under an obligation to show the actual effects of aid already granted in its decision, such obligation would ultimately favour Member States that pay aid without complying with the general duty to notify the aid, to the detriment of those that notify the aid at the proposal stage.[160] It follows directly that the Commission, in the case of illegal aid, only provides to the public a summary statement of grounds in respect of the effects of the State measures in question.

Generally, the Commission is not required to specify the numerous and complex facts on the basis of which a decision was adopted, provided that it refers to the general situation that led to its adoption and the general objectives that it pursues.[161]

Differentiating between an inaccurate statement of reasons and manifesting errors in the assessment is not always an easy task.[162] Still, in the ECJ's view, these are *distinct* pleas, each of which may be raised in proceedings under Article 263 TFEU. The first, alleging absence of reasons or inadequacy of the reasons stated, goes to an issue of infringement of essential procedural requirements within the meaning of Article 263 TFEU and, involving a matter of public policy, must be raised by the ECJ *motu proprio*. By contrast, the second, which goes to the substantive legality of the contested decision, is concerned with the infringement of a rule of law relating to the application

158. The ECJ did not take into account the arguments put forward by Unicredito during the hearing thereby adhering to a preliminary exception of the Commission. However, there is no mention of such a request in the final judgment.
159. Joined Cases C-15/98 and C-105/99, *Italy & Sardegna Lines v. Commission*, paras 68-69. A similar approach can be found in Case T-34/02, *EURL Le Levant 001 and Others v. Commission*, 22.2.2006, ECLI:EU:T:2006:59, and Joined Cases T-304/04 and T-316/04, *Italy and Wam S.p.A. v. Commission*, 6.9.2006, ECLI:EU:T:2006:239; appealed by the Commission on 30 Nov. 2006: Case C-494/06 P, *Commission v. Italy and Wam S.p.A*, 30.4.2009, ECLI:EU:C:2009:272.
160. Case T-55/99, *CETM v. Commission*, para. 103; Case T-214/95, *Vlaams Gewest v. Commission*, para. 67; Case C-301/87, *France v. Commission*, 14.2.1990, ECLI:EU:C:1990:67, para. 33.
161. Case T-243/94, *British Steel v. Commission*, para. 164. EU Courts seem to uphold even 'summary reasoning' provided that the decision is adopted in a well-known context and forms part of a consistent decision-making practice: *see* Joined Cases C-57/00 P and C-61/00 P, *Freistaat Sachsen v. Commission*, para. 77. On the contrary, 'if it goes appreciably further than the previous decisions, the Commission must give an account of its reasoning'. *See* Case C-73/74, *Groupement des fabricants de papiers peints de Belgique v. Commission*, 26.11.1975, ECLI:EU:C:1975:160, para. 31.
162. EU Courts have often examined jointly the pleas of inaccurate statement of reasons and that of manifest error of the assessment: for an example, Joined Cases T-371/94 and T-394/94, *British Airways and others v. Commission*, paras 43, 88 et seq., 259 et seq. and 432 et seq.

of the Treaty within the meaning of Article 263 TFEU and can be examined by the ECJ only if it is raised by the applicant.[163]

In a later ruling the Court has stated that the concept of State aid corresponds to an objective situation and that, accordingly, the Commission is not required to state the reasons why it changed the assessment of the regime in question in a decision as compared to its previous decisions on the same exact regime.[164]

The annulment of a Commission decision on the ground of inadequate statement of reasons may, however, prove to be a Pyrrhic victory for the applicant. For the Commission is not required to re-open the formal investigation procedure, since it can well take a new decision grounded on more accurate reasons on the basis of *the same* information as it had originally used.[165]

This occurred in the *Hytasa* case, where an earlier Commission decision prohibiting a State aid unlawfully granted by Spain to an undertaking in the textile sector was annulled by the Court as lacking sufficient reasons.[166] Subsequently, though the Commission had not re-opened the formal investigation procedure, it issued a *new*, more accurately reasoned decision, whereby it reiterated its finding that the measure in question was incompatible.[167] The Court of Justice endorsed the Commission's approach, holding that the implementation of the Court's earlier judgment did not require the Commission *to go through the whole* procedure provided for in Article 108 TFEU, since the reliability of the investigation measures had not been challenged by that judgment.[168]

The annulment of a Commission decision because of a manifest error of assessment engenders largely different consequences as, should the Commission intend to pursue the case further, it would have to commence the formal investigation procedure afresh, and only after the new procedure has been completed may it eventually delivery a new decision.[169]

163. Case C-367/95 P, *Commission v. Sytraval*, para. 67; Case C-166/95 P, *Commission v. Daffix*, 20.2.1997, ECLI:EU:C:1997:73, para. 24.
164. Case C-89/08 P, *'Eurallumina'*, para. 77.
165. This stems from the principle contained in Case C-331/88, *The Queen v. MAFF, ex parte Fedesa and Others*, 13.11.1990, ECLI:EU:C:1990:391, para. 34.
166. Commission Decision 92/317/EEC of 26 Jun. 1992 on State aid in favour of Hilaturas y Tejidos Andaluces SA, now called Mediterráneo Técnica Textil SA and its buyer, OJ 1992 L171/54 and Joined Cases C-278/92, C-279/92 and C-280/92, *Spain v. Commission*, 14.9.1994, ECLI: EU:C:1994:325.
167. Commission Decision of 18 Sep. 1996 amending Decision 92/317/EEC on State aid in favour of Hilaturas y Tejidos Andaluces SA, now called Mediterráneo Técnica Textil SA and its buyer, OJ 1997 L96/30.
168. Case C-415/96, *Spain v. Commission*, 12.11.1998, ECLI:EU:C:1998:533 (para. 34). *See also* the *Air France* increase in capital whereas a first decision of the Commission had been annulled: Joined Cases T-371/94 and T-394/94, *British Airways and others v. Commission. A month later*, the Commission adopted a *new* decision authorizing the aid but which took into account the criteria set out by the CFI. *See* Commission Decision 1999/197/EC of 22 Jul. 1998 concerning the notified capital increase of Air France, OJ 1999 L63/66.
169. *See* the enforcement of the judgment in Case C-169/84, *Cofaz v. Commission*.

§6.03 PRIVATE PARTIES' STANDING TO BRING ACTION

[A] The Beneficiaries of Aid

As a rule, showing a *direct interest* is not an insurmountable obstacle for aid recipients intending to prove their *locus standi* before the General Court.[170] Showing an *individual concern* is, however, known to be a challenging endeavour for prospective applicants.

It is undisputed that a decision declaring an *individual aid* to be incompatible with the common market is an act individually concerning the undertaking or undertakings specified in that decision.[171] This also applies to the potential beneficiary of an individual aid in respect of a decision declaring a proposed aid to be incompatible.[172]

As mentioned in subparagraph §6.02[B][3] of Chapter 6, the actual problem arises when the Commission has found an *aid scheme* to be inadmissible. The ECJ has appeared, in several judgments, inclined to take a restrictive approach to the problem, by dismissing actions brought by actual or potential beneficiaries of aid schemes against decisions that had found the schemes in question incompatible with the common market.

This leads to a fundamental distinction for the purposes of this paragraph: that between *potential beneficiaries* and *actual beneficiaries*. With respect to the former, early case law had adopted a restrictive approach, which basically consisted in the application of the '*Plaumann test*' to the actions brought by potential beneficiaries.[173]

Accordingly, in the *Van der Kooy* case, the Court of Justice held that:

> the contested decision is of concern to the applicants solely by virtue of their objective capacity as growers established in the Netherlands and qualifying for the preferential gas tariff on the same footing as any other grower in the same circumstances. With regard to them, therefore, the decision is a measure of general application [...].[174]

170. *See, ex multis*, Case C-370/79, *PhilipMorris BV v. Commission*, 17.9.1980, ECLI:EU:C:1980:209, para. 5, and Joined Cases C-296/82 and C-318/92, *The Netherlands and Leeuwarder Papierwarenfabriek v. Commission*, para. 13.
171. Case C-323/82, *Intermills v. Commission*, 14.11.1984, ECLI:EU:C:1984:345, para. 5; Joined Cases C-296/82 and C-318/92, *The Netherlands & Leeuwarder Papierwarenfabriek v. Commission*, para. 13; Case C-188/92, *Textilwerke Deggendorf GmbG (TWD) v. Germany*, 9.3.1994, ECLI:EU:C:1994:90, para. 14. *See also* Case T-72/98, *Astilleros Zamacona SA v. Commission*, 16.3.2000, ECLI:EU:T:2000:79, where the Commission did not contest the *locus standi* of the applicant.
172. Case C-730/79, *Philip Morris v. Commission*, para. 5.
173. *That is* the set of criteria introduced with the early *Plaumann* ruling: 'Applicants must show that the decision affects them by reason of certain attributes which are peculiar to them or by reason of circumstances in which they are differentiated from all other persons and by virtue of these factors distinguishes them individually just as in the case of the person addressed'; *see* Case C-25/62, *Plaumann v. Commission*.
174. *See* Joined Cases C-67/85, C-68/85, C-70/85, *Kwekeriij Van der Kooy and Others v. Commission*, 2.2.1988, ECLI:EU:C:1988:38. *See also* Case C-282/85, *DEFI v. Commission*.

Similar arguments formed the basis of the ECJ's declaration of inadmissibility in the *Federmineraria* case, wherein the Court stated that a decision cannot be considered to affect operators whose number or identity was fixed and ascertainable at the time of its adoption.[175] As early as in *DEFI*, the ECJ had introduced the principle whereby the aid plan does not determine which undertakings are to receive aid and, accordingly, stated that '*any undertaking wishing to bring an action in that connection is no more concerned by the commission decision than all the other traders in the sector in question*'.[176]

Though based on a principle in law similar to the one just described, the Court of First Instance reached a quite different conclusion (finding the action to be admissible) in *Mitteldeutsche Erdöl-Raffinerie*, where it determined that the applicant was in a situation that differentiated it from all other operators based on the following factors:[177] (i) the applicant undoubtedly qualified for the tax premium in question; (ii) the adoption of the aid scheme was prompted by the particular features of the applicant's situation; (iii) such specific situation had expressly been brought to the Commission's knowledge; and (iv) the German Government had proposed to the Commission that it would apply such aid scheme to the applicant only, and would individually notify any other cases wherein that scheme was applied.[178]

Subsequent case law confirmed this strict approach, further adding the following additional corollaries: first, an undertaking cannot, as a general rule, bring an action for annulment of a Commission decision prohibiting a sectoral aid scheme if it is concerned by that decision solely by virtue of the fact that it belongs to the sector in question and it is a potential beneficiary of the scheme.[179] Second, the appellant's participation in the formal investigation procedure is only one of the factors capable of establishing individual concern.[180]

The framework is different with respect to *actual beneficiaries* of an aid scheme, who benefit from a somewhat more open approach: an approach taken in cases such as *Sardegna Lines* – decided by the Court of Justice – and *Alzetta* and *CETM* – decided by the General Court.[181]

In the *Sardegna Lines* case, the applicant had a twofold individual concern with respect to the relevant Commission decision: on one hand, by virtue of it being an undertaking in the shipping sector in Sardinia – and thus a potential beneficiary of the aid scheme in force for Sardinian shipowners; on the other hand, also by virtue of being

175. Case C-6/92, *Federazione Sindacale dell'Industria Estrattiva and Others v. Commission*, 7.12.1993, ECLI:EU:C:1993:913.
176. Case C-282/85, *DEFI v. Commission*, para. 16.
177. Case T-9/98, *Mitteldeutsche Erdöl-Raffinerie v. Commission*, paras 77-78.
178. *Ibid.*, at paras 79-82.
179. *See, inter alia*, Case C-298/00 P, *Italy v. Commission*,; and the Order of the GC in Case T-400/11, *Altadis SA v. Commission*, 9.9.2013, ECLI:EU:T:2013:490, para. 25.
180. *See* Case T-86/96, *Arbeitsgemeinschaft Deutscher Luftfahrt-Unternehmen and Hapag Lloyd Fluggesellschaft v. Commission*, 11.2.1999, ECLI:EU:T:1999:25, with reference to an aid recipient. The *locus standi* of the aid recipient's competitors is discussed *infra*.
181. Joined Cases C-15/98 and C-105/99, *Italy and Sardegna Lines v. Commission*.

an actual beneficiary of the individual aid granted under that scheme, recovery whereof had been ordered by the Commission.[182]

According to Advocate General Alber, the decision must affect a '*closed group of persons that cannot be extended*'; aid recipients do not have to be specifically known to the Commission at the time that measure is adopted but it is sufficient for them to be identifiable by the national authorities called upon to implement the Commission's decision.[183] It follows that the focal element appears to be the existence of a recovery order in the Commission's decision.

The order for recovery exposes the recipients, from the time of the adoption of the decision, to the risk that the advantages they have received will be recovered, thus affecting their legal position. The possibility that, subsequently, the advantages declared illegal may not be recovered from their beneficiaries does not exclude individual concerns.[184] It is irrelevant whether the recovery order has effects at national level.[185]

It is worth noting that if the Member State concerned excludes an applicant from the procedure to recover the aid, the consequence could be dismissal for lack of interest in bringing an action, rather than for lack of individual concern.[186]

Therefore, the GC has issued several dismissal orders. For example, some Spanish applicants were not subject to a recovery obligation contained in a 2009 Commission decision (by virtue of the principle of legitimate expectations) but they claimed that the lack of a recovery order was not definitive.[187] According to the GC, the applicants confused the 'individual concern' requirement, which is determined only by the Commission decision, with the 'interest in bringing proceedings'. According to Advocate General Kokott in *Telefónica I*, the only risk of recovery from the contested decision may be seen where the decision is modified due to a third party's initiative: in this case, the applicant can bring an action against the new decision.[188]

---

182. *Ibid.*, para. 31. *See also* Case T-298/97, *Alzetta and Others v. Commission* 15.6.2000, ECLI:EU:T:2000:151; Case C-372/97, *Italy v. Commission* (the '*Alzetta* appeal'), 29.4.2004, ECLI:EU:C:2004:240, para. 39; and *see, inter alia*, Case T-136/05, *Salvat Père et Fils and Others v. Commission*, 29.9.2007, ECLI:EU:T:2007:295, para. 70; Case T-301/02, *AEM SpA v. Commission*, 11.6.2009, ECLI:EU:T:2009:191, para. 45. For a case of lack of evidence of any actual benefit from the scheme, *see* Case T-309/02, *Acegas -APS SpA v. Commission*, where the applicant was not able to state the amount received and the assessment to tax was nil.
183. *See* the Opinion of Advocate General Alber in Case C-372/97, *Italy v. Commission*, ECLI:EU:C:2003:275, paras 80-85.
184. *See* Joined Cases C-71/09, C-73/09 and C-76/09 P, *Comitato 'Venezia vuole vivere' v. Commission*, para. 56.
185. *See* the Order of the GC in Case T-174/11, *Modelo Continente Hipermercados v. Commission*, 21.3.2012, ECLI:EU:T:2012:143, para. 29.
186. Case T-228/00, *Gruppo Ormeggiatori Porto Venezia v. Commission*, 10.3.2005, ECLI:EU:T:2005:90.
187. This was due to an action brought before the GC by a competitor against the Commission's decision. *See* Case T-221/10, *Iberdrola SA v. Commission*, 8.3.2012, ECLI:EU:T:2012:112; Order of the GC in Case T-228/10, *Telefónica SA v. Commission ('Telefónica I') v. Commission*, 21.3.2012, ECLI:EU:T:2012:140.
188. Opinion in Case C-274/12 P, *Telefónica I*.

In its orders of 9 September 2013, issued in *Altadis SA*[189] and *Telefónica II*,[190] the GC ruled on cases concerning actual beneficiaries (which had applied the aid scheme to acquisitions of shareholdings) but not covered by the recovery obligation under the Commission decision. On that occasion, the General Court stated: '*The status of actual beneficiary of an aid scheme is not sufficient to identify that beneficiary individually, where the latter is not covered by the obligation to recover the aid paid under that scheme.*'[191]

A different outcome was reached in 2009 in *Koninklijke Friesland Campina*: although there was no recovery obligation in the decision (due to legitimate expectations), the appeal was deemed admissible.[192]

Summarizing the two cases – that of potential and that of actual recipients – the situation does not appear to follow a consistent criterion. According to traditional criticism, EU case law on admissibility of aid scheme recipients leads to greater rights for actual beneficiaries of illegal aids than for potential beneficiaries; this notwithstanding the fact that the former undertakings are under a duty to ascertain proper notification of aid by the relevant Member State.

Others argue that EU Courts might be giving unequal treatment to parties that deserve a similar – or even equal – degree of protection by consistently stating the principle that individual concern be '*determined only by the Commission decision*'.[193] This may be the case, for example, of actual beneficiaries whose recovery orders have no effects at national level and that of actual beneficiaries not covered by the recovery order in the decision – instances that appear in contrast with the legitimate expectation principle.

Finally, the current case law may have the effect of requiring the beneficiaries of the State aid to challenge the Commission decision immediately, even before knowing whether it would lead to a recovery order concerning them, with greater procedural burdens for the EU Courts; this argument has often been invoked by the Commission and has always been rejected in Luxembourg.

[B] The Beneficiary's Competitors

In analysing the situation of perspective applicants who are competitors of the aid beneficiary, case law of the ECJ has consistently been distinguishing two different situations, with accordingly different conditions of *locus standi* to be fulfilled: (i) decisions adopted by the Commission after a preliminary examination of the aid

189. Case T-400/11, *Altadis v. Commission*.
190. Case T-430/11, *Telefónica v. Commission ('Telefónica II')*, 9.9.2013, ECLI:EU:T:2013:489; on appeal: Case C-588/13 P, Information not available.
191. Case T-400/11 *Altadis v. Commission*, para. 34.
192. Case C-519/07 P, *Commission v. Koninklijke Friesland Campina*, 17.9.2009, ECLI:EU:C:2009:556.
193. Case T-221/10, *Iberdrola v. Commission*, para. 40. Similarly, *see* Case T-228/10, *Telefónica I*, para. 35.

pursuant to Article 108(3) TFEU; and (ii) decisions adopted by the Commission at the end of the formal investigation procedure *ex* Article 108(2) TFEU.[194]

In relation to challenges brought against the former group decisions, it suffices for a claimant to demonstrate its status of interested party; the latter group of decisions does, instead, warrant a higher threshold of standing, which must be met by applicants in order to successfully challenge them. The following paragraphs will, respectively, analyse the evolution of case law on the two points, at the same time giving an outline of the present situation.

[1] Decisions Issued at the End of Formal Investigation

The leading case in this regard is the *Cofaz* ruling,[195] where the Court held that two main (seemingly cumulative) conditions must be fulfilled, i.e.:

- the applicant must have been *substantially involved* in the procedure before the Commission; and
- his or her position on the market must be *substantially affected* by the aid in question.

The *Cofaz* requirements have undergone an evolution in subsequent case law: the condition of *procedural involvement* declined in importance, rapidly getting to the point where it was no longer held to be a *condicio sine qua non*, as '*an undertaking may be in a position to demonstrate by other means* [...] *that it is individually concerned*'.[196] In 2007 the ECJ expressly acknowledged that active participation in the procedure '*is not a necessary condition*' for there being individual concern.[197] This should not, at the other end of the spectrum, lead to hastily dismissing procedural involvement as a mere formality.[198]

The EU Courts have to date not provided a consistent definition of *sufficient involvement*: there is debate over whether it might be inferred from the mere submission of comments to the Commission,[199] or whether it is necessary for an applicant to be '*at the origin of the complaint which led to the opening of the procedure*'.[200]

---

194. *See* in particular Case C-198/91, *Cook v. Commission*; C-225/91, *Matra v. Commission*, para. 23.
195. Case C-169/84, *Cofaz v. Commission*.
196. Case T-435/93, *ASPEC v. Commission*, para. 64. *See also* Case T-11/95, *BP Chemicals Limited v. Commission*, 15.9.1998, ECLI:EU:T:1998:199; Case T-149/95, *Ducros v. Commission*.
197. Case C-260/05 P, *Sniace SA v. Commission*, para. 57.
198. One may note a more lenient approach to standing (and to the 'substantially affects' criterion) where an applicant shows an active involvement in the administrative procedure. *See* Case C-169/84, *Cofaz v. Commission*; Case T-36/99, *Lenzing AG v. Commission* 21.10.2004, ECLI:EU:T:2004:312 and Case T-146/03, *Asociación de Empresarios de Estaciones de Servicio de la Comunidad Autónoma de Madrid and Federación Catalana de Estaciones de Servicio v. Commission* (admissibility and active participation of the applicants), on the one hand; and Case T-11/95, *BP Chemicals v. Commission*; Case C-260/05 P, *Sniace v. Commission* and Case C-367/04 P, *Deutsche Post AG and DHL Express (Italia) v. Commission*, 21.02, 2006, ECLI: EU:C:2006:126 (dismissal of the action and minor or no role in the procedure) on the other.
199. Joined Cases T-371/94 and T-394/94, *British Airways v. Commission*.
200. Case T-36/99, *Lenzing v. Commission*; Case T-149/95, *Ducros v. Commission*.

With regard to the 'substantial affection' requirement, EU Courts have variously elaborated on the concept in the aftermath of *Cofaz*,[201] partly recovering criteria that had been set out in the earlier *Eridania* case:[202] an undertaking cannot rely solely on its status as a competitor of the aid recipient but shall also demonstrate the magnitude of the prejudice to its position on the market.[203] Such a test is to be conducted with reference to the beneficiaries of the aid measures from time to time at issue.[204]

A good example of the stricter approach is the *Deutsche Post/DHL Italia* case,[205] where the Court stated that neither the presence on the same market of the aid recipient, neither else its identification by name in the decision, nor the mere existence of over-capacity on the market, were sufficient.[206] Market shares proving that DHL were one of the largest competitors – the fifth, with more than 8% – of the aid recipient were also deemed irrelevant.[207] The Court interestingly added that the '*substantial affection*' criterion does not coincide with that of '*distortion of competition*' under Article 107 TFEU.

A more liberal stance was adopted in the *Lenzing* and *British Aggregates* cases. In these rulings, the ECJ held that the '*substantial affection*' requirement needs not necessarily be inferred from factors such as a significant decline in turnover, appreciable financial losses or a significant reduction in market share following the grant of the aid in question. Indeed, the grant of State aid can have an adverse effect on the competitive situation of an operator in other ways, either causing the loss of an opportunity or resulting in a development less favourable than it would have been the case without the aid.[208]

Likewise, the seriousness of such an effect is subject to variation depending on a large number of factors including, in particular, the structure of the market concerned

201. A stricter test was applied in cases such as Case T-11/95, *BP Chemicals v. Commission*; Case C-260/05, *Sniace v. Commission*. and Case T-36/99, *Lenzing v. Commission*; *see* Case T-442/93, *Association des Amidonneries de Céréales de la CEE (AAC) and Others v. Commission* [1995] ECR II-1329 and Case T-149/95, *Ducros v. Commission*.
202. Joined Cases C-10/68 and C-18/68, *Eridania v. Commission*, 10.12.1969, ECLI:EU:C:1969:66.
203. *See* Case C-106/98 P, *Comité d'entreprise de la Société française de production and Others v. Commission*, para. 41, followed by the GC in Case T-193/06, *Télévision française 1 SA (TF1) v. Commission*, 13.9.2010, ECLI:EU:T:2010:389 and in Case T-117/04, *Vereniging Werkgroep Commerciële Jachthavens Zuidelijke Randmeren and Others v. Commission*, 27.9.2006, ECLI: EU:T:2006:276. According to Kevin O'Higgins, *Overview of the Jurisprudence in State Aid Cases: Substance and Procedure – an Update*, European State Aid Law Quarterly 601(2011), the burden imposed on a competitor of a beneficiary of State aid to demonstrate that it is individually concerned by a Commission decision 'is comparable to the Alpe d'Huez stage of the Tour de France'.
204. T-354/05 – *TF1 v. Commission*, paras 78 and 81.
205. Order of the GC in Case T-358/02, *Deutsche Post AG and DHL International Srl v. Commission*, 25.5.2004, ECLI:EU:T:2004:159, upheld on appeal: Order of the ECJ in Case C-367/04, *Deutsche Post AG and DHL Express (Italia) v. Commission*. This was an appeal against a Commission decision authorizing a measure in favour of Poste Italiane.
206. *See also* Case T-375/04, *Scheucher-Fleisch v. Commission*, para. 59.
207. *Contra* Case T-146/03, *Asociación de Empresarios de Estaciones de Servicio de la Comunidad Autónoma de Madrid and Federación Catalana de Estaciones de Servicio v. Commission*, 12.12.2006, ECLI:EU:T:2006:386, although the applicants affected represented less than 3% of Spanish petrol stations.
208. *See* Case C-525/04 P, *Spain v. Commission*, paras 34-35.

or the nature of the aid in question.[209] The existence of an '*undefined number of other competitors*' suffering similar harm was also considered irrelevant.[210] In other words, the ECJ seems to have turned down the so-called *unique position test*, with the result that the fact that other competitors may have suffered similar harm cannot make an annulment action inadmissible.[211] The *Aiscat* case might be taken as another example of the ECJ's more liberal approach.[212]

In any case, the subsequent GC Orders seem to have departed from the ECJ's more favourable approach in *Lenzing* and *British Aggregates*, returning to a definitely more challenging burden of proof onto applicants – a sort of *probatio diabolica*.[213] The following cases are, *inter alia*, worth being recalled the following cases:

- *Vtesse Networks*: the procedure ended with a dismissal order because: (i) there were at least thirty-five competing operators on the relevant markets; (ii) the applicant did not indicate its market shares; and (iii) the applicant did not prove there being a causal link between the aid and the loss of a contract in favour of the recipient.[214]
- *Phoenix Reisen*: although applicants alleged that some of the aid beneficiaries would have disappeared from the market without the aid, the ECJ opted for dismissal.[215]
- *Mojo Concerts*: the GC examined the two markets affected by the aid and dismissed the action, as the applicants: (i) were unable to differentiate themselves from other competitors; and (ii) had grounded their action on '*hypotheses*' or '*simple suppositions*'.[216]

209. *Ibid.*, para. 35.
210. Case C-487/06, *British Aggregates v. Commission*, 22.12.2008, ECLI:EU:C:2008:757, para. 56. For a different approach, *see* Case T-117/04, *Werkgroep Commerciële Jachthavens Zuidelijke Randmeren and Others v. Commission*, where the market share of the applicants and the lack of decline in turnover were deemed relevant.
211. Case T-182/10, *Aiscat v. Commission*. *See* Bart Creve, Locus Standi *Requirements for Annulment Actions by Competitors: the Resurfacing 'Unique Position Test' Ought to Be Discarded*, in European State Aid Law Quarterly, 2014, 233.
212. This was an appeal against a Commission letter closing the file. The national measure was an award, with no call for tender, of the concession for the construction of the Passante di Mestre. The GC carried out quite a detailed market analysis. In application of the *Lenzing* principle, the applicants showed a less favourable development of their commercial results than would have been the case without the aid (para. 78 of the ruling), and this entailed the admissibility of the application on the basis of the criterion of substantial affection.
213. For another example of a strict application of the 'substantially affects' criterion, *see* paras 43-58 of Case T-488/11, *Scheepsbouwkundig Advies – en Rekencentrum (Sarc) BV v. Commission*, 12.6.2014, ECLI:EU:T:2014:497. *See contra* Case T-182/10, *Aiscat v. Commission*.
214. Case T-54/07, *Vtesse Networks Ltd v. Commission*, 25.1.2011, ECLI:EU:T:2011:15.
215. Order of the GC in Case T-58/10, *Phoenix- Reisen GmbH and Deutscher Reiseverband eV (DRV) v. Commission*, 11.1.2012, ECLI:EU:T:2012:3.
216. Order of the GC in Case T-90/09, *Mojo Concerts BV and Amsterdam Music Dome Exploitatie BV v. Commission*, 26.1.2012, ECLI:EU:T:2012:30.

- *UPS*: another dismissal despite the applicant's active role in the procedure, despite the allegation that the applicant was the '*main direct competitor*' of the recipient, and regardless of the very high amount of the aid.[217]
- *UOP*: the GC dismissed the appeal after having: (i) considered irrelevant the applicant's allegation that UOP was the 'world leader in aromatics technologies' and that it was one of the major competitors of the beneficiaries in each relevant market segment; (ii) contested the evidentiary value of the market shares; (iii) deemed the references to the applicant contained in the Commission's decision to be irrelevant; and (iv) rejected the applicant's references to the structure of the market based on invitations to tender, and its references to the nature (R&D) of the aid.[218]
- *Whirpool*: the action was dismissed based on the fact that: (i) there were a handful of competing undertakings and no tangible evidence was given that the beneficiary's exit from the market would have significantly increased the applicant's sales; (ii) even if a 1% increase in the competitor's market share in absence of the aid have been demonstrated, it would not have been sufficient, as further information is necessary in relation to the competitive situation in comparison to other market operators.[219]

[2] Decisions Issued at the End of the Preliminary Procedure

As it has been established above, the second scenario is that of an application brought by a recipient's competitor for the annulment of a decision based both on the Commission's refusal to open the formal investigation procedure and on the protection of the procedural guarantees under Article 108(2) TFEU.[220]

In light of the principles set out by the ECJ in the *Cook* and *Matra* cases,[221] applicants only need to show that they qualify as *parties concerned* for the purposes of Article 108(2); the rationale of this 'lighter' test can be found in the lack of information available to private parties in the pre-litigation phase.[222] Although this principle was confirmed by the ECJ in *ARE*, there is a great degree of inconsistency in the case law.[223]

217. Order of the GC in Case T-344/10, *UPS Europe and United Parcel Service Deutschland v. Commission*, 4.5.2012, ECLI:EU:T:2012:216. As correctly argued by Creve, Locus Standi *Requirements for Annulment Actions by Competitors*, 234, although the GC in *UPS Europe* dismissed the application brought before it, in doing so it followed an approach more consistent with Case C-487/06, *British Aggregates v. Commission*.
218. Case T-198/09, *UOP Ltd v. Commission*, 7.3.2013, ECLI:EU:T:2013:105.
219. Case T-118/16, *Whirlpool Europe BV v. Commission*, 22.6.2016, ECLI:EU:T:2016:365.
220. On this issue, *see* Pastor Merchante, *On the Rules of Standing to Challenge State Aid Decisions Adopted at the End of the Preliminary Phase*, European State Aid Law Quarterly 601 (2012) https://doi.org/10.21552/estal/2012/3/305.
221. Case C-198/91, *Cook v. Commission*; C-225/91, *Matra v. Commission* (para. 23).
222. *See* the Opinion of Advocate General Tesauro in Case C-198/91, *Cook v. Commission*, 31.3.1997, ECLI:EU:C:1993:122.
223. Case C-78/03 P, *Commission v. Aktionsgemeinschaft Recht und Eigentum e.V. (ARE)*, para. 35.

However, if the applicant calls into question the merits of the decision, the mere fact that it may be regarded as *concerned* suffices not to qualify the action as admissible. The applicant must further demonstrate that it has a particular status within the meaning of the *Plaumann/Cofaz* case law.[224]

Advocate General Jacobs stated in the *ARE* case that the jurisprudence in this regard is '*plainly unsatisfactory, complex, apparently illogical, and inconsistent*'.[225] He therefore suggested that the *individual concern test* - a broader type of *Plaumann* test - be applied in all cases, irrespective of the grounds on which the action is brought. The ECJ did however not follow suit on his opinion.

In the *Kronoply/Kronotex* case,[226] the Commission invited the ECJ to reconsider its case law and the compatibility with the Treaty of the *Cook* rule of standing, arguing that such a rule should be considered a sort of derogation to Article 263(4) TFEU. In *Kronoply/Kronotex*, Advocate General Jääskinen proposed the abolition of the distinction between procedural pleas and pleas related to the merits.[227] The ECJ, then again, declined the opportunity to clarify the issue. Consequently, the *Cook/Matra locus standi* rule is still deemed to be an application of Article 263(4), rather than an exception thereof.

Over time, a progressive broadening of the notion of *interested party* under Article 1(h) of Regulation 659/1999 became recurrent in decisions taken on appeal of first-instance rulings. As a result, the statutory definition of '*any persons, undertakings or associations whose interests might be affected by the granting of aid, that is, in particular competing undertakings and trade associations*' - a cohort that appears not to be far from 'an indeterminate group of addressees'[228] - could qualify as an interested party. This is much more the case considering that the requirement of being a direct competitor of the aid beneficiary has also been deemed unnecessary, as long as there is a '*sufficient relationship of competition*'.[229]

Finally, in *Kronoply/Kronotex* the General Court declared admissible an action brought by two undertakings that were plainly not competitors of the aid recipient, but rival purchasers of the raw material that the aid recipient also bought, and also for a different use.[230]

---

224. *Ibid.*, para. 37.
225. Opinion of Advocate General Jacobs in Case C-78/03 P, *Commission v. Aktionsgemeinschaft Recht und Eigentum e.V. (ARE)*, 24.1.2005, ECLI:EU:C:2005:106.
226. Case C-83/09 P, *Commission v. Kronoply GmbH & Co. KG and Kronotex GmbH & Co. KG*, 24.5.2011, ECLI:EU:C:2011:341. The applicants were deemed by the GC to have standing on the basis of *Cook* but not on the basis of *Cofaz*.
227. Opinion of the Advocate General Jaaskinen in Case C-83/09 P, *Commission v. Kronoply and Kronotex* 25.11.2010, ECLI:EU:C:2010:715.
228. Case C-367/95 P, *Commission v. Sytraval and Brink's France*, and Case C-78/03 P, *Commission v. Aktionsgemeinschaft Recht und Eigentum e.V. (ARE)*.
229. Case T-395/04, *Air One SpA v. Commission*, 10.5.2006, ECLI:EU:T:2006:123, where the applicant operated in the Italian market but not directly on the same routes as the aid recipient.
230. Case T-388/02, *Kronoply and Kronotex v. Commission*, upheld on appeal: Case C-83/09 P, *Commission v. Kronoply and Kronotex*. According to the GC, it was possible that the interests of the applicants could be adversely affected by the aid.

The so-called *explicit plea requirement*, as well as the *reinterpretation ban*, were formally confirmed, *inter alia*, by two 2011 ECJ rulings - *Kronoply/Kronotex* and *Belgium/Deutsche Post-DHL*. According to the Court:

> it is not for the EU judicature to interpret an action challenging exclusively the merits of an aid decision as seeking, in reality, to ensure the respect of the procedural rights [...], where the applicant has not expressly raised a plea to that effect. In such circumstances, the interpretation of the plea would be tantamount to re-defining the subject-matter of the action.[231]

Notwithstanding this vocal support, the explicit plea requirement has been applied on significantly looser terms in later case law. EU Courts have moved in the direction of an interpretation of the plea taking into account the arguments underlying the plea on the merits as well as on the '*actual wording of the application*' - as much as this may not contain a distinctly identifiable plea on procedural rights.[232]

From a substantial interpretation standpoint, applicants may invoke '*any plea*' in order to show that the assessment of the information and of the evidence the Commission had at its disposal during the preliminary examination phase should have raised doubts as to the compatibility of the aid. It follows that the key evidence seems to be directed at supporting the existence of doubts about compatibility.

In this sense, the *Smurfit Kappa* ruling[233] is noteworthy for its introduction of the rule whereby the admissibility of each plea and of the underlying arguments is to be examined on a case-by-case basis.[234] This case signals a further move away from the requirement of a stand-alone explicit procedural plea, which is in practice no longer necessary in order to benefit from the broad standing conditions provided for in *Cook*.[235]

In conclusion, the current standard seems to entail the existence of doubts about the classification of the measure as State aid and about its compatibility, regardless of the basis of the applicant's *locus standi*.[236]

It is arguable whether the rationale of the 'two-scenario approach' still holds valid in light of the above.[237] On the one hand, the aim pursued by the applicant is the

231. Case C-148/09 P, *Belgium v. Deutsche Post and DHL International*, 22.9.2011, ECLI: EU:C:2011:603.
232. A subtle distinction exists between pleas regarding the substance (inadmissible for *Cook*-based standing) and arguments alleging serious difficulties, which may be considered in support of a procedural plea. *See* Case T-388/02, *Kronoply and Kronotex v. Commission*.
233. Case T-304/08, *Smurfit Kappa Group v. Commission*.
234. *Ibid.*, para. 65.
235. Nevertheless, in Case T-182/10, *Aiscat v. Commission*, paras 44-47, the GC was unable to infer a procedural plea from the application on the grounds of a strict applicability of the explicit plea requirement.
236. Case T-388/02, *Kronoply and Kronotex v. Commission*, para. 59. A similar standard was proposed by Advocate General Mengozzi in Case C-487/06, *British Aggregates v. Commission*, 17.7.2008, ECLI:EU:C:2008:419.
237. As mentioned, strong criticism of this approach has been put forward by several Advocates General - namely Jacobs, then Mengozzi, Bot, Sharpston and Jääskinen. *See also* Andreas Bartosch, *Procedural Rights Denied for Too Long: Is Legal Conservativism Finally Heading for its Götterdämmerung?*, European State Aid Law Quarterly 579 (2011) https://doi.org/10.21552/estal/2011/4/256.

same regardless of whether it invokes the protection of procedural rights or challenges the merits of the decision: in both cases, its immediate aim is the initiation of a formal investigation procedure.[238] On the other hand, the current approach creates legal uncertainty as it is impossible both for the parties concerned – as well as for the General Court – to clearly identify which pleas are aimed at protecting procedural rights and which deal with the merits of the case.[239]

[C] Professional Associations

Professional associations – also referred to as 'representative bodies' – are entities that group and voice the positions of undertakings sharing a common denominator, typically their business sector or, less commonly, their geographic area. Such associations are considered entitled to bring actions for annulment in three situations: (i) in lieu of one or more affiliates who would have individually had standing to bring the action;[240] (ii) in special circumstances, including but without limitation to the case where the negotiating position of the association is affected by the measure at issue;[241] or (iii) by virtue of an express provision of law to that effect.[242] Save it for these cases, an association formed for the protection of the collective interests of a category of persons cannot be considered to be concerned, for the purposes of the fourth paragraph of Article 263 TFEU, by a measure affecting the general interests of that category.[243]

In the *AITEC* case, the Court of First Instance treated as admissible an action brought by an association representing the most part of Italian cement manufacturers. Based on the argument that the applicant had, in the context of a procedure under Article 108(2) TFEU, protected the interests of some of its members in accordance with

238. *See* the Opinion of Advocate General Bot in Joined Cases C-75/05 and C-80/05 P, *Kronofrance v. Germany*, 6.3.2008, ECLI:EU:C:2008:140.
239. *See* the Opinion of Advocate General Jääskinen in *Kronoply and Kronotex*.
240. *See* Case C-487/06, *British Aggregates v. Commission*, para. 53. *See also* C-282/85, *DEFI v. Commission*, para. 16; Case C-6/92, *Federmineraria v. Commission*, para. 17.
241. *See* Case T-117/04, *Werkgroep Commerciële Jachthavens Zuidelijke Randmeren and Others v. Commission*, para. 62; Case T-95/03, *Asociación de Empresarios de Estaciones de Servicio de la Comunidad Autónoma de Madrid and Federación Catalana de Estaciones de Servicio v. Commission* (*'Asociación de Estaciones de Servicio'*), 12.12.2006, ECLI:EU:T:2006:385, para. 42. *See also* the landmark cases: Case C-313/90, *CIRFS v. Commission*, paras 29 et seq.; Case T-55/99, *CETM v. Commission*, para. 23.
242. Case T-559/11, *Sdružení nájemníků BytyOKD.cz v. Commission*, 16.3.2013, ECLI:EU:T:2013:255, para. 29; Case T-170/04, *Confederazione nazionale dei consorzi volontari per la tutela delle denominazioni di origine e delle indicazioni geografiche tipiche dei vini italiani (FederDoc) and Others v. Commission*, 28.6.2005, ECLI:EU:T:2005:257, para. 49. *See* Case T-196/03, *European Federation for Cosmetic Ingredients (EFfCI) v. Parliament and Council*, 10.12.2004, ECLI:EU:T:2004:355, para. 42.
243. *See* the CFI Order in Case T-585/93, *Greenpeace and others v. Commission*, 9.8.1995, ECLI:EU:T:1995:147, para. 59, confirmed by the ECJ, Case C-321/95 P, *Greenpeace and others v. Commission*, paras 27-28; the ECJ Order in Case C-409/96 P, *Sveriges Betodlares and Henrikson v. Commission*, 18.12.1997, ECLI:EU:C:1997:635, para. 45. *See also* the ECJ Order Case C-59/79, *Fédération nationale des producteurs de vins de table et vins de pays v. Commission*, 11.7.1979, ECLI:EU:C:1979:188, para. 3; the CFI Order Case T-238/97, *Comunidad Autónoma de Cantabria v. Council*, para. 48, and Case T-86/96, *Arbeitsgemeinschaft Deutscher Luftfahrt-Unternehmen v. Commission*, para. 55.

the powers conferred on it by its statutes, without any objection from those members, and having successfully shown that a decision of the Commission was of direct and individual concern to those members, the applicant was regarded as individually concerned within the meaning of Article 263 TFEU.[244]

In general, the standard for assessing the concern of a representative organization is the same as that employed to assess the concern of individual applicants.[245] In the *Van der Kooy* and *CIRFS* cases, the Court ruled in favour of the applicant associations' standing, on grounds that they had served as negotiators or interlocutors on behalf of the represented undertakings – that is, they were held to have an own interest in the decision.[246,247] The Court has then returned on the point of these judgments stating that they were '*particular situations in which the applicant occupied a clearly* circumscribed position as negotiator which was intimately linked to the actual subject-matter of the decision, thus placing it in a factual situation which distinguished it from all other persons'.[248]

In the *Forum 187* ruling, an association of 'coordination centres' – what may be defined as a second-tier organization – was held to have standing notwithstanding some individual centres had already otherwise applied to the Commission in regard to

244. Joined Cases T-447/93, T-448/93, T-449/93, *AITEC v. Commission*, para. 62. In the same sense, *see* Case T-266/94, *Skibsværftsforeningen and others v. Commission*, para. 47, and Case T-55/99, *CETM v. Commission*, paras 24-25. For a case in which the action brought by an association has been deemed inadmissible as it was not proved that its members were entitled to bring an action for annulment *individually*, *see* Case T-69/96, *Hamburger Hafen und Lagerhaus AG v. Commission*, para. 49 – in that case the two associations represented the interests of German seaports.
245. Case T-182/10, *Aiscat v. Commission*, para. 60; *see* the grounds for rejection in the Case T-559/11, *BytyOKD v. Commission*.
246. In *Van der Kooy*, the applicants had challenged a Commission decision under Art. 108(2) TFEU, which had declared a system of preferential tariff charged to glasshouse-growers for natural gas in the Netherlands to be incompatible with the common market. One applicant – the *Landbouwschap* (agricultural board), a public organization formed to protect the interests of horticulturists in the Netherlands – represented glasshouse growers in the negotiations on tariff with gas distributors. The Court of Justice stated that, much as the *Landbouwschap* could not be considered to be individually concerned as a beneficiary of the aid, its *position of negotiator* on gas tariff on behalf of the growers was affected by the contested decision, and the *Landbouwschap* was, accordingly, individually concerned. *See*: Joined Cases C-67/85, C-68/85, C-70/85, *Van der Kooy v. Commission*, paras 21-23.
247. In *CIRFS* the ECJ found that the applicant – an association whose membership consisted of the main international manufacturers of synthetic fibres – had pursued, in the interest of those manufacturers, a number of actions connected with the policy of restructuring that sector. In particular, CIRFS had been the Commission's interlocutor with regard to the introduction of the aid measure in question and its extension and adaptation. Furthermore, during the administrative procedure prior to those proceedings, CIRFS had actively pursued negotiations with the Commission, in particular by submitting written observations to it and by keeping in close contact with the responsible departments. The Court then held that the application was admissible, since '[t]he position of CIRFS in its capacity as negotiator of the discipline is [...] affected by the contested decision'. *See* Case C-313/90, *CIRFS v. Commission*, paras 29-30. *See also* Case C-78/03 P, *Commission v. Aktionsgemeinschaft Recht und Eigentum e.V. (ARE)*, para. 56, wherein the ECJ held that during the procedure ARE had not been a negotiator of the same kind as the *Landbouwschap* in Joined Cases C-67/85, C-68/85, C-70/85, *Van der Kooy v. Commission*, or the Case C-313/90, *CIRFS v. Commission*.
248. Case T-236/10, *Asociación Española de Banca v. Commission*, 29.3.2012, ECLI:EU:T:2012:176, para. 43.

State aid;[249] in the *CBI* case, an association of private undertakings was held to have standing to challenge a decision approving the granting of aid to public undertakings operating in the same market.[250] This brief overview of case law has given a sample of the 'open' approach of the Court of Justice with respect to applications brought by representative associations: an impression further reinforced by the affirmed principle whereby an association needs not be formally mandated by its affiliates to bring the action in question.[251]

Certain limits do nonetheless exist: the General Court has stated that associations are unable to bring an action where the affiliates whose interests are supposedly represented have already filed individual actions regarding the same decision.[252] Associations are also required to have a certain minimum degree of representativeness of their relevant business or geographic area. This criterion is assessed in quantitative terms: in another case, an association representing only 6 out of over 1,200 undertakings in the relevant sector was deemed not to have, per se, sufficient standing to qualify for bringing action.[253]

[D] Annulment of 'Regulatory Acts' under Article 263(4) TFEU

The difficulties - examined to greater lengths hereinbefore - met by private applicants in demonstrating their individual concern in a decision they wish to challenge have long been a focal point in the debate on State aid proceedings in the EU: notwithstanding extensive criticism, the Court has been steadfast in upholding a very high threshold of concern.[254] This situation - and the perceived need to overcome it - have been reflected by drafters of the Treaty of Lisbon, who have waived the requirement of the individuality of concern for applicants who challenge a '*regulatory act*'.

The provision at issue is the last period of Article 263(4) TFEU, in particular, whereby applicants can bring action for annulment against '*a regulatory act which is of direct concern to them and does not entail implementing measures*'.

The focal points of the provision are, ostensibly, the notions of *regulatory act* and of *implementing measure*: upon enactment of the provision, presently expectations rose with academics and practitioners alike as to how the Court would have interpreted them.

249. Joined Cases C-182/03 and C-217/03, *Belgium and Forum 187 ASBL v. Commission*, 22.6.2006, ECLI:EU:C:2006:416, paras 53-64.
250. Case T-137/10, *Coordination bruxelloise d'institutions sociales et de santé (CBI) v. Commission*, 7.11.2012, ECLI:EU:T:2012:584, paras 61 et seq.
251. Case T-182/10, *Aiscat v. Commission*, paras 52 et seq.
252. Case T-236/10, *Asociación Española de Banca v. Commission*, paras 29-30.
253. Case T-117/04, *Werkgroep Commerciële Jachthavens Zuidelijke Randmeren and Others v. Commission*, para. 60.
254. *See supra* at §6.02[B][3].

With respect to the former notion, the first case of application was the order of the General Court *in re Inuit*.[255] This was an action for annulment of a regulation adopted through the ordinary legislative procedure banning trade in seal products from the EU markets. For purposes of the fourth paragraph of Article 263, the notion of *regulatory act* was held to include all acts of general application with the exception of legislative acts. This view was upheld on appeal before the Court of Justice, with the endorsement of Advocate General Kokott.[256]

The first case of successful application pursuant to the amended provision was the ruling of the General Court in the *Microban* case.[257] Applicants sought to annul a Commission decision addressed to the Member States which required them not to include a dangerous substance in a list of additives adopted in the exercise of their implementing powers. The General Court stated that the contested decision was of general application in that it applied to objectively determined situations and it produced legal effects with respect to categories of persons envisaged in general and in the abstract. The action was consequently held admissible.

The diverging outcomes of the two cases can be recollected from the different legislative techniques employed, entailing the lack of focus on the substance – in other words, the content of the act – and on the individual qualities of the applicant.[258]

That having been said, the next question is whether Commission decisions on a State aid scheme can be considered addressed to the grantor Member State as a *regulatory act* within the meaning of Article 263(4).

An affirmative answer was given by Advocate General Kokott.[259] In her view, although a regulatory act is not a legislative act[260] it is nevertheless of general application because, in spite of its being addressed only to the grantor Member State, it is binding on any organ of the addressee Member State and it produces legal effects with respect to potential beneficiaries – in other words, a category of persons outlined in general and the abstract terms.[261]

---

255. Case T-18/10, *Inuit Tapiriit Kanatami and Others v. Parliament and Council*, 6.9.2011, ECLI:EU:T:2011:419, upheld on appeal: Case C-583/11 P *Inuit Tapiriit Kanatami and Others v. Parliament and Council*.
256. C-583/11 P, *Inuit Tapiriit Kanatami and Others v. Parliament and Council*, on appeal of T-18/10, *Inuit Tapiriit Kanatami and Others v. Parliament and Council*, *see* in particular paras 51-61 therein.
257. Case T-262/10, *Microban International and Microban (Europe) v. Commission*, 25.10.2011, ECLI:EU:T:2011:623. In Case T-279/11, *T & L Sugars Ltd and Others v. Commission*, 6.6.2013, ECLI:EU:T:2013:299, paras 54-57, the GC held that the approach in *Microban* (with specific reference to the existence of measures implementing the contested regulations) could not be applied in the case before it.
258. Arjien Meij, *Standing in Direct Actions in the EU Courts After Lisbon*, in *Fundamental Rights and Principles: Liber Amicorum Pieter van Dijk* (Van Roosmalen and Others eds, Intersentia Uitgevers N. V, 2013), 141.
259. Opinion of the Advocate General in Case C-274/12 P *Telefónica I*, paras 17-29. *See also*, implicitly, the judgment of the ECJ in the same case and Cases C-132/12 P, *Stichting Woonpunt and Others v. Commission*, 27.2.2014, ECLI:EU:C:2014:100 and Case C-132/12 P, *Stichting Woonlinie and Others v. Commission*, 27.2.2014, ECLI: EU:C:2014:100.
260. Opinion in Case T-228/10, *Telefónica I*, paras 17-19.
261. *Ibid.*, paras 20-29. *See also* Case T-262/10, *Microban International and Microban (Europe) v. Commission*, para. 23.

This also finds confirmation in an earlier case, *Koninlijke Friesland Campina*, wherein the Court affirmed that decisions on sectoral aid could be seen as having a regulatory character, as they are addressed to the relevant Member State and aid beneficiaries are identified as a general and abstract category.[262]

As for the notion of *implementing measures*, a negative Commission decision on an aid scheme cannot, according to the General Court, be regarded by the beneficiaries as an 'act not entailing implementing measures'. The General Court dealt with the matter in the *Telefónica I, Iberdrola, Altadis* and *Telefónica II* cases, issuing dismissal orders in 2012 and then again in 2013.[263] In these cases, the contested decision itself referred not only to the existence of recovery/implementing measures (e.g., tax notices) but also to 'other' implementing measures, such as all the 'measures for implementing the incompatibility decision' (e.g., a rejection of the application for the tax advantage).

In addition, according to the GC, these measures can be challenged by the applicants before a national court, possibly leading to a preliminary reference on validity. Finally, the Court deemed it immaterial that the grantor Member State had no discretion in implementing the Commission's decision.[264]

The concept was further developed by Advocate General Kokott and the ECJ in *Telefónica I*,[265] where a pertinent issue was whether recovery measures and other measures implementing an incompatibility decision are 'implementing measures' for the purpose of Article 263(4). According to the Advocate General, on the one hand, the literal interpretation of the third category of Article 263(4) is not conclusive and, on the other hand, direct judicial protection is needed only when the act produces per se legal effects with respect to the private party – without need for implementing measures.

In light of the above, the recovery order is not a '*necessary implementing measure*' as it does not automatically follow incompatibility: conversely, a tax notice is necessary in order to specify the juridical effects for the recipient of the decision of incompatibility. What is more, a tax notice is challengeable before a national court by the means of a preliminary reference regarding its validity.

262. Case C-519/07, *Commission v. Koninlijke Friesland Campina*, para. 53.
263. Case T-221/10, *Iberdrola v. Commission*, paras 45-48; Case T-228/10, *Telefónica I*, paras 42-45; Case T-400/11, *Altadis v. Commission*, paras 42-50; Case T-430/11, *Telefónica II*, paras 48-54. In the same vein, but with reference to a Commission decision not in the field of State aid, *see* the Order of the GC in Case T-381/11, *Europäischer Wirtschaftsverband der Eisen - und Stahlindustrie (Eurofer) ASBL v. Commission*, 4.6.2012, ECLI:EU:T:2012:273, paras 41-64.
264. Interestingly, the lack of discretion is indeed a relevant criterion for the issue of direct concern. However, according to the GC, the requirement of an act which 'does not entail implementing measures' is a condition distinct from that of the requirement of direct concern. *See* Case T-400/11, *Altadis v. Commission*, para. 47; Case T-430/11, *Telefónica II*, para. 52; Case T-381/11, *Eurofer v. Commission*, para. 59. *Contra* the Opinions of Advocate General Wathelet in the two 'wocos' cases: Cases C-132/12 P, *Stichting Woonpunt and Others v. Commission*, para. 76 and note 28, and Case C-132/12 P, *Stichting Woonlinie and Others v. Commission*, para. 49 and note 19). As the Advocate General remarked in these cases, '*la condition liée à l'absence de mesure d'exécution n'est qu'une répétition de l'affectation directe*'.
265. *See* the Opinion of the Advocate General in Case T-228/10, *Telefónica I*, paras 30-56 and paras 27-39.

The ECJ shared the Advocate General's opinion and added that a negative decision does not define the specific consequences of a declaration of incompatibility for each recipient/taxpayer. Those consequences will be embodied in administrative documents (such as a tax notice), which constitute such an *implementing measure*.[266]

In conclusion, according to several orders of the General Court and of the ECJ, a negative Commission decision on an aid scheme should be regarded as a *regulatory act*, but one *entailing implementing measures*. In principle, this should be true for recipients of illegal aid with or without a recovery order.

Finally, the Court clarified some crucial aspects regarding the application of the final limb of the fourth paragraph of Article 263 in the State aid field, with reference to acts that do not imply a subsequent act challengeable at national level.[267]

In particular, the Court of Justice considered for the first time in *Montessori* the question of the admissibility of direct actions brought by competitors of beneficiaries of a State aid scheme against a positive decision of the Commission, declaring that the national scheme in question did constitute State aid, and acknowledging that the unlawful aid could not be recovered.[268]

The case concerned the exemption from municipal tax on real property (ICI) granted by Italy to non-commercial entities (including ecclesiastical or religious institutions) providing activities such as education or accommodation on the real property belonging to them. The Commission found the measure in breach of Article 108(3) TFEU. However, due to the particular circumstances of the case, related to the absence of cadastral and tax information allowing identification of the type of activity carried on in the building or to calculate objectively the amount of tax to be recovered, the Commission did not order the recovery of the aid, since it considered this to be absolutely impossible.[269]

The Court of Justice found the action brought by two competitors (a private education establishment and the owner of a tourist bed and breakfast establishment) to be admissible, stating that the Commission's decision: (i) is a 'regulatory act', that is, a non-legislative act of general application; (ii) of direct concern for the applicants; and (iii) does not entail implementing measures with respect to them.

Indeed, the Court noted that a Commission decision on an aid scheme is of general application, being applied to objectively determined situations and to address

---

266. Case T-228/10, *Telefónica* I, para. 35.
267. The ECJ has held that the question of whether a recovery order entails implementing measures should be addressed by reference to the position of the person pleading the right to bring proceedings. *See* Case T-228/10, *Telefónica* I, para. 30. It is therefore irrelevant whether the act in question entails implementing measures with regard to other persons.
268. Joined Cases C-622/16 P to C-624/16 P, *Scuola Elementare Maria Montessori Srl v. European Commission, European Commission v. Scuola Elementare Maria Montessori Srl* and *European Commission v. Pietro Ferracci*, 6.11.2018, ECLI:EU:C:2018:873. *See also* Edoardo Gambaro, Francesco Mazzocchi, *Private Parties and State Aid Procedures: A Critical Analysis of the Changes Brought by Regulation 734/2013*, 53(2) Common Market Law Review 385-417 (2016) https://doi.org/10.54648/cola2016035.
269. The Commission also found that the tax exemption provided for by the new Italian scheme of the single municipal tax (IMU), applicable in Italy as from 1 Jan. 2012, did not constitute State aid.

a category of persons defined in a general and abstract manner, given that the decision on an exemption to a general tax scheme holds the same effects of the original scheme with regard to potentially affected competitors.[270] Therefore, the positive decision was considered to fall within the scope of a 'regulatory act'.[271]

Moreover, the Court found that a positive decision without a recovery order does not need any implementing measure that could be challenged before national court. In fact, the principles established with regard to potential beneficiaries of aid schemes, who could challenge, for example, the tax notices, cannot be applied to the situation of competitors – such as applicants in *Montessori* – as the competitor/applicant usually would not be in the position to challenge an implementing act before a national court (and could prevail on the latter to request a preliminary ruling from the ECJ).[272] In fact, they could not be asked to make an artificial application just in order to challenge the denial and it is hard to imagine a situation where the competitor/applicant '*would have to break the law in order to have access to justice*'.[273]

Finally, as regards direct concern, the EU Court noted that the applicant must adequately show that the Commission's decision puts him in an unfavourable competitive position and produces effects on his legal situation.[274] This would require

270. A Commission's decision on individual aid cannot, in principle, qualify as a regulatory act; *see* Case T-353/15, *NeXovation v. Commission*, 19.6.2019, ECLI:EU:T:2019:434, para. 45. However, the qualification of an aid measure as 'aid scheme' does per se imply the qualification as 'regulatory act'. *See* case T-34/20, *Datenlotsen Infomationssysteme v. Commission*, 18.1.2021, ECLI:EU:T:2021:13 and T-373/15 *Ja zum Nurburgring v. Commission*, 19.6.2019, ECLI: EU:T:2019:432.
271. The principles stated in *Montessori* have been subsequently applied in other cases: *see* case T-69/18, *Verband Deutscher Alten- und Behindertenhilfe, CarePool Hannover GmbH v. Commission*, 14.4.2021, ECLI:EU:T:2021:189., paras 149-169; case T-223/18, *Casa Regina Apostolorum della Pia Società delle Figlie di San Paolo v. Commission*, 2.6.2021, ECLI: EU:T:2021:315, paras 72-102.
272. *See* Case T-228/10, *Telefónica I*, para. 28.
273. *See* the Order of the GC in Case T-381/11, *Eurofer v. Commission*, para. 59; Case T-228/10, *Telefónica I* (para. 27 of the ECJ's judgment and paras 40-41 of Advocate General Kokott's Opinion). *See also* Case T-601/11, *Dansk Automat Brancheforening v. Commission*, 11.7.2013, ECLI:EU:T:2014:839, paras 53-61. *See* Advocate General Wathelet Opinion, *Montessori*, 11.4.2018, ECLI:EU:C:2018:229, paras 79-80, where he explains the different outcome due to the fact that the Danish scheme did not provide for a tax exemption for certain beneficiaries, but laid down the taxes, including the higher levies for the undertakings that challenged the Commission's decision. Therefore, the tax notices were deemed adopted on the basis of a national legislation implementing the Commission's decision on the aid scheme. *See also* C-541/14 P, *Royal Scandinavian Casino Århus I/S v. European Commission*, 21.4.2016, ECLI:EU:C:2016:302. In any case, the fact that an individual affected by an EU measure might, in some instances, be able to raise issues as to the validity of the measure before the national courts (which might then submit a preliminary reference to the ECJ) by first violating the rules laid down by the measure would not be sufficient to secure for the applicant effective judicial protection. *See* the Opinion of Advocate General Jacobs in Case C-50/00 P, *Unión de Pequeños Agricultores v. Council*, para. 43; Case C-432/05, *Unibet (London) Ltd and Unibet (International) Ltd v. Justitiekanslern*, 13.3.2007, ECLI:EU:C:2007:163 (para. 64).
274. In particular, the recognition that some competitors of the addressees of an act '*may be directly affected by that act is justified, not by the purely economic effects of the act in question on their situation, but by the fact that that act affects the legal situation of those competitors, in particular their right under the Treaty on the Functioning of the European Union not to be subject to distorted competition*'; *see* Joined Cases C-622/16 P to C-624/16 P, *Scuola Elementare Maria Montessori Srl v. European Commission, European Commission v. Scuola Elementare Maria*

providing evidence that the applicant is active in the same product or service market and in the same geographical market as the beneficiary of the contested measure. To this end, however, it is not sufficient to point out that the products or services offered by the applicant are similar to those of the beneficiary.[275]

The subsequent *Trasta* case developed the above principles with reference to the legal standing of the shareholders to bring on their own right the action for annulment against the decision by the European Central Bank to revoke the banking licence of Trasta Bank.[276] In particular, the Court rejected the arguments raised by the shareholders on direct effect, stating that the intensity of the effects of the contested measures should not be confused with the production of legal effects. The ECB's decision in fact did not produce any direct effects on the legal situation of the shareholders, as their property rights were not affected, including their ability to participate in the management of the company and to receive dividends. In other words, the withdrawal of the banking licence as such did not impact their legal status, regardless of the subsequent economic losses suffered as a consequence.

In addition, the Court rejected the arguments concerning the criterion of the absence of discretion, by clarifying that the standing of competitors should be limited to acts infringing their right not to be subject to distorted competition, and it is not found when their mere economic interests are affected.[277]

§6.04 ARTICLES 278 AND 279 TFEU: APPLYING FOR INTERIM MEASURES

The general rule is that, in accordance with the presumption of legality of acts issued by EU institutions,[278] actions before the Court of Justice have no suspensory effects.[279] Actions for annulment of decisions on the matter of State aid before the General Court,

---

Montessori Srl and European Commission v. Pietro Ferracci, para. 45. The principle was later applied in the field of trade defence measures in case C-461/18 P, *Changmao Biochemical Engineering Co. Ltd v. Distillerie Bonollo SpA*, 3.12.2020, ECLI:EU:C:2020:979, para. 68. *See* Roberto Caranta, *Knock, and it shall be opened unto you: Standing for non-privileged applicants after* Montessori, 58, Common Market Law Review, 1, 163-186 (2021) https://doi.org/10.54648/cola2021007.

275. Case T-491/17, *Opere Pie d'Onigo v. Commission*, 24.9.2019, ECLI:EU:T:2019:692; case T-486/18, *Danske Slagtermestre v. Commission*, 1.12.2020, ECLI:EU:T:2020:576.

276. Joined Cases C-663, 665 & 669/17 P, *ECB v. Trasta Komercbanka et al.*, 5.11.2019, ECLI:EU:C:2019:923. *See* Marta Simoncini, *Different shades of legal standing and the right to judicial protection of private parties in the Banking Union: Trasta Komercbanka*, 57, Common Market Law Review, 6, 1867-1886 (2020) https://doi.org/10.54648/cola2020770.

277. In the case at issue, the liquidation of the company was the act directly affecting the rights of the shareholders, while the ECB's decision did not itself involve the automatic liquidation of the bank. Therefore, the shareholders rights were not prejudiced by EU law or on its necessary implementation under national law, but merely by national rules. Joined Cases C-663, 665 & 669/17 P, *ECB v. Trasta Komercbanka et al.*, paras 110-114.

278. *See*, lastly, Case T-79/10, *Colt Télécommunications France v. Commission*, 16.9.2013, ECLI:EU:T:2013:463, para. 16. *See* Case C-63/87, *Commission v. Greece*, 7.6.1988, ECLI:EU:C:1988:285, paras 10-12.

279. Article 278 TFEU.

as well as the proceedings on appeal thereof before the Court of Justice,[280] are no exception to this rule.[281]

Articles 278 and 279 TFEU do, however, provide for instruments to suspend the operation of a decision of the Commission pending the annulment proceedings –this possibility is, however, considered exceptional by case law, in light of the aforesaid presumption of legality.[282] Under the former provision, any Member State or private party may file an application for the suspension of the operation of the contested act; under the latter provision, the same subjects may file an application for the adoption of interim measures. These interim measures under Article 279 are atypical in nature, in that they encompass both the suspension of the contested decision and other interim measures.

Applications for interim relief, to be admissible, need to fulfil a series of procedural conditions:

(1) The relevant petition needs to be filed in compliance with the prescribed formal requirements. In particular, the relevant application needs to be filed in the form of a *separate document*, in the manner applicable to the memoranda filed to bring ordinary proceedings.[283] Consequently, an application for an interim measure made in the same document as the principal action is inadmissible.[284] The application needs to be specific in its content, to state the subject matter of the proceedings as well as the circumstances giving rise to urgency, as well as to point out the pleas of fact and law establishing a prima facie case for the interim measures applied for.[285]

(2) No application for the adoption of interim measures may be admitted unless there is a close link between the interim relief sought and the subject matter of the principal action;[286] interim relief may – accordingly – not be granted in cases where the scope of the application thereof exceeds that of the main proceedings.[287]

280. Case C-304/09, *Italy v. Commission*, 22.12.2010, ECLI:EU:C:2010:812, para. 52.
281. *See* Case C-213/85, *Commission v. Netherlands*, 2.2.1988, ECLI:EU:C:1988:39, para. 21.
282. Case T-62/06, *RENV R Eurallumina S.p.A. v. Commission*, 9.6.2011, ECLI:EU:T:2011:261, paras 17 et seq.
283. Article 83(3) of the Rules of Procedure of the ECJ, and Art. 104(3) of the Rules of Procedure of the General Court.
284. *See, ex multis*, the decision in Case T-298/97, *Alzetta and Others v. Commission*, paras 37-39.
285. This condition is also known as *fumus bonis iuris*; *see* Art. 83(2) of the Rules of Procedure of the ECJ, and Arts 105 and 106 of the Rules of Procedure of the General Court. In case law, *see* Case C-110/97 R, *Netherlands v. Council*, 21.3.1997, ECLI:EU:C:1997:185, para. 24; Case C-149/95 P(R), *Commission v. Atlantic Container Line*, 19.7.1995, ECLI:EU:C:1995:257, para. 22.
286. *See* Art. 83(1) of the Rules of Procedure of the ECJ and Art. 104(1) of the Rules of Procedure of the General Court.
287. *See, inter alia*, Case T-176/11, *Carbunión v. Commission*, 10.12.2013, ECLI:EU:T:2011:710, para. 2.

(3) The requirement of having an interest in the decision, which applies to the main action,[288] also applies to interim relief; the criterion of assessment is the same: the claimant party needs to be able to attain an advantage in case its petition to the Court be accepted.[289]

No time limit is specified for lodging applications for interim measures other than the inherent limit set by the main action: it follows directly that the application for interim relief needs to follow - if need be, to the point of being simultaneous - the principal application. Accordingly, the complainant is not precluded from submitting an application for interim measures pending a final decision.[290]

The proceedings for interim relief are of a summary nature. This is confirmed, *inter alia*, by the following facts: (i) decision-making powers are vested in the President of the proceeding Court - the ECJ or the General Court, as the case may be;[291] and (ii) a simplified procedure has been provided for.[292] Decisions on the application for interim measures take the form of an order. The order itself has an interim effect, without prejudice to the decision on the substance of the case, and is subject to lapsing upon delivery of the final judgment, unless the court mandates for a different, shorter time limit.[293]

From a substantial standpoint, it has already been pointed out how the application needs to contain an indication of the reasons that base the urgency and the *fumus boni iuris* - i.e., there being a prima facie case. These two conditions need to be both present in order for injunctive relief to be granted.[294] The evaluation of the substantive conditions is carried out in a manner which is established by the court - which has ample discretion to this effect - on a case-by-case basis,[295] taking into account, *inter alia*, a comparative weighing of the interests at stake.[296]

As for the *fumus boni iuris* requirement, the standard of evaluation of the court is consistent in applying a low threshold: it is generally sufficient that there is a

288. *See* §6.02[B][4] *supra*.
289. Case T-22/11, *Westfä lisch-Lippischer Sparkassen - und Giroverband v. Commission*, 2.3.2011, ECLI:EU:T:2011:64; *see* Case T-176/11, *Carbunión v. Commission*, para. 18.
290. However, an application for interim measures proposed in an advanced phase of the procedure has been deemed inadmissible: *see, for example,* for a case of an application brought *after* the oral procedure has come to an end, Joined Cases C-3/58 to C-18/58, C-25/58 and C-26/58, *Barbara Erzbergbau and Others v. High Authority*, 19.1.1960, ECLI:EU:C:1960:1.
291. The President can either decide the application himself or refer it to the Court. *See* Art. 85 of the Rules of Procedure of the ECJ and Art. 106 of the Rules of Procedure of the General Court.
292. Articles 84 and 85 of the Rules of Procedure of the ECJ, and Art. 104(2) of the Rules of Procedure of the General Court.
293. Article 86(3) and (4) of the Rules of Procedure of the ECJ, and Art. 107(3) and (4) of the Rules of Procedure of the General Court.
294. Case T-457/09 R, *Westfä lisch-Lippischer Sparkassen - und Giroverband v. Commission*, 18.3.2011, ECLI:EU:T:2011:96 para. 30; Case C-7/04 P(R), *Commission v. Akzo Nobel Chemicals Ltd and Akcros Chemicals Ltd.*, 27.9.2004, ECLI:EU:C:2004:566, para. 28; Case C-268/96 P(R), *Stichting Certificatie Kraanverhuurbedrijf and Federatie van Nederlandse Kraanverhuurbedrijven (SCK and FNK) v. Commission*, 14.10.1996, ECLI:EU:C:1996:381para. 30.
295. Case T-457/09 R, *Westfä lisch-Lippischer Sparkassen - und Giroverband v. Commission*, para. 31.
296. Joined Cases C-182/03 and C-217/03 R, *Belgium and Forum 187 ASBL v. Commission*, para. 97.

possibility of there being an error in law in the Commission's decision,[297] or any way that the position of the applicant does not appear entirely unfounded,[298] neither in the principal proceedings nor in the application for interim relief.[299]

As for the second requirement, that of urgency, the criterion employed by the Court of Justice is that of avoiding '*harm reparable only with difficulty*' onto the applicant[300] – who has the burden of proving his or her inability to wait.[301] Absolute certainty of the occurrence of damage in lack of interim relief would be hard to prove: accordingly, the Court has settled on a lower standard, whereby the applicant is required to demonstrate that the serious and irreparable damage is '*likely*' to happen if not for the interim measure.[302]

Case law has proven more stringent on the demonstration of the latter requirement as compared to the former. It is not infrequent, in practice, that assessments as to urgency be made before assessment as to *fumus bonis juris*, with the outcome of EU Courts turning down many such applications '*without it being necessary to consider whether the condition of* fumus boni iuris *is met*'.[303]

Pecuniary loss is, per se, hardly deemed sufficient to warrant the granting of injunctive relief, given its inherently reparable nature – in most cases, it can ultimately be the subject of financial compensation.[304] Exceptions have been made on instances where applicants were able to show that the pecuniary loss would have entailed additional and irreparable damage. An example to this effect could be that of an undertaking compelled to file bankruptcy proceedings on the account of the pecuniary loss. In any event, case law holds that assessments to this effect are to be carried out on a case-by-case basis,[305] taking into consideration, *inter alia*, the applicant's own financial position and that of the group of companies to which the applicant belongs.[306]

297. *See* Case T-378/02 R, *Technische Glaswerke Ilmenau GmbH v. Commission*, 1.8.2003, ECLI:EU:T:2003:216, para. 15.
298. *See* Case T-52/12 R, *Greece v. Commission*, 19.9.2012, ECLI:EU:T:2012:447, para. 13; Case T-378/02 R, *Technische Glaswerke Ilmenau v. Commission*, para. 75.
299. *See* Case T-27/11 R, *Rheinischer Sparkassen – und Giroverband v. Commission*, 2.3.2011, ECLI:EU:T:2011:65; Joined Cases T-195/01 and T-207/01 R, *Government of Gibraltar v. Commission*, 19.12.2001, ECLI:EU:T:2001:291, paras 47 and 55.
300. Joined Cases C-182/03 and C-217/03 R, *Belgium and Forum 187 ASBL v. Commission*, paras 130 and 141. *See* Joined Cases T-195 and 207/01 R, *Government of Gibraltar v. Commission*, para. 95.
301. *See* Case T-455/05 R, *Componenta Oyj v. Commission* [2006] ECR II-38, para. 34. Case T-181/02 R, *Neue Erba Lautex Weberei und Veredlung v. Commission*, 3.12.2002, ECLI:EU:T:2002:294, para. 82.
302. Case C-278/00 R, *Greece v. Commission*, 12.10.2000, ECLI:EU:C:2000:565, para. 15; *see* Case T-181/02 R, *Neue Erba Lautex v. Commission*, para. 83.
303. *See, ex plurimis*, the Orders of the CFI President in Case T-111/01 R, *Saxonia Edelmetalle GmbH v. Commission*, 2.8.2001, ECLI:EU:T:2001:197, para. 29 and Case T-455/05 R, *Componenta Oyj v. Commission*, para. 62.
304. *See* Case T-62/06 *RENV-R Eurallumina v. Commission*, paras 21 and 46; Case T-79/10, *Colt Télécommunications France v. Commission*, paras 37 and 44.
305. Order of the CFI President in Case T-181/02 R, *Neue Erba Lautex v. Commission*, paras 88-89.
306. For an isolated case of suspension (temporary and subject to conditions) of the operation of a State aid Commission decision, following to a detailed analysis of the financial situation of the applicant, *see* the Order of the CFI President Case T-198/01 R, *Technische Glaswerke Illmenau*

This high standard of proof is maintained with particular respect to State aid and is reflected in the scarcity of positive decisions. The Court tends to be very reluctant in granting interim relief to applicants: in 2011-2013 there have been twenty-five applications for an interim measure, which were granted only in one case – this makes for a 96% rejection ratio.[307]

This is probably linked to the fact that applications for a stay of execution are not admissible when they concern a *negative decision in the field of State aid*, as that suspension cannot have the effect of modifying the applicant's position.[308]

In a latter case, the Court did suspend the applicability of a Commission decision ordering the recovery of aid unlawfully granted – without prior notification – to Greek farmers.[309] The President argued that, in light of the difficult economic situation in Greece, it would have been likely that a significant part of the vast cohort of beneficiaries would have refused to pay voluntarily, and that the necessity to safeguard 'confidence in the public authority' would have made unpolitical to enforce collection of the due sum.[310] This argument was, however, set forth without making reference to the provisions of Article 107(3)(b) TFEU allowing for social unrest to be taken into account.

§6.05 ARTICLE 265 TFEU: ACTION FOR FAILURE TO ACT

Actions for failure to act are governed by Article 265 TFEU, which requires:

> Should the European Parliament, the European Council, the Council, the Commission or the European Central Bank, in infringement of the Treaties, fail to act, the Member States and the other institutions of the Union may bring an action before the Court of Justice of the European Union to have the infringement established. This Article shall apply, under the same conditions, to bodies, offices and agencies of the Union which fail to act.
>
> The action shall be admissible only if the institution, body, office or agency concerned has first been called upon to act. If, within two months of being so called upon, the institution, body, office or agency concerned has not defined its position, the action may be brought within a further period of two months.
>
> Any natural or legal person may, under the conditions laid down in the preceding paragraphs, complain to the Court that an institution, body, office or agency of the Union has failed to address to that person any act other than a recommendation or an opinion.

GmbH v. Commission, 8.7.2004, ECLI:EU:T:2004:222. The suspension has been upheld by two Orders of the CFI President [2003] ECR II-2895 and [2004] ECR II-1471.

307. The data are taken from the statistic information published by the Court on its website and available online.
308. *See* the Order of the ECJ President Case C-89/97 P (R), *Moccia Irme S.p.A. v. Commission*, 30.4.1997, ECLI:EU:C:1997:226.
309. Order of the President of the General Court of 20 Sep. 2012 *in re* Case T-52/12 R, *Greece v. Commission*, for suspension of the Commission Decision 2012/157/EU.
310. Paragraph 54 of the Order (*ibid.*), *see also* the Press Release No. 118/12 of 20 Sep. 2012. On this case, *see* Leigh Hancher, *State Aid Recovery: A New Public Order?*, in European State Aid Law Quarterly 1 (2013).

The majority of issues of procedures concerning actions for failure to act are modelled on what happens with respect to actions for annulment. Actions for failure to act are heard before the General Court; the ruling thereof is subject to appeal before the Court of Justice.[311] As far as procedure is concerned, actions for failure to act are subject to certain conditions in order to be admissible. In particular:

- The measure that the institution allegedly failed to take needs to be an act in the sense of Article 263 TFEU[312] - i.e., substantially modifying the legal situation of affected parties.
- Private applicants need to show a degree of individual concern with respect to the institution they claim has failed to adopt a measure that would have directly concerned them.[313] This requirement is considered to be satisfied by individuals who would have qualified as parties concerned by the measure that EU institutions allegedly failed to take, had they actually taken it.[314] The criteria to assess this concern are the same used to assess it in evaluating the admissibility of an action for annulment.[315]
- Actions for failure to act are admissible only if the institution concerned has first been called upon formally to act, and did not.[316] This 'call to action' has no particular formal requirements, but it needs to be sufficiently clear, so as to enable the Commission to ascertain clearly the content of the requested decision as well as the fact that it is thereby requested to take action.[317]

Case law has been consistent in interpreting the provisions of Article 265 TFEU as referring to failure to act in the sense of a material *failure to take a decision or to define* a position, and not in the sense of the adoption of a measure different from that desired or considered necessary by the persons concerned.[318]

311. Article 256(1) TFEU.
312. Case C-15/70, *Chevalley v. Commission*, 18.11.1970, ECLI:EU:C:1970:95, para. 6.
313. Like in the case of Art. 263(4) TFEU, whereby individuals are allowed to bring an action for annulment against a measure of an institution not addressed to them provided that the measure is of direct and individual concern to them, Art. 265(3) must be interpreted as entitling them to bring an action for failure to act against measures that would have concerned them in the same way. *See* Case T-167/04, *Asklepios Kliniken GmbH v. Commission*, 11.7.2007, ECLI:EU:T:2007:215, para. 45; Case C-68/95, *T Port GmbH & Co KG v. Bundesanstalt für Landwirtschaft und Ernahrung*, 11.7.1996, ECLI:EU:T:2007:215, para. 59; Case T-395/04, *Air One SpA v. Commission*, para. 25; Case T-95/97, *Gestevisión Telecinco SA v. Commission*, para. 58; the CFI Order Case T-41/01, *Rafael Pérez Escolar v. Commission*, 25.6.2003, ECLI:EU:T:2003:175, para. 29, confirmed by the ECJ Order of 1 Oct. 2004, Case C-379/03 P, 1.10.2004, ECLI:EU:C:2004:580.
314. *See* Case T-395/04, *Air One v. Commission*, paras 25-41. Case T-167/04, *Asklepios Kliniken GmbH v. Commission*, paras 80-81 and 90 et seq.; *see* Case T-17/96, *TF1 v. Commission*, para. 31.
315. *See supra* at §6.02[B][3].
316. *See*, in the State aid field, Case C-84/82, *Germany v. Commission*, 20.3.1984, ECLI:EU:C:1984:117, para. 23 and the ECJ Order in Case C-59/79, *Producteurs de vins*, para. 2.
317. Case T-442/07, *Ryanair v. Commission*, 29.9.2011, ECLI:EU:T:2011:547, para. 22.
318. Case C-8/71, *Deutsche Komponistenverband v. Commission*, 13.7.1971, ECLI:EU:C:1971:82, para. 2; Joined Cases C-166/86 and C-220/86, *Irish Cement Ltd. v. Commission*, 15.12.1988, ECLI:EU:C:1988:549, para. 17; Case T-107/96, *Pantochim SA v. Commission*, 17.2.1998,

Under Article 266 TFEU, the effect of a declaration of failure to act is that the defendant institution is required to take the necessary measures to comply with the judgment of the Court.[319] In any event, such judgment does not require the defendant EU institution – i.e., the Commission, in the case at stake – to take a specific conduct.[320] The Commission fulfils its duty of compliance with the judgment simply by adopting on the relevant point one of the decisions contemplated by applicable regulation.[321] This means that granting an action for failure to act provides no certainty as to the outcome of the case in the substance: after the adoption of such a decision, as much as it may be unfavourable to the complainant,[322] the subject matter of the actions ceases and, accordingly, cease the grounds for adjudication.[323]

Actions for failure to act are often brought by competitors of a purported aid beneficiary in cases where the Commission has not followed suit to their complaints. Competitors find actions for failure to act as a convenient initiative to take in various situations:

- the Commission has failed to act following a *complaint*, i.e., it has taken no decision to close the preliminary investigation procedure, having been elapsed a lengthy period of time. The, then, Court of First Instance has ruled that the Commission must, in the interests of the proper administration of the fundamental rules of the Treaty relating to State aid, conduct a diligent and impartial examination of a complaint alleging aid to be incompatible with the common market.[324] It follows, in particular, that the Commission cannot prolong *indefinitely* its preliminary investigation into State measures in relation to which there has been a complaint where it has agreed to initiate such an investigation;[325]

ECLI:EU:T:1998:36, para. 30; Case T-26/01, *Fiocchi Munizioni S.p.A. v. Commission*, 30.9.2003, ECLI:EU:T:2003:248, para. 82. *See also* the CFI Order in Case T-126/95, *Dumez v. Commission*, 13.11.1995, ECLI:EU:T:1995:189, para. 43.

319. *See, ex plurimis*, Joined Cases T-297/01 and T-298/01 *Sociedade Independente de Comunicação SA (SIC) SA v. Commission*, 19.2.2004, ECLI:EU:T:2004:48, para. 31.
320. *See* Case T-395/04, *Air One v. Commission*, para. 24; *see* Case T-127/98, *UPS Europe S.A. v. Commission*, 9.9.1999, ECLI:EU:T:1999:167, para. 50; Case T-74/92, *Ladbroke Racing (Deutschland) GmbH v. Commission*, 24.1.1995, ECLI:EU:T:1995:10, para. 75.
321. In particular, the Commission is to take one of the decisions provided by Regulation 659/1999. On the point *see* Case C-615/11 P, *Commission v. Ryanair*, 16.3.2013, ECLI:EU:C:2013:310, para. 67.
322. Case C-44/00 P, *Société de distribution mécanique et d 'automobiles (Sodima) v. Commission*, 13.12.2000, ECLI:EU:C:2000:686, para. 83.
323. *See* Joined Cases T-297/01 and T-298/01, *SIC v. Commission*, para. 31; Case T-105/96, *Pharos SA v. Commission*, 18.11.1998, ECLI:EU:C:1999:563, paras 41 et seq.
324. Case T-95/97, *Gestevisión Telecinco SA v. Commission*, paras 71 et seq.; Case T-17/96, *TF1 v. Commission*, para. 73; Case T-46/97, *SIC SA v. Commission*, para. 105. *See also* Case C-367/95 P, *Commission v. Sytraval*, para. 62.
325. Case T-95/97, *Gestevisión Telecinco SA v. Commission*, para. 74 and Case T-46/97, *SIC SA v. Commission*, para. 105. Time periods exceeding, respectively, thirty-three, thirty-one or twenty-six months have been held by the CFI to be too long for preliminary investigations. *See* Case T-46/97, *SIC SA v. Commission*, para. 106; Case T-17/96, *TF1 v. Commission*, paras 76 et seq.; Case T-95/97, *Gestevisión Telecinco SA v. Commission*, paras 80 et seq. On the contrary, in the Case T-395/04, *Air One v. Commission*, paras 62 et seq., the CFI held that by the time the

- the Commission fails to take a decision closing the formal investigation procedure, pursuant to Article 108(2) TFEU;[326]
- the Commission fails to open the requisite formal investigation procedure to revoke a previous decision.[327]

§6.06 ARTICLE 340 TFEU: ACTION FOR DAMAGES

Certain classes of subjects may, under certain circumstances, claim to have been damaged in relation to proceedings in the matter of State aid, and seek compensation thereof. Actions for damages in State aid cases against the Commission (or, in exceptional cases, against the Council) must be based on Article 340(2) TFEU, which reads as follows:

> In the case of non-contractual liability, the Union shall, in accordance with the general principles common to the laws of the Member States, make good any damage caused by its institutions or by its servants in the performance of their duties.

In theory, a competitor who has suffered damages by reason of illegal State aid may bring an action for damages against the Commission for not having commenced proceedings under Article 108 TFEU. To this effect, such an applicant would need to satisfy three conditions:[328]

(1) the Commission's conduct - be it amounting to action or to inaction - has to be unlawful. The standard of unlawfulness is that the Commission's conduct is to be affected by a sufficiently serious - i.e., there needs to be a manifest and grave disregard of the limits to institutional discretion[329] - breach of a rule of law intended to confer rights on individuals;[330]

Commission was given formal notice under Art. 265 TFEU the investigation had therefore been ongoing for less than six months and therefore its duration was not unreasonable. In that case, the CFI also considered that: (i) the Commission did not remain inactive; and (ii) the case was undeniably complex and displayed a certain novelty. *See also* Case T-442/07, *Ryanair v. Commission*, and Case T-167/04, *Asklepios Kliniken GmbH v. Commission*, wherein the Court deemed the time taken by the Commission to investigate into the matter to be reasonable.

326. It is worth noting that the period of eighteen months set forth in Art. 7(6) of Regulation 659/99 is not binding on the Commission ('[t]he Commission shall as far as possible endeavour to adopt a decision within a period of 18 months from the opening of the procedure'). One can assume that the applicant can bring an action ex Art. 265 TFEU in case of failure to adopt a formal decision *within two months from the Member State's request* (Art. 7(7) Regulation 659/99).
327. Article 9 of Regulation No. 659/1999.
328. Case T-88/09, *Idromacchine v. Commission*, 8.11.2011, ECLI:EU:T:2011:641, paras 23 et seq.; Case C-373/08, *Nuova Agricast v. Commission*, 24.5.2011, ECLI:EU:T:2011:237, summary publication (para. 50). *See* Case T-230/95, *Bretagne Angleterre Irlande (BAI) v. Commission*, 28.1.1999, ECLI:EU:T:1999:11, para. 29.
329. A mere infringement of law may however be sufficient to base an action for damages in cases where there is little discretion left to the relevant institution. *See* on the general requirement: Joined Cases T-362/05 and T-363/05, *Nuova Agricast and Cofra v. Commission*, 2.12.2008,

(2) actual damages need to have been suffered by the claimant; and
(3) a causal connection has to exist between the Commission's behaviour and the damage suffered.[331]

The most part of the – few – cases under Article 340 TFEU brought to date have not been successful. However, the Commission was ordered to compensate a company for damage to its reputation suffered as a consequence of a breach of the duty of confidentiality by the Commission; the Court did however turn down the claimant's requests for material damage.[332] Actions for damages may be brought also by a beneficiary of the national measure who has been damaged by an unlawful Commission decision.[333]

§6.07 ARTICLE 267 TFEU: PRELIMINARY RULING AS TO VALIDITY

The preliminary ruling mechanism provided for in Article 267 TFEU gives the Member States' tribunals an option, and their respective courts of last instance an obligation, to request the ECJ to issue a ruling on the interpretation or the validity of acts of EU institutions, if that tribunal or court considers that a decision on the question is necessary to enable it to issue a judgment.

National courts often submit questions concerning State aid to the ECJ; and, *inter alia*:

(1) questions of interpretation of EU provisions in the field of State aid submitted by national courts called upon to enforce the direct effect of Article 108(3) TFEU (e.g., upon request of competitors of the beneficiary of an aid unlawfully granted).[334] According to case law, a national court or tribunal may not, in a reference for preliminary ruling under Article 267 TFEU, ask the Court for guidance as to the compatibility with the common market of a given State aid or an aid scheme. The ECJ may nevertheless provide the national court with an interpretation of EU law with reference

ECLI:EU:T:2008:541, para. 72; Case C-373/08, *Nuova Agricast v. Commission*, para. 72. On the exception of limited discretion *see* Case T-88/09, *Idromacchine v. Commission*, para. 24.

330. *See* Case C-221/10 P, *Artegodan GmbH v. Commission and Germany*, 19.4.2012, ECLI: EU:C:2012:216.

331. In Case C-40/75, *Société des produits Bertrand SA v. Commission*, 21.1.1976, ECLI: EU:C:1976:4, paras 9-14, the ECJ dismissed the claim because the applicant was not able to prove the causal link between the aid granted to its Italian competitors and the loss in its sales. Similarly, *see* Case T-230/95, *BAI v. Commission*, para. 34.

332. Case T-88/09, *Idromacchine v. Commission*.

333. *See* Cases T-344/04 *Bouychou v. Commission*, 19.7.1997, ECLI:EU:T:2007:234 and T-360/04 *FG Marine v. Commission*, 19.7.1997, ECLI:EU:T:2007:235. The applicants claimed that the unlawfulness of Commission Decision 2000/513/EC (annulled by the Court on 16 May 2002) was sufficient to engage the Commission's non contractual liability under Art. 288 EC. On 19 Jul. 2007 the CFI rejected both appeals and held that there was no causal connection between the Commission's behaviour and the damage suffered.

334. On this issue *see* more in detail Ch. 7. *See also* the Commission Notice on the enforcement of State aid law by national courts, OJ 2009 C85/1.

to, on the issue of compatibility, the interpretation of Article 107 TFEU;[335] and

(2) questions as to the *validity* of a Commission decision ordering recovery of State aid, in relation to an issue raised in this respect in proceedings brought by an aid recipient.

This section will only take into account the case referred to under point (2), above, i.e., in connection with references for preliminary rulings as to validity.

The *direct* remedy of actions for annulment positively interacts with the *indirect* remedy provided by references for a preliminary ruling on validity:[336] the two lines of remedy are far from being separate and independent fields. Conversely, EU case law considers the two procedures to be *complementary* to each other within the comprehensive system of judicial remedies provided for by the Treaty.[337]

In the *Rau and others v. BALM* case,[338] the Court of Justice had taken a definitely liberal approach, by allowing any person who has brought an action for the annulment of an act issued by an EU to *concurrently* request, in proceedings pending before a national court, an order of reference for a preliminary ruling *on the validity* of that same act.[339]

In its *TWD* judgment,[340] the Court of Justice has partially revised this approach, though, by stating that the beneficiary of a State aid could not, in proceedings pending

335. For a case of redrafting of preliminary references concerning State aid matters *see* Case C-34/01, *Enirisorse S.p.A. v. Sotacarbo S.p.A.*, 27.11.2003, ECLI:EU:C:2003:640, paras 23-25. For a wide interpretation of the jurisdiction of the Court in a State aid case *see* the opinion of Advocate General Tizzano in Joined Cases C-393/04 and C-41/05, *Air Liquide Industries Belgium SA v. Ville de Seraing*, 30.3.2006, ECLI:EU:C:2006:216, paras 23-34, upheld by the Court, at paras 20-26 of the judgment.

336. Respectively Arts 263 and 267 TFEU.

337. *See* the opinion of Advocate General Ruiz-Jarabo Colomer in Joined Cases C-346/03 and C-529/03, *Atzeni and others v. Regione Autonoma della Sardegna*, 28.3.2005, ECLI:EU:C:2005:256, paras 84-85.

338. Joined Cases C-133/85 to C-136/85, *Walter Rau Lebensmittelwerke and Others v. Bundesanstalt für Landwirtschaftliche Marktordnung (BALM)*, 21.5.1987, ECLI:EU:C:1987:244. In this case, the Court held: 'there is nothing in Community law to prevent an action from being brought before a national court against a measure implementing a decision adopted by a community institution where the conditions laid down by national law are satisfied. When such an action is brought, if the outcome of the dispute depends on the validity of that decision the national court may submit questions to the Court of Justice by way of a reference for a preliminary ruling, without there being any need to ascertain whether or not the plaintiff in the main proceedings has the possibility of challenging the decision directly before the Court', then proceeded on to affirm 'that the possibility of bringing a direct action under the second paragraph of Article 173 of the EEC Treaty [now 263 TFEU] against a decision adopted by a Community institution does not preclude the possibility of bringing an action in a national court against a measure adopted by a national authority for the implementation of that decision on the ground that the latter decision is unlawful'.

339. In the same sense, *see* Case C-216/82, *Universitat Hamburg v. Hauptzollamt Hamburg-Kehrwieder*, 27.9.1983, ECLI:EU:C:1983:248, paras 7-11; implicitly, *see* Case C-314/85, *Foto -Frost v. Hauptzollamt Lü beck-Ost*, 22.10.1987, ECLI:EU:C:1987:452, where the ECJ stated on questions concerning the validity of a decision that the applicant in the main proceeding could certainly appeal *ex* Art. 230 EC. *See also* Case C-16/65, *Schwarze v. Einfuhr – und Vorratsstelle für Getreide und Futtermittel*, 1.12.1965, ECLI:EU:C:1965:117.

340. Case C-188/92, *TWD v. Germany*.

before a national court, object to the invalidity of a Commission decision that was addressed to the Member State that had granted the aid and required it to recover such aid. The ECJ held so precisely because the undertaking in question, which could, in its being entitled to do so, have challenged that decision pursuant to Article 173 TEC – now Article 263 TFEU of the Treaty, *had, in fact, allowed the mandatory time limit laid down therein to expire.*[341] And so:

The Court of Justice itself considers the reference to *TWD* to be 'irrelevant', except in the case of a company that was *undoubtedly* entitled, and that had been informed that it was entitled, to bring an action for annulment of the act whose validity it was challenging before a national court.[342]

In general, except for the specific circumstances underlying the *TWD* judgment, case law precedents allowing for bringing parallel proceedings – direct actions under Article 263 TFEU and indirect actions under Article 267 TFEU – against the same EU act seem to remain applicable.

In the *Unicredito* case, the ECJ found a reference for a preliminary ruling (including as to validity) to be admissible, in respect of a Commission decision concerning State aid, precisely because the individual concerned had *duly brought action* before the Court of First Instance.[343] The very fact that the Commission had, in the parallel actions brought pursuant to Article 263 TFEU, raised a number of objections as to admissibility played a decisive role in leading to the judgment in question. Precisely from the Commission's attitude, it emerged that those same private parties could not be 'undoubtedly' deemed to have *locus standi* under Article 230 EC.[344]

That the *TWD* judgment is no longer regarded as reliable precedent has conclusively been confirmed by the ECJ's judgment in *Atzeni and others*.[345] In that case, some owners of agricultural undertakings had brought an action before the Court of First Instance seeking annulment of a Commission decision relating to State aid. By its order

341. In the proceeding at issue, the Court held that: 'accept that in such circumstances the person concerned could challenge the implementation of the decision in proceedings before the national court on the ground that the decision was unlawful would in effect enable the person concerned to overcome the definitive nature which the decision assumes as against that person once the time-limit for bringing an action has expired'.
342. Case C-241/95, *The Queen v. Intervention Board for Agricultural Produce*, ex parte *Accrington Beef Co. Ltd and Others*, 12.12.1996, ECLI:EU:C:1996:496, paras 14-16; Case C-178/95, *Wiljo NV v. Belgische Staat*, 30.1.1997, ECLI:EU:C:1997:46, para. 21. *See also* the CFI Order, Case T-228/00, *Gruppo Ormeggiatori del Porto di Venezia v. Commission*, paras 31-33 and Case T-141/03, *Sniace SA v. Commission*,para. 40.
343. In that case the appeal before the CFI had been brought by ABI (Associazione Bancaria Italiana) also on behalf of Unicredito. *See* Case C-148/04, *Unicredito v. Agenzia delle Entrate*, and the opinion of Advocate General Stix-Hackl, *Unicredito v. Agenzia delle Entrate*, 8.9.2005, ECLI: EU:C:2005:522, paras 26-32 of the opinion.
344. In the *Unicredito* case the Commission itself recognized – in its written observations under Art. 267 TFEU – that the *TWD* judgment was not applicable. According to the Commission, such inapplicability was due to: (i) the position taken by the Commission in the suspended proceedings before the CFI where it had insisted for the inadmissibility of the direct actions brought by the banks; and (ii) the fact that Unicredito had duly proposed an appeal under Art. 263 TFEU.
345. Joined Cases C-346/03 and C-529/03, *Atzeni and others*, paras 30-34.

of 29 May 2002, Case T-21/02, *Atzeni and others v. Commission*, the Court of First Instance dismissed the action as inadmissible *because it had been brought after the time limit, without, however, ruling on a second ground* of inadmissibility raised by the Commission, relating to *the applicants' lack of standing to bring proceedings* before the Court of First Instance.

Despite the fact that the action for annulment had been brought belatedly, the ECJ held the relevant applications for a preliminary ruling to be *admissible*. This because:

> unlike the circumstances giving rise to the judgment in *TWD* [...], it was not self-evident that an action for annulment brought against the contested decision brought by the recipients of the four aid measures would have been admissible.[346]

It should further be pointed out that a general principle of EU law is that *any person lacking standing to institute direct proceedings pursuant* to Article 263 TFEU must have the right to bring indirect actions before the relevant national court to challenge the validity of acts of EU institutions, based on the argument that such persons must not be deprived of what might be the only remedy available to them.

In its judgment in *BPP*,[347] the ECJ interpreted again the ruling in *TWD* by adding that:

- the *TWD* principle applies only as regards a party which invokes the unlawfulness of an EU measure before a national court, whereas it could undoubtedly have brought an action under Article 263 TFEU for the annulment of that measure, but failed to do so within the prescribed period.[348] Consequently, the fact that the Portuguese State did not bring an action for annulment of that decision before the General Court was deemed irrelevant;
- it does not follow from the judgment in *TWD* that the admissibility of a question referred for a preliminary ruling concerning the validity of an EU measure is conditional upon an application having been made for suspension of operation of that measure pursuant to Article 278 TFEU.

346. *Ibid.*, at para. 34. The ECJ in any case has warned that 'if [the applicants] had had standing to bring proceedings but had merely failed to bring their action within the prescribed time-limits, the present references for a preliminary ruling, relating to the validity of the contested decision, would be inadmissible before this Court' (para. 30 of the judgment). In the same sense, *see* the opinion of Advocate General Ruiz-Jarabo Colomer, at paras 93-100.
347. *See* Case C-667/13, *Estado português v. BPP SA*, 5.3.2015, ECLI:EU:C:2015:151, paras 26-32.
348. It may be worth noting that by the time of the ECJ's judgment, the General Court had *already* dismissed the beneficiary's challenge (*see* Case T-487/11, *Banco Privado Português, SA*, 12.12.2004, ECLI:EU:T:2014:1077).

CHAPTER 7

Unlawful State Aid: Protection Before National Courts

Alberto Tedoldi

§7.01 THE NOTION OF UNLAWFUL AID

The last sentence of Article 108(3) TFEU definitely forbids Member States from putting any form of aid into effect until the Commission's authorization procedure has resulted in a final decision. This is the 'standstill obligation' further affirmed by Article 3 of Council Regulation (EU) No. 1589/2015 of 13 July 2015,[1] to the effect that aid notifiable pursuant to Article 2(1) shall not be put into effect before the Commission has taken, or is deemed to have taken, a decision authorizing such aid.

An aid is deemed to have been 'put into effect' not only when it has actually been paid but also when the regulatory process empowering a governmental authority to award it to the intended beneficiaries has been completed without the need for further action.

Thus, the authorization procedure before the Commission is an incidental sub-procedure, as a pre-requirement for, and pre-condition to, the validity of the process of national law leading to the grant of aid.[2]

---

1. *See* OJ L 248, 2015. As for the concept of 'unlawful aid', *see also* Ch. 3 *supra* and *Commission Notice on the notion of State aid as referred to in Article 107(1) of the Treaty on the Functioning of the European Union* of 19 Jul. 2016, OJ C-262.
2. *See* Ornella Porchia, *Il procedimento di controllo degli aiuti pubblici alle imprese tra ordinamento comunitario e ordinamento interno* pp. 146 et seq. (Naples, 2001). *See also* Cristina Schepisi, *Aiuti di Stato e tutela giurisdizionale* pp. 10 et seq. (Turin, 2012), specifically with regard to the Commission's State Aid Action Plan and the strengthening of public enforcement; Luigi Daniele, *Private enforcement in materia di aiuti di Stato e ruolo dei giudici nazionali: la nuova Comunicazione della Commissione europea* (Schepisi ed.), *La 'modernizzazione' della disciplina sugli aiuti di Stato. Il nuovo approccio della Commissione europea e i recenti sviluppi in materia di public e private enforcement* pp. 159 et seq. (Turin, 2011); *see also* Alice Pisapia, *Aiuti di stato:*

Hence, the notion of 'unlawful aid', which includes:[3]

(1) aid not notified to the Commission;
(2) notified aid put into effect before being authorized by the Commission; and
(3) aid granted by a Member State in breach of the terms and conditions of the authorization given by the Commission.

§7.02 DIRECT APPLICABILITY OF ARTICLE 108(3) EC, LAST SENTENCE: THE NATIONAL COURTS' ROLE COMPLEMENTARY TO, AND DISTINCT FROM, THE COMMISSION'S

It is settled Community case law that the last sentence of Article 108(3) TFEU can be applied directly by the Member States' national courts.[4] Thus, it amounts to a provision of law apt to vest individual parties with rights and obligations that can be directly pleaded before the courts and tribunals of the respective national legal systems.[5]

National tribunals and courts have thereby been given a role complementary to that of the Commission in the field of State aid.

On the one hand, the Commission exercises its power to assess aid for compatibility with the internal market by taking views of an economic nature with some discretion. The European Court of Justice's (ECJ) judicial control over Commission decisions relating to State aid is restricted to testing them for compliance with the applicable rules of procedure and establishing the grounds for each decision and the material accuracy of facts or misuse of power since the ECJ is barred from substituting its own assessment for the Commission's.[6] However, the European court tends, in fact, to do more than that, by reviewing the Commission's decision-making process and assessing the definition of the relevant market and that market's structure, the presence of competitors, the fairness of the recipient undertaking's restructuring plans, the extent of distortion of competition relative to common interests, and so forth.[7]

---

profili sostanziali e rimedi giurisdizionali (Padova, 2013); Giovanni Luchena & Biancamaria Raganelli, *Concorrenza e aiuti di Stato in Europa*, (Torino, 2022).

3. *See* Art. 1(f) of Regulation No. 1589/2015. *See also* Leonardo Bellodi & Daniele Grespan, *La procedura in materia di aiuti* (Tosato, Bellodi eds), *Il nuovo diritto europeo della concorrenza* 353 (Milan, 2004).
4. Since the Judgment in Case C-6/64, *Costa v. ENEL*, 15.7.1964, ECLI:EU:C:1964:66; *see also* Case C-120/73, *Lorenz GmbH v. Bundesrepublik Deutschland and Others*, 11.12.1973, ECLI:EU:C:1973:152 and Case C-354/90, *Fédération nationale commerce extérieur des produits alimentaires et syndicat national des négociants et trasformateurs de saumon v. France*, 21.11.1991, ECLI:EU:C:1991:440.
5. As for the notion of 'direct applicability' *see, ex multis*, Riccardo Luzzatto, *La diretta applicabilità nel diritto comunitario* pp. 33 and 91 et seq. (Milan, 1983).
6. *See*, among many others, Case C-399/08, *Commission v. Deutsche Post*, 2.9.2010, ECLI:EU:C:2010:481.
7. *See* Case C-303/88, *Italy v. Commission* ('*Lanerossi I*'), 21.3.1991, ECLI:EU:C:1991:136 para. 34 and Case C-301/87, *France v. Commission* ('*Boussac*'), 14.2.1990, ECLI:EU:C:1990:67. As for the notion of syndicate of legitimacy, *see* Case C-105/99, *Italy and Sardegna Lines v. Commission*, 19.10.2000, ECLI:EU:C:2000:570.

On the other hand, the national courts have the duty to require compliance with the standstill clause, the infringement of which can by no means be remedied by a final decision of the Commission declaring aid compatible with the internal market. Any other interpretation would have the effect of according a favourable outcome to the non-observance by the Member State concerned and would deprive Article 108(3)'s last sentence of its direct effect.[8]

The mutually complementary, albeit distinct, character of the roles the Commission and the national judicial authorities have to play is borne out by the Commission being barred from ordering recovery of aid just because that aid was found to be unlawful, i.e., either not notified or put into effect prior to authorization. Unlawful aid is not synonymous with incompatible aid, though. The Commission is obliged to examine the aid and determine whether it is compatible with the internal market, much as it has been unlawfully granted, but cannot order the recovery of a non-notified aid, subject, however, to the Commission's power to issue an interim decision requiring the Member State to suspend immediately the payment of such aid pending the outcome of the examination of the aid.[9]

In turn, national courts have the power to order that the grant of aid be suspended or the aid repaid merely by reason of the infringement of the standstill clause implied in Article 108(3) TEC.

In other words, while the Commission has the exclusive duty to examine the compatibility of State aid with the internal market, the national courts' duty is to observe the applicable rules of procedure and, above all, to ensure compliance with the prohibition to grant a State aid not previously authorized by the Commission. It follows that the national judge is required to play a complementary role in the furtherance of the Commission since it is called upon to ensure the full effectiveness of the exercise by the Commission of its powers.[10] Unlike the Commission, which is obliged to make an evaluation as to compatibility before ordering recovery, the national court may, indeed, merely determine whether the measure constitutes State aid and whether the standstill obligation applies.[11]

8. *See* Case C-354/90, *Fédération nationale commerce extérieur des produits alimentaires and Others v. France,* 21.11.1991, ECLI:EU:C:1991:440 and Case C-39/94, *Syndicat français de l'Express international (SFEI) and Others v. La Poste and Others,* 11.7.1996, ECLI:EU:C:1996:285. *See also* Art. 16(1) of Regulation No. 1589/2015, under which a negative decision on unlawful aid should result in a decision from the Commission that the Member State concerned take all necessary measures to recover the aid from the beneficiary.
9. *See* Case C-301/87, *Boussac,* 14.2.1990, ECLI:EU:C:1990:67.
10. *See* Ornella Porchia, *Il procedimento di controllo degli aiuti pubblici alle imprese tra ordinamento comunitario e ordinamento interno,* p. 160, *supra*; and Cristina Schepisi, *Aiuti di Stato e tutela giurisdizionale,* pp. 157 et seq., *supra.*
11. *See Commission Notice on the enforcement of State aid rules by national courts* of 30 Jul. 2021, OJ C-305, 30 Jul. 2021, paras 41 et seq. About the 2021 Notice *see* Cristina Schepisi, *Aiuti di Stato e giudici nazionali nella Bozza di nuova Comunicazione della Commissione: alcune riflessioni a prima lettura* (*Eurojus,* 2-2021); Francesco Maria Salerno & Federico Macchi, *Il* private enforcement *in materia di aiuti di Stato in Europa* (*Eurojus,* 3-2021).

§7.03 LEGAL QUALIFICATION OF SPECIFIC STATE AID AS A PRELIMINARY QUESTION, CAPABLE ALSO OF BEING ADDRESSED EX OFFICIO

In applying the last sentence of Article 108(3) TFEU, the national court must necessarily deal with the problem of whether a specific measure brought to its attention qualifies as State aid liable to prior notification to, and prior authorization by, the Commission.

Legally qualifying a specific measure in terms of State aid is a *preliminary question* that the court may also raise ex officio, since it would result in the voidance of the measure that granted the aid, making it a matter that the parties must discuss, pursuant to Article 101(2) of the Code of Civil Procedure, with a failure to do so resulting in the judgment being void.[12] In a broad sense, preliminary qualification is both a concept of a logical nature and an intellective step the judge takes in reaching a final decision. If such a step is not disputed, a mere *preliminary point* will come up. If it brings about a dispute, it turns into a *preliminary question* the judge will have to settle incidentally, without this leading to its effectiveness as res judicata. Where the question must further be decided by judgment as res judicata, by the operation of law or at the parties' request, then it becomes a self-standing issue in judicial proceedings and changes into a *preliminary cause of action.*[13]

In general, a distinction is usually made between 'logical preliminary qualification' and 'legal preliminary qualification'. The concept of *logical preliminary qualification* applies to any questions and issues (whatever their contents in fact or in law, whether they are procedural or substantive) that are as many logical antecedents to the decision. *Legal preliminary qualification* refers, however, to any question that, in addition to constituting a logical antecedent to the decision, may become itself a separate cause of action.[14]

In terms of legal preliminary qualification, which regards the substantive legal situation with which the trial is concerned, that is, the substantive case, a further distinction is made between 'technical preliminary qualification' and 'logical-and-legal preliminary qualification'. The former applies when the nexus of preliminary status with dependence occurs between two distinct legal relationships, one of which contributes to the constituting specificity of the other (e.g., the right to alimony

12. *See*, among many others Italian Supreme Court, tax section, *Agenzia delle Entrate v. Logistics Service Scarl.*, 23 May 2014, No. 11453, *Giust. Civ. Mass.*, 2014. On the complex issues around the identification, decision and effectiveness of a judgment upon contractual voidances, *see* Italian Supreme Court, unified bench, *Bettio Antonio and Another v. Sandi Ferdinando and Another* and *Vanni Antonio v. Fascioli Licia and Others*, 12 Dec. 2014, Nos 26242 and 26243, both in *Giust. Civ. Mass.* 2014.

13. *See* Francesco Menestrina, *La pregiudiciale nel processo civile* pp. 139 et seq. (Milan, 1904), reprised by Giuseppe Chiovenda, *Istituzioni di diritto processuale civile*, I pp. 332 et seq. (Naples) *See also* Stefano Recchioni, *Pregiudizialità processuale e dipendenza sostanziale nella cognizione ordinaria* pp. 55 et seq. (Padua, 1999).

14. *See* Enrico Tullio Liebman, *Manuale di diritto processuale civile*, VI, p. 161 (Colesanti, Merlin, Ricci eds, Milan, 2002); *see also* Giuseppe Chiovenda, *Istituzioni di diritto processuale civile*, I, p. 333, *supra*.

depends on the existence of kinship relationships as well as other constituting factors). The latter applies when the nexus of preliminary status with dependence occurs between the individual effect and the underlying legal relationship (e.g., the right to take delivery of the thing sold and purchased as related to the underlying purchase agreement).[15]

From a systematic perspective, the specific notion of 'State aid', as introduced by European law, primarily through Articles 107 and 108 TFEU, falls within the domain of logical-and-legal preliminary questions. It is, in fact, a unifying notion embracing the plurality of effects it is bound to generate, each of which is capable of forming the subject matter of separate proceedings in the European courts, or in the national administrative, civil or tax courts, as the case may be.[16]

The preliminary nature of the legal qualification of a specific measure as State aid has been acknowledged unequivocally by the Commission, according to which a national court will have to consider whether the 'proposed measures' constitute State aid within the meaning of Article 107(1) before reaching a decision as to the standstill obligation laid down in the last sentence of Article 108(3).[17]

§7.04 QUALIFICATION BY NATIONAL COURTS OF SPECIFIC MEASURES AS STATE AID

Since the 'State aid' notion originated from within Community law, national courts called upon to adjudicate infringements of the standstill clause are faced with the problem of how to interpret such notion and to assess whether a specific State measure constitutes aid in a technical sense:[18]

> The first question which national courts have to consider in an action under the last sentence of Article 108(3) is whether the measure constitutes new or existing State aid within the meaning aid of Article 107(3) TFEU. The second question to be answered is whether the measure has been notified either individually or under a scheme and if so, whether the Commission has had sufficient time to come to a decision.[19]

---

15. *See* Francesco Luiso, *Diritto processuale civile*, I pp. 160 et seq. and 267 et seq. (Milan, 2014).
16. According to the Italian Supreme Court, the existence of a pending case before the European courts concerning the annulment of a decision by which the Commission found the incompatibility with the common market ex Art. 87 TEC of a State measure implies the necessary stay (*sospensione necessaria*) - pursuant to Art. 295 of the Italian Civil Procedure Code - of the national proceeding regarding the recovery of the aid granted (even if the latter proceeding concerns parties not involved in the pending European case). *See* Italian Supreme Court, *Inps v. Ditta Marangon*, 21 Jun. 2006, n. 14411, *Foro it.*, I, 2007, pp. 1886 et seq., with a critical comment by Porreca. In the same sense, *see*, Italian Supreme Court, *Inps v. Soc. D'Amico navigazione*, 9 Oct. 2006, n. 21635, *Foro it., Mass.*, pp. 1754 et seq.
17. *See* Art. 29 of Regulation No. 1589/2015 and *Commission Notice on the enforcement of State aid rules by national courts*, OJ 2021 C-305, paras 7 et seq.
18. *See* Case C-189/91, *Kirsammer-Hack v. Nurhan Sidal*, 24.11.1993, ECLI:EU:C:1993:905 para. 14 and Case C-78/76, *Steinike und Weinlig v. Federal Republic of Germany*, 22.3.1977, ECLI: EU:C:1977:52 para. 14.
19. *See* Art. 29 of Regulation No. 1589/2015 and *Commission Notice on the enforcement of State aid rules by national courts*, OJ 2021 C-305, paras 41 et seq.

Since State aid is a European notion, the national judge may only construe it in terms of European law, by applying the provisions of that law as interpreted by the case law of the ECJ. The classification of the particular measure as State aid must, in short, be reached in light of European law, and the approaches laid down by the ECJ.[20]

However, the national court is not required either to decline jurisdiction or to stay proceedings until the Commission takes a decision on the measure apt to constitute State aid.[21] As indicated above, the national court's scope for cognizance is limited to establishing compliance with the rules of procedure relating to State aid and is far removed from the Commission's power to assess the compatibility of State measures with the internal market. On the contrary, the national court is obliged in any event to intervene to impose a penalty upon a breach of the standstill obligation under Article 108(3) TFEU, without awaiting any opinion it may have sought from the Commission, under principles of loyal cooperation between European institutions and the bodies of Member States.[22]

An especially interesting instance in this respect is an ordinance delivered by the Regional Administrative Tribunal (*TAR*) of Lombardy, Chamber of Brescia, concerning airport fees and dues, which, as it is unpublished, deserves reproduction at length below, as an example of the national court's proper *modus procedendi* in a case of unlawful State aid:[23]

> In general, State aid prohibited by Article 107 TFEU shall be deemed to be any aid granted by public agencies which 'distorts or threatens to distort competition by favoring certain undertakings or the production of certain goods'. In this respect, the European Court of Justice, by its judgment of 2 August 1974 in C-173/73, clarified that the concept of State aid does not include general measures of economic policy so long as they are not intended to benefit a specific productive sector. Subsequently, by its judgment of 15 March 2001 in C-265/99, the Court of Justice stressed that an apparently general and abstract set of measures formally intended for a whole sector may constitute State aid where it benefits one or more specific undertakings.
>
> In light of the foregoing, the temporary regime in issue in these proceedings is intended, by providing for a general reduction in fees and dues, to transfer the benefit of reduced fees to airlines operating in Italian airports, thereby charging the associated costs to the Italian State as the entity collecting such fees. This has been

20. *See* especially Case C-280/00, *Altmark Trans GmbH and Regierungspräsidium Magdeburg v. Nahverkehrsgesellschaft Altmark GmbH*, 24.7.2023, ECLI:EU:C:2003:415; and Case C-399/08, *Commission v. Deutsche Post AG*, 2.9.2010, ECLI:EU:C:2010:481.
21. Case C-39/94, *SFEI and Other*, 11.7.1996, ECLI:EU:C:1996:285, para. 44, *supra*.
22. *Commission Notice on the enforcement of State aid rules by national courts* paras 17 et seq., *supra*.
23. *See* TAR Lombardia, Brescia, *SACBO and Assaeroporti v. Ministry of Infrastructures and Transports, Ministry of Economy and Finances, E.N.A.C and Alitalia Linee Aeree S.p.A.*, Order of 21 Mar. 2006, not published. Such *interim* order was overruled by a subsequent judgment of TAR Lazio of 17 May 2007. In that ruling, the TAR Lazio made wrongful application of the ECJ case law in the field of State aid by declaring that Italian law 248/2005 was *not* a State aid. In particular, TAR Lazio omitted to consider the de facto selective nature of the measure (in favour of national air carriers) which could be easily inferred by the following issues: (i) the national airlines (*in primis*, Alitalia, the national flag airline) hold the great majority of the Italian air market and of the main air routes; (ii) Law 248/2005 provides a double advantage to carriers operating national routes; (iii) the Italian press had named the said law 'Alitalia-rescue Decree'.

> borne out by the very act of grant, which has, as indicated above, introduced such reduction with a view to 'ensuring economic neutrality to airport operators and aligning reductions in dues with reductions in fees'... and has otherwise provided for a 'differential', itself to be charged to the governmental authority, for the recovery of any shortfalls. This conclusion is further supported on the fact that the effect of the temporary regime so introduced is not the gradual introduction of the new provisions, but the immediate entry into force of the financially most significant measures levied on airport operators, quite far from the rebalancing, itself provided for in respect of all of their assets, expected to arise from such regime in full operation.
>
> The benefit so awarded to airlines abstractly applies to any airlines, whether Italian or otherwise, which operate on Italian airports. Yet, it cannot be denied in practice that the main beneficiary of such measures is the Italian State-controlled airline, Alitalia, which uses national airports to a greater extent than its competitors. Therefore, as the things now stand, assuming that an aid has been granted to it is not manifestly ungrounded, even the more so as the measure in issue has been regarded by Alitalia itself to be an effective remedy for its present, difficult financial situation (...). More explicitly, the daily Press... has termed such measure the 'Alitalia-rescue Decree', and this is not without significance, since Community case law has, thought for partly different purposes, deemed media reports to be indicators relevant to categorizing a transfer of State resources as State aid (*see* the European Court of Justice's judgment of 16 May 2002 in Case C-482/99).
>
> This having been said, it is indisputably true that the typical censure in a case of unlawful payment of State aid is the European Commission's intervention. Contrary to the argument offered by defendant Alitalia, that is not, however, the only penalty available, since Community case law has conceded that, under special circumstances, a private entity – such as SACBO in this specific case – has standing to bring action before the national judge to claim that that aid is unlawful aid.
>
> In regard to the foregoing, if the measure in issue is found to be, in fact, State aid, it would fall within the category of aid put into effect without prior notification to the European Commission – because this appears to be the case – and, consequently, it should be liable to the standstill obligation, i.e. the prohibition for the Member State concerned to put the aid into effect (*see* the ECJ's *Lorenz* judgment of 11 December 1973 in C-120/72). Further, according to Community case law, specifically the ECJ's judgment of 21 November 1991 in C-354/90 ('*French Salmon*'), national operators alleging to have been harmed by an aid may bring action before national courts to have the standstill clause enforced, and this is why SACBO should abstractly be deemed to have standing.
>
> SACBO's material interest in bringing action arises from SACBO's allegation that it would be harmed by the measure in issue. In this respect, it cannot be denied that the immediate result is that SACBO will be paid the relevant airport dues only to a reduced extent, whilst, in case the reduction in such dues is found to be out of balance with the reduction in fees, the 'differential' discussed above would be paid at a future time – without no date certain having being fixed. Further, the reduction in night-flight dues and the additional 10 per cent reduction indicated above have immediate effect, with no compensation as to charges, so that there is certainly the abstract possibility for SACBO to be prejudiced as a result thereof.

Notwithstanding the preliminary nature of the question of whether a national measure qualifies as State aid, the Italian judge is prevented from ordering the 'necessary' stay of proceedings, within the meaning of Article 295 of the Italian Code of

Civil Procedure, for at least two reasons: (a) because it is not a case of technical preliminary qualification, which, alone, allows for necessary stay;[24] and (b) because it is not a case of two concurrent actions pending before two different courts, but of one action pending before a national court and another, administrative action pending before the European Commission.

Moreover, the risk of a mismatch between judicial decisions is very real and may result in mutually contrasting legal qualifications by different Community bodies and national authorities.

The likelihood of a practical conflict between decisions by the national courts and those of the Commission is aggravated by the fact that, as a result of the exemptions provided by Council Regulation (EC) No. 1588/2015 of 13 July 2015 on the application of Articles 107 and 108 TFEU to certain categories of horizontal State aid,[25] or under Commission Regulation (EU) No. 651/2014 of 17 June 2014, which declares certain categories of aid compatible with the internal market in application of Articles 107 and 108 TFEU,[26] the national courts are called upon to establish not only whether the relevant measures are State aid but also whether or not they fall within the scope of those Regulations, or within a specific notified and authorized aid scheme, or represent existing State aid, with a view to exemption from notification and standstill obligations.[27]

The national courts have often misconstrued their role, and pushed past the limits established by European law as to their cognizance, by pushing forward, beyond the mere qualification of specific measures as State aid, to rule, albeit incidentally, on whether State aid measures are compatible with the internal market, which is a prerogative that is by its nature reserved, moreover exclusively, to the Commission.

That was the case, for example, when the Italian Supreme Court found that an aid was compatible with the meaning of Article 107(3)(a) and/or (c), to the extent it was intended to foster economic development in areas in which the standard of living was abnormally low and/or to facilitate the development of certain activities - thereby exercising powers reserved to the Commission.[28]

---

24. Italian Supreme Court, Sez. Un., *Craparo v. Inps*, 26 Jul. 2004, n. 14060, *Giust. civ.*, 2005, 5, I, p. 1168.
25. *See* OJ L 248, 2015.
26. In OJ L 187, 26.6.2014, as amended by Commission Regulation (EU) No. 1315/2023 of 23 Jun. 2023, OJ L 167, 30.6.2023.
27. *See* Ornella Porchia, *Il procedimento di controllo degli aiuti pubblici alle imprese tra ordinamento comunitario e ordinamento interno* pp. 160 and 162, *supra*, footnotes 96 and 102.
28. *See* Italian Supreme Court, *Fall. soc. traghetti Mediterraneo v. Soc. Tirrenia navigaz. and Min. of Transports*, 19 Apr. 2000, n. 5087, *Foro it.*, 2000, I, p. 2824. *See also* Court of Genoa, *Soc. ind. aeronautiche meccaniche Piaggio v. Soc. costruz. Less*, 15 Nov. 1999, *Giur. it.*, 2000, 782, *Dir. fallim.*, 2000, II, p. 618, with a comment by Ronco, *Giur. comm.*, 2000, II, p. 472 with a comment by Montanari. In that case the Court of Genoa considered Prodi Act on the extraordinary administration of great firms in crisis compatible with the common market. A comment of '*exorbitant*' pronunciations is provided by Cinthia Pinotti, *Gli aiuti di stato alle imprese nel diritto comunitario della concorrenza* pp. 350 et seq. and 369 et seq. (Padua, 2000). *See also* Ornella Porchia, *Il procedimento di controllo degli aiuti pubblici alle imprese tra ordinamento comunitario e ordinamento interno* p. 162, *supra*, footnote 103.

European case law has constantly treated the notion of aid within a quite broad scope, with a view to giving the Commission wide control over government measures apt to affect competition. Since it is for the Commission alone to establish whether aid is compatible with the internal market, its exclusive jurisdiction must also be observed when national courts are called upon to assess whether some form of State aid subject to prior notification and standstill obligations has or has not occurred.[29]

§7.05 EXTRAORDINARY SUSPENSION AND INTERIM MEASURES PENDING A DECISION BY THE COMMISSION ON THE LAWFULNESS OF STATE AID

There exists a theoretical derogation from the prohibition upon ordinary suspension of proceedings in the national court pending resolution of a preliminary question in the formal sense, under Article 295 of the Code of Civil Procedure, referred to above in section §7.03, although its use would be wholly exceptional. That would be to await the outcome of the assessment as to the State aid's compatibility before issuing the ultimate decision, while taking such interim measures, essentially on a precautionary basis, as would be required to punish the breach of the standstill obligation under Article 108(3) TFEU.

This is an atypical example of an extraordinary stay of proceedings, discretionary in nature and reserved to the court that is making the ultimate decision (sitting as a tribunal, where that is required by Italian law), and also interim applications for the preservation of assets that were issued by the court responsible for overseeing the matter's preparation for trial under Article 669*quater* of the Code of Civil Procedure, so as to ensure that the implementation of the definitive order by the national court would not be prejudiced pending the Commission's decision on the aid's compatibility.

In the event of such extraordinary suspension, the *Commission notice on the enforcement of State aid law by national courts* suggests (in its paragraph 62) that funds corresponding to the unlawful aid be paid onto a blocked account. In the event that:

(1) the Commission declares the aid incompatible, then the national court would order the funds on the blocked account to be returned to the State aid granting authority (the aid, plus interest for the period of the unlawful grant); or
(2) the Commission declares the aid compatible, then this would release the national court from its Community law obligation to order full recovery, and the court may therefore order the aid amount to be released to the beneficiary, in accordance with the domestic procedural rules. The national court will, however, remain under a Community law obligation to order recovery of the illegality interest that accrued for the period for which

29. *See* the Opinion of Advocate General Lenz in Case C-40/85, *Belgium v. Commission,* 10.7.1986, ECLI:EU:C:1986:305. On the complex meaning of State aid *see* Vincent Roberti, *Le contrôle de la Commission des Communautés européennes sur les aides nationales*, in *Actualité Juridique* pp. 398 et seq. (1993).

> the standstill obligation under Article 108(3) TFEU was breached, and that sum will be paid by the beneficiary to the national State aid granting authority, at the interest rate set annually by the Commission under Article 9 of Commission Regulation (EC) No. 794/2004 of 21 April 2004[30] implementing Council Regulation (EC) No. 659/1999.

Once the Commission's decision on the compatibility of State aid has been issued, the proceedings before the Italian court may go forward, without having to wait for the Commission's decision to become definitive with the expiry of the period in which the decision could be challenged in the Luxembourg court by direct application under Article 263 TFEU, or with a ruling by that court that it has become res judicata. On the one hand, such an extraordinary suspension will be subject, *a fortiori*, to the principle established by the Italian Supreme Court, sitting as a unified bench, for ordinary suspension and discretionary suspension, under Articles 295 and 337(2) of the Code of Civil Procedure, respectively;[31] on the other, Article 669*novies*, final paragraph, part (2), of the Code of Civil Procedure, does not make the effectiveness of a foreign judgment on the interim measure subject to the ruling becoming definitive: it follows that the proceedings suspended before the Italian court pending the Commission's decision may be reinstated even before that decision has become irrevocable, or confirmed by the ECJ, with a ruling that is res judicata, ordering in accordance with (1) or (2) above, that is to say, confirming, revoking or amending the provisional interim measure, possibly before, or pending, the decision under Article 669*decies* of the Code of Civil Procedure, since the decision by the Commission on the State aid's compatibility clearly amounts to a 'change of circumstances' of the kind required by that Article.

The national court retains the ability to order that the matter be referred to the Court of Justice for consideration of its validity or interpretation, pursuant to Article 267 TFEU.[32]

---

30. In OJ L 140, 30.4.2004, 1-134.
31. Judgment of the Italian Supreme Court, Unified Bench, *Broda v. Bruno and Another*, 19 Jun. 2012, No. 10027, *Corriere giur.*, 2012, p. 1178, with a note by Sergio Menchini, *Le sezioni unite sui rapporti tra gli art. 295, 297 e 337, 2° comma, c.p.c.: una decisione che non convince*, in *Riv. dir. proc.*, p. 683 (2013), and a note by Beatrice Zuffi, *Le sezioni unite ammettono la sola sospensione discrezionale del processo sulla causa dipendente allorché la causa pregiudiziale sia stata decisa con sentenza di primo grado impugnata*, in *Corriere giur.*, p. 1322 (m) (2012), with a note by Elena D'Alessandro, *Le sezioni unite e la tesi di Liebman sui rapporti tra art. 295 e 337 c.p.c.: much ado about nothing?*, in *Giur. it.*, p. 2601 (2012), with a note by Maria Cristina Vanz, *Azione di stato e petizione d'eredità: rapporto di pregiudizialità e sospensione necessaria del processo tra antichi dubbi e nuovi principi*, in *Famiglia e dir.*, p. 450 (2013), suggesting that where proceedings are prejudiced by other proceedings and those latter proceedings are not res judicata, the proceedings in the prejudiced claim may be suspended only where that is required by a specific provision, or otherwise only under Art. 337(2) of the Code of Civil Procedure, where the court considers that it will not rely on the ruling in the first set of proceedings; the prejudiced case, where suspended pursuant to Art. 295 of the Code of Civil Procedure, may recommence immediately following publication of the first-instance judgment in the other proceedings, and need not await those other proceedings becoming res judicata.
32. *See* 2009 Notice to national courts, para. 90.

§7.06 COOPERATION BETWEEN THE COMMISSION AND NATIONAL COURTS ON STATE AID MATTERS: ARTICLE 29 OF REGULATION NO. 1589/2015 AND THE 2021 COMMISSION NOTICE ON THE ENFORCEMENT OF STATE AID RULES BY NATIONAL COURTS

In light of all this complexity, the Commission has sought a way to provide support to national courts on how they discharge their duties on the procedural rules for State aid matters, in particular, the standstill obligation under the final sentence of Article 108(3) TFEU.

Already in its *Notice on cooperation between national courts and the Commission in the State aid field* of 23 November 1995,[33] the Commission explicitly invited the national courts to contact its offices, where the application of Article 87(1) or 88(3) (now Articles 107(1) and 108(3) TFEU) created difficulties over classifying a measure as State aid or establishing whether it was new or existing aid.[34]

The comprehensive *Commission Notice on the enforcement of State aid law by national courts of 9 April 2009*[35] replaced the 1995 Notice and followed the *State Aid Action Plan – Less and better targeted state aid: a roadmap for state aid reform 2005-2009*[36] and the *Study on the enforcement of State aid law at national law.*[37] It clarified the importance of the role of the national courts in applying the standstill obligation under Article 108(3) TFEU (ex 88(3) TEC) and after providing guidance for the proper interpretation and effective application of the European rules on State aid, it provides two fundamental tools to assist the courts – the transmission of information, and requests for opinions regarding the application of State aid rules.

Pursuant to Article 29 of Regulation 1589/2015, for the application of Article 107(1) and Article 108 TFEU, the courts of the Member States may ask the Commission to transmit to them information in its possession or its opinion on questions concerning the application of State aid rules. Where the coherent application of Article 107(1) or Article 108 TFEU so requires, the Commission, acting on its own initiative, may submit written observations to the courts of the Member States that are responsible for applying the State aid rules. It may, with the permission of the court in question, also make oral observations. The Commission shall inform the Member State concerned of its intention to submit observations before formally doing so. For the exclusive purpose of preparing its observations, the Commission may request the relevant court of the Member State to transmit documents at the disposal of the court, necessary for the Commission's assessment of the matter.

33. OJ C-312, 23.11.1995.
34. On this second aspect, and the difficult distinction between new and existing aid, *see* Case C-44/93, *Namur-Les assurances du crédit SA v. Office national Ducroire*, 9.8.1994, ECLI: EU:C:1994:311.
35. OJ C-85, 9.4.2009.
36. COM (2005) 107 final. *See also* the Communication from the Commission on EU State Aid Modernization, of 8 May 2012, COM (2012) 209 final.
37. Available at: https://op.europa.eu/en/publication-detail/-/publication/801bf70b-c64b-4fa8-bef 6-2ec17204b1f1.

Applying Article 29 of Regulation No. 1589/2015 the *Commission Notice on the enforcement of State aid rules by national courts of 30 July 2021* (OJ C305 of 30 July 2021) replaced the 2009 *Commission Notice*. In providing assistance to the national courts, the Commission must comply with its duty of professional secrecy, and safeguard its own functioning and independence, remaining neutral and objective. The Commission's assistance to national courts is part of its duty to defend the public interest, and the Commission should not serve the private interests of the parties involved in the case pending before the national court, or hear any of the parties involved in the national proceedings regarding its assistance to the national court. Moreover, this is without prejudice to the national courts' ability or duty or seek a preliminary ruling regarding the interpretation of Community law or the validity of the Commission's decisions, under Article 267 TFEU.[38]

Above all, the national courts may approach the Commission for the following kinds of information:

(1) information concerning a pending Commission procedure which may include information, *inter alia*, on whether:
   - a procedure regarding a particular aid measure is pending before the Commission;
   - a certain aid measure has been duly notified in accordance with Article 108(3) TFEU;
   - the Commission has initiated a formal investigation; and
   - whether the Commission has already adopted a decision, and if it has not, to clarify when such a decision is likely to be adopted.

In addition, national courts may ask the Commission to transmit documents in its possession, including copies of existing Commission decisions to the extent that these decisions are not already published on the Commission's website, factual data, statistics, market studies and economic analyses.

To ensure efficiency in its cooperation with national courts, requests for information will be processed as quickly as possible by the Commission, which will endeavour to satisfy them within a month of its receipt of the request. Where the Commission needs to ask the national court for further clarifications, this one-month period starts to run from the moment the clarification is received. Where the Commission has to consult third parties who are directly affected by the transmission of the information (e.g., for certain types of information submitted by a private person, or where information submitted by one Member State is being requested by a court in a different Member State), the one-month period starts from the conclusion of this consultation.

In transmitting information to national courts, the Commission must uphold the guarantees given to natural and legal persons under Article 339 TFEU, which prevents

38. *See* 2021 Notice, paras 101 et seq., *supra*.

members, officials and other servants of the Commission from disclosing information covered by professional secrecy, including business secrets.

Compliance with professional secrecy does not constitute an absolute prohibition upon the Commission transmitting information covered thereby to the national courts. As the European case law has confirmed, the duty of loyal cooperation requires the Commission to provide the national courts with whatever information they seek, including information covered by professional secrecy. Where it does intend to provide information covered by professional secrecy, however, the Commission will remind the national court of its obligations under Article 339 TFEU. It will ask the national court whether it can and will guarantee the protection of that confidential information, and business secrets - and where it cannot, the Commission will not transmit the relevant information to the national court. Where the national court can and will do so, the Commission will transmit the information requested.[39]

There are other scenarios in which the Commission may be prevented from disclosing information to a national court. In particular, the Commission may refuse to transmit information to the national courts for overriding reasons regarding the need to safeguard its own interests, or where such transmission would interfere with the functioning and independence of the Communities. This would be the case where disclosure would jeopardize the accomplishment of the tasks entrusted to the Commission (e.g., information concerning the Commission's internal decision-making process).[40]

When called upon to apply State aid rules to a case pending before it, a national court must respect any relevant Community rules in the area of State aid and their interpretation in the existing case law of the Community courts. In addition, a national court may seek guidance in the Commission's decision-making practice and in the notices and guidelines concerning the application of the State aid rules issued by the Commission. However, there may be circumstances in which these tools do not offer the national court sufficient guidance on the issues at stake. In the light of its obligations under Article 10 of the Treaty and given the important and complex role which national courts play in State aid enforcement, the Commission therefore gives national courts the opportunity to request the Commission's *opinion* on relevant issues concerning the application of the State aid rules, which may in principle cover all economic, factual or legal matters which arise in the context of the national proceedings.

Possible subject matters for Commission opinions include whether:

(1) a certain aid measure qualifies as State aid within the meaning of Article 107 TFEU, and if so, how the exact amount of aid is to be calculated; such opinions may relate to each of the criteria under Article 107 TFEU (namely,

39. Case T-353/94, *Postbank v. Commission*, 18.9.1996, ECLI:EU:T:1996:119, paras 64 and 93 and with a note by Luciano Vasques, *Limiti al diritto d'accesso e tutela delle parti nei procedimenti antitrust italiani e comunitari*, in *Foro it.*, IV, p. 159 (1997); Case C-2/88, *Zwartveld and Others*, 13.7.1990, ECLI:EU:C:1990:315, paras 10, 11, and 16-22.
40. *See* 2021 Notice, paras 112 et seq., *supra*.

the existence of an advantage, granted by a Member State or through State resources, possible distortion of competition and effect on trade between Member States);

(2) a certain aid measure meets a certain requirement of a Block Exemption Regulation so that no individual notification is necessary and the standstill obligation under Article 108(3) TFEU does not apply;

(3) a certain aid measure falls under a specific aid scheme which has been notified and authorized by the Commission, or otherwise qualifies as existing aid, and if in such cases the standstill obligation under Article 108(3) TFEU does not apply;

(4) there are exceptional circumstances[41] which would prevent the national court from ordering full recovery under Community law;

(5) where a national court is required to order the recovery of interest, it may ask the Commission for assistance as regards the interest calculation and the interest rate to be applied; and

(6) the legal prerequisites for damages claims under Community law and issues concerning the calculation of the damage incurred.[42]

Moreover, the information and opinions provided by the Commission do not regard assessing the compatibility of an aid measure with the internal market but are limited to contributing to the legal classification of the measure, in terms of State aid. Indeed, the assessment of the compatibility of an aid measure with the internal market pursuant to Article 107(2) and 107(3) TFEU falls within the exclusive competence of the Commission, and national courts are not competent to assess that compatibility. While the Commission cannot, therefore, provide opinions on compatibility, this does not prevent the national court from requesting procedural information as to whether the Commission is already assessing the compatibility of a certain aid measure (or intends to do so) and, if so, when its decision is likely to be adopted.

When giving its opinion (within four months of receipt of the request or such clarifications as may have been sought), the Commission will limit itself to providing the national court with the factual information or the economic or legal clarification sought, without considering the merits of the case pending before the national court.

The opinions do not bind the courts that sought them but operate as a form of moral suasion, a kind of argument from authority that may apply even before the highest courts of the Member State, which may persuade them to seek a preliminary ruling from the Court of Justice, mandatory in principle where the court is one against whose decision there is no judicial remedy under national law.[43]

41. As set out in Case C-39/94, *SFEI and Others*, 11.7.1996, ECLI:EU:C:1996:285 paras 70 and 71, *supra*.
42. *See* 2021 Notice, para. 115, *supra*.
43. *See* the 2021 Notice, paras 117 et seq., *supra*. A reference for a preliminary ruling is not even mandatory for the national court of final instance, when the proper interpretation of the European law is clear from the existing case law, or where there is no room for any reasonable doubt (*see* Case C-283/81, *Cilfit v. Ministero della Sanità*, 6.10.1982, ECLI:EU:C:1982:335, paras 14-20, also reported with notes by Antonio Tizzano and Francesca Capotorti, in *Riv. dir.*

For example, in one case, following the submission in court of an opinion delivered by the Commission, according to which the contested measures were not aid, the *Avvocatura dello Stato* waived grounds for appeal to the Italian Constitutional Court against a regional law, for infringement of Article 88(3) TEC (now 108(3) TFEU) and, consequently, of Article 11 of the Italian Constitution.[44]

The Italian courts' duty to ask the Commission to provide information may be deemed to fall within their general duty to request information, whether at the parties' request or ex officio, from the public administration, pursuant to Article 213 of the Italian Code of Civil Procedure, where relevant to the case at hand. This power entails not so much the acquisition of evidence of facts in judicial examination, as is properly the case with a request for information from public authorities under Article 213 of the Italian Code of Civil Procedure, as the acquisition of expert opinions or technical appraisals with a view to the legal characterization of a specific measure as State aid. Thus, that is a power of a more consultative than strictly evidentiary nature, in the same way as the powers provided for in the first paragraph of Article 14 of Act No. 218 of 31 May 1995, relating to the reform of the Italian system of private international law, according to which an Italian court may, in taking cognizance of the applicable foreign law, rely both on any instruments available under national provisions of law and on information obtained through the Italian Ministry of Justice, and even consult experts or – as in the case under scrutiny – such specialized institutions as the European Commission. This power must be exercised in adversarial proceedings, with the parties' indispensable cooperation (*see* Articles 101(2) and 183(5) of the Italian Code of Civil Procedure, and Article 14(2) of Act No. 218/1995, where reference is made to the parties' assistance).[45]

The application for an opinion may be seen, on one side, in the context (*mutatis mutandis*) of the powers under Article 14(1) of Act No. 218/1995, allowing the courts to seek out experts and specialist institutions; and on the other, as evoking the notion of amicus curiae,[46] offering support and impartial assistance to the courts with its complete, accurate and detailed knowledge of the law, favouring the positivist myth of the omniscient judge (on matters of law as well as on relevant matters of fact) that has done so much to make the Italian civil process so asymmetrical, bureaucratic, and authoritarian, instead of even-handed and liberal.

---

internaz. privato e proc., p. 159 (1983), with a note by Roberta Catalano, in *Giust. civ.*, 1983, I, 3, with a note by Francesca Capotorti, in *Giur. it.*, I, 1, 1008 (1983); and Joined Cases C-428/06 to C-434/06, *Unión General de Trabajadores de La Rioja and Others v. Juntas Generales del Territorio Histórico de Vizcaya and Others*, 11.9.2008, ECLI:EU:C:2008:488, paras 42 and 43).

44. Italian Constitutional Court, *Commissario Stato Reg. Sicilia v. Reg. Sicilia*, 29 Apr. 1996, n. 134, in *Foro it.*, 1996, I, p. 2979 para. 6.
45. *See*, albeit with reference to foreign law, Nerina Boschiero, *Commentario alla legge 31 maggio 1995, n. 218* (Bariatti ed.), *Le nuove leggi civili commentate* p. 1041 (1996); and Sergio Maria Carbone, *La conoscenza del diritto straniero e il giudice italiano*, in *Dir. comm. internaz.* pp. 193 et seq. (2009).
46. On which *see*, with regard in particular to common law jurisdictions, Fabrizio Criscuoli, Amicus curiae, in *Enc. giur. Treccani*, II (Roma, 1988); Francesco De Franchis, Amicus curiae, in *Dig. civ.*, I, pp. 301 et seq. (Turin, 1987). The Commission's function as an amicus curiae for the national courts is to some degree confirmed by the email address to which requests for information and opinions are sent: *ec-amicus-state-aid@ec.europa.eu*.

To be clear, the task is not one of identifying, gaining knowledge of, or construing foreign laws, and certainly cannot substitute the residual extent to which Italian laws are to be applied, pursuant to Article 14(2) of Act No. 218/1995, where the judge is unable to ascertain the applicable foreign law, even with the parties' assistance. For European rules form an integral part of the Italian legal system, and indeed, where conflicts arise, the primacy of EU law prevails, all the more so where those European rules can immediately be applied by national courts, as is the case with the last sentence of Article 108(3) TFEU. As foreign laws must be applied according to their own criteria for interpretation and application over time (*see* Article 15 of Act No. 218/1995),[47] that must be the case, *a fortiori*, for EU rules, which automatically become part of Italian law and are subject, for all purposes, to the *iura novit curia* principle laid down in Article 113 of the Italian Code of Civil Procedure. Accordingly, they must be construed and applied in compliance with the European interpretative tests derived from the case law of the Court of Justice, the practice and communications of the Commission, and making use of all the information the European system makes available to national courts.

While waiting for a response from the Commission, the national court is not allowed to stay proceedings, since there is no ground for suspension pending preliminary qualification. Indeed, the general obligation of the national court, that it must safeguard individual rights under Article 108(3) TFEU, applies also in the period during which the Commission prepares the information or draws up its opinion, irrespective of whether its intervention has been sought. As explained in the previous section, the national court may exceptionally stay proceedings pending a decision by the Commission on the lawfulness of State aid but will have to adopt any preliminary and interim measures that are capable, by freezing the current situation, and protecting the parties from any possible harm, as is the case with a reference to the ECJ for a preliminary ruling, of which more in section §7.07, below.

It must be reiterated that, in any case, any information from the Commission, even regarding statistics or economic analyses, must be used by the national court only to determine the issue of preliminary qualification of the relevant measure as State aid, for the application of the penalties for breach of the procedural obligations as to prior notice and authorization, and the standstill obligations under Article 108(3) TFEU, but it may never allow that court to extend its determination to the compatibility of aid with the internal market, which is a matter for the Commission alone.

§7.07 PRELIMINARY REFERENCES TO THE COURT OF JUSTICE

Even if the Commission has failed to give its view about the lawfulness of an aid measure, the national courts can always be guided, in interpreting European law and correctly qualifying a specific case in legal terms, by the case law of the General Court and the Court of Justice, as well as by the Commission's previous decisions and general

47. *See* Italian Supreme Court, *Regoli v. Etchi*, 26 Feb. 2002, n. 2791, *Foro it.*, 2002, I, p. 1712, with a comment by Andreoni.

notices. In giving its answer to the requesting national court, the Commission must make it clear that its view is not definitive and that the national court's right to request a preliminary ruling from the Court of Justice is unaffected.[48]

Indeed, a national court is not precluded, even without requesting the Commission to give its view in advance, from referring a question on the interpretation of the State aid notion to the Court of Justice, pursuant to Article 267 TFEU, if it considers that a decision thereon is necessary to enable it to give judgment in domestic proceedings. In fact, through reference for a preliminary ruling, the Court of Justice may be requested not to assess an aid for compatibility with the internal market (which is only for the Commission to decide), but only to give an interpretation of Article 107 TFEU, with a view to determining whether that measure is effectively State aid, which ought as such to have been a matter of prior notice to and authorization from the Commission.[49]

Reference for a preliminary ruling also proves instrumental in requesting the Court to determine whether the limits laid down in Commission decisions authorizing certain forms of aid have been complied with.[50]

It is appropriate to mention that, pursuant to the last paragraph of Article 267 TFEU, where proceedings are pending before a national court - against whose decisions no appeal can be made under the national laws - that national court must apply to the ECJ for a ruling unless the interpretation of European law may be clearly deduced from the existing case law or there is no scope for reasonable doubt.[51]

The proceedings in the national court will be stayed, but the national court will be required, also where it refers a question to the ECJ for a preliminary ruling, to take interim precautionary measures in order to safeguard the interests of the parties pending final judgment in the original proceedings and the ruling from the Court of Justice.[52]

In truth, the legal protection guaranteed by European law includes the right of individuals to induce national courts, as a preliminary issue, to refer questions to the Court of Justice for a preliminary ruling. That right would be compromised if, pending delivery of a judgment of the Court, individuals were not in a position, where certain conditions are satisfied, to obtain a decision granting suspension of enforcement that would make it possible for the effects of the disputed measure to be rendered, for the

---

48. *See* 2021 Notice to national courts, paras 112 et seq.
49. *See* Case C-78/76, *Steinike und Weinlig*, 22.3.1977, ECLI:EU:C:1977:52, *supra*, para. 15 and Case C-295/97, *Industrie Aeronautiche e Meccaniche Rinaldo Piaggio SpA v. International Factors Italia SpA (Ifitalia), Dornier Luftfahrt GmbH and Ministero della Difesa ('Piaggio')*, 17.6.1999, ECLI:EU:C:1999:313.
50. *See Consiglio di Stato*, section VI, *Soc. Fonderia A. v. Cassa conguaglio settore elettrico*, 16 Mar. 1992, n. 167, *Giur. it.*, 1992, III, 1, p. 789.
51. *See* Case C-283/81, *Cilfit v. Min. sanità*, 6.10.1982, ECLI:EU:C:1982:335, paras 14-20, *supra* and with notes by Antonio Tizzano and Francesca Capotorti, in *Riv. dir. internaz. privato e proc.*, p. 159 (1983), with a note by Roberta Catalano, in *Giust. civ.*, 1983, I, 3, with a note by Francesca Capotorti, in *Giur. it.*, I, 1, p. 1008 (1983); Joined Cases C-428/06 to C-434/06, *Union General de trabajadores de la Rioja*, 11.9.2008, ECLI:EU:C:2008:488, *supra* paras 42 and 43 also in *Giust. civ.*, 2009, I, p. 795.
52. *See* Case C-39/94, *SFEI and Others*, para. 53, *supra*.

time being, inoperative as regards them. Thus, a national court may only order interim suspension and take such interim measures as are appropriate, pending the ruling from the Court of Justice. Where the Court has not already been referred to, the national judge must order a reference to it for a preliminary ruling.[53]

Where however a question relevant to the qualification of a measure as State aid is already pending before the Court of Justice, the national court may stay proceedings on the substance of the case until judgment is delivered by the Court of Justice, without the need for reference for a preliminary ruling.

§7.08 CONFLICTS BETWEEN NATIONAL COURTS AND THE COMMISSION IN CLASSIFYING A MEASURE AS STATE AID

However much caution is taken, a failure in coordination, and as a result, a conflict may often occur between Commission decisions and national courts' judgments as to whether a measure constitutes State aid.

For example, a national court may have ruled that a State measure was not aid, and the Commission subsequently reached the opposite conclusion. Conversely, a national court may classify as aid a measure the Commission later finds to be not State aid.[54]

In either case, the national court's contrary decision may still be called into question. If proceedings on the substance of the case are still pending before the national court, then the latter must take into account the Commission's decision, though retaining the power to refer a question to the Court of Justice for a preliminary ruling, pursuant to Article 267 TFEU, and to stay proceedings accordingly.[55] The suspension of national proceedings, along with the taking of interim precautionary measures, will be all the more necessary where the interested parties have contested the Commission's decision in the European courts. Reference of a question to the ECJ for a preliminary ruling may also concern the validity of an act of an institution of the Community within the meaning of Article 267(1)(b) TFEU, provided the parties were not entitled (or unable) to bring an application directly, under Article 263 TFEU, or did not do so within the period in which they could.[56]

53. Joined Cases C-143/88 and C-92/89, *Zuckerfabrik Süderdithmarschen AG v. Hauptzollamt Itzehoe and Zuckerfabrik Soest GmbH v. Hauptzollamt Paderborn*, 21.2.1991, ECLI: EU:C:1991:65; *see also* Case C-465/93, *Atlanta Fruchthandelsgesellschaft mbH and others v. Bundesamt für Ernährung und Forstwirtschaft*, 9.11.1995, ECLI:EU:C:1995:369.
54. Ornella Porchia, *Il procedimento di controllo degli aiuti pubblici alle imprese tra ordinamento comunitario e ordinamento interno* pp. 168 et seq., *supra*.
55. For an example of preliminary reference to the ECJ in the State aid field *see Pretore di Padova, Nalon v. Ente poste*, 17 Dec. 1997, *Il lavoro nella giur.*, p. 233 (1998), with a comment by Zampini.
56. *See* Case C-188/92, *TWD Textilwerke Deggendorf v. Germany*, 9.3.1994, ECLI:EU:C:1994:90, para. 13; Case T-228/00, *Gruppo Ormeggiatori del Porto di Venezia Soc. Coop. a.r.l. and others v. Commission*, 10.3.2005, ECLI:EU:T:2005:90; Italian Supreme Court, tax section, *Agenzia Entrate v. Fondaz. Cassa risp. La Spezia*, 2 Apr. 2010, No. 8082, *Giust. civ. Mass.*, 2010, 4, p. 497 under which the Commission's decisions as to the compatibility of aid granted by Member States with the common market do not give rise to a definitive and unimpeachable evaluation regarding the

Thus, an aid recipient will not be precluded, in national proceedings for the recovery of State aid, from pleading the invalidity of the decision ordering recovery, in support of an action against the enforcement of measures issued by national authorities, insofar as the recipient has contested such decision pursuant to Article 263 TFEU. That is the case because, where the legality of a decision ordering recovery of State aid is contested under Article 263 TFEU, the national court is not bound by the definitive nature of that decision and thus remains entitled to order suspension of proceedings and to refer a question to the Court of Justice for a preliminary ruling as to the validity of that decision by the Commission, under Article 267 TFEU. The national court may, in the interests of the proper administration of justice, order that proceedings be stayed pending a ruling of the case at the Court of First Instance made on the direct application of the interested party.[57]

§7.09 AN OVERVIEW OF THE POWERS AND ROLE OF NATIONAL COURTS IN THE FIELD OF STATE AID: THE PRIMACY, EQUIVALENCE AND EFFECTIVENESS OF EUROPEAN LAW – AND HOW THAT PRIMACY MAY DEFEAT RES JUDICATA

The last sentence of Article 108(3) TFEU is immediately applicable. Member States are, therefore, precluded from putting into effect any form of aid to undertakings, whether directly or indirectly, unless the Commission has been given prior notice thereof and has taken, or is deemed to have taken, a decision authorizing such aid, save in the case that aid falls within the scope of an exemption regulation (Articles 2 and 3 of Regulation No. 659/1999.

Failure to comply with the standstill obligation under Article 3 of Regulation No. 1589/2015 entails the suspension of the unlawful aid or its recovery from the recipient undertaking, irrespective of the subsequent Commission decision on whether the relevant measure is or is not compatible with the common market. The Commission's injunctions for suspension or recovery of aid must be enforced by the national courts, which have a role complementary to the Commission's and are required to take appropriate measures in discharging their responsibility for implementing provisions of EU law. The Commission itself will assess the compatibility of an aid with the internal market, but it is barred from ordering recovery merely because the aid had not been notified or had been put into effect before the authorization procedure was completed. In turn, the national courts are called upon to ensure compliance with the standstill obligation, by ordering suspension or recovery of any aid deemed unlawful because it was not notified, or put into effect before time.

---

aid's compatibility, and may be the subject of an *ex ufficio* preliminary reference as to validity, even where not challenged by those entitled to do so. Among the academic authorities, *see* Cristina Schepisi, *Aiuti di Stato e tutela giurisdizionale* pp. 117 et seq., *supra*, which include further references to academic and case law sources regarding the importance of the entitlement to bring a direct application under Art. 263 TFEU on preliminary references for validity under Art. 267 TFEU.

57. *See* Case T-34/02 R, *B. v. Commission*, 27.2.2002, ECLI:EU:C:2002:123; *see also* Case T-181/02 R, *Neue Erba Lautex GmbH v. Commission*, 3.12.2002, ECLI:EU:T:2002:294.

However, the national court may not in any circumstances assess an aid for compatibility with the internal market, for such assessment falls within the jurisdiction of the Commission, whose decision is subject to appeal before the European Courts. In applying the last sentence of Article 108(3) TFEU, the national courts are required to settle the preliminary question as to whether the relevant measure should or should not be categorized as new State aid not included in an exemption regulation, but they may not, in doing so, also assess the aid for compatibility with the internal market, which is a technical determination reserved to the Commission.

Thus, a boundary has been set, in an *actio finium regundorum* of a sort, to the cognizance of the case by the national judges, who are oftentimes led to exceed the scope and technical purport of the State aid concept, which by definition involves economic and statistical notions. How the national courts have to settle preliminary questions depends on the application of European law and related interpretation methods, which require the national judge, when he has even the least doubt, to cooperate closely with European institutions – first with the Commission in consultative forms free of strict legal constraints, pursuant to Article 29 of the Regulation No. 1589/2015 and to the *Commission Notice on the enforcement of State aid rules by national courts* of 30 July 2021, then with the Court of Justice, by references for preliminary rulings pursuant to Article 267 TFEU, which is the quintessence of the European judicial system.[58] National proceedings, whether brought for full or summary cognizance, will be stayed, and the national judge will take any necessary provisional and urgent measures to protect the parties' substantive interests.

The national courts are in any event obliged to apply the standstill obligation under Article 108(3) TFEU and to protect the rights of individuals against unlawful State aid. In principle, national procedural rules apply to such proceedings. However, based on general principles of EU law, the application of national law in these circumstances is subject to two essential conditions:

(1) national procedural rules applying to actions under Article 108(3) TFEU may not be less favourable than those governing actions under domestic law (the 'principle of equivalence');[59]

58. *See* Joined Cases T-12/99, T-63/99, *Uk Coal plc v. Commission*, 12.7.2001, ECLI:EU:T:2001:188: 'The possibility for individuals to assert the rights which they derive from Community law before the national courts, which have the power to grant interim relief and, where appropriate, to make a reference for a preliminary ruling, constitutes the very essence of the Community system of judicial protection.'

59. Case C-368/04, *Transalpine Ölleitung in Österreich GmbH and Others v. Finanzlandesdirektion für Tirol and Others*, 5.10.2006, ECLI:EU:C:2006:644, para.45; Joined Cases C-392/04 and C-422/04, *i-21 Germany GmbH and Arcor AG & Co. KG v. Bundesrepublik Deutschland*, 19.9.2006, ECLI:EU:C:2006:586, para. 57, also in *Dir. proc. ammin.*, 235 (2007), with a note by Giuliano Grüner.

(2) the national procedural rules may not render the exercise of the rights conferred by EU law virtually impossible or excessively difficult (the 'principle of effectiveness').[60]

Given the primacy of EU law, the national courts must leave national procedural rules unapplied if doing otherwise would violate the principles of equivalence and effectiveness.[61]

Thus, for example, the principle of effectiveness has a direct impact on the standing of prospective litigants in the national courts under Article 108(3) TFEU. European law requires that national rules on legal standing not undermine the right to effective judicial protection – accordingly, the national rules cannot limit legal standing only to the beneficiary's competitors, and third parties who are not affected by the distortion of competition resulting from the aid measure may also have a sufficient legal interest of a different character (as has been recognized in tax cases) to bring proceedings before a national court.[62]

Thus it has been established that EU law may prevent the application of a national rule, such as Article 2909 of the Italian Civil Code, on res judicata, to the extent that the rule's application would prevent recovery of State aid granted against EU law, and whose incompatibility with the internal market has been declared in a decision by the Commission that has become final.[63] This does not call into question the principle

60. Case C-368/04, *Transalpine Ölleitung in Österreich*, 5.10.2006, ECLI:EU:C:2006:644, *supra*; Case C-174/02, *Streekgewest Westelijk Noord – Brabant v. Staatssecretaris van Financiën*, 13.1.2005, ECLI:EU:C:2005:10 and with a note by Ceraso, in *Riv. it. dir. pubbl. comunitario*, p. 975 (2005).
61. 2009 Notice to national courts, paras 70 et seq.
62. Case C-174/02, *Streekgewest*, 13.1.2005, ECLI:EU:C:2005:10, paras 14-21, *supra*; and previously, Case C-142/87, *Belgium v. Commission ('Tubemeuse')* 21.3.1990, ECLI:EU:C:1990:125, in particular the conclusions by AG Tesauro in the *Tubemeuse* case (19 Sep. 1989, *ibid.*) that 'any person having an interest in doing so may rely before the national courts on the incompatibility with Community law of the measure granting the aid, where it is envisaged to implement it without Community control and, in any event, on the unlawfulness of the implementing measures adopted for that purpose'.
63. Case C-119/05, *Min. ind. v. Soc. Lucchini*, 18.7.2007, ECLI:EU:C:2007:434 and with a note by Enrico Scoditti, *Giudicato nazionale e diritto comunitario*, in *Corr. giur.*, p. 1221 (2007); Case C-2/08, *Amministrazione dell'Economia e delle Finanze and Agenzia delle entrate v. Fallimento Olimpiclub Srl.*, 3.9.2009, ECLI:EU:C:2009:506 and, Case C-40/08, *Asturcom Telecomunicaciones S L v. Nogueira* 6.10.2009, ECLI:EU:C:2009:615, and with a note by Giovanni Raiti, *Le pronunce Olimpiclub ed Asturcom Telecomunicaciones: verso un ridimensionamento della paventata ' crisi del giudicato civile nazionale' nella giurisprudenza della corte di giustizia*, in *Riv. dir. Proc.*, p. 670 (2010); Case C-453/00, *Kühne & Heitz NV v. Produktschap voor Pluimvee en Eieren*, 13.1.2004, ECLI:EU:C:2004:17.

    See, among the academic authorities, Claudio Consolo, *La sentenza Lucchini della Corte di giustizia: quale possibile adattamento degli ordinamenti processuali interni e in specie del nostro?*, in *Riv. dir. proc.*, pp. 224 et seq. (2008); Claudio Consolo, *Il percorso della Corte di giustizia, la sentenza Olimpiclub e gli eventuali limiti di diritto europeo all'efficacia esterna ultrannuale del giudicato tributario (davvero ridimensionato in funzione antielusiva Iva del divieto comunitario di abusi della libertà negoziale?)*, in *Riv. dir. trib.*, pp. 1143 et seq. (2010); Annalisa Negrelli, *Il primato del diritto comunitario e il giudicato nazionale; un confronto che si poteva evitare o risolvere altrimenti*, in *Riv. it. dir. pubbl. com.*, pp. 1217 et seq. (2008); Andrea Andolina, *Crisis of res judicata and new techniques for dispute resolution: (selfstanding anticipatory) provisional measures on the merits*, in *I quaderni europei*, pp. 5 et seq., (February 2009); Giovanni Raiti, *The crisis of civil* res iudicata *in the EC legal system*, in *I quaderni europei*,

of res judicata, which is fundamental to the certainty of law, but regards situations in which a party has abused its right to a defence, failing to exercise remedies against the Commission's decision in the European courts, and the national court has in turn failed to seek a preliminary ruling from those courts, under Article 267 TFEU. In such circumstances, the rules on State aid would be evaded, and the national ruling would not hold essential value for the effective protection of private rights in terms of legal certainty, since, in order to safeguard that principle, the national court would be obliged to give a decision that was in clear contrast with Community law, and simply acknowledge the ruling that had been reached.

In other words, the primacy of EU law applies also in relation to a national ruling that is res judicata, where there is an attempt unreasonably to extend the positive effectiveness of the ruling to situations beyond the scope of the claim and the proceedings, and thereby evade the mandatory nature of the rules on matters of State aid, the exclusive jurisdiction of the Commission to decide upon the compatibility of aid with the internal market, and the definitive nature of the Commission's decision, which cannot be directly appealed, or, where permitted, there is a reference for a preliminary ruling on validity, under Article 267 TFEU.[64]

§7.10 LEGAL ISSUES ARISING FROM INFRINGEMENTS OF THE STANDSTILL CLAUSE: THE ALLOCATION OF JURISDICTION

Infringement of the standstill clause may result in a range of legal situations. European law does not recognize the division between subjective rights and legitimate interests, which may be reflected in the allocation of jurisdiction between ordinary courts, administrative courts and tax courts, depending upon the form the State aid took.

The Court of Justice's milestone judgment in *Costa v. ENEL*, which finally established, albeit by way of an *obiter dictum*, that the last sentence of Article 108(3) TFEU might be applied directly by national courts, briefly referred to individual rights without any qualification whatsoever.[65]

The last sentence of Article 108(3) TFEU has an essentially procedural content, i.e., the prohibition for a Member State to put an aid measure into effect until approval is given by the Commission. This prohibition is a constituent element – or a prerequisite, if you wish – of the process leading to the grant of the aid under the national system of laws. The infringement of this procedural obligation by the Member State in exercising its authoritative powers may result in the respective legal positions of the beneficiary and of its competitors being qualified as legitimate interests.

---

pp. 9 et seq. (February 2009); Giovanni Marino, *The wane of the res judicata in the Italian enforcement proceedings*, in *I quaderni europei*, pp. 14 et seq. (February 2009); Giovanni Amoroso, *Diritto comunitario v. giudicato interno. La sentenza Lucchini a un triennio dalla sua emanazione*, in *Rass. dir. pubbl. eur.*, pp. 187 et seq. (2011); Giangiacomo D'Angelo, *Giudicato tributario (esterno) e diritto comunitario: un equilibrio difficile*, in *Riv. dir. trib.*, pp. 285 et seq. (2009).

64. *See* Cristina Schepisi, *Aiuti di Stato e tutela giurisdizionale* pp. 348 et seq., *supra*.
65. *See* Case C-6/64, *Costa v. ENEL*, *supra*.

The divide rests on the binding or non-binding character of the administrative activity. The clarity and accuracy of the last sentence of Article 108(3) TFEU, which prevents an unnotified or unauthorized State aid from being put into effect, exclude any discretion for the Member State's administrative authorities, whose powers are closely restricted. Therefore, infringing the standstill clause generates subjective rights for the interested parties, according to the restricted-activity/subjective rights module.

Accordingly, the position of the parties interested in or otherwise affected by the State aid is a subjective right when EU or national measures directly and automatically bring about public-law obligations, without any room being left for assessment or appreciation. When, however, the grant of contributions and their possible recovery are not a direct result of the establishment of binding pre-requirements, but arise from the exercise of a discretionary public-law function, then the relevant controversy will fall under the general jurisdiction of the administrative judge over legitimacy, in that it relates to positions of legitimate interests arising from rules of action as opposed to rules of relation.[66]

Conversely, the public administration has a wider discretion in assessing situations governed by exemption regulations, since it is required to assess whether the conditions laid down in those regulations for the exclusion of the duty of prior notification have been fulfilled. Thus, in each such case, there will be rather legitimate interests than subjective rights.

Where Member States' authorities have some discretion in establishing compliance with the conditions for the grant of a benefit contemplated by EU rules, a subjective right under Community law becomes tantamount to a legitimate interest. Thus, jurisdiction over the issue will be vested in the administrative court.[67]

Quite beyond a rigid, dogmatic contraposition, it is advisable to take a straightforward approach to the judicial protection of substantive situations, by distinguishing between the different causes of action in any proceedings individuals may bring in matters of unlawful aid. The emphasis will then be shifted to the specific object of such protection and the specific interest pursued, in furtherance of a functionalist approach better suited to modern reading of legal and judicial systems.

Generally, what matters is how the allocations are made, based on the nature of the subjective situations, as follows:

(1) where the dispute arises in relation to the time of the aid's grant, or the collection of a subsidy based on an alleged breach by the beneficiary, the ordinary court has jurisdiction, even where the issue regards acts such as

66. *See Consiglio di Stato, Reg. Umbria v. Soc. Castel dell'Aquila,* section IV, 12 Apr. 2001, n. 2224, *Dir. e giur. agr. e ambiente,* 2001, p. 733; *see also* Italian Supreme Court, section IV *Reg. Umbria v. Gnoni Maravelli,* 14 May 2004, n. 3040, *Giur.it.*, 2004, p. 1732. *See also* Pietro Virga, *Diritto amministrativo – Attività e prestazioni,* IV, pp. 13 et seq. (Milan, 1990); Ornella Porchia, *Il procedimento di controllo degli aiuti pubblici alle imprese tra ordinamento comunitario e ordinamento interno* pp. 186 et seq., *supra, Contra,* as a minority opinion, *see* Belotti, *Gli aiuti di Stato nel diritto comunitario della concorrenza – della tutela dei terzi,* in *Dir. com. sc. int,* pp. 469 et seq. (1995).

67. *See Lante v. Reg. Veneto,* Order of *TAR Veneto* of 1 Jun. 1991, n. 432, *Foro amm.*, 1992, p. 858.

revocation, cessation or termination, because they are based upon an alleged breach of the obligations the beneficiary assumed in return for the grant;

(2) a private party has subjectively a legitimate interest, and the administrative court thus has jurisdiction, where the dispute regards a procedural stage prior to the measure that conferred the benefit, or where following the benefit's grant, the measure was cancelled or revoked because of defects in its legitimacy, or because it *a priori* conflicted with the public interest.[68]

Finally, it should be noted that since the former barriers that traditionally complicated seeking compensation of legitimate interests harmed by the conduct of general government bodies as authorities have long since fallen,[69] and given the way the ordinary and the administrative courts now have their jurisdictions divided on the basis of subject matter, the importance of the distinction between subjective rights and legitimate interests has been on the decline.

[A] Actions That May Be Brought in the Event of Unlawful Aid: Issues of Jurisdiction and Procedure

Action before the national courts constitutes a fundamental means for competitors and other third parties to protect their rights, where they have been harmed by unlawful State aid.

The available remedies include:

(1) preventing the payment of unlawful aid;
(2) recovery of unlawful aid (independent of its compatibility);
(3) recovery of interest for the period of the unlawful aid;
(4) damages for competitors and other third parties; and
(5) interim measures against unlawful aid.

68. *Consiglio di Stato, T.C.L.V. s.r.l v. Prov. Siena, Reg. Toscana, Agea ed altro*, 10 Nov. 2010, No. 7994, *Foro amm.-Cons. Stato*, 2010, p. 2361 (m); Italian Supreme Court, unified bench, *Cons. AN.SA.PE v. Min. politiche agr.*, 21 Nov. 2011, No. 24409, *Riv. it. dir. pubbl. comunitario*, p. 175 (2012).

69. 'In relation to the tortious liability of the person who committed an act injurious towards legally material interests, the formal classification of the legal position of the injured party is not crucial. It should thus be held that legitimate interests may be compensated wherever injured as a result of the unlawful and culpable activity of general government (with a finding that, where it is a matter for the ordinary jurisdiction, arises irrespective of any prior annulment decision by the administrative court), as may the interest in the good to which the legitimate interest relates, and always providing that that interest in the good is deserving of protection under the positive law; in that light, the raising of an issue regarding whether legitimate interests may be compensated does not give rise to an issue of jurisdiction, but goes to the substance of the claim', the famous dictum in Italian Supreme Court, unified bench, *Com. Fiesole v. Vitali*, 22 Jul. 1999, No. 500/SU, *Foro it.*, 1999, I, 2487, with notes by Palmieri and Pardolesi.

Before dealing with some of the actions that may be brought in the event of unlawful aid – thus, aid in relation to which the standstill obligation under Article 108(3) TFEU was breached – we should attempt to shed some light on the series of interventions that the Italian legislature has made since 2008, the overall effect of which has been to complicate rather than clarify the procedure.

Under Articles 1 and 2 of Law Decree 59/2008, containing urgent measures for the implementation of Community obligations and the execution of judgments from the Court of Justice, later Act No. 101/2008 (as amended), procedures were introduced for the recovery of State aid following a decision by the Commission issued under Article 14 of the Procedural Regulation (EC) No. 659/1999 (now Article 16 of the Procedural Regulation No. 1589/2015), through the civil and tax courts (with the addition of an Article 47*bis* into Legislative Decree 546/1992 on tax proceedings).

Article 9 of Legislative Decree 150/2011 on procedural simplification then brought in a new procedure for the recovery of State aid through the civil courts which made use of the employment procedure, and amended Article 1 of Law Decree 59/2008 accordingly.

That approach did not last long, however. Articles 48 et seq. of Act No. 234/2012 (as amended by Law No. 122/2016), containing general provisions on Italy's participation in the formation and implementation of the European Union's rules and policies, further accelerated the procedure for the recovery of State aid following a Commission decision. Under the new system, enforceable rights would be created by administrative means, which meant a decree of the Minister with jurisdiction for the particular matter (or, where the aid was granted by a local authority, by that authority's legal representative), with the decree identifying the persons obliged to repay the aid, establishing the amounts payable, and determining the terms of payment. Collection would be carried out in a form similar to tax collection, and handled by Agenzia Entrate-Riscossione.[70]

Disputes related to acts and measures that grant State aid in breach of Article 108(3) TFEU, and disputes regarding acts and measures taken pursuant to a recovery decision under Article 16 of the Procedural Regulation (EC) No. 1589/2015, are now solely under the jurisdiction of the administrative courts, under Article 133(z-sexies) of the Code of Administrative Procedure (Legislative Decree 104/2010. This is the case irrespective of the form of the aid, and the entity by which it was granted. Pursuant to Article 119(1)(m-*quinquies*) of that Code, in proceedings before an administrative court regarding acts and measures adopted in the implementation of a recovery decision by the Commission pursuant to Article 16 of the Procedural Regulation (EC) No. 1589/2015, the accelerated procedure applies. This means all the ordinary

70. The previous procedures under Arts 1 and 2 of Law Decree 59/2008, that is, respectively, Art. 9 of Legislative Decree 150/2011, for proceedings in the civil court, and Art. 47-*bis* of Legislative Decree 546/1992 in the tax court, will continue to apply only to proceedings pending on 19 Jan. 2013, when Act No. 234/2012 (published in the Official Gazette, 4 Jan. 2013, No. 3) came into force. Moreover, the new domestic collection procedures for State aid for which the Commission has ordered recovery apply also with respect to recovery decisions adopted before Act No. 234/2012 came into force. The amendments made by Law No. 122/2016 to Act No. 234/2012 apply to the recovery decisions serviced from 1 Jan. 2015.

statutory periods are halved, including that for appealing judgments. The only exceptions are, at first instance, the periods for the service of the original claim, any cross-claim, and any additional grounds; and the period for an interim appeal against a decision by the Regional Administrative Court on the inhibitory of the execution of acts and measures taken pursuant to a recovery decision (Article 62(1) of the Code of Administrative Procedure).

Article 50 of Act No. 234/2012 added that measures granting State aid in breach of Article 108(3) TFEU may be challenged in the Regional Administrative Court with geographical jurisdiction. Clearly, the period of sixty days in which such a challenge may be brought before that court will run, for the beneficiary's competitor and for third parties, from the day on which they become fully aware of the act, or of its harmfulness.

What was previously referred to as the 'administrative prejudice', which meant any claim for compensation had to be preceded or accompanied by an action overturning the unlawful administrative act, no longer applies. Nonetheless, an injured party that does not pursue such an action will have its conduct evaluated, pursuant to Article 1227 of the Civil Code and the principle of bona fides, for the purpose of quantifying the damages that may be compensated on the basis of contributory negligence by the claimant.[71] Such a stance is puzzling when it comes to unlawful State aid, granted in breach of EU rules, which do not admit any mitigation or limitation of the sanctions to be imposed by the national courts, under the aforementioned principles of primacy, equivalence and effectiveness of EU law and its instruments.

The legislature thus appears to have intended to confer upon the administrative courts sole jurisdiction over all State aid matters, whether the action was brought by the beneficiary or by its competitors, irrespective of the substantive nature of the situations involved.[72] The issue remains that State aid may arise in a wide variety of

71. *See Consiglio di Stato, Fall. soc. Rem v. Soc. Enel distribuz.*, 23 Mar. 2011, No. 3, *Corr. giur.*, 2011, p. 979, with a note by Franco Gaetano Scoca and with a note by Annalaura Giannelli, *La pregiudiziale amministrativa rinasce dalle proprie ceneri: la mancata impugnazione dell'atto illegittimo recide il nesso di causalità tra provvedimento illegittimo e lesion*, in *Foro it.*, III, p. 31 (2012); *Consiglio di Stato, Soc. S. v. Com. Roma e altro*, 31 Oct. 2012, No. 5556, in *Diritto e Giustizia online* (2012) which considered an application for the annulment of an act and a claim for compensation of the unfair losses caused by unlawful exercise by general government of administrative activity, and the failure to carry on their mandatory activity, under Arts 30 et seq. of the Code of Administrative Procedure. The court found the legislation had not taken up the notion of administrative prejudice, nor that the two remedies were completely independent of one another, but had opted for an intermediate solution, which would consider a failure to bring an application for the annulment of the injurious measure in good time as not precluding an application for compensation, but rather as conduct that should form part of an overall assessment of the parties' conduct, and as such may authorise the court to exclude compensation, or reduce its amount, where it finds that a prompt application for annulment of the injurious act would have avoided or limited the damages therefrom. With regard to the issue of administrative prejudice, which obviously arises only where there is injury deriving from the unlawful measure, the claim for compensation should thus be considered admitted, in accordance with the principles set out in the judgment, also irrespective of the challenge to the (allegedly) unlawful and injurious measure.
72. *See*, for some early observations, Enrico Altieri, *Prime impressioni sulla giurisdizione del giudice amministrativo in materia di aiuti di Stato*, in *Riv. dir. trib.*, I, pp. 197 et seq. (2013).

forms, not necessarily translating into administrative acts or measures of the kind that may be brought before the administrative court, and that court will in such circumstances also have to deal with the award of damages. There thus remains an area of ordinary jurisdiction, in circumstances in which the unlawful aid did not arise out of an administrative decision that might be contested on its own basis.

Another chapter of this book deals with the procedures for recovering State aid from beneficiaries (*see* Chapter 4). Here, however, we will examine the instruments available to competitors and third parties affected by the unlawful aid.

Certainly, the confusion over jurisdictions and processes in connection with State aid is further evidence of the fundamental need to eliminate the distinctions between national courts, and finally move to a single national jurisdiction, duly subdivided into specialist sections, each with highly trained, qualified and expert judges. This would deal once and for all with the division of jurisdiction between administrative, tax and accounting sectors, which still continues in the twenty-first century, reminiscent more of an *ancien régime* than a modern State governed by a rule of law. It would bring matters into line with the *procès equitable* contemplated by the European Convention on Human Rights (in its Article 6), which Italy ratified in the 1950s and which is now an integral part of European law, under Article 6 TEU.[73]

[B] The Judicial Actions Against Unlawful Aid Open to Competitors and Third Parties: Challenging Administrative Measures Granting Aid

As State aid is heterogeneous in nature, it may take a variety of forms, as was mentioned earlier.

When State aid arises from an administrative measure issued in the implementation of a national law, any of the aid beneficiary's competitors or a third party affected by the unlawful aid may challenge that measure before the administrative court to have it declared invalid on the ground of infringement of the standstill obligation.

According to one approach, this leads to the assumption that the act in question can be annulled so far as the action is brought in due time and the grounds of appeal are specifically stated. Still, once an action has been brought in good time before the administrative court, the infringement of the applicable European rule may be raised by the national court ex officio even in the absence of a specific statement of grounds. This is the case because:

> whilst the imposition on litigants of a period is not objectionable *per se*, Community law precludes application of a domestic procedural rule whose effect, in procedural circumstances such as those in question in the main proceedings, is to

73. On relations between European and Italian law, including the European Convention on Human Rights and the ECJ's case law, *see* Maurizio Pedrazza Gorlero, *Alla ricerca della 'forma condizionante'. Introduzione ai rapporti fra Corti costituzionali nazionali e Corti europee dopo il Trattato di Lisbona*, (Pedrazza Gorlero ed.), *Corti nazionali e corti europee dopo il Trattato di Lisbona*, pp. 3 et seq. (Naples, 2010); Eduardo Gianfrancesco, *Incroci pericolosi: CEDU, Carta dei diritti fondamentali e Costituzione italiana tra Corte costituzionale, Corte di Giustizia e Corte di Strasburgo, ivi*, pp. 167 et seq.

> prevent the national court, seized of a matter falling within its jurisdiction, from considering of its own motion whether a measure of domestic law is compatible with a provision of Community law when the latter provision has not been invoked by the litigant within a certain period.[74]

In any case, the sixty-day period must be deemed to start, as regards the aid beneficiary's competitor or the third party, on the day on which the competitor had full knowledge of the measure in question. When the sixty-day period begins thus depends on the circumstances, and the applicant must specify when they gained knowledge of the measure and be ready to provide evidence thereof.

Under a different approach, an administrative act adopted on the basis of a national law contrasting with European law appears to be neither void nor voidable, but merely as well liable to be misapplied by the national administrative judge as that domestic law.[75] Both the court and the public administration may, of their own motion, establish the unlawfulness of that administrative act at any time, and take any necessary measures to restore the *status quo ante*.

What both the ECJ and the Italian Constitutional Court demand is for the administrative act to be removed forthwith, instead of it being allowed to stand pending removal. Thus, both the national court and the national public authority involved are expected to disapply the provision of law underlying the aid measure and to establish the resulting unlawfulness of that measure ex officio.[76]

The latter approach suggests the aid beneficiary's competitor or the third party may instead of taking action against the administrative measure, enjoin the public administration to withdraw the contested measure and to take any necessary steps to recover the aid. Should the public administration fail to do this, the competitor might bring action before the administrative court, seeking the appointment of a 'commissioner *ad acta*', who will take all necessary steps in lieu of the public authority involved, if the latter has failed to comply even within such additional period as is granted by the administrative court.

If the administrative act is not based on a provision of domestic law but is itself incompatible with the standstill obligation under Article 108(3) TFEU, then unlawfulness results in the possibility, not to have the contested act disapplied, but to have it set

74. *See* the operative part of Case C-312/93, *Peterbroeck v. Belgium*, 14.12.1995, ECLI:EU:C:1995:437. With regard to the compatibility with European law of national rules stating 'reasonable' terms of appeal subject to forfeiture *see* Case C-33/76, *Rewe-Zentralfinanz eG and Rewe-Zentral AG v. Landwirtschaftskammer für das Saarland*, 16.12.1976, ECLI:EU:C:1976:188. *See also* Case C-126/97, *Eco Swiss China Time ltd. v. Benetton International N V*, 1.6.1999, ECLI:EU:C:1999:269. For a specific case, *see Consiglio di Stato*, s. VI, *SEA v. Pres. Cons.*, 1 Apr. 2000, n. 1885, *Foro it.*, 2001, III, p. 71 para. 11.1.
75. *See TAR Veneto*, 10 Jun. 1991, n. 432, *Giur.it.*, 1992, III, pp. 434 et seq. *See also* Roberto Caranta, *Giustizia amministrativa e diritto comunitario*, pp. 373 et seq. (Naples, 1992).
76. In this sense, Antonio Tizzano, *La tutela dei privati nei confronti degli Stati membri dell'Unione europea*, in *Foro it.*, IV, p. 21, footnote 8 (1995).

aside in an action the competitor concerned may bring before the national administrative court within sixty days of gaining full knowledge of that act,[77] as Article 50 of Act No. 234/2012 now expressly states.

The beneficiary or at least one of several beneficiaries of the aid must, in its quality as a party directly concerned by the aid measure, be called in to plead defences in adversarial proceedings.

Where the administrative court seized of the matter finds that the last sentence of Article 108(3) TFEU has been infringed, in that the relevant measure was new State aid not falling within the scope of an exemption regulation, it will inhibit, or order the suspension of, such grant of aid and order the public authority granting the aid to take all suitable steps to recover it.

At the complainant's request, the administrative judge may issue the most appropriate interim measures to provisionally secure the effects of the decision on the case, by ordering that the unlawful aid be suspended and recovered. Any such provisional measure will be issued in the form of an interim order open to challenge before the *Consiglio di Stato*, and it must be based on the assumption that there exists, in addition to *fumus boni juris*, a serious, irretrievable prejudice arising from the implementation of the contested administrative act. Such *periculum in mora* may well be identified in the competition-distorting effects of the grant of that aid, which effects cannot always and adequately be remedied or retrieved by way of equivalent monetary compensation.

The public authority involved will have to comply with the administrative court's order, by taking any necessary administrative measures to recover the amounts paid in aid. If the public administration fails to act, then the interested party may request the administrative judge, in exercising his powers in actions for compliance, to take any appropriate measures for enforcement, by specifying the manners in which the order must be executed and, if need be, the entity required to take action to that effect:

> The complainant in administrative proceedings for the granting of measures relating to State aid, to the extent they create obligations for the administration, shall be deemed to have subjective rights, and the relevant action for compliance shall be deemed to fall within the exclusive jurisdiction of the administrative court.[78]

The declaration of illegality of an administrative act for non-compliance with the obligation to suspend the aid under the last sentence of Article 108(3) TFEU will invalidate any subsequent acts of whatever nature.

---

77. *See, exempli gratia, TAR Campania*, section I, *De Capua v. Min. ind.*, 13 Apr. 1989, n. 196, *Riv. it. dir. pubbl. comunitario*, p. 209 (1991). *See also* Ornella Porchia, *Il procedimento di controllo degli aiuti pubblici alle imprese tra ordinamento comunitario e ordinamento interno*, pp. 194 et seq., *supra*.
78. *See Cons. Stato, Consiglio di Giustizia Amministrativa per la Regione Sicilia, Judicial Division, Reg. Sicilia v. L.I.C.*, 3 Mar. 1999, n. 60, 1999, I, p. 502.

[C] Challenging General Meetings' Resolutions for Unlawfulness of the Object

Unlawful aid may well be put into effect in the absence of an actual administrative act or measure. For example, aid may be granted in the form of a new issue of equity by a limited company in which the State has a holding.

In that case, illegality can be pleaded before an ordinary court on the grounds of unlawfulness of the object, in that the relevant measure goes against the mandatory and immediately applicable terms of the last sentence of Article 108(3) TFEU. Actions for annulment can be brought by any interested persons, but are now subject to a limitation period (three years) – which becomes even shorter (180 days) in the case of a resolution for a share capital increase – under Article 2379 and 2379*ter* introduced by the Italian Company Law Reform Act (Legislative Decree No. 6 of 17 January 2003).

The day starting from which an action for annulment may be brought tends to be rather the date on which the relevant resolution is entered in the Companies Registry than the date on which the interested party has taken full knowledge of that resolution, as is the case with actions against administrative acts discussed above. Moreover, a resolution for a capital increase by a company that uses equity capital markets for funding may not be declared invalid after a statement has been recorded in the Companies Registry, pursuant to Article 2444 of the Italian Civil Code, to the effect that the whole or any portion of such increase has been paid in (Article 2379*ter*, paragraph 2, of the Italian Civil Code).

Even in case the required limitation period has elapsed without any action having been brought, the interested parties' right to be paid damages for losses resulting from that resolution will remain unaffected (Article 2379*ter*, paragraph 3, of the Italian Civil Code).

There is still room to wonder whether such a strict limitation period is compatible with third parties' right to obtain, then and there, the removal of the aid granted without the standstill clause having been complied with. For awarding damages to the interested third party is not sufficient remedy to secure the effectiveness of the prohibition arising from the last sentence of Article 108(3) TFEU. As a result, a conflict may arise between the limitations provided for by the Italian Civil Code in relation to actions for the annulment of company resolutions pursuant to Articles 2379 et seqq. and Article 108(3) TFEU, which must be fully enforced by national courts.

The declaratory judgment that a company meeting's resolution is invalid may be supplemented with items of judgment *in rem* ordering that the aid be recovered and the previous situation restored.

[D] Actions for Unfair Competition

The standstill obligation in the last sentence of Article 108(3) TFEU is imposed upon Member States, whose bodies, including local governmental bodies, are barred from granting aid that has not been notified to and authorized by the Commission. Since the beneficiary has received the aid from a State authority, he cannot be held liable for any violation, since he has not breached any of his legal obligations under the law:

> The machinery for reviewing and examining State aids established by Article 93 of the Treaty does not impose any specific obligation on the recipient of aid ... That being so, Community law does not provide a sufficient basis for the recipient to incur liability where he has failed to verify that the aid received was duly notified to the Commission.[79]

Notwithstanding his right to bring action against the grant of unlawful aid and to pray national courts to enforce recovery orders upon the State, the recipient's competitor is not allowed to bring an action for non-contractual liability for an unlawful act against the aid recipient, unless the use the recipient directly or indirectly makes of the aid is found to be conduct contrary to professional fairness principles and apt to harm another person's business (*see* Article 2598, indent 3, Italian Civil Code):[80]

> Infringing a provision of civil law, whether of Community origin or otherwise, is not, in itself, tantamount to an abstract, self-standing case of unfair competition. In other words, a mere violation of a civil-law rule cannot automatically be taken also to imply that that conduct is unfair in terms of competition. Therefore, for an unlawful conduct to be deemed to be a violation of competition rules, it must preliminarily be established whether the interests underlying the rule so violated also include interests aimed at governing competition and fair trading, and it must further be established whether that rule of civil law was also violated with a view to affecting directly the existing competitive situation, as a result of which that act has directly or indirectly caused the deterioration of another person's position in the market. Thus, the conduct so violating civil-law rules must be an element of a broader anticompetition activity, which must be measured by any competition-distorting effects it might have to the detriment of a competitor.[81]

Under this approach, the violation of a civil-law rule has been deemed to be an illegal act if it directly caused the diminishing of another business's goodwill or it has, by itself, even without a specific conduct in the market, generated a competitive advantage that would not have occurred had that rule been observed.[82]

In fact, violations of competition law have an objective trait, in the sense that – once anti-competitive acts have been established, especially in terms of the injurious effects caused to a competitor's business by a conduct contrary to professional fairness standards – negligence is presumed, pursuant to the last paragraph of Article 2600 of

79. *See* Case C-39/94, *SFEI and Others*, paras 73 and 74, *supra*.
80. With regard to the utilization of Art. 2598(3) of the Italian Civil Code in case of violation of antidumping norms or extra-community subsidies *see* Alberto Santa Maria, *European Economic Law*[3], p. 269 (2014).
81. *See* Court of Naples, *Soc. Lidchi International v. Soc. Haas dal 1811*, 6 Feb. 2003, *Arch. civ.*, 2003, p. 947; Court of Milan, *Soc. ed. A. Mondadori v. Associaz. naz. videonoleggiatori it.*, 30 Aug. 1996, *Giur. it.*, 1997, I, 2, p. 444; Court of Genoa, *Soc. Corsica Line v. Soc. Navarma*, 5 Jul. 1989, *Giur. dir. ind.*, 1989, p. 491 and Court of Appeal of Bologna, *Soc. Muzzi v. Com. Bologna*, 31 Jul. 1984, *Giur. dir. ind.*, 1984, p. 587.
82. *See* Italian Supreme Court, *Chiarella v. Musso*, 27 Apr. 2004, n. 8012, *Dir. Industrial*, 2005, p. 203; Court of Milan, *Soc. Bristol Myers Squibb v. Parke Davis*, 2 Jul. 1999, *Rass. dir. farmaceutico*, 1999, p. 677.

the Italian Civil Code. Unlawful State aid results, by itself, in a distortion of the competitive environment. For example, where an undertaking uses unlawful aid to make discounts on prices, thereby raiding a competitor's customer base, it commits a violation of competition law, which some have deemed to exist *in re ipsa*.[83]

These statements of principle have not, however, been followed in case law by the application of the prohibition to use non-notified State aid to the detriment of competitors.

Case law on the merits and on issues of law has sometimes gone beyond the cognisance boundaries European law has imposed on national courts that were described above, and pushed on as far as to assess aid for compatibility with the internal market, though this is a task exclusively reserved to the Commission. For example, the existence of a case of unfair competition has been excluded in lower-tariff policies put into effect through non-notified State aid, even though such policies were apt to result in customer raiding.

Thus, in one case, the Italian Supreme Court found State aid to be compatible with the internal market when it is designed to foster economic development in regions where the standard of living is abnormally low or underemployment raises serious concerns. In this respect, the Italian Supreme Court observed that State aid in itself, in addition to being permissible on occasions, is invariably bound to affect competition. In fact, State aid is an exception to the rule, on the argument that, if competition were left to play unchecked in the market by way of an undertaking seeking approaches better suited to achieve cost-effectiveness in its operations, it may leave certain common interests unprotected. Therefore, while State aid measures are prohibited in their being a technique that distorts competition by their sheer nature, they are or might be compatible, as the case may be, precisely when free competition must be adjusted with a view to the fulfilment of needs that could not be served otherwise.[84]

The boundaries of the national judge's cognisance of the case were clearly crossed in this judgment by the Italian Supreme Court, much as national courts, far from being allowed to assess State aid for compatibility with the internal market, are only expected to establish whether a measure likely to qualify as State aid has or has not been notified to the Commission and previously authorized by it, whether expressly or implicitly, under Article 108(3) TFEU.

Conversely, where an aid has been authorized by the Commission subject to certain conditions, the national judge may determine whether the fact that the aid recipient exceeded the limits imposed by the authorization has or has not resulted in an act of unfair competition. Yet, even then, the national court may not restrict its task to establishing whether the limits set in the authorization decision were exceeded, but it must also specifically determine whether this has resulted in a violation of the

83. *See* Court of Genoa, *Grandi Traghetti di Navigazione SpA v. Viamare di Navigazione,* 26 Apr. 1993, *Il dir. Marittimo,* 1993, pp. 772 et seq., which, however, excluded the existence of a State aid.

84. *See* Italian Supreme Court, *Fall. soc. traghetti Mediterraneo v. Soc. Tirrenia navigaz. and Min. of Transports,* 19 Apr. 2000, n. 5087, *supra.*

professional fairness requirements laid down in Article 2598(3) of the Italian Civil Code, which violation is apt to harm another person's business:

> For example, liability for unfair competition has been excluded in the case of an entrepreneur who had installed a watercraft hoisting system through financial contributions from the European Community and the Italian State, within the scope of an aid plan for fisheries, and had subsequently used such system for non-fishing vessels as well. In this specific case, the financing instrument failed to refer expressly to an exclusive destination of the equipment for the stated purposes of the aid plan. Thus, the entrepreneur in receipt of the aid could not be deemed to have committed an act of unfair competition by violating civil-law rules, unless it was proved that he was not already engaged in the handling of non-fishing watercraft before installing the equipment through public loans, or that he did not prevailingly use such equipment for the handling of vessels other than fishing boats, or else that he even had this goal in mind at the time he applied for such grant of public aid.[85]

The legal remedy an aid recipient's competitor is entitled to apply for pursuant to Article 2598(3) of the Italian Civil Code may be intended – including in an urgency, within the meaning of Article 700 of the Italian Code of Civil Procedure, when an imminent, irretrievable prejudice is threatened – to obtain judicial measures enjoining the aid recipient from engaging in unfair competition and ordering him to pay damages.

[E] Actions for Damages Against the State

Precisely because the standstill clause implied in the last sentence of Article 108(3) TFEU is addressed to the Member States of the European Union and is immediately applicable in national legal systems, a State infringing that clause is liable to be sued for damages by the injured parties.

That a Member State is liable for infringing any rules of European law has become a firmly rooted principle, at least since the milestone *Francovich* judgment, which established the right on the part of individuals to obtain reparation for losses incurred because of the Member State's delay in implementing a European directive. In fact, the principle whereby a State must be liable for loss and damage caused to individuals by breaches of European law for which the State can be held responsible is inherent in the system of the Treaties. Were it not so, the full effectiveness of European rules would be impaired and the protection of the rights that they grant to individuals would be weakened:

> Where ... a Member State fails to fulfil its obligation under ... the Treaty to take all the measures necessary to achieve the result prescribed by a directive, the full effectiveness of that rule of Community law requires that there should be a right to reparation provided that three conditions are fulfilled. The first of those conditions is that the result prescribed by the directive should entail the grant of rights to individuals. The second condition is that it should be possible to identify the

85. *See* Court of Trapani, 10 Jul. 2000, *Soc. off. meccanica navale Drepanum v. Soc. cantiere navale Trapani, Giur. dir. ind.*, 2000, p. 1046.

> content of those rights on the basis of the provisions of the directive. Finally, the third condition is the existence of a causal link between the breach of the State's obligation and the loss and damage suffered by the injured parties. ... [I]t is on the basis of the rules of national law on liability that the State must make reparation for the consequences of the loss and damage caused.[86]

Therefore, individuals may, without the need to await the European judicature's prior judgment on State liability, bring action against the State, pursuant to Article 2043 of the Italian Civil Code, to be awarded damages for any loss incurred by them.

In principle, for an act of the State to be deemed to be illegal and damaging, the plaintiff must prove that: (a) a rule of European law granting individuals immediately applicable rights was breached; (b) such breach is manifest and serious; and (c) there exists a causal link between the breach of the State's obligation and the loss suffered.

Moreover:

> Reparation from Member States for loss or damage caused to individuals as a result of breaches of Community law must be commensurate with the loss or damage sustained. In the absence of relevant Community provisions, it is for the domestic legal system of each Member State to set the criteria for determining the extent of reparation. However, those criteria must not be less favourable than those applying to similar claims based on domestic law and must not be such as in practice to make it impossible or excessively difficult to obtain reparation. National legislation which generally limits the damage for which reparation may be granted to damage done to certain, specifically protected individual interests not including loss of profit by individuals is not compatible with Community law.[87]

Where unlawful aid is granted, the aid recipient's competitor, or any injured third party (such as the creditors of a firm that became insolvent following unlawful aid to a competitor, closing down as a consequence of the undue advantage afforded to the beneficiary) may bring proceedings against the State, not only to seek an order from the national court for the recovery of non-notified aid but also to compensate for losses incurred as a result of the State's unlawful conduct.

The purport of the last sentence of Article 108(3) TFEU is so cogent and specific that any breach thereof by a Member State may well be viewed as 'manifest and serious' in itself. In fact, the requirement that a breach of a European obligation or prohibition must be sufficiently serious is met wherever the State is under a specific result obligation. This is the case with all provisions imposing on the Member States precise, clearly identified obligations to refrain from some conduct, such as all the standstill clauses.[88]

In determining whether a breach of European law is sufficiently serious, the ECJ has emphasized the discretion that the national authorities may exercise. If the

---

86. *See* Joined Cases C-6/90 e C-9/90, *Andrea Francovich and Others v. Italy*, 19.11.1991, ECLI: EU:C:1991:428, paras 39-42.
87. *See* Joined Cases C-46/93 and C-48/93, *Brasserie du Pêcheur SA v. Bundesrepublik Deutschland and The Queen v. Secretary of State for Transport, ex parte: Factortame Ltd and others*, 5.3.1996, ECLI:EU:C:1996:79, para. 5.
88. *See* the Opinion of Advocate General Tesauro of 28 Nov. 1995 in Case C-48/93, *Brasserie du pêcheur & Factortame III*, 5.3.1996, ECLI:EU:C:1996:79, paras 71 and 80.

authority in question does not have any discretion, the mere breach of EU law may be sufficient to establish that the breach was sufficiently serious. Indeed, so far as Article 108(3) TFEU is concerned, the authorities within Member States do not have any discretion that would allow them not to notify a State aid measure. They in principle have an absolute obligation to notify any measure of that sort, prior to its implementation. While the ECJ at times considers breaches of EU law forgivable,[89] where it is a matter of State aid, the national authorities cannot as a matter of principle argue that they were not aware of the standstill obligation. This is due to the existence of both extensive case law and the Commission's own Guidelines on the application of Article 107(1) and Article 108(3) TFEU. In the event of doubt, Member States can always notify a measure to the Commission, to have certainty over the law.[90]

However, in the case of an exemption regulation, the national courts are called upon to ensure and test compliance with the criteria laid down in the appropriate European provisions, by determining not only whether a measure is State aid but also whether it falls within the scope for application of the relevant regulation, with a view to establishing eligibility for exemption from notification and standstill obligations. In each such case, the national authority granting the aid enjoys a wider scope for assessment than merely determining compliance with the standstill clause, and so the serious and manifest character of the breach of the exemption regulation alleged against the Member State will have to be specifically assessed by the national court through accurate investigation, without automatically applying conventional standards.

The subjective element of intentionality as opposed to negligence, which abstractly qualifies any violation provided for by Article 2043 of the Italian Civil Code, can be deemed implied and must, in fact, be presumed whenever an unlawful regulatory or administrative act is being implemented, insofar as that act goes contrary to European rules or to a Commission decision, whether because of the indisputably voluntary character of any measure issued by public authorities or because of a violation of the legality principles any public authority is unfailingly required to observe.

In summary, for a Member State to be found liable for infringing its obligations under European law, an investigation into the possible existence of negligence as the subjective component of unlawful conduct has no relevance at all. Accordingly, the national court cannot make reparation of loss or damage incurred by individuals conditional upon fault (intentional or negligent) on the part of the organ of the State responsible for the breach, going beyond that of a manifest and sufficiently serious breach of EU law.[91]

89. *See* judgment in Case C-39/94, *SFEI and Others*, para. 73, *supra*.
90. *See* Case C-278/05, *Carol Marilyn Robins and Others v. Secretary of State for Work and Pensions*, 25.1.2007, ECLI:EU:C:2007:56; Case C-424/97, *Haim v. Kassenzahnärztliche Vereinigung Nordrhein*, 4.7.2000, ECLI:EU:C:2000:357, and with a note by Fabio Ferraro in *Riv. it. dir. pubbl. comunitario*, p. 407 (2001); Case C-5/94, *The Queen v. Ministry of Agriculture, Fisheries and Food*, ex parte: *Hedley Lomas* (Ireland) *Ltd*, 23.5.1996, ECLI:EU:C:1996:205 and with a note by Roberto Caranta in *Riv. it. dir. pubbl. comunitario*, p. 1003 (1996).
91. *See also* the Opinion of Advocate General Tesauro of 28 Nov. 1995 in Case C-48/93, *Brasserie du pêcheur & Factortame III*, para. 85, *supra*.

Of all the constituting elements of a violation of provisions of civil law, only damage and the causal link, if any, between damage and the breach of a standstill obligation can be claimed in court. A plaintiff seeking compensation for damages from the State will have to discharge the fundamental burden of proof imposed on him in relation to these aspects of his claim for damages.

With respect to proving and quantifying the losses causally connected with the unlawful aid, account should be had to the following:[92]

(1) By virtue of the principles on the equivalence and effectiveness of Community law, the national rules may not exclude a Member State's liability for loss of profit. There may be a loss under European law both where the breach resulted in a loss of an asset for the claimant, and where it prevented the claimant from improving its asset position. Where loss of profit is not a loss that may be compensated under the national legislation, the national court must not apply the provision related to the compensation of losses, pursuant to Article 108(3) TFEU.
(2) Determination of the actual amount of lost profit will be easier where the unlawful aid enabled the beneficiary to obtain a contract or a specific business opportunity from the claimant. In that case, the national court may calculate the revenue that the claimant was likely to generate under that contract. In the event that the contract has already been performed by the beneficiary, the national court would also take account of the actual profit generated.
(3) More complicated damage assessments are necessary where the aid merely leads to an overall loss of market share. One possible way of dealing with such cases could be to compare the claimant's actual income situation (based on the profit and loss account) with the hypothetical income situation had the unlawful aid not been granted.
(4) There may be circumstances where the damage suffered by the claimant exceeds the lost profit. This could, for example, be the case where, as a consequence of the unlawful aid, the claimant is forced out of business (through insolvency, for example).

National procedural rules will sometimes allow the national court to rely on reasonable estimates for the purpose of determining the actual amount of damages to be granted to the claimant (*see*, for example, Article 1226 of the Civil Code). Where that is the case, and provided the principle of effectiveness is respected, the use of such estimates would also be possible in relation to damages claims arising under Article 108(3) TFEU.

The legal prerequisites for damages claims under European law and issues of damages calculation can also form the basis of requests for Commission assistance (in

92. 2021 Notice, paras 87 et seq., *supra*.

the form of information, or opinions) pursuant to the 2009 Commission Notice to national courts.

The ability to seek compensation for damages is as a matter of principle independent from any parallel Commission investigation concerning the same aid measure's compatibility with the internal market. That there is such an investigation ongoing does not release the national court from its obligation to safeguard individual rights under Article 108(3) TFEU. Since the claimant may be able to demonstrate that he suffered a loss due to the premature implementation of the aid, and, more specifically, as a result of the beneficiary's unlawful time advantage, successful damages claims are also possible where the Commission has already approved the aid by the time the national court decides.[93]

Moreover, any decision that the Commission may take on the aid's compatibility with the internal market, while immaterial in legal terms with respect to the failure to comply with the standstill obligation that the national court must address, including through the award of compensation against the State, may affect the establishment of the causal nexus, and the damages suffered by the competitor. In other words, since the breach of the prohibition upon implementation of the aid prior to the Commission's authorization amounts to an unlawful act that ceases when the Commission approves the measures, compensation of damages must take into consideration only the period from the premature (and for that fact unlawful) grant of the aid, up to the Commission's authorization, which as we discussed in section §7.02, neither remedies nor retrospectively eliminates the breach of the mandatory rule under Article 108(3) TFEU, last sentence.

Claims for the compensation of losses against the State or a local authority for the grant of unlawful aid must be brought in the administrative court, where the State aid flows from an administrative act or measure that is capable of being contested by the competitor or third party. Article 133(z-*sexies*), which was introduced by Act No. 234/2012, provides that the administrative courts have exclusive jurisdiction over disputes related to acts and measures that grant State aid in breach of Article 108(3) TFEU, and Article 50 of Act No. 234/2012 states that such measures may be challenged in the Regional Administrative Court with geographical jurisdiction.

As mentioned earlier, what was previously referred to as the 'administrative prejudice', which meant any claim for compensation had to be preceded or accompanied by an action overturning the unlawful administrative act, no longer applies. Nonetheless, an injured party that does not pursue such an action will have its conduct evaluated, pursuant to Article 1227 of the Civil Code and the principle of bona fides, for the purpose of quantifying the damages that may be compensated on the basis of contributory negligence by the claimant.[94] Such a stance is puzzling when it comes to

93. Case C-199/06, *Centre d'exportation du livre français (CELF) and Ministre de la Culture et de la Communication v. Société internationale de diffusion et d'édition (SIDE)*, 12.2.2008, ECLI: EU:C:2008:79, with a note by Luca Terminiello, in *Dir. pubbl. comparato ed europeo*, p. 933 (m) (2008).
94. *See Consiglio di Stato, Fall. soc. Rem v. Soc. Enel distribuz.*, 23 Mar. 2011, No. 3, *Corr. giur.*, 2011, p. 979, with a note by Franco Gaetano Scoca and with a note by Annalaura Giannelli, *La pregiudiziale amministrativa rinasce dalle proprie ceneri: la mancata impugnazione dell'atto*

unlawful State aid, granted in breach of Community rules, which do not tolerate any mitigation or limitation of the sanctions that may be imposed by the national courts, under the aforementioned principles of the primacy, equivalence and effectiveness of Community law and its instruments.

When the unlawful aid does not flow from such an administrative measure, but instead from a tax measure or a measure of another kind (such as the subscription of shares in publicly-owned companies), jurisdiction will lie with the tax courts, or the ordinary courts, as the case may be.

Naturally, where a claim for compensation is based upon a breach of Article 108(3) TFEU, as here, there should also be a claim for the failure on the part of the State to implement any decision declaring the aid incompatible and ordering its recovery. Once the period granted for its implementation has passed, the Commission's decision ordering recovery in fact produces a direct effect with respect to the competitor, which could raise the breach of that decision by the State as a basis for prejudice to its competitive position – indeed, the loss would certainly be greater, because it continues from the initial grant without notification, to the date of actual recovery.[95]

§7.11 INTERIM RELIEF AND THE REFORM OF PRECAUTIONARY MEASURES

As indicated above in sections §7.05 and §7.06 of this chapter, when a national court decides to consult the Commission or to raise a preliminary question before the Court of Justice pursuant to Article 267 TFEU, it is required to adopt any necessary interim relief or precautionary measures to protect the parties' interests pending ordinary proceedings on the substance, while awaiting a reply from the European institution to which it has applied.

This is an established principle in the European case law, reaffirmed in a number of judgments of the Court of Justice, that a national court called upon to decide a case

illegittimo recide il nesso di causalità tra provvedimento illegittimo e lesione, in *Foro it.*, III, 31 (2012); *Consiglio di Stato, Soc. S. v. Com. Roma e altro*, 31 Oct. 2012, No. 5556, *supra*, which considered an application for the annulment of an act and a claim for compensation of the unfair losses caused by unlawful exercise by general government of administrative activity, and the failure to carry on their mandatory activity, under Arts 30 et seq. of the Code of Administrative Procedure. The court found the legislation had not taken up the notion of administrative prejudice, nor that the two remedies were completely independent of one another, but had opted for an intermediate solution, which would consider a failure to bring an application for the annulment of the injurious measure in good time as not precluding an application for compensation, but rather as conduct that should form part of an overall assessment of the parties' conduct, and as such may authorize the court to exclude compensation, or reduce its amount, where it finds that a prompt application for annulment of the injurious act would have avoided or limited the damages therefrom. With regard to the issue of the damage, which obviously arises only where there is injury deriving from the unlawful measure, the claim for compensation should thus be considered admitted, in accordance with the principles set out in the judgment, also irrespective of the challenge to the (allegedly) unlawful and injurious measure.

95. *See* 2021 Notice, para. 93, *supra*.

concerning Community law must disapply the national rule that precludes it from granting interim relief.[96]

Interim legal protection is instrumental in ensuring the effectiveness of the judicature's workings both at the European level and under Articles 24 and 111 of the Italian Constitution. The ECJ has, in fact, been led to concede that national courts may take precautionary measures even in the face of European acts challenged before the judges in Luxembourg, where: (a) the national judge entertains serious doubts as to the validity of the European measure (*fumus boni juris*); and (b) there is urgency, in the sense that interim measures are necessary to prevent the applicant from incurring serious and irreparable damage (*periculum in mora*). In any event, the national court must take due account of the interests of the Community and of the presumption that European measures are valid. Further, where that Community measure has not been challenged, the national court must raise a preliminary question of validity before the Court of Justice by way of a reference for a preliminary ruling, pursuant to Article 267(b) TFEU, and adopt any interim measures as are necessary to protect the parties' interests pending proceedings.[97]

Italian case law has closely followed these guidelines:

> Where a preliminary question is raised as to the interpretation of Community rules or the validity of acts of Community institutions, pursuant to Article 267 TFEU, in an action for interim relief [in Italy], the judge may, pending a decision from the European Court of Justice, take adequate interim measures to protect each party's interests, much as he is required to defer adjudication of the parties' requests for precautionary orders.[98]

Therefore, when the national judge in interlocutory proceedings deems it necessary to consult with the Commission or to raise a preliminary question before the ECJ as to the interpretation of Article 107 TFEU, in order to correctly qualify a State measure as State aid, he may take any appropriate interim measures to protect the parties' interests in urgency, pending the relevant procedure, by issuing injunctions inhibiting the grant or continuation of the aid or by ordering recovery if that aid has already been paid.

Technically, the national court will grant an interim measure, refer the case to the ECJ and stay interlocutory proceedings before issuing an order to confirm, vary or

96. *See* Case C-213/89, *The Queen v. Secretary of State for Transport,* ex parte: *Factortame Ltd and Others,* 19.6.1990, ECLI:EU:C:1990:257.
97. *See* Joined Cases C-143/88 and C-92/89, *Zuckerfabrik Süderdithmarschen and Zuckerfabrik Soest v. Hauptzollamt Itzehoe and Hauptzollamt Paderborn,* 21.2.1991, ECLI:EU:C:1991:65, *supra. See also* Case C-465/93, *Atlanta Fruchthandelsgesellschaft mbH and Others v. Bundesamt für Ernährung und Forstwirtschaft, supra.* and Case C-314/85, *Foto-Frost v. Hauptzollamt Lübeck-Ost,* 16.6.1966, ECLI:EU:C:1966:34, para. 19 in which the Court added that the general rule by which national courts may not themselves declare community acts invalid may be derogated in certain circumstances, for example, in the case of proceedings relating to an application for interim measures. *See also* Case C-344/98, *Masterfoods Ltd. v. HB Ice Cream Ltd.,* 14.12.2000, ECLI:EU:C:2000:689.
98. *See TAR Lombardia, Unione comm. prov. Milano e altro v. Com. Milano,* 5 Apr. 1994, n. 267, *Trib. amm. reg.,* 1994, I, p. 1853 and Italian Supreme Court, section IV, *Min. fin. v. Soc. Philip Morris Belgium e altro,* 25 Aug. 1991, n. 962, *Riv. it. dir. pubbl. com.,* pp. 298 et seq. (1992).

discharge such interim measure. Thus, the national court will be able to take account of the Court of Justice's preliminary ruling for the purposes of a subsequent decision confirming, varying or discharging its order.[99]

The mechanism is clear from two rules that have since been abolished and may be applied only to claims that were pending on 19 January 2013 (*see* Article 61 of Act No. 234/2012). They regarded litigation for the recovery of State aid following an order from the Commission, and are Article 9 of Legislative Decree 150/2011, for proceedings in the civil court, and Articles 47*bis* of Legislative Decree 546/1992, for proceedings in the tax court. For example, under Article 9 of Legislative Decree 150/2011, in civil proceedings regarding a court order for payment consequent to a recovery decision, the court may upon application suspend the enforceability of the order, if all of the following conditions are satisfied: (a) there are serious grounds for the recovery decision's unlawfulness, or patent error in the identification of the person obliged to repay the State aid, or in the calculation of the amount to be recovered, to the extent of that error; and (b) the risk of an imminent and irreparable prejudice. Where the application for suspension is upheld on grounds related to the unlawfulness of the recovery decision, the court should immediately refer the matter for a preliminary ruling to the ECJ, if the question of the Community act's validity has not already been so referred. An application for suspension cannot be upheld on grounds related to the legitimacy of the recovery decision where the applicant would be entitled to contest the recovery decision directly, under Article 263 but has not done so; has done so but has not sought suspension of the recovery decision, under Article 278 TFEU; or has sought its suspension, but has been unsuccessful.

A civil or administrative court hearing a dispute (whether in relation to an interim application, or the substantive case) over the grant of unlawful aid in breach of Article 108(3) TFEU, that intends to seek the Commission's assistance or raise a preliminary issue of interpretation or validity before the Court of Justice, must act similarly, *mutatis mutandis*, and suspend the proceedings. In the meantime, it must issue appropriate interim measures, which may also be atypical in nature, but it may not raise a preliminary issue of validity, or uphold an interim application, where the parties were clearly capable of taking the matter to the European courts, by a direct application under Article 263 TFEU, thereby achieving full coordination between national courts and European bodies, and between the court remedies provided by the national and by the European courts.

Interim measures in respect of State aid may be intended to preserve assets or as a preventative measure, and may also be atypical in nature. For example, while awaiting the Commission's assistance, or a judgment from the Court of Justice on a preliminary issue of interpretation or validity, the national court may order payment of funds corresponding to the aid onto a blocked account, whereafter it will order restitution to the national authority or payment to the beneficiary, as the case may be, subject to the restitution in any event of aid received prior to the Commission's

99. *See* Case C-388/85, *Pardini v. Ministry of commerce with foreign Countries*, 21.4.1988, ECLI: EU:C:1988:194.

authorization (and interest thereon), because such aid would in any event be unlawful, for its breach of Article 108(3) TFEU.[100]

The adoption of orders under Article 700 of the Italian Code of Civil Procedure, with a view either to inhibiting or recovering aid unlawfully granted or, in actions for unfair competition, to enjoining the aid beneficiary from engaging in anti-competitive conduct through unlawful State aid, will make proceedings on the substance of a case unnecessary, as the last three paragraphs of Article 669*octies* of the Italian Code of Civil Procedure reveal, leaving the parties free to elect whether or not to bring proceedings for full cognisance. Moreover, the interim relief anticipatory of a final judgment on the substance will survive even if the action is extinguished. This has resulted in the widely shared view that interlocutory orders that are apt to anticipate the effects of a final judgment on the merits are characterized by 'instrumentality' or, rather, 'attenuated temporariness'.

Interim applications in the administrative courts will be subject to Articles 55 et seq. of the Code of Administrative Procedure, which allows interim measures to apply also prior to trial, where the matter is exceptionally serious and urgent, and allows the substantive case to be determined at the end of the interim hearing (Article 60 of the Code of Administrative Procedure).

§7.12 PROBLEMATIC QUALIFICATION OF ACTIONS FOR DAMAGES BROUGHT BY AID RECIPIENTS AGAINST THE STATE

Accommodating an aid beneficiary among the parties entitled to claim damages from the State for breach of European rules is quite a difficult endeavour where that aid measure was implemented without the standstill obligation under the last sentence of Article 108(3) TFEU having been complied with.

An undertaking in receipt of State aid is bound to wonder whether the aid is compatible with European law. This is so, not so much because of the principle that *ignorantia legis non excusat*, as because the undertaking's very position in a free-market economy prevents it from overlooking the potential implications of measures that are apt to distort competition in any case.

In other words, when an undertaking receives a non-notified State aid, it must comply with its duties of fairness and due care, and deal with the problem of compliance with Community rules of its own motion. If it fails to do so, it can only blame itself for any losses it will incur from being forced to repay aid unlawfully granted by the State.

As can be inferred, in principle, from Article 1227 of the Italian Civil Code, the beneficiary's conduct may be relevant to the causal link between the unlawful act and the harmful event. As the beneficiary undertaking was under an obligation to make sure that Community obligations had been observed when the aid was first granted, it cannot plead losses and claim damages if it is unexpectedly forced to give back what it had unlawfully been granted. For it must be stressed that, even where the Commission

100. *See* 2021 Notice, paras 95 et seq., *supra*.

finds the aid to be compatible with the internal market, this is not sufficient to cure infringement of the standstill clause, and not even in this case might the aid beneficiary complain for being forced to repay aid untimely, thus unlawfully, granted in breach of the last sentence of Article 108(3) TFEU.

Only in exceptional cases might the State be deemed to have Aquilian liability to the beneficiary of an aid unlawfully granted, when the public administration's conduct has been such as to relieve and exempt the aid beneficiary from any natural, autonomous duty of care. One of several examples given in literature was the case of an aid beneficiary that had been expressly assured by the State that the aid was irrelevant under Article 107 TFEU, or that the applicable aid measures could be deemed to be compatible with the internal market because of general exemption regulations.[101] All such questions obviously border upon the issue of the legitimate expectations an aid beneficiary may plead as defendant in an action for aid recovery, an issue already discussed in Chapter 4 above.

101. *See* Ornella Porchia, *Il procedimento di controllo degli aiuti pubblici alle imprese tra ordinamento comunitario e ordinamento interno, supra,* footnote 98 at p. 231.

CHAPTER 8

Insolvency Proceedings

Claudio Biscaretti di Ruffia

§8.01 STATE AID FOR FIRMS IN DIFFICULTY AND INSOLVENCY PROCEEDINGS: THE EUROPEAN UNION LEGISLATION

In the context of the European legislation on State aid, rescue and restructuring aid for firms in difficulty is considered to be among the most distortive. However, in certain cases, firms in difficulty could carry out restructuring, abandoning loss-making activities and reorganizing the remaining activities. In this case, restructuring should, in principle, take place without State aid.

In some cases, however, if all other market options are exhausted, the firms concerned may be eligible to receive public aid if such aid is intended to achieve a well-defined objective of common interest.[1] Based on these considerations, the European Commission adopted the Guidelines on State aid for rescuing and restructuring non-financial undertakings in difficulty, the latest version of which was published on 31 July 2014.[2] It replaced the previous Guidelines originally adopted in 2004, whose expiry had been repeatedly postponed.[3] The new Guidelines came into force on 1 August 2014 and should have been applied until 31 December 2020. Even in relation to

1. *See*, in this regard, Camera dei deputati, *Gli aiuti di Stato, Parte speciale, Principali orientamenti della Commissione*, n. 67/1, 26 Oct. 2023, pp. 41 et seq.
2. Communication from the Commission – *Guidelines on State aid for rescuing and restructuring non-financial undertakings in difficulty* (2014/C249/1). For a critical examination of these Guidelines *see* Giulia Sonderegger, *A Critical Analysis of Rescue and Restructuring Aid* in *ESALQ*, pp. 264 et seq. (2019) https://doi.org/10.21552/estal/2019/3/6; *see also* Geoffrey Mamdani and Simone Ritzek-Seidl, *Rescue and restructuring*, in *EU Competition Law*, IV, 2, pp. 745 et seq. (Pesaresi, van de Casteele, Flynn and Siaterli, Deventer-Leuven eds, 2016); Piet Jan Slot, *Rescue and restructuring Aid*, in *EU State Aid*, pp. 1013 et seq. (Hancher, Ottervanger and Slot eds, London, 2016).
3. *See*, lastly, Commission communication concerning the prolongation of the application of the *Community guidelines on State aid for rescuing and restructuring firms in difficulty of 1 Oct. 2004*

them, however, the period of application has been extended several times, most recently with the Commission Communication of 29 November 2023, which extended the period of application until 31 December 2025.[4]

The Guidelines set the conditions that must be satisfied for State aid to non-financial undertakings in difficulty to be considered compatible with the internal market, under Article 107(3)(c) TFEU. In particular, subparagraph 20.(c) of the Guidelines, as part of its definition of undertakings in difficulty – after stating that an undertaking is considered to be in difficulty where, without intervention by the State, it would almost certainly be condemned to go out of business – goes on to include within that scope situations *'where the undertaking is subject to collective insolvency proceedings or fulfils the criteria under its domestic law for being placed in collective insolvency proceedings at the request of its creditors'*. The other circumstances in which undertakings are considered to be in difficulty under paragraph 20 of the Guidelines regard limited liability companies for which more than half of the subscribed share capital has disappeared as a result of accumulated losses; companies in which at least some members have unlimited liability for the debt, and more than half of its capital as shown in the company accounts has disappeared as a result of accumulated losses; and undertakings that are not SMEs where for the past two years: (i) the undertaking's book debt-to-equity ratio has been greater than 7.5; and (ii) the undertaking's EBITDA interest coverage ratio has been below 1.0.[5]

Paragraph 7 of the Guidelines states that where parts of a failing undertaking remain essentially viable, an insolvency procedure may also return a viable undertaking to the market *'by way of acquisition by third parties, whether of the undertaking as a going concern or its various production assets'*.

The Guidelines apply to all undertakings in difficulty, including any in the fisheries and aquaculture sector, subject, however, to the specific provisions set out in the guidelines for the examination of national aid in the fisheries and aquaculture sector, and to the agricultural sector, including the primary agricultural production sector.[6]

(OJ C 296/3 2012). In relation to these Guidelines *see* Maurizio Orlandi, *La disciplina degli aiuti di Stato* (Tizzano ed.), *Il diritto privato dell'Unione europea*, II, pp. 1668 et seq., especially pp. 1693 et seq. (Turin, 2006).

4. Communication from the Commission amending the *Guidelines on State aid for rescuing and restructuring non-financial undertakings in difficulty, as regards the period of application*, 29 Nov. 2023 (C/2023/1212).
5. *See* the Guidelines, subparas 20.(a), 20.(b) and 20.(d). On the special nature of the concept of an undertaking in difficulty, and the manner of its identification by the Commission, *see* Joined Cases T-267/08 and T-279/08, *Région Nord-Pas-de-Calais v. Commission*, 12.5.2011, ECLI: EU:T:2011:209; Case T-102/07, *Freistaat Sachsen e.a. v. Commission*, 3.3.2010, ECLI: EU:T:2010:62.
6. *See* Guidelines, para. 18. 'Primary agricultural production' means production of the agricultural and livestock products set out in Annex I TFEU that have not been processed to change their nature.

They do not, however, apply to the coal and steel sectors as well as to firms governed by specific rules for financial institutions. They are, however, without prejudice to the specific rules for firms in difficulty in a particular sector.[7]

There is a special scheme for SMEs and smaller State-owned undertakings, which may be granted temporary restructuring support, in the form of liquidity support for the restructuring of an undertaking, enabling the beneficiary to draw up and implement action to restore long-term viability.[8] As in the previous Guidelines, the other kinds of aid are forms of rescue aid, which by nature is urgent and temporary; and of restructuring aid, intended to restore long-term viability.[9]

Finally, the Guidelines under consideration here do not apply to newly established companies, that is, in the first three years of a company's operation in a particular sector.

Regarding the criteria for compatibility of aid, it should first be recalled that aid under the '*one time, last time*' principle can only be granted to an enterprise once every ten years.

That said, in order to assess whether the aid is compatible under Article 107(3)(c), the Commission must assess whether it complies with the following criteria: (a) whether it makes an effective contribution to the achievement of an objective of common interest; (b) whether the State intervention is necessary in order to bring about a tangible improvement that the market, without aid, would not be able to provide; (c) whether the aid measure is appropriate in the sense that other, less distortive aid measures would not achieve the same result; (d) whether the proposed aid measure has a real incentive effect, and, that is, whether without it the objective of common interest would not have been achieved; (e) whether the aid is actually proportional (and, that is, limited to the minimum necessary) to achieve the objective of common interest.

Finally, as to the length of the procedure for granting the aid, there is a one-month time limit for rescue aid decisions that comply with all of the compatibility conditions outlined above, provided that the amount of each individual aid is limited to a maximum of EUR 10 million and that the situations envisaged in paragraphs 72.(b) and (c) of the Guidelines do not arise in the specific case, namely:

> (b) where rescue aid or temporary restructuring support has been granted in accordance with these guidelines and that aid was not followed by restructuring aid, if:

7. *See*, among others, *Community guidelines on State aid for railway undertakings* (2008/C 184/07). The Commission recently (18 Jun. 2024) launched a public consultation (until 20 Sep. 2024) on its draft amendment to the Guidelines for railway undertakings.
8. With reference to the SMEs, *see* Geoffrey Mamdani and Simone Ritzek-Seidl, *Rescue and restructuring, supra*, pp. 807 et seq.
9. *See* para. 2 of the Guidelines. On restructuring aid, the General Court has found, in considering restructuring aid's compatibility with the internal market, that the Commission must in principle examine the cumulative effect of that aid with any earlier aid which has not yet been recovered, as the advantages conferred by the grant of earlier incompatible aid which has not yet been recovered continue to produce effects on competition (*see* Joined Cases T-115/09 and T-116/09, *Electrolux and Whirlpool v. Commission*, 14.2.2012, ECLI:EU:T:2012:76).

(i) it could reasonably have been believed that the beneficiary would be viable in the long term when the aid pursuant to these guidelines was granted, and

(ii) new rescue or restructuring aid becomes necessary after at least five years due to unforeseeable circumstances of which the beneficiary is not responsible.

(c) in exceptionable and unforeseeable circumstances for which the beneficiary is not responsible.[10]

By referring generally to firms in difficulty, European Union case law has established some core principles under which State aid measures should be assessed for compatibility with the common market. First, it ruled that the term '*insolvency proceedings*' covers all insolvency proceedings relating to enterprises provided for under national law whether they are initiated ex officio by national administrative or judicial authorities or on the initiative of the enterprise concerned. That said, if an enterprise is in the conditions provided by national law for the opening of insolvency proceedings against it, this circumstance is sufficient to prevent the granting, in respect of it, of State aid.[11] Furthermore, European Union case law has indicated the *private investor criterion*, under which it should be established whether a private investor, under comparable circumstances, would have made investments in the same amount as those actually made by the public body involved.[12]

European Union case law has also specified that the conduct of a private investor, with which the intervention of the public investor must be compared, need not be the conduct of an ordinary investor laying out capital with a view to realizing a profit in the relatively short term, but it must at least be the conduct of a private holding company or a private group of undertakings pursuing a structural policy, whether general or sectoral and guided by prospects of profitability in the longer term.[13]

A further criterion the European Union (EU) Courts have identified is the *private creditor criterion*, according to which a national government or any public body that has issued a loan should act as a diligent private creditor trying to recover at least a marginal amount of its claim. The conformity of each specific case to the general private creditor criterion must be assessed on the basis of comparable circumstances.[14]

10. For an effective summary of the Guidelines under consideration here, *see* Camera dei deputati, *Gli aiuti di Stato, Parte speciale, supra*, pp. 41 et seq.
11. *See* Case C-245/16, *Nerea S.p.A. v. Regione Marche*, 6.7.2017, ECLI:EU:C:2017:521.
12. Case T-209/11, *MB System v. Commission*, 3.7.2013, ECLI:EU:T:2013:338; Joined Cases C-214/12 P, C-215/12 P and C-223/12 P, *Land Burgerland v. Commission*, 24.10.2013, ECLI: EU:C:2013:682. Previously, *see* Case C-399/00, *Sim 2 Multimedica S.p.A. v. Commission*, 8.5.2003, ECLI:EU:C:2003:252; Case T-296/97, *Alitalia v. Commission*, 12.12.2000, ECLI: EU:T:2000:289 and Case C-256/97, *Déménagements-Manutention Transport SA (DTM)*, 29.6.1999, ECLI:EU:C:1999:332. On the *private investor criterion, see also* Gianluca Contaldi, *La nozione di aiuto di Stato*, 3, pp. 107 et seq., in *Eurojus* (2019).
13. *See, ex multis*, Case C-278/92, *Spain v. Commission*, 14.9.1994, ECLI:EU:C:1994:325, para. 14; and also Case C-39/94, *Syndicat français de l'Express international (SFEI) v. La Poste and Others*, 11.7.1996, ECLI:EU:C:1996:285, para. 60; Case T-358/94, *Air France v. Commission*, 12.12.1996, ECLI:EU:T:1996:194.
14. *See* Case C-300/16 P *Commissione v. Frucona Košice*, 20.9.2017, ECLI:EU:C:2017:706; on this judgment, which clarified the *private creditor criterion, see* Oliver Geiss and Tatiana Siakka,

More specifically, the EU Courts have decided cases of State aid granted in connection with individual insolvency proceedings, by stating a general principle of non-discrimination between undertakings operating under comparable conditions in the same market. In this respect, the European Court of Justice has decided that within the scope of insolvency proceedings (the case at issue involved the Spanish insolvency law), the national authorities may only enter into debt waiver and rescheduling agreements with individual undertakings insofar as such agreements are potentially applicable to any other undertaking in that condition.

In the specific case under scrutiny, the charge alleged against the Spanish government related to the conduct of State authorities (specifically the Spanish Tax Authority) following the opening of insolvency proceedings and the conclusion of debt waiver and rescheduling agreements. The European Court of Justice granted the Commission's contention and accordingly held that the Spanish Tax Authority had failed to take specific, separate measures available under Spanish law and to act as a private creditor trying to recover its claim.[15]

Prior to that judgment, the European Court of Justice had also been called upon to determine the compatibility of the Spanish insolvency law with the common market in connection with the provision pursuant to which the debts of undertakings that have been declared insolvent cease to produce interest.[16] The Court held that such a rule, to the extent it is justified by the common interest of all the creditors in not burdening the insolvent undertaking's assets with new debts likely to worsen the situation, and applies to all creditors alike, private or public, in all procedures of this kind, *has no discriminatory character*. The ECJ also specified that this rule, taking account of the legislation's objective, the absence of any discrimination in its application and the fact that it applies only to interest falling due *after* the declaration of insolvency on aid unlawfully received *before* that declaration, cannot be regarded as rendering the recovery of aid required by European Union law virtually impossible.

The Court of First Instance (now General Court), by its order of 3 December 2002, held that the commencement of bankruptcy proceedings, or even only the risk for an undertaking to become liable to bankruptcy, does not, by itself, remove the obligation to repay an aid regarded as incompatible with the common market.[17] In the weighing of interests, the interest of the European Community (now European Union) must take precedence over the interest of the aid recipient in avoiding enforcement of the obligation to repay. In particular, in the General Court's view, it is necessary to show, while waiting for a judgment on the merits, that there are serious and exceptional circumstances justifying the grant of a suspension of the obligation to recover aid.

Redrawing the Market Economy Operator Test: EU State Aid Law Post Frucona, pp. 297 et seq. in ECLR, (2018); previously, Case C-276/02, *Spain v. Commission*, 14.9.2004, ECLI:EU:C:2004:521; and Case T-36/99, *Lenzing v. Commission*, 21.10.2004, ECLI:EU:T:2004:312.

15. *Ibid.*
16. *See* Case C-480/98, *Spain v. Commission*, 12.10.2000, ECLI:EU:C:2000:559.
17. *See* the CFI Order in Case C-181/02, *Neue Erba Lautex v. Commission*, 3.12.2002, ECLI:EU:T:2002:294.

§8.02 STATE AID AND EXTRAORDINARY ADMINISTRATION OF LARGE COMPANIES IN DIFFICULTY IN ITALY: FROM THE PRODI ACT TO THE MARZANO ACT

The provisions of law applicable to the Italian procedure for the 'extraordinary administration' of large companies in difficulty stand out for their complexity among those being reviewed both by the EU Courts and (as will be seen below) by the Commission in connection with the European Union's State aid rules. The relevant procedure was instituted in Italy by Law Decree No. 26 of 30 January 1979, as amended and enacted into law by Act No. 95 of 3 April 1979 (the Prodi Act), as repeatedly amended and finally repealed under Legislative Decree No. 270 of 8 July 1999, which provided for a new set of rules on the matter (the Prodi-bis Act). These pieces of legislation were later supplemented with Act No. 39 of 18 February 2004 (the Marzano Act), containing specific rules for undertakings with an especially large number of employees and high debt, as first amended by Act No. 166 of 5 July 2004, then by Law Decree No. 281 of 29 November 2004, relating to 'Amendments to provisions of law for the restructuring of large firms in crisis', as enacted into law by Act No. 6 of 28 January 2005 and by Decree No. 22 of 28 February 2005, as enacted into law by Act No. 71 of 29 April 2005.[18] The regulations under consideration here, first enacted to deal with the bankruptcy of Parmalat S.p.A., have since been repeatedly amended to allow their application to other cases such as, for example, *ILVA S.p.A.* and *Alitalia S.p.A.*, which are discussed below.[19]

The main purpose of the extraordinary administration procedure is to permit the continuation of an enterprise's productive activity and the maintenance of the unity of its business complex with a view to preserving its existing employment and production levels (the 'preservation objective'). An ancillary objective is the satisfaction of creditors' claims.

Originally, Article 1 of the Prodi Act identified the firms subject to extraordinary administration on the basis of two criteria: (a) no fewer than three hundred workers employed for at least one year; and (b) debt exposure exceeding five times the enterprise's paid-up capital, corresponding to an amount to be updated on a year-to-year basis, as indebtedness towards credit institutions, special credit institutions, social welfare and social security institutions or bodies in which the State had a majority holding.

Since 1993, Article 1*bis* of the Prodi Act had extended the extraordinary administration procedure to yet other categories of firms. The former version of Article 1 required that, once a firm's state of insolvency or its failure to pay at least three month's wages and salaries had been established in court, the Minister for Industry, Commerce and Craft Trades should, in agreement with the Minister for the Treasury, issue a decree for the extraordinary administration of that firm. The relevant procedure would

18. These amendments to the Marzano Act were approved in occasion of the insolvency of the Italian airlines company Volare S.p.A.
19. *See* the recent Law No. 28 of 15 Mar. 2024, on urgent provisions on the extraordinary administration of enterprises of a strategic nature.

be carried out by one or three 'commissioners' to be appointed by, and under the supervision of, the Minister for Industry.

Pursuant to Article 2 of the Prodi Act, the Minister for Industry had discretion, through the decree ordering the extraordinary administration procedure, to authorize the *continuation of the enterprise's operations* for an initial period of two years (which could be extended for up to two additional years). Within the scope of a rehabilitation plan compatible with the general national industrial policy directions, the appointed commissioner or commissioners were required to draw up a business plan, which was to be filed after, not before, the decision to open the extraordinary administration procedure.

Under Article 2*bis*, the Minister for the Treasury could guarantee some or all of the debts contracted by undertakings under special administration to banking institutions to finance current operations and to reactivate or complete plant, buildings and industrial equipment.

Article 3 of the Prodi Act required that the same extraordinary administration procedure should apply to corporate groups, including controlled companies, companies controlling companies under extraordinary administration and companies subject to the same management as companies under extraordinary administration, much as any such company were not individually in the conditions provided for in respect of the admission to the extraordinary administration procedure.

Pursuant to the original Prodi Act, the extraordinary administration procedure came to an end if a composition was accepted, if total assets were distributed, if credit was exhausted, if there were insufficient assets or if the firm was once again able to fulfil its obligations and hence return to financial equilibrium.

As indicated above, Act No. 95 of 3 April 1979, as amended, was repealed by Legislative Decree No. 270 of 8 July 1999, headed 'New rules for the extraordinary administration of large firms in insolvency, pursuant to Article 1 of Act No. 274 of 30 July 1998'. By Legislative Decree No. 270/1999, the Italian lawmakers intended to respond to the Commission's objections, specifically in relation to the Treasury's guarantee for public loans granted, reduced rates of tax and waiver of social security contributions. One exception was the transitional scheme under Article 106 of Legislative Decree No. 270/1999, whereby extraordinary administration procedures pending at the time such decree entered into force were allowed to continue their course. This transitional scheme was expressly referred to in Article 7 of Act No. 273 of 12 December 2002, relating to 'Measures to encourage private initiative and the development of competition', which converted 'older' extraordinary administration procedures into compulsory administrative liquidation procedures.

The matter developed further following the entry into force of Law Decree No. 347 of 23 December 2003, as amended and enacted into law by Act No. 39 of 18 February 2004, relating to 'Measures for the restructuring of large firms in crisis' (commonly referred to as the Marzano Act). In particular, the first version of that act, which incorporated the provisions of the Prodi-*bis* Act to the extent compatible, was applicable to undertakings that simultaneously met the following requirements: (a) not fewer than 1,000 workers under subordinate employment contracts, including workers eligible for unemployment insurance benefits, employed for at least one year; and (b) debts aggregating at least EUR 1 billion, including liabilities for guarantees issued. Apparently, this act had previously been discussed by Minister Marzano with the then-Commissioner for Competition, Prof. Monti, who, in a press release dated 29 January 2004, specified that the procedural alterations contained in the new legislative instrument raised no problems in connection with the Community's State aid rules.[20]

The subsequent Law Decree No. 119 of 3 May 2004, as amended and enacted into law by Act No. 166 of 5 July 2004, relating to 'Provisions correcting and supplementing measures for large firms in crisis', introduced some corrections to the Marzano Act, specifically concerning composition with creditors, along with specific measures applicable to road-transport undertakings.

Afterwards, Law Decree No. 281 of 29 November 2004, as enacted into law by Act No. 6 of 28 January 2005 (on the occasion of the insolvency of Volare Group), lowered the applicability ceilings under the Marzano Act to provide for undertakings with at least 500 employees and at least EUR 300 million debt. More alterations, not as relevant to the matter here under scrutiny, were introduced by Law Decree No. 22/2005, as enacted into law by Act No. 71 of 29 April 2005.

§8.03 PROCEEDINGS BEFORE THE COMMISSION IN RELATION TO THE PRODI ACT

The issue of whether the Prodi Act was or was not, in its original version, compatible with the European Community principles had already emerged a few years after its entry into force. Apparently, after the Commission had taken knowledge of the Act in 1992, it had, at first, accepted the Italian representatives' 'verbal' undertaking that the act was a merely exceptional measure and had, by then, exhausted its functions.[21]

Later on, faced with yet more cases of application of the Prodi Act, the Commission issued Notice E 13/1992 and initiated to monitor the proceedings, in accordance with the rules applicable to *existing aid* (i.e., constant review, within the meaning of Article 88(1) EC, now Article 108(1) TFEU), in that the contested measures had been qualified as such.[22] Most likely, the Commission had taken this decision under the influence, on the one hand, of its own inactivity for fourteen years or so before initiating monitoring proceedings, and, on the other, of the reliance made by the undertakings concerned on the Prodi Act and of the practical impossibility to obtain refund of recoverable amounts (if any).

20. *See* Commission Press Release MEMO/04/19 of 29 Jan. 2004.
21. The history of the relationship between the Commission and the Italian Government in this matter is described at paras 1-17 of Commission Decision, OJ L 79/29, 2001.
22. *See* letter of 30 Jul. 1992, OJ C 395/4, 1994. On that occasion, the Commission stated that the application of the extraordinary administration for enterprises with at least 300 employees and the grant of a guarantee by the Treasury Ministry have to be considered State aid according to Art. 92 (now Art. 107), para. 1, TFEU, excluding the application of exceptions. For a criticism of the extensive application by the Commission of Art. 107 TFEU, *see* Alberto Santa Maria, *European Economic Law*, pp. 504 et seq., Alphen aan den Rijn (2019).

In early 1995, the Commission requested the Italian government to notify all cases of application of the Prodi Act, thus complying with the principles the Commission had laid down in the *Community guidelines on state aid for rescuing and restructuring firms in difficulty* then in force. In their reply of 9 March 1995, the Italian authorities agreed only to notify cases in which State guarantees were granted and refused to regard the other measures provided for in the Prodi Act as aid.

Only by its letter of 25 March 1997, did the Commission first initiate formal proceedings against Italy under Article 88(2) of the EC Treaty (now Article 108(2) TFEU), in respect of the scheme provided for in the Prodi Act.[23] Following the Court of Justice's *Ecotrade* and *Piaggio* judgments, the Commission, by its letter of 12 August 1999, withdrew its two previous decisions (including the former commencement of the procedure) and initiated proceedings under Article 88(2) in respect of the aid scheme in question, which was thenceforth categorized as *non-notified new aid*.[24] The proceedings ended with Commission Decision 2001/212/EC of 16 May 2000, of which more is below.

§8.04 THE *ECOTRADE* AND *PIAGGIO* JUDGMENTS OF THE EUROPEAN COURT OF JUSTICE

As indicated above, within just a few months, from December 1988 to June 1999 – shortly before the Prodi Act was repealed by Legislative Decree No. 270/1999, that is – the European Court of Justice took a position in the matter on two occasions, in its judgments settling the *Ecotrade* case and the *Piaggio* case following two references for a preliminary ruling ordered by the Italian Supreme Court and the Tribunal of Genoa, respectively.[25]

In the *Ecotrade* case, the ECJ established that a prohibited aid (pursuant to Article 4(c) of the ECSC Treaty in that specific instance) should be deemed to exist if an undertaking:

- has been permitted to continue trading in circumstances in which it would not have been permitted to do so if the rules of ordinary law relating to insolvency had been applied; or
- has enjoyed one or more advantages, such as a State guarantee, a reduced rate of tax, exemption from the obligation to pay fines and other pecuniary penalties or waiver in practice of public debts wholly or in part, which could not have been claimed by another insolvent undertaking in connection with the application of the rules of ordinary law relating to insolvency.

23. OJ C 192 1997.
24. OJ C 245 1999.
25. *See* Case C-200/97, *Ecotrade v. Altiforni and Ferriere di Servola*, 1.12.1998, ECLI:EU:C:1998:579 and Case C-295/97, *Industrie Aeronautiche e Meccaniche Rinaldo Piaggio SpA v. International Factors Italia SpA (Ifitalia), Dornier Luftfahrt GmbH and Ministero della Difesa ('Piaggio')*, 17.6.1999, ECLI:EU:C:1999:313.

In substance, the Court of Justice, far from holding that the Prodi Act was, by itself, tantamount to a national aid measure, ruled that this could only be the case when placing a firm under special administration and allowing it to continue trading did entail an additional burden for the State, compared to the situation that would have arisen had the usual insolvency rules been applied. As this implied an assessment of actual facts, it was for the national courts to make a determination.

In its later *Piaggio* decision, the ECJ, after blaming the Commission for considering the measures under the Prodi Act to be rather existing aid than new aid, endorsed the purport of the *Piaggio* judgment, much as, based on the *Lorenz* precedent, it specified that:

> since it is established that a system such as that established by Law No. 95/79 is in itself capable of giving rise to the grant of State aid within the meaning of Article 92(1) of the Treaty (now Article 107(2) TFEU), that system cannot be put into operation unless it has been notified to the Commission and, if it has been so notified, before the Commission has made a decision acknowledging that the aid plan is compatible with the common market, or, if the Commission takes no decision within a period of two months from the notification, before that period has expired.

The two judgments quoted above have raised some interpretational issues. In particular, according to one interpretation, the Court appears to have held that, failing notification to the Commission, the Prodi Act itself ought to be disapplied.[26] Even the Tribunal of Genoa, in delivering its reference order concerning *Rinaldo Piaggio*, expressed the belief that contravention to the Treaty was enough to rule out the applicability of the Prodi Act altogether:

> also in connection with insolvency proceedings (...) and, in particular, with the applicability of the provisions relating to the setting-aside of the acts contemplated in Article 67 of the Insolvency Act.[27]

Conversely, when the *Piaggio* judgment is read throughout, it emerges that the ECJ intended to re-affirm the judgment it had delivered in the *Ecotrade* case, in the sense that it did not oppose Act No. 96/1979 as a whole, but just those individual provisions thereof which it believed actually apt to result in an additional burden for the public authorities. This is quite clearly evidenced by the statement that:

26. In this sense, Giorgio Tarzia, *Disapplicazione della legge Prodi per contrasto con la disciplina comunitaria*, in *Fallimento*, p. 517 (2000); Edoardo Staunovo Polacco, *'La Legge Prodi' dopo la decisione della Commissione* CE 16 *maggio* 2000 *e gli altri provvedimenti degli organi comunitari*, in *Fallimento*, p. 464 (2001); Luigi Costato, *La legge Prodi e la Corte di giustizia*, in *Studium iuris*, p. 156 (2001). In this comment the author considered that the European Court of Justice – which could not declare, in a preliminary reference procedure ex Art. 234 EC (now Art. 267 TFEU), the Prodi Act to be contrary to the EC Treaty (now TFEU) – acted within its power according to that procedure in order to obtain the same practical result.
27. *See* Court of Genoa of 15 Nov. 1999, *Giur. comm.*, 2000, II, c. 47.

> if it were in fact established that the State or public bodies were among the principal creditors of the undertaking in difficulties, all the more so because, by definition, that undertaking owes debts of considerable value.[28]

Nonetheless, the two national courts that ordered reference in the *Ecotrade* and *Piaggio* cases (the Italian Supreme Court and the Tribunal of Genoa, respectively) reached different conclusions.

Based on its construction of the European Court of Justice's judgment in the *Ecotrade case*, The Italian Supreme Court held that:

> in order to determine whether the decree for admission to the [extraordinary administration] procedure can be identified as prohibited State 'aid' (...) and should be disapplied, the fact-finder must establish the circumstances surrounding the subjection of the firm to the procedure, examine the decree and the consequent acts that provided for advantages to be awarded to the firm, and compare the effects of extraordinary administration to those predictably arising from bankruptcy if the firm had been subjected thereto.[29]

Since such scrutiny involves an examination of the merits of the case and escapes ruling as to legitimacy, the Italian Supreme Court provided no assessment as to the lawfulness or unlawfulness of the Prodi Act.[30]

Conversely, the Tribunal of Genoa assumed (wrongly) that the European Community Court had considered Act No. 95/179 as a whole to be *new* aid not notified to the Commission, and accordingly ruled that the entire act should be disapplied. Hence, the judgment rejected the clawback action brought by the extraordinary administrator of the undertaking concerned.[31]

§8.05 THE COMMISSION'S DECISION OF 16 MAY 2002 ON THE PRODI ACT: SURVIVAL OF PRODI ACT PROVISIONS UNDER ARTICLE 106 OF LEGISLATIVE DECREE NO. 270 OF 8 JULY 1999

Just a few months after the second of the ECJ's two judgments quoted above about Act No. 95/1979, the Commission also expressed its view of the matter in Decision 2001/212/EC of 16 May 2000, clarifying the procedure initiated by its letter of 12 August 1999 (i.e., after Act No. 95 of 3 April 1979, as amended, had been repealed by

28. *See* Case C-200/97, *Ecotrade v. Altiforni, supra*, para. 41 and Case C-295/97, *Piaggio, supra*, para. 40.
29. *See* Italian Supreme Court, 11 Sep. 1999, n. 9681, *Fallimento*, 2000, p. 503.
30. *See* Court of Appeal of Trieste, 10 Feb. 2004, *Corr. giur.*, 2005, pp. 96 et seq., with a comment by Bruno Nascimbene, *Una disapplicazione 'condizionata' della legge Prodi?* pp. 98 et seq. In its judgment, after the referral made by the Italian Supreme Court, the Court of Appeal did not examine the legal case. On the contrary, it analysed the Prodi Act and decided that it was contrary to EC Law.
31. Some commentators have suggested a '*third way*'. It consists in the verification whether the decree of admission of the company to the procedure of extraordinary administration had been previously notified to the Commission. Yet, this criterion has not been used in the two mentioned judgments neither by the Italian Supreme Court nor by the Court of Genoa. On this topic *see* Giorgio Tarzia, *Disapplicazione della legge Prodi per contrasto con la disciplina comunitaria, supra*, p. 517.

Legislative Decree No. 270 of 8 July 1999), on the aid scheme implemented under that act, since it had deemed such scheme to be non-notified aid.[32] In its decision, the Commission stated that the first task was to identify, within the legal framework of Act No. 95/1979, the measures that were not general measures and then to decide whether they were covered by Article 87(1) of the EC Treaty (now Article 107(1) TFEU). In this connection, the Commission pointed out that the act under examination refers back, in certain respects, to the general rules of Italian bankruptcy law and, where it provides for the application without derogation of the latter's mechanisms, the mechanisms and procedures 'constitute general measures and are not in any way selective'. Further, in the Commission's view, the Prodi Act contained specific provisions, including the granting to identifiable recipients of a number of special advantages involving public resources. Such cases, and only such cases, would constitute State aid within the meaning of Article 87(1) EC Treaty.

The Commission then referred to the principles laid down in the *Ecotrade* judgment (the same principles as those set out in the *Piaggio* judgment) to conclude that some advantages arising from the Prodi Act constituted an aid scheme within the meaning of Article 87(1) EC Treaty. Thus, the decision of the Minister for Industry to place the firm in difficulties under extraordinary administration and to authorize it to continue trading could only be assumed to involve an additional burden for the public authorities if it were established that the State or other public bodies were among the chief creditors of that firm. True, the continuation of the bankrupt's economic activity is also provided for under the ordinary bankruptcy procedure, but the extraordinary administration procedure may well involve the risk that the State if it were one of the firm's chief creditors, might intentionally waive its claims for reasons of general economic policy. Even more so as, in this case, the condition of selectivity or specificity, which is one of the necessary requirements of the State aid notion, would be fully met, in view of the special class of undertakings covered (large firms in crisis) and of the wide scope for discretion enjoyed by the Minister for Industry under the Prodi Act.[33]

The Commission, as well as the Court of Justice before it, also identified the following advantages in the Prodi Act, which it regarded as incompatible with the common market:

(1) the grant of a State guarantee under Article 2*bis* of the Prodi Act;
(2) extension of the prohibition and suspension of all individual actions for enforcement to tax debts and penalties, interest and increases in cases of belated payment of company tax pursuant to Article 4 of Act No. 544/1981;
(3) exemption from the obligation to pay fines and pecuniary penalties in the case of failure to pay social security contributions pursuant to Act No. 19 of 6 February 1987; and

32. OJ L 79/29, 2001.
33. *See* Case C-241/94, *France v. Commission*, 26.9.1996, ECLI:EU:C:1996:353, paras 23-24. *See also*, Case C-200/97, *Ecotrade v. Altiforni, supra*, para. 40; Case C-295/97, *Piaggio, supra*, para. 39 and Commission Decision, point 53.

(4) application of a preferential rate where all or part of the firm is transferred pursuant to Article 5*bis* of the Prodi Act.

In examining the issue of compatibility by derogation, the Commission ruled that the derogations in Article 87(2) and (3) EC Treaty (now Article 107(2) and (3) TFEU) were clearly not applicable in the case of Act No. 95/1979.

Yet, much as the application of derogations had been ruled out and the case involved unlawful (non-notified) aid, the Commission avoided delivering an order to recover the aid granted under the scheme on account of the legitimate expectation the scheme had created.

Even more exceptional, in light of the Commission's practice, was that legitimate expectations were recognized not only to the undertakings concerned but also to the State that had issued an aid scheme - one not even notified, in fact. However, the Commission had erroneously created the legitimate expectation that the aid under the Prodi Act was existing aid, as itself conceded at points 72 and 73 of Decision 2001/212/EC, in addition to having in fact protracted its review of the legislation involved for over twenty years.

It should be noted that, as the Commission itself acknowledged, the aid scheme under Act 95/1979 had been abolished by Legislative Decree No. 270/1999, pending the examination procedure, even prior to the opening of infringement proceedings.

Lastly, Article 2 of the conclusions of the Decision tersely reads:

> the scheme ... is unlawful and incompatible with the common market.

Merely reading the conclusions of the Decision might lead one to believe that the Commission took a more restrictive stance than the European Court of Justice had taken. The laconic phrase quoted above has, in fact, been understood by some to convey a condemnation of the entire set of rules provided for by the Prodi Act, without exceptions.[34] This view is by no means justified if one considers the reasons for the Decision, particularly the sentences in which the Commission qualified the scope of its assessment by distinguishing between general measures, deemed to be consistent with bankruptcy law principles and, as such, lawful, and *specific* provisions that, however, constituted a prohibited aid scheme.

In fact, the selective approach is only one in line with the Commission's role in the matter of State aid. For the Commission may only, lest it should incur misuse of power, require the annulment of any individual rules of domestic law it may deem to clash with the provisions of Articles 87 et seq. of the EC Treaty (now Articles 107 et seq. TFEU). Once the disapplication of Act 95/1979 as a whole has been ruled out, what remains to do is to identify which provisions in that legislation do not constitute State aid measures in the Commission's and the ECJ's view, and to preserve the applicability of the rules that are distinctive of the Italian extraordinary administration procedure and are not derogations from the general provisions of bankruptcy law.

34. *See* Edoardo Staunovo Polacco, *'La Legge Prodi' dopo la decisione della Commissione* CE 16 *maggio* 2000 *e gli altri provvedimenti degli organi comunitari*, *supra*, p. 464.

Due consideration should also be given to the relevance the principle of legitimate expectation has, as the Commission itself has conceded, for national authorities called upon to implement the Commission's decision.[35]

The decision here under scrutiny was not impugned by the Italian State. The issue of how it should be implemented arose, however, in connection with extraordinary administration proceedings still pending, because of the 'ultra-activity' (survival of provisions) of Act No. 95/1979 pursuant to Article 106 of Legislative Decree No. 270/1999.

In this respect, Italian case law has taken different views as to the effects of the Commission's decision, i.e., as to determine which provisions of the Prodi Act the Italian courts ought to disapply, in their being in contrast with European Community legislation, as opposed to the provisions still deemed compatible.

A minority approach in Italian case law, based on the assumption that the Commission had finally established the clash of the entire Act No. 95/1979 with the European Community State aid rules, has resulted in its being *disapplied in its entirety*.[36]

A different group of judgments have, more correctly – in line with the Italian Supreme Court's view following the ECJ's *Ecotrade* judgment – held that the incompatibility of the Prodi Act with the European Community rules does not affect the relevant legislation as a whole, but only the *individual provisions* under which the incompatible aid was put into effect.[37]

---

35. As for the application of the principle of legitimate expectations *see* Case T-326/07, *Cheminova and Others v. Commission*, 3.9.2009, ECLI:EU:T:2009:299, and Case T-145/06, *Omya v. Commission*, 4.2.2009, ECLI:EU:T:2009:27; specifically on State aid *see* Case C-382/99, *The Netherlands v. Commission*, 13.6.2002, ECLI:EU:C:2002:363.
36. Beyond the above mentioned decision of the Court of Genoa, 15 Nov. 1999, *see* in the same sense: Court of Trieste, 2 May 2001, *Fallimento*, 2001, pp. 1167 et seq. with a comment by Adelmo Cavalaglio, *Requiem per la Prodi: ... e adesso?* pp. 1168 et seq.; Court of Trieste, 14 Jan. 2002, *Fallimento*, 2002, p. 441, with a comment by Giorgio Tarzia, *Il regime transitorio della nuova legge sull'amministrazione straordinaria al vaglio della Corte di Giustizia CE*, pp. 450 et seq.; Court of Padova, 28 Jun. 2002, *Fallimento*, 2003, pp. 645 et seq., with a comment by Filippo Lamanna, *Incompatibilità tra il 'regime di aiuti di Stato' introdotto dall'ex 'legge Prodi' e la normativa comunitaria: disapplicazione ed effetti conseguenti*, pp. 647 et seq. With these decisions national Judges have rejected the clawback request proposed by the commissioner or they have emitted a decision not to proceed. There are also some decisions in which judges affirmed the need to transmit *ex officio* acts of the cause to Bankruptcy Courts (*Tribunale Fallimentare*), according to Art. 8 of Insolvency Law, in all cases of misapplication of the law. In the same sense *see also*: Court of Genoa, 6 Apr. 2001 and Court of Trieste, 8 Apr. 2001, *Banca, borsa tit. cred.*, 2001, II, pp. 732 et seq. *See also* Court of Trieste, 14 Jan. 2002. Concerning opposition to the passive state of the procedure of extraordinary administration, in order not to consider admissible, *see* Court of Lecco, 6 Mar. 2002, *Fallimento*, 2002, pp. 1141 et seq. In the same sense, *see also*, Court of Genoa, 31 May 2003, *Foro it.*, 2003, *Rep. sub, Liquidazione coatta amministrativa*, n. 68; Court of Appeal of Venezia, 26 Jun. 2003, *Fallimento*, 2004, pp. 566 et seq.; Court of Appeal of Trieste, 10 Feb. 2004, Corr. giur., 2005, pp. 96 et seq.
37. In the same sense, *see* Court of Turin, 22 Jun. 2000, *Fallimento*, 2001, pp. 691 et seq., with a comment by Pierdomenico De Gioia- Carabellese, *Compatibilità della legge fallimentare con la disciplina comunitaria*, pp. 694 et seq.; Court of Turin, 7 Jul. 2000, *Giur. it.*, 2001, c. 776 et seq.; Court of Turin, 11 Sep. 2000, *Giur. it.*, 2000, c. 1304; Court of Turin, 31 Oct. 2000, *Giur. it.*, 2000, c. 484 et seq.; Court of Turin, 24 Jan. 2001, *Giur. it.*, 2002, c. 1007 et seq.; Court of Turin, 22 Jan. 2002, *Giur. it.*, 2002, c. 787 et seq.; Court of Appeal of Turin, 12 Feb. 2002 and 23 May 2002, *Giur.*

Thus, it should not come as a surprise that an additional order of reference for a preliminary ruling on the Prodi Act was submitted to the European Court, specifically concerning the 'ultra-activity' of law pursuant to Article 106 of Legislative Decree No. 270/1999.[38] This was what the Tribunal of Catania did, raising doubts as to whether the previous provisions of law should be disapplied without first establishing whether the transitional scheme was or was not compatible with Community law. It did so by addressing two, almost identical, orders of reference to the ECJ on 16 July and 21 October 2001, requesting answers to the following questions:

(1) whether following the interpretation of Articles 87 et seq. of the EC Treaty (now Articles 107 et seq. TFEU), the transitional scheme laid down by Article 106 of Legislative Decree No. 270/1999 constitutes a new aid scheme;
(2) whether, once the scheme in question has been qualified either as new State aid or as the modification of an existing aid scheme, it might be regarded as compatible with the Treaty; and, lastly
(3) whether the transitional scheme might be regarded as compatible with the Treaty in light of the general principles of European Community law and, in particular, the principles of legal certainty and the protection of legitimate expectations, the principles of non-discrimination and proportionality and the principle of effectiveness.

---

comm., 2003, II, c. 351, with a brief comment by Luca Jeantet, '*Legge Prodi*': *aiuto di Stato integrale ed effettivo ovvero parziale? Il dibattito prosegue*, pp. 359 et seq.; Court of Appeal of Turin, 4 Apr. 2002, *Giur. it.*, 2003, c. 729; Court of Turin, 19 Jan. 2005, *Giur. it.*, 2005, c. 510 et seq. *See also*, with partially different reasoning, Court of Bologna, 8 Feb. 2001, Court of Piacenza, 17 Jan. 2001 and Court of Appeal of Venezia, 12 Mar. 2001, *Banca, borsa tit. cred.*, 2001, II, pp. 733 et seq., with a comment by Vigo and Macrì; Court of Piacenza, 9 Jul. 2001, *Dir. comm.*, 2001, pp. 2092 et seq., with a comment by Angelo Bertolotti, *Non ha fine il tormentato rapporto della legge Prodi con le norme comunitarie*; Court of Appeal of Bari, 30 Jan. 2002, *Fallimento*, 2002, pp. 2092 et seq. *See also* Court of Milan, 19 Mar. 2003, *Foro it.*, 2003, *Rep.*, *Liquidazione coatta amministrativa*, n. 64; Court of Bologna, 6 Apr. 2004, not edited. In the same direction, with reference to the Marzano Act, *see Tribunale amministrativo regionale del Lazio* (hereinafter, TAR Lazio), 12 Jul. 2004, n. 6805 and TAR Lazio, 16 Jul. 2004, n. 6998, *Foro it.*, 2004, III, c. 615, with a comment by Massimo Fabiani. This author analyses the theme of possible competence conflicts among insolvency procedures in different countries with reference to European Community Regulation n. 1346/2000 on insolvency procedures. Concerning this topic *see* Patrizia De Cesari, *Diritto internazionale privato dell'Unione europea*, pp. 255 et seq. (Turin, 2011); Stefania Bariatti, *Filling in the Gaps of EC Conflicts of Law Instruments: the Case of Jurisdiction over Actions Related to Insolvency Proceedings* (Venturini, Bariatti eds), *Nuovi strumenti del diritto internazionale privato*, pp. 23 et seq. (Milan, 2009); and Luigi Carbone, *Il Regolamento* (CE) 1346/2000 *relativo alle procedure di insolvenza* (Carbone, Frigo, Fumagalli eds), *Diritto processuale civile e commerciale comunitario*, pp. 89 et seq. (Milan, 2004). Finally, for a 'reasoned' application of the Prodi Act, in the sense of excluding only those cases whose benefits were incompatible with the EC law, *see* judgments of the Italian Supreme Court, 19 Mar. 2004, n. 5561, *Foro it. Mass.*, 2004, p. 405; Italian Supreme Court, 21 Sep. 2004, n. 18915, *Foro it.*, 2004, I, c. 3310 et seq.; Italian Supreme Court, 10 Nov. 2005, n. 21823, *Fallimento*, 2006, pp. 779 et seq.; Italian Supreme Court, 24 Feb. 2006, n. 4206, *Fallimento*, 2006, pp. 771 et seq., both with a comment by Massimo Cataldo, *Amministrazione straordinaria delle grandi imprese in stato di insolvenza e disciplina della concorrenza nella Comunità europea*, pp. 790 et seq.

38. In this sense, *see* the orders of referral of the Court of Catania of 16 Jul. 2001, *Banca, borsa tit. cred.*, 2001, II, pp. 733 et seq. and of 22 Oct. 2001, *Foro it.*, 2002, I, c. 3242 et seq., with a comment by Cosio.

Regardless of any comments as to how these questions were set out (both orders appear to be misstated, in that the last two questions asked the European Court to enter a ruling on the compatibility of a specific aid scheme with the common market, much as any such ruling falls within the exclusive competence of the Commission or the Council), such questions did not reflect the real issue, which was to determine in fact whether which provisions of Act No. 95/1979 derogated from the rules of bankruptcy law, and, once these had been identified, which of them could be deemed to be caught by the notion of 'State aid scheme'.

§8.06 THE ECJ'S ORDERS OF 24 JULY 2003 AND 27 JANUARY 2004: THE SCOPE OF THE TRANSITIONAL SCHEME

By its orders of 24 July 2003 and 27 January 2004, the European Court of Justice answered the questions in the Tribunal of Catania's orders of reference, by ruling that the transitional rules introduced by Article 106 of Legislative Decree No. 270/1999, in extending the applicability of a new aid scheme – as the one contained in Act No. 95/1979 had already considered to be by the Court's case law –, in themselves constituted a new aid scheme, which ought to be notified, as such, to the Commission pursuant to Article 88(3) EC Treaty (now Article 108(3) TFEU).[39]

Such a ruling appears incorrect. For neither Article 106 of Legislative Decree No. 270/1999, extending Act 95/1979 in respect of extraordinary administration procedures still pending, nor the reference later made by Article 7 of Act No. 273/ 2002 to Article 106 should be considered to convey *new* State aid. For they confirm the applicability of the Prodi Act *solely* in respect of existing extraordinary administration procedures. What was involved was, therefore, a mere *prorogatio* granted to undertakings that had already benefited from the applicable special legislation, i.e., recipients previously determined and identified. The notion of a 'new aid scheme' is, instead, contingent upon the abstract, *pro-futuro* character of the State measure involved.[40]

Moreover, the ECJ failed to consider that the provisions of law relating to extraordinary administration procedures pending on the date of entry into force of Article 106 of Legislative Decree No. 270/1999 (8 July 1999, that is) were already covered at European Community level by the previous decision of the Commission of

39. *See* the ECJ Order, 24 Jul. 2003 in Case C-297/01, *Sicilcassa S.p.A. v. IRA Costruzioni S.p.A. and others*, 24.7.2003, ECLI:EU:C:2003:416. On 27 Jan. 2004, the ECJ delivered another order to answer to the Court of Catania's referrals. The operative part of this order, Case C-428/01, *Fratelli Costanzo v. Elettrica S.p.A.*, 22.6.1989, ECLI:EU:C:1989:256, is the same of the *Sicilcassa* case.

40. *See* Mario Barcellona, *Amministrazione straordinaria e aiuti di Stato: sulla compatibilità della disciplina transitoria dell'art.* 106, *d.lgs.* n. 270/1999 *con gli artt.* 87 *e* 88 *del Trattato* CE, in *Europa e diritto privato*, 1, pp. 228 et seq. (2002). In the sense of the superfluity of the preliminary reference *see* Giorgio Tarzia, *Il regime transitorio della nuova legge sull'amministrazione straordinaria al vaglio della Corte di Giustizia CE, supra*, p. 454, in which the author supports the thesis of the misapplication *in toto* of the Prodi Act and therefore of the transitory regime. *See also* Court of Trieste, 14 Jan. 2002, *Fallimento*, 2002, p. 441.

16 May 2000.[41] Lastly, as aptly argued by the Italian government in the observations it submitted during the proceedings before the European Court of Justice, Article 7 of Act No. 273/2002 offered the correct interpretation of Article 106 of Legislative Decree No. 270/1999, when it observed that the effects of Law No. 95/79, retained by Article 106 of Legislative Decree No. 270/99, related only to the procedural aspects of a liquidation, not to the part of the law that instituted the State aid held to be incompatible with the Treaty. This observation seems to have been endorsed by the ECJ, which held that it was for the referring national court to establish the scope of Article 106 of Legislative Decree No. 270/99, 'if necessary, in light of Article 7 of Law No. 273/2002'.[42]

The European Court deemed the second and third questions referred to be inadmissible, in that they were intended to ask the Court for an assessment of the compatibility of an aid scheme with the common market – an assessment falling, as indicated above, within the exclusive competence of the Commission.

The following considerations can be drawn from the relevant orders of the Court of Justice:

- the extension of aid formerly granted under the Prodi Act to undertakings involved in extraordinary administration procedures pending on the date of entry into force of Article 106 of Legislative Decree No. 270/1999 was not deemed to clash with the Decision of the Commission of 16 May 2000, whereby 'the Commission expressly declined to require recovery of aid granted under Law No. 95/79, even though it regarded such aid as incompatible with the common market';[43]
- the Court then requested the national court, based on the direct applicability of Article 88(3) EC (now Article 108(3) TFEU), to order the recovery of any aid granted under Act No. 95/79 *after the Prodi Act was repealed*, even if granted to undertakings already in special administration when Legislative Decree No. 270/99 entered into force;[44] and
- therefore, the national court is expected to apply selectively, not to disapply, the extension at issue. Besides, the Court clarified, in its order, that the national court called upon to interpret the relevant extension provision (and, if necessary, of Article 7 of Act No. 273/2002) must do so, in so far as possible, consistently with Community law and having regard also for the judgment in *Piaggio* (...) and Decision 2001/212.[45]

41. In the same sense, Mario Barcellona, *Amministrazione straordinaria e aiuti di Stato, supra*, pp. 217-218; Ornella Porchia, *L'esecuzione degli obblighi comunitari da parte delle autorità nazionali: il caso della legge Prodi*, in *Contratto e Impresa/Europa*, pp. 745 et seq. (2002).
42. *See* the ECJ Order of 24 Jul. 2003 (para. 44).
43. *Ibid.*, at para. 40.
44. *Ibid.*, (para. 42).
45. *Ibid.*, at para. 44.

§8.07 THE PROVISIONS IN THE PRODI ACT THAT HAVE BEEN CONSIDERED STATE AID AS OPPOSED TO THOSE DEEMED LAWFUL: HOW THAT DISTINCTION IS REFLECTED IN THE MARZANO ACT

As observed above, only some of the provisions of Act No. 95/1979, as specifically detailed by the ECJ and referred to by the Commission, were deemed to be incompatible with Community law. For each such provision gave the recipients advantages that, in the Commission's view, amounted to a State aid scheme in their being realistically apt to generate an additional burden for the public authorities.

The issue now appears to be greatly simplified if the approach that considers such advantages to be denied extension under Article 106 of Legislative Decree No. 270/1999 is accepted.[46] Under this approach, neither the 'new' extraordinary administration procedures nor those still 'pending', within the meaning of the *first* Prodi Act, would enjoy such advantages 'at risk'.

As for the prohibition on individual actions for enforcement (for any debts other than tax liabilities) following the decree opening an extraordinary administration procedure, it must be observed that such prohibition, in its being intended for the protection of the general body of creditors, represents a *common* rule among the general rules of bankruptcy law and it is not, accordingly, apt to generate a burden on State resources. In the words of the Court of Justice:

> the possible loss of tax revenue for the State as a result of the application of the system of special administration, on account of the absolute prohibition on individual actions for enforcement and the suspension of interest on all debts owed by the undertaking in question, and the correlated reduction in creditors' profits (...).

is a consequence deemed to be:

> an inherent feature of any statutory system laying down a framework for relations between an insolvent undertaking and the general body of creditors.

without serving as a justifiable reason to infer automatically that an additional financial burden has been generated.[47]

Specifically in respect of clawback actions in bankruptcy (*revocatoria fallimentare*) under Italian law, it is appropriate to state at the outset that even the European Court of Justice, in its *Piaggio* judgment, expressly conceded the nonselective character of such actions, in their being a common feature of the ordinary insolvency procedure.[48]

---

46. In this sense, *see* Mario Barcellona, *Amministrazione straordinaria e aiuti di Stato, supra*, pp. 210 et seq.
47. *See* Case C-200/97, *Ecotrade v. Altiforni, supra*, para. 36, which refers to Joined Cases C-72/91 and C-73/91, *Sloman Neptun*, 17.3.1993, ECLI:EU:C:1993:97, para. 21.
48. *See* Case C-295/97, *Piaggio, supra* (para. 26). *See also* the Opinion of the Advocate General Ruiz-Jarabo Colomer of 4 Mar. 1999, in Case C-295/97, *Piaggio, supra* (para. 22): 'The fact that the payments made during that period are ineffective has nothing to do with the insolvency

That is why I entirely share settled case law based on the decision whereby the Commission departed from the judgment of the Tribunal of Genoa in *Piaggio* to reject both the 'Community objection' to the entire Act No. 95/1979 and the objection to the admissibility of clawback actions. According to these precedents, bringing clawback actions is not State aid if, once the firm's business operations have ceased under the relevant ministerial decree, the procedure becomes *comparable to a liquidation procedure*.[49] Nor could the exclusion of clawback actions be justified within the scope of a procedure now solely designed to liquidate the debtor's assets in order to satisfy the body of creditors – thus being in no way different from a clawback action brought in ordinary bankruptcy proceedings.[50]

A conclusion similar to that of the 'selective' application of the Prodi Act by national courts can also be reached through the application of the general principles of European Union law, specifically the principle of the protection of legitimate expectations.[51] This principle is worth being also upheld before national courts when the Commission's decisions on State aid are to be enforced, though only under exceptional circumstances.

That the circumstances were exceptional in the case of the Prodi Act was expressly recognized by the Commissions at points 70-73 of its decision of 16 May 2000, where it held it could not order the recovery of the aid on account of the legitimate expectation of the Italian authorities, as well as that of the recipient undertakings, that the aid was existing aid.

Now, the choice made by some Italian courts to disapply all pending extraordinary administration procedures is paradoxically tantamount to ordering silent recovery of a sort of aid already awarded – a recovery that, in fact, the Commission had intentionally declined to order.

The Court of Justice itself confirmed such a view in its *Sicilcassa* order, where it referred to aid granted under the Prodi Act until the entry into force of Legislative Decree No. 270/1999 to rule that:

---

procedure, whether ordinary or extraordinary, since it is a general measure found in the majority of insolvency systems. The declaration that such payments are ineffective is therefore completely extraneous to the particular characteristics of extraordinary administration provided for in the special Italian law.'

49. *See* Court of Turin, 22 Jun. 2000, *Fallimento*, 2001, pp. 691 et seq. The reference to a 'biphasic' structure (managerial-conservative phase and liquidative phase) is connected to principle enounced by *the* Italian Supreme Court, 27 Dec. 1996, n. 11519, *Giust. civ.*, 1997, I, c. 3129, with a comment by D'Alessandro, confirmed also by the Italian Supreme Court, 23 Jun. 2000, n. 8539, *Foro it.*, 2001, I, c. 1302, with a comment by Anselmo Barone e Massimo Fabiani, *La difficile convivenza della revocatoria fallimentare con l'amministrazione straordinaria*.
50. On this topic, but with reference to a case of compulsory winding up, *see* Case C-362/89, *D'Urso e altri v. Ercole Marelli Elettromeccanica Generale S.p.A. and Others*, 25.7.1991, ECLI: EU:C:1991:326, para. 31. *See also* Italian Supreme Court, 21 Sep. 2004, n. 18915, for which the clawback action, in the procedure of extraordinary administration, does not represent a State aid if it is promoted after the liquidation phase has begun.
51. Concerning the importance of principles in the European Union practice *see*, Roberto Adam e Antonio Tizzano, *Manuale di diritto dell'Unione europea*, pp. 123 et seq. (Turin, 2022); Giuseppe Tesauro, *Manuale di diritto dell'Unione europea*, pp. 170 et seq. (edited by De Pasquale and Ferraro, Naples, 2021); Girolamo Strozzi e Roberto Mastroianni, *Diritto dell'Unione europea, Parte istituzionale*, pp. 213 et seq. (Turin, 2013).

> it is for the national court to decide whether, by reason of the fact that it has not been notified, any such new aid should be recovered or not. In this connection, the national court will take account of the general principles of its internal law, including the principle of the protection of legitimate expectations, the circumstances of the case and especially Decision 2001/212.[52]

It should also be stressed that recovering an aid scheme that has already generated most of its effects is apt to alter the marketplace equilibrium even more deeply than maintaining it in operation.[53]

In light of the foregoing considerations about the compatibility of the Prodi Act with Community law, it is now possible to offer some reflections on the same subject with respect to the Marzano Act.[54]

It must first be observed that the four advantages identified by the Commission in connection with Act No. 95/1979 were undoubtedly State aid in a technical sense (*see* §8.05, above).

By the Marzano Act, the provisions of the Prodi-*bis* Act that had led the Commission to establish incompatibility were set aside. In fact, as indicated above, the body of rules newly introduced seems to have been a result of negotiations between the Commission and the Italian State, precisely with a view to making the relevant national legislation compatible with the Community rules governing State aid.

The objectives of the Marzano Act, as specified in the *Relazione* annexed thereto, are: (i) to permit faster commencement and completion of insolvency procedures for especially large firms; (ii) to ensure effective restructuring; and (iii) to pursue as well the preservation of that firm's goodwill and market position as its creditors' interests. As the Marzano Act was modelled on the Prodi-*bis* Act in many respects, it did not predictably contain elements likely to let it be regarded as an unlawful ad scheme within the meaning of Article 107(1).[55]

Furthermore, the Communication from the Commission of 2004 - *Community guidelines on State aid for rescuing and restructuring firms in difficulty* - substantially confirmed this point by the already cited new *Guidelines on State aid for rescuing and restructuring non-financial undertakings in difficulty* - specified that, for a restructuring aid to be approved, its grant must be made conditional on the implementation of a restructuring plan, the duration of which must be as short as possible, which must be endorsed by the Commission and made the object of the Commission's constant review

52. *See* the ECJ Order of 24 Jul. 2003, para. 41.
53. In Case C-295/97, *Piaggio, supra,* at para. 45, beyond legitimate expectations, the European Court of Justice also argued that 'the impossibility in practice of obtaining repayment of the sums which might be recoverable' would have induced the European Commission to qualify the State aid as 'existing'. On this issue, one must recall that case law has never upheld the ground concerning the absolute impossibility to recover an unlawful State aid. *See*, for all, Case C-404/97, *Commission v. Portugal,* 27.6.2000, ECLI:EU:C:2000:345.
54. On the compatibility between the Marzano Act and EC legislation and for a biography of works on these topics, *see* the comment of Massimo Fabiani to *TAR Lazio*, 12 Jul. 2004, n. 6805 and *TAR Lazio*, 16 Jul. 2004, n. 6998, both cited in n. 30.
55. Expressly in this direction, *see TAR Lazio*, 12 Jul. 2004, n. 6805, *supra*; on the lack of conflict, in principle, between Law Decree n. 347/2003 and EC legislation, *see also TAR Lazio*, 16 Jul. 2004, n. 6998, *supra*. Both decisions mention, in support of their reasoning, Commissioner Monti's declaration, dated 29 Jan. 2004, cited in §8.02 of this chapter.

based on regular detailed reports communicated by the Member State concerned. A further condition the new Guidelines of 2014, in line with the Commission's decision of 2000, seem to impose on the grant of a derogation, is that any aid actually awarded to a large enterprise must be notified *individually* to the Commission. For no awards of general rescue or restructuring aid schemes can be authorized by the Commission except in the case of small or medium-sized enterprises. In conclusion, even large enterprises may benefit, by individual notification, from the derogation indicated above, even where the measures provided for in a restructuring plan are categorized as State aid by the Commission.

No problems seem, however, to arise if the approach alternative to a restructuring plan is taken, i.e., the transfer of business complexes within the meaning of Article 27(2)(a) of Legislative Decree No. 270/1999, in which case notifying the Commission of the plan specifically drawn up by the special administrator seems to be unnecessary.

§8.08 CLAWBACK ACTIONS UNDER THE MARZANO ACT: THE PARMALAT CASE

A quite different line of reasoning should be followed in examining the rules governing clawback actions, which are permitted by the Marzano Act, insofar as clawback results in advantages for the firm's creditors. In particular, Article 49(1) of Legislative Decree 270/1999 (the Prodi-*bis* Act) provides that:

> any actions to be brought for any acts prejudicial to creditors to be declared unenforceable and set aside, as provided for in Section III, Chapter III of Title I of the Bankruptcy Act, may only be proposed by the extraordinary commissioner if the implementation of a plan for the transfer of business complexes has been authorized except in the case of conversion of the procedure in bankruptcy.

In the terms of this provision, a clawback action brought within the scope of an extraordinary administration procedure is by no means different from an action brought under the usual rules of insolvency law.[56]

The first version of the Marzano Act, however, permitted clawback actions to be brought even within the scope of a firm's restructuring plan, provided they were aimed, in the creditors' best interests, at accomplishing the goals of the plan. Yet, that particular provision was quite ambiguously worded as far as the relationship between the creditors' interests and the accomplishment of the goals of the plan was concerned. This ambiguity was soon detected by the law-makers, whose revised, final text of the act provides that:

> the extraordinary commissioner may bring any of the clawback actions provided for in Articles 49 and 91 of Legislative Decree No. 270, even in case the

56. On the EC legitimacy of clawback action in the scheme considered, *see* Italian Supreme Court, 21 Sep. 2004, n. 18915 and Italian Supreme Court, 10 Mar. 2006, n. 5301, *Foro it.*, 2006, I, c. 1639 et seq.

implementation of the restructuring plan has been authorized, insofar as they result in an advantage for creditors.[57]

Thus, it was the law-makers' intention that clawback actions should be essentially regarded as an asset-reinforcing tool to satisfy the firm's creditors, and they were no longer referred to as an asset-reinforcing tool apt to permit the continuation of a business activity that would otherwise have come to an end.[58]

The persisting ambiguity of how the provision quoted above was worded did not escape the attention of the parties affected by the many clawback actions the extraordinary administrator of the Parmalat Group had brought. The defendant organizations in such actions raised some preliminary objections as to the incompatibility of the entire Marzano Act, or its Article 6, with Articles 87 and 88(3) (now Articles 107 and 108(3) TFEU) and/or Articles 3, 10 and 82 (now Articles 3-6 TFEU, Article 4, paragraph 3 TEU and Article 102 TFEU), as well as the unconstitutional character of Article 6 of the Marzano Act under Articles 3 and 41 of the Italian Constitution.[59]

By its judgment dated 18 November 2005 in Action RGN 117/2005, the Tribunal of Parma held – contrary to the prevailing approach that the 'Community argument' should take precedence over the constitutional argument – that the issue of the constitutional lawfulness of Article 6 of the Marzano Act was relevant and not manifestly ungrounded in relation to Articles 3 and 41 of the Italian Constitution, to the extent Article 6 permitted the clawback actions provided for in Articles 49 and 91 of Legislative Decree No. 270/1999 to be brought even in case the firm concerned was being restructured and its business operations allowed to continue.[60]

Specifically in respect of Article 3 of the Constitution, the Tribunal of Parma held that the principle of equal treatment prevented the law-makers from arbitrarily discriminating between persons in identical or comparable conditions (i.e., an undertaking subject to the Prodi-*bis* Act as opposed to one subject to the Marzano Act in the case at issue).

In respect of Article 41 of the Constitution, the Tribunal of Parma held that discretion in bringing clawback actions in implementing a restructuring plan compounded the unreasonable purport of the provision in question, because of the unequal treatment of undertakings operating in the marketplace, which clashed with the principle of free competition laid down in Article 41.[61]

---

57. *See* Art. 6, para. 1, of the Marzano Act.
58. On this topic, Lino Guglielmucci, *Lezioni di diritto fallimentare*, pp. 382 et seq. (Turin, 2014).
59. The Marzano Act was adopted in order to save the Parmalat Group. According to press news, clawback actions, brought by Parmalat in extraordinary administration period, against many banks, had the aim to recover about EUR 7.5 billion.
60. *See* Court of Parma, 18 Nov. 2005, *Fallimento*, 2006, p. 277. On the priority of the EU exception on the 'constitutional' one, *see* Giuseppe Tesauro, *Diritto dell'Unione europea*, pp. 301 et seq. (Padua, 2012); *see also* the Order of the Italian Constitutional Court 9 Nov. 2011, n. 298, *GU 1 st Special Series – Consitutional Court*, 2011, n. 48; previously *see* Marta Maria Carla Cartabia, *Considerazioni sulla posizione del giudice comune di fronte a casi di 'doppia pregiudizialità'*, in *Foro it.*, V, c. 222 et seq. (1997).
61. This procedure concerns Parmalat S.p.A. in extraordinary administration and HSBC Bank plc. By Order of 27 Dec. 2005, the Court of Parma raised the same questions of not constitutionality with

With unprecedented rapidity, the Italian Constitutional Court adjudicated these objections as unconstitutionality in its Judgment No. 172 of 21 April 2006, whereby it held such objections to be ungrounded. As for the issue relating to Article 3 of the Constitution, the Constitutional Court preliminary stated that the argument that it was for the insolvent debtor alone to choose whether to rely on the Marzano Act or on the Prodi-*bis* Act was not supported by any provision of law. It was deemed to be so because the insolvent undertaking's petition must first pass the Ministry for Industry's screening (with a view to the decree for admission to the procedure) and then the Tribunal's (with a view to the declaration of insolvency). According to the Italian Constitutional Court, such a process did not affect the requisite control guarantees, and the decision as to which procedure should be applied was only contingent on the requirements as to the size it was expected to meet.

On this basis, the Italian Constitutional Court pointed out that the Marzano Act provided, in fact, for an array of different sub-proceedings within the scope of those available under the Prodi-*bis* Act. The latter pursues the objective of preserving the debtor's productive assets through either a business transfer plan or a restructuring plan. In particular, the purpose of a restructuring plan is to allow the insolvent undertaking to recover its ability to discharge its obligations as and when due. The Marzano Act, though listing the insolvent debtor's willingness to rely on a restructuring plan among the requirements for admission to the extraordinary administration procedure, does not exclude the possibility for the restructuring process to evolve towards plans with a different purpose and different goals. Indeed, a restructuring plan may well be replaced with a plan for the transfer of the debtor's business complexes or, if no such plan appears feasible, the undertaking concerned may be declared bankrupt.

Within this context, composition arrangements may be entered into as provided for by Article 4*bis* of the Marzano Act, whereby a contracting third party (an *assuntore*) may be called upon to take over all of the insolvent undertaking's assets, along with an obligation to perform the relevant composition arrangements. In the alternative, no third party is involved or, at the very best, a third party may be asked to guarantee the fulfilment of any obligations the insolvent debtor has undertaken under the composition agreement. It was the Constitutional Court's view that the two approaches to composition with creditors correspond to those provided for in Article 124 of Royal Decree No. 267 of 16 March 1942 (the Italian Insolvency Law), which permits clawback actions to be assigned to a third-party contractor taking over the obligation to perform

reference to the procedure between Parmalat S.p.A. in extraordinary administration and other eighteen banks. The abovementioned questions were discussed before the Italian Constitutional Court on 4 Apr. 2006. Further orders of referral to the Italian Constitutional Court have been delivered by Court of Parma (always related to Parmalat facts), orders n. 95, 164, 165, 166, 328 and 329/2006, with reference to Arts 3 and 41 and 42 of the Italian Constitution. The Constitutional Court has rejected, even in these circumstances, the objections raised by the Court of Parma. *See* Constitutional Court, orders of 28 Dec. 2006, n. 456 and 5 Apr. 2007, n. 118, *Fallimento*, 2007, pp. 515 et seq.

the relevant composition arrangements from the bankrupt and the bankrupt's guarantors – thus even in the case of composition arrangements subject to a third party's guarantees.[62]

In conclusion, Article 6(1) of the Marzano Act must be construed in the sense that clawback actions are only admissible where the extraordinary administration procedure has evolved towards a liquidation of a sort, i.e., through either composition subject to a contracting party's guarantees (as in the Parmalat case) or the transfer of business complexes within the meaning of Article 27(2)(a) of the Prodi-*bis* Act, or else a bankruptcy declaration. No such action is, instead, permitted in any other case.

The Constitutional Court also rejected the objection as to constitutionality in relation to Article 41 of the Italian Constitution. In this connection, the Court held that the case of an undertaking being reorganized through a restructuring plan pursuant to the Prodi-*bis* Act was incomparable to the case of an undertaking being reorganized in composition through a contracting party pursuant to Article 4*bis* of the Marzano Act – which would, in fact, dispel the fear of unequal treatment between two comparable conditions. Furthermore, the insolvent undertaking would by no means have an opportunity to benefit from forced financing (on account of any moneys recovered through clawback actions), an opportunity that would result in distorting competition and impairing equal conditions between undertakings. This is because, in a composition through a contracting part as well as in bankruptcy, secured creditors must be satisfied in full. Unsecured creditors will, however:

> see their claims extinguished upon being paid what is stated in the proposal (accepted by them) for composition arrangements approved by the Tribunal. Thus, the fact that the proceeds from clawback actions cannot be apportioned – within the meaning of Articles 113 and 117 of the Insolvency Act in relation to distribution of moneys – among creditors is a natural feature of composition, which reflects the fact that the contracting party's proposal for settlement – as well as the acceptance thereof by creditors – is also benchmarked, where the agreement submitted to the creditors for approval provides for the assignment of clawback actions to the contracting party, to the predictable outcome of such actions, which are themselves part of the assets for which the contracting party has paid the agreed price.[63]

In substance, clawback actions in composition proceedings through a contracting party have been deemed to discharge both their redistributive function and their recovery function, and the argument that the proceeds there from would go rather to

62. The Italian Constitutional Court argued that the modifications of Bankruptcy Act introduced by Legislative Decree of 9 Jan. 2006, n. 5 provided for 'modalities of satisfaction of creditors identical to those provided by the Marzano Act'.

63. *See* Italian Constitutional Court, 21 Apr. 2006, with a comment by Matteo Rescigno, *Le leggi Parmalat al vaglio della Corte Costituzionale*, in *Corr. Giur.*, p. 1237 (2006); with a comment by Francesco Macario, *Compatibilità costituzionale delle azioni revocatorie promosse nel corso del piano di ristrutturazione dell'impresa in crisi e sistema della responsabilità patrimoniale: cronaca di una frattura annunciata?*, in *Banca, borsa*, II, p. 440 (2006); with a comment by Andrea Penta, *L'azione revocatoria fallimentare nell'Amministrazione straordinaria delle grandi imprese alla luce della recente sentenza n. 172 del 21 aprile 2006 della Corte costituzionale*, in *Dir. fall.*, II, p. 834 (2006).

shareholders than to creditors, seems to be irrelevant. For creditors, by approving composition arrangements, thereby forfeiting most of their claims, have accepted to become shareholders of a company into whose assets the proceeds from clawback actions would inevitably flow. Conversely, the third-party defendants in clawback actions claim the right to be treated on equal footing with composition creditors, thus to be satisfied to an equal extent.

Since the Marzano Act appears only to bring about such consequences, in the same way as the general provisions of insolvency law do in respect of composition through a contracting party, the relevant legislation seems to escape any objections as to unconstitutionality even in this respect.

§8.09 THOUGHTS ON JUDGMENT NO. 172 OF 21 APRIL 2006 BY THE ITALIAN CONSTITUTIONAL COURT

The Italian Constitutional Court's judgment outlined above - a core ruling for the implementation of the composition arrangements of the Tribunal of Parma endorsed by Judgment 22/2005, *Vol. Jurisd.*, of 1 October 2005 - does not, however, overcome all of the doubts arising from the wording of Article 6(1) of the Marzano Act. In particular, it should be noted that this provision was 'salvaged' by the Constitutional Court through a restrictive interpretation according to which no clawback actions should be permitted except in the cases specified above - composition through a contracting party among them.[64]

This interpretation has, however, been challenged in doctrine. For it has been objected that the composition arrangements contemplated in Article 4*bis* of the Marzano Act appear to belong to the restructuring plan and could not, accordingly, be counted among the ways in which the extraordinary administration procedure may evolve towards liquidation. This might, at most, result from the Tribunal denying endorsement to the composition agreement. Further, as to the assignment of clawback actions within the scope of composition arrangements, it has been observed that this would be contingent upon whether such actions can or cannot be brought beforehand, i.e., if the composition is one of the ways in which a liquidation plan, and not a restructuring plan, can be implemented - the divide being not whether or not a contracting party has been called in. Therefore the inequality of treatment between creditors and third parties under both the Marzano Act and the Prodi-*bis* Act appears to persist, contrary to the view taken by the Italian Constitutional Court, even in composition proceedings through a contracting party.[65]

---

64. Luciano Panzani, *Parità di trattamento tra creditori e tutela della concorrenza*, in *Fallimento*, pp. 761 et seq., in particular at p. 770 (2006) refers to a 'creative' interpretation, which somehow modifies the Marzano Act. In the same sense, *see* Stefano Poli, *Il giudizio di costituzionalità dell'art. 6 della 'legge Marzano': la Corte riconosce la legittimità delle revocatorie fallimentari nelle procedure di ' risanamento oggettivo'*, in *Corr. giur.*, pp. 1232 et seq. (2006).
65. *See*, in agreement, Giorgio Tarzia, *Amministrazione straordinaria delle grandi imprese in stato di insolvenza*, in *Dir. e pratica del fall.*, 3, pp. 45 et seq. (2006). For a criticism of clawback action in a reorganization procedure *see, previously*, Massimo Fabiani, *Dai pomodori ai latticini, ovvero dalla regola all'eccezione: un testo unico per l'amministrazione straordinaria e la gestione dei*

Finally, it has been objected that the assumption on which the Constitutional Court has grounded its conclusions is that clawback actions may not be brought so long as a restructuring plan is underway.[66]

In the light of both the findings set forth in the previous paragraphs of this Chapter and the interpretation of Article 6 offered by the Constitutional Court in its Judgment No. 172/2006, it should be stressed that the Marzano Act as such seems to not be conflicting with the EU rules governing State aid. For it has not introduced a special, selective scheme generating an undue advantage for the recipient undertakings, as has been confirmed in the (unusual) press release dated 29 January 2004 from the then-Commissioner for Competition, prof. Monti.

Likewise, it does not seem that a violation or threatened violation of Article 82 EC Treaty (now Article 102 TFEU), providing for the abuse of a dominant position within the internal market or in a substantial part of it, can be inferred merely from the requirements for the applicability of the Marzano Act to enterprises of a large size both in terms of numbers employed and in financial terms.

As for the rules applying to clawback actions, it is appropriate to start from decisions taken in Italian case law in the light of the European Court's rulings on the Prodi-*bis* Act, e.g., as follows:

> [Since] clawback actions in bankruptcy may, as a rule, be brought during insolvency proceedings, no selective character in the form of State aid may be deemed to exist where a clawback action is brought at the liquidation stage of the extraordinary administration procedure for the only purpose of protecting *par condicio creditorum* in the same way as in bankruptcy proceedings.[67]

Accordingly, the issue of whether or not the clawback action provided for by the Marzano Act is compatible with the EU rules governing State aid is settled upon the extraordinary administration procedure turning into bankruptcy, pursuant to Article 4(4) of the Marzano Act. The same occurs where a plan for the transfer of business complexes is adopted pursuant to Article 27(2)(a) of the Prodi-*bis* Act.

Even the case that led the Tribunal of Parma to issue the order of reference to the Italian Constitutional Court discussed above, i.e., the approval of a composition agreement in association with the transfer to a contracting party of the assets of the undertakings concerned, and the assignment to it of clawback actions, pursuant to

---

gruppi transnazionali, in *Foro it.* I, c. 1567 et seq. (2004). *See also*, Carmine Punzi, *Le procedure di amministrazione straordinaria nel sistema delle procedure concorsuali*, in *Dir. fall.*, I, pp. 268 et seq. (2005) and Edoardo Staunovo Polacco, *Art. 6. Azioni revocatorie* (Castagnola, Sacchi eds), *La legge Marzano. Commentario*, pp. 231 et seq. (Turin 2006). Again on the judgment of the Italian Constitutional Court, *see* the critical comment of Cottino, in *Giur. it.*, pp. 1423 et seq. (2006) and Matteo Rescigno, *Le leggi Parmalat al vaglio della Corte costituzionale*, *supra*, pp. 1237 et seq.

66. *See* Luciano Panzani, *Parità di trattamento tra creditori e tutela della concorrenza*, *supra*, p. 769.

67. *See* Italian Supreme Court, 21 Sep. 2004, n. 18915. *See also* Italian Supreme Court, 28 Oct. 2005, n. 21083, *Fallimento*, 2006, pp. 1162 et seq., with a comment by Patrizia De Cesari, *Amministrazione straordinaria, Aiuti di Stato – Revocatoria: la Cassazione torna a distinguere tra fase conservativa e liquidatoria*, in *Fallimento*, pp. 1168 et seq. (2006). Subsequently, the Italian Supreme Court underlined that also business concern transfer has a liquidation function (*see* Italian Supreme Court, 10 Mar. 2006, n. 5301, *Foro it.*, 2006, I, c. 1639 et seq.).

Article 4*bis* (1)(c) of the Marzano Act, was deemed by the Constitutional Court to be tantamount to liquidation. In the light, and within the boundaries, of such interpretation (though it has been challenged in doctrine, including in relation to the phase in which clawback actions were supposedly brought), bringing clawback actions in the cases offered above does not appear to meet the conditions under which a State aid can be identified. Moreover, no difference is to be found in this respect with the case of a clawback action brought within the scope of a transfer plan pursuant to the Prodi-*bis* Act – which the European Commission has not contested so far.[68]

§8.10 AMENDMENTS TO THE MARZANO ACT, DECISIONS BY THE COMMISSION AND JUDGMENTS BY THE EUROPEAN COURTS RELATING TO ALITALIA

When Italy's national carrier Alitalia was hit by crisis, the Marzano Act was swiftly amended, by Law Decree No. 134 of 28 August 2008, which was subsequently converted as Law No. 166 of 27 October 2008. Shortly afterwards, the company Tributi Italia S.p.A. faced insolvency, and the law was again amended, by Law Decree No. 40 of 25 March 2010, converted as Law No. 73 of 22 May 2010, and as a result the Marzano Act's scope was expanded to include local authorities' revenue collection companies.[69]

There were then further changes to the extraordinary administration procedure and, recently, with law 15 March 2024, n. 28.[70]

68. In analogous sense, *see* Luciano Panzani, *Parità di trattamento tra creditori e tutela della concorrenza, supra*, p. 770, who observes that the person who carries out the composition with creditors operates in the market; for this reason, in a composition with creditors procedure all entrepreneurs would be potential competitors for the acquisition of the company, thereby taking advantages from the proceeds of clawback actions. According to Edoardo Staunovo Polacco, *Art. 6. Azioni revocatorie, supra*, p. 236, a clawback action brought within the Marzano Act cannot constitute a 'State aid' for it does not imply burdens, in whichever form, for the Italian State.
69. In relation to these changes, *see* Giovanni Battista Fauceglia, in *Fallimento*, pp. 1177 et seq. (2010).
70. On the various changes that have been made to the extraordinary administration procedure over the years, *see* Giorgio Meo, *L'amministrazione straordinaria delle grandi imprese in crisi*, in *Le altre procedure concorsuali*, pp. 1061 et seq. (Turin, 2014). *See also* Law Decree 5 Jan. 2015, No. 1, converted with modifications by Law 4 Mar. 2015, n. 20, The Marzano Act has been modified again in order to include also those companies that 'manage at least an industrial plant of national interest', with a clear and explicit reference to the ILVA S.p.A. plant located in Taranto and active in the iron and steel sector. In particular, it should be noted that ILVA S.p.A. was admitted to the extraordinary administration procedure by Ministerial Decree of 21 Jan. 2015.

    After several years of events involving both the Institutions of the European Union (most recently with the 25 Jun. 2024 ruling in Case C-626/22, *ILVA S.p.A. et al*, 25.6.2024, ECLI: EU:C:2024:542, in which the Court of Justice ruled that the Court of Milan may suspend the operation of the Taranto steel plant if it determines that the Taranto steel plant poses serious and significant dangers to the environment and human health), and the European Court of Human Rights (ECHR). The European Commission, on 12 Jul. 2024, approved the bridging loan, amounting to EUR 320 million, that the Italian government wants to make to the company Acciaierie d'Italia S.p.A. under extraordinary administration (formerly Ilva S.p.A.), in order to restart production and find a new buyer for the Taranto plant.

With regard to Alitalia, faced with the company's evidently insolvent position, the Italian government granted the carrier a loan of EUR 300 million, under Law Decree No. 80 of 23 April 2008.[71] The government did not notify the measure to the European Commission, pursuant to Article 88(2) of the EC Treaty (now Article 108(2) TFEU), then in force. The Commission received a number of complaints from Alitalia's competitors that the loan constituted State aid, and on 11 June 2008, the Commission decided to pursue a formal investigation under Article 88(2) and notified the Italian authorities to that effect.[72]

Alitalia had in the meantime entered extraordinary administration under the terms of the Marzano Act, which had been amended especially. Specifically, under Law No. 166/2008, an Extraordinary Administrator could, *inter alia*: (a) present a programme for the sale of operating assets as an alternative to a restructuring programme; (b) where the business was operating essential public services, make privately-negotiated sales of assets, a derogation from Article 62 of the Prodi-*bis* Act which required that sales could only be made following '*appropriate forms of public disclosure*'. The legislation also established, again in relation to companies operating essential public services, that concentrative transactions made no later than 30 June 2009 would not require authorization from Italy's competition regulator, the Autorità Garante della Concorrenza e del Mercato (AGCM), as such transactions would '*meet pre-eminent general interests*'.[73]

Finally, the Italian government notified the Commission of the offer that Compagnia Aerea Italiana had made to purchase some of Alitalia's assets, and of its appointment of a bank as an independent expert to examine whether the sale price of the assets was fair, relative to market value.

The Commission reached two separate decisions on the measures that the Italian government had taken, both dated 12 November 2008. The first found that the EUR 300 million loan that Alitalia had been granted constituted unlawful State aid, incompatible with the internal market, and accordingly to be recovered by the State.[74]

In the second, it decided that the sale of Alitalia assets did not imply the grant of State aid to the purchasers, provided the Italian government complied with its commitment that the sale would be at market prices.[75] The Commission also took the opportunity to examine the changes that had been made to the rules governing extraordinary administration between 2003 and 2008 but did not find provisions that amounted to State aid.

71. Law Decree 2008/80, *Urgent measures to ensure a public air transport service* (*Official Gazette*, No. 97 of 24 Apr. 2008).
72. *See* Letter from the Commission to the Italian government (D/203822) dated 12 Jun. 2008.
73. *See* Art. 4*quinquies* of Law Decree 347/2008. It was stated to be subject to the law of the European Union on concentrations between undertakings. The provision in question was found to be constitutional in relation to Arts 3 and 41 of the Italian Constitution (*see* Constitutional Court, 22 Jul. 2010, No. 270, *Corriere giur.*, 2011, pp. 787 et seq., with a comment by Mastrorilli), on application from the Lazio regional administrative court (TAR).
74. Decision 2009/155/EC of 12 Nov. 2008, in (2009) OJ L 52/3.
75. Decision (2008) 6745 of 12 Nov. 2008, concerning State aid No. 510/2008 Italia (not published in the OJ).

The two decisions were contested in the European courts by Ryanair Ltd, a competitor of Alitalia's. In a detailed judgment of 28 March 2012, the General Court dismissed the Irish carrier's claim, and found, specifically, that the Commission had in that case correctly applied the 'private investor' principle.[76] Ryanair appealed the judgment of the General Court to the Court of Justice. That court too upheld the Commission's decision, in a judgment of 13 June 2013.[77]

The private investor principle was used by the Commission also in its decision of 22 January 2014, regarding aid that the Region of Sardinia had provided to Saremar, a company that the private shipping firm Società Tirrenia di Navigazione had controlled but sold to the Region.[78] Specifically, the Commission found that no private investor operating under market conditions would have participated in the share capital increase that Saremar had announced for EUR 6.1 million, but into which only EUR 824,309.69 had been paid in on 11 July 2012. Similarly, the Commission found that EUR 10 million paid to Saremar in two instalments on 6 November and 3 December 2012, by way of compensation for services on two routes linking Sardinia to the mainland, pursuant to Regional Law No. 15 of 7 August 2012, constituted State aid.

The Commission also found that two patronage letters to Saremar (one of which was authorized by the Region under its resolution 52/119 but never issued) did not guarantee any financial obligation of Saremar and that promotional activities that the company had carried on were paid for at market prices. Accordingly, those measures did not constitute State aid.

---

76. Case T-123/09, *Ryanair v. Commission*, 28.3.2012, ECLI:EU:T:2012:164. The court had dealt previously with Alitalia – first, in its judgment of 12 Dec. 2000 in Case T-297/97, *Alitalia v. Commission ('Alitalia I')*, 12.12.2000, ECLI:EU:T:2000:289, overturning the Commission's 1997 decision on Alitalia's recapitalization (97/789/EC); and later in its judgment of 9 Jul. 2008, in Case T-301/01, *Alitalia – Linee aeree italiane SpA v. Commission ('Alitalia II')*, 9.7.2008, ECLI:EU:T:2008:262, which upheld the Commission's 2001 decision on another Alitalia recapitalization (2001/723/CE). On these complex affairs, *see* Cristoforo Osti, *Alitalia: la dolorosa storia. I puntata*, in *Merc. Conc. Reg.*, pp. 317 et seq. (2008).
77. Case C-287/12, *Ryanair v. Commission*, 13.6.2013, ECLI:EU:C:2013:395, with a commentary from Milligan, Sales, *Appeal against Alitalia State Aid Decision by Ryanair Dismissed*, in *Eur. State Aid Law Quart.*, pp. 98 et seq. (2014) https://doi.org/10.33278/sae-2014.vol.1. For an analysis of the interplay between the Commission and the Alitalia group prior to the Court of Justice's recent judgments, *see* Davide Diverio, *Gli aiuti di Stato al trasporto aereo e alle banche*, Milan, pp. 20 et seq. (2010).
78. Commission Decision of 22 Jul. 2014, C (2013) 9101 final, on aid measures SA. 32014 (2011/C), SA. 32015 (2011/C), SA. 32016 (2011/C). The measure had its origin in Decision C (2011) 6961 final, adopted on 5 Oct. 2011 (OJ C 28 of 1 Feb. 2012, 18), under which the Commission began a formal investigation in relation to some measures that Italy had taken in relation to companies of the former Tirrenia group. In 2013, the Region asked the Commission to spin out the investigation into Saremar from its broader enquiries, in light of the plans for that company's privatization. As a result, that decision regarded only the measures adopted in favour of Saremar.

In conclusion, the Commission decided that Italy should recover the amounts considered State aid, an amount of EUR 10,824,309.69, *'in order to re-establish the situation that existed on the market prior to the granting of the aid'*.[79]

The complex affair concerning Alitalia, meanwhile admitted in 2017 to extraordinary administration proceedings and replaced in 2021 by ITA Trasporto Aereo S.p.A. (ITA Airways, which acquired its brand name), now seems to be drawing to a close as the Commission, in a decision dated 3 July 2024, approved under the EU Merger Control Regulation the proposed joint acquisition of ITA Airways by Deutsche Lufthansa AG and the Italian Ministry of Economy and Finance.[80] In particular, according to the parties' commitments to the Commission, they will only be able to carry out the takeover transaction after they have activated the corrective measures agreed upon for each of the commitments related to short-haul and long-haul routes and Milan Linate Airport.

79. Decision C (2013) 9101 final, para. 305. On the evolution of the private investor principle in the case law of the Court of Justice, *see* Davide Maresca, *Dell'investitore privato al debitore privato: l'evoluzione del modello di operatore economico in materia di aiuti di Stato*, in *Eurojus.it*, 2, pp. 228 et seq. (2022).
80. European Commission – Press release, 3 Jul. 2024, case number M.11071.

CHAPTER 9

The Recovery and Resilience Plans of the EU: A Test Case for the Tightness of EU's State Aid Rules

Pietro Missanelli

§9.01 HISTORY AND PURPOSE OF THE RECOVERY AND RESILIENCE PLANS

The Recovery and Resilience Plans (RRPs) are detailed national plans providing for investments and reforms established in response to the unprecedented challenges posed to the Union by the COVID-19 outbreak. Such plans are possible by virtue of the Recovery and Resiliency Facility (RRF), a temporary instrument established through a specific regulation (RFF Regulation), by which the Commission may raise funds made subsequently available to EU Member States.[1]

The economic and social impacts of the pandemic needed a comprehensive strategy to support EU Member States in their recovery efforts.[2] The primary reason for the establishment of such new instruments was thus to address the economic downturn caused by the pandemic, which threatened the stability and growth of EU economies. Eventually, the RRPs turned out to be a central component of the broader NextGenerationEU initiative, designed not only to repair the immediate damage

1. Regulation (EU) No. 2021/241 of the European Parliament and of the Council of 12 Feb. 2021 establishing the Recovery and Resilience Facility, OJ L 57, 18.2.2021.
2. For more information, *see* Francesco Corti, Alessandro Liscai, Tomas Ruiz, *The Recovery and Resilience Facility: Boosting Investment in Social Infrastructure in Europe?*, 15 Italian Labour Law e-Journal, 15, 30, n. 1S (2022), where the authors examine a sample of six countries and investigate the extent to which the social investments included in the plans could be considered truly additional, finding that the RRF de facto fast-forwarded the implementation of investments in social infrastructure.

brought by COVID-19 but also to enhance the efforts towards green and digital transitions.

In fact, the introduction of the EU legal framework was driven by the need for a coordinated and robust response that could mitigate the economic shock caused by the outbreak, while also paving the way for long-term reforms. The goals of the RRPs had to take into account the long-term EU's strategic priorities: the European Green Deal, which seek to transform Europe into the first climate-neutral continent by 2050, as well as the Digital Strategy, which focuses on boosting the EU's digital capabilities.

The EU and its Member States historically faced various crises that have required substantial economic interventions, but it would not be unfair to say that the COVID-19 pandemic was unique in its scale and impact. For this reason, the Commission quickly recognized that the recovery from such a widespread disruption would require unprecedented financial support and innovative policy measures: a support that was never granted before, not even in the framework of the banking and financial crisis of 2008.

The RRPs were thus crafted to be comprehensive, focusing not only on immediate recovery but also on driving long-term structural reforms and investments, fostering sustainable growth, enhancing economic stability, and improving social resilience across the Union, reflecting the EU's commitment to solidarity and cohesion.[3]

The setting up of the RRPs also drew from lessons learned from previous EU financial mechanisms and programs, such as the European Structural and Investment Funds (ESIF), which provided a valuable reference for designing the RRPs, ensuring that funds would be allocated efficiently and transparently.[4]

Moreover, the Stability and Growth Pact (SGP) has also historically provided mechanisms for coordinating fiscal policies and monitoring economic performance across Member States;[5] the RRPs build on these foundations by incorporating the principles of fiscal discipline and macroeconomic stability, while also introducing a more flexible and forward-looking approach to economic governance.

Finally, the birth of the RRPs was also influenced by the EU's commitment to sustainable development and the United Nations' 2030 Agenda: it is evident, in most of the RRPs, the emphasis put on achieving the Sustainable Development Goals (SDGs),

3. Cf. Silvia Rainone, *From Deregulatory Pressure to Laissez Faire: The (Moderate) Social Implications of the EU Recovery Strategy*, 15 Italian Labour Law e-Journal, 31, 52, n. 1S (2022), where the author interestingly assesses the impact of the EU recovery strategy in (re)aligning the EU with the pursuit of social objectives, focusing on the major innovations introduced by the NextGenerationEU (NGEU) plan and SURE (a temporary instrument aimed at mitigating unemployment risks during the pandemic).
4. Cf. Radu, C., Radu, L. (2023), *From the Next Generation EU to the National Recovery and Resilience Plan*, 14 Romanian Review of Social Sciences, 50, 64 n. 1. Cf. also Dimitrios Skiadas, *Trade-offs in Auditing the EU Recovery and Resilience Facility – Flexibility vs Compliance: A Greek Case Study*, Eucrim – The European Criminal Law Associations' Forum (2024) https://doi.org/10.30709/eucrim-2023-033.
5. Cf. Diane Fromage, Günter Herzig, Paul Weismann, *The way forward in the EMU: inflation, public debt and reforms for the next generation (Part III)*, EU Law Live: Weekend Edition, No. 141 (2023), special issue Madrid: EU Law Live, 2023.

particularly those related to economic growth, social inclusion, and environmental sustainability.

§9.02 KEY ELEMENTS OF THE RECOVERY AND RESILIENCE PLANS

The RRPs submitted by EU Member States outline their proposed reforms and investments to be funded under the RFF, which forms the financial backbone of the RRPs, offering up to EUR 723.8 billion in grants and loans to support the Member States' initiatives.[6]

Specifically, Member States must present investments and reforms as organized into coherent components. According to the Commission's guidance to Member States on RPPs, a component is a constituent element or a part of the recovery and resilience plan; each component reflects the priorities in policy areas, sectors, activities or themes, forming a coherent package with complementary measures.[7]

The RRPs are structured around six pillars (or objectives): green transition, digital transformation, smart, sustainable, and inclusive growth, social and territorial cohesion, health and economic, social, and institutional resilience, and policies for the next generation (i.e., children and youth):[8]

(1) a significant emphasis is placed on the green transition, which aligns with the EU's commitment to becoming climate-neutral by 2050. This pillar includes investments in renewable energy, energy efficiency improvements, and sustainable transport systems, to reduce carbon emissions and foster sustainable economic growth. Specific projects under this pillar may include the development of wind and solar energy farms, retrofitting buildings to improve energy efficiency, and expanding electric vehicle charging infrastructure;

(2) the digital transformation pillar seeks to ensure that the EU is at the forefront of the digital age. This involves investments in digital infrastructure, such as the expansion of high-speed broadband and 5G networks, as well as initiatives to enhance digital literacy and skills among the EU population. The focus is on ensuring that also rural and underserved areas are provided access to modern digital services, thereby reducing the digital divide;

(3) the pillar on smart, sustainable, and inclusive growth aims to boost economic growth that is both environmentally sustainable and socially inclusive. This includes support for small and medium-sized enterprises (SMEs), fostering innovation, and ensuring that economic growth benefits all segments of society;

(4) social and territorial cohesion is another critical pillar, addressing disparities between different regions and social groups within the EU (which would

6. *See* the report of the EU Court of Auditors for 2023.
7. *See* Commission staff working document guidance to Member States recovery and resilience plans of the European Commission of 22 Jan. 2021, SWD (2021) 12 final.
8. Article 3 of the RRF Regulation.

include investments in infrastructure, healthcare, education, and social services);

(5) the health and economic, social, and institutional resilience pillar focuses on enhancing the EU's capacity to respond to future crises. This involves strengthening healthcare systems, improving crisis response mechanisms, and building resilient infrastructure that can withstand future shocks (e.g., through the development of advanced healthcare facilities, the creation of strategic reserves of medical supplies, as well as the implementation of robust disaster response plans);

(6) finally, the policies for the next generation, children, and youth pillar emphasize investments in education, training, and employment opportunities for young people. The aim is to equip the younger generation with the skills and opportunities needed to thrive in a rapidly changing world (e.g., initiatives to improve the quality of education, provide vocational training, and create job opportunities for young people).

To ensure transparency and accountability, the Commission requires Member States to provide detailed timelines, milestones, and targets for each component of their RRPs. Regular monitoring and reporting mechanisms are in place to track progress and ensure that the funds are used in accordance with the agreed-upon timings.

The practical implementation of the RRPs involves a close collaboration between national governments and EU institutions. Member states are required to submit periodic progress reports, which are reviewed by the Commission to ensure compliance with the agreed targets and milestones. Additionally, the European Court of Auditors plays a critical role in auditing the use of funds and ensuring that they are spent in accordance with EU rules and regulations.[9] Finally, the European Parliament also monitors the implementation of RRPs, for instance, through regular dialogues with and written questions to the European Commission, by producing internal studies and expressing its views on the RRF implementation through the approval of parliamentary resolutions.

§9.03 THE ROLE OF STATE AID IN THE RECOVERY AND RESILIENCE PLANS

The interrelation between the Recovery and Resilience Plans (RRPs) and State aid is a critical aspect of ensuring that the EU's recovery efforts are both effective and compliant with the Union's legal framework: recital 8 of the RFF Regulation expressly provides that Member States must ensure that all reforms and investments outlined in the RRPs comply with the applicable EU State aid rules and follow the required State

9. Annual report on the implementation of the EU budget of the European Court of Auditors of 2023. Retrieved from https://www.eca.europa.eu Ch. 3, para. 4.

aid procedures.[10] This implies that measures entailing State aid must be notified to and approved by the Commission to ensure compliance with relevant EU State aid rules.

The Commission has provided updated practical guidance[11] and templates[12] to assist Member States in designing plans that are compliant with EU State aid rules. EU Member States are encouraged to utilize the updated templates and guidance provided by the European Commission to ensure their measures can be approved swiftly.

For instance, in compliance with the current framework on State aid, most of the available templates directly specify or indirectly assume that the following measures do not constitute State aid:[13]

(i) those aimed at supporting activities that are not of an economic nature;
(ii) those not involving the transfer of public resources;
(iii) those of general application and do not favour specific undertakings or sectors (i.e., non-selective measures);
(iv) those that have no effects on trade between Member States and do not distort competition.

Moreover, the practical guide distinguishes between four types of support measures:

(i) Those aid measures that do constitute State aid and thus need to be notified to the Commission for approval. In relation to those State aid measures that are included in the RFF plans, the Commission committed to assess notifications within six weeks;
(ii) Those new measures which, although constituting aid, do not need to be notified to the European Commission because they fall within the scope of an exemption regulation (e.g., *de minimis* aid or aid covered by the GBER);
(iii) Those measures that qualify as State aid but do not need to be notified to the Commission as they are part of existing aid schemes that have already been approved;
(iv) Those measures that do not constitute State aid (e.g., direct financial support to consumers), which do not fall within the scope of Article 107 TFEU.

---

10. Cf. Sara Gobbato, *Fate Presto: Italy Starts Discussions on the National Recovery and Resilience Plan*, 19 European State Aid Law Quarterly, 528, 530 n. 4 (2020), where the author points out that 'Member States should bear in mind that all investments provided within the NRRPs must comply with the EU State aid rules and follow all regular procedures and rules. Investments should not cover areas that are already satisfactorily covered by the market but should address market failures and, to the extent possible, aim at attracting private investors.'
11. Practical guidance to Member States for a swift treatment of State aid notifications in the framework of the Recovery and Resilience Facility of the European Commission. Retrieved from https://competition-policy.ec.europa.eu/system/files/2022-02/practical_guidance_to_MS_for_notifications_under_RRF.pdf.
12. The templates are available on the website of the Commission, here: https://competition-policy.ec.europa.eu/state-aid/legislation/rrf-guiding-templates_en?prefLang=it.
13. For a more in-depth analysis *see* the guidance issued by Assonime, circolare 18/2022.

When drafting the RFF plans, EU Member States have to specify whether or not the reform or investment support in question is to be qualified as State aid, as well as whether it is included in an aid scheme or exemption regulation or, in the alternative, whether such aid required a re-notification, an indication of when it would be pre-notified or notified to the Commission.

In any case, the inclusion of this information in the RFF plans does not constitute (and does not replace) the notification of the aid measure to the Commission. Similarly, the authorization of the national RFF plan by the Commission does not constitute clearance of the State aid measures contained therein regarding their compatibility with the internal market.

In order to ensure compliance with State aid rules, the practical guidance outlines that the Commission will engage directly with Member States regarding the reforms and investments included in their national RRPs.[14]

The informal contacts with DG Competition will allow the start of a dialogue for the preparation of a complete notification of the State aid measure in question. Such pre-notification contacts will also cover the legal and economic aspects of a proposed measure. Once the set of information is deemed complete, Member States are invited to file the formal notification form in the usual State aid notification system.

If all the steps have been duly followed by the Member States, the Commission will use a fast-tracking path for the approval of the State aid measures included in the RRPs, aimed at ensuring the timely deployment of recovery funds within six weeks.[15] This prioritization may be essential for the swift implementation of critical investments and reforms needed to address the immediate economic and social challenges posed by the pandemic.

As anticipated, other measures can benefit from *de minimis* thresholds or block exemptions, which help speed up the implementation of essential projects.[16] The block exemptions apply to aid that meets specific criteria set out in the General Block Exemption Regulation (GBER), which covers areas such as aid for environmental protection, research, development and innovation, and aid to SMEs.[17]

Although the measures not necessitating a notification are probably a majority, the number and importance of the measures approved by the Commission is quite remarkable. For instance:

(a) on 11 April 2022, the Commission approved, under EU State aid rules, a EUR 250 million aid measure, made available to Portugal through the RFF, to further capitalize the promotional institution Banco Português de Fomento.

14. *Ibid.*, section 2, para. 2.
15. National Recovery and Resilience Plans: Latest state of play of the European Parliament of June 2023, PE 749.781, section 3, para. 1. Retrieved from https://www.europarl.europa.eu.
16. Sara Gobbato, *Italy COVID-19: Liquidity Support in the Cura Italia Decree*, 19 European State Aid Law Quarterly, 92, 94, n. 1 (2020), p. 93. Retrieved from https://www.jstor.org/stable/10.2307/48685474.
17. *See* the relevant chapter of this book.

Such a measure was aimed at developing the Portuguese economy by facilitating access to finance, particularly for small and medium enterprises;[18]

(b) on 7 July 2023, the Commission had approved, under EU State aid rules, a EUR 350 million Spanish scheme, made available through the RFF, to support the construction and operation of electricity storage facilities. As highlighted by the Commission: 'Such a measure will contribute to achievement of the European Green Deal targets while helping to reduce dependence on Russian fossil fuels and fast forward the green transition in line with the REPowerEU Plan';[19]

(c) on 22 November 2023, the Commission approved, under EU State aid rules, a scheme for about EUR 5.7 billion made to support the production and self-consumption of renewable electricity. The scheme will be partly funded by the RRF, following the Commission's positive assessment of Italy's Recovery and Resilience Plan and its adoption by the Council;[20]

(d) on 16 February 2024, the Commission approved a German scheme of about EUR 4 billion made available in part through the RFF to help companies to decarbonize their industrial production processes;[21]

(e) on 27 June 2024, the Commission approved a Swedish State aid measure for about EUR 265 million partly funded under the Recovery and Resilience Facility to support a green steel plant.[22]

Despite several successful initiatives, recent reports highlighted the existence of several obstacles to the implementation of the recovery and resiliency plans.[23] For instance, it was highlighted that investment bottlenecks emerged in relation to the long time for the State aid notification process and the lack of clarity in the case of cross-border projects. In particular, the lengthy State aid notification process appears to remain the major challenge of the implementation of IPCEIs, with an average time of 1.5 years for receiving authorization, the timeline for IPCEIs remains uncertain.

This said, overall the implementation of RFF is progressing. Recent statistics (February 2024) show that over 1,150 milestones and targets have been successfully fulfilled with nearly EUR 225 billion disbursed to support Member States' economies. Additionally, around EUR 150 billion in additional support for Member States h been provided through new financing for the REPowerEU chapters of recovery plans and additional loan support.

Furthermore, twenty-seven recovery plans have been revised to enhance their impact, address emerging challenges and speed up implementation in 2024, while

18. European Commission Press Release IP/22/2401 of 11 Apr. 2022.
19. European Commission Press Release IP/23/3382 of 7 Jul. 2023.
20. European Commission Press Release IP/23/5787 of 22 Nov. 2023.
21. European Commission Press Release IP/24/845 of 16 Feb. 2024.
22. European Commission Press Release IP/24/3468 of 26 Jun. 2024.
23. *See*, for instance, the study supporting the mid-term Evaluation of the Recovery and Resilience Facility Prepared by ECORYS, CEPS, CSIL, NIESR, and Wavestone for the European Commission, Directorate-General for Economic and Financial Affairs, December 2023.

twenty-three REPowerEU chapters have been endorsed by the Council, which will imply over EUR 100 billion in disbursements are expected in 2024.

The results, from a practical point of view, are also remarkable: 28 million megawatt hours (MWh) saved in annual primary energy consumption due to RRF support, with about 9 million people benefitting from protection from environmental disasters and further about 8.7 million people whose education benefitted from the RFF. As for youth, 5.8 million young people aged 15-29 are receiving monetary and in-kind support for education, training and employment globally, 308 million citizens are benefitting from new or improved public digital services and 5.6 million additional houses have been provided with internet access via very high-capacity networks.

Lastly, it is important to highlight that the recent report prepared by Mario Draghi on EU competitiveness stressed the importance of using the Next Generation EU in order to build a new model for the regular issuance of common debt, so as to enable joint investment projects among Member States and increase the EU's competitiveness.[24] In fact, facing the challenges of the coming decades only through State aid measures would inevitably lead to a fragmentation of the single market, a phenomenon accelerated by the extensive use of temporary frameworks and subsidies in response to the US Inflation Reduction Act.[25] Such a risk of fragmentation, as emphasized also by Enrico Letta in his report on the single market, can be prevented with innovative solutions that could 'balance a stricter enforcement of State aid at national level and the progressive expansion of EU level funding support'.[26]

24. Mario Draghi, *The future of European competitiveness, Part A. A competitiveness strategy for Europe*, Report, September 2024, p. 62.
25. Annual Report 2022 on competition policy of the European Parliament of 8 May 2023, (2022/2060(INI)), A9-0183/2023, PE740.653v02-00, pp. 7 and 17.
26. Enrico Letta, *Much more than a market – Speed, Security, Solidarity. Empowering the Single Market to deliver a sustainable future and prosperity for all EU Citizens*, Report addressed to the European Council, April 2024, p. 11. On this point, it is worth highlighting that the reasoning behind such consideration is the assumption that funds disbursed by EU institutions are less distortive than State aid measure (*see* Péter Staviczky, *Analysis of the State Aid-Related Proposals in the Letta Report*, 23 European State Aid Law Quarterly, n. 3, pp. 258, 267, (2024)) https://doi.org/10.21552/estal/2024/3/4. This is probably the case, if we take as examples recovery plans and we consider the fact that their content is agreed with the EU Commission and the measures contained therein are also scrutinized under EU State aid rules.

CHAPTER 10

The EU Foreign Subsidy Regulation: A New Arrow to the EC's State Aid Bow?

Edoardo Gambaro & Stefania Nardelli

§10.01 INTRODUCTION

This chapter presents the Foreign Subsidy Regulation (FSR), the new instrument created by the European Union (EU) to address distortions caused on the EU internal market by State aid granted by a non-EU Government ('foreign subsidies') and is structured as follows. Sections 10.01 and 10.02 introduce, respectively, the geopolitical context justifying the need for this instrument and the legal procedure and legal bases explaining the FSR's unique features and hybrid nature, in-between EU State aid law and international trade rules. Section 10.03 describes the main features of the FSR, which take inspiration from both sets of rules, and focuses on its main substantive legal concepts, like the balancing test. Section 10.04 provides an overview of the procedure (the mandatory notifications and the different phases of the investigation), which might lead to commitments or measures countering the distortions caused by the foreign subsidies. Before the conclusion, section 10.06 describes the first cases launched by the European Commission based on the FSR.

§10.02 A NEW INSTRUMENT FOR A CHANGED GEOPOLITICAL CONTEXT

Historically, the idea behind fair competition is that tearing down barriers to trade has to be accompanied by the elimination of distorting practices.[1] From the EU internal market's perspective, EU competition rules complement the benefits of the free

1. Andreas Reindl & Isabelle Van Damme, *The EU Foreign Subsidies Regulation*, 1 (Concurrences 2024), (Foreword by Arancha Gonzales Laya).

movement of people, goods, services, establishment and capital by ensuring a level playing field.[2] From an international trade perspective, EU trade defence rules were introduced to complement free trade rules: they deter and counterbalance unfair competition from non-EU countries, when imports cause damage to the EU industry on the internal market. The EU internal market is, therefore, at the heart of both sets of rules: during more than thirty years, thanks to around 450 million consumers and the legal certainty created by EU rules for companies and investors, the internal market has fostered economic and social development[3] in the EU and provided it with a stronger voice on the global arena.

In more recent years, the pandemic and the following economic crisis, the tensions between the EU and its main economic partners – USA and China (and between those two) – the Russian war of aggression to Ukraine and the resulting energy crisis led to a general sentiment of uncertainty and a strong push for inward-looking economic policies. Governments intervened with subsidies to rescue companies from the above-mentioned economic crises while supporting in some cases environment-friendly policies (like, in the USA, with the Inflation Reduction Act). This resulted, inevitably, in a subsidy race.[4]

Eventually, this new geopolitical context has cast a long shadow on the simple idea that globalization benefits the EU internal market and the EU companies, workers and consumers. It became even more evident that the level playing field on the EU market cannot be achieved without taking due account of the weaknesses of modern globalized economies. These crises showed the other side of the coin of globalization, namely the risks embedded in the deeply integrated global value chains and in the economic interdependencies between countries acting, one day, as economic partners and, the other, as rivals.

The crisis of the main multilateral economic forum happened in parallel: the inability of the World Trade Organisation (WTO) to guarantee the level playing field among its members has now been acknowledged also by the EU, while its reform is

2. Lena Hornkohl, *Protecting the Internal Market from Subsidisation With the EU State Aid Regime and the Foreign Subsidies Regulation: Two Sides of the Same Coin?*, 3 Journal of European Competition Law & Practice 14, 137-151 (Gianni De Stefano e Paolo Ibanez Colombo eds, Oxford University Press 2023) https://doi.org/10.1093/jeclap/lpad005.
3. According to Art. 3(3) TEU and Protocol No. 27 on the internal market and competition, the EU internal market consists of an open, highly competitive social market economy with free and undistorted competition.
4. It has been argued that the EU has an ambivalent stance on subsidies since 'the EU does not shy away from subsidisation itself'. *See* Jan Blockx & Pierfranco Marriolo, *The Foreign Subsidies Regulation: Calling Foul While Upping the Ante?*, 28 European Foreign Affairs Review, Special Issue, 67-70 and 73 (2023) https://doi.org/10.54648/eerr2023014. In fact, it is rather for the EU and not for foreign countries to decide which subsidies are allowed or not on the EU market. In this perspective, the FSR is not ambivalent and replies in a coherent way to the EU needs of economic security. It is China's instrumentalization of trade and investment relations to its (geo)political purposes and legislation such as the United States Chips and Science Act or the Inflation Reduction Act which triggered the subsidy race. *See* Thomas Verellen, Alexandra Hofer, *The Unilateral Turn in EU Trade and Investment Policy*, 28 European Foreign Affairs Review, Special Issue, 4-5 (2023) https://doi.org/10.54648/eerr2023011.

taking forever (not being a priority for other important members, like the USA).[5] As a result, the EU took a more autonomous and assertive stance in the global arena by introducing the new economic concepts of Open Strategic Autonomy[6] and, more recently, Economic Security.[7] These concepts have in common the idea that, while the EU market needs to remain open to the benefits of international trade and investments, the EU needs to secure access to strategic resources and, where necessary, protect itself from unfair and abusive practices[8] especially when it comes to critical infrastructures and sectors. For example, availability of semiconductors is essential for industry and national security alike. Given the currently fragile state of global supply chains, expanding fabrication within the EU and ensuring fair competition on the global and internal markets are of paramount importance for the EU's tech sovereignty.[9]

The changed geopolitical context eventually showed the urgency to fill a rather relevant and long-standing regulatory gap in EU law: EU State aid rules restrict EU Member States from subsidizing their domestic companies, while third countries may provide unlimited support to their players even if they are active in the EU.[10] The EU is closely intertwined with the global economy: trade in goods and services accounted in 2019 for 16.4% of overall global trade and for almost 35% of the EU's gross domestic product (GDP), with 35 million jobs in the EU dependent on exports. In this context, it is rather understandable that the EU tries to stop third-country subsidies, which are used to finance company acquisitions in the EU and interfere with public procurement.[11]

5. The FSR has been defined as 'a unilateral initiative which precisely aims to circumvent the paralysis of the WTO': *Ibid.*, 65.
6. Communication from the Commission to the European Parliament, the Council, the European Economic and Social Committee and the Committee of the Regions – Trade Policy Review – An Open, Sustainable and Assertive Trade Policy, 18.2.2021 COM(2021) 66 final. The analysis of the interaction between the concept of strategic autonomy and WTO rules and State-Owned Enterprises (SOEs) show that the unilateral, bilateral, and multilateral approaches are strictly intertwined as far as they reveal a shift in the most recent EU trade policy objective in relation to the role of State in the market. *See* Nerina Boschiero & Stefano Silingardi, 24 German Law Journal, 151-178 (2023).
7. Joint Communication to the European Parliament, the European Council and the Council on 'European Economic Security Strategy' Join/2023/20 Final. *See also* Lorenza Mola, *The Securitisation of International Economic Law and 'Global Security': An Analysis of the EU Law Approach Through the Prism of the Common Commercial Policy*, 12 Cambridge International Law Journal, 1, 105-128 (2023) https://doi.org/10.4337/cilj.2023.01.07; Christopher Yukins, *State Aid, Protectionism and Public Procurement: An Uneasy New World Order*, 22 European State Aid Law Quarterly, 2 181-187 (2023) https://doi.org/10.21552/estal/2023/2/8.
8. White paper on levelling the playing field as regards foreign subsidies, Brussels, 17.6.2020 COM(2020) 253 final, 4. *See also* Krenek, Filip, and Eddy De Smijter. *From a White Paper to a Proposal for a Regulation on Foreign Subsidies: Filling a Regulatory Gap in Protecting the EU Internal Market*, Springer International Publishing, 129-148 (2022). Jürgen Kuling et al., *Third-Country State Aid Regulation: The European Debate on Foreign Subsidies – Necessity and Possibilities of a Reform*, Springer International Publishing, 149-161 (2021).
9. Andreas Haak & Barbara Thiemann, *Fostering Tech Sovereignty with a Level Playing Field on State Aid and Foreign Subsidies*, European State Aid Law Quarterly, 21, 1, 20-30 (2022) https://doi.org/10.21552/estal/2022/1/4.
10. Ulrich Soltész, *Foreign Subsidies Control: A Bureaucratic Monster?*, 7, European State Aid Law Quarterly, 22, II, 175-180 (2023).
11. *Ibid.*

The EU co-legislators, namely the European Parliament and the Council of the EU, have also raised the issue of foreign subsidies on several occasions. Also, the European Council, which sets the priorities of the EU, called for 'further instruments to address the distortive effects of foreign subsidies in the single market'. In its report on competition policy, the European Parliament called on the Commission to look for 'appropriate investigative tools in cases where a company is deemed to have engaged in distortionary behaviour due to government subsidies'. Forty-one members of the European Parliament expressed in a letter to the Commission strong support for an instrument to tackle 'companies from third countries that have received substantial state support'.[12]

The Foreign Subsidy Regulation (FSR) was conceived to close such regulatory gap in the merit-based competition in the EU[13] and integrate the EU trade defence 'toolbox'. This new instrument, like the other trade tools addressing the new geopolitical context,[14] marks a small revolution in EU trade and investment policy due to its unilateral nature:[15] it originates from EU rules which do not transpose any international agreement and is the concrete application of the idea that the EU shall not be naïve anymore in its international trade relations (*see* above the concepts open strategic autonomy/economic security).

§10.03 A HYBRID INSTRUMENT FILING A GAP IN EU AND INTERNATIONAL LAW

Until mid-January 2023, subsidies from non-EU countries could be granted to companies active in the EU, thereby distorting the level playing field[16] on the EU market, while the same subsidies granted by EU Member States would be problematic pursuant

12. Proposal for a Regulation of the European Parliament and of the Council on foreign subsidies distorting the internal market, COM/2021/223 final.
13. Eddy De Smijter, *There's a New Kid in Town: The Foreign Subsidies Regulation*, 13 Journal of European Competition Law & Practice 8, 529 (2022) https://doi.org/10.1093/jeclap/lpad001.
14. In occasion of the entry into force of the revised Enforcement Regulation (No. 2021/167) allowing the EU to react against unfair trade practices despite the blockage of the judiciary function of the WTO, Executive Vice-President and Commissioner for Trade, Valdis Dombrovskis, said: 'The European Union must be able to defend itself against unfair trading practices. These new rules will help protect us from those trying to take advantage of our openness. We continue to work towards our first preference, which is a reformed and well-functioning multilateral rulebook with an effective Dispute Settlement System at its core. But we cannot afford to stand defenseless in the meantime. These measures allow us to respond resolutely and assertively.' Regulation 2023/2675 on the protection of the European Union and its Member States from economic coercion (the Anti-Coercion Instrument) enables the EU to take action in cases of economic coercion of the EU or its Member States by non-EU countries. The objective is to deter coercion, and if necessary, to respond to it.
15. *See* the brief, non-exhaustive overview of the unilateral trade instruments the EU has either modernized or introduced in the 2017-2023 period, in Thomas Verellen & Alexandra Hofer, *The Unilateral Turn in EU Trade and Investment Policy*, 28 European Foreign Affairs Review, Special Issue, 1-14 (2023) https://doi.org/10.54648/eerr2023011.
16. Wolfgang Weiß, *The Regulation on Foreign Subsidies Distorting the Internal Market A Path to a Level Playing Field?* SpringerBriefs in Law, Springer Cham (2024).

to EU competition rules.[17] These foreign subsidies may indeed be used, for instance, to finance economic activities, such as participation in public procurement procedures,[18] or the acquisition of undertakings, including those with strategic assets such as critical infrastructure and innovative technologies (Recital 2 FSR).

This rather unfortunate situation can be explained by the lack of EU rules and global rules and political agreement at the EU and global level to cover such scenario for its implications in terms of sovereignty and national industrial policy.[19] On the one hand, EU State aid rules apply only to subsidies granted by EU Member States. On the other hand, WTO rules on countervailing measures[20] cover subsidies granted by a Government to an exporting company distorting the competition in another country, but they do not cover the case of subsidies granted by the Government of a third country to a company established in the country where the distortion takes place. In other terms, trade defence instruments enable the Commission to act when subsidized goods are imported into the Union, but not when foreign subsidies take the form of subsidized investments (Recital 5 FSR).

For instance, WTO rules allow the EU to impose a duty to countervail the subsidy granted by the Chinese government to a Chinese company exporting solar panels to the EU in order to offset the non-competitive advantage created by the subsidy and the consequent economic damage caused to the EU producers of solar panels. However, neither WTO rules nor EU competition rules allow the EU to counterbalance the non-competitive advantage created by a subsidy granted by the Chinese Government to an EU company despite it causing economic damage to other EU companies producing solar panels and distorting the competition in the internal market.

Then, on 12 January 2023, new rules on foreign subsidies distorting the EU internal market came into force. These new rules had been agreed upon, following the EU ordinary legislative procedure, by the EU co-legislators, the Council of the European Union and the European Parliament, in December 2022, namely only nineteen months after the Commission presented its proposal. The speed of the legislative process was

17. Commission Communication, *White paper on levelling the playing field as regards foreign subsidies*, Brussels, 17.6.2020 COM(2020) 253 final, 5.
18. Some criticized the need for new rules when it comes to public procurements. Anke Meskens, *Mind the (Regulatory) Gap: The Commission's Legislative Proposal on Levelling the Playing Field in Public Procurement for Foreign Subsidies*, 17 European Procurement & Public Private Partnership Law Review, 2, 94-106 (2022) https://doi.org/10.21552/epppl/2022/2/6.
19. China has been 'going global' for many years for example with the investment under its Belt and Road Initiative. The concerns that Chinese companies establishing themselves in third countries would be unfairly advantaged by the financing they receive under China's expansionist strategy is not new. Victor Crochet and Vineet Hegde tried to reply to the question whether such financing could be disciplined under the World Trade Organization Agreement on Subsidies and Countervailing Measures. *See* Victor Crochet & Vineet Hegde, *China's 'Going Global' Policy: Transnational Production Subsidies Under the WTO SCM Agreement*, 23 Journal of International Economic Law, 841-863 (2020) https://doi.org/10.1093/jiel/jgaa029.
20. The level playing field in international trade is governed by international trade rules agreed by some countries, which are members of the WTO, and then transposed by each of them in its own legislative system (with some inevitable differences and inconsistencies). In case of subsidies, the relevant rules can be found in the WTO Agreement on Subsidies and Countervailing Measures.

rather extraordinary,[21] showing the strong political will and urge of the EU co-legislators to fill an important gap in EU and WTO law.

The FSR instrument is openly conceived as a protective measure on the part of the EU against the inability to reach a more comprehensive agreement at the international level on the regulation of subsidies to companies, which could limit unfair competition, and, on the other hand, as an instrument of political pressure on third Countries and the WTO itself. First, Recital 43 of the Regulation clearly states that this instrument 'should complement the Union's efforts to improve multilateral rules on distortive subsidies'. Second, the text of the Regulation itself provides for the possibility for the Commission to propose the abrogation of the FSR itself, 'if the Commission considers that multilateral rules to address foreign subsidies distorting the internal market have rendered this Regulation fully redundant'.[22] However, Article 44(9) of the FSR states clearly that the EU rules must respect WTO rules and 'no action shall be taken under this Regulation which would amount to a specific action against a subsidy within the meaning of the WTO Agreement on Subsidies and Countervailing Measures and granted by a third country which is a member of the World Trade Organisation'.

On the one hand, the FSR is thus strongly 'commercial' in nature, which prevents it from being treated exclusively as a competition policy instrument. This is clear from its function as an instrument of political pressure on third countries and the WTO, as mentioned above. On the other hand, the FSR has an undeniable impact on competition policy and the internal market and is expressly aimed at ensuring a level playing field between EU and foreign companies (Article 1.1 FSR). As a result, the FSR necessarily presents two faces.

The legal basis for the FSR is also twofold:[23] Article 207 TFEU, which allows foreign subsidies to be regulated under the EU common commercial policy, and Article 114 TFEU, as the FSR affects the freedom of establishment and the free movement of goods and services. That dichotomy has not been exempt from criticism, pointing out that it would have been more appropriate to opt either for Article 207 TFEU alone, for competition provisions or the open clause of Article 352 TFEU.[24] Such criticisms seem

---

21. Eddy De Smijter, *There's a New Kid in Town: The Foreign Subsidies Regulation*, 13 Journal of European Competition Law & Practice, 8, 529 (2022) https://doi.org/10.1093/jeclap/lpad001.
22. Article 52(2)(e) FSR.
23. The legislative process involved different services of the European Commission and included months of negotiations inside the European Parliament in order to identify the Committee in charge for this hybrid new instrument.
24. It has been argued that the use of Art. 114 TFEU is not correct given that this provision concerns the harmonization of existing or future national rules. However, this would be inconsistent with the interpretation of Art. 207 TFEU, which classifies foreign subsidies as an area of exclusive EU competence. Furthermore, there are those who argue that the foreign *subsidies* legislation should be more properly framed in the context of competition policy, an element that the regulation does indeed mention among its objectives, but which also falls within the exclusive competence of the EU. In this sense, there are those who have put forward the hypothesis of using only Art. 207 TFEU as a legal basis, arguing that the restoration of competition is only a consequence of the regulation of trade. Again, there are those who have referred to Art. 352 TFEU, i.e., the so-called open clause of the Treaty, because of the primarily competitive nature of the rules on *foreign subsidies* and the inadequacy of Arts 103 and 109 TFEU as legal bases. *See* J.S. Wolski, *Legal Basis of the Proposal for Regulation on Foreign Subsidies*, EStAL, 2, 153-172 (2022) https://doi.org/10.21552/estal/2022/2/6.

in our view to be excessively formalistic, given that Article 207 TFEU expressly refers to '*standardisation of measures*' concerning foreign subsidies and it cannot be denied that the conditions of fair trade are intrinsically linked to the dynamics of competition in the single market, thus also falling within the scope of Article 114 TFEU. At the same time, the FSR is clearly a tool for common commercial policy as it concerns *foreign* subsidies: the duality of its legal basis is echoed in the key concepts of the FSR (*see* below).

Trade policy, based on Article 207 TFEU, is an exclusive competence of the EU. By contrast, the measures for the internal market, based on Article 114 TFEU, normally fall in an area of shared competence with the Member States, unless the objectives of the instrument could be better achieved at the EU level. This is the case for the FSR, where several Member States, as mentioned above, had called on the Commission to propose draft legislation in this area. The situation is indeed comparable to State aid granted by EU Member States, which by nature has effects on more than one Member State. Addressing distortive foreign subsidies at the EU level allows also potential beneficiaries of foreign subsidies to know in advance the rules that the Commission will use to assess the existence of foreign subsidies and possible distortions they may cause (legal certainty).[25]

Therefore, also under the FSR, not the national authorities but the European Commission is tasked to investigate financial contributions granted by non-EU governments to companies active in the EU and can impose measures to redress their distortive effects: the Commission is, therefore, the sole enforcer of the FSR. In particular, the Directorate-General for Competition (DG COMP) is responsible for enforcing the FSR as regards concentrations and the Directorate-General for Internal Market, Industry, Entrepreneurship and SMEs (DG GROW) is responsible for enforcing the FSR as regards financial contributions in public procurement procedures.[26] The Directorate-General in charge of trade, including trade defence, (DG TRADE) remains involved in the inter-service consultations, due to the major geopolitical implications of this instrument. This conferral of powers to the Commission is meaningful and justified by the need to ensure a level playing field throughout the internal market and consistency in the application of the Regulation (Recital 8, FSR). However, the implementation of the Regulation is without prejudice to the right of each Member State to protect its essential security interests (Recital 10, FSR).

---

25. The dual legal basis is well justified in the Proposal for a Regulation of the European Parliament and of the Council on foreign subsidies distorting the internal market, COM/2021/223 final.
26. In case of questions regarding the application of the FSR on concentrations, an email can be sent to DG COMP's Foreign Subsidies Registry functional email address: comp-fsr-registry@ec.europa.eu. In case of questions regarding the application of the FSR on public procurement procedures, an email can be sent to DG GROW's functional email: grow-fsr-pp-notifications@ec.europa.eu.

§10.04 MAIN FEATURES OF THE FSR: A MIX OF EU COMPETITION AND TRADE DEFENCE RULES

As mentioned, the FSR is indebted[27] respectively to EU competition rules (antitrust, merger, and State aid control) and trade defence instruments (anti-dumping and anti-subsidy regulations): neither of these two sets of rules seemed indeed sufficient on its own to face the current challenges caused by foreign subsidies distorting the competition on the EU internal market. The main features of the FSR described below take inspiration from both sets of rules with some adjustments. Indeed, the economic rationale of both State aid and foreign subsidy control are overlapping since they address the same distortions interfering with the normal competition on the market based on the competitive advantage of the different companies and try the re-establish the level playing field. On the one hand, State aid rules concern subsidies granted by a State who wants to foster economic development in its own market to the detriment of another State. On the other hand, foreign subsidies, similarly to countervailable subsidies in WTO terms, operate on the market of another State which can be detrimental to the interest of the State granting the subsidy. It is important to stress this element of 'extra-territoriality' because of its implications for the conception of this new instrument and its enforcement setup.

'Foreign subsidy': The scope of application of FSR is based on the notion of 'foreign subsidy' distorting the internal market, the definitions of which are laid down in the same regulation. Pursuant to Article 3(1) FSR, a foreign subsidy is deemed to exist 'where a third country provides, directly or indirectly, a financial contribution which confers a benefit on an undertaking engaging in an economic activity in the internal market and which is limited, in law or in fact, to one or more undertaking or industry'. The starting point for understanding the notion of foreign subsidy is thus that of financial contribution, which is not defined in a general way. In fact, the FSR provides only a non-exhaustive list of measures that are to be considered as financial contributions,[28] including the transfer of funds and liabilities (e.g., capital injections, grants, loans and guarantees),[29] the waiver of revenues otherwise due (e.g., tax exemption)[30] and the provision or purchase of goods and services.[31] As for timing, a

---

27. *Ibid.*, 529.
28. Article 3.2.a FSR.
29. Such category includes also setting off operating losses, compensation for financial burdens imposed by public authorities, fiscal incentives, debt for equity swap, debt forgiveness or rescheduling.
30. Similarly to State aid law, a financial contribution can be found even if the government has not incurred in a cost. In case of tax exemption, the assessment would require the comparison between the tax treatment granted to the company with the ordinary system of taxation chosen and applied by the third country. Other examples may come from previous Commission's anti-subsidy practice, which has qualified as tax reductions measures like accelerated depreciation, exemption from income sale taxes, import duty exemptions, favourable income taxes for specific undertakings or industries. *See inter alia* Commission Decision 284/2000/ECSC of 4 Feb. 2000 imposing a definitive countervailing duty on imports of certain flat rolled products of iron or non-alloy steel, of a width of 600 mm or more, not clad, plated or coated, in coils, not further worked than hot-rolled, originating in India and Taiwan and accepting undertakings offered by certain exporting producers and terminating the proceeding concerning imports originating in

foreign subsidy would be considered granted when the beneficiary obtains an entitlement to receive a financial contribution, while the actual disbursement is not required.[32] The subsidy recipient must be an individual undertaking engaging in an economic activity in the internal market (Articles 1(2) and 3(1) FSR). One could assume that the respective jurisprudence of competition and State aid law on the concept of undertaking can be transposed to FSR: for example, a subsidy paid to the parent company is deemed to benefit also its subsidiary.[33] A specificity condition is also established, as the benefit shall be 'limited in law or in fact to one or more undertaking or industries', which would possibly recall the case law developed by EU Courts in State aid law.

However, in the case of FSR, the general principles of trade defence law apply: the fact that a subsidy is paid by a third country to the parent company does not trigger as such any countermeasure unless it causes a distortion on the EU internal market. Indeed, third countries are not subject to EU rules on State aid.

Moreover, the measure at issue shall confer a 'benefit' to the undertaking concerned, which can be determined based on comparative benchmarks, such as the practice of market operators or the terms available on the market or comparable tax treatment. When comparable treatments are not available, adjusted or alternative benchmarks can be established based on generally accepted assessment methods.[34] The FSR thus recalls the same methods of State aid law in relation to the use of benchmarks and the market economy operator principle (MEOP).

The benefits conferred by a financial contribution to a company not active in the internal market may be passed on to an entity engaging in an economic activity in the EU, for instance in the case of internal transfers within the same control group, of government payments made for indirectly benefitting a specific recipient.[35]

South Africa, OJ L 31, 5.2.2000, pp. 44-78; Commission Regulation (EU) No. 1261/2010 of 22 Dec. 2010 imposing a provisional countervailing duty on imports of certain stainless steel bars originating in India, OJ L 343, 29.12.2010, pp. 57-75; Commission Implementing Regulation (EU) 2022/433 of 15 Mar. 2022 imposing definitive countervailing duties on imports of stainless steel cold-rolled flat products originating in India and Indonesia and amending Implementing Regulation (EU) 2021/2012 imposing a definitive anti-dumping duty and definitively collecting the provisional duty imposed on imports of stainless steel cold-rolled flat products originating in India and Indonesia, C/2022/1515, OJ L 88, 16.3.2022, pp. 24-180.

31. A subsidy can occur in case, for instance, that the sale-purchase relationship between the State and a company can artificially lower production costs or if the State provides training for skills related to the production of a certain product for free or at below-market rates, or if the State assign infrastructure or assets to a company for its exclusive use for a certain period of time.
32. Recital 15 FSR. In case that an undertaking is entitled to payments under a grant, a financial contribution is deemed to occur only when the condition has materialized and the recipient is entitled to the payment. In any case, please mind that in the context of FSR notification (further detailed below), the determination of whether thresholds have been met is based only on financial contributions received in the three years prior to the notification.
33. Hornkohl, *supra* n. 2.
34. The provisions or purchase of goods and services carried out following a competitive, transparent and non-discriminatory tender procedure is presumed to be in line with normal market conditions (Recital 13, FSR).
35. Recital 13, FSR.

'*Provided by a third country*': With regard to the source of the financial contribution by the public authority of the third country, the FSR explains that this includes not only the central government of the third country and all other levels of public authorities but also any public and private entity whose behaviour can be referred to the third country, in light of the characteristics of the entity and the legal and economic environment prevailing in the state where the entity operates, including the role of the government in the economy.[36] While the condition of imputability overlaps in State aid law and in FSR, the latter did not borrow the condition of State resources.[37] Similar to the EU anti-subsidy regulation,[38] for the FSR the imputability of the subsidy on the State does not require the government granting the subsidy to incur any costs and can also mean financing at preferential terms from foreign banks directly upon instructions of a foreign State.[39] Like in trade defence, the Commission would not have anyhow any investigating powers to look into the costs incurred by a third country granting the subsidy.

In light of the above, the notion of foreign subsidy provided for in the FSR lies somewhere in between that of State aid and subsidy within the meaning of the WTO framework. On the one hand, the definition in the FSR does not refer to the EU State aid law criteria of State resources, advantage and selectivity but recalls the criteria contained in the WTO Agreement on Subsidies of 'financial contribution', 'benefit' and 'specificity'. The latter, as interpreted by the case law of the WTO Appellate Body, is broader and could lead to a definition of foreign subsidy under FSR wider than that of State aid.[40] On the other hand, the FSR contains several references to concepts typical of State aid rules, such as the assessment of benefits based on benchmarks, and prescribes that the rules should be interpreted in accordance with EU law, including State aid law.[41] In addition, it cannot be overlooked that both EU courts and the Commission (especially DG COMP) are likely to be influenced by the concepts of the State aid rules when applying the FSR rules.

'*Distortion of competition*': while the distortion of competition is presumed under State aid law, in the FSR – like in trade defence – the Commission must prove a distortion (Article 4 FSR).[42] In particular, the Commission needs to establish a relationship between the foreign subsidy and the activities of the undertaking in the internal market.[43]

---

36. Article 3.2.b FSR.
37. Hornkohl, *supra* n. 2.
38. Regulation (EU) 2016/1037 of the European Parliament and of the Council of 8 Jun. 2016 on protection against subsidized imports from countries not members of the European Union (OJ L 176, 30.6.2016, p. 55).
39. Commission Communication, *White paper on levelling the playing field as regards foreign subsidies*, Brussels, 17.6.2020 COM(2020) 253 final, 8.
40. Morris Schonberg, *The EU Foreign Subsidies Regulation: Substantive Assessment and Open Issues*, 2 EStal, 145 (2022) https://doi.org/10.21552/estal/2022/2/5.
41. Recital 9 FSR.
42. Hornkohl, *supra* n. 2.
43. For instance, according to the Commission, a prima facie connection exists 'in the case of an interest-free loan provided by a third country directly to an EU entity active in the internal market', while a relationship with the internal market is not apparent 'in the case of a foreign subsidy that has been granted to a subsidiary not active in the Union, where that subsidy has

This requires a deep economic examination of the impact of the subsidy, proving the recipient's improved competitive position and harm to competition, on the basis of a non-exhaustive list of indicators (Article 4(1) FSR).[44] Recital 19 FSR provides additional details on the evaluation of such indicators, such as the part of the purchase price covered by the foreign subsidy in a concentration, the greater distortive nature of subsidies granted for operating costs rather than for investment costs, the lower impact of subsidies to SMEs compared to those to large companies.[45]

The condition of the effect on trade between Member States, which is relevant under State aid law, is not part of the list: the inter-Union dimension seems indeed presumed in the case of a foreign subsidy (international dimension) when it is above a certain *de minimis* threshold.

More specifically, under the M&A tool, the distortive effect would have to be 'limited to the concentration concerned'[46] and could possibly be established regarding competition in the market for corporate control 'where such concentrations are fully or partially financed through foreign subsidies',[47] as well as on the downstream product markets on which the parties will be active post-merger, provided that the distortive effects are resulting specifically from the merger.[48] As for the public procurement tool, Article 27 FSR establishes that a distortive effect is found in case a foreign subsidy enables an economic operator to submit a tender 'that is unduly advantageous in relation to the works, supplies or services concerned'.[49]

---

been granted and effectively used in order to develop the local activity of the subsidiary in a third country'. In any case, the Commission states that 'foreign subsidies with no apparent relationships with an activity in the internal market can still be considered distortive, for instance where they are used in the group to cross-subsidise activities in the internal market'. *See* Commission Staff Working Document, *Initial clarifications on the application of Article 4(1), Article 6 and Article 27(1) of Regulation (EU) 2022/2560 on foreign subsidies distorting the internal market*, Brussels, 26 Jul. 2024, SWD(2024) 201 final, 1 (Working Document).

44. Such indicators include the amount and nature of the foreign subsidy, as well as its purpose, conditions and intended use on the internal market, the situation of the undertaking, including its size and the markets or sectors concerned, the level and evolution of economic activity of the undertaking on the internal market. Commission is not required to assess all these criteria in each FSR investigation. In fact, 'the Commission will assess each case on its merits and will use the relevant indicators as appropriate to assess the distortive effect of the subsidy'. In addition, in the case of subsidies falling under Art. 5(1) FSR a detailed assessment based on indicators is not required. *See* Commission Staff Working Document, *Initial clarifications on the application of Article 4(1), Article 6 and Article 27(1) of Regulation (EU) 2022/2560 on foreign subsidies distorting the internal market, supra* n. 2.
45. Additional guidance can also be found in the Commission's White Paper, which refers to a collection of indicators related to the subsidized acquisition and the relevant market situation. *See* White Paper COM (2020) 253 final (n 9) 26.
46. Article 19 FSR.
47. Recital 4 FSR.
48. The Commission specified that foreign subsidies received by the acquirer are more critical than those received by the target or the seller. However, '[s]ubsidies granted to the target (or in some circumstances, even to the seller) may also be relevant'. *See* Commission Staff Working Document, *Initial clarifications on the application of Article 4(1), Article 6 and Article 27(1) of Regulation (EU) 2022/2560 on foreign subsidies distorting the internal market, supra* n. 2, 5.
49. As detailed in the Working Document, the 'unduly advantage' is a twofold criterion: (i) the tender shall be 'advantageous', following a comparison between the allegedly subsidized tender with the other bids submitted in the procurement procedure, in lights of the documents showing the assessment of the competing bids by the contracting authority; if the allegedly subsidized

'Most likely distortive foreign subsidies': As indicated by Article 5, a number of specific types of foreign subsidies are to be considered 'distortive', absent any specific evidence to the contrary,[50] some of them would also be considered incompatible with the internal market under EU State aid law (i.e., rescue and restructuring subsidies to an undertaking in difficulty without a restructuring plan and unlimited guarantees).[51]

A recipient undertaking can rebut the presumption of distortion by demonstrating that the subsidy does not improve the competitive position of the undertaking in the UE nor negatively affects competition in the internal market, for instance by providing evidence of the absence of effects of the benefit on the operations of the undertaking within the EU.[52]

'Non-distortive foreign subsidy': There are two thresholds and one exception in the FSR that introduce presumptions of non-distortive foreign subsidies, which have different implications.[53]

According to Article 4(2) FSR, a foreign subsidy is *unlike to distort* the internal market if its total amount does not exceed EUR 4 million over any consecutive period of the financial year (*de minimis* threshold) – meaning that some room of discretion is left to the investigating authority, the Commission, which carries the burden of proof to reverse the presumption.

According to Article 4(3) FSR, a foreign subsidy below the threshold of EUR 200,000 under Article 3(2) of the De Minimis Regulation under State Aid law *shall not be considered to distort* the internal market – meaning that subsidies below this threshold never qualify as distortions.

According to Article 4(4) FSR, foreign subsidies making good damages from natural disasters or exceptional occurrences *may be considered non-distortive* – meaning that once again room for discretion is left to the Commission. This provision differs substantially from the similar provision under State Aid law (Article 107(2) TFEU) which does not give the Commission any discretion by stating that disaster aid *shall be considered compatible* with the internal market.[54] The greater discretion granted to the Commission and the fact that disaster subsidies are not part of the balancing test under the FSR (*see* below) seems directly linked to the experience of the many State aid

tender is lower than competing bids, all other things being equal, it will likely be deemed 'advantageous'; (ii) the advantage must be 'undue'. On this point, the Commission will consider possible justifications based on other factors than the subsidy itself, while the recipient undertaking will be able to provide defensive arguments, e.g., based on the criteria set out by the EU procurement Directives in relation to 'abnormally low tenders'.

50. These include a foreign subsidy granted to ailing undertakings, unlimited guarantees for debts or liabilities, export financing measures not in line with OECD Agreement on officially supported export credits, a foreign subsidy directly facilitating a concentration or enabling an undertaking to submit an unduly advantageous tender.
51. *See* Communication from the Commission – Guidelines on State aid for rescuing and restructuring non-financial undertakings in difficulty, OJ C 249, 31.7.2014, pp. 1-28; and Commission Notice on the application of Arts 87 and 88 of the EC Treaty to State aid in the form of guarantees, OJ C 155, 20.6.2008, pp. 10-22.
52. Andreas Reindl & Isabelle Van Damme, *The EU Foreign Subsidies Regulation*, 60 (Concurrences 2024).
53. Hornkohl, *supra* n. 2.
54. *Ibid.*

decisions authorized during the COVID-19 pandemic and the litigations that followed.[55]

'Balancing test': the conception and the construction of the balancing test in the FSR deviates from State Aid law and is inspired directly by the 'Union interest test' used in trade defence investigations. In trade defence law, such test tries to assess whether the imposition of a duty on certain dumped or subsidized imports is in the interest of the European Union, as a whole. The 'Union interest test' requires the Commission, before imposing a countervailing duty,[56] to compare positive against negative economic effects on the internal market of such duty.

The 'Union interest test' is an additional procedural layer imposed pursuant to EU law, as compared to the obligations imposed by international rules (WTO Agreements). The EU's more restrictive rules result from the negotiations between the EU co-legislators and reflect the final compromise between Member States and political groups in the European Parliament. This background can explain why a similar test has spilt over to the FSR: foreign subsidies have an important external trade component insofar as they are granted by third countries and are not 'generally prohibited' (Recital 17, FSR), so the exemption-based approach of State aid rules would not be fitting.

Pursuant to the FSR, following the same logic of trade defence law, the Commission will: (1) investigate whether a foreign subsidy exists, (2) assess on a case-by-case basis whether it distorts the internal market (Recital 17, FSR), (3) apply the balancing test before imposing a counterbalancing measure or commitment. Therefore, the Commission will not look at whether a foreign subsidy is prohibited or incompatible with the internal market in the abstract but will assess whether concretely it causes negative effects on the development of relevant subsidized economic activity on the internal market outbalancing its positive effects (Article 6(1) FSR).[57] It may also consider other broader positive effects in relation to the relevant policy objectives of the Union. Based on such assessment, as mentioned above, the Commission will decide whether to impose redressive measures or to accept commitments and the nature and level of those measures or commitments.

The wording used for the balancing test in the FSR implies that foreign subsidies may have indeed both positive and negative effects on the relevant economic activity on the internal market. It reflects the complexity of the concept of 'Open Strategic Autonomy': the EU needs to be open to investments in so far as they serve its strategic objectives and the EU is not dependent on them in critical sectors. Openness to trade and investment underpins Europe's prosperity and competitiveness, but trade relations

55. *Ibid.*
56. Before applying the Union interest test, it is noteworthy to stress that, according to EU rules, anti-dumping and anti-subsidies duties are already set at the lowest level possible offsetting the economic impact on the EU industry caused by the dumped or subsidized import (so-called lesser duty rule). As a result, unlike in the USA, EU trade defence duties can be set at a level lower ('lesser duty') than the actual subsidization and dumping benefiting foreign exporters.
57. According to Art. 6(1) FSR, the Commission may balance the negative effects of a distortive foreign subsidy against its positive effects on the development of relevant subsidized economic activity on the internal market.

must be mutually beneficial to ensure the EU economy's resilience.[58] Member States, as well as any natural or legal persons, can submit evidence on the positive effects of a foreign subsidy. Additionally, the Commission may perform its balancing test, while considering other positive effects of the foreign subsidy 'such as the broader positive effects in relation to the relevant policy objectives, in particular those of the Union' (Article 6(1)). The relevant policy objectives (in particular those of the Union) can include a high level of environmental protection and social standards, and the promotion of research and development (Recital 21 FSR) but these are not exhaustive examples. In other terms, the positive effects of a foreign subsidy will outweigh its negative effects only if they serve the policy objectives of the Union. When the effects of a foreign subsidy serve the policy objectives of the State granting it, they would normally be negative for the EU, since such policy objectives would foster the economic development in the territory of the granting State. In particular, the Commission Staff Working Document refers to the possibility of relying on all 'positive effects on the internal market have been acknowledged under the EU State aid rules'.[59]

The Commission shall publish, at the latest on 12 January 2026 (and regularly update thereafter) guidelines regarding the application of the balancing test in accordance with Article 6 (Article 46(1)b FSR). So far, this test has not yet been used in any concrete case, which could be provided as an example, but it is questionable that EU and WTO jurisprudence on the 'Union interest test' will be applicable by analogy to the balancing test introduced by the FSR.

§10.05 THE PROCEDURES UNDER THE FOREIGN SUBSIDY REGULATION

The FSR introduces three procedures: two notification-based procedures to investigate respectively concentrations and bids in public procurement procedures above certain thresholds, and an ex officio procedure to investigate all other market situations, where the Commission can start a review on its own initiative. The following investigation for the review of the foreign subsidies is divided into two phases: the preliminary review and the subsequent 'in-depth investigation'. In the end, the Commission may: (i) accept commitments proposed by the company if they fully and effectively remedy the distortion, (ii) impose a redressive measure including the prohibition of the transaction, or (iii) issue a no-objection decision.

[A] Two Types of Mandatory Notifications

FSR introduces two types of mandatory notification: the first, addressed to DG COMP, relates to mergers that exceed a double set of thresholds, based on both turnover and

58. Commission Communication, White Paper on levelling the playing field as regards foreign subsidies, Brussels, 17.6.2020, COM(2020) 253 final, 4.
59. Commission Staff Working Document, *Initial clarifications on the application of Article 4(1), Article 6 and Article 27(1) of Regulation (EU) 2022/2560 on foreign subsidies distorting the internal market*, *supra* n. 2, 6.

the level of foreign subsidies received ('M&A Tool');[60] the second, addressed to DG GROW, concerning bids in public procurement procedures involving financial contributions from non-EU governments, when thresholds on the value of the contract and the level of subsidies received are exceeded (Public Procurement Tool).[61]

If the relevant thresholds are exceeded, the parties are subject to a notification obligation, accompanied by a standstill obligation on the conclusion of the concentration or the award of the public contract until the outcome of the procedure.[62] The Commission may also request ad hoc notifications even if the thresholds are not exceeded if it suspects the existence of distortive foreign subsidies.[63]

[1] M&A Tool

The M&A Tool operates in parallel to the EU merger control regime and mirrors its rules under many aspects.[64]

For instance, the notion of a notifiable concentration is similar to that of the Regulation (EC) 139/2004 (EUMR),[65] based on change of control on a lasting basis, including the creation of a full-function JV.[66] The principles expressed in the context of the EUMR and in the Jurisdictional Notice therefore apply.[67] As far as the turnover thresholds are concerned, unlike the EUMR, the FSR provides that the relevant entity is established in the EU, including the case in which it has a single subsidiary in the EU.[68]

60. In particular, notification of a concentration is due when the acquired company, one of the merging parties or the joint venture is established in the EU and generates an EU turnover of at least EUR 500 million and the parties have received foreign financial contributions of more than EUR 50 million in the last three years.
61. A tender notification is due when the estimated value of the contract is at least EUR 250 million and the tender involves a foreign financial contribution of at least EUR 4 million per third country over the last three years.
62. In the case of gun jumping, fines of up to 10% of the total turnover of the parties are foreseen. In two cases, similar to what is established under EU merger control rules, an exemption from the standstill obligation is possible: in the case of a takeover bid or a series of securities transactions, provided that the transaction is notified without delay and that the acquirer does not exercise its voting rights on the acquired shares.
63. The Commission cannot require the notification of transactions that do not constitute concentrations, but only of sub-threshold concentrations. However, the Commission may review different transactions under the ex officio investigation tool.
64. The specific rules of the M&A Tool are provided under Arts 20-26 FSR, while a specific form for notification is provided under Annex 1 FSR (Form FS-CO).
65. Council Regulation (EC) No. 139/2004 of 20 Jan. 2004 on the control of concentrations between undertakings (the EC Merger Regulation) (Text with EEA relevance), OJ L 24, 29/01/2004, pp. 1-22.
66. Unlike the EUMR, the turnover of the buyer or the parents of a JV is not relevant for the calculation of turnover under FSR thresholds. Therefore, the creation of a new greenfield JV cannot meet FSR thresholds.
67. This has been expressly confirmed by the Commission in FSR Q&A, Question 6, n. 31.
68. *See* FSR Form CO section 4, fn 4 and the ECJ case law referred therein. The Commission clarifies that the requirement of the establishment in the EU includes the incorporation of a subsidiary or a permanent business establishment in the Union. This requirement, which does not apply to EUMR turnover thresholds, is explained by the different rationale of the two instruments: FSR

Under the FSR, the concept of turnover is broad and includes revenue generated from assets located in the EU, as well as revenue from sales or services provided to other entities or consumers located within the EU, including revenue generated with sales in the EU by entities of the same group without an established presence within the Union. Therefore, the M&A Tool could possibly apply to foreign-to-foreign transactions, insofar as an EU permanent presence within the same group is established.

It shall also be noted that, in case of JVs, the turnover of the acquirer or the parents is not relevant for the calculation of the FSR turnover thresholds. This entails that the creation of a greenfield JV cannot trigger FSR notification requirements.[69]

As regards the threshold for contributions, there is no requirement of nexus with the EU, so it is possible that the benefit was received, directly or indirectly, anywhere in the world. The relevant contributions are those received in the three years prior to the conclusion of the agreement, the announcement of the public bid or the purchase of the controlling interest (not from the date of notification). Also, the subjects whose contributions received are relevant are different from those provided for the calculation of turnover: in fact, in the event of acquisition, the contributions received from the purchasers and the acquired entity are considered; in the case of mergers, by merging parties; in the case of a JV, by the parties creating the JV and the JV itself.

In any case, the FSR allows the Commission to initiate ex officio investigation in case information indicates the possibility that a foreign subsidy distorting the internal market exists, even if the transaction does not meet the above-mentioned thresholds.

The relevant moment to notify a transaction is similar under FSR and EUMR,[70] and a standstill obligation is established as well, until receiving the Commission's clearance or the expiry of the maximum terms for review (twenty-five days after formal notification or ninety days after the start of an in-depth investigation).[71]

---

concerns the acquisition of assets in the EU facilitated by subsidies, whereas EUMR concerns the assessment of the competitive effects of a merger on markets, beyond a formal presence of the companies concerned in the EU.

69. *See* Commission FSR Q&A, Question 2, n. 31. The criteria for calculating turnover for FSR also differ from those of the EUMR in that the threshold of EUR 500 million refers to the turnover of a single party, i.e., the acquired or merging entity or the JV, unlike merger control where the thresholds consider all the turnover of the parties concerned. This is due to the different function of the two instruments: the FSR aims to avoid acquisitions that benefit from illegitimate competitive advantages of major players active in Europe, while the EUMR wants to assess the future competitive impact of an operation.

70. Under Art. 21 FSR, parties shall notify a transaction 'prior to their implementation and following the conclusion of the agreement, the announcement of the public bid, or the acquisition of a controlling interest', as well as 'when they demonstrate to the Commission a good faith intention to conclude an agreement or, in the case of a public bid, where they have publicly announced their intention to make such a bid'.

71. Article 24 FSR. Similarly to EUMR, the FSR does not prevent the implementation of '*a public bid or of a series of transactions in securities*' provided that the concentration is notified '*without delay*' and '*the acquirer does not exercise the voting rights attached to the securities in question or does so only to maintain the full value of its investments based on a derogation granted by the Commission*'.

[2] *Public Procurement Tool*

The Public Procurement Tool applies to public procurement procedures falling under the EU public procurement Directives listed by Article 2 FSR.[72] Notification to the Commission is due based on the value threshold, while the contribution threshold determines whether a full form or a less detailed form is required.

The relevant entities whose contributions shall be taken into account under the Public Procurement Tool differ from those of the M&A Tool and include the economic operator, including its subsidiary companies without commercial autonomy, its holding companies, and, where applicable, its main subcontractors and suppliers involved in the same public procurement project.

Contracting authorities, when publishing a contract notice for new public works, supplies or service contracts, shall state the economic operators will be subject to the FSR. In case of negotiated proceeding, the economic operator shall inform the Commission of all financial contributions received. However, this information will not be considered a notification under FSR and will not be subject to the review procedure.

Pending Commission's review, public authorities and economic operators are subject to a standstill requirement, prohibiting the award of the procedure, although allowing for the implementation of all other procedural steps.

In case the economic operator has not submitted an FSR notification, the contracting authority may request to make the filing within ten working days, subject to exclusion from the procedure. Such notice is necessary in order to declare the request to participate or tender irregular.

The notification under the Public Procurement Tool is structured according to the type of procedure: in case of a one-stage procedure, the filing is performed when submitting the bid; in multi-stage procedures the submission is performed twice, following the request to participate and following the final bid, reflecting any changes occurred. Therefore, there can be more than one notifying party for a procedure.

[B] The Different Phases of the Investigation

Following a mandatory notification or the starting of an ex officio procedure, the FSR investigation is structured in two phases: the preliminary review and the subsequent 'in-depth investigation'. In the first one, it is assessed whether the benefitting measure constitutes a foreign subsidy distorting the internal market, while in the second one, a more in-depth analysis of the distortive effect is carried out, if necessary. In addition,

72. Such list includes: (i) any type of award procedure covered by Directive 2014/24/EU for the conclusion of a public contract or Directive 2014/25/EU for the conclusion of a supply, works and service contract; (ii) a procedure for the award of a works or a service concession covered by Directive 2014/23/EU; (iii) procedures for awarding contracts falling under Directive 2009/81/EC, unless exempted by Member States on the basis of Art. 346 TFEU; procedures for the award of contracts referred to in Art. 10(4), point (a) of Directive 2014/23/EU, Art. 9(1), point (a) of Directive 2014/24/EU or Art. 20(1), point (a) of Directive 2014/25/EU.

the Commission encourages the initiation of a 'pre-notification' phase before formal notification is submitted.

The first stage starts from the moment the Commission considers the notification complete. It is not expected to be published in the EU Official Journal, unlike notifications under the EUMR. In the event of incomplete information or documentation, the Commission may send RFIs to the parties and, in the absence of a complete response, the review deadlines are suspended.

If the Commission does not take a decision at the end of Phase I (lasting a maximum of twenty-five or twenty working days for the M&A Tool and the Public Procurement Tool respectively), the transaction is deemed to have been approved and can be implemented by the parties. Otherwise, the Commission may take the formal decision to initiate an in-depth investigation, which is published in the Official Journal inviting comments.

Following the decision to open phase II, the Commission review can last up to 90 - under the M&A Tool - or 110 - under the Public Procurement Tool - working days, which can be extended in some cases.[73]

Under the Public Procurement Tool, contracting authorities shall notify the Commission of any decision relating to the cancellation of the procedure, the rejection of the tender of the notifying operator, the submission of a new tender by the same operator or the award of the public contract pursuant to Article 32(2) FSR.

The scheme is mirroring State aid procedure. The intermediate step between the two phases is similar under the two frameworks, i.e., a Commission decision ordering the opening of Phase 2, in which the relevant facts and main legal issues are to be summarized.

The nature of the addressee will of course be different: a Member State in the State aid decision, the undertaking concerned under the FSR. Similarly, in contrast to aid procedures, where the addressee of any information request is the Member State,[74] under FSR it is instead the undertaking concerned that is the subject of requests for information and inspections, while the foreign State cannot be obliged to cooperate in the investigation procedures.[75]

The nature of the powers which can be applied by the Commission at the end of the two phases is also different, given the broader powers provided for in the FSR.[76] In Phase 1, the Commission may carry out investigations and then either initiate Phase 2 or close the investigation in a negative sense (no subsidy or no actual or potential

73. For instance, for the M&A Tool, such period is automatically extended by fifteen working days in case the parties offer commitments; following the parties' request, if made within fifteen days from the opening of phase II; by agreements between the Commission and the parties for maximum twenty working days.
74. Requests for information may be made directly to the aid beneficiary with the consent of the Member State concerned pursuant to Art. 7(2) b of the Procedural Regulation.
75. Of course, the Commission has no coercive instruments at its disposal against a third state. In the case of inspections at the premises of the undertaking concerned outside the EU require the consent of the undertaking and the State concerned.
76. In State aid procedures, at the end of stage 1 the Commission may declare that the measure does not constitute aid, that the aid is compatible or that, at the end of stage 2, the measure may not be adopted.

distortion of competition), but no commitments or other measures can be imposed. In Phase 2, the Commission is subject to an obligation to carry out in-depth investigations and then it may either impose redressive measures, adopt a commitment decision or a decision not to raise objections.

In both Phase 1 and Phase 2, the FSR states that the Commission may decide on the basis of the available information if the interested party and/or third state does not cooperate with a request for information or inspection. If an undertaking fails to provide the requested information, the burden of proof is reversed in favour of the Commission, meaning that a benefit is presumed to have been conferred. These rules clearly appear stricter than those provided under State aid legislation but are dictated by the greater difficulty of conducting an investigation procedure against a foreign undertaking.[77]

[C] Measures under the Foreign Subsidy Investigation

Under the FSR, the Commission is entrusted with a vast set of decision-making powers: during the review period, it can issue requests for information, conduct interviews, carry out inspections, and impose interim measures; at the end of its review, it can decide not to raise objections, to prohibit the transaction, adopt redressive measure or accept commitments by the undertaking concerned.

The balancing test can lead to the conclusion not to impose redressive measures where the positive effects of the foreign subsidy outweigh its negative effects. If the negative effects prevail, the balancing test can help to determine the appropriate nature and level of the commitments or redressive measures. In any event, given that the balancing test considers the positive effects of a foreign subsidy, applying that balancing test should not lead to an outcome for the undertaking that would be worse than if the balancing test had not been applied. Where the Commission carries out a balancing test, 'it should set out its reasoning in the decision closing an in-depth investigation' (Recital 21 FSR).

Commitments and redressive measures in the FSR are mostly inspired by State Aid law and based on the internal market logic, while duties, which are the typical counterbalancing measures in trade defence law, are not excluded but less likely to be used. They can consist of behavioural or structural remedies: offering fair and non-discriminatory access to infrastructures, reducing market presence, licensing assets acquired under FRAND condition, repaying the foreign subsidy, providing public access to R&D elements, divestments, and undoing the transaction. The Commission cannot of course prohibit a third Country not to grant the subsidy and to recover it, as under State aid law, but can only deploy measures to offset the adverse effect on the internal market. Greater flexibility is thus needed in order to be able to develop tailored-made solutions.

77. W. Weis, *Ex Officio Third Country Subsidies' Review: Similarities and Differences to State Aid Procedure*, 2 EStal 136 (2022) https://doi.org/10.5771/1435-439x-2022-3-467.

Interim measures can also be adopted under FSR in case there is an indication that a financial contribution constitutes a foreign subsidy and distorts the internal market and if there is a serious risk of substantial and irreparable damage to competition on the internal market. The threshold for applying interim measures is thus lower than under State aid rules, where there should be no doubts about the aid character of the measure concerned. Moreover, in State Aid Commission can order the suspension or provisional recovery of the aid, while under FSR interim measures they can be much more varied depending on the case.

Finally, like in anti-subsidy regulation, the Commission may perform a market investigation leading to a report, which can then be used for all investigations under the FSR in a particular sector (Article 36 FSR). This is the practice used in trade defence, where, for example, the findings of several investigations on subsidized imports from China have been compiled in a report (recently reviewed in April 2024).[78]

§10.06 FIRST PROCEEDINGS BASED ON THE FOREIGN SUBSIDY REGULATION

In April 2024, the Commission opened two in-depth investigations under the FSR in the solar panel photovoltaic sector. Two bidders in a public procurement procedure in the EU are owned and controlled, respectively, by a Chinese company listed on the Hong Kong Stock Exchange and by a Chinese State-Owned Enterprise. They receive from their Chinese controlling companies subsidies, which may have allowed them to submit an unduly advantageous offer in reply to a tender. Such an offer could distort the competition on the internal market by causing other companies, participating in the public procurement procedure, to lose sales opportunities. In line with the FSR, once the investigation is concluded, the Commission may accept the commitments proposed by the company if it fully and effectively remedies the distortion, prohibits the award of the contract, or issues a no-objection decision. The Commission has 110 days to make a decision from the date of submission of their views by the companies investigated.

As Thierry Breton, at the time Commissioner for Internal Market, put it: 'solar panels have become strategically important for Europe: for our clean energy production, jobs in Europe, and security of supply. The two new in-depth investigations on foreign subsidies in the solar panel sector aim to preserve Europe's economic security and competitiveness by ensuring that companies in our Single Market are truly competitive and play fair'. Margrethe Vestager, at the time Executive Vice-President for Europe Fit for the Digital Age, further stressed that fair competition is fundamental to attracting research and investment on the European solar market.[79]

---

78. Commission Staff Working Document on Significant Distortions in the Economy of the People's Republic of China for the Purposes of Trade Defence Investigations, SWD(2024)91; there is a similar report also on Russia (SWD(2020)242).
79. Commission press release, *Commission opens two in-depth investigations under the Foreign Subsidies Regulation in the solar photovoltaic sector*, 3 Apr. 2024 (https://ec.europa.eu/commission/presscorner/detail/en/IP_24_1803).

The European solar industry has a long history of trade disputes and has long been exposed to cheaper Chinese imports with many EU manufacturers shutting down plants and calling for more funding and fair competition. In addition, it is a fast-growing market in the EU thanks to the Green Deal, which combined with US tariffs against Chinese imports, channels excess Chinese productions to Europe. An EU solar charter was signed on 15 April 2024, setting out a series of voluntary actions to be undertaken to support the EU photovoltaic sector[80] aiming at rapid implementation of the EU's Net Zero Industry Act's non-price criteria in energy auctions and public procurement. These investigations send a strong warning: companies who benefit from foreign subsidies and are bidding for European tenders must factor in the risk that the Commission will investigate them to counter possible competition distortions. It means that a bidder should take very seriously their notification obligations under the FSR or could find itself excluded from a tender process; otherwise, they should withdraw from their bid, like the Chinese train maker CRRC Corp which was faced with the prospect of the first ever FSR investigation into its funding.[81]

Also in April 2024, EU officials performed unannounced inspections at the offices of Chinese security equipment maker Nuctech, which makes and sells baggage security scanners for airports and other equipment in Europe. The European Commission stated that it 'has indications that the inspected company may have received foreign subsidies that could distort the (EU's) internal market pursuant to the FSR'.[82] These unannounced inspections were a preliminary investigative step into suspected distortive foreign subsidies. The Commission officials were accompanied by their counterparts from the national competition authorities of the Member States where the inspections were carried out, namely Poland and the Netherlands. The China Chamber of Commerce to the EU, whose members include Chinese state-owned and private firms, expressed its 'strong dissatisfaction' about the raids, which it said had been conducted 'without prior notice and without solid evidence': 'The European side manifested its intention to weaponize the Foreign Subsidies Regulation as a tool to suppress lawfully operating Chinese companies in Europe', the lobby group said in a statement.[83]

As solar panels, x-ray scanners also have already been at the centre of the trade disputes between the EU and China. In 2013, a WTO panel report (DS425) found that

80. European Solar Charter, signed by the Commission, EU Member States and the representatives of the solar PV value chain, in particular wholesale, distribution and manufacturing parts, in Brussels, on 15 Apr. 2024 (https://energy.ec.europa.eu/topics/renewable-energy/solar-energy/european-solar-charter_en).
81. The investigation was launched on 16 Feb. 2024. The Bulgarian Ministry of Transport and Communication public procurement tender, with an estimated value of EUR 610 million (USD 657 million), is for twenty electric 'push-pull' trains and for their maintenance over fifteen years. *See* Commission press release, Commission opens first in-depth investigation under the Foreign Subsidies Regulation, 16 Feb. 2024, (https://ec.europa.eu/commission/presscorner/detail/en/ip_24_887).
82. Commission press release, Commission carries out unannounced foreign subsidies inspections in the security equipment sector, 23 Apr. 2024 (https://ec.europa.eu/commission/presscorner/detail/en/mex_24_2247).
83. Press release, CCCEU expresses serious concern over the European side's unannounced raids on Chinese companies Operating in Europe, 24 Apr. 2024 (http://en.ccceu.eu/2024-04/24/c_4219.htm).

China's anti-dumping duties on imports of X-ray security scanners from the EU were in breach of WTO anti-dumping rules, marking a clear victory for the EU in a long dispute that started several years before. China had retaliated against the EU anti-dumping duty on imports of certain cargo scanning systems originating in China produced by Nuctech by imposing similar, but unjustified, duties on the imports from the EU producer and competitor who had complained about Nuctech's unfair practices and requested and obtained trade defence measures.[84] So, it is not surprising that, in June 2024, Nuctech appealed to the General Court of the EU against the European Commission's decision to inspect Nuctech's offices pursuant to the FSR: this case needs to be followed because the decision will most likely have an impact on the extension of investigating powers of the Commission under the FSR. This case has clear geopolitical implications given also that, in 2020, the US government added Nuctech to a list of entities subject to stricter license requirements 'for its involvement in activities that are contrary to the national security interests of the United States'.[85]

In July 2024, China launched a trade and investment barrier investigation into the FSR based on the complaint received by the China Chamber of Commerce for Import and Export of Machinery and Electronic Products (CCCME). The Chinese Commerce Ministry (MOFCOM) will examine whether the investigations of Chinese enterprises launched by the EU under the FSR amounted to 'trade barriers'.[86] EU's investigations allegedly 'have caused impediments to the entry of Chinese products or services into the European market ... and damaged the competitiveness of Chinese enterprises, constituting trade barriers', the chamber said in its application. The products mentioned in the MOFCOM statement range from rail locomotives and photovoltaics to wind power and security equipment goods. The investigation will last until January 2025 and could be extended to April 2025, under special conditions.

The press reports about Chinese experts calling the EU to respect multilateralism and urging it to stop its short-sighted behaviour, as 'only a close cooperative relationship with China is the most beneficial long-term solution for the EU's industrial development'.[87] At the same time, as already mentioned, Chinese retaliatory practices and the use of trade to create pressure on the EU are not new. It is noteworthy that the announcement from MOFCOM on the probe into the FSR comes just days after the

84. Commission Regulation (EU) No. 1242/2009 of 16 Dec. 2009 imposing a provisional anti-dumping duty on imports of certain cargo scanning systems originating in the People's Republic of China, OJ L 332, 17.12.2009, pp. 60-72; Council implementing Regulation (EU) No. 510/2010 of 14 Jun. 2010 imposing a definitive anti-dumping duty and collecting definitively the provisional duty imposed on imports of certain cargo scanning systems originating in the People's Republic of China, OJ L 150, 16.6.2010, pp. 1-16.

85. Department of Commerce, Bureau of Industry and Security, 15 CFR Part 744, [Docket No. 201215-0347], RIN 0694-AI37, *Addition of Entities to the Entity List, Revision of Entry on the Entity List, and Removal of Entities From the Entity List Federal Register*, Vol. 85, No. 246/Tuesday, 22 Dec. 2020.

86. *See* Ministry of Commerce of the People's Republic of China, communiqué no. 28: (mofcom.gov.cn/zwgk/zcfb/art/2024/art_d2a237a0cd204ea6b89559470a630744.html); Ministry of Commerce of the People's Republic of China Regular Press Conference (11 Jul. 2024).

87. *See* Global Times, *China launches probe into EU's actions on Chinese firms under FSR. Move to protect legitimate interests, uphold true multilateralism: experts*, 10 Jul. 2024, 11:23 PM https://www.globaltimes.cn/page/202407/1315812.shtml.

provisional additional duties on imports of Chinese-made EVs into the EU came into effect (China also launched a case at the WTO).[88] Just one day after definitive duties on EVs have been imposed (on 21 August 2024), China has opened an investigation into imported EU dairy products (it is investigating also pork and French Cognac imported from the bloc).[89] Given the countries and the topic involved, the geopolitical nature of the FSR is once again confirmed.

Finally, in October 2024, the Commission adopted its first clearance decision, subject to commitments, under the FSR in relation acquisition of parts of PPF Telecom by Emirates Telecommunications (e&), owned by the Emirates Investment Authority (EIA). The Commission considers that there are sufficient indications that e& has received foreign subsidies distorting the EU internal market in the form of an unlimited guarantee from the UAE and a loan from UAE-controlled banks directly facilitating the transaction. According to the Commission, the foreign subsidies did not have negative effects on the acquisition process itself, given that e& was the sole bidder in the acquisition process and could have financed the transaction with its own resources. However, the Commission found that there was a risk of potential distortions in the EU internal market after the transaction, as the potential subsidies – and the unlimited guarantee in particular – would confer an advantage to the operator in engaging in investments or acquisitions. Therefore, e& and EIA offered the following commitments for ten years, which may be extended by another five years: (i) the exclusion of the unlimited state guarantee, by ensuring compliance of e&'s articles of association with ordinary UAE bankruptcy law; (ii) the prohibition upon e& and EIA of financing PPF's activities in the EU – save for exceptions, such as emergency funding – as well as the undertaking that other transactions should also be on market terms; (iii) an obligation for e& to report to the Commission any future acquisition that is not notifiable under the FSR.

§10.07 CONCLUSION

The President of the European Commission, Ursula Von der Leyen, in her political guidelines 2024-2029 published on 18 July 2024 (the day of her re-election by the European Parliament), mentions among other things 'A new economic foreign policy' based on the increasingly thin line between economy and security: 'in today's world geopolitics and geoeconomics go together. Europe's foreign and economic policy must do the same'.[90] The FSR is a clear expression of this new concept of economic foreign policy, in so far as it provides a tool for a more assertive response in protecting the EU's economy from security concerns through a trade instrument.

---

88. Financial Times, *China challenges Brussels' electric car tariffs with WTO complaint*, 9 Aug. 2024.
89. Laura He, *China examining if EU is putting up 'trade barriers' as tensions intensify*, CNN (10 Jul. 2024, 8:01 AM EDT) https://edition.cnn.com/2024/07/10/business/china-eu-probe-trade-barriers-intl-hnk/index.html; Thomas Moller-Nielsen, *EU rebuffs threat of Beijing probe, stands by foreign subsidies law*, Euractiv (1 Jul. 2024, 13:51) https://www.euractiv.com/section/competition/news/eu-rebuffs-threat-of-beijing-probe-stands-by-foreign-subsidies-law/.
90. Ursula von der Leyen, *Europe's Choice, Political guidelines for the next European Commission, 2024-2029*, 18 Jul. 2024, 26.

As already mentioned, the FSR is meant to preserve fair competition on the EU internal market which is 'much more than a market': it is an instrument to deliver a sustainable future and prosperity for all EU citizens and for this reason, its further empowerment will be a priority in the next legislative term, as suggested by Enrico Letta in its report committed by the Council of the Union.[91] Indeed, the Single Market is the 'robust platform' that supports the Union's economic security.

The idea of a new economic foreign security is based on the consultations and on the common ideas discussed with the democratic forces in the European Parliament[92] but will need to take into consideration the evolutions in the geopolitical contest and also the reaction of the EU stakeholders. The impact of the EU trade tools, like the FSR, trying to 'export' the EU rules and values beyond the EU borders, are and will be subject to scrutiny and criticism by the EU trade partners. In particular, EU laws having an impact on non-EU countries (so-called extraterritorial effect) might lead to reactions, which will need to be addressed, possibly by helping these countries adjust to and, where possible, benefit from those laws.[93] The FSR already foresees the involvement of non-EU countries in the procedure through a dialogue to explore options aimed at obtaining the cessation or modification of the foreign subsidies under investigation (Article 37 FSR).

Some fear that the FSR will increase the costs and the administrative burden for many EU and non-EU companies[94] and hope that the Commission will use it exclusively to catch 'the big fish', meaning that it will focus on major distortions (possibly beyond the thresholds mentioned above) while keeping the compliance burden in particular on smaller entities as low as possible.[95] Others note in particular that assessing what constitutes a 'subsidy' is especially difficult because government support for contractors is often tied to government policy goals, which go well beyond the contractors themselves, and that the extraterritorial application of the SFR might further undo the economy and efficiencies of a transnational network of secure

---

91. Enrico Letta, *Much more than a Market, SPEED, SECURITY, SOLIDARITY – Empowering the Single Market to deliver a sustainable future and prosperity for all EU Citizens*, report presented to the European Council on 18 Apr. 2024.
92. Ursula von der Leyen, *Europe's Choice, Political guidelines for the next European Commission, 2024-2029*, 18 Jul. 2024, 5.
93. *Ibid.*, 26-28.
94. From October 2023 to the end of July 2024, the Commission engaged in pre-notification talks on FSR filings in 106 cases. A formal notifications was submitted in 76 cases, 63 of which were unconditionally approved after phase I (Source: Commission, EU Competition Policy brief, September 2024).
95. Ulrich Soltész, *Foreign Subsidies Control: A Bureaucratic Monster?*, 22 European state aid law quarterly, 2, 175-180 (2023), also Massimo Merola and Alessandro Cogoni analyse the quantity and type of information required in the notification process with regard to foreign subsidies/financial contributions received by the notifying undertaking in the previous three years in the context of concentrations and public procurement procedures and conclude by proposing a reasonably balanced solution. *see* Massimo Merola & Alessandro Cogoni, *Foreign Subsidies and Financial Contributions: Much Fine-Tuning Ahead*, 8 Competition Law & Policy Debate, 1, 1-3 (2023) https://doi.org/10.4337/clpd.2023.01.01.

suppliers.[96] Moreover, concern is growing regarding also investments from the EU into third countries (outbound investments) when they relate to critical technologies and can put at risk the EU technology and know-how (this concerns notably technologies suitable for enhancing military and intelligence capabilities).[97]

In conclusion, DG COMP, DG GROW and DG TRADE will need to continue to cooperate between themselves and possibly with Third Countries' national authorities. The Commission shall present an annual report to the EU co-legislator on the implementation of the FSR (Article 52 FSR) and will publish at the latest by January 2026 guidelines (Article 46 FSR) to fine-tune this instrument[98] based on the cases launched and the experience gained also in the interaction with the EU main economic partners. However, things might go faster than foreseen depending on the elections in the USA and Chinese retaliatory practices. Josep Borrell, the EU's outgoing High Representative for Foreign Affairs and Security Policy, has warned that a trade war between the EU and China 'may be unavoidable'.[99]

96. Christopher Yukins, *State Aid, Protectionism and Public Procurement: An Uneasy New World Order*, 22 European State Aid Law Quarterly, 2, 181-187 (2023) https://doi.org/10.21552/estal/2023/2/8.
97. The Commission has published a White Paper on outbound investments and, on 23 Jul. 2024, DG TRADE published results of targeted consultation on outbound investment: https://policy.trade.ec.europa.eu/news/dg-trade-publishes-results-targeted-consultation-outbound-investment-2024-07-23_en.
98. Useful and regularly updated information is available in the Q&A section on DG COMP's website: https://competition-policy.ec.europa.eu/foreign-subsidies-regulation/questions-and-answers_en.
99. Carl Deconinck, *Borrell warns for 'systematic confrontation' between EU and China*, brusselssignal.eu (21 Aug. 2024) https://brusselssignal.eu/2024/08/eus-borrell-warns-eu-china-trade-war-could-be-unavoidable/.

CHAPTER 11

From Aid to Subsidy: The New UK System of Public Spending Control

Andrea Biondi

§11.01 INTRODUCTION

Famously, in probably one of the most celebrated early days cases, the European Court of Justice held that 'the concept of aid is nevertheless wider than that of a subsidy because it embraces not only positive benefits, such as subsidies themselves, but also interventions which, in various forms, mitigate the charges which are normally included in the budget of an undertaking and which, without, therefore, being subsidies in the strict meaning of the word, are similar in character and have the same effect'.[1] This was the beginning of a long journey that made State aid control one of the cornerstones of the European economic integration project. After over fifty years of nearly impeccable application of the EU provisions, the UK, in the aftermath of its withdrawal from the EU, has recently adopted its own domestic version of public spending control. Significantly 'State aid' disappeared being replaced by 'subsidy': on 4 January 2023, the Subsidy Control Act 2022 (SCA) entered into full force. The SCA provides the framework for UK-wide subsidy control, a brand new domestic system that should guarantee that UK public authorities are not adopting measures that could distort competition and that should ensure compliance with UK international obligations. This chapter is structured chronologically around the trajectory of EU State aid control in the UK: in the first place, the position of EU State aid control in the immediate post-Brexit scenario will be analysed, followed by an exam of the new current regulatory framework and, finally, it concludes with an assessment of the first year or so of its application. An attempt will be made therefore to verify whether the UK

1. Case 30/59, *De Gezamenlijke Steenkolenmijnen in Limburg v. High Authority*, 23.2.1961, EU:C:1961:2.

Government's stated aims have been truly achieved and whether the new system is actually working. In short, whether to replace 'aid' with 'subsidy' was such a good idea.

§11.02 THE IMMEDIATE AFTERMATH OF BREXIT AND STATE AID CONTROL

State aid law has been undoubtedly one of the most fiercely contested areas of EU law in the post-Brexit scenario. State aid rules are indeed a very sensitive area as they essentially concern the introduction of checks on public spending, so they are often perceived either as an obstacle to national governments pursuing their own industrial and economic policies or as a constraint to further deregulation and market liberalisation. The UK Government, especially under PM Johnson, expressed its own profound disgust towards the whole EU machinery and restated its own intention to simply get rid of any form of control.[2] Such a political stance was particularly curious as the UK has always been a staunch supporter of State aid rules, as it considered them essential to preserve a competitive and fair internal market, favouring the emergence of the most innovative companies. Not only the level of UK aid has also been consistently lower when compared with other large EU Member States, but it was also mostly due to the UK influence and its grip on DG Competition that State aid control has over the years gradually morphed into a State aid policy akin to some form of antitrust regulation, that would come into play only if, and in so far as, State aid rules can reduce anti-competitive distortive effects by preventing inefficient undertakings surviving in an artificially competitive market.[3] '*Value for money*' was essentially a British slogan. Further, differently from other Member States, the UK has been very rarely involved in infringement proceedings: the EU has enforced State aid rules against the UK only four times in the last twenty years, compared to twenty-nine enforcement actions against France, forty-five against Italy and sixty-seven against Germany. The British Government has also always been very efficient in using the procedure imposed by the Treaty requiring an *ex ante* notification to the European Commission of any plan to grant aid. The European Commission, making the UK one of the biggest winners in the State aid arena, has approved most of the UK's notifications.[4] In the new post-referendum madness, such a glorious past did not count, as accepting a continuous application of State aid control would have simply meant accepting also the concurrent continuous role of the European Commission in supervising national spending policies. State aid

2. Prime Minister Boris Johnson's speech in Greenwich, 3 Feb. 2020, Transcript available at: https://www.gov.uk/government/speeches/pm-speech-in-greenwich-3-february-2020.
3. For a more detailed analysis, *see* Massimo Merola, The Forces Shaping State Aid Control in the EU, in Luca Rubini & James Hawkins (eds) 'What Shapes the Law? Reflections on the History, Law, Politics and Economics of International and European Subsidy Disciplines', (EUI/University of Birmingham, 2016), 101, available at: http://cadmus.eui.eu/bitstream/handle/1814/42404/WhatShapesLaw_2016.pdf?sequence=3.
4. *See* further Ciara Barbu-O'Connor & Andrea Biondi, *State Aid & National Enforcement: United Kingdom* in Jacques Derenne, Denis Jouve, 2 Mar. 2023, e-Competitions State Aid & National Enforcement.

had to go; certain laws or rights had to be removed as they 'refer to the involvement of an EU institution or be predicated on UK membership of, or access to, an EU regime or system. Once we have left the EU, this legislation will no longer work'.[5] Thus, eventually and for some time, the UK decided not to keep any State aid provisions in domestic law.[6] However, the other side, the European Union was immediately very consistent in insisting that any future form of collaboration would have to include some form of State aid control. As stated in the EU Council Guidelines as early as 23 March 2018 '[g]iven the UK's geographic proximity and economic interdependence with the EU27, the future relationship will only deliver in a mutually satisfactory way if it includes robust guarantees which ensure a level playing field. The aim should be to prevent unfair competitive advantage that the UK could enjoy through undercutting of levels of protection with respect to, *inter alia*, competition and state aid, tax, social, environment and regulatory measures and practices.'[7] As reality started kicking in, some compromises had to be found. First of all, to avoid legal chaos, the EU and the UK Government rapidly agreed to buy some time and concluded the EU-UK Withdrawal Agreement (WA) that not only dealt with some pressing divorce settlement issues but also extended the application of EU law until 11 pm on 31 December 2020 (the so-called IP completion day).[8] Thus, Article 92 WA provides that the Commission remains competent to resolve any State aid investigation that has been allocated by the end of transition period. Further, Article 93 WA provides that the Commission remains competent to initiate new State aid procedures for up to four years after the transition ends for aid granted before 31 December 2020. Any possible recovery action would then be still actionable if it refers to past aid. The continuous application of State aid rules to the first interim phase is by no means irrelevant. From a 'constitutional' perspective, it should be reminded that Article 87(1) of the Withdrawal Agreement also extended the Court of Justice of the European Union's (CJEU) jurisdiction in actions brought before it by the Commission under Article 258 TFEU within four years after the end of the transition period. Thus, in a recent judgment, one of the many chapters of the *Micula* saga, the Court of Justice robustly reminded the UK Supreme Court of its obligations under EU law.[9] In particular, the Court found that by ordering the enforcement of an ICSID arbitral award which was instead considered a State aid by the European Commission, the UK Supreme Court violated several fundamental principles of EU law such as the duty of loyal collaboration and the duty to refer a question of interpretation under Article 267 TFEU, being the Supreme Court a court of last resort.

5. HM Government, Our approach to the Future Relationship with the EU. The UK's Approach to Negotiations (CP 211, 2020), available at: https://www.gov.uk/government/publications/our-approach-to-the-future-relationship-with-the-eu.
6. 1 Dec. 2020 through the State aid (Revocations and Amendments) (EU Exit) Regulations 2020.
7. *See* European Council, 'Guidelines on the framework for the future EU-UK relationship', 23 Mar. 2018, EUCO XT 20001/18, para. 12.
8. Agreement on the withdrawal of the United Kingdom of Great Britain and Northern Ireland from the European Union and the European Atomic Energy Community 2019/C 384 I/01 (OJ C 384I, 12.11.2019, pp. 1-177). The UK implemented such an agreement with the European Union (Withdrawal Agreement) Act 2020 ('EUWAA 2020').
9. Case C-516/22, *Commission v. United Kingdom (Judgment of the Supreme Court)*, 14.3.2024, EU:C:2024:231.

The CJEU did not pass the opportunity to remind the UK that 'the application of the rules of EU law on State aid laid down in Articles 107 and 108 TFEU is based on an obligation of sincere cooperation between, on the one hand, the national courts, and, on the other hand, the Commission and the Courts of the European Union, in the context of which each acts on the basis of the role assigned to it by the Treaty'.[10] From a 'substantive' perspective, despite the generally compliant attitude toward State aid rules, one specific area has always been rather problematic for the UK: fiscal aid. Indeed the amount of aid granted in the form of fiscal measures, that is tax benefits, tax reductions or deductions, has been approximately calculated at a staggering GBP 93 billion. The UK has therefore often been embroiled in cases concerning fiscal measures as State aid. Very recently, the CJEU has closed (maybe) an extremely long-running dispute between the UK Government and the European Commission concerning whether or not the UK's tax regime, as regards the profits of controlled foreign companies (CFCs), gave rise to unlawful State aid. The Commission found that the exemption of certain types of profits from tax (non-trading financial profits arising from qualifying loans) constituted aid to UK-domiciled parent companies. The UK Government applied to annul the Commission's decision on various grounds. In particular, the Commission had misunderstood UK law and identified the wrong reference framework. The Commission found that the exemptions were a derogation from the CFC Rules; the UK Government argued that the proper reference framework was the general corporation tax system of the UK. The General Court found in favour of the Commission.[11] On appeal, instead, the Court annulled the GC decision and found that the interpretation advanced by the UK was consistent with the general interpretation of its domestic system, so the UK measures could not be considered selective.[12] Intriguingly, as many actions of recovery stemming from the original Commission decision had been already enforced it remains to be seen what the UK Treasury will do to compensate the companies affected. Further, the issue of possible violation of State aid rules via aggressive use of tax exemptions is likely not to go away. For instance, the Commission has decided to bring the UK before the CJEU for failing to implement a Commission decision taken before the end of the transition period ordering the recovery of fiscal aid granted by Gibraltar in the form of an exemption for passive interest and royalties.[13]

[A] The Continuous Application of EU State Aid Law: The Northern Ireland Protocol

As it is well known, Northern Ireland is subject to specific arrangements applicable to that part of the UK only. The Northern Ireland Protocol provides for the establishment

10. *Ibid.*, para. 95.
11. T-363/19 and T-456/19, *United Kingdom and ITV v. Commission*, 8.6.2022, EU:T:2022:349.
12. Joined Cases C-555/22 P, C-556/22 P and C-564/22 P, *United Kingdom and Others v. Commission*, 19.9.2024, EU:C:2024:763.
13. *See* State aid: Commission refers United Kingdom to European Court for failure to fully recover illegal tax exemption aid of up to around €100 million in Gibraltar, European Commission – Press release, 19.3.2021, available at: https://ec.europa.eu/commission/presscorner/detail/en/ip_21_1266.

of a sort of tailored custom area that also includes the preservation of State aid rules. Article 10 of the Protocol provides that State aid provisions continue to apply to the UK 'in respect of measures which affect that trade between Northern Ireland and the Union which is subject to this Protocol'. The Commission later clarified in a Notice to Stakeholders on the application of the Northern Ireland Protocol that an effect on trade cannot be merely hypothetical or presumed but has to be demonstrated.[14] The EU and UK recently reached a political agreement on resolving certain issues in Northern Ireland, the so-called Windsor Framework. Still, the State aid provisions have been left untouched. The Framework simply restates that 'for a measure to be considered to have a genuine and direct link to Northern Ireland and thus to have an effect on the trade between Northern Ireland and the Union that is subject to the Windsor Framework, that measure needs to have real foreseeable effects on that trade. The relevant real foreseeable effects should be material, and not merely hypothetical or presumed'.[15] It then lists some factors that can be considered to determine the materiality of the effect such as the size of the undertaking, the size of the subsidy, and the market presence of the undertaking in the relevant market in Northern Ireland. The possible implications of the application of Article 10 of the Northern Ireland Protocol were discussed before the UK High Court in *R (British Sugar) v. Secretary of State for International Trade*.[16] The case concerned the imposition of an autonomous tariff quota (ATQ) applicable to imports of raw cane sugar into the UK. Its effect was basically to allow raw cane sugar to be imported duty-free into the UK. One sugar company argued that the ATQ was essentially going to be applied to just one competitor and thus constituted a selective advantage. The applicant relied on a possible violation of Article 10 of the Northern Ireland Protocol. The Court, in our view, rightly dismissed such a claim, holding the measure as non-selective. It also found that the companies involved were not in a legally and factually comparable situation. Thus, Article 10 of the Northern Ireland Protocol was inapplicable, as the measure did not constitute State aid. Interestingly, the Court felt compelled to clarify that to trigger the application of Article 10, a 'genuine and direct' effect on trade had to be proven which was not the case in the proceedings because the measure had a very indirect effect as it involved 'at best very small volumes and is premised on the unproven assertion that the ATQ is liable to lead to the displacement of EU refined sugar from Northern Ireland'.[17]

---

14. Communication from the Commission, Notice to stakeholders on the withdrawal of the United Kingdom and EU rules in the field of state aid 2023/C 202/04 (OJ C 202, 9.6.2023, pp. 25–29), available at: https://eur-lex.europa.eu/legal-content/EN/TXT/HTML/?uri=CELEX:52023XC0609(03).
15. Joint Declaration of the Union and the United Kingdom in the Joint Committee established by the Agreement on the withdrawal of the United Kingdom of Great Britain and Northern Ireland from the European Union and the European Atomic Energy Community of 24 March 2023 on the application of Art. 10(1) of the Windsor Framework (OJ L 102, 17.4.2023, pp. 88–89).
16. *R (British Sugar) v. Secretary of State for International Trade* [2022] EWHC 393 (Admin).
17. *Ibid.*, para. 123.

§11.03 STATE AID VERSUS SUBSIDY IN POST-BREXIT UK: THE SUBSIDY CONTROL ACT – ESSENTIAL FEATURES

A second compromise between the two very different negotiating positions was eventually found – rather surprisingly – in what is now Chapter 3 of the EU-UK Trade and Cooperation Agreement (TCA).[18] The surprise element was caused by the fact that this specific chapter devoted to the regulation of subsidies is one of the most extensive and comprehensive parts of the TCA: thirteen pages and thirteen articles![19] Most importantly, the TCA in its Article 371 requires the parties to set an *effective* domestic regime of subsidies control. The TCA clearly takes for granted that the EU has such a system, thus it was up to the UK to properly implement the TCA provisions. As mentioned, Chapter 3 provides a very detailed framework that encompasses provisions on the definition of what constitutes a subsidy, the monitoring system and its enforcement, leaving not too much of a manoeuvring space for the UK. Eventually, the new system was unveiled: the Subsidy Control Act received Royal Assent on 28 April 2022 and entered into full force on 3 January 2023.[20] The Subsidy Control Act tends to be nearly a copy and paste of the TCA structure: scope, monitoring and enforcement. These are the fundamental features of the SCA: in terms of scope of application, the definition of what constitutes a subsidy contained in section 2 faithfully replicates that of Article 363(1)(b) of the TCA and consists in four limbs: 'subsidy' means financial assistance which:

(a) is given, directly or indirectly, from public resources by a public authority,
(b) confers an economic advantage on one or more enterprises,
(c) is specific, that is, is such that it benefits one or more enterprises over one or more other enterprises with respect to the production of goods or the provision of services, and
(d) has, or is capable of having, an effect on—
  (i) competition or investment within the United Kingdom,
  (ii) trade between the United Kingdom and a country or territory outside the United Kingdom, or
  (iii) investment as between the United Kingdom and a country or territory outside the United Kingdom.

Thus, as for the definition of what constitutes a subsidy, the SCA – as the TCA in the first place – is a pick and mix of elements derived both from EU State aid law and from international regulation of subsidies. For instance, the notion of 'enterprise' is exactly the same as the notion of undertaking in EU law as the SCA refers to 'the

18. Trade and Cooperation Agreement between the European Union and the European Atomic Energy Community, of the one part, and the United Kingdom of Great Britain and Northern Ireland, of the other part OJ L 149, 30.4.2021, pp. 10-2539.
19. For this author take on Ch. 3 TCA, *see* Andrea Biondi, *Preserving the Playing Field: Subsidies Regulation in the TCA*, in Federico Fabbrini (ed.), *The law and politics of Brexit*, 4 vol., OUP, 2024, 218.
20. Subsidy Control Act 2022 (c. 23).

provisions of goods or services, or the purchase of goods or services'. The expression 'specificity' is instead definitively resonant from Article 2 of the ASCM but, for instance, the SCA – implementing again the TCA – includes also a bespoke definition of specificity that outlaws subsidies that may confer a discriminatory advantage, a provision nearly identical to the EU fiscal aid *acqui*.[21] Still, there are some novel elements as well. One of the criteria for a national measure to qualify, as a subsidy is that it should come from '*public resources*' given by '*a public authority*'. Section 6 of the SCA defines 'public authority' in a negative form as it simply lists those entities that are *not* public authorities, such as the Houses of Parliament. Thus, the specific identification of what constitutes a public authority is left hanging out and it will depend on the future characterisation (by whom? the courts?) of the functionality of a myriad of local and devolved authorities, many central government bodies and hybrid authorities may be privately funded but exercising statutory powers or providing a public service. The UK Government guidance on the application of the SCA simply states that the notion of public resources should include 'public funds that are administered by the UK Government, the devolved administrations or local authorities, whether they are given directly, through other public bodies, or through private bodies',[22] a quasi 'imputability' criteria.[23] Still, in terms of the definition of scope, the SCA seems wide enough to cover a wide range of measures thus in line with accepted practice both in EU State aid law as well as international trade law. The key provisions are contained in Schedule 1 SCA, once again modelled on Article 366 TCA. Schedule 1 lists seven principles that need to be verified in order to establish whether a certain measure constitutes a subsidy. These principles are:

(A) Subsidy should pursue a specific policy objective in order to—
  (1) remedy an identified market failure or
  (2) address an equity rationale (such as local or regional disadvantage, social difficulties or distributional concerns).

(B) Subsidies should be proportionate to their specific policy objective and limited to what is necessary to achieve it.

(C) (1) Subsidies should be designed to bring about a change of economic behaviour of the beneficiary.
  (2) That change, in relation to a subsidy, should be—
    (a) conducive to achieving its specific policy objective, and
    (b) something that would not happen without the subsidy.

(D) Subsidies should not normally compensate for the costs the beneficiary would have funded in the absence of any subsidy.

---

21. *See*, for instance, Commission Notice on the notion of State aid as referred to in Art. 107(1) of the Treaty on the Functioning of the European Union (OJ C 262, 19.7.2016, pp. 1–50), point 5.4. *See also* Case C-374/17, *A-Brauerei*, 19.12.2018, EU:C:2018:1024; Case C-203/16 P, *Andres (Insolvenz Heitkamp BauHolding) v. Commission*, 28.6.2018, EU:C:2018:505.
22. Draft Statutory Guidance on the SCA at https://www.gov.uk/government/consultations/statutory-guidance-on-the-subsidy-control-act-2022 pp. 21 et seq.
23. C-482/99, *France v. Commission*, 16.5.2002, EU:C:2002:294, para. 55.

(E) Subsidies should be an appropriate policy instrument for achieving their specific policy objective and that objective cannot be achieved through other, less distortive, means.

The SCA is however innovative with respect to the TCA as it does introduce a further layer:

(F) Subsidies should be designed to achieve their specific policy objective while minimising any negative effects on competition or investment within the United Kingdom.
(G) Subsidies' beneficial effects (in terms of achieving their specific policy objective) should outweigh any negative effects, including in particular negative effects on—
  (1) competition or investment within the United Kingdom;
  (2) international trade or investment.

These principles are all familiar concepts in EU State aid control as they are modelled on the Commission's practice on compatibility. However, the truly innovative feature is that compliance with these principles is left to each and every public body in the UK granting a subsidy. Thus, all public authorities are now in charge of deciding whether or not a measure would be considered a subsidy and thus unlawful. Another relevant provision is section 10 of the Act that allows the UK Government to put in place 'streamlined subsidy schemes' with a view to allowing 'lower-risk subsidies to be given by public authorities more quickly and easily, without their needing to assess compliance with the principles or other subsidy control requirements'.[24] These are a sort of UK – GBER-styled provisions that de facto exempt certain awards if they fall within certain policy areas. So far, the Government identified SME, R&D and Energy Usage as the first three routes.[25] In terms of monitoring, the SCA places a lot of faith in transparency. The SCA requires that public authorities should 'enter' their decision in a publicly accessible subsidy database with information on the amount of the subsidy, the identity of the beneficiary, the subsidy's legal basis and the policy objective, which it pursues. Under the SCA the subsidy value threshold for publishing all the relevant information is GBP 100,000 and the time limit is three months from the decision to grant a subsidy. Finally, as for enforcement, the TCA contains a truly innovative element. Article 372 TCA commits the parties to confer on their courts and tribunals the power to review any decisions either of the authority in charge of controlling subsidies or any granting public authority to verify the lawfulness of the subsidies granted. Courts and tribunals are given the jurisdiction to grant any appropriate remedy including the suspension, prohibition, or requirement of action by the granting authority, the award of damages, and the recovery of a subsidy from its beneficiary. Very significantly, Article 372(2) TCA allows either party to intervene in the domestic judicial process. Once again the EU judicial system of State aid control is

24. Subsidy Control Bill, Explanatory Notes, para. 46.
25. *See* https://www.gov.uk/government/publications/subsidy-control-act-2022-streamlined-routes.

presumed to be TCA compliant, thus it was up to the UK to devise an entirely new jurisdiction. The SCA provides then that any interested parties can bring a judicial review action before the Competition Appeal Tribunal (CAT).[26] The CAT jurisdiction is usually on appeals on the merits in respect of decisions made under the Competition Act 1998 by the CMA and the regulators in the telecommunications, electricity, gas, water, railways, air traffic services, payment systems, healthcare services, and financial services sectors. The CAT is now entitled to review a stand-alone subsidy and a scheme, including those falling within the scope of one of the streamlined routes. In terms of the scope and extent of review, the CAT applies the standard rules of judicial review.

§11.04 THE SCA ONE YEAR ON: A FIRST ASSESSMENT

According to the UK Government, the SCA should enable 'UK public authorities, including devolved administrations and local authorities, *to give subsidies that are tailored to their local needs, and that drive economic growth while minimising distortion to UK competition and protecting our international obligations.*' Further, the SCA will bring *about a dynamic and less bureaucratic system allowing an efficient allocation of public resources.*[27] Despite the rhetoric, one year on, the shortcomings of the SCA are many and easy to spot: public authorities are struggling to comply with the new rules, which are opaque and lack effective control by an independent body.

[A] The Weaknesses of the 'Self-Certification' Model

[1] A Heavy Burden on Public Authorities

Under the SCA system, every public body in the UK granting a subsidy of any amount has autonomy over its decisions. On its face, this seems to attempt to introduce a form of 'localism'; a bottom-up model that encourages targeted and tailored decision-making. But the new system is placing public authorities under considerable stress: all public authorities must ensure that any of their decisions involving disbursements of public resources are in line with the SCA rules and need to decide if they can be considered a subsidy and thus lawful or whether any exceptions apply. Any public authority must therefore carry out an assessment involving a complex analysis of whether the seven subsidy control principles are satisfied. These principles include, for example, the requirement that subsidies should only be granted to remedy a market failure or to remedy a local or regional disadvantage, social difficulties or distributional concerns and that subsidies should be an appropriate instrument to promote a public policy. Most importantly, subsidies should be designed to achieve their specific policy objective while minimising any negative effects on competition or investment within

26. SCA, pt 5 section 70.
27. The UK Subsidy Control Regime at https://www.gov.uk/government/collections/subsidy-control-regime.

the United Kingdom. Compliance with the seven subsidy principles, therefore, requires a complex legal and economic analysis. For instance, under the seventh subsidy principle, any public authority is obliged to carry out a full analysis on how to calculate whether the likely benefits of a certain subsidy outweigh the risks to fairness of competition law. Thus, basic antitrust tools such as an analysis of market characteristics, the extent of market concentrations, and above all the definition of a relevant market should be the relevant benchmarks. The statutory guidance to the SCA indeed specifically refers to the need for public authorities to use decisions in the fields of antitrust and merger control that have considered the product or services in question.[28] While the application of these principles may be sort of routine for antitrust authorities or for economic consultants, public authorities may not be necessarily equipped as they would require expertise, the gathering of a huge amount of evidence and information, collecting data, and so on.[29] In theory, such a heavy burden could be alleviated by exploring the possibility of adopting streamlined routes that are block-exempted areas. The scope and usage of streamlined routes should however be regularly reviewed and expanded where necessary. Streamlining is actually one of the most effective ways of balancing the apparently competing interests of empowering public authorities on the one hand while providing certainty to public authorities to a degree that is sympathetic to the resource restrictions within which they perform their role under the SCA, on the other hand. Political expediency prevented so far from gaining useful experience from the EU system. Actually, a specific assertion has been inserted in the forward of the three current streamlined routes adopted so far, that these are not intended to replace the GBER system. The opposite would have been much more useful: GBER provisions were comprehensively applied by the UK in many and varied contexts, from art and cultural heritage measures to aid to innovation or risk finance investment. In 2020, the number of GBER measures in the United Kingdom reached 57.6% of the total number of measures, with 58.9% of all newly implemented measures falling under the GBER (as at the last State aid scoreboard before Brexit took effect). Two 'lessons' should have been kept in mind: the GBER is a 'living instrument' based on the assumption that its content can be changed and new categories of aid exempted according to the evolution of the markets and the experience gained by the European Commission. The same dynamic can be transposed in the UK context. First, the experience gained in over a year can be used to identify further categories that can be added to the very thin list of existing streamlined routes. Second, the streamlined routes need to be more ambitious in terms of their financial thresholds that are generally considered to be too low. In terms of distribution of spending decisions, in the EU State aid regime, the balancing test on whether the benefits of an aid outweigh the negative effects is carried out by the European Commission. For better or worse, the Commission acts as a supranational referee between the different Member States, gradually developing the 'common European interest' as a benchmark through sixty

28. *See* UK Subsidy Control Statutory Guidance, section 3.58 (18 Dec. 2023). It should be noted that the SCA, under section 79(6), compels all relevant stakeholders to have regard to the guidance.
29. *See* Andreas Stephan, *Will the New UK Subsidy Control Regime Help Level Up the Economy*? 87 MLR 172 (2024) https://doi.org/10.1111/1468-2230.12835.

years of applying State aid law. All UK authorities involved will have now to undertake the same process, as they would need to gradually identify a UK-wide 'common interest'. The SCA introduces in its section 18 an anti-delocalisation provision requiring that subsidies should not be 'given to an enterprise subject to a condition that the enterprise relocates all or part of its existing economic activities' and where 'the relocation of those activities would not occur but for the giving of the subsidy'. However, under the subsidies control principles, public authorities are entitled to take into account socio-economic factors when deciding whether or not to grant a subsidy – for instance, on how to redress disadvantage or deprivation in specific areas. There are therefore real risks that without any central coordination, regions or different authorities can simply engage in subsidies wars to attract businesses in their own region. Finally – despite its outlook – the SCA reaffirms the centralised character of the UK public law system, as control of distortive and harmful subsidies has actually been made a reserved matter for the government without any involvement of Scotland, Wales and Northern Ireland. The devolved Parliaments are mentioned only as entities that should not be considered public authorities, but nowhere else in the SCA. There is, therefore, a discrepancy between primary legislation of devolved governments that is brought within the scope of the SCA, and Acts of the Westminster Parliament, which are instead subject only to limited obligations, such as the requirement to enter legislation on the subsidy database.

[2] Transparency, What Transparency?

As to guarantee the effectiveness of the system, the TCA is very empathic as far as transparency is concerned. Article 369 commits the parties to ensure a full and effective system of transparency, a system that would allow competitors and other authorities to 'check' the behaviour of those authorities granting a subsidy. Thus, parties under their respective regulatory systems should provide information on certain key information relating to the grant of a subsidy, including its legal basis, the policy objective being pursued, the identity of the recipient and the amount of the subsidy in question must be made publicly available. Under the new SCA system, the Transparency for Subsidies Database is the main tool to ensure transparency. Just a cursory look at the entries submitted reveals, however, the total inadequacy of the database, as many authorities tend not to record all awards, and the entries are often minimal, missing key information. This lack of transparency goes unsanctioned, as no specific penalties can be imposed. Thus, the features of the SCA system – the complexity of the decision-making required by the SCA, the vast range of authorities that it applies to, the inconsistent recording of subsidy decisions and the lack of effective independent oversight – create an environment in which authorities may struggle effectively to comply with it. In turn, this means the lawfulness of decisions about public spending may be called into question or, alternatively, that decisions are not taken at all, for fear of falling foul of the rules. Once again, the EU experience can turn out to be useful. The EU State aid system, as shaped by the GBER, is heavily reliant on stringent transparency obligations, and most notably Article 10 GBER provides that failure to comply with transparency requirements may lead to a Commission decision that all, or some, future aid measures adopted by the Member State in question are to be notified to the Commission and sanctions are to be ordered. In terms of enhancing transparency and accountability, the SANI (State Aid Notification Interactive) system could provide a possible model for public authorities as to a clear reporting requirement (annual reports on schemes, effective record keeping on aid schemes once implemented and so on). Overall, increased transparency, especially in the context of streamlined subsidies, could be beneficial to the UK regime by ensuring coherent application of the rules and consequently reducing legal costs for both public authorities and beneficiaries and reducing the risk of challenge from competitors or other interested parties.

[3] The (Limited) Role of the CMA

Public authorities are, in theory, not entirely on their own, as for certain kinds of subsidies it would be possible for them to seek an opinion from the Competition Marker Authority (CMA) the hugely respected UK competition authority. Within the CMA, a specific unit – the Subsidy Unit Advice (SUA) – has been set up and tasked to prepare a report on the public authority's subsidy control compliance assessment. The public authority can decide whether or not to seek the advice of the SUA if the measure concerns a subsidy of interest. Only in cases where the SCA defines 'a subsidy of particular interest', a public authority would have an obligation to ask the SUA to prepare such a report. The distinction between a subsidy of interest and a subsidy of particular interest is based on financial thresholds: a general one of GBP 10 million for subsidies of particular interest (SOPI) and GBP 5 million for subsidies of interest (SOI). Subsidies in excess of GBP 10 million would be subject to mandatory referral to the CMA, while subsidies between GBP 5 million and GBP 10 million would be subject to voluntary referral.[30] For specific sensitive sectors where there is evidence of global overcapacity or a record of international trade disputes, the lower GBP 5 million threshold will be enough to consider them as of 'particular interest'. Once the request has been filed, the CMA would normally be required to prepare its report within thirty working days from receipt of the required information from the public authority. The Act further allows the Secretary of State to *direct* public authorities to request a CMA report in relation to a proposed subsidy or scheme where the Secretary of State considers that there is a risk of non-compliance or of 'negative effects' on competition or investment within the UK arising.[31] It should be acknowledged that the SUA took its role seriously with around forty reports already delivered in over a year. There is also evidence that after the publication of a not-so-favourable report, the public authority concerned decided to withdraw the measure for fear of legal challenge. Still, the

30. 'Consultation on subsidies and schemes of interest and of particular interest' at https://assets.publishing.service.gov.uk/government/uploads/system/uploads/attachment_data/file/1063355/ssopi-and-ssoi-consultation.pdf accessed September 2022.
31. Sections 55 and 58.

experience so far has been rather disappointing:[32] in its very first report published in March 2023, the SUA stated how its report had to be considered as advisory only and that it did not directly assess whether the subsidy scheme referred complied 'with the subsidy control requirements, nor is its purpose to make a recommendation on whether the scheme should continue to be implemented'.[33] Thus, the SUA reports do not state whether the proposed measures are compliant with the subsidy principles. The SUA limits itself to possible recommendations on how a public authority to improve its assessment in terms of its reasoning and use of evidence but it never goes as far as to clearly state whether the proposed subsidy itself could be in violation of the SCA. Such a narrow reading of the SUA tasks is not due to institutional timidity only but it is borne out by the simple fact that the SUA does not have any real powers; its opinions are only advisory and non-binding. In short, the CMA SUA cannot, under the SCA terms, perform the role of an independent regulator.

[4] The Role of the Courts

So far, only one case has been brought before the CAT with just another one in the pipeline. Thus, it is impossible to predict whether the new head of jurisdiction is going to be effective. Certainly, there seems not a great appetite for litigation and the case decided so far, *MaxRecycle*,[34] could be hardly described as of great importance. Still, certain brief observations can be derived from this very first decision. The CAT clearly signalled that it is its intention not to limit itself to a review of whether the measure adopted by the public authority was lawful. It instead focused on the merits of the authority decision and on whether the subsidy principles have been satisfied. On the specific question of whether the Durham County Council was distorting the market, by being able to offer a subsidised cheaper commercial waste collection service – using Council employees and vehicles for less than the fair market price – the CAT rather rudimentarily held that there was no violation of the SCA. Essentially, there was no subsidy where the benefit was conferred by a public authority to itself – not exactly a finding in line with EU law. Actually, despite the parties' submission, the CAT found that there was no need to rely on the case law of the Court of Justice. The CAT also refused to grant permission to appeal, which was disappointing, as the CAT itself recognised that 'guidance from the Court of Appeal might be of assistance on the construction of the new subsidy control regime under the [SCA] and its relationship to EU state aid law'.[35]

32. For an opposite view, *see* David du Parc Braham and Maria Marsden, *The UK's Subsidy Control Regime Subsidy Advice Unit Referrals – Tips and Best Practice*, European State Aid Law Quarterly, 4 (2023) https://doi.org/10.21552/estal/2023/4/5.
33. Subsidy Advice Unit Report on Contracts for Difference (AR5) 22 Feb. 2023, para. 2.6.
34. *The Durham Company Limited v. Durham County Council* [2023] CAT 50.
35. *Ibid.*

§11.05 CONCLUSIONS

It has been documented how UK spending on subsidies as a proportion of GDP has increased very significantly post-Brexit, even taking into account the COVID-19 impact.[36] Needless to say, that such a trend is in line with the increase in aid granted by all EU Member States. Of course, subsidies are not necessarily bad; on the contrary, they may be necessary or even desirable to pursue various virtuous policies. However, the risk of using them to distort competition and trade is ever so present. The SCA was supposed to provide an effective system to prevent those risks. There are, in my view, serious doubts about whether the SCA can do so. It would indeed benefit from a better framework on both the transparency and accountability of spending decisions, a serious rethinking about the lack of an independent authority and what mechanisms can be introduced to contribute to ensuring geographic solidarity between the different areas of the UK. Finally, the Subsidy Control Act has been drafted and approved so as to directly comply with specific obligations imposed by the Trade and Cooperation Agreement concluded between the EU and the UK. However, the SCA is quite shy in this respect, limiting the references to the TCA to the strictly necessary. Although one of the subsidy control principles is that a public authority needs to check if the beneficial effects of a measure outweigh its negative effects having regard to 'international trade or investment', in most cases, the main statutory focus seems to be on the impact on competition or investment within the UK. For instance, the SAU at the CMA is expressly directed to consider only the effects of the proposed subsidy or scheme on competition or investment within the UK. There is no escape from concluding that the SCA has thus a very distinct 'local' flavour and may not be enough to ensure UK international obligations. It is true that EU State aid control is also going through several transformations and thus there may not be an appetite to confront the inadequacies of the UK system, for instance by relying directly on the TCA and its other state-to-state enforcing mechanisms. Whatever the merits of the arguments developed above, the question however remains the same: after so many years of discussion, debate and so on, was it really worth the effort to replace aid with subsidy?

36. https://www.aoshearman.com/en/insights/uk-almost-triples-spending-on-subsidies-since-leaving-the-european-union.

CHAPTER 12

Overview of State Aid to Particular Sectors: Agriculture and Fishery

Claudio Biscaretti di Ruffia

§12.01 STATE AID TO AGRICULTURAL AND FISHERY UNDERTAKINGS: AN INTRODUCTION

Under Title II of the third part of the TFEU, entitled 'Agriculture and Fisheries', competition and State aid are dealt with in Article 42.[1]

1. On State aid applicable to agricultural undertakings *see*, Nina Maksimović Sekulić, Maja Kovačević & Radislav Jovičić, *The EU State aid Regime in Agriculture – Legal Aspect*, in *Economics of Agriculture*, 2024, No. 1, pp. 239 et seq.; Luigi Costato & Luigi Russo, *Corso di diritto agrario italiano e dell'Unione europea*, Milan, 2023, pp. 94 et seq.; Claudio Biscaretti di Ruffia, *Gli aiuti di Stato a favore delle imprese agricole*, in *Scritti in onore di Anna Marzanati*, Milan, 2018, pp. 27 et seq.; Carlo Eugenio Baldi, *La disciplina degli aiuti di Stato*, Santarcangelo di Romagna, 2018, pp. 523 et seq.; Russo, *Art. 42*, in Fausto Pocar & Maria Caterina Baruffi, *Commentario breve ai Trattati dell'Unione europea*, Padua, 2014, pp. 315 et seq.; Orlandi, *Art. 42*, in Antonio Tizzano, *Trattati dell'Unione europea*, Milan, 2014, pp. 645 et seq.; and earlier, Erlbacher, *Arts 175-179* and Markovicova, *Arts 180-182a*, both in Mögele Rudolf & Friedrich Erlbacher (eds.), *Single Common Market Organisation*, München-Oxford, 2011, pp. 775 et seq.; Antonio Iannarelli, *Aiuti comunitari e aiuti di stato*, in *Dir. e giur. agr. alim. amb.*, 2009, pp. 375 et seq.; Fabio Gencarelli, *La nouvelle politique communautaire en matière d'aides d'Etat en agriculture*, in *Rev. du droit de l'Union eur.*, 2008, pp. 5 et seq.; Foszczynski & Agnieszka Stobiecka-Kuik, *Agriculture*, in Wolfgang Mederer, Nicola Pesaresi & Marc Van Hoof, *EU Competition Law*, Vol. IV, *State Aid*, Leuven, 2008, pp. 1511 et seq.; Daniele Bianchi, *La politica agricola comune (PAC)*, Ghezzano, 2007, pp. 350 et seq.; Antonio Iannarelli, *Pluralismo definitorio dell'attività e dell'impresa agricola tra diritto comunitario e diritto interno*, in *Studi sull'integrazione europea*, 2007, pp. 469 et seq., in particular pp. 484 et seq.; Erhart, *State Aid in the Field of Agriculture*, in Michael Sanchez Rydelski, *The EC State Aid Regime: Distortive Effects of State Aid on Competition and Trade*, London, 2006, pp. 477 et seq.; Conor Quigley & Anthony Collins, *EC State Aid Law and Policy*, Oxford-Portland, 2003, pp. 209 et seq.; Jean-Paul Keppenne, *Guide des aides d'État en droit communautaire*, Brussels, 1999, pp. 507 et seq.; Giancarlo Olmi, *Politique agricole commune, Commentaire Mégret*, Brussels, 1991, pp. 284 et seq.; Barthelemy, *La politique communautaire en matière d'aides dans le secteur agricole*, in *Rev. droit rur.*, 1988, 201.

Specifically, the first part of Article 42 provides that the rules on competition under Articles 101-109 TFEU apply to the production of and trade in agricultural products: (a) only to the extent determined by the European Parliament and the Council (previously, by the Council alone, prior to the amendments made to that article by the Lisbon Treaty); (b) within the framework and in accordance with the approval procedure for agricultural matters set out in Articles 43(2) and 43(3) TFEU; and (c) with account being taken of the objectives of the Common Agricultural Policy (CAP), set out in Article 39 of that Treaty.

Unlike the first part of Article 42, which deals both with competition proper and State aid, the second part deals only with the latter. It provides that the Council may, upon the Commission's proposal (not a requirement prior to the changes introduced by the Lisbon Treaty), authorize the grant of aid in two specific cases: (a) for the protection of enterprises handicapped by structural or natural conditions; and (b) within the framework of economic development programmes.

It should be noted that the expression regarding 'enterprises handicapped by structural or natural conditions', under Article 42 part (a), reflects the terms of Article 39(2)(a), which states that in working out CAP, account shall be taken of the particular nature of agricultural activity, which results from the social structure of agriculture and the structural and natural disparities between the various agricultural regions.[2]

This provision emphasizes the specific favour the European Union legislation shows towards these two categories of aid but, in truth, it does not seem to add much to what is already set out in the first part of Article 42, which already allows the Parliament and the Council to authorize aid in particular situations.[3]

On 4 April 1962, the Council used the powers it had under the version of Article 42 then in force to issue Regulation No. 26/62, regarding the application of competition rules to the production of and trade in agricultural products.[4] That Regulation was subsequently amended and later abolished and replaced as part of the codification of Community law, by Regulation (EC) No. 1184/2006 of 24 July 2006.[5] With respect to State aid, Article 3 of that latter Regulation (which reflected the content of Article 4 of the previous Regulation No. 26/62) provides that aid granted to the production of and

2. *See* Luigi Costato & Luigi Russo, *Corso di diritto agrario, supra*, p. 95.
3. The difference between Arts 42(1) and 42(2) is thus that, under the former, aid is authorized under the ordinary procedure (i.e., to say, by the Parliament and the Council); and under the latter, by the Council, at the Commission's proposal. On this, *see* Russo, *Art. 42*, in Fausto Pocar, Maria Caterina Baruffi, *Commentario breve, supra*, c. 320; and Orlandi, *Art. 42*, in Antonio Tizzano, *Trattati dell'Unione europea, supra*, p. 653.
4. Article 4 of Regulation (EEC) No. 26/62 provided that 'the provisions of Art. 93(1) and of the first sentence of Art. 93(3) [now 108(3)] of the Treaty shall apply to aids granted for production of or trade in the products listed in Annex II to the Treaty'.
5. Council Regulation (EC) No. 1184/2006 of 24 Jul. 2006 (has been amended several times and, lastly, by Regulation (EU) No. 1379/2013 of the European Parliament and of the Council of 11 Dec. 2013), applying certain rules of competition to the production of, and trade in, agricultural products. On the competition rules under Regulations 26/62 and 1184/2006, *see* Claudio Biscaretti di Ruffia, *Introduzione alle regole di concorrenza dell'Unione europea per le imprese del settore agricolo*, in *Scritti in onore di Giuseppe Tesauro*, II, *Diritto e politiche dell'Unione europea*, Naples, 2014, pp. 1409 et seq.

trade in agricultural products detailed in Annex I to the TFEU is subject to the terms of Article 108(1) and the first sentence of Article 108(3) of that Treaty.

That means, first, that plans to grant or alter aid must be notified to the Commission in sufficient time for it to submit its comments (Article 108(3), first sentence); and second, that the Commission must keep under constant review all systems of aid in the Member States, in cooperation with those States. The Commission also proposes appropriate measures to the Member States as required by the progressive development or the functioning of the internal market (Article 108(1)).[6]

It should be observed however that Regulation No. 1184/2006 has over the years become more and more limited in the scope of its application, as specific Regulations have been approved for a variety of agricultural products. It thus has a residual application, dealing with those matters not covered by the regulations established by the Common Market Organizations (CMOs) concerning those agricultural products.

That the Regulation applies only to products not subject to a CMO and, subsequently, the products not subject to Regulation (EC) No. 1234/2007, means two things. First, in relation to those products, the Commission would be able to submit comments upon aid, once it had been notified, but could not prohibit its grant. Second, in relation to the constant review of existing aid, the Commission would be able to propose 'appropriate measures required by the progressive development or by the functioning of the internal market', but could not make use of the procedure under Article 108(2) TFEU.[7] In the event that a State did not comply with the remarks submitted by the Commission regarding aid that the State had planned and notified, the Commission

6. *See* Fabio Gencarelli, *La politica agricola comune nella giurisprudenza comunitaria*, Padua, 2000, p. 36, which points out how, aside from the general provisions summarized here, the articles of the Treaty (now TFEU) that govern State aid have been made fully applicable by the regulations on each of the individual common market organizations. Consequently, only those products for which no individual CMO was provided prior to the 2007 reforms have remained outside the complete application of those articles. In substance, those products were subject exclusively to the rules of Regulations 26/62 and, later, 1184/2006. *See* on this the judgment of the Court of Justice in Joined Cases C-346/03 and C-529/03, *Atzeni and Others v. Regione autonoma della Sardegna*, 2006, ECLI:EU:C:2005:256 (paras 37-42 and 48); and Thibaut Kleiner, *Preferential Loans in favour of Agricultural Undertakings: Admissibility, Legal Basis, Legitimate Expectations*, in *Eur. State Aid Law Quart.*, 2006, 423. More recently, the Court of Justice has emphasized the broad discretion that the Council has under Art. 108(2), third sentence, TFEU – *see* judgments in *Commission v. Council* C-111/10 and others [2013] ECLI:EU:C:785;786;787;784. Finally, as regards the jurisprudence concerning the notion of State aid in the agricultural sector, *see* the judgments of the Court of Justice in Case C-467/15, *Commission v. Italy* ECLI:EU:2017:99 (subsequent corrected by the order of 21 Nov. 2017, ECLI:EU:C:2017:904) and in Case C-431/14 P, *Hellenic Republic v. Commission*, 8.03.2016, ECLI:EU:C:2016:145.
7. That provision of course allows the Commission to decide that a Member State must abolish or modify aid within a stated period where, after notifying the State that it should submit its comments, it finds that the aid is incompatible with the internal market under Art. 107. If the State does not comply with its decision within that stated period, the Commission, or other Member States, may refer the matter to the Court of Justice directly, in derogation from Art. 258 TFEU (or, for the Member States, from Art. 259).

   In relation to the solution adopted by Art. 3 of Regulation No. 1184/2006, *see* Fabio Gencarelli, *La nouvelle politique communautaire en matière d'aides d'Etat en agriculture*, *supra*, p. 7, who describes it as a 'solution minimaliste ne permettant à la Commission que d'examiner, d'une part, les aides existantes et, d'autre part, d'être informée sur les projets d'aides, avec possibilité de proposer aux Etats membres des mesures utiles'.

could make use of the procedure under Article 258 of the Treaty. That is to say, it could deliver a reasoned opinion, after giving the State concerned the opportunity to submit its observations. It could then bring the matter before the Court of Justice if the State did not comply with the opinion within the period laid down by the Commission.[8]

For products subject to a CMO, previously under Regulation (EC) No. 1234/2007 and now under Regulation (EU) No. 1308/2013, Articles 107-109 of TFEU apply, as described in more detail below.

Prior to the entry into force of Regulation (EC) No. 1234/2007, the Court of Justice had emphasized another consequence of the creation of individual CMOs – namely, that in such circumstances, the Commission had, in the context of the CAP, to take on any issues that arose in the sector regulated by those CMOs. The Member States on the other hand had to avoid introducing any unilateral measures, even if that measure was intended to support the Union's common policy.[9] Unsurprisingly in that light, the Court of Justice has found State aid to be unlawful where it had the effect of derogating from regulation by the European Union.[10]

§12.02 STATE AID UNDER REGULATION (EU) NO. 1308/2013 AND THE MOST RECENT REGULATIONS CONCERNING THE COMMON AGRICULTURAL POLICY (CAP) FROM 2023 TO 2027

The entry into force on 1 January 2014 of Regulation (EU) No. 1308/2013 of the European Parliament and of the Council, establishing a common organization of the markets in agricultural products and repealing, *inter alia*, Council Regulation (EC) No. 1234/2007, further reduced the scope of application of Regulation No. 1184/2006. The new Regulation, modified several times in subsequent years and most recently by Regulation (EU) No. 1143/2024 of the European Parliament and of the Council of 11 April 2024 was unlike Regulation No. 1234/2007 in that it applied to all the products 'listed in Annex I to the treaties [the TEU and the TFEU], with the exception of the fishery and aquaculture products as defined in Union legislative acts on the common organization of the markets in fishery and aquaculture products'.[11]

8. *See* on this, Russo, *Art. 42, supra*, p. 319; Agnieszka Stobiecka-Kuik, *Agriculture, supra*, p. 295; and Erhart, *State Aid in the Field of Agriculture*, in Michael Sanchez Rydelski, The *EC State Aid Regime, supra*, pp. 479 et seq. The latter author underlines how the Commission has followed the procedure and taken decisions recommending to States that they not grant a particular form of aid, and that Member States have nonetheless failed to follow that recommendation; and that there appear to have been no cases in which the Commission has brought the matter to the Court of Justice under Art. 258 TFEU after a Member State had refused to comply with its recommendation.
9. *See* the judgment of the Court of Justice in Case C-173/02, *Spain v. Commission* [2004] ECLI:EU:C:2004:617 and Cosimo's commentary thereon, in *OCM e adempimento degli obblighi comunitari: alcuni spunti di riflessione*, in *Dir. pubbl. comp. ed eur.*, 2005, 522; Previously, the judgment of the Court of Justice in Case C-86/89, *Italy v. Commission* [1990] ECLI:EU:C:1991:142.
10. *See* judgments of the Court of Justice, in Case C-113/00, *Spain v. Commission*, 2002, ECLI:EU:C:2002:507 and in Case C-11/00, *Spain v. Commission*, 2002, ECLI:EU:C:2003:395 and the comments by Diman, in *I 'crediti di gestione' al settore agricolo al vaglio della Corte di giustizia*, in *Dir. pubbl. comp. ed eur.*, 2003, 486.
11. Article 1, Regulation No. 1308/2013.

The rules on State aid regarding the 'first pillar' of the CAP, that is to say, agricultural and forestry policy, consisting of a number of instruments connected with the functioning of agricultural markets and the food supply chain, are contained above all in Articles 211-218 of Regulation (EU) No. 1308/2013.[12]

Article 211(1) provides that Articles 107-109 TFEU apply to the production of, and trade in, agricultural products. The next sub-article describes some exceptions to that general rule. In particular, Article 211(2)(a) provides that these articles do not apply to payments made by Member States pursuant to and in conformity with the measures provided for in this Regulation, partly or wholly financed by the Union; and Article 211(2)(b) provides that Articles 107-109 TFEU do not apply to payments made by Member States under the circumstances contemplated in Articles 213-218 of Regulation (EU) No. 1308/2013.

Article 213 regards payments made by Finland and Sweden for the production and marketing of reindeer and reindeer products; Article 214 authorizes Finland to make certain payments to sugar beet growers, for a sugar marketing campaign;[13] Article 216 regards national payments to wine producers in justified cases of crisis; Articles 215 and 218 authorize States to make payments to the apiculture sector and to nut farmers; and, finally, Article 217 regards payments made for the distribution of agricultural products to schoolchildren.

The articles examined above have been only marginally modified by the new regulations concerning the 2023-2027 CAP and, in particular, by Regulation (EU) No. 2117/2021 of the European Parliament and of the Council of 2 December 2021 amending Regulation (EU) No. 1308/2013 establishing a common organization of the markets in agricultural products, (EU) No. 1151/2012 on quality schemes for agricultural products and foodstuffs, (EU) No. 251/2014 on the definition, description, presentation, labelling and the protection of geographical indications of aromatized wine products and (EU) No. 223/2013 laying down specific measures for agriculture in the outermost regions of the Union.[14]

The other basic regulations of the 2023-2027 CAP are: Regulation (EU) No. 2115/2021 of the European Parliament and of the Council of 2 December 2021 establishing rules on support for strategic plans to be drawn up by (CAP Strategic Plans) and financed by the European Agricultural Guarantee Fund (EAGF) and by the

12. On Regulation No. 1308/2013, *see* Luigi Costato & Luigi Russo, *Corso di diritto agrario, supra*, pp. 155 et seq.; On the rules of the previous CAP 2014-2020, *see* Nemeckova, *Agriculture and Forestry*, in *EU Competition Law*, edited by Nicola Pesaresi, Koen Van de Casteele, Leo Flynn, Christina Siaterli & Deventer-Leuven, 2016, IV, 2, pp. 1199 et seq.; Ferdinando Albisinni, *La definizione di attività agricola nella nuova PAC, tra incentivazione e centralizzazione regolatoria*, in *Riv. it. dir. pubbl. com.*, 2014, pp. 967 et seq.
13. Again, with reference to Finland, Art. 214(a) (as replaced by Regulation (EU) No. 2117/2021) provides that, under certain conditions and subject to authorization by the Commission, Finland may continue to grant national aids which it granted in 2022 to producers, on the basis of this article, for the period 2023-2027.
14. For a summary of CAP 2023-2027 *see* European Commission, *The Common Agricultural policy at a glance*. For a critical examination of the structure of the new CAP *see* the collective work, Herve Guyomard, et al., *How the Green Architecture of the 2023-2027 Common Agricultural Policy could have greener*, in *Ambio*, 2023, 52, pp. 1327 et seq.

European Agricultural Fund for Rural Development (EAFRD) and repealing Regulations (EU) No. 1305/2013 and (EU) No. 1307/2013[15] and Regulation (EU) No. 2116/2021 of the European Parliament and of the Council of 2 December 2021 on the financing, management and monitoring of the common agricultural policy and repealing Regulation (EU) No. 1306/2013.[16] Only the first of these regulations contains, in Article 145, a rule on State aid, according to which: '1. Save as otherwise provided for in this Title, Articles 107, 108 and 109 TFEU shall apply to support under this Regulation.

2. Articles 107, 108 and 109 TFEU shall not apply to support provided by Member States pursuant to and in accordance with this Regulation, or to additional national financing referred to in Article 146 of this Regulation, falling within the scope of Article 42 TFEU'.

Other exceptions to the general principle that Articles 107-109 TFEU apply to the production of and trade in agricultural products are contained in other regulations connected with the CAP.

More specifically:

- Under the terms Article 23 of Regulation (EU) No. 228/2013, laying down specific measures for agriculture in the outermost regions of the Union, amended lastly with Regulation (EU) No. 2117/2021 of the European Parliament and of the Council, the Commission may authorize State aid under Article 108 TFEU, in the sectors producing, processing and marketing the agricultural products covered by Annex I TFEU. That aid is intended to alleviate the specific constraints on farming in the outermost regions as a result of their isolation, insularity and extreme remoteness, and may regard, *inter alia*, sugar, plant health programmes, wine, milk, livestock, and tobacco production.
- Other aid is permitted under Article 17 of Regulation (EU) No. 229/2013, laying down specific measures for agriculture in favour of the smaller Aegean islands. In particular, such aid may be authorized by the Commission, under Article 108 TFEU, with a view to alleviating difficulties resulting from the islands' insularity, small size, mountainous terrain, climate, economic dependency on a smaller number of products and distance from markets.
- Also Commission Regulation (EU) No. 651/2014 of 17 June 2014 declaring certain categories of aid compatible with the internal market in application of Articles 107 and 108 of TFEU contains some rules that are relevant to our purposes. Specifically, in its Article 1, concerning the scope of the Regulation, it specifies in paragraph 3 that it does not apply to aid granted in the fisheries and aquaculture sector, which is governed by Regulation (EU) No. 1379/2023 except for the cases specifically listed. Equally, the Regulation does not apply

15. Regulation (EU) No. 2115/2021 has been amended, lastly, by Regulation (EU) 2024/1468 of the European Parliament and of the Council of 14 May 2024.
16. Regulation (EU) No. 2116/2021 has been amended, lastly, by Regulation (EU) 2024/1468 of the European Parliament and of the Council of 14 May 2024.

to aid granted in the primary production of agricultural products, except for the cases specifically listed in the text.[17]

The so-called second pillar of the CAP – so named as opposed to the 'first pillar' mentioned earlier – which is rural development policy, is intended to improve competitiveness in the agricultural sector, the sustainable management of natural resources, also as a function of climate change, and balanced development of rural areas.

In this regard, it should be pointed out that, as mentioned above, Regulation (EU) No. 2115/2021 repealed, *inter alia*, Regulation (EU) No. 1305/2013 and, with it, Articles 81 and 82 thereof, which contained specific rules on State aid in the matter in consideration here.[18]

Under Regulation (EU) No. 2115/2022, Member States can grant aid under rural development programmes that are co-financed by the EU.

§12.03 GUIDELINES FOR STATE AID IN THE AGRICULTURAL AND FORESTRY SECTORS AND IN RURAL AREAS FOR THE PERIOD FROM 2023 TO 2027

Upon their natural expiry on 31 December 2020, the Guidelines for the period 2014 to 2020 were extended until 31 December 2022 and adjusted to take into account the COVID-19 pandemic.[19] With the subsequent Communication from the Commission, 'Guidelines for State aid in the agriculture and forestry sectors and in rural areas' [(2022/C) 485 of 14 December 2022] the new Guidelines for the period 2023-2027 were adopted.[20] They concern all notified aid measures on which the Commission is called upon to take a decision after 1 January 2023, even if the aid measures were notified before that date.

17. Regulation (EU) No. 651/2014 has been amended lastly by Commission Regulation (EU) 2023/1315 of 23 Jun. 2023. In relation to its interpretation *see*, lastly, European Court of Justice, Case C23-22 *Caxamar – Comércio* e *Indústria* de *Bacalhau SA v. Autoridade Tributária* e *Aduaneira*, 15 Dec. 2022, ECLI:EU:C:2022:994; and Case C-347/20, *SIA Zinatnes parks v. Finanšu ministrija*, 27 Jan. 2022, ECLI:EU:C:2022:59.
18. For a review of the rules regarding State aid and rural development policy, *see* Luigi Costato & Luigi Russo, *Corso di diritto agrario, supra*, pp. 137 et seq.; previously, Fabio Gencarelli, *La nouvelle politique communautaire en matière d'aides d'Etat en agriculture, supra*, pp. 11 et seq. and Nicolaides Phedon, Mihalis Kekalekis, Maria Kleis, *State Aid Policy in the European Community*, Alphen aan den Rijn, 2008, pp. 271 et seq.
19. *See* the Communication Notice amending the European Union Guidelines for State aid in Agricultural and Forestry Sectors and in Rural Areas 2014 to 2020 as regards their period of application and making temporary adaptation to take in the account the impact of the COVID-19 pandemic (2020/C 424/05).
20. The Guidelines 2023 to 2027 have been amended, on 5 Mar. 2024, by the Communication from the Commission correcting the Guidelines in question (C/2024/1902). On the mandatory value, for the Commission, of the guidelines it has issued, *see* Court of Justice, *Hellenic Republic v. Commission*, Case C-431/14P, ECLI:EU:C:2016:145; previously, Court of Justice, *Holland Malt v. Commission*, Case C-464/09P, ECLI:EU:C:2010:733.

The new Guidelines also apply to all notifiable aid measures, which, therefore, do not fall within the scope of Regulation 2022/2472/EU 'ABER', i.e., the General Block Exemption Regulation, examined below.

On the one hand, they set out the criteria to be used in the sector under scrutiny to assess State aid under the conditions of Article 107(3) TFEU. If this is the case, State aid may be considered compatible with the internal market. On the other hand, the Guidelines determine when aid to compensate for damage caused by natural disasters or exceptional occurrences is considered compatible with the internal market on the basis of Article 107(2)(b) TFEU.

The Commission considers, first, that State aid granted under Article 107 TFEU must be consistent with the support for farmers under the CAP. Therefore, the application and interpretation of the Guidelines under consideration here will have to be carried out taking into account the rules under the CAP.[21]

In addition, the new Guidelines have been aligned with the EU's strategic priorities as defined in the CAP, the European Green Deal[22] and, finally, in 'farm to fork' strategies[23] and in the Biodiversity Strategy.[24]

The main changes compared to the 2014 to 2020 Guidelines first concern new incentives for farmers to join schemes that prescribe higher environmental standards than the current provisions. Second, the new Guidelines provide for an extension of the scope of measures against animal diseases and plant pests. This broadening allows aid to be granted for emerging animal diseases and certain invasive exotic species. Finally, from a procedural point of view, the new Guidelines provide for a simplified procedure, both for the authorization of aid and for measures co-financed under the CAP.[25]

As for the scope of application, the new Guidelines, like their predecessors, provide that no State aid may be granted to companies in difficulty, subject to specific exceptions.[26] Therefore, the Guidelines on State aid for rescuing and restructuring non-financial firms in difficulty, the period of application of which was extended until 31 December 2025 by the Communication from the Commission amending the

---

21. Camera dei Deputati, *Gli aiuti di Stato, Parte Speciale, Principali Orientamenti della Commissione*, n. 67/1, 30 Jan. 2024, pp. 70 et seq.
22. On such matter, *see* the Communication from the Commission to the European Parliament, the European Council, the Council, the European Economic and Social Committee and the Committee of the Regions – The European Green Deal (COM [2019] 640 final).
23. *See* Communication from the Commission to the European Parliament, the Council, The European Economic and Social Committee and the Committee of the Regions – A Farm to fork Strategy for a fair, healthy, and environmentally – friendly food system (COM [2020] 381 final).
24. *See* Communication from the Commission to European Parliament, the Council, the European Economic and Social Committee and the Committee of the Regions – EU Biodiversity Strategy for 2030 'Bringing nature back into our lives' (COM [2020] 380 final). On these communications *see*, for a general overview, Luigi Costato & Luigi Russo, *Corso di diritto agrario, supra*, pp. 137 et seq. *See also*, for a criticism of the strategy underlying the new CAP 2023 to 2027, Herve Guyomard et al, *How the Green Architecture, supra*, pp. 1307 et seq.
25. Camera dei Deputati, *Gli aiuti di Stato, Parte Speciale, supra*, pp. 70 et seq.
26. *See Guidelines for State Aid, supra*, Part I, para. 2.2 *Scope of application* (23).

Guidelines in question of 29 November 2023, must be applied to undertakings in difficulty.[27]

They do not, however, apply to aid for agricultural products within the meaning of Annex 1 to the Agreement on Agriculture of the *World Trade Agreement*, which constitutes an export subsidy as defined in that Agreement.[28] Finally, the new Guidelines do not apply to aid for agricultural products that constitute financial support for export, provided by a government or any public body, within the scope of the Ministerial Decision of the *World Trade Agreement* of 19 December 2015.[29]

On the contrary, the State aid rules apply to all co-financed interventions, both by the EAFRD and the State; they also apply to those complementary national funding measures that do not fall within the scope of Article 42 TFEU but do fall within the scope of Regulation (EU) No. 2115/2021, i.e., interventions in support of activities in rural areas and interventions in the forestry sector.

As regards the applicability criteria, in general, on the basis of Article 107(3)(c) aid measures may be declared compatible with the internal market provided that the positive condition that the aid must facilitate the development of an economic activity and the negative condition that the aid must not adversely affect trading conditions to an extent contrary to the common interest of the EU are met.

The Guidelines also provide for more specific and detailed compatibility criteria, which are described in Part II. They concern: (a) aid in favour of undertakings active in the primary production, processing and marketing of agricultural products; (b) aid for the forest sector; (c) aid in rural areas which is co-financed by the EAFRD or granted as additional financing such co-financed interventions.[30]

Finally, it should be noted that the Commission may decide to revise or amend the new Guidelines if it considers this necessary for reasons related to competition policy, or to take account of other Union policies, while Member States, for their part, must submit annual reports to the Commission and keep records for ten years for all aid measures granted, making them available to the Commission if requested.[31]

§12.04 STATE AID UNDER COMMISSION REGULATION (EU) 2022/2472 (AGRICULTURAL BLOCK EXEMPTION REGULATION, ABER)

Among the rules related to the 2023-2027 CAP reform, an important role is played by Commission Regulation (EU) No. 2472/2022 of 14 December 2022, which declares

27. Communication from the Commission (C/2023/1212). *See*, about them, Baldi, *La disciplina*, *supra*, pp. 532 et seq.
28. *See Guidelines for State Aid*, *supra*, Part I, para. 2.2, *Scope of application* (24).
29. WT/MIN (15)/45-WT/L/980.
30. A clear summary of the compatibility criteria for State aid in the agricultural sector is contained in Camera dei Deputati, *Gli aiuti di Stato, Parte speciale*, *supra*, pp. 74 et seq.; on Regulation (EU) No. 2472/2022, *see* also Nina Maksimović Sekulić, Maja Kovačević & Radislav Jovičić, *The EU State aid Regime*, *supra*, pp. 240 et seq.; The authors underline, among other observations, that the amendments to Agriculture and Fisheries Block Exemption Regulations include a significant extension of the measures covered by the Block Exemption.
31. *See Guidelines for State Aid*, *supra*, Part III, *Procedural matters*, para. 1, *Duration of aid schemes and evaluation* (650 et seq.).

certain categories of aid in agriculture and forestry and rural areas compatible with the internal market pursuant to Articles 107 and 108 of the Treaty on the Functioning of the European Union (ABER). The aforementioned regulation replaces the previous Commission Regulation (EU) No. 702/2014 from 1 January 2023.[32] The latter, however, continues to apply until 31 December 2025 to aid granted in accordance with Regulation (EU) No. 1305/2013 of the European Parliament and of the Council.

In turn, Regulation (EU) No. 2472/2022, under consideration here, will apply until 31 December 2029 (Article 64).[33]

It, like previous regulations in the field, aims to identify and regulate the categories of aid that may be exempted from the *ex ante* notification procedure, as well as the regulations concerning small amounts of aid, i.e., the '*de minimis*' regulations, which will be examined below.

That said, the scope of the ABER Regulation includes: (a) aid for micro-enterprises and small and medium-sized enterprises (SMEs) active in the agricultural sector and also, under certain conditions, in non-agricultural activities in rural areas; (b) aid for environmental protection in agriculture (concerning only enterprises active in primary agricultural production); (c) investment aid for the preservation of the cultural and natural heritage present on farms and in forests; (d) aid to remedy the damage caused by natural disasters in the agricultural sector; (e) aid for research, development and innovation in the agricultural and forestry sectors; and (f) aid for the forestry sector.

Article 4 of the Regulation provides the aid thresholds above which State aid must be notified. These thresholds are numerous and range from a few hundred euros for aid for organic farming, to EUR 600,000 concerning investments in farms related to primary agricultural production, to EUR 7.5 million per project, concerning aid for research and development in the agricultural and forestry sectors.

The aids, which must be transparent (Article 5) and have an incentive effect under Article 6 of the Regulation, may be combined with each other under certain conditions specified in Article 8.

Chapter II of the ABER Regulation deals with certain procedural requirements for obtaining exemption of Article 108 TFEU notification of aid granted. In this regard, Article 10 specifies that if they do not meet the conditions set forth in Chapters I, II and III of the Regulation the Commission, after allowing the Member State to express its views, may adopt a decision stating that all, or part, of the future aid measures

32. On Regulation (EU) No. 702/2014 amended, lastly, by Commission Regulation (EU) 2020/2008 of 8 Dec. 2020, *see* Claudio Biscaretti di Ruffia, *Gli aiuti di Stato, supra*, pp. 27 et seq. and Carlo Eugenio Baldi, *La disciplina, supra*, pp. 327 et seq. Regarding the interpretation and application of Regulation (EU) No. 702/2014, *see* Case C-251/21, *Piltenes meži SIA v. Lauku atbalsta dienests*, 28 Apr. 2022, ECLI:EU:C:2022:311 and Case C-128/19, *Azienda sanitaria Provinciale di Catania v. Assessorato della Salute della Regione Sicilia*, 20 May 2021, ECLI:EU:C:2021:401.

33. Commission Regulation (EU) No. 2472/2022 has been amended by Commission Regulation (EU) No. 2607/2023 of 22 Nov. 2023. On the main changes made to the matter by Regulation (EU) No. 2472/2022, *see* the summary in Camera dei Deputati, *Gli aiuti di Stato, Parte Generale, Principali Orientamenti della Commissione*, n. 67/1, 26 Oct. 2024 *supra*, p. 32, note (49); *see also* ić- Nina Maksimović Sekulić, Maja Kovačević & Radislav Jovičić, *The EU State aid, supra*, pp. 240-241.

approved by the Member State concerned must be notified to it under Article 108(3) TFEU.

For the purpose of the Commission's control of the regularity of aid, on the one hand, the States must transmit to the Commission summary information concerning each aid measure granted within twenty working days of its entry into force (Article 11); on the other hand, Member States must keep detailed records containing all the information and supporting documents necessary to verify compliance with the conditions set forth in the Regulation (Article 13).

Finally, Article 63 specifies that the Regulation applies to individual aid granted before the date of its entry into force, provided that such aid fulfils the conditions set forth in the Regulation, except as provided in Article 9, concerning the publication and information that States must provide in connection with aid granted. However, as an exception to this rule, at the end of the period of validity of the Regulation, aid schemes that fall within the scope of Regulation (EU) No. 2115/2021 and are co-financed by the EAFRD or supplementary national funding for such co-financed measures, shall remain exempt for the duration of the programming period in accordance with the same Regulation (EU) No. 2115/2021.

§12.05 STATE AID IN THE AGRICULTURAL SECTOR UNDER COMMISSION REGULATION (EU) NO. 1408/2013 (*DE MINIMIS* REGULATION)

Commission Regulation (EU) No. 1408/2013 of 18 December 2013, which has been amended several times and most recently by Commission Regulation (EU) No. 2391/2023 of 4 October 2023, concerns the application of Articles 107 and 108 of the TFEU to small-scale aid granted to undertakings engaged in the primary production of agricultural products.[34]

In particular, the scope of application of the Regulation under consideration, according to its Article 1(1), concerns: (a) aid the amount of which is fixed on the basis of the price or quantity of the products marketed; (b) aid concerning activities related to exports to third countries or Member States, i.e., aid directly linked to the quantities exported, to the establishment and management of a distribution network or to other current expenses related to the export activity; and (c) aid conditional on the use of domestic products as opposed to imports.

However, the second and third paragraphs of the same Article 1 provide for some exceptions, among which it is worth mentioning the one concerning the hypothesis for which an enterprise operating in the primary production of agricultural products also operates in the primary production of fishery and aquaculture products. In this case, Commission Regulation (EU) No. 717/2014, which will be examined below, applies to the aid granted, provided, however, that the Member State concerned ensures that the

34. Commission Regulation (EU) No. 1408/2013 of 18 Dec. 2013 on the application of Arts 107 and 108 of the Treaty on the Functioning of the European Union to *de minimis* aid in the agriculture sector. For a summary of the Regulation under consideration here, *see* Camera dei Deputati, *Gli aiuti di Stato, Parte Generale, supra*, pp. 43 et seq.

primary production of agricultural products does not benefit from *de minimis* aid granted in accordance with the same Regulation.

Article 3 of the Regulation specifies, on the one hand, that the total amount of *de minimis* aid granted by a Member State to an enterprise may not exceed EUR 20,000 over a period of three fiscal years; on the other hand, the total amount of *de minimis* aid granted by a Member State to enterprises engaged in the primary production of agricultural products, over a period of three fiscal years, may not exceed the national limit set forth in Annex I of the Regulation. Article 3(3 *bis*) below, however, specifies that Member States may decide that, under certain conditions, the above thresholds may be exceeded.[35]

The subsequent Article 4 stipulates that the Regulation under consideration here applies only to 'transparent aid', i.e., aid in respect of which it is possible to calculate precisely the gross grant equivalent *ex ante*, without the need for a risk assessment. Regulation (EU) No. 1408/2013 then provides that *de minimis* aid granted under it can, under certain conditions, be cumulated with *de minimis* aid granted for other sectors of activity (Article 5).

Article 6 governs the regime of controls regarding the proper use of de *minimis* aid granted on the basis of the Regulation at issue. It provides that where Member States grant *de minimis* aid under Article 3(3a) they must have a central register of such aid.

Member States must, however, record all information regarding the application of Regulation (EU) No. 1408/2013 and must retain such data for ten fiscal years.In any case, upon a written request from the Commission, Member States must submit, within twenty days or the different period specified in the request, all information concerning aid that is requested from them.

The following Article 7 provides some transitional provisions. In particular, the first paragraph of this article should be emphasized, whereby 'This Regulation shall apply to aid granted before its entry into force if the aid fulfils all the conditions laid down in this Regulation. Any aid which does not fulfil those conditions will be assessed by the Commission in accordance with the relevant frameworks, guidelines, communications and notices.'

Subsequent subsections of Article 7 then concern *de minimis* aid granted between 1 January 2005 and 30 June 2014, which, under the conditions indicated, will be exempt from the notification requirement of Article 108(3) TFEU.

Finally, the Regulation (EU) No. 1408/2013 will apply until 31 December 2027 (Article 8).[36]

---

35. On the basis of this article, the Italian Government, with Ministerial Decree (MIPAAF) of 19 May 2020, has established, among other things, that the total amount of *de minimis* aid granted to an enterprise engaged in the primary production of agricultural products shall not exceed EUR 25,000 over three fiscal years.
36. However, it should be noted that in June 2024, the Commission launched a public consultation on the proposal to, among other things, raise the *de minimis* aid threshold for agriculture to EUR 37,000 over three years and extend the application of the Regulation at issue until 2032.

§12.06 COMMISSION REGULATION (EU) 2023/2831 OF 13 DECEMBER 2023 ON THE APPLICATION OF ARTICLES 107 AND 108 OF THE TREATY ON THE FUNCTIONING OF THE EUROPEAN UNION TO *DE MINIMIS* AID

On 1 January 2024, this Regulation entered into force, which contains a reform of the framework regarding *de minimis* State aid for all economic sectors except for specific cases, including the primary production of agricultural, fishing and aquaculture products.[37] On the contrary, the sectors of processing and marketing of agricultural products, on the one hand, and fishing and aquaculture, on the other hand, fall within the scope of the Regulation, unless the amount of aid is determined on the basis of the price or quantity of the products purchased or marketed or, but with reference exclusively to the hypothesis of processing and marketing of agricultural products, if the aid is conditional on the fact of being partially or entirely transferred to primary producers.[38]

The other hypotheses in which the Regulation under consideration here does not apply concern: (a) aid for activities related to exports to third countries or Member States, i.e., aid directly linked to the quantities exported, to the establishment and management of a distribution network, or to other current expenses related to the export activity; (b) aid conditional on the use of domestic products and services as opposed to imported ones.The new Regulation stipulates in Article 3(2) that the total amount of *de minimis* aid granted shall not exceed EUR 300,000 over three years per enterprise, or single enterprise as defined in Article 2(2). Subsequent paragraph (7) of the same Article 3 then stipulates that if the granting of new *de minimis* aid results in the above total amount being exceeded, the new aid will not benefit from Regulation (EU) 2023/2831.

It should still be made clear that the total amount applies regardless of the form or objective of the aid and regardless of whether the aid granted is financed wholly or partly with resources from the EU.

The very detailed Article 4, after specifying that the Regulation under review applies only to aid in relation to which it is possible to precisely calculate the gross grant equivalent *ex ante*, without any need to undertake a risk assessment (transparent *de minimis* aid), contains the provisions that specifically address: (a) aid comprised of grants or interest rate subsidies; (b) aid comprised of loans; (c) aid comprised of capital injections; (d) aid comprised of risk finance measures taking the form of equity or quasi-equity investments; (e) aid comprised of guarantees; and (f) aid received by a financial intermediary implementing one or more *de minimis* aid schemes which shall be available on equal terms to financial intermediaries operating in the Member State concerned. Finally, Article 4(8) provides that 'Aid comprised of other instruments shall be considered as transparent de minimis aid if the instrument provides for a cap that

37. In relation to these sectors, *see* respectively, Regulation (EU) No. 1408/2013 and Regulation (EU) No. 717/2014.
38. Regulation (EU) No. 2831/2023, Art. 1. For an exhaustive summary of the Regulation in question, *see* Camera dei Deputati, *Gli aiuti di Stato, Parte generale, supra*, pp. 38 et seq.

ensures the ceiling laid down in Article 3 (2) of this Regulation.' Regulation (EU) No. 2831/2023, following the pattern of other regulations in the field, then deals with the issues of cumulation, monitoring and reporting concerning *de minimis* aid granted. In the first aspect, Article 5(1) and (2) provide, respectively, that de *minimis* aid granted under this Regulation may be cumulated with *de minimis* aid granted under Commission Regulation (EU) 2023/2832[39] and that it may be cumulated with *de minimis* aid granted under Commission Regulations (EU) No. 1408/2013 (examined above) and (EU) No. 717/2014 (examined below) up to the total amount provided for in Article 3(2) of Regulation (EU) No. 2831/2023.

In the second aspect, Article 6 primarily requires Member States to ensure that as of 1 January 2026, all information on *de minimis* aid granted is entered into a central register at the national or EU level. In addition, Member States must keep the information recorded and related to *de minimis* aid for a period of ten years from the date the aid was granted.Finally, according to Article 7, the Regulation under consideration here also applies to aid granted prior to its entry into force provided that it meets all the conditions set forth therein. Furthermore, at the end of the period of application of Regulation (EU) 2023/2831, *de minimis* aid that meets the conditions prescribed in the Regulation itself may be lawfully granted for an additional period of six months.

Finally, according to Article 8, Commission Regulation (EU) 2023/2831 shall apply until 31 December 2030.

§12.07 THE PROVISIONS ON THE APPLICATION OF STATE AID TO UNDERTAKINGS ACTIVE IN THE PRODUCTION, PROCESSING AND MARKETING OF FISHERY AND AQUACULTURE PRODUCTS: AN INTRODUCTION

As noted at the beginning of this chapter, the fishery and aquaculture sector falls under Part Three, Title III, of TFEU entitled, precisely, 'Agriculture and Fisheries'.

However, given its wholly unique characteristics, the implementing provisions of the aforementioned Title III (Articles 38-44) TFEU concerning fisheries and aquaculture are autonomous from those concerning agriculture and forestry.

For the purposes of their examination, it is good to start with Regulation (EU) No. 1379/2013 of the European Parliament and of the Council of 11 December 2013 on the common organization of the markets in fishery and aquaculture products.[40]

Said Regulation, in regulating the sector under consideration, as well as the already examined Regulation No. 1308/2013 for agricultural products, contains, in Chapter V, rules on competition that reaffirm, first, the application of Articles 101 to

39. Commission Regulation (EU) 2023/2832 of 13 Dec. 2023 on the application of Arts 107 and 108 of the Treaty on the Functioning of the European Union to *de minimis* aid granted to undertakings providing services of general economic interest.
40. Regulation (EU) No. 1379/2013 has been amended, lastly, by Regulation (EU) 2020/560 of the European Parliament and of the Council of 23 Apr. 2020. For a clear distinction between '*processing activities of fishery and aquaculture products*' and '*processing activities of agricultural products*', *see* Court of Justice, *Caxamar – Comércio e Indústria de Bacalhau SA v. Autoridade Tributária e Aduaneira*, Case C-23/22, ECLI:EU:2022:994.

106 TFEU – insofar as their application does not hinder the functioning of the Common Fisheries Policy (CFP) and does not jeopardize the achievement of the objectives set forth in Article 39 TFEU[41] – to agreements concerning the production and marketing of fishery and aquaculture products (Article 40). Next, Article 41 regulates exceptions to the application of competition rules concerning certain agreements, decisions and practices of producer organizations and interbranch organizations that meet certain conditions.[42]

Regulation (EU) 2013/1379, however, does not contain provisions specifically concerning State aid. Instead, the topic is the subject of Article 10 of Regulation (EU) 2021/1139 of the European Parliament and of the Council of 7 July 2021 establishing the European Maritime Fisheries and Aquaculture Fund and amending Regulation (EU) 2017/1004.[43] This article provides that Articles 107-109 TFEU apply to aid granted by Member States to undertakings in the sector at issue, except where payments made by Member States under and in accordance with Regulation (EU) No. 508/2014 fall within the scope of Article 42 TFEU.

Paragraph (3) of the article under consideration then stipulates: 'National provisions setting up public financing going beyond the provisions of this Regulation concerning payments referred to in paragraph 2 shall be treated as a whole on the basis of paragraph 1.'

Finally, Article 10 of Regulation (EU) 2021/1139 provides, in paragraph 4, that for fishery and aquaculture products, to which Articles 107-109 TFEU apply, the Commission may authorize, in accordance with Article 108, operating aid in the outermost regions referred to in Article 349 TFEU, within the sectors of production, processing and marketing of fishery and aquaculture products, in order to reduce the specific difficulties of those regions, linked to their isolation, insularity or great distance.

41. That is, following the principle of the primacy of the Common Agricultural Policy over the objectives of the TFEU in the area of competition, a principle already established by the European Court of Justice in its judgment of 29 Oct. 1980 in *Maizena v. Council* C139/79, ECLI:EU:C:1980:250, and reaffirmed several times thereafter. On the Court of Justice's ruling in the *Maizena* case and, more generally, on the relationship between competition rules and the Common Agricultural Policy, *see* Claudio Biscaretti di Ruffia, *Introduzione alle regole di concorrenza, supra*, pp. 1417 et seq.
42. On the common fisheries and aquaculture policy, *see*, for a general overview, Roberto Adam & Antonio Tizzano, *Manuale di diritto dell'Unione europea*, Turin, 2017, pp. 475 et seq. For an examination of State aid under the CAP 2014-2020, *see* Noë, *Fisheries*, in *EU Competition Law, supra*, pp. 1221 et seq.
43. The European Maritime Fisheries and Aquaculture Fund (EMFAF) is a new financial instrument to support the fisheries and aquaculture sector for the period 2021-2027. It entered into force on 14 Jul. 2021 with the objective of contributing to: (a) food security through the supply of fish products; (b) the growth of a sustainable marine economy; (c) the maintenance of healthy, safe, and sustainably managed seas and oceans (*see* https://oceans-and-fisheries.ec.europa.eu).

§12.08 GUIDELINES FOR STATE AID IN THE FISHERY AND AQUACULTURE SECTOR FOR THE PERIOD FROM 2023 TO 2027

As with the agriculture and forestry sector, the Commission, upon the expiration of the previous Guidelines in the fishery and aquaculture sector,[44] adopted new Guidelines with a communication.[45] They set out the conditions under which State aid granted by Member States can be considered compatible with the relevant EU provisions and are part of a package of rules concerning the agriculture, forestry, fisheries and aquaculture sectors. The aim of the new Guidelines is to align State aid to businesses with the Union's strategic priorities, including the new Common Fisheries Policy, the European Maritime Fisheries and Aquaculture Fund, the European Green Deal, as well as the Farm to Fork Strategy and the Biodiversity Strategy.[46]

The new Guidelines, which apply to all enterprises operating in the sectors at issue, cover aid granted to those sectors, including regional aid components and all other aid granted to the same sectors under EU funds. They do not, however, apply to undertakings in difficulty, with exceptions concerning: (a) aid to compensate for losses or damage caused by natural disasters and exceptional occurrences, provided that such aid is compatible with the internal market under Article 107(2)(b) TFEU; (b) aid (subject to certain conditions) intended to compensate for losses or damage caused by adverse climatic events, which can be assimilated to a natural disaster, animal diseases and infestations by invasive exotic species and protected animals; (c) aid (subject to certain conditions) for the prevention, control and eradication of animal diseases in aquaculture; and (d) aid relating to information actions for promotion measures of a generic nature, provided that they are covered in Part I, Chapter 2, section 2.3 of the Guidelines.

In Part I, Chapter 3, of the Guidelines, the Commission specifies that under Article 107(3)(2) it may consider aid to facilitate the development of certain economic activities or certain economic regions to be compatible with the internal market, provided that it does not adversely affect trading conditions to an extent contrary to the common interest. For this reason, in order to assess whether State aid can be considered compatible with the internal market, the Commission: (a) will have to determine whether the aid measure facilitates the development of a certain economic activity (first condition); and (b) whether it alters trading conditions to an extent contrary to the common interest (second condition). To this end, the Commission will

---

44. Communication from the Commission – *Guidelines for the examination of State aid to the fishery and aquaculture sector*, of 2 Jul. 2015 (2015/C217/01).
45. Communication from the Commission – *Guidelines for State aid in the fishery and aquaculture sector* (2023/C107/01). For a summary of the new Guidelines, *see* https://eur-lex.europa.eu/EN/legal-content/summary/guidelines-for-state-aid-in-the-agricultural-and-forestry-sectors-and-in-rural-areas.html.
46. For further information *see* Confagricoltura, *State Aid: Commission adopts new rules for agriculture, forestry, fisheries and aquaculture sectors*, available at https://www.confagricoltura.it/ita/europa/news/aiuti-di-stato-la-commissione-adotta-nuove-norme-per-i-settori-dell-agricoltura-della-silvicoltura-della-pesca-e-dell-acquacoltura, 14 Dec. 2022.

have to assess whether state intervention is necessary, appropriate, proportionate and transparent.

Finally, the Commission specifies that, under certain conditions, aid may also be granted under several aid schemes or cumulated with aid granted ad hoc.

In Part II of the Guidelines, the categories of permissible aid are specified. They are: (a) aid for risk and crisis management; (b) aid in the outermost regions; and (c) aid for measures concerning the fleet and cessation of fishing activities.

As for procedural aspects, these are dealt with in the third and final part of the Guidelines. In this regard, the Commission states that it is willing to authorize only aid schemes whose period of application does not exceed seven years. It adds, then, that for certain aid schemes that are large in amount or have innovative features or are aimed at significant technological, regulatory or market changes, it may require an *ex post* evaluation.

In the second paragraph of Part III, it is specified that a review clause will have to be provided for the commitments made by undertakings benefiting from the measures covered by implementing regulations by category in order to ensure that these commitments are adjusted in the event of a change in the rules of the mandatory conditions set out in Articles 38 and 39 of Regulation (EU) 2022/2473 (examined below).

Finally, in the fifth and sixth paragraphs of Part III, it is specified, on the one hand, that Member States are required to submit annual reports to the Commission and, on the other hand, that the Commission reserves the right to revise or amend the Guidelines at any time, should it be deemed necessary.

§12.09 STATE AID UNDER COMMISSION REGULATION (EU) 2022/2473 (FISHERY AND AQUACULTURE BLOCK EXEMPTION REGULATION

The Commission has recently published a new block exemption regulation in the fisheries and aquaculture sector. This is the Commission Regulation (EU) 2022/2473 which entered into force on 1 January 2023 with an expected expiration date of 31 December 2029.[47]

It replaces Commission Regulation (EU) No. 1388/2014, which applied until 31 December 2022.[48]

47. Commission Regulation (EU) 2022/2472 of 14 Dec. 2022 declaring certain categories of aid to undertakings active in the production, processing and marketing of fisheries and aquaculture products compatible with the internal market in application of Arts 107 and 108 of TFEU, amended, lastly, by Commission Regulation (EU) 2023/2603 of 22 Nov. 2023.
48. Commission Regulation (EU) No. 1388/2014 of 16 Dec. 2014 declaring certain categories of aid to undertakings active in the production, processing and marketing of fishery and aquaculture products compatible with the internal market in application of Arts 107 and 108 of Treaty on the Functioning of the European Law.

The purpose of the new Regulation is to determine the categories of aid that are compatible with State aid rules by exempting them from the requirement of prior notification to the Commission.[49]

It applies, first and foremost, to aid: (a) to micro-enterprises and small and medium-sized enterprises (SMEs) active in the production, processing and marketing of fisheries products; (b) to municipalities participating in participatory local development projects; (c) to fishing ports, landing places, auction halls and fishing shelters; (d) in favour of enterprises active in the sector under consideration here – regardless of the size of the enterprise – whose objective is to remedy the damage caused by natural disasters, or events assimilated to them, repair the damage caused by protected animals, and to innovate the fishing and aquaculture sector. Aid granted under the Regulation must meet the requirement of transparency (Article 5) and must also have an incentive effect (i.e., there must be a potential beneficiary who has submitted a written application for aid to the Member State concerned before starting work on the project or activity) (Article 6). Finally, aid granted must be published on national and Commission websites (Article 9).

The cases to which the Exemption Regulation does not apply, however, are listed in Article 1, paragraphs 3-7. Among them, it should be noted that the Regulation under review does not apply, with specific exceptions, to aid undertakings in difficulty (Article 1(4)). It also does not apply to individual aid for projects with eligible expenses exceeding EUR 2.5 million, or where the gross grant equivalent of the aid exceeds EUR 1.25 million per company and per year (Article 3, which also specifies that the thresholds set by it may not be circumvented by artificial splitting of aid schemes or aid projects).

As for procedural requirements, Article 10 stipulates that where a State has granted aid without fulfilling the conditions set forth in Chapters I, II and III of the Regulation, the Commission, after hearing the Member State concerned, may withdraw, in whole or in part, the benefit of the block exemption. Member States must, in addition, submit to the Commission an annual report on the application of the Regulation under consideration here (Article 11).

According to the following Article 12, as of the date of entry into force of the Regulation at issue, aid schemes whose expenditure exceeds EUR 150 million in any one year or EUR 750 million over the life of the scheme, must be subject to an *ex post* evaluation.

Finally, Member States must keep detailed records containing the information and supporting documents necessary to verify compliance with the conditions set out in the Regulation.

49. For a summary of Commission Regulation (EU) 2022/2472, *see State aid – fishery and aquaculture sectors*, available at https://eur-lex.europa.eu/EN/legal-content/summary/state-aid-fishery-and-aquaculture-sectors.html (15 Oct. 2024).

§12.10 STATE AID IN THE FISHERY AND AQUACULTURE SECTOR UNDER COMMISSION REGULATIONS (EU) NOS 717/2014 AND (EU) 2023/2831 (*DE MINIMIS* AID)

On 1 July 2014, Commission Regulation (EU) No. 717/2014 of 27 June 2014, on the application of Articles 107 and 108 of the Treaty on the Functioning of the European Union to *de minimis* aid in the fishery and aquaculture sector, which replaces the previous Regulation (EC) No. 875/2007 and was to remain in force until 31 December 2020, entered into force.[50] However, due to subsequent amendments, it will apply until 31 December 2029.[51]

This Regulation applies to the primary production of fishery and aquaculture products, albeit with numerous exceptions, listed in Article 1. The total amount of *de minimis* aid granted by a Member State to a single enterprise may not exceed EUR 30,000 over a period of three fiscal years (Article 3(2)). However, as an exception to this provision, the subsequent paragraph (*2a*) of the same Article 3 provides that a Member State may decide that the total amount of *de minimis* aid granted to a single enterprise shall not exceed EUR 40,000 over a period of three fiscal years (thus increasing the aid ceiling), provided that the Member State has established a national central register of State aid in accordance with Article 6(2). Also under the amendments made by Commission Regulation (EU) 2023/2391, the cumulative amount of *de minimis* aid granted to undertakings engaged in the primary production of fishery and aquaculture products may not exceed the national limit set out in the Annex to the above Regulation, which is EUR 38,524 million over three fiscal years.

Further rules of the (EU) Commission Regulation at issue (rules common to all recent regulations in the matters examined here) concern: (a) the circumstance that aid granted must be 'transparent aid', that is, aid with respect to which it is possible to calculate precisely the gross grant equivalent *ex ante* without the need to carry out a risk assessment (Article 4); (b) the specific conditions to which aid is subject when it is granted to undertakings that, in addition to operating in the sector under consideration here, are also active in the sectors covered by Regulations (EU) No. 1407/2013 and (EU) No. 1408/2013.

Regulation (EU) No. 717/2014 also requires States to monitor individual and national ceilings, to keep central records of aid granted for ten years, and to provide the Commission with the information it requests within twenty working days, or such longer period as the Commission may specify.

Finally, among the transitional provisions, in Article 7, paragraph 4 should be emphasized, that at the end of the application of the Regulation, it will continue to

50. For a summary of Commission Regulation (EU) No. 717/2014, *see State aid – fishery and aquaculture sectors,* available at https://eur-lex.europa.eu/EN/legal-content/summary/state-aid-fishery-and-aquaculture-sectors.html (15 Oct. 2024), *supra. See also* Claudio Biscaretti di Ruffia, *Gli aiuti di Stato, supra*, pp. 42 et seq.
51. Commission Regulation (EU) No. 717/2014 has been lastly amended by Commission Regulation (EU) 2023/2391 of 4 Oct. 2023. For a summary of such Regulation *see* Camera dei Deputati, *Gli aiuti di Stato, Parte generale, supra*, pp. 45 et seq.

apply for an additional period of six months to all *de minimis* aid schemes that meet the conditions laid down in the same Regulation.

Before ending this paragraph, it should be mentioned that, as we have already written in paragraph 6 of this chapter, Commission Regulation (EU) 2023/2831, which contains a general reform of the *de minimis* State aid, entered into force on 1 January 2024. In its Article 1, the new Regulation states that it is applicable 'to aid granted to undertakings in all sectors', but with certain exceptions. Among them, we have already mentioned aid granted to undertakings engaged in the primary production of fishery and aquaculture products, which remains governed by Commission Regulation (EU) No. 717/2014 and also, with reference to undertakings engaged in the processing and marketing of fishery and aquaculture products: '(i) where the amount of aid is fixed on the basis of the price or quantity of such products purchased from primary producers or put on the market by undertakings concerned; (ii) where the aid is conditional on being partly orientively passed on to primary producers'.

To what has already been written above on the Commission Regulation (EU) 2023/2831, it is only worth adding that, with the recent reform of the State aid framework, the sector of processing and marketing of fishery and aquaculture products has been separated from that of primary production and can, today, take advantage of the higher aid ceilings provided for in the new General Regulation on *de minimis* aid.[52]

§12.11 THE TEMPORARY CRISIS FRAMEWORKS FOR STATE AID MEASURES TO SUPPORT THE AGRICULTURE SECTOR AND THE FISHERY AND AQUACULTURE SECTOR

The State aid frameworks concerning agriculture and fishery have been enriched as a result of the complex crises that have affected the economies of the entire world and also of EU Member States in recent years. First, the financial crisis at the end of the first decade of the century; then, the crisis caused by the COVID-19 pandemic; and finally, the crisis resulting from Russia's invasion of Ukraine. The European Commission's response, in order to enable Member States to protect their economies and aid economic recovery, has relied, in particular, on Article 107(2)(b) and 107(3)(b) TFEU, the first concerning public aid aimed at repairing damage caused by natural disasters or other exceptional occurrences (aid that is, in itself, compatible with the internal market); the second, concerning aid intended to remedy a serious disturbance in the economy of a Member State (aid that may be compatible with the internal market but must be authorized by the Commission). Based on these articles, the Commission has adopted some Temporary Frameworks for State aid measures over the years. As far as we are interested here, it is worth mentioning the Communication from the Commission – '*Temporary Crisis Framework for State Aid measures to support the economy following the aggression against Ukraine by Russia*' (2022/L 131 1/01) published on 24 March 2022, following the invasion of Ukraine by Russia.

52. *See*, in this regard, Camera dei Deputati, *Gli aiuti di Stato*, 31 Jan. 2024, p. 8.

It was intended to address the liquidity shortage of undertakings directly or indirectly affected by the severe disruption of the economy following that war, the sanctions imposed by the European Union and its international partners on Russia, and the related countermeasures taken by Russia.[53] The Temporary Framework under consideration was later supplemented by the Commission in July 2022 (COM 2022/C 280/01) and again supplemented and extended on 28 October 2022 (2022/C 426/01).

Subsequently, given the prolongation and escalation of the conflict in Ukraine, it was replaced by a new Temporary Crisis and Transition Framework, approved on 9 March 2023.[54] Finally, on 2 May 2024, the Commission, after a consultation open to Member States, adopted a limited extension of section 2.1 of the Temporary Crisis and Transition Framework, with reference to aid granted to the primary agriculture, fishery and aquaculture sectors, until 31 December 2024.[55] This section covers limited amounts of aid, which may be granted under Article 107(3)(c) TFEU to undertakings damaged by Russia's aggression against Ukraine.

The extension does not include an increase in the ceilings set for aid that can be granted under section 2.1 under consideration here. They will, therefore, remain at EUR 280,000 for the agriculture sector and EUR 335,000 for the fishery and aquaculture sector, as under previous versions of the Temporary Crisis and Transition Framework.

The other provisions of such document, concerning various economic sectors, remain unchanged. It is to be expected, however, should the current war not come to an end, that the Commission will put in place, in future, additional interventions in favour of the European undertakings.

53. *See* Camera dei Deputati, *Gli aiuti di Stato, Parte generale, supra*, pp. 54 et seq.
54. Communication from the Commission – *Temporary Crisis and Transition Framework for State Aid measures to support the economy following the aggression against Ukraine by Russia*, Bruxelles, 9.3.2023 [C(2023)1711 final]. The Temporary Crisis and Transition Framework has been amended by the Communication from the Commission of 21 Nov. 2023 (C/2023/1188).
55. Communication from the Commission – *Second amendment of the Temporary Crisis and Transition Framework for State Aid measures to support the economy following the aggression against Ukraine by Russia* (C/2024/3113). *See* European Commission – *Press release*, Brussels, 2 May 2024.

CHAPTER 13
Banking and Finance

Luigi Santa Maria & Edoardo Gambaro

§13.01 EARLY RESPONSES TO THE FINANCIAL CRISIS

The first signs of the financial crisis emerged in 2007 when the US subprime mortgage market began to collapse. Shortly afterwards it reached Europe, where the impairment of securitization markets, the decrease in bank assets due to exposure to subprime mortgages and the fall of assets prices triggered a spiral of uncertainty on bank's exposure to toxic assets. It soon became clear that a crisis of such size would require swift and determined action if contagion was to be avoided within the banking system.

When the crisis reached Europe, there were no sectorial regulations concerning State aid to banks in place.[1] In the early stage of the crisis, the Commission assessed national measures of support to banks under the Guidelines on State Aid for Rescuing and Restructuring Firms in Difficulty (the 'R&R Guidelines').[2] Application of the R&R Guidelines – designed for undertakings facing economic difficulties in whichever sector of the economy – to troubled financial institutions soon proved inefficient.[3] In

1. Before the crisis, State aid rules had been applied to the financial sector in a very limited number of cases. *See*, for instance, the Commission Decision 95/547/EC of 26 Jul. 1995 giving conditional approval to aid that France granted to the bank *Crédit Lyonnais* 95/547/EC OJ 1995 L308/92; Commission decision 2005/345/EC of 7 Apr. 2004, State Aid C28/2002 *Bankgesellschaft Berlin* OJ 2005 L116/1.
2. *See* the Guidelines on State Aid for Rescuing and Restructuring Firms in Difficulty OJ 2004 C244/2, repealed and replaced by the Guidelines on State Aid for Rescuing and Restructuring Non-Financial Undertakings in Difficulty OJ 2014 C249/1. The legal basis of the R&R Guidelines is Art. 107(3)(c) TFEU, exempting: 'aid to facilitate the development of certain economic activities or of certain economic areas, where such aid does not adversely affect trading conditions to an extent contrary to the common interest'.
3. The R&R Guidelines distinguish between two categories of aid: (i) rescue aid, which is urgent and temporary, and has the primary objective of making it possible to keep an ailing undertaking afloat for the time needed to work out a restructuring or liquidation plan; and (ii) restructuring aid, which is aimed at restoring the long-term viability of the beneficiary, through more enduring

particular, after the collapse of Lehman Brothers in September 2008 there was no longer any question over the need to introduce a State aid policy that focused especially upon the banks, as a means of responding to a crisis that was assuming systemic dimensions.

In October 2008, the Council highlighted the need for the Commission to be swift and flexible when deciding upon the compatibility of State aid to troubled banks, but at the same time emphasized the necessity of ensuring adherence to the principles of the single market and State aid legislation.[4] The task of the Commission was two-folded: on the one hand, it had to act quickly, trying to avoid the typical procedural obligations upon the Member States (as to prior notification, and the standstill obligation)[5] resulted in a timetable that was incompatible with the urgency of the measures; on the other, the Commission could not deviate from the underlying principles of State aid control and had to limit the adverse effects such measures could have upon competition.

On this background, the Commission adopted a series of communications, beginning in October 2008 on State aid to banks (the 'Crisis Framework'). The Crisis Framework implied a shift in EU policy on State support to financial institutions, which resulted in an unprecedented expansion of State aid to the financial sector. From 1 October 2008 to 1 October 2014, the Commission took more than 450 decisions authorizing State aid measures for the financial sector, both in the form of aid schemes and ad hoc individual interventions in favour of certain financial institutions.[6]

The Crisis Framework distinguishes between four categories of aid: guarantees on liability, liquidity measures, recapitalizations and impaired asset measures. The most frequently used instruments were guarantees and recapitalization measures. Regarding guarantees on liabilities, between 1 October 2008 and 1 October 2014, the Commission authorized a total aid of EUR 3,892.6 billion (29.8% of EU GDP in 2013) with banks utilizing about a quarter of the amount approved. The outstanding amount reached its peak in 2009 totalling EUR 835.8 billion (6.39% of EU 2013 GDP).[7] Recapitalization is the second most commonly used instrument to support the financial sector with the Commission approving EUR 821.1 billion (6.3% of EU 2013 GDP) over the last six years. From 2008 to 2013, Member States were granted an overall amount of EUR 448 billion (3.4% of EU 2013 GDP) in recapitalization measures.

assistance. Rescue aid requires an accompanying commitment from the relevant Member State that within six months of authorization, a restructuring plan, a liquidation plan, or proof that the loan has been reimbursed in full shall be submitted to the Commission.

4. *See* the Council Conclusion – Ecofin Council of 7 Oct. 2008 – Immediate responses to financial turmoil (13930/08) and Ecofin Declaration on a concerted European action plan of the European countries of 12 Oct. 2008.
5. *See supra*, Ch. 3, on the procedural aspects of State aid monitoring.
6. Since the beginning of the financial crisis, 112 banks in the EU representing around 30% of the EU banking system by assets, have received State aid. *See* The Competition State Aid Brief Issue 2015-1 Feb. 2015.
7. *Source*: State Aid Scoreboard 2014, available on the Commission website.

§13.02 THE CRISIS FRAMEWORK

The Commission adopted seven communications dealing with aid to financial institutions:

(i) The Banking Communication of 25 October 2008.
(ii) The Recapitalization Communication of 15 January 2009.
(iii) The Impaired Assets Communication of 26 March 2009.
(iv) The Restructuring Communication of 22 July 2009.
(v) The First Prolongation Communication of 2011.
(vi) The Second Prolongation Communication of 2012.
(vii) The Banking Communication of 1 August 2013, which replaced the original Banking Communication of 2008.

The legal basis of these communications is Article 107(3)(b) TFEU, which provides that State aid may be considered compatible with the internal market where it serves 'to remedy a *serious disturbance* in the economy of a Member State'.[8]

In its 2013 Banking Communication, the Commission underlined 'the persistent risk of a serious disturbance in the economy of Member States', concluding that the requirements for the application of Article 107(3)(b) TFEU to State aid in the financial sector continued to be satisfied.[9]

The decision-making process of the Commission under the Communications mentioned above was characterized by a peculiar 'fast track procedure', relying heavily on close cooperation between the Commission and the Member State.[10] In particular, pre-notification talks with the Member States have significantly contributed to shortening the length of the proceedings between notification and the decision. Moreover, in order to speed up the procedure, the Commission adopted a simplified internal consultation procedure, agreed on simplified linguistic requirements and temporarily empowered the Commissioner for Competition to authorize 'emergency rescue measures', whereas usually decisions must be adopted by the College of Commissioners acting collectively.

---

8. When the first symptoms of the financial crisis emerged, the Commission refused to apply the derogation provided by Art. 107(3)(b) TFEU and assessed a number of bailout cases on the basis of the Rescue and Restructuring Guidelines. *See* the Commission Decision in Case NN 70/07, *Northern Rock*, in OJ 2007 C43/51, where the Commission decided that the aid in question were not intended to remedy a disturbance affecting a whole Member State, but rather problems specific to the position of the UK bank. The same approach was adopted also in several decisions in the first half of 2008. *See* Commission Decision of 31 Jul. 2008, Case NN 36/2008, *Roskilde Bank*, OJ 2008 C238/5; Commission Decision 2009/341/EC, *Sachsen LB* in OJ 2009 C135/21.
9. According to the Commission: 'The application of that derogation remains, however, possible only as long as the crisis situation persists, creating *genuinely exceptional circumstances* where financial stability at large is at risk' (Emphasis added). *See* Communication from the Commission on the application, from 1 Aug. 2013, of State aid rules to support measures in favour of banks in the context of the financial crisis ('Banking Communication') OJ 2013 C216/1 (para. 6).
10. This procedure must not be confused with the Simplified Procedure explained in Ch. 3, which concerns 'standard' measures (straightforward cases, 'safe harbor' cases, established case law cases). *See* in this regard Werner, Maier, *Procedure in Crisis? Overview and Assessment of the Commission's State Aid Procedure*, in EStAL 2/2009, p. 177.

Typically, the authorization process for State aid to financial institutions followed a two-phase assessment, borrowed from the system for rescue aid under the R&R Guidelines. The Commission granted temporary approval to restructuring aid on a rescue basis, with a final decision as to their compatibility put off to a later date. That full decision would follow a detailed examination of a restructuring plan for the beneficiary, aimed at allowing the undertaking to restore its profitability and enable the repayment of the State aid or its remuneration upon normal market terms.[11]

Although this 'emergency' approach helped prevent the collapse of the financial sector as a whole, the restructuring efforts of individual beneficiaries were often delayed. In some cases, delayed action to address banks' issues led to a higher final cost to the taxpayers.[12] The 2013 Banking Communication marked a change of approach. The Commission said that henceforth a bank would be able to benefit from 'structural' State aid (whether a recapitalization or an impaired asset measure) *only* once the bank's restructuring plan is approved:[13]According to the Commission, this approach aims to ensure that the amount of aid is better tailored to the situation and that the underlying causes of the bank's problems are identified and addressed at an early stage.

[A] The 2008 Banking Communication

The Banking Communication issued in October 2008 was the first measure in the Crisis Framework. The Communication provided guidance on Treaty-compatible criteria relevant for general schemes as well as ad hoc interventions by Member States, dealing in particular with liability guarantees, as well as recapitalization measures and liquidity assistance.[14] The Communication drew a distinction between fundamentally sound banks, whose viability problems related to the exceptional circumstances in the

---

11. *See*, for an example of individual recapitalization aid, the Commission Decisions on State aid to Banca Monte dei Paschi di Siena of 17 Dec. 2012 and 27 Nov. 2013, State aid No. SA. 36175 (2013/N) – *Italy MPS Restructuring.* In December 2012, the Commission temporarily approved a EUR 3.9 billion capital injection through hybrid instruments (the so-called Monti Bonds) that Italy planned to grant to MPS, to enable it to comply with European Banking Authority (EBA) requirements, subject to the notification of a restructuring plan, which was notified by Italy to the Commission in June 2013 and updated it in November 2013. The Commission approved the aid in view of the nineteen MPS commitments attached to the restructuring plan, which included the obligation to execute a capital increase of at least EUR 2.5 billion within 2014 and to redeem the full share of State bonds within five years. For examples of approvals of recapitalizations schemes, *see* the Decision of 23 Dec. 2008 in Case N-648/08, *Recapitalisation measures in favour of the financial sector in Italy*, in OJ 2009 C88; the Decision of 13 Oct. 2008, in Case N-507/08, *Financial Support Measures to the Banking Industry in the UK*, in OJ 2008 C290/4; and the Decision of 27 Oct. 2008 in Case N-512/08, *Rescue package for credit institutions in Germany*, in OJ 2008 C293/2.
12. *See* the Banking Communication of 1 Aug. 2013 (para. 23).
13. However, measures may exceptionally be authorised by the Commission on a temporary basis as rescue aid before a restructuring plan is approved, 'if such measures are required to *preserve financial stability*'. [Emphasis added].
14. *See* para. 5 of the Communication. *See also* para. 15 that sets out the features of the support measures, which must be well-targeted, proportionate and designed in order to minimize negative effects on competitors and other sectors or States.

financial sector, and unsound (or distressed) banks facing problems of endogenous nature, the causes of which might lie in a variety of factors, such as poor management and risky strategies. The latter category of banks would require far-reaching restructuring and, as a consequence, distortions of competition might be substantial.[15]

The Communication set eligibility criteria for aid to financial institutions[16] and required that any State support should be limited in time and scope.[17] Furthermore, the Communication highlighted the need to ensure the private sector made a significant contribution[18] and introduced the possibility of imposing behavioural constraints on the beneficiaries such as restrictions on commercial conduct as well as adjustment measures.[19]

In terms of the speed of its decision-making, the Commission said it took steps to ensure swift response, if necessary, within twenty-four hours or over a weekend.[20]

[B] Recapitalization Communication

The Recapitalization Communication was published a few months after the Banking Communication and deals with aid in the form of recapitalization measures, including the purchase by the State of various capital instruments issued by the recipient.[21]

The Commission made clear the need, when assessing recapitalization schemes, to take into account possible distortions of competition at three different levels: (i) first, recapitalization by one Member State of its own banks should not provide those banks with an unfair competitive advantage over banks in other Member States; (ii) second, recapitalization schemes which are open to all banks within a Member State without adequate differentiation based on risk could unfairly favour distressed or less-performing banks over fundamentally sound ones; and (iii) third, public recapitalization, in particular its remuneration, should not place banks that do not rely on public funding - yet seek additional capital on the market - at a significant competitive disadvantage.

The Communication set out the general principles of the different types of recapitalization[22] and focuses on the elements of recapitalizations such as the importance of ensuring that capital injections by States[23] and incentives for State capital redemption[24] were appropriately priced.

---

15. Paragraph 14.
16. Paragraph 18.
17. Paragraph 24.
18. Paragraphs 25 and 26.
19. Paragraph 27.
20. Paragraph 53.
21. Such as equity, other Tier 1 capital (such as hybrid securities) or Tier 2 capital (e.g., cumulative preferences shares or debt instruments).
22. Paragraphs 19-25.
23. Paragraphs 26-30.
24. Paragraphs 31-34.

Furthermore, the Commission stated that the recapitalization of banks that were not fundamentally sound should be subject to stricter conditions and must include compensatory measures.

[C] Impaired Assets Communication

In early 2009, several Member States announced their intention to complement their existing support measures with some form of relief for impaired bank assets. Indeed, uncertainty about the valuation and location of impaired and toxic assets was indicated as one of the reasons for a sharp deceleration in credit expansion to the real economy.

To prevent excessive financial exposure on the part of Member States as a result of taking on such risks, the Impaired Assets Communication required the State intervention to be appropriately targeted and accompanied by behavioural safeguards imposed upon the beneficiaries. Furthermore, in order to limit the impact of such measures upon Member States' own finances, it suggested that governments should ensure asset relief measures were sustainable for the public finances.[25]

The Communication set out the following basic principles on asset relief measures: (i) applications for such aid would be subject to full *ex ante* transparency and disclosure of impairments by eligible banks;[26] (ii) costs related to impaired assets should be shared between State, shareholders and creditors;[27] and (iii) enrolment in the asset relief programme should not be available for more than six months unless there are exceptional circumstances occur, as a means of ensuring that banks did not delay disclosures in the hope of higher levels of relief at a later date.[28]

[D] Restructuring Communication

The Restructuring Communication provided a framework for the assessment of restructuring requirements for banks receiving aid in the financial crisis.

A restructuring plan submitted under the Communication was required to outline how financial institutions that had received State aid intended to return to viability without reliance on State support, or, failing that, liquidation plans for their orderly winding-up. The methods of assessment followed those contained in the R&R Guidelines, namely: (i) the plan had to include a thorough diagnosis of the bank's problems, with a view to restoring viability;[29] (ii) Member States and the beneficiary banks had to share the costs of restructuring (the burden-sharing principle);[30] (iii) compensatory measures might be applied to prevent distortions of competition that could harm banks not receiving aid.[31]

25. Paragraph 3.
26. Paragraph 5.1.
27. Paragraph 5.2.
28. Paragraph 5.3.
29. Paragraphs 2 and 9.
30. Paragraph 3.
31. Paragraph 4.

[E] The Prolongation Communications

By the First Prolongation Communication, issued in 2010, the Commission kept the four previous Communications – which had been intended to last only as long as the 'serious disturbance in the economy' caused by the crisis – in play until 31 December 2011.[32] The Communication acknowledged that markets were still facing a situation of stress and the need to keep supporting firms that were still facing difficulties.

The Communication abandoned the distinction between sound and distressed banks that had been introduced by the 2008 Banking Communication: what would matter in determining whether a bank had to submit a restructuring plan would not be whether the bank would be treated as unsound, but rather, the amount and the nature of the aid received.

The Second Prolongation Communication, published in the latter half of 2011, extended the application of the four Communications indefinitely – in recognition of the long-term nature of the crisis and the impossibility of predicting when its effects would cease.

[F] The 2013 Banking Communication

The 2013 Banking Communication replaced the original Banking Communication, issued in 2008. It emphasized how, despite the unprecedented monetary and fiscal efforts of European Institutions and Member States to respond to the financial crisis, the markets still remained stressed and extremely volatile and the risk of spillover effects persisted. In addition, the Commission acknowledged that the public debt of many States had increased, due to the support offered to banks and non-financial firms during the crisis.

Although the Communication did not repeal the Recapitalization Communication, Impaired Asset Communication, Restructuring Communication or the two Prolongation Communications, it did alter in several respects the substantive assessment of the various types of crisis aids addressed in those earlier Communications.

First of all, Communication acknowledged that structural and long-term interventions rather than immediate and emergency measures are required to restore market efficiency.

Moreover, the Commission underlined the need to increase the degree of *burden-sharing* by shareholders and creditors, in order to make support to banks more sustainable for Member States.[33] In the first year of the crisis, the majority of the Member States did not go beyond the minimum requirements set by State aid rules with regard to burden-sharing, and only a few required bail-ins of investors and creditors,

32. Only the Restructuring Communication had an expiry date, initially set at 31 Dec. 2010.
33. On this topic *see* Lienemeyer, Kerle, Malikova, *The New State Aid Banking Communication: The Beginning of the Bail-in Era Will Ensure a Level Playing Field of Enhanced Burden-Sharing*, in *EStAL* 2/2014, p. 289.

which meant a divergent approach to this issue among Member States. The Communication stated that the bank and its capital holders should contribute to any restructuring as much as possible with their own resources, provided that the minimum requirements for burden-sharing should be raised. In particular, the Communication envisaged that losses would be inflicted at all levels of the bank's capital structure up to (but not including) senior debt holders. In principle, said the Commission, banks whose capital ratio remains above the EU regulatory minimum should normally be able to restore their capital shortfalls on their own. Where structural aid is necessary for such banks, subordinated debt should be converted into equity before State aid is granted. For banks whose capital ratio are below the minimum regulatory requirements, structural aid should be granted until equity, hybrid capital and subordinated debt have 'fully contributed to offset any losses'.[34] There is, however, a significant exception: the requirement to inflict such losses on investors can be avoided where the adoption of those measures would endanger financial stability or lead to disproportionate results.[35]

This approach to burden-sharing is consistent with the key principle of the new EU resolution framework for banks set out in the Directive (EU) 2014/59 ('BRRD')[36] and in Regulation (EU) 806/2014[37] establishing the Single Resolution Mechanism ('SRM'), which is to minimize public intervention in distressed banks by requiring private parties (and shareholders first) to bear an appropriate part of the losses.

As mentioned earlier, the Commission established the principle that recapitalization and impaired assets measures can be authorized only once the bank's restructuring plan is approved. Conversely, under the new Communication, guarantees and liquidity support can be granted before a restructuring plan is approved, but only after notification and temporary approval by the Commission. However, guarantees and liquidity support schemes will be available only to banks which have no capital shortfall, as defined by the competent supervisory authority.[38]

The Commission's new approach met with an important first endorsement from the Court of Justice in the *Kotnik* case,[39] concerning a reference for a preliminary ruling

34. Paragraph 44.
35. Paragraph 45. In any case, the 'no-creditor worse off principle' must be applied, meaning that creditors should not receive less in economic terms than their instruments would have been worth if no State aid had been granted.
36. Directive 2014/59/EU of the European Parliament and of the Council of 15 May 2014 establishing a framework for the recovery and resolution of credit institutions and investment firms.
37. Regulation (EU) No. 806/2014 of the European Parliament and of the Council of 15 Jul. 2014 establishing uniform rules and a uniform procedure for the resolution of credit institutions and certain investment firms in the framework of a Single Resolution Mechanism and a Single Resolution Fund and amending Regulation (EU) No. 1093/2010.
38. Banking Communication of 1 Aug. 2013 (paras 56-58). A 'capital shortfall' for the purposes of this Communication refers to a capital shortfall established in a capital exercise, stress-test, asset quality review or an equivalent exercise at Union, euro area or national level, where applicable confirmed by the competent supervisory authority.
39. *See* Court of Justice, case C-526/14, *Tadej Kotnik and Others v. Državni zbor Republike Slovenije*, ECLI:EU:C:2016:570, 19.7.2016. *See* Gianni Lo Schiavo, *Burden Sharing Arrangements vs. Shareholders and Creditors: Kotnik, Dowling and the Current State Aid Policy in the Banking Sector*, in European Business Organization Law Review v 19 n 3 (2018): 581-613 https://doi.org/10.1007/s40804-018-0114-6. *See also* Ana Vlahek, Matija Damjan, *European Commission's*

from the Slovenian Constitutional Court. The main issues concerned the interpretation of the 2013 Banking Communication adopted by the Commission under Article 107(3)(b) TFEU, the conformity of the principle of burden sharing with the aid rules (107/108 TFEU), as well as the compatibility of the principles contained in the 2013 Banking Communication with the principle of legitimate expectations and the right to property. In particular, the national court asked whether the conversion or write-down of hybrid capital and subordinated debt instruments is a prerequisite for the granting of aid and whether it should be proportionate.

A restrictive approach was taken by Advocate General Wahl,[40] who pointed out that 'the Commission's unjustified refusal to derogate from the provisions contained in its Banking Communication could be legitimately challenged before the Luxembourg Courts'.

Conversely, the Court emphasized the non-binding nature of the 2013 Banking Communication vis-à-vis Member States. In particular, where the measure notified by the State does not meet the criteria set forth in the Banking Communication, the Commission may nevertheless authorize the granting of aid if the State in question demonstrates the existence of '*specific exceptional circumstances*' under Article 107(3)(b) TFEU.[41]

Regarding the burden sharing, the Court noted that Articles 107 to 109 TFEU should be interpreted as not conflicting with points 40 to 46 of the 2013 Banking Communication, as these points require burden-sharing by shareholders and subordinated creditors as a prerequisite for the authorization of State aid.[42] The Court emphasized that burden-sharing helps mitigate so-called moral hazard and ensure that, prior to the grant of any State aid, the banks with a capital shortfall take steps, alongside their investors, to reduce that shortfall. In fact, without such burden-sharing measure, banks whose shareholders and subordinated creditors had not contributed to the reduction of the capital shortfall would receive State aid of an amount greater than that which would have been necessary to overcome the remaining shortfall.[43]

Finally, the Court concluded for the absence of violation of the principle of legitimate expectation and the right to property. As for legitimate expectation, the Court considered that, although in the first phases of the international financial crisis, the subordinated creditors were not called upon to contribute to the rescue of credit institutions, such circumstance could not be regarded as a precise, unconditional and consistent assurance capable of engendering a legitimate expectation burden-sharing

---

Banking Communication Question of Validity in the Slovenian Banking Bail-in Puzzle Annotation of the Judgment of the Court (Grand Chamber) of 19 July 2016 C-526/14 *Tadej Kotnik and Others v. Državni zbor Republike Slovenije*, 15 European State Aid Law Quarterly, 3 (2016): 458-467; and Łukasz Stępkowski, *Judgment of the Court of Justice in* C-526/14 *Tadej Kotnik and Others v. Državni zbor Republike Slovenije and permissibility of granting State aid to financial institutions*, 6 Polish Review of International and European Law 2, 89-105 (2018).

40. Opinion of AG Nils Whal, case C-526/14, *Tadej Kotnik and Others v. Državni zbor Republike Slovenije*, ECLI:EU:C:2016:102, 18.2.2016.
41. *Ibid.* (para. 41).
42. *Ibid.* (para. 60).
43. *Ibid.* (paras 56-57).

measures would not be applied in the future.[44] Furthermore, the overriding interest in the EU's financial stability overcomes the possible need for a transitional period following the entry into force of the Banking Communication.[45]

With regard to the right to property, the Court emphasized that the extent of losses incurred by shareholders of distressed banks would, in any event, remain the same, regardless of whether those losses result from a court-ordered insolvency due to the absence of State aid or from a State aid procedure that requires burden-sharing as a prerequisite.[46] Similarly, the burden-sharing measures on which the grant of State aid in favour of a bank would not cause any detriment to the right to property of subordinated creditors that those creditors would not have suffered within insolvency proceedings that followed such aid not being granted.[47]

[G] The Case of the Italian Regional Bank Crisis

The Commission's change of approach in 2013 created significant issues, especially for the Italian banking market, which at that time was facing major crises involving regional banks, which later ended with very different outcomes: on the one hand, the rescue of Banca Tercas[48] and subsequent litigation with the European Commission; on the other hand, the resolution of Banca Marche, Banca Etruria, Carife and Carichieti.[49]

As for Banca Tercas,[50] the latter was placed under extraordinary administration on 30 April 2012. The extraordinary commissioner identified a regional bank, BP Bari, as a possible buyer of Tercas and, on 27 July 2014, the Tercas shareholders' meeting ordered the partial coverage of losses by zeroing the capital and cancelling all outstanding ordinary shares and the increase of capital up to EUR 230 million by issuing new ordinary shares reserved for BPB.

The Interbank Deposit Protection Fund ('FITD'), i.e., the Italian deposit guarantee scheme, intervened in the operation allowing the transfer of the ownership to BP Bari, but such intervention was not notified by the Italian State to the Commission, since it was deemed by the entities involved as not constituting State aid. Conversely,

44. *Ibid.* (paras 65-66).
45. *Ibid.* (paras 67-69).
46. *Ibid.* (para. 75).
47. *Ibid.* (para. 78).
48. Commission Decision (EU) 2016/1208 of 23 Dec. 2015 on State aid granted by Italy to the Bank Tercas (Case SA.39451 (2015/C)).
49. Decisions in SA. 39543 (2015/N) – Resolution of Banca delle Marche S.p.A., SA.41134 (2015/N) – Resolution of Banca Popolare dell'Etruria e del Lazio Soc. Coop, SA.41925(2015/N) – Resolution of Cassa di Risparmio di Ferrara S.p.A and SA.43547 (2015/N) – Resolution of Cassa di Risparmio della Provincia di Chieti S.p.A. of 22.11.2015 and amendments of 29.4.2016, 7.10.2016, 30.4.2017 and 29.6.2017.
50. Grazia Vitale, *The General Court's Ruling in Tercas: Between Imputability of the Aid to the State and Use of State Resources*, in European Papers v 2019 4 n 3 (20200101): 895-905. Irene Mecatti, *The Role of Deposit Guarantee Schemes in Preventing and Managing Banking Crises: Governance and Least Cost Principle*, in European Company and Financial Law Review v 17 n 6 (2020/12/01): 657-669 https://doi.org/10.1515/ecfr-2020-0029.

departing from its precedent on the matter,[51] the Commission took the opposite advice, for two basic reasons:

(a) Although the resources used to allow the acquisition of Tercas by BP Bari were private, (as the FITD is financed by the resources of the member banks), a number of indications seemed to show, in the Commission's view, that they were under the control of the State (in particular, of the Bank of Italy). Following this perspective, the FITD was thus acting under a 'public mandate'.[52]
(b) The intervention consisted of measures that were considered not to be 'on market terms', according to the private investor criterion.[53]

The measures in question were then deemed incompatible, essentially for the reason that the write-down of subordinated securities (but only share write-downs) mandated by the 2013 Communication was not foreseen and the restructuring plan had not been notified in advance.[54] In the Commission's view, only the s.c. 'voluntary' schemes of the FITD, i.e., those schemes to which banks can adhere on a contractual

51. This was the consequence of the Commission Decision 2000/600/EC of 10 Nov. 1999, conditionally authorizing the aid granted to Banco di Sicilia and Sicilcassa 1999 OJ L 256/21, where the Commission excluded the public nature of the FITD after having examined its composition and decision-making process.
52. Specifically, as to the imputability requirement, the Commission argued, *inter alia*, that the Italian authorities (and in particular the Bank of Italy) had decisively influenced the FITD's decision. With regard to the 'state resources' requirement, the Commission highlighted the mandatory nature of the contributions made to the Fund by member banks, arguing that they were under the control of the Italian authorities.
53. Specifically, the measures put in place by the FITD that were found to be incompatible State aid were:

    (i) a grant of EUR 265 million to partially cover Tercas' capital deficit;
    (ii) a EUR 35 million guarantee to cover the credit risk associated with certain Tercas exposures;
    (iii) a guarantee of EUR 30 million to partially cover the possible additional costs and losses associated with the tax treatment of the 265 million contribution referred to in (*i*) above.

54. Another case of the Commission's approval of the measures is the intervention for Banca Romagna. On 13 Nov. 2013, Banca Romagna is placed under extraordinary administration; as of 31 May 2015, losses amount to EUR 111.3 million. The ICCREA banking group is awarded part of the sold *assets*, the rest is covered by the support intervention of the Fondo Interbancario di Tutela dei Depositi del Credito Cooperativo (FITDCC). In a decision dated 2 Jul. 2015, C(2015)4599 *final*, the Commission approves the rescue of Banca Romagna – resolution aid (through the 'orderly liquidation' of the Bank – prior to the entry into force of the BRRD). The Commission considers the FITDCC intervention to be imputable to the Italian state (and therefore 'aid') but nevertheless considers it compatible because:

    (i) will allow an 'orderly' liquidation of the bank;
    (ii) distortions of competition are limited;
    (iii) shareholders and subordinated bond holders contribute as much as possible (shareholders fully written down; subordinated debt holders will unlikely benefit from the proceed of liquidation);
    (iv) allows long-term viability to be restored through sale to ICCREA.

and voluntary basis, did not constitute State aid. A litigation on the *Tercas* case then started before the Luxembourgish Courts.

The Commission's position on FITD interventions was maintained during its interlocutions with the Italian Ministry of Economics and Finance ('MEF') on the crisis of several regional banks and, in particular, of Banca Marche, Banca Etruria, Carife and Carichieti, as well as reiterated in a letter dated 19 November 2015, signed by Commissioners Margrethe Vestager and Jonathan Hill, respectively in charge of competition and financial services in the EU.

In that letter, which was picked up by various international news agencies, the Commissioners stated that, in order not to deprive Directives 2014/49/EU on BRRD and 2014/59/EU on bank resolution of their '*effect utile*', FITD interventions would be subject to State aid rules and that this would imply that shareholders and subordinated creditors would have to share the burden of the rescue of the banks.

The political clash between the MEF and the Commission ended up undermining the use of FITD interventions for the restructuring of several regional banks, playing a decisive role in the drop in confidence that, within a few months, would affect the Italian banking system.

With particular reference to Banca Marche, Banca Etruria, Carife and Carichieti, in the impossibility of a FITD intervention, such banks were subject to an intervention by the newly created Resolution Fund, allowing the transfer of assets and bonds to four new bridge entities, as well as the capitalization of the latter; the Resolution Fund provided a guarantee with respect to these assets. On 22 November 2015, with four separate decisions, the Commission approved the resolution plans of such small Italian banks and acknowledged their compliance with EU state aid rules (in particular, with the Communication of 2013).[55] The position of the MEF was subsequently summarized in a note published on its website, from which the differences between its views and those of the Commission appear very clear.[56]

Subsequently, the Commission's position on the qualification as State aid of FITD interventions was refuted by the judgment of the General Court in *Tercas*,[57] first, and then by the ECJ.[58]

On 19 March 2019, the General Court pointed out that the evidence gathered during the Commission's investigation was not sufficient to prove the involvement of the Italian authorities in the FITD's decisions, nor the control over its resources. This was due to the fact that FITD is a private consortium, whose elective bodies are composed exclusively of representatives of the member banks, and the Bank of Italy's supervision over its interventions is merely for prudential supervision purposes. According to the General Court, in the absence of an organic link between the State and the FITD, the Commission could not simply allege, as it did, that it was unlikely that the

55. Commission press release, State aid: Commission approves resolution plans for four small Italian banks Banca Marche, Banca Etruria, Carife and Carichieti, 22.11.2015.
56. MEF, Aiuti di Stato, risoluzioni bancarie e FIDT, 23.12.2015, available here https://www.mef.gov.it/inevidenza/Aiuti-di-Stato-risoluzioni-bancarie-e-FITD/.
57. Judgment of the General Court, Joined Cases T-98/16, T-196/16 and T-198/16, *Italian Republic and Others v. European Commission*, ECLI:EU:T:2019:167 19.3.2019.
58. Case C-425/19 P, *Commission v. Italy and Others*, ECLI:EU:C:2021:154, 2.3.2021.

national authorities were not involved in the FITD's decisions. On the contrary, in the case of entities endowed with a private status, the Commission is under an '*even more significant*' obligation to specify and give reasons for concluding in the sense of public control over the resources used and the imputability of the measures to the State.

Subsequently, in its appeal of the General Court's judgment, the Commission argued that in so deciding, the former had improperly raised the evidentiary standard required of the latter by EU case law (and in particular the *Stardust Marine* precedent). In addition, the Commission alleged that the Tribunal had made an atomistic, rather than a global, assessment of the evidence collected by the Commission, thus depriving it of evidentiary value.

However, the Court definitively rejected the Commission's arguments, confirming its lack of grounds for its defences.[59] On the evidentiary standard, the Court clarified that if the aid-granting entity is private in nature, the evidence capable of proving the imputability of the measure to the State must be 'different' (and stronger) than that required in the case where the aid-granting entity is a public enterprise. Thus, the Commission cannot simply allege the unlikelihood of the State's non-involvement. This constitutes clarification of the scope of application of the *Stardust Marine* precedent, whose methodological framework remains unchanged.

§13.03 CONCLUSIVE REMARKS

EU State aid rules were flexible enough to address the challenges arising from the financial and economic crisis and globally the EU institutions were able to set up a new, coherent framework for the banking system, although several controversial issues sometimes would arise from the parallel application of rules on State aid and those on the recovery and resolution of banks.[60] In particular, the role of deposit guarantee schemes in the rescue of banks and the qualification of their intervention as a State aid case was finally rejected by the Luxembourgish Courts, not without consequences for the final shaping of the EU financial framework.[61]

59. For more information on the case, *see* Grazia Vitale, *The General Court's Ruling in Tercas: Between Imputability of the Aid to the State and Use of State Resources*, in European Papers 2019 4 n 3, 895-905; Andrea Vignini, *State Aid and Deposit Guarantee Schemes, The CJEU Decision on Tercas and the Role of DGSs in Banking Crises*, Legal Papers, Quaderni di Ricerca Giuridica della Consulenza Legale, Bank of Italy, 2019; Edoardo Gambaro, Pietro Missanelli, *La Corte di Giustiza annulla la decisione della Commissione Ue: L'intervento di sostegno a Banca Tercas non era 'aiuto di Stato'*, NT Diritto (12 Mar. 2021) La Corte di Giustiza annulla la decisione della Commissione Ue: L'intervento di sostegno a Banca Tercas non era 'aiuto di Stato' | NT + Diritto (ilsole24ore.com).
60. Ginevra Bruzione, Miriam Cassella, *The Interplay of State Aid Control, Bank Supervision and Resolution: Rethinking the European Framework*, in 24 Concorrenza e Mercato, 2017, 'oltre la crisi: regolazione, concorrenza e aiuti di stato nei settori bancario e finanziario'.
61. Andrea Pezza, *Which role for deposit guarantee schemes in the financial crisis? An analysis of the Italian situation*, and Alessandro Zenca, *Il ruolo dei sistemi di garanzia dei depositi nel nuovo quadro regolamentare e il loro inquadramento nella normativa degli aiuti di Stato*, both in 24 Concorrenza e Mercato, 2017, 'oltre la crisi: regolazione, concorrenza e aiuti di stato nei settori bancario e finanziario'.

Recently, a public consultation was launched by the Commission to evaluate the State aid rules for banks in difficulty,[62] and the EU Parliament stressed the need to review the 2013 Banking Communication, considered 'long-overdue', as it was issued before the entry into force of the Bank Recovery and Resolution Directive.[63]

62. This consultation (from 17 Mar. 2022 to 15 Jul. 2022) aims at gathering evidence and views on the effectiveness, efficiency, relevance, coherence and EU added value of State aid rules for banks in difficulty. More information are available at https://competition-policy.ec.europa.eu/public-consultations/2022-sa-banking-rules_en#results-of-consultation-and-next-steps.
63. European Parliament resolution of 11 Jul. 2023 on Banking Union – annual report 2022 (2022/2061(INI)).

CHAPTER 14
Digital Transition

Bertone Biscaretti Di Ruffia

§14.01 THE PLACE OF STATE AID IN A DIGITAL SOCIETY

Supporting the transition to a digital economy has been at the heart of the Union's industrial policies since the adoption of the Lisbon Strategy in 2000.[1] On such occasion, the European Council called on the Commission to reduce the general level of State aid, focusing on 'horizontal objectives of Community interest'.[2]

At the end of the following decade, having decided on a number of cases related to the roll-out of high-speed digital services since 2003,[3] the Commission adopted its first Guidelines for the application of State aid rules in relation to the rapid deployment of broadband networks (Broadband Guidelines),[4] noting that well-targeted State intervention in the broadband sector could contribute to the reduction of the digital divide,[5] an 'objective of common [EU] interest' soon included in the Digital Agenda for Europe adopted in 2010.[6]

1. Presidency conclusions, Lisbon European Council, 23 and 24 Mar. 2000, section 8, *An Information Society for All.*
2. Since then, State aids has remained stable or increased slightly in almost all sectors until 2013, and then increased sharply until the steep rise following the COVID-19 and the war in Ukraine crises. *See* the Scoreboard State Aid data – New dissemination tool for statistics (2000-2022), published by the Commission at: https://competition-policy.ec.europa.eu/state-aid/scoreboard/scoreboard-state-aid-data_en.
3. *See* Commission Decision n. 282/2003 of 10 Dec. 2003, United Kingdom, 'Cumbria Broadband – Project Access – Advancing Communication for Cumbria and Enabling Sustainable Services', available at: https://ec.europa.eu/competition/state_aid/cases/133982/133982_477578_33_2.pdf.
4. Commission Communication, 'Community Guidelines for the application of State aid rules in relation to rapid deployment of broadband networks', OJ 2009 C235/04: https://eur-lex.europa.eu/legal-content/EN/ALL/?uri=CELEX%3A52009XC0930%2802%29.
5. Digital divide is defined as the gap between those who have access to information technologies and those that do not. On the considerations which led the Commission to adopt specific

Contribution to a 'well-defined objective of common interest' was a key element in the balancing test that the Commission would carry out under the 2009 Broadband Guidelines to assess the compatibility of a State aid measure under Article 107(3) TFEU (ex-Article 87(3) TEC), with the existence of market failures addressed by such measure being considered the rationale for public intervention.[7]

Since then, technological, economic, and social progress has only increased the focus of EU Institutions on supporting the overall digital transition of European society and economy.[8]

The great costs required for the development of digital infrastructures, the existence of market failures that may discourage private investment, and the need to strengthen the security and resilience of technological infrastructures have led the Commission to conclude that a massive scale-up of investments in the digital transition is required to narrow the global investment gap in this strategic sector[9] and that coordination of funding efforts by Member States, along with EU financial support, is necessary to leverage private investments.[10] In addition, particularly in light of geopolitical developments in recent years, EU Institutions are aiming to strengthen the Union's digital sovereignty to ensure reliable supply chains for the digital sector, with the purpose of avoiding bottlenecks and limiting the dependence of the EU digital market on a few foreign suppliers.[11]

In this context, State aid became an increasingly central instrument of EU industrial policy in the digital sector. In 2021, in its Communication 'A Competition Policy fit for the new Challenges', the Commission expressly identified State aid policy as a key and complementary tool to enable the digital transition and strengthen the resilience of the Digital Single Market.[12]

---

guidelines for State aid in the broadband sector, *see* Broadband Guidelines 2009, para. 1. *See* also Communication from the Commission 'State aid Action Plan – Less and better targeted State aid: a roadmap for State aid reform 2005-2009', para. (I.1).

6. *See* Communication from the Commission '*A Digital Agenda for Europe*', of 19 May 2010, COM/2010/0245 final.
7. *See, inter alia,* Decision C(2012) 3488 of 25 May 2012 concerning State aid No. 33807, Italy, *National broadband plan Italy*. Contribution to the achievement of objectives of common interest was *de facto* a necessary condition for a measure to be considered compatible under Art. 107(3) TFEU also before 2009: *see* Decision C(2008) 8368 of 10 Dec. 2008, on State aid No. 508/2008, United Kingdom, *Provision of remote Broadband services in Northern Ireland*.
8. *See* European Parliament and Council Decision (EU) 2022/2481 of 14 Dec. 2022 establishing the Digital Decade Policy Programme 2030, OJ L 323, 19.22.2022, available at: https://eur-lex.europa.eu/eli/dec/2022/2481/oj. On the relevance of digital infrastructures for European economic policies, *see* also White Paper of the Commission, 'How to master Europe's digital infrastructures needs?', of 21 Feb. 2024, para. I.
9. *See* Ockenfels et al., *Investment and funding needs for the Digital Decade connectivity targets*, Publications Office of the European Union, 2023.
10. In the 2020 Communication 'Shaping Europe's digital future', the Commission stressed that 'Europe needs to invest in connectivity, deep tech and human capital, as well as in smart energy and transport infrastructures', and that 'for digital infrastructure and networks alone, the EU has an investment gap of EUR 65 billion per year'.
11. *See* Poli and Fahey, *The Strengthening of European Technological Sovereignty and its legal bases in the Treaties*, in Eurojus, 2, 2022, pp. 147 et seq.
12. Communication from the Commission 'A Competition Policy fit for the new Challenges' of 18 Nov. 2021, COM(2021) 713, para. 3. On this topic, *see* Editorial Comment, *The EU's integrated*

This view lies at the heart of the State Aid Modernization (SAM) reform implemented in 2014,[13] which led to a relaxation of State aid control and an accelerated revision of the General Block Exemption Regulation (GBER)[14] and of rules regarding State aid for, *inter alia*, important projects of common European interest (IPCEI), research development and innovation (R&D&I), the deployment of broadband networks, and environmental protection and energy, all relevant for the EU Digital Strategy.

In the Commission's view, the review of the GBER, Broadband Guidelines and the State aid framework for research and development and innovation (R&D&I Framework) aimed at further facilitating the roll-out of secure and performant networks where private investment is lacking, and boosting private-sector investments, supporting technological and market developments essential for the twin Digital and Green transitions.[15]

From the trend outlined above, a vision of State aid emerges as a tool for channelling Member States' investments towards the EU Digital Strategy, going beyond the nature of State aid control as a tool for safeguarding competition.[16]

This view might have been undermined by the well-known Hinkley decision of September 2020, whereby the Grand Chamber of the ECJ followed the Opinion of Advocate General Hogan in concluding that Article 107(3)(c) TFEU does not make the compatibility of aid dependent on its pursuing an objective of common interest.[17]

The Commission has since removed from both the revised 2022 R&D&I Framework[18] and 2023 Broadband Guidelines[19] any express requirements that State aid must pursue an objective of common interest to be deemed compatible, replacing it with a more literal reference to the facilitation of the development of an economic activity, in line with the wording of Article 107(3)(c) TFEU.

---

policy approach towards competitiveness: The interplay between State aid control and industrial policies, in Common Market Law Review, 61, pp. 1-12, 2024, https://doi.org/10.54648/cola2024001; *see also* E. Fazio, *Adapting Competition Law to the Digital Transition. Two Challenges*, in EU Forum, 7/2022, pp. 981 et seq.

13. One of the main SAM objectives was fostering positive aid, capable of contributing to objectives of common interest and to rectifying market failures. *See* COM(2012)209, 'EU State Aid Modernization (SAM)', at. p. 5.
14. Commission Regulation (EU) No 651/2014 of 17 Jun. 2014 declaring certain categories of aid compatible with the internal market in application of Arts 107 and 108 of the Treaty, OJ L 187, 26.6.2014.
15. *See* Communication from the Commission 'A Competition Policy fit for the new Challenges', para. 3.3.
16. On the role attributed to State aid control in the context of the State Aid Modernization reform *see* J. Piernas López, *The Transformation of EU State Aid Law ... and Its Discontents*, in Common Mark. Law Rev., 60, pp. 1623-1654, 2003 https://doi.org/10.54648/cola2023118. On the same topic *see also* Editorial Comment, *The EU's Integrated Policy Approach Towards Competitiveness: The Interplay Between State Aid Control and Industrial Policies*, in Common Mark. Law Rev., 61, pp. 1-12, 2024, https://doi.org/10.54648/cola2024001.
17. Case C-594/18 P, *Austria v. Commission*, EU:C:2020:742.
18. Communication from the Commission 'Framework for State aid for research and development and innovation', of 28 Oct. 2022, 2022/C 414/01.
19. Communication from the Commission 'Guidelines on State aid for broadband networks', of 31 Jan. 2023, 2023/C 36/01.

In any case, reference to the instrumentality of State aid in pursuit of objectives identified by the European institutions has only been attenuated. For instance, the 2022 R&D&I Framework expressly states that wider R&D&I-related positive effects can be considered to assess the necessity of the relevant State aid, where they reflect the aims embodied in Union policies such as the European Green Deal and Digital Strategies.[20]

Even though State aid control guidelines regarding deployment of broadband networks and R&D&I economic activities are clearly designed to facilitate public funding to support digitization, the main purpose of such rules remains that of preventing unduly distortions of the level playing field in the Digital Single Market, as it is apparent from the overall system rooted on the General Incompatibility Principle under Article 107(1) TFEU.

The enormous amount of investment required to support the digital transition and the need to reduce the investment gap with the EU's competitors make State aid a necessary complementary instrument to realize policies of common interest, especially in the light of the relatively greater capacity of Member States' finances compared to EU resources. However, using state aid control rules to over-facilitate and channel public funding from Member States entails serious risks of market distortions and subsidy races between single States, favouring those with the greatest fiscal capacity, and thus disrupting the EU internal market.

Against this background, one of the solutions advocated by the Commission in recent years is to increase the recourse to common budgetary instruments to stimulate private investment in the technology and digital sectors through common financing solutions, limiting the role of State aid in the deploying of EU's industrial policies.[21]

§14.02 STATE AID AND THE EU DIGITAL STRATEGY

[A] The Digital Transition in EU's Industrial and Political Strategies

Following the Lisbon Strategy adopted in 2000, the digital transition has been increasingly central to EU policies. The 2010 Digital Agenda for Europe[22] underscored Information and Communication Technologies as pivotal for achieving the EU's objectives. In 2015, ensuring better access to digital goods and services across Europe and fostering optimal conditions for digital networks were explicitly addressed in the Communication from the Commission 'A Digital Single Market Strategy',[23] while the centrality of the digital transition as a common strategic goal continued to be emphasized in the 2020 Communication 'Shaping Europe's digital future' whereby the

20. *See* 2022 R&D&I Framework, paras 133 et seq. A similar concept is expressed in the 2023 Broadband Guidelines. *See ibid.*, para. 43.
21. *See* the keynote speech by Commissioner for Internal Market Thierry Breton at the European Policy Center of 10 Jan. 2024, 'A Europe that protects its citizens, transforms its economy, and projects itself as a global power'.
22. Communication from the Commission '*A Digital Agenda for Europe*', of 19 May 2010, COM/2010/0245 final.
23. Communication from the Commission '*A Digital Single Market Strategy for Europe*', of 6 May 2015, COM(2015) 192.

Commission identified three groups of objectives for years 2020-2025 to shape the development and use of digital technologies for the benefit of EU citizens.[24]

Lastly, the European Parliament and the Council have set ambitious digital targets to be achieved by 2030 establishing the 'Digital Decade Policy Programme 2030', focusing on enhancing digital skills, infrastructures, business transformation, and public services.[25] To do so, EU institutions aim to support coordination efforts by Member States to facilitate joint investments and establish multi-country projects to tackle market failures or sub-optimal investment situations.[26]

State aid is still seen as a key instrument to support the EU Digital Strategy, despite the risks this approach poses to the integrity of the internal market.

[B] EU's Strategic Tools for State Aid to Support Its Digital Strategy

Following the SAM reform, the EU has several hard and soft law instruments at its disposal to shape State aid as a means to pursue its Digital Strategy, in addition to Broadband Guidelines and the R&D&I Framework.

Just to mention the most relevant of these, which will not be discussed in detail in the following sections of this chapter but are more extensively dealt with in other chapters of this book, reference can be made to the GBER, to IPCEI and to the European Chips Act Regulation.

The GBER exempts Member States from notifying State aid for R&D&I and broadband infrastructure to the Commission if it meets the thresholds and conditions set out therein.[27]

The Commission's IPCEI Communication[28] provides guidance on the assessment of IPCEIs under Article 107(3)(b) TFEU. It states that a project must represent a concrete, clear and identifiable important contribution to the Union's objectives, having a significant impact on sustainable growth. Supporting the European Green Deal and the Digital Decade strategies are expressly mentioned as examples that fulfil such condition.[29]

IPCEIs play an important role in the EU's industrial policies, including the Digital Strategy. They often involve considerable technological and financial risks, addressing

24. With reference to the first of the three sets of objectives, entitled 'Technology that works for people' and focused on the digital transition, the Commission emphasized that EU and Member States must pool their investments in research and innovation and that public funding has to be used to leverage private investment. *See* Communication from the Commission, 'Shaping Europe's digital future', of 19 Feb. 2020, COM(2020) 67.
25. Decision (EU) 2022/2481 of the European Parliament and of the Council of 14 Dec. 2022 establishing the Digital Decade Policy Programme 2030, OJ L 323, 19.12.2022.
26. *See ibid.*, Whereas no. 41.
27. *See* GBER, sections 4 and 10.
28. Communication from the Commission 'Criteria for the analysis of the compatibility with the internal market of State aid to promote the execution of important projects of common European interest', of 30 Dec. 2021, 2021/C 528/02.
29. *See ibid.*, para. 14.

market failures in the industry such as coordination failures, difficulties in appropriating positive externalities and failure to address negative externalities, thus enabling the financing of economic activities that the market would not otherwise finance.[30]

State aid rules for IPCEIs[31] apply to projects in all economic sectors. The fact that an IPCEI should normally involve at least four Member States and that its benefits should not be limited to the financing States, in addition to the role that the Commission can play in designing and managing it, makes IPCEIs a potentially more compatible industrial policy instrument with the integrity of the internal market.

The European Chips Act[32] aims to increase the EU's share of global semiconductor production, reduce dependency on external suppliers, and enhance the resilience of the European semiconductor supply chain, ensuring that the EU remains competitive in key digital sectors such as artificial intelligence, 5G, and autonomous vehicles.

In addition to the 'direct' funding intervention of the Union, the second pillar of the Chips Acts includes provisions for State aid to support research, development, and production of semiconductors. Where not covered by the exemptions already provided for in the existing guidelines, public financing of production facilities will be assessed by the Commission on a case-by-case basis under Article 107(3)(c) TFEU as an aid to promote specific economic activities.

In particular, Chapter III of the Chips Act provides a framework for Member States to support measures and provide administrative support to integrated production facilities[33] and open EU foundries.[34] On 20 August 2024, the Commission adopted dedicated Guidelines on the requirements and further elements that are assessed to

30. In December 2023, the Commission approved State aid of up to EUR 1.2 billion from seven Member States for an IPCEI on Next Generation Cloud Infrastructure and Services (IPCEI CIS) which is expected to leverage a further EUR 1.4 billion of private investment. *See* Commission Decision on 'IPCEI on Next Generation Cloud Infrastructure and Services – RRF', of 5 Dec. 2023, C(2023) 8552. In June 2023, the Commission approved another IPCEI to support research, innovation and early industrial deployment of microelectronics and communication technologies across the value chain (IPCEI ME/CT), involving fourteen Member States and providing EUR 8.1 billion in public funds to leverage EUR 13.7 billion in private investment. *See* Commission Decision on 'IPCEI on Microelectronics/Communication Technologies', of 8 Jun. 2023, C(2023) 3817.
31. Communication from the Commission 'Criteria for the analysis of the compatibility with the internal market of State aid to promote the execution of important projects of common European interest', of 30 Dec. 2021, 2021/C 528/02.
32. Regulation (EU) 2023/1781 of the European Parliament and of the Council of 13 Sep. 2023 establishing a framework of measures for strengthening Europe's semiconductor ecosystem and amending Regulation (EU) 2021/694, OJ L 229, 18.9.2023, pp. 1-53.
33. *See* Art. 13 of the Chips Act, 'Integrated production facilities shall be first-of-a-kind facilities for semiconductor manufacturing, and, where relevant, including design, or for the production of equipment or key components for such equipment predominantly used in semiconductor manufacturing in the Union, which may integrate other steps of the supply chain, and that contribute to the security of supply and the resilience of the Union's semiconductor ecosystem and in addition they may, where relevant, contribute to the security of the global semiconductor supply chains.'
34. *See* Art. 14 of the Chips Act, 'Open EU foundries shall be first-of-a-kind facilities for semiconductor manufacturing in the Union that offer production capacity to unrelated undertakings and thereby contribute to the security of supply for the internal market and the resilience of the Union's semiconductor ecosystem and in addition they may, where relevant, contribute to the security of the global semiconductor supply chain.'

provide an undertaking with the integrated production facility or open EU foundry status pursuant to Article 15 of the Chips Acts,[35] including: (i) the 'first-of-a-kind' nature of the applying facility, which must provide innovation with regard to the manufacturing process or final product that is not yet substantively present or committed to be built within the Union; (ii) commitment to comply with the criteria set out in Article 13(3) or in Article 14(3) of the Chips Act; (iii) the business plan evaluating the financial and technical viability of the facility; (iv) documentation regarding the experience of the applicant in installing and operating similar facilities; (v) the readiness of the Member States(s) on whose territory the facility would be built to facilitate its establishment; (vi) the existence of appropriate policies, including technical protection and implementing measures, aimed at ensuring the protection of undisclosed information and IP rights; (vii) commitment to prioritize orders in time of crisis, when a semiconductor crisis stage is activated under Article 23 of the Chips Act due to risk of serious disruption in the supply of semiconductors.

§14.03 STATE AID FOR RESEARCH, DEVELOPMENT AND INNOVATION

Support for research and development has been enshrined in the European Treaties since the Single European Act, under Article 163 TEC (now Article 179 TFEU).[36] State aid rules have traditionally been supportive of public funding of R&D, and the 1996 Community Framework for State Aid for R&D justified this approach on the basis of its importance for the economy and the considerable costs and risks involved.[37] Successive revisions of this framework by the Commission over the years have gradually extended its scope and provided a justification for public intervention in this field on the basis of market failures preventing the market from delivering efficient levels of R&D&I.

Since 2008 the R&D&I Framework (Framework) is complemented by the GBER which covers a broad range of aid categories, including R&D&I, setting out general conditions and thresholds for aid to be exempt from notification. Aid measures that fall within the scope of the GBER and meet its conditions can be implemented without prior notification to the Commission, streamlining the process for Member States.[38] For aid

35. Communication from the Commission on the Guidance on the application for an undertaking to obtain the status of integrated production facility and open EU foundry pursuant to Art. 15 of the Chips Act Regulation (EU) 2023/1781, of 20 Aug. 2024, C/2024/4911.
36. Article 179(1) TFEU states that: 'The Union shall have the objective of strengthening its scientific and technological bases by achieving a European research area in which researchers, scientific knowledge and technology circulate freely, and encouraging it to become more competitive, including in its industry, while promoting all the research activities deemed necessary by virtue of other Chapters of the Treaties.'
37. Information from the Commission, Community Framework for State aid for Research and Development, of 17 Feb. 1996, OJ C 045, pp. 5-16.
38. Notification thresholds for R&D&I are set forth under Art. 4(1)(i)-(m) of the GBER. Specific conditions regarding support to research and development projects, research infrastructures, innovation clusters, SMEs, process and organizational innovation, and research and development in the fishery and aquaculture sector are set forth under Arts 25 et seq. GBER. On the General Block Exemption Regulation *see supra*, Ch. 1.

measures that do not fall within the GBER's scope or exceed its thresholds, the 2023 Framework provides the necessary guidelines for Member States to notify the Commission and seek approval.

[A] The R&D&I Framework and the Notion of State Aid

The latest Framework was adopted in 2022 and it provides guidance on how the Commission assesses the compatibility of State aid in this sector on the basis of Article 107(3)(c) TFEU. It applies to R&D&I economic activities in all sectors governed by the TFEU, including those sectors which are subject to specific Union rules on State aid, with the exception of aids in favour of firms in difficulty[39] and measures fulfilling the conditions laid down in a block exemption Regulation adopted by the Commission pursuant to Article 1 of Council Regulation (EU) No. 2015/1588.[40]

Considering that any measure meeting the criteria set out in Article 107(1) TFEU constitutes State aid and recalling that the Notice on the notion of State aid clarifies how the Commission understands the notion of State aid in general,[41] the Framework provides indications regarding situations typically arising in the field of R&D&I activities.

For an aid measure to be covered by Article 107(1) TFEU, its beneficiary must be qualified as an undertaking, which is determined by the fact that it carries out an economic activity.

Primary activities of research organizations and research infrastructures are generally considered of non-economic nature. This includes knowledge transfer activities carried out by the same, or jointly with, or on behalf of other such entities, where all profits from those activities are reinvested in their primary activities. Primary activities include education,[42] independent R&D and wide dissemination of research results on a non-exclusive and non-discriminatory basis.[43]

Where the same entity carries out both economic and non-economic activities, there must be a clear separation between the two types of activities in order for public funding to the non-economic activity not to be considered State aid. This must be done in such a way as to effectively avoid cross-subsidization of the economic activity. Where a research organization or infrastructure is used almost exclusively for a non-economic activity, its funding may fall outside State aid rules in its entirety if the

39. As defined in the Community guidelines on State aid for rescuing and restructuring firms in difficulty, is excluded. *See* 2022 R&D&I Framework, para. 11.
40. Council Regulation (EU) 2015/1588 of 13 Jul. 2015 on the application of Arts 107 and 108 of the Treaty on the Functioning of the European Union to certain categories of horizontal State aid (codification), OJ L 248, 24 Sep. 2015.
41. The Commission Notice on the notion of State aid as referred to in Art. 107(1) of the Treaty on the Functioning of the European Union, OJ C 262, 19.7.2016.
42. Education is considered to be non-economic when it is financed entirely or mainly by the state, insofar as the public education system is aimed a fulfilling the state's duties towards its population and is funded from the public purse and not by pupils or their parents. *See* Case 263/86, *Belgian State v. René Humbel*, (1988) ECLI:EU:C:1988:451, para. 18.
43. *See* Framework, para. 20.

economic use remains purely ancillary and does not exceed 20% of the beneficiary's overall annual capacity.[44]

Where research organizations or research infrastructure are used to perform economic activities, public funding of those activities will be considered State aid, unless the beneficiary acts as a mere intermediary for passing on to the final recipients the totality of the public funding and any advantage acquired through it.

[B] Compatibility Assessment of R&D&I Aid

The Commission outlines a series of measures for which State aid may be compatible with the internal market, indicating the kind of market failures they could address:

(1) aid for R&D projects supports fundamental and applied research (industrial research and experimental development) to address knowledge spillovers, imperfect information, and coordination failures;
(2) aid for feasibility studies helps overcome market failures related to imperfect and asymmetric information;
(3) aid for research infrastructures addresses coordination difficulties and imperfect information, facilitating high-quality research by overcoming high upfront investment costs;
(4) aid for testing and experimentation infrastructures tackles imperfect information and coordination failures, with high initial costs and uncertain client bases making market financing difficult. Publicly funded infrastructures must be accessible on a transparent and non-discriminatory basis;
(5) aid for innovation activities targets market failures like knowledge spillovers and coordination difficulties, especially for SMEs, supporting patents, personnel secondment, and advisory services;
(6) aid for process and organizational innovation focuses on positive externalities and coordination difficulties, mainly for SMEs, with large enterprises needing to collaborate with SMEs to qualify;
(7) aid for innovation clusters aims to resolve coordination problems within and between clusters, supporting shared infrastructures and operations to enhance collaboration and learning.[45]

Such measures can be considered compatible with internal market if they meet the conditions laid out by Article 107(3)(c) TFEU. In assessing whether the measure facilitates the development of an economic activity, the Commission verifies whether the aid is likely to change the behaviour of the undertaking concerned so that it engages in additional activity which, in the absence of the aid, would not be carried out or would be carried out in a different way, in a smaller scale or in a different location

44. *See ibid.*, para. 21.
45. *See ibid.*, paras 13 et seq.

(incentive effect). It also assesses that the aid does not contravene the relevant rules and principles of EU law.

To assess whether the R&D&I aid does not unduly affect trading conditions to an extent contrary to the common interest, the Commission considers the following aspects: (a) the existence of a need for State intervention to bring about a material development where the market fails to deliver an efficient outcome; (b) the appropriateness of the aid measure; (c) its proportionality; (d) its transparency; (e) its negative effects on competition.

As per the necessity test, Member States should explain how the measure can mitigate well-identified market failures and the Commission shall consider positive effects of the aid on the supported economic activity.

Finally, the Commission weighs, on the one hand, the distortive effects of the measure and its negative effects on trade between Member States, and, on the other hand, its positive effects on economic activities, the economy or society in the Union and considers State intervention compatible with the internal market if the positive effects outweigh the negative effects.

The RDI framework ensures that aid is proportionate to market failures it addresses by setting maximum aid intensities and eligible costs based on the activity, size of the enterprise, and the severity of the market failure.[46]

Transparency rules require Member States to publish the text of individual aid-granting decisions and information on beneficiaries and aid amounts for awards over EUR 100,000.[47] Additionally, Member States must conduct *ex post* evaluations for aid schemes exceeding EUR 150 million annually or EUR 750 million in total and maintain detailed records of all aid measures for ten years.[48]

§14.04 STATE AID TO THE GREEN DIGITAL SECTOR

EU Institutions consider reducing the digital divide in the Union's economy and society pivotal not only for the EU's economic growth, innovation and competitiveness but also for fostering the Green Transition. Digitalization is presented as a fundamental tool in the race to carbon neutrality, a goal that the EU aims to achieve by 2050, as set out in the European Green Deal and enshrined in the European Climate Law.[49] For this reason, digital and green transitions are considered and referred to as 'twin transitions', two parallel strategic policies that can reinforce each other.

46. Intensities and eligible costs are listed by activity and size of enterprise basing on closeness of the aid to the market, size of the beneficiary and acuteness of any market failure. *See ibid.*, para. 95 and Annex II.
47. *See ibid.*, paras 100 et seq.
48. *See ibid.*, paras 146 et seq.
49. *See* Communication from the Commission, 'The European Green Deal', COM(2019) 640 final of 11 Dec. 2019, and Regulation (EU) 2021/1119 of the European Parliament and of the Council of 30 Jun. 2021 establishing the framework for achieving climate neutrality and amending Regulations (EC) No 401/2009 and (EU) 2018/1999, OJ L 243, 9.7.2021.

That said, these two political priorities intended to shape the future of the Union are not automatically aligned.[50] On the one hand, ICT-based solutions could lower greenhouse gas emissions by, for example, reducing commuting and favouring a more efficient – and therefore limited – employ of energy and natural resources; on the other hand, the development of digital infrastructures could lead to a significant increase in energy consumptions, with a corresponding environmental footprint that could undermine the Union's green policies.[51]

In 2024, digital technologies account for a relevant percentage of the Union's energy consumption and greenhouse gas emissions, largely due to the resources required to manufacture and operate digital infrastructures such as the huge data centres that represent the necessary physical foundations of the otherwise dematerialized data-based economy.[52] It is therefore necessary to aim at the greening of the digital sector itself.

To achieve this goal, the Union launched and planned a series of measures and initiatives based on the interplay between the Digital and Green Transitions.[53]

With reference to State aid control, by its 2022 R&D&I Framework, the Commission recalled that public funding to R&D&I may bring about positive effects identified in the Union's objectives and strategies, including the European Green Deal wherein the Commission clearly stated that new technologies are critical to achieving the Union's green objectives.[54]

R&D&I Framework applies to all technologies, industries and sectors, hence compatibility with Article 107(3)(c) TFEU of an economic activity aimed at developing innovative solutions to green digital technologies and infrastructures can be assessed by the Commission under such set of guidelines.[55]

50. On the possible effects of digitalization on energy efficiency *see* I. Benedetti, G. Guarini and T. Lauretti, *Digitalization in Europe: A Potential Driver of Energy Efficiency for the twin Transition Policy Strategy*, in Socio-Economic Planning Sciences, 89, October 2023, https://doi.org/10.1016/j.seps.2023.101701. For a critical view on the implications of digitalization for environmental sustainability *see also* T. Santarius et al., *Digitalization and Sustainability: A call for a Digital Green Deal*, in Environmental Science & Policy, 147, September 2023, pp. 11 et seq., https://doi.org/10.1016/j.envsci.2023.04.020. For an analysis of the twin transition strategy as a policy discourse to reframe tensions between conflicting economic and sustainability policy aims, *see* Z. Kovacic et al., *The twin green and digital transition: High-level policy or science fiction?*, in Environment and Planning E: Nature and Space, *0(0)*, 17 Jun. 2024, https://doi.org/10.1177/25148486241258046.
51. *See* S. Muench et al., *Towards a green and digital future*, Publications Office of the European Union, 2022: https://publications.jrc.ec.europa.eu/repository/handle/JRC129319.
52. *See ibid.*, pp. 27 et seq.
53. For an overview of existing and planned instruments *see* 'Green cloud and green data centers', https://digital-strategy.ec.europa.eu/en/policies/green-cloud, 'Green Digital Sector', https://digital-strategy.ec.europa.eu/en/policies/green-digital, and 'European Green Digital Coalition', https://digital-strategy.ec.europa.eu/en/policies/european-green-digital-coalition, on the European Commission's website.
54. *See* Communication from the Commission, 'The European Green Deal', COM(2019) 640 final of 11 Dec. 2019, section 2.2.3.
55. *See* 2023 Broadband Guidelines, para. 4.

Guidelines on State aid for climate, environmental protection and energy 2022[56] (CEEAG) are also relevant. They do not apply to State aid for research, development and innovation but, once an innovative solution has been successfully searched and developed, its application to an economic activity in a manner that improves environmental protection can be subject to such specific set of rules under the conditions set forth therein.[57]

As a side note, the transition from 4G to 5G broadband networks can allow for a significant reduction in energy consumption.[58] Given the horizontal nature of the R&D&I Framework and the specific scope of the Broadband Guidelines, an economic activity aimed at developing a technological solution to provide more efficient broadband networks would fall within the scope of the former set of rules, while State aid to support the deployment of such improved networks would be assessed by the Commission under the latter Guidelines.

§14.05 BROADBAND SECTOR IN THE EUROPEAN STATE AID POLICY

[A] The Commission's Broadband Guidelines

Connectivity, the ability of an IT device to connect to other devices or to the Internet, is fundamental to digital transformation, as access to broadband is essential for citizens and businesses to benefit from digital services. For this reason, the Union set ambitious connectivity objectives in the Gigabit Communication,[59] the Communication Shaping Europe's digital future, the Digital Compass Communication[60] and the Digital Decade Policy Programme 2030.[61]

The first Broadband Guidelines were adopted in 2009 and were largely the result of the Commission's State aid assessments of the first support projects notified for State aid approval since 2003.[62] New Guidelines were adopted in 2013 and, finally, in 2023, when the Commission published its latest Broadband Guidelines.

---

56. Communication from the Commission, 'Guidelines on State aid for climate, environmental protection and energy 2022', OJ C 80, 18.2.2022.
57. For an overview of State aid control in the Green and Energy sectors, *see infra*, Ch. 15.
58. *See* '5G: Questions and answers', https://digital-strategy.ec.europa.eu/en/faqs/5g-questions-and-answers, on the European Commission website.
59. Communication from the Commission, 'Connectivity for a Competitive Digital Single Market – Towards a European Gigabit Society' of 14 Sep. 2016, COM(2016) 587 final (Gigabit Communication).
60. Communication from the Commission, 'Digital Compass Communication', of 9 Mar. 2021, COM/2021/118.
61. In particular, according to the Gigabit Communication, by 2025 all households should have internet speeds of at least 100 Mbps, upgradeable to 1 Gbps; key socio-economic entities like schools and hospitals should have 1 Gbps speeds; and all urban areas and major transport paths should have uninterrupted 5G coverage. The Digital Compass Communication states, as the connectivity objective for 2030, that all Union households should be covered by a Gigabit network, and all populated areas should be covered by 5G.
62. *See* Commission Decision n. 282/2003 of 10 Dec. 2003, United Kingdom, 'Cumbria Broadband – Project Access – Advancing Communication for Cumbria and Enabling Sustainable Services'.

Considering that State interventions that do not fulfil one of the conditions of Article 107(1) TFEU do not constitute State aid and are not subject to the compatibility assessment by the Commission, 2023 Broadband Guidelines provide guidance on how the compatibility of State aid for the deployment and take-up of fixed and mobile broadband networks and services are assessed on the basis of Articles 106(2) and 107(3)(c) TFEU.

[B] Types of Broadband Networks

For the purposes of assessing State aid, Broadband Guidelines distinguish between:

- fixed access networks delivering broadband services of at least 100 Mbps download speed (fixed ultrafast access networks);[63]
- wireless communications network that provides connectivity to end users at any location in the area covered by the network using one or several International Mobile Telecommunications standards (mobile access networks); and
- the parts of networks that connect the access network to the backbone network, where the traffic of end users is aggregated (blackhaul networks). These networks are necessary inputs to sustain both fixed and mobile access networks.

Market for fixed broadband services is considered separate from the market for mobile broadband services, due to significant qualitative differences between the two technologies.[64]

The Guidelines differentiate between the different types of networks in terms of the assessment of the existence of market failure and the existence of a step change, which is relevant to assess the appropriateness of the aid as a policy instrument, as well as in terms of the mapping and analysis of coverage necessary to assess the need for State intervention.

[C] Compatibility Assessment under Article 106(2) of the Treaty

If the four cumulative conditions of the Altmark judgment are met, compensation for costs incurred to deploy a network providing services of general economic interest (SGEI) does not amount to State aid. Compensation for the provision of such broadband services that constitute aid is assessed under the rules applicable to State aid in the form of public service compensation (the SGEI package).[65]

63. All speeds mentioned in the 2023 Broadband Guidelines are intended under peak-time conditions, at the hour of the day where the network load is usually at its maximum.
64. *See* Case M.8808 – T-Mobile /UPC Austria, Commission decision pursuant to Art. 6(1)(b) of Council Regulation N. 139/2004 and Art. 57 of the Agreement on the European Economic Area.
65. For an overview of the SGEI package *see supra*, Ch. 1.

Considered that Member States cannot attach specific public service obligations to services that are already provided or can be provided satisfactorily and under conditions consistent with the public interest under normal market conditions when assessing the absence of manifest error in the classification of a broadband service as an SGEI, the Commission considers the following:

- the measure should target areas where private investors cannot provide adequate broadband services. Adequate service levels are defined by each Member State based on national conditions and the minimum bandwidth necessary for social inclusion and participation in the digital economy;
- the relevant network must offer universal and affordable broadband services for all premises in the target area, not just businesses, and be technologically neutral;
- the SGEI provider must offer open wholesale access on a non-discriminatory basis; and
- if the service provider is vertically integrated, Member States must implement safeguards to avoid conflicts of interest, undue discrimination, and hidden indirect advantages.[66]

[D] Compatibility Assessment under Article 107(3)(c) of the Treaty

The Commission can evaluate whether a State aid measure is compatible with Article 107(3)(c) TFEU when it contributes to the deployment of fixed or mobile networks that can increase the offer of connectivity and access to performant broadband services, hence growing the economic competitiveness of a targeted area.

Having established that a measure constitutes State aid under Article 107(1) TFEU and that it facilitates the development of an economic activity,[67] the Commission must carry out a 'balancing test' to evaluate whether the aid unduly affects trading conditions to an extent contrary to the common interest. To do so, it considers whether the aid: (a) is capable of bringing about positive effects, and how;[68] (b) is necessary to bring about material improvement that the market alone cannot deliver;[69] (c) is appropriate to address the identified market failure and to achieve the objectives

66. *See* 2023 Broadband Guidelines, paras 26 et seq.
67. The Commission assesses whether the aid in question has changed the behaviour of the beneficiaries and their investment patterns in the target areas (incentive effect).
68. Member States can design State interventions to reduce the digital divide by addressing social or regional inequalities and achieving equity objectives. These interventions should aim to improve access to essential communication means, enhancing social and territorial cohesion.
69. Member States must conduct detailed mapping and public consultation to assess the performance of existing or planned fixed, mobile, and backhaul networks within the targeted area and relevant time horizon. While Member States have significant discretion in setting target areas, they are encouraged to consider economic, geographical, and social conditions when making these determinations. *See ibid.*, para. 70.

pursued by the aid;[70] (d) is proportionate and limited to the minimum necessary to induce the additional investment or activity in the area concerned;[71] (e) complies with the principle of technological neutrality;[72] (f) supports an activity that grants wholesale access for third parties to the funded networks;[73] (g) may have negative effects in terms of market distortions and impact on trade between Member States.[74]

70. State-funded fixed and mobile networks must offer significantly enhanced characteristics compared to existing networks, ensuring a 'step change'. This step change is achieved if the deployment involves a significant new investment, and the State-funded network introduces substantial new capabilities in terms of availability, capacity, speeds, and competition in broadband services. In the case of State aid to fixed access networks, the existence of a step change is assessed on the basis of a distinction between types of target areas, categorized as White, Grey, or Black areas depending on the growing presence of fixed ultrafast networks. *See ibid.*, paras 95 et seq.
71. State aid granted through a competitive selection procedure that attracts a sufficient number of participants is considered to be proportionate and limited to the minimum necessary. Member States must entrust the evaluation of the winning bid (including cost calculations) to an independent auditor if the number of participants or eligible bids is insufficient. Depending on the circumstances, different procedures might be appropriate. In the case of highly technically complex measures, Member States may choose to organize a competitive dialogue with potential tenderers in order to ensure the best design of the measure. *See ibid.*, paras 116 et seq.
72. Public intervention, both in the selection of beneficiaries and in the provision of wholesale access, must not favour or exclude any particular technology, given the existence of different technological solutions. Bidders should be free to propose the provision of the required services using or combining the technologies they consider most appropriate. This does not affect the possibility for Member States to define the desired performance, including energy efficiency of networks, in advance of the procedure and to award priority points to the most appropriate technological solution or mix of technological solutions on the basis of objective, transparent and non-discriminatory criteria. *See ibid.*, paras 125 et seq.
73. Effective wholesale access for third parties to the funded networks is an essential condition of any State aid measure in the sector of broadband networks deployment. In particular, wholesale access allows third parties to compete with the selected bidder, thus increasing choice and competition in the areas covered by the measure. The creation of regional service monopolies is also avoided through wholesale access. *See ibid.*, paras 129 et seq.
74. The Commission assesses the importance of distortion of competition and effect on trade in terms of impact on competitors and crowding out of private investment, also considering the risk that public support encourages local service providers to use services provided by the public network instead of those provided on market terms. Moreover, if the aid beneficiary is likely to be an undertaking already dominant or likely to become dominant due to the public investment, the aid could weaken competitive constraints on competitors. Cumulative effects are considered by the Commission to assess the overall level of distortions. *See ibid.*, para. 169.

CHAPTER 15

Energy/Environment/Green Transition/Sustainability

Guendalina Catti De Gasperi & Ester Latorre

§15.01 INTRODUCTION

Over the past decade, environmental protection (including energy savings) has repeatedly overtaken regional development as the most subsidized horizontal objective, accounting, in 2022, for about 37% of all non-crisis aid earmarked for horizontal objectives and 18.2% of the overall expenditure at EU level, albeit, compared to 2021, the relevant support measures strongly decreased.[1] Moreover, as a result of the onset of the energy crisis in 2021 and the outbreak of the war in Ukraine in 2022, the share of Member States' public interventions in the energy sector in the same year increased dramatically to reach an estimated amount of EUR 390 billion, including approximately EUR 123 billion of fossil fuel subsidies. This, although energy subsidies already followed a gradually increasing trend in the previous years, rising from EUR 177 billion in 2015 to EUR 216 billion in 2021.[2]

That trend has been strengthening over recent years notwithstanding the Commission's long-stated intention to apply a more rigorous stance towards State support to the energy sector following the opening-up of the energy market and the alleged failure of environmental aid measures to generate the required incentive effect.[3] The positive outcome still being that, in 2022, 39% of electricity was generated by

1. *See*, the Commission State Aid Scoreboard 2023 at http://ec.europa.eu/competition/state_aid/scoreboard/index_en.html.
2. *See*, the 2023 Report on Energy Subsidies in the EU (COM(2023) 651 final) of 24 Oct. 2023 prepared by the Commission, p. 2.
3. *See*, DG Competition Report on Energy Sector Inquiry of 10 Jan. 2007, SEC (2006) 1724, pp. 323 et seq.

renewable sources and, in May 2023, the EU produced more electricity from wind and solar than from fossil fuels.[4]

The breadth of the subject means that an in-depth analysis of all the relevant topics is impossible. This Chapter will therefore describe the key issues arising out of the application of State aid rules to environmental measures in general and the non-nuclear energy sector in particular, with a particular focus on the most recent developments.

§15.02 THE NOTION OF AID AND THE ENERGY SECTOR

As with any State measure, in order for environmental and energy-related measures to fall within the scope of Article 107(1) TFEU, all the conditions set out therein must be met. With respect to measures adopted in the energy sector, however, the *transfer of State resources* continues to be the most controversial requirement and, as the constant stream of case law confirms, the definition of the so-called indirect resources category – i.e., the category covering private resources under the permanent control of the State – is still work in progress. Indeed, such requirement keep gaining further importance given the increasingly stricter approach adopted with respect to the compatibility assessment of energy-related schemes. Consequently, this chapter focuses on this element of the notion of aid.

The long-lasting debate over the above requirement may be traced back to the *PreussenElektra* ruling, where the Court established that measures imposing obligations to purchase green electricity at fixed minimum prices did not involve any transfer of State resources to the extent that they were financed through private resources.[5] While the latter approach is legally sound and environmentally efficient, it has been extensively criticized for providing a somewhat formalistic legal distinction and moving away from the traditional effect-based and economic-oriented approach to State measures.[6] Indeed, the economic effects of a *PreussenElektra*-type measure and of a State aid scheme are substantially alike.

This has, in turn, generated an incentive for Member States to devise schemes potentially eluding the application of State aid rules, by taking advantage of the *PreussenElektra* ruling loophole.[7] The Commission has then struggled to resist such unorthodox practices, by setting boundaries between *PreussenElektra*-type measures and other measures involving a transfer of State resources. The key distinction was identified in the establishment of mechanisms allowing public authorities to exercise

4. *See*, the State of the Energy Union Report 2023 (COM(2023) 650 final) of 24 Oct. 2023 prepared by the European Commission, p. 3.
5. *See*, Case C-379/98, *PreussenElektra AG v. Schleswag AG*, 13.3.2001, ECLI:EU:C:2001:160 (paras 58-66).
6. *See*, *ex plurimis*, J. B. Cruz, F. C. De la Torre, *A Note on PreussenElektra*, in 26 *ELRev*, 2001, 489.
7. *See*, *contra*, AG Jacobs's Opinion delivered on 26 Oct. 2000 in Case C-379/98, *PreussenElektra*, *supra* (para. 158), providing an interesting reasoning as to why the risk of circumvention was not as grave as suggested by Commission in the case.

control over market participants' resources, which shall otherwise flow directly between them for a measure to be considered a *PreussenElektra*-type measure.[8]

Examples of such mechanisms in the context of feed-in-tariff (FIT) schemes include, *inter alia*: (i) parafiscal levy systems to finance the costs of the purchase obligation, administered by public bodies or a State-controlled private entity;[9] and (ii) levelization mechanisms whereby an intermediary supervised by the State collects and redistributes the funds according to the electricity suppliers' market shares.[10]

With respect to green certificates (GC) schemes, in its decision in *Belgium Green Certificates*, the Commission has clarified that the issuance, free of charge, of intangible assets with no market value – such as tradable emission documents merely providing official proof of the generation of electricity from renewable energy sources ('RES-e' or 'green electricity') – cannot be considered a waiver of revenue by the State.[11] It has then gone further to rule that the *PreussenElektra* rationale is applicable to GC systems imposing obligations to purchase GC at fixed minimum prices. Therefore, mechanisms whereby entities controlled by the State are entrusted with collection and redistribution tasks in relation to revenues from fines imposed under the GC schemes do involve State resources.[12]

PreussenElektra has also been relied upon as regards tradable emission credits issued under both Member States' National Allocation Plans for the first two trading periods of the European Emission Trading System (EU ETS) and pre-EU ETS trading schemes. In its decision on the Dutch NOx trading scheme, the Commission has explicitly distinguished emission allowances from GC, emphasizing that the former are intangible assets embodying a market value and that the existence of a market for this kind of pollution documents evidences their monetary worth. Consequently, where they are granted below their market value or allocated free of charge, as opposed to being sold or auctioned, State revenues are foregone.[13]

---

8. *For example*, Commission Decisions of 22 May 2002, Aids NN 27/2000 and 68/2000, on German feed-in laws for renewable electricity and for CHP installations, OJ 2002 C164/3. For an interesting insight on the *PreussenElektra* case and the consequences thereof, *see* A. Biondi, E. Righini, *An Evolutionary Theory of EU State Aid Control*, in Arnull, Chalmers, *The Oxford Handbook of European Law*, Oxford, 2015, p. 2015.
9. *For example*, Commission Decision of 4 Jul. 2006, Aids NN 162/A/2003 and N 317/A/2006, *Austrian Green Electricity Act for renewable electricity*, OJ 2006 C221/8, and Commission Decision 2011/528/EU of 8 Mar. 2011, Aid C-24/09, OJ 2011 L235/42, concerning the successor Austrian scheme and which findings were upheld by the General Court in Case T-251/11, *Austria v. Commission*, 11.12.2014, ECLI:EU:T:2014:1060.
10. Examples include public funds, private law entities appointed by concession, accounts managed by the State. *See*, for instance, Commission Decisions of 14 Apr. 2010, Aid N 94/2010, UK feed-in tariffs, OJ 2010 C166/1.
11. Commission Decision of 25 Jul. 2001, Belgium Green Certificates, Aid N 550/2000, OJ 2001 C330/3. Similarly, *inter alia*, Commission Decision of 2 Aug. 2002, Aid N 14/2002, Belgian offshore wind energy, OJ 2002 C309/14.
12. *For example*, Commission Decision of 28 Nov. 2001, Aid N 504/2000, British scheme, OJ 2002 C30/12. *Contra*, Commission Decision of 24 Oct. 2006, Aid N 254/2006, Belgium Panneaux photovoltaïques, OJ 2006 C314/80, where a penalty mechanism in which funds flowed directly between market participants did not constitute State aid.
13. The Commission Decision of 24 Jun. 2003 (Aid N 35/2003, OJ 2003 C227/19) was upheld, on this point, on appeal by both the General Court and the ECJ. *See*, respectively, Case T-233/04,

Finally, the *PreussenElektra* rationale has also been applied with respect to stranded costs compensation systems, adopted by many Member States to offset the losses incumbent electricity undertakings suffer as a result of the liberalization of the electricity sector.[14] In fact, it has been precisely in that context that the EU Courts have ultimately embraced, with respect to the energy sector, the Commission's approach, as outlined above.[15] In addition to the foregoing, both the ECJ in *Essent* and the General Court in *Iride* have tried to shed some further light on the legal differences between what the Commission had already considered deceptively similar arrangements, i.e., the measures under the cases at hand and the *PreussenElektra*-type measures.[16]

It was, however, only in the *Association Vent De Colère* ruling that the ECJ provided an economically sound explanation for differentiating measures that looked very similar from an effect-based perspective, by asserting that the distinction between the *PreussenElektra*-type and the *Essent*-type measures rests on the degree of risk borne by electricity suppliers, which is very low in the first case and high in the second.[17] Interestingly, such reasoning appears to simply complement Advocate General Jacobs' Opinion in *PreussenElektra* by adding a comparative perspective.[18]

The following case law further elaborated on the above by providing that, when applying the 'indirect' resources category, the issue is essentially how the State is involved in the measure: that is to say, it should be assessed if the State established a mechanism to compensate the additional costs incurred by the private companies obliged to purchase/sell energy at a given price and/or is able to exercise a certain degree of control over the relevant funds and/or the entities mandated to manage them.

In the *ENEA* judgment, the ECJ dealt with a Polish scheme that imposed on both private and public electricity suppliers a purchase obligation in favour of generators of electricity from cogeneration. The ECJ found that the advantage conferred upon such generators was not granted through State resources for two main reasons: (i) the Polish legislation did not impose a compulsory contribution/charge or a levy on final

---

Netherlands v. Commission, 10.4.2008, ECLI:EU:T:2008:102 (paras 63-78) and Case C-279/08, *Commission v. Netherlands*, 8.9.2011, ECLI:EU:C:2011:551 (paras 106-112).

14. *For example*, Commission Decision of 27 Feb. 2002, Aid N 661/1999, *UK Competitive Transition Charge*, OJ 2002 C113/3 where a stranded costs system mirroring the *PreussenElektra*-type measure did not constitute State aid.

15. *See*, Case C-206/06, *Essent Netwerk Noord and Others v. Aluminium Delfzijl BV*, 17.7.2008, ECLI:EU:C:2008:413 and Case T-25/07, *Iride and Iride Energia v. Commission*, 11.2.2009, ECLI:EU:T:2009:33, whereby compensation schemes in which the relevant amounts were under public control constituted State aid.

16. *Ibid.*, respectively, paras 66-69 and 74-75 and paras 24-28.

17. According to the ECJ, 'the funds at issue [in *PreussenElektra*] could not be considered a State resource since [...] there was no mechanism, such as the one [...] in the present case [...] for offsetting the additional costs arising from that obligation to purchase and through which the State offered those private operators the certain prospect that the additional costs would be covered in full'. *See*, Case C-262/12, *Association Vent De Colère! And Others v. Ministre de l'Économie, des Finances et de l'Industrie*, 19.12.2013, ECLI:EU:C:2013:851 (para. 36).

18. AG Jacobs, indeed, stated that '[n]o public authority enjoys at any moment any rights with regard to [the] sums [at issue in *PreussenElektra*]. If one of the undertakings refuses to comply with its obligations under the StrEG 1998 the other has to go to court'. *See*, AG Jacobs's Opinion, delivered on 26 Oct. 2000 in Case C-379/98, *PreussenElektra*, *supra* (para. 166).

consumers; and (ii) there was no controlling influence of the State over the private resources involved in that they were not managed by an entity entrusted by the State with collection, administration and redistribution duties in accordance with the provisions of the legislation and under the supervision of public authorities.[19]

The same rationale was applied, *inter alia*, in the *Achema and Others* and the *DOBELES* judgments – where both the (not cumulative) elements under items (i) and (ii) above were satisfied and, thus, the measures qualified as State aid – and in the *EEG 2012* ruling, where, instead, the ECJ excluded a dominant influence of the State in the management of the relevant resources in that the financial mechanism was managed by the private TSOs, although it was strictly regulated and monitored by public authorities and bodies.[20]

§15.03 A REVISED FRAMEWORK FOR 'ENERGY EXEMPTION'

Environmental and energy-related measures that meet the conditions set out under the new general and SGEI *de minimis* Regulations, and that do not exceed the ceilings set therein, are exempt from the prior notification requirement mandated by Article 108(3) TFEU.[21] Where, however, this is not the case, there may still be scope for exemption from the prior notification obligation for environmental and energy aid measures complying with the requirements under the General Block Exemption Regulation, as last amended in June 2023 (GBER).[22]

The amendments to the GBER were actually aimed at: (i) reflecting the changes to the previous Guidelines on State aid for environmental protection and energy (the 'EEAG')[23] provided under the new Guidelines on State aid for climate, environmental protection and energy (the 'CEEAG');[24] (ii) tackling some of the economic effects stemming from the energy crisis and the war in Ukraine; and (iii) making it easier for the Member States to grant support for clean tech production in Europe and to sectors that are key for the transition to climate neutrality and to a net-zero industry, in line

19. *See*, Case C-329/15, *ENEA S.A. v. Prezes Urzędu Regulacji Energetyki*, 13.9.2017, ECLI: EU:C:2017:671 (paras 23-37). Case C-206/06, *Essent Netwerk Noord and Others v. Aluminium Delfzijl BV*, 17.7.2008, ECLI:EU:C:2008:413.
20. *See*, Case C-706/17, *Achema and Others*, 15.5.2019, ECLI:EU:C:2019:407 (paras 57-72), Joined Cases C-702/20, *DOBELES HES*, and C-17/21, *Sabiedrisko pakalpojumu regulēšanas komisija*, 12.1.2023, ECLI:EU:C:2023:1 (paras 34-43), and Case C-405/16 P, *Germany v. Commission, 28.3.2019*, ECLI:EU:C:2019:268 (paras 65-86). *See also* C-850/19 P, *FVE Holýšov I and Others v. Commission*, 16.9.2021, ECLI:EU:C:2021:740, where the ECJ clarified, *inter alia*, the meaning of its *EEG 2012* judgment.
21. *See* Commission Regulations (EU) No. 2023/2831 and No. 2023/2832, [2023] OJ L of 15 Dec. 2023.
22. Commission Regulation (EU) No. 651/2014, [2014] OJ L 187/1, as last amended by Commission Regulation (EU) No. 2023/1315, [2023] OJ L 167/1. A consolidated version of the GBER is available at https://eur-lex.europa.eu/legal-content/EN/ALL/?uri=CELEX:02014R0651-20230701.
23. For a comprehensive overview of the Commission decisional practice under the EEAG, *see* E. Righini and G. Catti De Gasperi, *Survey – The Application of EU State Aid Law in the Energy Sector*, 10(1) Journal of European Competition Law & Practice (2019): 53-68 https://doi.org/10.1093/jeclap/lpy082.
24. Communications from the Commission, respectively, [2014] OJ C 200/1 and [2022] OJ C 80.

with the Green Deal Industrial Plan ('Green Deal' and, altogether, the 'Green Deal GBER Amendment').[25]

Given that the successive guidelines specifying the criteria for the Commission *ex ante* assessment of non-exempt environmental and energy-related measures have been increasingly rigorous and demanding, and that aid measures covered by the GBER can be implemented without prior Commission scrutiny, the changes introduced thereunder are of considerable relevance for both Member States and potential beneficiaries. Indeed, such changes provide more flexibility for granting authorities that intend to devise measures meeting the exemption requirements.

More specifically, the Green Deal GBER Amendment: (i) increased the notification thresholds for green projects; (ii) block exempt aid measures aimed at regulating energy prices; and (iii) enhanced and streamlined the possibilities for granting environmental and energy aid[26] to support the rollout of renewable energy, decarbonization projects, green mobility and biodiversity, as well as to facilitate investments in renewable hydrogen and energy efficiency projects.

In that respect it is worth recalling that, under the GBER adopted in 2014 as part of the State Aid Modernization (SAM) initiative,[27] the scope of the environmental and energy aid category was already comprehensive,[28] the notification thresholds and maximum allowable aid intensities were set at very high levels, the methodology for calculating eligible costs was duly refined and the relevant exemptions were applicable to all the sectors governed by the Treaty, including the steel and the coal sectors. Indeed, in order to counterbalance the above pro-aid provisions, for large aid schemes[29] the exemption from the prior notification requirement is limited to a six-month period, which may be extended by the Commission upon approval of an evaluation plan notified by the Member State. Moreover, the main conditions for environmental and energy-related aid measures to be automatically exempt[30] were already largely inspired by the assessment criteria set out under the EEAG, the main

25. Communication from the Commission of 1 Feb. 2023, *A Green Deal Industrial Plan for the Net-Zero Age*, COM/2023/62 final.
26. *See* Arts 36-49 and section 16 of the GBER.
27. *See*, Communication from the Commission of 8 May 2012, COM(2012) 209 final.
28. More specifically, as later amended, the GBER covers aid for the facilitation of energy performance contracting, aid for studies and consultancy services on environmental protection and energy matters, operating aid for the promotion of energy from renewable sources and of renewable hydrogen in small projects and renewable energy communities, as well as investment aid for: (i) the promotion of RES-e, renewable hydrogen and high-efficiency cogeneration; (ii) energy infrastructure; (iii) energy efficiency measures in buildings and other than in buildings; (iv) energy efficient district heating and/or cooling; (v) resource efficiency and for supporting the transition towards a circular economy; (vi) environmental protection, including decarbonization; (vii) recharging or refuelling infrastructure; (viii) the acquisition of clean vehicles or zero-emission vehicles and for the retrofitting of vehicles; and (ix) the remediation of environmental damage, the rehabilitation of natural habitats and ecosystems, the protection or restoration of biodiversity and the implementation of nature-based solutions for climate change adaptation and mitigation.
29. That is aid schemes with an average annual budget exceeding EUR 150 million.
30. The common principles and administrative requirements applicable to all the categories of aid covered by the GBER are spelt out under Chs I and II of the GBER. Ch. III, section 7, then, sets out the specific conditions applicable to the different types of environmental aid measures.

differences in respect to the CEEAG still being the smaller aid intensities permitted under the GBER and the procedural and substantive simplifications provided therein to increase Member States' reliance on that instrument.

§15.04 ENERGY AID AND THE COMPATIBILITY TEST

[A] The New Climate, Energy and Environmental Aid Guidelines

Environmental and energy aid measures which do not qualify for block exemption, either under the new *de minimis* Regulations or under the GBER, may still be authorized under Article 107(3)(c) TFEU where they meet the eligibility and compatibility criteria and conditions outlined under the CEEAG. This holds true also in relation to those State aid measures included in the Member States' recovery and resilience plans (RRPs) and supported by the Recovery and Resilience Facility (RRF) which are not block-exempt.[31] Indeed, funds from the RRF are under the control of Member States and may, therefore, qualify as State aid. Actually, almost half of the relevant notification templates prepared by the Commission and of the support measures included in the RRPs that, in the period 2021-July 2024, required *ex ante* approval encompassed environmental, climate and energy aid measures.[32]

The CEEAG purport to provide Member States and companies with a framework to support the European Green Deal objectives,[33] including climate neutrality by 2050, climate change adaptation, resource and energy efficiency, circularity, zero pollution, recovery of biodiversity, etc., all goals requiring significant investments. The scope of the CEEAG have been, thus, widened to such a degree that it now covers, along with the GBER, most of the measures, technologies, investments and flexibilities national granting authorities should support, carry out and take advantage of in order to be able to reach the above objectives while ensuring that competition and the integrity of the Internal Market are not distorted and impaired. The new GBER that will be adopted in the near future may still address the potentially remaining funding gaps.

More specifically, while the individual notification thresholds have been increased – and may be further increased – in the context of the GBER, the common assessment principles have remained substantially alike and, alongside the revisions regarding the scope of the individually notifiable aid measures, the CEEAG has elaborated on the additional specific assessment criteria for evaluating the compatibility of the relevant measures. Indeed: (i) as provided below, the categories of investments, instruments (e.g., contracts for difference are now covered) and technologies that Member States may support were broadened; (ii) cross-cutting measures have

31. The RRF is the key, temporary, funding instrument of the NextGenerationEU set up by the European Union. *See* https://commission.europa.eu/strategy-and-policy/eu-budget/eu-borrower-investor-relations/nextgenerationeu_en.
32. *See* the guiding templates and the list of notified aid provided in the relevant documents accessible at the following link: https://competition-policy.ec.europa.eu/state-aid/legislation/rrf-guiding-templates_en.
33. Communication from the Commission of 11 Dec. 2019, *The European Green Deal*, COM(2019) 640 final.

been aggregated and a simplified assessment is provided under single sections; (iii) where support is granted through a competitive bidding process – which shall now qualify as the default process for a wide range of aid measures and should be technology-neutral, although there are circumstances in which technology specific tenders are allowed – aid amounts may be increased to cover up to 100% of the funding gap; (iv) smaller players, as renewable energy communities and SMEs, may be exempt from the competitive tendering requirement and the latter can also benefit from increases in aid intensities in relation to a number of aid categories; (v) the limitations of maximum aid intensities (i.e., the maximum amount of aid in relation to eligible costs that Member States are allowed to pay) have been lowered for a wide range of measures as compared to the EEAG; (vi) where specific conditions are met, Member States may fund up to 100% of the eligible costs for decarbonization projects; and (vii) there is no more a requirement to notify individual large green projects within previously approved aid schemes.

On the other side, to ensure that the above described objectives are properly pursued and the common assessment criteria are satisfied: (a) in order to verify the need for support, Member States are required to carry out public consultations on schemes and projects that exceed certain thresholds in terms of budget; (b) the quantification of the environmental benefit of the measure – in terms of CO_2 abatement cost – is also required; (c) support for the most polluting fossil fuels is excluded, while State aid for projects involving natural gas is still possible but subject to a number of safeguards and commitments aimed at avoiding 'lock in' effects, discouraging aid measures, as well as ensuring their phasing-out and the compatibility with the EU's 2030 and 2050 climate targets; and (d) certain categories of schemes may still be made subject to a requirement of *ex post* evaluation, whereby the Commission may limit their duration allowing Member States to re-notify their prolongation afterwards.

As a result of the above-described streamlining exercise on and rearrangement of existing rules, the CEEAG now cover the following categories of aid.

Aid for the reduction and removal of greenhouse gas emissions including through support for renewable energy and energy efficiency: the CEEAG now provide for a 'catch-all' provision for RES-e aid, covering all relevant technologies.

Aid for the improvement of the energy and environmental performance of buildings, which is similar to the same category of investment aid provided under the GBER but may be cumulated with any support measure that improves the energy or environmental performance of buildings.

Aid for clean mobility, which now encompasses, in addition to aid for the purchase of clean vehicles and retrofitting of vehicles, aid to the deployment of recharging and refuelling infrastructure for all transport modes (including aviation). The relevant provisions also provide stricter requirements for vehicles to be considered as 'clean' and increased flexibility for Member States to determine the eligible costs and the amount of support that is necessary.

Aid for resource efficiency and for supporting the transition towards a circular economy, which is no longer limited to waste management.

Aid for the prevention or the reduction of pollution other than from greenhouse gases.

Aid for the remediation of environmental damage, the rehabilitation of natural habitats and ecosystems, the protection or restoration of biodiversity and the implementation of nature-based solutions for climate change adaptation and mitigation.

Aid for studies or consultancy services on matters relating to climate, environmental protection and energy.

Aid in the form of reductions from electricity levies for energy-intensive users and aid in the form of reductions in taxes or parafiscal levies, which also allow support to energy-intensive users to avoid carbon leakage and relocation issues, falls foul of the *polluter pays* principle and is no longer limited to levies financing the support of RES-e. This form of aid is now conditional upon commitments by the beneficiaries to reduce their carbon footprint through specific actions.

Aid for the security of electricity supply, which addresses generation adequacy issues while running the risk of hindering the phasing-out of environmentally and economically harmful subsidies. The CEEG further limit the potential for fossil fuels to benefit from the relevant support measures.

Aid for energy infrastructure, also aiming at accommodating concerns with respect to security of supply, as well as ensuring the completion of the European internal energy market.

Aid for district heating and cooling.

Aid for the closure of power plants using coal, peat or oil shale and of mining operations relating to coal, peat or oil shale extraction, a new form of aid encompassing also support to cover exceptional costs resulting from the closure.

Hence, the nuclear sector still falls outside the scope of the GBER and the CEEG.

[B] The Interaction Between the EEAG and a Plurality of Other Grounds for Authorization

The vast majority of environmental and energy aid measures so far authorized have been assessed under Article 107(3)(c) TFEU in light of the criteria set out in the various environmental and energy aid guidelines that have applied over time. As a result of the broad scope of the CEEAG, this has also been the case in the last two years in relation to major projects where aid had to be granted over a long duration and will continue to be true when all the temporary frameworks expire. However, in the last years, a large volume of aid schemes and ad hoc measures aimed at supporting consumers, suppliers and energy-intensive users have been – and will keep being – addressed and declared compatible under Article 107(3)(b) TFEU in light of the Temporary Crisis and Transition Framework (the 'TCTF'),[34] which so far allowed Member States to bypass the

34. *See*, Communication from the Commission of 9 Mar. 2023, Temporary Crisis and Transition Framework for State Aid measures to support the economy following the aggression against Ukraine by Russia, [2023] OJ C 101/3, as later amended. The consolidated version of the TCTF is provided at the following link: https://eur-lex.europa.eu/legal-content/EN/TXT/?uri=CELEX%3A02023XC0317%2801%29-20240502.

stricter conditions provided under the CEEAG without even requiring the phasing-out of fossil fuels.[35]

The TCTF was adopted to foster the objectives of the Green Deal and partially amended and extended the Temporary Crisis Framework (TCF), introduced in March 2022 to enable Member States to support their economies in the context of Russia's aggression against Ukraine.[36] More specifically, while the most potentially contentious provisions under the TCTF/TCF have now been phased out, until 31 December 2025 Member States may still grant, thereunder, aid to foster the transition to a net-zero economy: i.e., aid aimed at decarbonizing industrial production processes and at accelerating the rollout of renewable energy and energy storage, as well as investment support for the manufacturing of certain essential clean technologies,[37] their key components and critical raw materials.

Climate, environmental and energy-related aid measures may also be authorized under Article 107(3)(b) TFEU in light of the common and specific eligibility and compatibility criteria provided under the new Communication on important projects of common European interest ('IPCEIs' and, altogether, the 'new IPCEIs Communication'),[38] which have substantially remained unchanged. More specifically, in relation to the environmental and energy sectors, the new IPCEIs Communication expressly covers any project of major importance for, *inter alia*, the European Green Deal, the New Industrial Strategy for Europe and the Next Generation EU.[39] In this respect, it is worth noting that, in order to accelerate the EU's green transition, as with the CEEAG the new IPCEIs Communication now requires Member States to provide evidence of compliance of the notified projects with the 'do no significant harm' principle.

These new provisions, however, do not represent all the applicable rules. The new IPCEIs Communication is, in fact, without prejudice to the analysis of IPCEIs under the CEEAG, although is certainly better placed to deal with large projects of a

35. *See* the list of authorized aid provided in the relevant document accessible at the following link: https://competition-policy.ec.europa.eu/state-aid/temporary-crisis-and-transition-framework_en. *See, inter alia*, SA.102454 and SA.102569, where support in relation to part of the fuel costs incurred by fossil fuel power plants was also allowed.
36. *See*, Communication from the Commission of 23 Mar. 2022, Temporary Crisis Framework for State Aid measures to support the economy following the aggression against Ukraine by Russia, [2022] OJ C 131 1/01, as later amended.
37. Namely, batteries, solar panels, wind turbines, heat pumps, electrolysers and carbon capture and storage devices.
38. *See*, Communication from the Commission, *Criteria for the analysis of the compatibility with the internal market of State aid to promote the execution of important projects of common European interest*, [2021] OJ C 528/10.
39. *See*, respectively, Communications from the Commission of 11 Dec. 2019, COM(2019) 640 final; of 10 Mar. 2020 and 5 May 2021, COM(2020) 67 final and COM(2021) 350 final; and of 27 May 2020, COM(2020) 456 final. *For example*, the Commission found that the Hydrogen IPCEIs (*see* the list of authorized IPCEIs at https://competition-policy.ec.europa.eu/state-aid/ipcei/approved-ipceis_en) – i.e., projects aimed at supporting he development of an innovative and sustainable European hydrogen industry – contributed to the objectives of the European Green Deal, the EU Hydrogen Strategy and the REPowerEU Plan.

transversal nature and 'integrated projects'.[40] Moreover, its application might be the preferable option, because it allows a greater diversification of support instruments and aid at higher levels than would otherwise apply under the CEEAG.

Notwithstanding the broad scope of application of the CEEAG to aid measures potentially falling within Article 107(3)(c) TFEU, specific compatibility criteria have also been established for certain energy aid measures under the new EU ETS Guidelines,[41] which apply to national schemes intended to compensate electro-intensive users particularly affected by the changes to the EU ETS in effect from 2021 onwards. More precisely, the new EU ETS Guidelines explain the Commission's approach to some temporary measures allowed under the EU ETS Directive[42] in connection with electricity generation and consumption, such as aid: (i) compensating indirect emission costs – i.e., EU ETS allowance costs passed on in electricity prices – borne by energy-intensive industries operating in sectors deemed vulnerable to carbon leakage; and (ii) in the form of transitional free allocations for the modernization of electricity generation.

Environmental and energy aid measures that do not qualify for block exemption and are not covered by the CEEAG, the new IPCEIs Communication or the new EU ETS Guidelines may nonetheless be authorized on the basis of other available grounds for authorization. In particular, they can be directly approved under Article 107(3)(c) TFEU or Article 107(3)(b) TFEU.

So far, most of the Commission decisions directly authorizing environmental and energy-related aid measures under the former pertained to kinds of aid not included in the EEAG or in the previous environmental aid guidelines, for the Commission not being familiar with such measures or due to political reasons. These cases show, first, that the Commission systematically applies the common assessment principles provided under the environmental guidelines in force at the relevant time and, second, that the Article 107(3)(c) TFEU exemption might be a valuable tool in future cases concerning innovative measures.[43] This holds also true with respect to the exemption under Article 107(3)(b) TFEU, which to date has not been widely directly employed but

---

40. *See*, Commission Decision on Aid N 416/2001 (OJ 2001 C88/16), where, as the UK Emission Trading Scheme, failed to fulfil the conditions for the public financing of IPCEIs, the Commission assessed it according to the EAG provisions on Art. 107(3)(c) TFEU exemption.
41. *See*, Guidelines on certain State aid measures in the context of the system from greenhouse gas emission allowance trading post-2021, [2020] OJ C 317/5.
42. *See*, Directive 2003/87/EC of 13 Oct. 2003, establishing a system for greenhouse gas emission allowance trading within the Union, [2003] OJ L 275/32, as later amended.
43. *See*, for instance, Commission Decision of 28 Jun. 2021 on regulatory support for the storage of natural gas in French (SA.49414, [2022] OJ L 090/122), where the Commission did not consider any specific objectives but applied the other common principles under the EEAG and secured several commitments to minimize distortions of competition; Commission Decision of 8 Oct. 2014 on the UK support plan for the construction and operation of the Hinkley Point nuclear power plant (SA.34947, [2015] L 109/44), where, although the nuclear sector still falls outside the scope of the GBER and the relevant compatibility guidelines notwithstanding the extensive and long-lasting debate on the matter, the Commission applied the common assessment principles at the time established under the EEAG; and Commission Decision of 13 Jul. 2009, Aid N 629/2008, *UK Carbon Reduction Commitment (CRC)*, OJ 2009 C238/1, where, given its innovative character, a trading system providing CRCs for energy-intensive sectors not covered by the EU ETS was considered to fall outside the scope of the category of 'aid in the form of

proved to be useful (albeit on a temporary basis) as a means for authorizing aid schemes for the production of green products complying with the conditions provided under the 2009 and 2010 Temporary Framework Communications for State aid measures to support access to finance.[44]

In principle, energy aid measures can be authorized also on the basis of the SGEI exemption under Article 106(2) TFEU. Indeed, the successive electricity directives applicable from time to time and the EU's past decisional practice have included the supply of electricity among the universal services and security of supply obligations imposed by Member States upon prospective candidates for public service obligation status.[45] However, the decision-making practice on the application of Article 106(2) TFEU in the energy sector has not always been consistent: while some Member States have successfully invoked Article 106(2) TFEU despite the measures in question not meeting the *Altmark* conditions,[46] in other cases the Commission and the ECJ have essentially relied upon those conditions to conclude that, as they were not met, the relevant schemes could not be cleared directly under the abovementioned provision.[47]

Other grounds for authorization that may potentially apply to aid measures in the non-nuclear energy sector include the new Framework for State aid for research and development and innovation[48] and the new Guidelines on regional State aid and on State aid for rescuing and restructuring non-financial undertakings in difficulty.[49] The interaction of different guidelines and frameworks that may be applicable to the same measure has indeed led to some difficulties in certain cases. A trend may however be detected as regards the interplay between the Guidelines on regional State aid and the CEEAG.[50] While a considerable number of support mechanisms of a purely environmental nature have been approved under Article 107(3)(a) TFEU by applying the criteria set out in past regional aid guidelines, with respect to the energy sector the

---

tradable permit schemes' covered by the environmental aid guidelines applicable at the time, but was authorized under Art. 107(3)(c) TFEU.

44. *See*, Communications of the Commission, [2009] OJ C83/1 and [2011] OJ C6/5, respectively, at paras 4.5 and 2.5 Aid measures for the design and manufacture of environmentally friendly products have been, in fact, explicitly excluded from both the EAG and the EEAG coverage.
45. *See*, now, Directive 2009/72/EC of 13 Jul. 2009, concerning common rules for the internal market in electricity, [2009] OJ L211/55, Art. 3, and, *ex plurimis*, Case C-159/94, *Commission v. France*, 23.10.1997, ECLI:EU:C:1997:501 (paras 68-88).
46. *See* Case C-280/00, *Altmark Trans GmbH and Regierungspräsidium Magdeburg v. Nahverkehrsgesellschaft Altmark GmbH*, 24.7.2003, ECLI:EU:C:2003:415, paras 88-93. Examples include Commission Decision of 29 Sep. 2010, Aid N 178/2010, Spanish indigenous coal power plants, OJ 2010 C312/6, paras 77-103.
47. *See*, for *example*, Case C-706/17, *Achema and Others*, *supra* (paras 104-121), on several energy-related measures, and Commission Decision 2009/609/EC of 4 Jun. 2008, Aid N C45/2005, Hungarian PPAs, OJ 2009 L225/53, paras 255-275 and 433-436.
48. [2022] OJ C 414/1. *For example* Commission Decisions of 14 Dec. 2010 and 26 Jan. 2011, Aids N 276/2010 and N 240/2010, respectively, Swedish GoBiGas and Domsjo R&D projects, OJ 2011 C196/2 and C180/1.
49. Respectively, [2021] OJ C 153/1 and [2014] OJ C 249/1. *For example*, Commission Decisions of 6 Dec. 2006 and 2 Jul. 2008, Aids N 14/2006 and C 11/2007, Italy, Ottana Energia, respectively, OJ 2007 C68/5 and 2009 L259/22.
50. Such interaction has been addressed in Commission Decision of 15 Sep. 2010, Aid C 8/2009, Fri-El Acerra, OJ 2011 L46/28, on appeal Case T-551/10, *Fri-El Acerra v. European Commission*, 13.9.2013, ECLI:EU:T:2013:430.

Commission has so far relied mostly on Article 107(3)(c) TFEU and environmental aid guidelines, by examining the peculiar regional circumstances in its assessment under this framework.[51]

§15.05 CONCLUDING REMARKS

The past and more recent developments of the State aid regime and the related temporary frameworks show the considerable efforts the European Union has made when seeking to reconcile the conflicting interests and the various EU policies that any wide-ranging reform to government intervention in energy markets and in relation to environmental measures must take into consideration. While the Commission's strategy of trying to please all parties would appear to be the only realistic option at the present time, it is not without its risks or contradictions.

The strategy has in fact been pursued along three lines. First, by introducing and keeping pro-aid provisions that benefit energy-intensive undertakings, the Commission has sought to both allay concerns over security of supply, capacity, competitiveness and carbon leakage and address shortcomings in infrastructure and networks that it considers to be hindering the completion of the internal electricity market.

Second, several provisions still deal with the substantiated claims that in the last years, pro-RES policies have further exacerbated, by generating cost-inefficiencies, market distortions and overcompensation issues. Hence, under the CEEAG, renewables are not treated as favourably as they were under the previous regime, meaning that the different energy sources are now treated more evenly, which again benefits energy-intensive sectors.

Thirdly, several safeguard mechanisms have been introduced to limit the side-effects that the above-described pro-aid reforms produce with respect to, *inter alia*, the objectives under the Green Deal, the effectiveness of the *polluter pays* principle, the liberalization of the internal electricity market and the phasing-out of environmentally harmful subsidies. Some of these safeguards may, in turn, have a major impact on existing aid schemes and increase the administrative burden that the wide-ranging changes introduced by the GBER are meant to reduce.

With respect to the GBER, although the expansion of its scope is very welcome precisely for the reduction in administrative costs it should imply, it may emphasize the legal certainty issues that cautious Member States have so far overcome by electing to notify risky measures. Additionally, the broad terms of the New GBER may encourage Member States to devise exemptible aid measures that do not generate the required incentive effect, at the expense of both environmental objectives and competitiveness.

Nonetheless, the CEEAG have yet to be put to the test of practice because, in the first two years of implementation, the crisis frameworks – which were not aimed at granting 'less and better targeted State aid' – have clearly impaired its evaluation. The

51. *For example* Commission Decision of 18 Jul. 2001, Aid N 660/A/2000, Exemption from climate change levy for Northern Ireland, OJ 2001 C263/10. *Contra*, Commission Decision of 5 Aug. 2009, Aids N 434-5-6/2008, OJ 2009 C234/1, where the Commission applied the guidelines on regional aid to measures for green energy production.

changes they introduce will surely lead to the dawn of a new era for EU climate and energy policies in the State aid arena. It is still unclear, however, whether the sun will rise in the east or in the west.

CHAPTER 16

Sport

Luigi Santa Maria & Francesco Mazzocchi

§16.01 INTRODUCTION: SPORT AND COMPETITION LAW

Sport officially became an area of European Union policy with the Lisbon Treaty. Article 165(1) TFEU, within Title XII (*Education, Vocational Training, Youth and Sport*) expressly recognizes its social and cultural value and specificity, stating:

The Union shall contribute to the promotion of European sporting issues while taking account of the specific nature of sport, its structures based on voluntary activity and its social and educational function.[1]

However, sport's special nature does not put it beyond the reach of the Treaty's rules on the internal market,[2] competition and the free movement of people and services,[3] at least to the extent that it amounts to economic activity.

---

1. In truth, the declaration made in the Lisbon Treaty of sport's particular status was not breaking entirely new ground. The European Court of Justice (ECJ) had made statements of this sort on more than one occasion (*See*, among others, Case C-36/74, *B.N.O. Walrave and L.J.N. Koch v. Association Union cycliste internationale, Koninklijke Nederlandsche Wielren Unie and Federación Española Ciclismo*, 12.12.1974, ECLI:EU:C:1974:140).
2. *See* Case C-36/74, *Walrave and Koch v. Association Union cycliste international and Others*, *supra* (para. 4), Case C-13/76, *Gaetano Donà v. Mario Mantero*, 14.7.1976, ECLI:EU:C:1976:115 (para. 12); Case C-415/93, *Bosman, Royal club liégeois SA v. Jean-Marc Bosman and Others and Union des associations européennes de football (UEFA) v. Jean-Marc Bosman*, 15.12.1995, ECLI: EU:C:1995:463 (para. 73); Joined Cases C-51/96 and C-191/97, *Christelle Deliège v. Ligue francophone de judo et disciplines associées ASBL, Ligue belge de judo ASBL, Union européenne de judo and François Pacquée*, 11.4.2000, ECLI:EU:C:2000:199 (para. 4); and Case C-176/96, *Jyri Lehtonen and Castors Canada Dry Namur-Braine ASBL v. Fédération royale belge des sociétés de basket-ball ASBL (FRBSB)*, 13.4.2000, ECLI:EU:C:2000:201 (para. 32).
3. A leading case in this regard is *Bosman*, Case C-415/93, '*Bosman*', *supra* (para. 75) in which the Court found that the rules of FIFA and UEFA governing player transfers, under which a fee would be paid by the new club to the old club, came within the scope of the Treaty's rules. In that case, the rules in question were considered unjustified restrictions on the free movement of professional footballers. While it recognized 'the difficulty of severing the economic aspects from the

On the contrary, the courts of the European Union have placed increasing emphasis on the economic dimension of sport, effectively coming to treat sport as they do any other economic sector,[4] and gradually eroding the distinction, introduced by the earliest European case law, between those aspects that purely regard sport, and as such lay beyond the application of the Treaty's rules, and economic aspects, which as such are subject to the EU's legislation.[5]

Generally, that change in stance has reflected the growing importance of sport as an industry, and of the related markets.

This chapter provides a brief analysis of the applicability of the main rules on EU competition to sport, and football in particular. In §§8.03 et seq. it then concentrates on the subject of State aid, with a particular focus on infrastructural aid and aid to individual football clubs.

§16.02 SPORT AND COMPETITION IN EUROPE

The ECJ has recognized not only that clubs constitute undertakings for the purposes of competition law, where they carry on economic activities,[6] but also that individual sportsmen and women,[7] and the various sporting federations and associations both domestic and international may constitute associations of undertakings, and as such, be subject to the competition rules, including Articles 101 and 102 TFEU.

---

sporting aspects of football', the Court emphasized the principle that rules in sport which are justified on non-economic grounds, which relate to the particular nature and context of certain competitions, lay outside the scope of the Treaty's application. Nonetheless, such a restriction on the scope of application could not be relied upon to exclude the whole of a sporting activity from the scope of the Treaty.

4. *See* Case T-313/02, *Meca-Medina and Majcen v. Commission*, 30.9.2004, ECLI:EU:T:2004:282 (para. 44): 'high level sport has become, to a great extent, an economic activity'.
5. *See*, for instance, Case C-13/76 *Gaetano Donà v. Mario Mantero*, 14.7.1976, ECLI:EU:C:1976:115, the Court was asked for a preliminary ruling on the compatibility with European law of a provision in the rules of the Italian Football Federation which meant that in principle affiliation was restricted to players of Italian nationality. The Court found that the rule was incompatible with the prohibition on discrimination and the rules of the Treaty on free movement, but that, nonetheless, the Treaty's terms were not concerned with domestic rules that relate to the '*particular nature and context of such matches*', as they are '*of sporting interest only*'. *See also* Case C-36/74, *Walrave and Koch v. Association Union cycliste international and Others, supra* the Court was drawing a distinction between 'economic' rules and sporting rules, and finding that domestic regulations (in this case, the rules of the *Union Cycliste Internationale*) that were based solely on purely sporting interest had nothing to do with economic activity. Also, Case C-519/04 P, *Meca-Medina and Majcen v. Commission*, 18.7.2006, ECLI:EU:C:2006:492 (para. 22).
6. The Court of Justice has defined the term 'undertaking' broadly to include 'every entity engaged in an economic activity, regardless of the legal status of the entity and the way in which it is financed'. Bayern Munich, one of the most profitable football clubs in the world, is organized as a registered club, a structure that in Germany is basically reserved to non-economic organizations.
7. Joined Cases C-51/96 and C-191/97, *Deliège, supra* (paras 56 and 57). In the same judgment the European Court of Justice stated that the amateur status of athletes does not necessarily place them outside the scope of economic activities. In *Bosman*, however, Advocate General Lenz considered that football players employed by a football club do not themselves constitute undertakings. Similarly, *see also* the answer given on 14 Apr. 2003 by Mr Monti on behalf of the Commission, to written question E-537/03 by Erik Meijer of 14 Feb. 2003, OJ C 280E/65.

Recent judgments have addressed in detail the topic of the interplay of sports and EU competition law, particularly with reference to the application of the competition rules on sport's governing bodies' statutes.[8]

In such judgments, the Court reiterated that in so far it constitutes an economic activity, the practice of sports is subject to EU competition law.[9]

The ECJ seems to have to some extent 'downplayed' the importance of Article 165 TFEU, underlining that it authorizes the Union to exercise a mere *supporting competence*, with the exclusion of any harmonization of the provisions adopted at a national level and without any obligation to integrate or take into account the objectives listed in Article 165 TFEU in the application of the other rules of the Treaty (e.g., competition rules, freedom of movement of persons, services, and capital)[10] In spite of this, sport's specificity, which according to the Court might be found not only in amateur sport but also in the pursuit of sport as an economic activity, is not completely disregarded, but can be a factor to be taken into account when examining the question whether a particular type of agreement should be considered as having as its 'object' or 'effect' of restricting competition under Article 101 TFEU.[11] To measure, the ECJ seems to argue, the 'degree of harm' of a certain conduct.[12]

Moreover, in exceptional cases, the ECJ stated that agreements between undertakings or decisions by associations of undertakings in the sports domain may *escape tout court* the application of the competition rules, in cases involving agreements or decisions taking the form of rules adopted in the view to pursuing certain ethical or principled objectives and, more broadly, to regulate the exercise of a professional activity if the association/undertaking concerned demonstrates that certain specific conditions are satisfied. For instance, in the *Meca-Medina* case, then, ECJ argued that, while all sporting rules must be scrutinized in the light of competition law, anti-doping rules may escape the prohibitions established by Articles 101 and 102 TFEU.[13]

---

8. Case C-124/21 P, *International Skating Union v. Commission*, 21.12.2023, ECLI:EU:C:2023:1012; Case C-680/21, *UL and SA Royal Antwerp Football Club v. Union royale belge des sociétés de football association ASBL*, 21.12.2023, ECLI:EU:C:2023:1010; Case C-333/21, *European Superleague Company SL v. Fédération internationale de football association (FIFA) and Union of European Football Associations (UEFA)*, 21.12.2023, ECLI:EU:C:2023:1011.
9. *See*, to that effect, Case C-36/74, *Walrave and Koch v. Association Union cycliste international and Others*, *supra* (para. 4); Case C-325/08, *Olympique Lyonnais SASP v. Olivier Bernard and Newcastle UFC*, 16.3.2010, ECLI:EU:C:2010:143 (para. 27). *See also* Case C-680/21, *UL and SA Royal Antwerp Football Club*, *supra* (para. 54), according to which 'only certain specific rules which were adopted solely on non-economic grounds and which relate to questions of interest solely to sport per se must be regarded as being extraneous to any economic activity. That is the case, in particular, of those on the exclusion of foreign players from the composition of teams participating in competitions between teams representing their country or the determination of ranking criteria used to select the athletes participating individually in competitions'.
10. Case C-333/21, *European Superleague Company SL*, *supra* (paras 95-107).
11. Case C-124/21 P, *ISU*, *supra* (paras 91-96).
12. *Ibid.*
13. On the substance, the Court found that even where the anti-doping rules were restrictive, they were not in the particular case in violation of Art. 101(1) TFEU, in that they were justified by a legitimate objective, inherent in the organization and the proper conduct of competitive sport, and their very purpose was to ensure healthy rivalry between athletes. Also on anti-doping measures, *see* the Commission Decision (EU) C(2009)7809 of 12 Oct. 2009 on COMP/39471 *Certain joueur de tennis professionnel/Agence mondiale antidopage, ATP Tour Inc. et Fondation*

In this respect, the ECJ underlined that the examination on whether a rule adopted by a sports association infringed the competition rules should take place on the basis of the principles established by the judgment in *Wouters* (which had regarded members of the legal and other professions in the Netherlands), and in particular, the following factors: (a) the overall context in which the rule was adopted or produced its effects and its objectives; (b) whether the restrictions caused by the rule were inherent in the pursuit of the objectives; and (c) whether the rule was proportionate in light of the objective pursued.

In a nutshell, therefore, the specificity and cultural and social value of sport may potentially be taken into account not only (i) to exclude, in exceptional circumstances, certain conduct from the application of competition law (e.g., in the doping domain) but also (ii) to assess the scope and extent of a violation of competition rules, for instance, when examining the question of whether a particular type of conduct should be considered having as its 'object' or, failing that, 'effect', the prevention, restriction or distortion of competition, in light of the economic and legal context of which it forms a part and the actual conditions or context that characterize the structure and functioning of the sector concerned.[14] Moreover, to add a further layer of complexity, the possibility always remains open, under the general principles, that an agreement that restricts competition can be justified on the basis of the efficiency gains generated by it pursuant to Article 101(3) TFEU[15] or an abusive unilateral conduct can be justified

Conseil international de l ' arbitrage en matière de sport, in which the Commission recognized the ATP could be considered an undertaking subject to competition rules, but nonetheless stated, 'la lutte contre le dopage dans le tennis est un objectif légitime au sens de l'arrêt Meca-Medina. La Commission va démontrer ci-dessous qu'il semble improbable que les règles en question ainsi que la sanction imposée au plaignant aillent au-delà de ce qui est nécessaire au sens de la jurisprudence Meca-Medina et qu'une violation de l'article 81, paragraphe 1, semble donc très improbable'.

14. *See* Case C-124/21 P, *ISU, supra* (para. 111), where the Court clarified that such an assessment may involve taking into account, for example, the nature, organization or functioning of the sport concerned and, more specifically, how professionalized it is, the manner in which it is practised, the manner of interaction between the various participating stakeholders and the role played by the structures and bodies responsible for it at all levels, with which the Union is to foster cooperation, in accordance with Article 165(3) TFEU.

15. If, in other terms, it is proved that the agreement at issue contributes to improving the production or distribution of goods or to promoting technical or economic progress, while allowing consumers a fair share of the resulting benefit, without however (a) imposing on the undertakings concerned restrictions which are not indispensable to the attainment of these objectives; (b) afford such undertakings the possibility of eliminating competition in respect of a substantial part of the products in question. *See* in this regard Case C-680/21, *UL and SA Royal Antwerp Football Club, supra* (paras 118 et seq.); Case T-193/02, *Laurent Piau v. Commission*, 26.1.2005, ECLI:EU:T:2005:22. It is interesting to note that in order to exempt the agreement in the sport sector, the Court rarely did make use of the exceptions available under Art. 101(3) TFEU, and the related 'technical' criteria but ended its evaluation at a logically *prior* stage, in connection with Art. 101(1) TFEU, drawing largely upon considerations regarding compliance with the principle of proportionality. That no use was made of Art. 101(3) TFEU may perhaps be explained by the fact that the cumulative conditions set out therein were originally conceived for application to anti-competitive agreements between competing undertakings in 'genuinely economic' sectors, and considerations of a social or educational nature do not in principle fit very well into the exemptions under Art. 101(3) TFEU (*see, for example*, the extensive debate on the application of Art. 101(3) TFEU to competition-restricting agreements that produce beneficial effects for the environment and in terms of sustainability).

under Article 102 TFEU when the said conduct is objectively necessary, or the exclusionary effect produced may be counterbalanced or even outweighed by advantages in terms of efficiency which also benefit the consumer.[16]

In conclusion, the assessment of the interplay between sports and competition law seems to be deferred to a case-by-case analysis, with little certainty for undertakings and operators.

[A] Sporting Rules and the Organization of Sports

The Courts of the European Union have repeatedly been called upon to consider the compatibility between the rules and regulations adopted by sporting federations and other sports bodies, and the Treaty's rules. In particular, the earliest case law examined those rules in the light of the Treaty provisions on free movement of people and services, on the assumption – stated repeatedly by the Court – that their substantially 'private' nature was irrelevant.[17]

More recently, the ECJ dealt with such issue with specific reference to antitrust law (Articles 101 and 102 TFEU), in the judgment *International Skating Union* (ISU), in relation to the rules related to the prior authorization of other skating events and the eligibility of athletes in ISU-organized events[18] and in the judgment *Superleague*, in relation to a set of rules by which FIFA and UEFA on the prior approval of 'competing'

16. *See* Case C-333/21, *European Superleague Company SL, supra* (paras 202 et seq.). Consistently with what is provided for in Art. 101(3) TFEU, it follows from the Court's case law relating to Art. 102 TFEU that an undertaking holding a dominant position may show that conduct liable to come within the scope of the prohibition laid down in that article may yet be justified. *See* Case C-209/10, *Post Danmark A/S v. Konkurrencerådet*, 27.3.2012, ECLI:EU:C:2012:172 (para. 40); Case C-377/20, *Servizio Elettrico Nazionale and Others*, 12.6.2022, ECLI:EU:C:2022:379 (para. 46). In particular, an undertaking may demonstrate, to that end, either that its conduct is objectively necessary, or that the exclusionary effect produced may be counterbalanced or even outweighed by advantages in terms of efficiency which also benefit the consumer (Case C-209/10, *Post Danmark A/S, supra* (para. 41); Case C-377/20, *Servizio Elettrico Nazionale and Others, supra* (paras 46 and 86)).
17. *See* Case C-438/05, *International Transport Workers' Federation and Finnish Seamen's Union v. Viking Line ABP and OÜ Viking Line Eesti*, 11.12.2007, ECLI:EU:C:2007:772 (para. 33); Case C-379/09, *Maurits Casteels v. British Airways plc.*, 10.3.2011, ECLI:EU:C:2011:131 (para. 19); Case C-325/08, *Olympique Lyonnais SASP v. Olivier Bernard and Newcastle UFC*, 16.3.2010, ECLI:EU:C:2010:143 (para. 30); Case C-519/04 P, *Meca-Medina and Majcen v. Commission, supra* (para. 24); Case C-309/99, *J.C.J. Wouters, J.W. Savelbergh e Price Waterhouse Belastingadviseurs BV v. Algemene Raad van de Nederlandse Orde van Advocaten*, 19.2.2002, ECR I-1577 (para. 120); Case C-415/93, *'Bosman', supra* (para. 82); Case C-36/74, *Walrave and Koch v. Association Union cycliste international and Others, supra* (paras 16 et seq.).
18. Namely, according to the rules at stake, the organizers of such a competing competition must submit to ISU financial, technical, commercial and sporting information (including the venue of the planned event, value of the prizes to be awarded, business plan, budget, television coverage), as well as a declaration confirming that it accepts the ISU's Code of Ethics. The eligibility rules concern the athlete's eligibility to compete in an ISU organized event. In a nutshell, an athlete can lose this eligibility, for a specific period or for life, when they compete in a non-approved event. It is worth underlying that the case law stems from a complaint by two professional skaters who considered that the rules adopted by the International Skating Union (ISU) infringed Arts 101 and 102 TFEU.

international football competitions to that organized by UEFA and possible sanctions for the clubs joining such alternative projects.[19]

The ECJ recalled that only certain specific rules which were adopted solely on non-economic grounds and which relate to questions of interest solely to sport per se must be regarded as being extraneous to any economic activity. That is the case, in particular, of those on the exclusion of foreign players from the composition of teams participating in competitions between teams representing their country or the determination of ranking criteria used to select the athletes participating individually in competitions.[20]

Apart from those specific rules, the rules issued by sporting associations and, more broadly, the conduct of the associations which adopted them come within the scope of the Treaty provisions on competition law where the conditions of application of those provisions are met.[21]

On those grounds, the Court recalled that the rules on a sporting association's exercise of powers governing prior approval for sporting competitions, the organization and marketing of which constitute an economic activity for the undertakings involved come, in that capacity, within the scope of the TFEU provisions on competition law.[22]

In the ISU case, the ECJ underlined that, also in the sport sector, only certain types of coordination between undertakings which reveal a sufficient degree of harm to competition shall be deemed to restrict competition 'by object' under Article 101 TFEU,

19. The European Super League is an international interclub football competition project promoted by several professional football clubs, e.g., FC Barcelona, Real Madrid C.F., AC Milan and Manchester City. Following the launch of the project, FIFA and UEFA were heavily opposed to it. The clubs then brought an action before the Commercial Court in Madrid seeking protective measures against FIFA and UEFA. The Commercial Court in Madrid referred to the CJEU regarding the interpretation of Arts 101 and 102 TFEU in light of FIFA's and UEFA's statutes. FIFA's statutes provide for, *inter alia*, (i) UEFA to ensure that international leagues or other groups of clubs shall not be formed without FIFA's and UEFA's consent and approval (Art. 22 FIFA Statutes), (ii) no international match or competition takes place without the prior permission of FIFA and UEFA (Art. 71 FIFA Statutes), (iii) FIFA's and UEFA's authorization for associations/leagues/clubs affiliated to a Member Association to take part in competitions on another FIFA member association's territory (Art. 73 FIFA Statutes). Further, FIFA's statutes concern the exploitation of various rights emanating from the organization of professional football competitions. UEFA's statutes provide for, *inter alia*, (i) UEFA's sole jurisdiction to organize or abolish international football competitions in Europe, in which Member Associations and/or their clubs participate (Art. 49 UEFA Statutes); (ii) prior approval for international matches, competitions or tournaments not organized by UEFA but played on UEFA's territory (Art. 49 UEFA Statutes); (iii) UEFA's mandatory permission for forming combinations or alliances between UEFA Member Associations, leagues or clubs (Art. 51 UEFA Statutes); (iv) a Member Association's mandatory permission for playing or organizing matches outside a Member Association's territory (Art. 51 UEFA Statutes).
20. *See* Case C-36/74, *Walrave and Koch v. Association Union Cycliste Internationale and Others, supra* (para. 8); Case C-415/93, *'Bosman', supra* (paras 76 and 127); Joined Case C-51/96, C-191/97, *Deliège, supra* (paras 43, 44, 63, 64 and 69).
21. *See* Case C-519/04 P, *Meca-Medina and Majcen v. Commission, supra* (paras 30-33), which means that those associations may be categorized as 'undertakings' within the meaning of Arts 101 and 102 TFEU or that the rules at issue may be categorized as 'decisions by associations of undertakings' within the meaning of Art. 101 TFEU.
22. Case C-36/74, *Walrave and Koch v. Association Union cycliste international and Others, supra.*

i.e., those that by their very nature, as being injurious to the proper functioning of normal competition and for which it is not necessary to assess their effects.[23]

In order to determine, in a given case, whether an agreement, a decision by an association of undertakings or a concerted practice in the sport sector reveals, by its very nature, a sufficient degree of harm to competition that it may be considered as having as its object the prevention, restriction or distortion thereof, it is necessary to examine, first, the content of the agreement, decision or practice in question; second, the economic and legal context of which it forms a part; and, third, its objectives.[24]

A similar exercise shall be carried out in the context of Article 102 TFEU (the rule prohibiting the abuse of dominant position) which pursues distinct objectives and has distinct scopes but can apply simultaneously to the same conduct, where the respective conditions for their application are satisfied.[25]

Interestingly, in those judgments the ECJ, relying on the case law on undertakings holding exclusive or special rights granted by the State under Article 106 TFEU,[26] recalled the notion of 'equal of opportunity', and 'conflict of interest', concepts that are not usual when applying antitrust rules (Articles 101 and 102 TFUE).

Namely, the ECJ argued that the maintenance or development of undistorted competition in the internal market can be guaranteed only if equality of opportunity is ensured between undertakings.

To entrust an undertaking (such as ISU, FIFA and UEFA) which exercises a given economic activity the power to determine, de jure or even de facto, which other undertakings are also authorized to engage in that activity and to determine the conditions under which that activity may be exercised gives rise to a conflict of interests and puts that undertaking at an obvious advantage over its competitors, by

23. *See*, to that effect, Case C-56/65, *Société Technique Minière v. Maschinenbau Ulm GmbH*, 30.6.1966, ECLI:EU:C:1966:38 (para. 249); Case C-179/16, *F. Hoffmann-La Roche and Others v. Autorità Garante della Concorrenza e del Mercato*, 23.1.2018, ECLI:EU:C:2018:25 (para. 78); Case C-307/18, *Generics (UK) Ltd and Others v. Competition and Markets Authority*, 30.1.2020, ECLI:EU:C:2020:52 (para. 67).
24. *See* Case C-67/13 P, *CB v. Commission* [2014] EU:C:2014:2204 (para. 53); Case C-179/16, *F. Hoffmann-La Roche and Others, supra* (para. 79).
25. *See*, to that effect, Case C-66/86, *Ahmed Saeed Flugreisen and Others v. Zentrale zur Bekämpfung unlauteren Wettbewerbs e.V.*, 11.4.1989, ECLI:EU:C:1989:140. The ECJ underlined that a given conduct may be categorized as 'abuse of a dominant position' not only where it has the actual or potential effect of restricting competition on the merits by excluding equally efficient competing undertakings from the market(s) concerned, but also where it has been proven to have the actual or potential effect – or even the object – of impeding potentially competing undertakings at an earlier stage, through the placing of obstacles to entry or the use of other blocking measures or other means different from those which govern competition on the merits, from even entering that or those market(s) and, in so doing, preventing the growth of competition therein to the detriment of consumers, by limiting production, product or alternative service development or innovation. *See* Case C-333/21, *European Superleague Company SL, supra* (para. 131); Case C-307/18, *Generics (UK) Ltd and Others, supra* (paras 154-157); Case C-66/86, *Ahmed Saeed Flugreisen and Others v. Zentrale zur Bekämpfung unlauteren Wettbewerbs, supra* (para. 32); Joined cases C-395/96 P, C-396/96 P, *Compagnie Maritime Belge Transports SA and Others v. Commission*, 16.3.2000, ECLI:EU:C:2000:132 (para. 33); Case C-307/18, *Generics (UK) Ltd and Other, supra* (para. 146).
26. *See*, to that effect, Case C-49/07, *MOTOE v. Elliniko Dimosio*, 1.7.2008, ECLI: EU:C:2008:376.

enabling it to deny them entry to the relevant market or to favour its own activity and, also, in so doing, to prevent the growth of competition therein.[27]

Consequently, according to the Court, such a power may be conferred on a given undertaking only on condition that it is subject to restrictions, obligations and review, irrespective of whether that power originates from the grant, by a Member State, of exclusive or special rights placing the undertaking on which it is conferred in a dominant position on the relevant market,[28] or from the autonomous behaviour of an undertaking in a dominant position.

Consequently, these regulatory powers – enabling that undertaking to prevent potentially competing undertakings from accessing that market or related or neighbouring market – must be subject to restrictions, obligations and review that are capable of eliminating the risk of abuse of its dominant position (102 TFEU) and agreements restricting competition (101 TFEU).

For these reasons, while sports governing bodies are in principle allowed to adopt, apply and ensure compliance with rules relating to the organization of the sporting discipline concerned according to the ECJ, there is a need for previously enacted and accessible *transparent, clear and precise substantive criteria,* circumscribing that regulatory power. These criteria must ensure that the power is exercised without discrimination and that sanctions are objective and proportionate. In addition to such substantive criteria, the regulatory power must be subject to transparent and non-discriminatory procedural rules.[29]

According to the ECJ, the ISU's prior authorization rules and eligibility rules – conferring the ISU to authorize, control and set conditions of access to the relevant market and to determine both the degree and conditions of competition – did not contain such substantive criteria and procedural rules that would have circumscribed and controlled the ISU's regulatory power.[30]

Therefore, according to the Court, the ISU rules restricted competition by their object. While the Court left the door open to possible exemption under Article 101(3) TFEU, it did not specifically address the matter, since Article 101(3) TFEU was not the subject of the ISU's appeal.[31]

---

27. *See*, to that effect, Case C-8/88, *Federal Republic of Germany v. Commission*, 12.6.1990, ECLI:EU:C:1990:241 (para. 25); Case C-163/96, *Raso and Others*, 12.2.1998, ECLI:EU:C:1998:54 (paras 28-29); Case C-49/07, *MOTOE v. Elliniko Dimosio, supra* (paras 38, 49, 51 and 52).
28. *See* Case C-49/07, *MOTOE v. Elliniko Dimosio, supra* (paras 50 and 53).
29. Case C-124/21 P, *ISU, supra*, para. 135.
30. *Ibid.*, paras 136-149. The CJEU held that the prior authorization rules and eligibility rules allow the ISU, *inter alia*: (i) to exclude any competing undertaking from the market for organizing skating competitions, (ii) to restrict the creation and marketing of alternative and new competitions, and (iii) to deprive athletes of the opportunity to participate in alternative or new competitions as well as spectators of the opportunity to attend or watch alternative or new competitions. *See also* C-333/21, *European Superleague Company SL, supra* (para. 176).
31. Interestingly, the ECJ argued that the three stages of the so-called Meca-Medina test (i.e., the conduct must pursue a legitimate objective of public interest, the specific conduct must be genuinely necessary to pursue the objective, and the conduct's competition-restricting effects do not eliminate all competition), *see also Case C-1/12, Ordem dos Técnicos Oficiais de Contas v. Autoridade da Concorrência, 28.2.2013, ECLI:EU:C:2013:127* (paras 93-100); Case C-124/21 P,

Similarly, the ECJ found that the FIFA and UEFA rules on prior approval and participation which are, in a general way, not subject to restrictions that are capable of eliminating the risk of abuse of a dominant position and – more specifically, where there is no framework for substantive criteria and detailed procedural rules for ensuring that they are transparent, objective, precise and non-discriminatory – must be held to infringe Article 102 TFEU.

Notwithstanding the above, the ECJ left it to the national court to determine if those rules might be justified by efficiency gains. The Court emphasized that the four conditions for an efficiency defence – (1) the existence of efficiency gains, (2) efficiency gains counteracting the harmful effects, (3) conduct is necessary for achieving the efficiency gains, and (4) no elimination of effective competition – apply both in the context of Article 102 TFEU as well as in the context of Article 101(3) TFEU.[32] While the 'efficiency defence' always remains available, these conditions are difficult to meet, especially the fourth, as effective competition is already at risk due to the undertaking's dominant position as such.[33]

Another recent example of regulation adopted by a sporting association deemed in violation of EU and competition law can be found in the recent judgment by the Court of Justice in Case C-650/22, *FIFA v. BZ*, a preliminary reference brought by the Cour d'Appel de Mons (Belgium) regarding the compatibility of FIFA's 'Regulations on the Status and Transfer of Players' with the free movement of workers and competition law.[34]

The rules in question applied, *inter alia*, in cases where players terminated their employment without 'just cause' before the relevant contract's normal term of expiry. In such cases, the FIFA rules provided that both the player involved and the club wishing to employ him should have been held jointly liable to compensate the club for losing the player. The rules also provided for an additional sporting sanction to the hiring club, consisting of being banned from registering any new players for a given period. Lastly, the rules prohibited the issuance of the required International Transfer Certificate as long as disputes regarding the contract termination would still be in place.

The Court held that the relevant FIFA rules amounted to an unjustified violation of the free movement of professional footballers wishing to develop their career by moving to a club established in another Member State and an infringement of Article

---

ISU, supra (para. 111) only applies to '*by effect*' restrictions of competition. As the ISU's rules were regarded as '*by object*' restrictions of competition, the CJEU did not apply the three-pronged Meca-Medina test.

32. Case C-333/21, *European Superleague Company SL, supra* (paras 204-208).
33. *See* in this regard, T. Lichtenberg, '*International Skating Union, European Super League and Royal Antwerp: The beautiful game and skating before the CJEU*', 8 Jan. 2024, in competitionlawblog.kluwercompetitionlaw.com.
34. Case C-650/22, *FIFA v. BZ*, 4.10.2024, ECLI:EU:C:2024:824. For a national case *see* the Italian Competition Authority decision of 1 Jul. 2024 in Case A562 – *Sanzione alla Figc per abuso di posizione dominante* where the Authority found that the Italian Football Federation (FIGC) put in place a complex exclusionary strategy to reinforce its dominant position in the organization of youth football competitions of a competitive nature and to extend it also to the amateur-football market, in which it competes with a number of sports promotion associations.

101 TFEU.[35] According to the Court of Justice, the FIFA rules entailed a decision of an association of undertakings having their object the restriction, and even prevention, of cross-border competition which could be pursued by all clubs established in the European Union, by unilaterally recruiting players under contract with another club or players about whom it is alleged that the employment contract was terminated without just cause.[36] While also in this case the ECJ left the door open for a possible application of Article 101(3) TFUE by the referring judge, again a justification based on efficiency gains seems extremely difficult.

[B] Media Rights and Ticket Sales Connected with Sporting Activities

Many economic activities connected with sport have been the subject of deliberation in terms of their relationship with competition law.

Above all, the Commission has been involved in examining issues connected with sales of television transmission rights to sporting events. Specifically, the Commission considered the competition law aspects of the centralized sales and negotiation of television rights to matches of the UEFA Champions League,[37] the Bundesliga and the Premier League. The Commission put forward a series of observations and adjustments to the initial sales and negotiating models as initially put forward, and once these were implemented the Commission found that the agreements – while in principle restrictive, constituting joint selling on an exclusive basis, and thus reducing outputs and limiting price competition – contributed to the improvement of production and distribution of the 'products', allowing the creation of a branded product of high quality, to the benefit of the media organizations, the football clubs, and, ultimately, consumers.[38]

Generally, one might say that the Commission considers the sale of collective rights compatible with competition law, under Article 101(3) TFEU, where the

35. The Court was observed that rules of the kind inhibited international transfers as they imposed interested parties to face the critical combination of considerable legal risks, unforeseeable and potentially very high financial risks as well as major sporting risks regarding the player's position. Against this background, the Court still considered that, on a general basis, restrictions on the free movement of professional players could be justified by overriding reasons such as ensuring the regularity of interclub football competitions and maintaining a certain degree of stability in the player rosters of professional football clubs. In this respect, the Court nonetheless considered on a preliminary basis that the contested FIFA rules appeared to go beyond the usual 'proportionality and objective necessity' requisite in relation to the aims pursued by the rules.
36. In that regard, the Court has recognized the essential role of competition among clubs in the football sector on the professional 'workforce' (i.e., trained players); so that any rule restricting that kind of cross-border competition should be considered in the same way as any other harmful no-poach agreement, as ultimately having the effect of immutably fixing the distribution of workers between employers and cloistering the markets.
37. Commission Decision (EU) of 23 Jul. 2003 on COMP/C.2 37.398 – *Joint selling of the commercial rights of the UEFA Champions League*, OJ L 291, 8.11.2003.
38. In Italy as well the competition authority, the AGCM, has abandoned some initial doubts and come out in favour of centralized sales of television rights. *See* AGCM decision of 21 Dec. 2006, No. 16280.

following conditions are satisfied: (i) a transparent, non-discriminatory, sales procedure that is not subject to unreasonable conditions; (ii) a reasonable number of sales 'packages' into which transmission rights are divided; (iii) the need to avoid sales criteria that favour 'dominant' operators; (iv) the grant of rights only for a limited term (generally, not more than three years); and (iv) the ability to offer content through a variety of different media and in a range of ways, including the internet, mobile phones and other devices.

The judgment in the *Murphy* case must surely be considered important. The ECJ gave a very detailed judgment on the broadcast rights negotiated between the rights-holders, and the broadcasters, under agreements that established territorial exclusivity for different EU countries.[39] In terms of the competition law aspects, the Court worked from the premise that the territorial restrictions associated with exclusivity, where intended to partition the markets, must in principle be considered anti-competitive agreements for the purpose of Article 101(1) TFEU. In the Court's view, however, the fact that this segmented the EU into its various national markets was not sufficient to constitute a breach of competition law.[40] There was a breach of competition rules by the exclusivity provisions where the broadcasters were required 'not to supply decoding devices giving access to that right holder's protected subject-matter outside the territory covered by the [...] agreement concerned'.[41] In substance, it appears to be these supplementary obligations - the prohibition upon supplying transmission devices, such as decoders and subscription cards - that bring the exclusivity arrangements closer to a breach, in that they would result in absolute territorial protection of a kind that would mean no competition whatsoever among the broadcasters.

A further aspect that has repeatedly been scrutinized in competition law is the sale and supply of tickets to sporting events. One only has to think of the breaches that the Commission alleged against a series of companies, and FIFA and the Italian Football Federation, regarding an agreement under which a company had worldwide exclusive access to the entrance tickets to stadiums, which it used to put together package tours for the 1990 World Cup. At the time of the 1998 World Cup in France too, the Commission concluded that the French organizing committee had abused its dominant position by imposing commercial terms that were unfair, with ticket purchases requiring an address in France and a booking system that clearly penalized customers outside France. Again, at the time of the 2006 World Cup finals, the Commission was only able to consider the system for the sale of entry tickets

39. Case C-403/08, *Football Association Premier League Ltd & Others v. QC Leisure and Others, Karen Murphy v. Media Protection Services Ltd*, 4.10.2011, ECLI:EU:C:2011:631. The case arose when Karen Murphy, a Portsmouth bar-owner, sought to avoid the costs of Sky's annual subscription fees to show Premier League matches on the premises by buying a Greek decoder and subscription. The Premier League took action against Murphy for breach of copyright, and the case went as far as the ECJ, which was asked to decide upon eighteen separate issues.
40. In doing so, it moved away from the earliest case law, which had doggedly defended the internal market, finding that arrangements that sought to offer absolute geographical protection within individual Member States were restrictive by 'object', and the most blatant restrictions of competition law, without the need to consider their effects.
41. *Ibid.* (para. 146).

compatible with competition rules after FIFA agreed to alter its terms so that persons resident within the EEA but outside the Eurozone could purchase tickets by making a bank transfer in their countries' own currency, without having to bear the substantial costs associated with having to make a cross-border bank transfer denominated in euros.[42]

§16.03 STATE AID IN THE SPORT SECTOR

Public intervention has often an important role in situations that arise within the sport sector.

In particular, the peculiar status of the football market, and its importance throughout Europe not just economically but especially socially, has put central and local government authorities under pressure to find ways to address the financial needs of sports clubs (especially football clubs) that are more often than not unable to cope with their costs. One might say that many sports clubs depend upon financial support from public bodies in order to run their sporting activities.

Public bodies can provide financial support to professional sports clubs in a variety of ways. These may include favourable tax rates, guarantees and loans at low interest rates. Other examples are the opportunity to rent or acquire a sporting facility for a price below the real market value. Public authorities can also grant the undertakings direct subsidies from public funds or make sales, donations or exchanges of land upon terms that a private investor would have difficulty offering.

Until the first years of the new millennium, the Commission showed very little interest in considering such matters under the State aid provisions, with the exception of a few isolated cases. For example, it took a stance in relation to the Italian legislation on financial reporting by professional sports clubs in 2004-2005, which received heavy media coverage at the time. On that occasion, the Commission opened a formal investigation under Article 108(2) TFEU against Italy, in relation to an accounting rule that allowed sports clubs to recognize depreciation of long-term rights in professional players' services on the balance sheet (the so-called *salva calcio* law). The Commission's procedure ended in a decision under Article 7(3) of Regulation No. 659/99 because the measure 'no longer constituted State aid' following the Italian authorities' agreement to modify the measures with a view to eliminating any effect on taxation.[43]

---

42. *See* Commission Press Release IP/05/519 of 2 May 2005.
43. Alberto Santa Maria was leading counsel of the *Lega Nazionale Professionisti* and the Italian Government with regard to its defence of the '*salva-calcio*' law in the formal procedure opened by the Commission. For further details, *see also* the A. Santa Maria, *Lo sport professionistico e la concorrenza*, in *Giurisprudenza Commerciale*, 2004, 945. The Commission also opened an infringement procedure against Italy pursuant to Art. 226 CE (now Art. 258 TFEU) relating to the same matter. In July 2004, the Commission formally requested that Italy amend its '*salva-calcio*' law. Negotiations with the Italian government led to the repeal of the law, by Legislative Decree No. 115 of 30 Jun. 2005, as confirmed by Law No. 168 of 17 Aug. 2005, and the Commission closed both procedures (under Arts 108(2) and 258 TFEU). However, the Italian Government 'saved' a five-year effectiveness of the '*salva-calcio*' law (half of the period set forth by the original text). *See* Commission Press Release IP/05/1271 of 13 Oct. 2005.

Generally, however, notification of aid in sport has in the past been lacking, and so has the Commission's enforcement activity in this sector.

The situation has changed in the last decade when the Commission began pursuing a number of State aid procedures against football clubs pursuant to Article 108(2) TFEU[44] that, as outlined in section [B] below, mainly concerned certain Spanish football clubs.

Moreover, during the COVID-19 pandemic, the Commission approved different measures through which Member States supported sports events and sport-related industries under the State Aid Temporary Framework[45] and Articles 107(2)b, 107(3)b and 107(3)c TFEU.

The following analysis considers three broad categories of aid based on the initiatives the Commission has pursued: (i) the financing of football stadiums and multifunctional arenas; (ii) aid to individual football clubs; and (iii) training aid to professional clubs.

[A] Aid to Sport Infrastructure

The use of public resources for the implementation of infrastructure policies in connection with sport generally and professional football in particular is certainly no new phenomenon. One only has to think of the UK experience[46] and the structural measures that the British government funded under the Taylor Act after the Hillsborough disaster in Sheffield in April 1989.

The reforms that the Taylor Report[47] outlined were accompanied by robust incentives from the State. In March 1990, the then-Chancellor of the Exchequer, John

---

44. These procedures followed a letter of October 2012 from the Commission to all Member States, seeking an overview of the financing of professional football in EU and an assessment of the possible impact of the application of the State aid rules under the TFEU upon such financing. In its letter, the Commission underlined that professional football clubs, regardless of their legal forms, have to be considered 'undertakings' for the purpose of competition law and should receive no exceptional treatment compared to other undertakings as regards financial relationships with the Member States. The Commission's new focus on State aid was triggered in part by the entry into force of the UEFA 'financial fair play' rules, which sought to encourage financial responsibility among the clubs, especially in relation to controlling costs through the application of a 'live-within-your-means' or 'breakeven' rule. While the Commission's State aid rules obviously operated at a different level to UEFA's own rules, the Commission has supported the initiative vigorously, emphasizing that it was fully consistent with the aims and objectives of European Union policy in the field of State aid.
45. Communication from the Commission, Temporary Framework for State aid measures to support the economy in the current COVID-19 outbreak - 2020/C 91 I/01. *See*, among others, Commission Decision (EU) of 19 Aug. 2020 on SA.58208 (2020/N) Italy - *COVID-19: Aid in the form of guarantees on loans and subsidised interest rates managed by the 'Istituto per il Credito Sportivo' as provided by Article 14, Para 1 and 2 of Law Decree of 8 April 2020, no. 23*; Commission Decision (EU) of 4 May 2023 on SA.102405 (2022/N)The Netherlands - *COVID-19: Compensation scheme for organisers of top-level sports competition and events*; Commission Decision (EU) of 22 Jul. 2020 on SA.57614 (2020/N) Czechia - *Compensation scheme for sport organisations, facilities and cancellation of sport events related to COVID-19* (the 'COVID - Sport Programme').
46. Discussed in more detail in the previous version of this book, pp. 295 et seq.
47. The UK government commissioned Taylor LJ, later Baron Taylor of Gosforth, to undertake an inquiry into the causes of the tragedy, and measures that would improve safety within stadiums.

Major, announced a tax cut for football clubs of 2.5%, which effectively released around GBP 100 million over five years for the construction and restructuring of stadiums and other facilities. This tax relief was extended to 2000, and thus it was worth approximately GBP 200 million in total.

Additionally, in October 1990, the Football Trust, a governmental body set up with the aim of improving safety in sports facilities, provided the clubs with another GBP 40 million for infrastructural works over the next five years. Where two or more different clubs shared facilities, the Football Trust offered additional benefits, provided the resources were used to build new stadiums.

In just the first year of the new measures' implementation, the Football Trust received 76 applications for funds, regarding 120 different projects. In 1997, English and Scottish clubs invested around GBP 500 million in programmes for the modernization and restructuring of stadiums and the construction of new facilities, with the Football Trust contributing approximately 30% of that amount.

One of the first opinions given by the Commission on public financing to large sports infrastructure projects were letters sent in the late 1990s to the national authorities of Germany and the United Kingdom. The Commission approved the public financing of the stadiums of Hannover and Wembley on the basis that they would not be used exclusively by a specific undertaking. No 'selective' advantage was therefore implied, according to the Commission, since the stadiums would both be open to various football events and to events other than football matches ('polyvalent' and 'multifunctional' use).[48]

Moreover, the Commission made clear that most infrastructure is local in nature and is unlikely to have an effect on trade between Member States and therefore does not have State aid relevance.[49] Typically, this is the case where the promoted activity is not capable of capturing demand from another Member State.[50] This conclusion was reached, for example, in the case of a local swimming pool in Germany, and cableways in ski resorts with a small number of installations and/or limited accommodation capacity for tourists.[51]

While the Report had its origins in an emergency, the recommendations were structural in nature, with the most significant change being the requirement to have all-seater stadiums.

48. These letters have not been published.

49. *See* Ch. 1.

50. *See* Commission Decision (EU) of 21 Dec. 2000 on State Aid N 258/00, Germany – *Leisure Pool Dorsten*, OJ 2001 C172/16, 16.6.2001 and Commission Press Release IP/00/1509 of 21 Dec. 2000, *On application by Germany, Commission decides that municipal aid for public swimming is not state aid*. The assessment might be different, however, for leisure parks, for example, advertised nationally or internationally. these also the Commission Notice on the notion of State aid as referred to in Art. 107(1) of the Treaty on the Functioning of the European Union, C/2016/2946, OJ C 262, 19.7.2016, para. 197. *See also*, C 10/2003 – Netherlands – *Non-profit harbours for recreational crafts*, OJ L 34, 6.2.2004 (p. 63); Commission Decision (EU) of 29 Apr. 2015 on SA.37963 United Kingdom – *Alleged State aid to Glenmore Lodge*, OJ C 277, 21.8.2015 (p. 3); Commission Decision (EU) of 29 Apr. 2015 on SA.38208 United Kingdom – *Alleged State aid to UK member owned golf clubs*, OJ C 277, 21.8.2015 (p. 4).

51. *See* Commission Communication to the Member States and other interested parties concerning State aid N 376/01 – *Aid scheme for cableways*, OJ 2002 C172/2, 18.7.2002. *See also* Commission Decision (EU) of 7 May 2004 on State Aid N 676/2002 Italy – *Cableways Valle d'Aosta*, OJ 2005 C131/12, 7.5.2004; Commission Decision (EU) of 11 Nov. 2003 on State Aid N 397/2003 Italy –

Moreover, if the beneficiary does not carry on economic activity, no State aid will be involved: as a general proposition, amateur football clubs are not considered to be 'undertakings' and therefore fall outside the scope of Article 107 TFEU.[52]

As a consequence, under certain strict conditions, financial support for stadiums may be considered not to constitute aid and, therefore, fall outside the scope of Article 107(1) TFEU.[53]

In more recent times the approach of the Commission to the financing of infrastructure that could be used for sports events in general and by football clubs in particular has shifted and become more nuanced. Its decisions appear to have been influenced by the judgment of the Court of Justice in the *Leipzing/Halle*[54] case. Therein, the Court found that not only did the operation and management of infrastructure constitute economic activity, but also the construction of infrastructure, which cannot be separated from its later operation. In other words, the economic character of the later use of the infrastructure determines the nature of the construction. Therefore, if the stadium is used for economic purposes, there needs to be an assessment of whether there is State aid to the various entities with roles in the project (e.g., the owner, the operator, and the user).[55]

On the one hand, this approach, by focusing the assessment on whether there is any commercial exploitation of the infrastructure (which in principle could apply to any kind of sports facility) has made the Commission's analysis on selectivity and impact on trade between Member States more cursory, which means an expansion in the scope of application of Article 107(1) TFEU. On the other, this approach has enabled the Commission to make wider use of compatibility testing for aid, under Article 107(3) TFEU.[56] It should be remembered that even if all the cumulative

Cableways Trento 2003, OJ 2004 C34/8; Commission Decision (EU) of 14 Dec. 2004 on State Aid N 476/2004 Italy – *Public contribution to cableways Prada-Costabella*, OJ 2005 C131/14.

52. Commission Decision (EU) of 9 Aug. 2016 on SA.43983 Germany – *BLSV Sportcamp Nordbayern*, 2015. *See* however the position expressed by the Court in Joined Cases C-51/96 and C-191/97, *Deliège*, *supra*.
53. *See also* whereas seventy-four of the Regulation (EU) No. 652/2014 of the Commission of 17 Jun. 2014 declaring certain categories of aid compatible with the internal market in application of Arts 107 and 108 of the Treaty Text with EEA relevance, OJ L 187, 26.6.2014 (the Block Exemption Regulation). 'In the sport sector a number of measures taken by Member States may not constitute State aid because the beneficiary does not carry out an economic activity or because there is no effect on trade between Member States. This could be, under certain circumstances, the case for aid measures which have a purely local character, or which are taken in the field of amateur sport.'
54. Joined Cases T-443/08, T-455/08, *Freistaat Sachsen and Land Sachsen-Anhalt and Mitteldeutsche Flughafen AG and Flughafen Leipzig-Halle GmbH v. Commission*, 24.3.2011, ECLI: EU:T:2011:117.
55. *See* Commission Decision (EU) of 2 May 2013 on SA.33618 – Sweden – *Uppsala Arena*, OJ L 243, 12.9.2013; Commission Decision (EU) of 9 Nov. 2011 on SA.31722 Hungary – *Sport infrastructure development scheme*, Commission Decision 9 Nov. 2001 on SA. 31722 – *Supporting the Hungarian sport sector via tax benefit scheme*, OJ C 364, 14.12.2011 (paras 35 and 73).
56. This is the case of Commission Decision (EU) of 24 May 2017 on SA.46530 – Slovakia – *Construction of Bratislava National Football Stadium*, OJEU C/354/2017 of 20.10.2017, where the aid was granted to the undertaking carrying the project outside of any competitive allocation public mechanism to a specific entity. The Commission briefly mentioned that, aside of the subject owning and managing the facility, the selective criterion importantly regards the

conditions to State aid are met,[57] financing of infrastructure that is also open for the general public may still be found to be compatible with the internal market. The 'open' and multi-purpose nature of a certain infrastructure has been emphasized in several Commission's decisions, when assessing the compatibility of a certain aid measure, in the light of the positive social and economic effects of a certain infrastructural initiative.[58]

Before the entry into force of Commission Regulation (EU) No. 651/2014 of 17 June 2014, there were no horizontal or sectorial guidelines covering this type of aid, and the Commission considered that the assessment of compatibility of the aid with EU State aid rules should be based directly on Article 107(3)(c) TFEU, which states that 'aid to facilitate the development of certain economic activities or of certain economic areas, where such aid does not adversely affect trading conditions to an extent contrary to the common interest' is considered compatible with the internal market.

In particular, in order to assess whether a measure is compatible under Article 107(3)(c) TFEU, the Commission balances the positive and negative effects of the aid. In applying the balancing test, the Commission considers the following:

(1) Is the aid measure aimed at a well-defined objective of common interest, i.e., does the proposed aid address a market failure or other objective?
(2) Is the aid well designed to deliver the objective of common interest? In particular: (i) is State aid an appropriate policy instrument, i.e., are there other, better-placed instruments? (ii) is there an incentive effect, i.e., does the aid change the behaviour of undertakings? (iii) is the aid measure proportional, i.e., could the same change in behaviour be obtained with less aid?
(3) Are the distortions of competition and the effect on trade limited, so that the overall balance is positive?[59]

Such a test leaves the Commission with a wide margin when assessing the overall impact of the measures. Applying its terms, the Commission has authorized State aid for a series of multifunctional stadiums in the form of both individual aid, and aid

multifunctional character of a facility allowing a wide spectrum of users to benefit from it. The assessment testing the compatibility of the aid under Art. 107(3)(c) was indeed primarily based on the common interest objective pursued, being not limited to sporting events and commercial activity.

57. Namely, (i) the measure has to be granted out of State resources; (ii) it has to confer an economic advantage to undertakings; (iii) the advantage is selective and must distort or threaten to distort competition; and (iv) the measure has to affect intra-Community trade. *See* Ch. 1.

58. *See* Commission Decision (EU) of 31 Mar. 2022 on SA.62831 Lithuania – *Individual aid for the development of the multifunctional health, education, culture and business support complex in Vilnius*, OJEU C/387/2022, 7.10.2022; Commission Decision (EU) of 31 Jul. 2017 on SA.47683 (2017/N) Finland – *Tampere Arena*; Commission Decision (EU) of 24 May 2017 on SA.46530 – Slovakia – *Construction of Bratislava National Football Stadium*, OJEU C/354/2017, 20.10.2017; Commission Decision (EU) of 13 Jul. 2023 on SA.58891 – Czechia – *Aid for the construction of a multifunctional hall in Brno*, OJEU C/4507/2024 of 15.7.2024.

59. *See* Commission Decision (EU) of 20 Nov. 2013 on SA.37109 (2013/N) Belgium – *Football stadiums in Flanders*, para. 28.

schemes: in France (stadiums for Euro 2016);[60] Belgium (a football stadium in Flanders);[61] Hungary (tax benefit schemes for infrastructural projects and individual aid);[62] Sweden (the Uppsala Arena);[63] Germany (the Jena Stadium[64] and the Erfurt Stadium[65]); Slovakia (the National Football Stadium);[66] Lithuania (multifunctional complex in Vilnius)[67] and, more recently, Czech Republic (multifunctional hall in Brno)[68]

For example, in a seminal decision of 13 October 2011, the Commission authorized a measure entitled 'Supporting the Hungarian sport sector via tax benefit scheme'. The measures formed part of a broader 'national sport development strategy',[69] but the main focus regarded exemptions and tax subsidies for sports companies, clubs, associations and other undertakings that intended to make investments in building or restructuring sports infrastructure. The aid scheme, renovated through the years and now set to continue until 2029, was originally expected to result in an aggregate tax saving for the affected undertakings of approximately EUR 455 million.[70]

The Commission's favourable assessment was based upon, *inter alia*, the following factors: (i) the measures sought to remedy a clear market failure, given the absence of suitable alternatives to public aid; (ii) the measures' objectives were of common interest, and formed part of a wider project for enhancing Hungarian sport;

---

60. Commission Decision (EU) of 18 Dec. 2013 on SA.35501 France – *Financement de la construction et de la renovation des stades pour l'EURO 2016*.
61. Commission Decision (EU) of 20 Nov. 2013 on SA.37109 (2013/N) – Belgium – *Football stadiums in Flanders*.
62. Commission Decision (EU) of 9 Nov. 2011 on SA.31722 – Hungary – *Supporting the Hungarian sport sector via tax benefit scheme*, OJ C 364, 14.12.2011. The measure has been prolonged twice under Commission Decisions (EU) of 5 May 2017 on SA.46615 Hungary – *Sport support scheme – prolongation*, OJ C 142, and of 16 Feb. 2023 on SA.104802, Hungary – *Prolongation of the Hungarian Sport Support Scheme* (2023-2029).
63. Commission Decision (EU) of 2 May 2013 on SA.33618 Sweden – *Uppsala Arena*, OJ L 243, 12.9.2013.
64. Commission Decision (EU) of 20 Mar. 2013 on SA.35440 – Germany – *Multifunktionsarena der Stadt Jena*, OJEU C/140/201, 18.5.2013.
65. Commission Decision (EU) of 20 Mar. 2013 on SA.35135 – Germany – *Multifunktionsarena der Stadt Erfurt*, OJEU C/140/2013, 18.5.2013.
66. Commission Decision (EU) of 24 May 2017 on SA.46530 – Slovakia – *Construction of Bratislava national football stadium*, OJEU C/354/2017, 20.10.2017.
67. Commission Decision (EU) of 31 Mar. 2022 on SA.62831 Lithuania – *Individual aid for the development of the multifunctional health, education, culture and business support complex in Vilnius*, OJEU C/387/2022, 7.10.2022.
68. Commission Decision (EU) of 13 Jul. 2023 on SA.58891 – Czechia – *Aid for the construction of a multifunctional hall in Brno*, OJEU C/4507/2024 of 15.7.2024.
69. Paragraph 4 of the Commission's decision states, 'The National Sport Strategy involves initiatives concentrating on the supply side (such as renovating and building sport facilities, improve the availability of sport facilities and equipment for local citizens, increase the safety of sport infrastructures for the general public, etc.) and also on the demand side (for instance, by focusing on the training of the new generation, promoting amateur sports and mass sport events, increasing the number of physical education classes in primary and secondary schools, etc.).'
70. The scheme provides for the set-up of a 'Controlling Authority' which will monitor the implementation of the infrastructural investments, and the prices for the use and operation of stadiums, almost all of which are in public ownership. Few of the stadiums would be newly built, the Hungarian government said, and the investments would be directed mostly to modernizing existing facilities.

(iii) the aid was proportionate to the objectives that had been established, and the execution of the investments would be monitored by an independent authority; (iv) the measures' ultimate objective would be to bring the public back into the stadiums; and (v) the facilities would be multifunctional in character.

The Commission also authorized, pursuant to Article 107(3)(c) TFEU, the financing in France for the construction and renovation of nine of the ten stadiums designated as venues for the 2016 UEFA European Championship. The funding involved State measures (most of which were not previously notified to the Commission) totalling approximately EUR 1,052 million, made up of EUR 152 million in grants from the central government (through *Le Centre National pour le Développement du Sport*) and an estimated EUR 900 million from local authorities.

As for the owners of the stadium, eight of them were local authority-owned.[71] In the case of the privately owned Lyon stadium, the Commission decided there were clear objectives of common interest (the project was part of a major regeneration of East Lyon), and despite the presence of a EUR 20 million grant, the Commission appreciated the way the aid was limited, in amount and duration. Also, commitments were obtained from the private owner/operator/user that it would undertake community activities. On that basis, the aid was exempted.

With regard to the future users, the Commission stated that there might be State aid if the rent they had to pay was lower than the rent for the use of comparable infrastructure under normal market conditions.[72] In this respect, the Commission acknowledged that France would set up a system to control the prices paid by the resident clubs, in order to ensure they were used upon market terms. Since however operating conditions and future use, including the rents payable by future users, were not fully defined, the decision was limited to the aid needed for the development of the stadiums.

In the compatibility assessment, the Commission accepted that, in addition to the way in which such works would enhance Euro 2016 as an event, there was a common need for the modernization and enlargement of the stadiums, i.e., the works would not result in the duplication of facilities, and this would not occur without State intervention, i.e., there was a market failure.

The Commission emphasized that while the nine stadiums would principally be used for football, they would also host other events for the public (such as cultural and social events) and thus contribute to cultural diversity, in line with Article 167(4)

71. Even if some of them are not directly managed by public authorities. *See* paras 218-219 of the Decision.
72. *See* para. 249 of the Decision. The Commission has taken a specific approach in order to ensure no State aid is passed on; for example, in *Multifunktionsarena der Stadt Erfurt*, there was no State aid where rent was based on fees paid by nearby, comparable clubs, and set at the high end of the range. A similar benchmarking approach was adopted in the *Football stadiums in Flanders* case. According to the Commission the benchmarking method was 'not sufficiently precise … to guarantee that … prices [would] adequately reflect the cost of use for the stadium'. The approach was, however, important in enabling exemption of the aid: 'a part of the advantage … may be clawed back in the form of higher rents … [T]his pricing mechanism … will serve to limit distortion of competition vis-à-vis privately owned and funded football infrastructures'.

TFEU.[73] In line with its most recent practice, the Commission praised the multifunctional nature of the stadium, not in terms of the measure's selectivity (a requirement for the application of Article 107(1))[74] but, rather, in its assessment of the measure's compatibility under Article 107(3) TFEU.

There was also similar approval from the Commission of Stadiums in Flanders (a scheme for the investment of EUR 8 million in the renovation and construction of stadiums in Flanders and Brussels-Capital Region).[75] The Commission emphasized the 'high social return' of the projects, the multifunctional use of the infrastructures and its character as an 'open stadium'.

As may be seen, the Commission looks favourably upon public measures intended to support the construction or restructuring of sports facilities and stadiums. While unquestionably such measures are ultimately capable of favouring particular sports clubs,[76] the Commission has shown a certain leniency in assessing them under the rules on State aid. Broadly speaking, it would appear that the Commission tends to consider such measures to be compatible with the internal market provided they have a 'social' purpose, the facilities host a variety of events and initiatives and are open to use by third parties, even if that is only a potential use.[77]

Initiatives that give national public support to infrastructure policies for sports facilities will accordingly have to take such considerations into account.[78]

---

73. Article 167(4) TFEU provides, 'The Union shall take cultural aspects into account in its action under other provisions of the Treaties, in particular in order to respect and to promote the diversity of its cultures.'
74. *See* Ch. 1.
75. Aid under the measure consists of a one-time grant of 10% of the investment amount, with a maximum of EUR 2.5 million for the construction of new stadiums, and of EUR 750,000 for renovation projects.
76. That has been the case, for instance, in the recent Commission Decision (EU) of 24 Apr. 2017 on SA.46530 Slovakia – *Construction of Bratislava National Football Stadium*, OJEU C/354/2017, 20.10.2017, where the beneficiary of the aid was, ultimately, NFŠ, a.s. – owned by ŠK Slovan Bratislava futbal a.s., the only first league football club in Bratislava.
77. It should be noted that the UEFA rules on Financial Fair Play also create an incentive (albeit indirectly) to football clubs investing in infrastructural works. Costs related to facilities' construction and restructuring are not included in the calculation used to establish compliance with the breakeven rule, and neither are costs that might be considered 'ancillary' thereto, such as costs linked to 'social activities', financial expenses linked to property construction, tax charges, and some costs related to non-football activities.
78. In Italy, for example, Legislative Decree No. 38 of 28 Feb. 2021 introduced some administrative simplifications for the construction and renovation of stadiums, thus only providing a reference framework for possible interventions, including public ones. To apply for the construction or restructuring of sporting infrastructures, clubs have to submit a feasibility study in the form of a preliminary project and a business plan, to the relevant municipal government. The law provides that in order to ensure the achievement of the overall economic and financial balance of the initiative, as well as in order to ensure adequate levels of bankability and the possible involvement of public and private banking and financial operators, that 'the feasibility document may contemplate the recognition of a price, the issuance of guarantees, support measures by the municipality or other public administrations or entities, the transfer of the surface right or the right of usufruct over them, or the transfer of the surface right or the right of usufruct over other real estate owned by the public administration, as well as the transfer of ownership of the same to the amateur or professional sports association or club that uses the facility. In any case, such measures, which to date do not seem to have been used by the main clubs for the

In this respect, it should be noted that 'aid for sport and multifunctional recreational infrastructures' represents a specific category of block-exempted aid. Under the 2023 Amending Regulation,[79] Article 4, paragraph 1, letter (bb) of the Block Exemption Regulation has been revised in order to raise the relevant thresholds set for the applicability of the block exemption to investment aid in sports and multifunctional infrastructures. The regime applies for: (i) investment aids to sport and multifunctional infrastructures below EUR 33 million, (ii) investment aids provided for projects whose total costs did not exceed EUR 110 million per project, and (iii) operating aid for sport infrastructure below EUR 2.2 million per infrastructure per year.[80]

More particularly, State measures meeting the following conditions are considered compatible without any need for prior notification:[81]

1. Aid for sport and multifunctional recreational infrastructures shall be compatible with the internal market within the meaning of Article 107(3) of the Treaty and shall be exempted from the notification requirement of Article 108(3) of the Treaty, provided that the conditions laid down in this Article and in Chapter I are fulfilled.
2. Sport infrastructure shall not be used exclusively by a single professional sport user. Use of the sport infrastructure by other professional or non-professional sport users shall annually account for at least 20% of time capacity. If the infrastructure is used by several users simultaneously, corresponding fractions of time capacity usage shall be calculated.
3. Multifunctional recreational infrastructure shall consist of recreational facilities with a multi-functional character offering, in particular, cultural and recreational services with the exception of leisure parks and hotel facilities.
4. Access to the sport or multifunctional recreational infrastructures shall be open to several users and be granted on a transparent and non-discriminatory basis. Undertakings which have financed at least 30% of the investment costs of the infrastructure may be granted preferential access under more favourable conditions, provided those conditions are made publicly available.
5. If sport infrastructure is used by professional sport clubs, Member States shall ensure that the pricing conditions for its use are made publicly available.
6. Any concession or other entrustment to a third party to construct, upgrade and/or operate the sport or multifunctional recreational infrastructure shall be assigned on an open, transparent and non-discriminatory basis, having due regard to the applicable procurement rules ....

---

construction of new infrastructures and the renovation of existing ones, will always have to be granted in compliance with State aid legislation'.

79. Regulation (EU) No. 2023/1315 of the Commission of 23 Jun. 2023, OJ L 167, 30.6.2023, amending the Commission's Block Exemption Regulation (EU) No. 651/2014.
80. The aid may take the form of: (a) investment aid, including aid for the construction or upgrade of sport and multifunctional recreational infrastructure; (b) operating aid for sport infrastructure. Investment aid consists of costs in tangible and intangible assets, while operating aid stands for the eligible costs for the provision of services by the infrastructure. Those operating costs include costs such as personnel costs, materials, contracted services, communications, energy, maintenance, rent, administration, etc., but exclude depreciation charges and the costs of financing if these have been covered by investment aid. With respect to operating aid, Art. 55, para. 12 of the Block Exemption Regulation sets the maximum amount of aid at 80% of eligible costs, as long as the operating aid does not exceed EUR 2.2 million.
81. Under Art. 55 of Regulation (EU) No. 651/2014 of the Commission of 23 Jun. 2023, OJ L 167, 30.6.2023, as amended.

[B] Aid to Individual Clubs

The Commission has also opened a number of formal investigation procedures pursuant to Article 108(2) TFEU with regard to (non-notified) public measures granted in favour of individual clubs.[82]

Many football clubs are financially vulnerable, as there is a structural imbalance between income and expenditure. Clubs are facing higher costs for player contracts and for grounds, while the revenues from sponsorship agreements and, especially, television rights have been declining.

Against this background, the Commission investigated a variety of dealings between local government entities in the Netherlands and professional football clubs in the country's first and second division[83] – such as reductions to the rent some clubs pay for stadiums, sales and leasebacks of land, the waiver of certain claims, and other arrangements.

Many Spanish football clubs were also the addressees of negative decisions by the European Commission in 2016, relating to tax treatments and other financings. The decisions were challenged before the EU Courts and gave rise to eight judgments. Out of three decisions by the Commission, two were annulled by the ECJ and only one was confirmed.[84]

For most of those measures, it was the analysis of whether there had been an economic advantage that was crucial, as the public actions were assessed under the market economy operator principle.

In principle, where the Commission has doubts over the compatibility of aid measures, that is assessed in the light of the Guidelines on State aid for rescuing and restructuring firms in difficulty (the 'R&R Guidelines').[85] The Commission has stated the view that so long as professional clubs meet the tests provided therein and qualify

82. For a summary of the many cases of public aid to professional football clubs not scrutinized under the State aid rules, please *see* the previous edition of this book, pp. 294-295.
83. Commission Decision (EU) of 6 Mar. 2013 on SA.33584 Netherlands – *State aid to Dutch football clubs*, OJEU C/116/2013 of 23.4.2013 and later developments in: Commission Decision (EU) of 4 Jul. 2016 on SA.41612 – Netherlands – *Aid to Dutch Football Club MVV*; Commission Decision (EU) of 4 Jul. 2016 on SA.41614 Netherlands – *Aid to Dutch Football Club Den Bosch*, OJEU L/306/2016, 15.11.2016; Commission Decision (EU) of 4 Jul. 2016 on SA.41617 – Netherlands – *Aid to Dutch Football Club NEC*, OJEU L/320/2016, 26.11.2016; Commission Decision (EU) of 4 Jul. 2016 on SA.41613 – Netherlands – *Aid to Dutch Football Club PSV*, OJEU L/282/2016, 19.10.2016.
84. Case T-865/16, *Fútbol Club Barcelona v. Commission*, 26.2.2019, ECLI:EU:T:2019:113, Case T-679/16, *Athletic Club v. Commission*, 26.2.2019, ECLI:EU:T:2019:112, Case T-766/16, *Hércules Club de Fútbol v. Commission*, 20.3.2019, ECLI:EU:T:2019:173, Case T-791/16, *Real Madrid Club de Fútbol v. Commission*, 22.5.2019, ECLI:EU:T:2019:346, Case T-732/16, *Valencia Club de Fútbol v. Commission*, 12.3.2020, ECLI:EU:T:2020:98, Case T-901/16, *Elche Club de Fútbol, SAD v. Commission*, 12.3.2020, ECLI:EU:T:2020:97. Both the *Fútbol Club Barcelona* and *Valencia Club de Fútbol* Court rulings were appealed in front of the Court of Justice (respectively, cases C-362/19 P and C-211/20 P), being decided upon respectively in 2021 and 2022.
85. Communication from the Commission 2014/C 249/01 – Guidelines on State aid for rescuing and restructuring non-financial undertakings in difficulty, replacing the 2004 version and still valid until 2025 after the Amending Communication (c/2023/1212) from the Commission regarding the period of application of the R&R Guidelines.

as undertakings in difficulty, they qualify for rescue and restructuring aid, like undertakings in any other sectors.[86] Interestingly, this view has been contested by an applicant in one of the cases regarding aid to Spanish football clubs, which will be briefly outlined below.[87] In challenging the Commission's decisions on the existence of an incompatible aid, Hercules F.C. argued that due to the peculiarities of sport protected by Article 165 TFEU, communications and notices by the Commission such as the R&R Guidelines should not be applied to the football sector, being the latter '(...) essentially characterised by a greater capacity of firms to raise capital and debt, regardless of their financial situation, and by a greater volatility in their revenue and assets, which are essentially linked to their sporting results'.

Both the General Court and the Court of Justice dismissed this argument and confirmed that the Commission Guidelines, including the R&R and the Notice on Guarantees, were fully applicable to the sports sector.[88]

On merit, said guidelines require there to be compensatory measures, which should be in proportion to the distortive effects of the aid and should work in favour of the competing undertakings (i.e., the other clubs) that did not receive aid.

The Commission has suggested the following as examples of possible compensatory measures: (i) limiting the number of registered players at the club for one or more seasons; (ii) accepting a cap on the ratio of salaries to revenues that is below that in the Financial Fair Play rules; (iii) banning the payment of transfer fees for a certain period; and (iv) offering additional expenditure on 'pro bono' activities, for the benefit of the community and training of amateurs.

This reading by the Commission seems, however, overly simplistic. The football market has a peculiar nature: public demand does not easily switch from one competitor to another. That means it does not readily lend itself to compensatory measures. Additionally, those measures will have to apply within what is a highly regulated activity, with strict disciplinary rules. Having different criteria apply only to a few individual clubs risks undermining the nature of the competition.

As mentioned, Spanish football has found itself the focus of attention, with three separate cases. The first concerned preferential corporate tax treatment for Real Madrid, Atletico Bilbao, Osasuna and Barcelona, which were benefitting from the tax regime afforded to non-profit entities.[89] The Commission ended up stating the incompatibility of the aid with the internal market and required Spain to end the selective

---

86. In particular, the Commission is willing to assess, in the context of the formal procedure pursuant to Art. 108(2) TFEU, whether the aid measures comply with the conditions set out in the Guidelines for restructuring aid.

87. Case T-766/16, *Hércules Club de Fútbol v. Commission, supra* (paras 44 and 56).

88. The Court recalled (Case T-766/16, *Hércules Club de Fútbol v. Commission, supra*, para. 40) that 'in the specific area of State aid, the Commission is bound by the guidelines and notices that it issues, inasmuch as they do not depart from the rules in the Treaty and are accepted by the Member States. In particular, those texts cannot be interpreted in a way which reduces the scope of Articles 107 and 108 TFEU or which contravenes the aims of those articles'.

89. Under Art. 19(1) of Spanish Law 10/1990 on sport, all Spanish professional sports clubs were obliged to convert into public limited sports companies aiming at more responsible financial management. However, an exception was provided for professional sports clubs that had achieved a positive financial balance in the years preceding the adoption of the law. The law in

treatment of the four clubs and recover the aid.[90] After being the decision appealed from the different clubs involved,[91] the General Court dismissed the action brought by *Athletic Club*, but upheld the action brought by *F.C. Barcelona* and annulled the decision. In the General Court's view, in essence, annulment was justified as the Commission did not prove the existence of an advantage procured to the beneficiary of the aid. According to the General Court, the tax regimes for non-profit entities did not invariably lead to a more favourable tax burden for the four football clubs.[92] The CJEU, however, backed the Commission's approach, according to which the advantage in State aid regimes 'must be examined on an ex-ante basis, having regard to the information available at the time the intervention was decided upon'[93] and set aside the judgment of the General Court.[94]

The ECJ argued that in the case of an aid scheme – as opposed to a single aid – the Commission must 'merely [to] study the characteristics of the scheme at issue in order to assess (...) whether the latter gives an advantage to beneficiaries' and that, concerning aid schemes, the analysis of the aid granted in individual cases is relevant only at the stage of recovery of the aid. So that, ultimately, the Commission had rightly assessed in advance the unconditional effects of the aid scheme, as foreseeable at the beginning of a tax year, ignoring those aspects of the aid scheme which 'depend[ed] on the subsequent occurrence of random and variable circumstances'.

The second investigation concerned a State guarantee granted to three clubs in the Valencia area (Valencia, Hercules and Elche). As regards the Valencia football club, aid was granted in the form of a guarantee provided by the Regional Government of Valencia for a bank loan to Fundación Valencia, a non-profit organization aiming to the

question provided that the exempted clubs paid corporate tax for their commercial income at a reduced rate of 25% instead of the general rate of 30%. *See* para. 7 of the Commission Decision (EU) of 18 Dec. 2013 on SA.29769 (2013/C) Spain – *State aid to certain Spanish professional sports clubs*.

90. Commission Decision of 4 Jul. 2016. The total amount to be recovered consisted of the difference between the corporate tax they actually paid and the corporate tax to which they would be subjected, had they had the legal form of a sport limited company, as of the tax year 2000.
91. Case T-865/16, *Fútbol Club Barcelona v. Commission, supra*; Case T-679/16, *Athletic Club v. Commission, supra*.
92. In particular, the General Court held that the Commission: (i) had not sufficiently established the existence of an 'advantage', having not proved whether the lower nominal tax rate could be offset by capping tax deductions at a level less beneficial for non-profit entities than for public limited sports companies (the legal form into which other clubs were obliged to transform); and (ii) failed to request Spain the necessary information in that regard (GC, para. 59). The General Court assessed whether the tax regime for non-profit entities had consistent traits of an advantage for the beneficiaries, considering that the various components of a tax regime for non-profit entities must be evaluated as an indivisible whole. In order to do so, the crux of the matter was found by the General Court with regard to the relationship between the non-profit entities' favourable tax regime as compared to their disadvantages in the treatment of tax deductions and consequently in the reinvestment of extraordinary profits. Indeed, the beneficiaries of the aid could produce evidence of a period whereby their overall tax regime was more disadvantageous because of a less favourable treatment in tax deductions, even more so considering the latter as a significant voice in player transfers.
93. Commission Notice on the notion of State aid as referred to in Art. 107(1) of the Treaty on the Functioning of the European Union (2016/C 262/01), para. 78.
94. Case C-362/19 P, *Commission v. Fútbol Club Barcelona*, 4.3.2021, ECLI:EU:C:2021:169.

promotion of sport, culture and social aspects of the professional club Valencia CF.[95] On a total amount of EUR 75 million that Fundación Valencia needed to acquire 70.6% of the shares in the club, the guarantee covered 100% of the loan including also interest and related costs. The guarantee premium amounted to a mere 0.5% annual return, and as such was deemed insufficient to remunerate the risk carried by the Regional Government, especially in view of the fact that Valencia was a company in difficulty. For this reason, the guarantee was found to produce an undue advantage for the beneficiary. The General Court however annulled[96] the decision of the Commission on the grounds of a lack of proof to the requisite legal standard, as the Commission, departing from the Commission Notice on the treatments of guarantees,[97] did not verify a guarantee premium benchmark on the financial markets before recurring to the reference rate. The General Court's decision was upheld by the Court of Justice in 2022.[98]

The third case regarded the seemingly endless saga of real estate swaps between Madrid's city government and Real Madrid.[99] The Court of Justice annulled the General Court's judgment (and the Commission's decision)[100] on the grounds of a lack of full proof to the requisite standard that the measure at issue conferred an advantage on the applicant.

The judgments of the Spanish cases marked an important step in the enforcement of aid in sport. They focused, albeit with different nuances, on the assessment of the

95. Commission Decision (EU) of 18 Dec. 2013 on SA.36387 – Spain – *Alleged aid in favour of three Valencia football clubs*, OJ C 69, 7.3.2014. In its final Decision of 4 Jul. 2016, the Commission found that the 2009 and 2010 aids in favour of the three clubs were granted in breach of Art. 108(3) TFEU. The Commission also considered that the measures did not meet the conditions required by the 2004 R&R Guidelines and the Commission Notice on the application of State aid to guarantees (2008/C 155/02 – 'Guarantee Notice') and hence deemed the aid as not compatible with the internal market, subsequently imposing the recovery of the aid.
96. Case T-732/16, *Valencia Club de Fútbol v. Commission, supra.*
97. Under para. 3.2, letter d) of the Notice: '(...) risk-carrying should normally be remunerated by an appropriate premium on the guaranteed or counter-guaranteed amount. When the price paid for the guarantee is at least as high as the corresponding guarantee premium benchmark that can be found on the financial markets, the guarantee does not contain aid. If no corresponding guarantee premium benchmark can be found on the financial markets, the total financial cost of the guaranteed loan, including the interest rate of the loan and the guarantee premium, has to be compared to the market price of a similar non-guaranteed loan.

    In both cases, in order to determine the corresponding market price, the characteristics of the guarantee and of the underlying loan should be taken into consideration. This includes the amount and duration of the transaction; the security given by the borrower and other experience affecting the recovery rate evaluation; the probability of default of the borrower due to its financial position, its sector of activity and prospects; as well as other economic conditions'.
98. Case C-211/20 P, *Valencia Club de Fútbol v. Commission*, 10.11.2022, ECLI:EU:C:2022:862.
99. Commission Decision to initiate formal investigations of 18 Dec. 2013 on SA.33754 (2013/C) – Spain – *Real Madrid de Fútbol*, OJ C 69, 7.3.2014.
100. Case T-791/16, *Real Madrid Club de Fútbol v. Commission, supra*, upholding the Commission's Decision of 4 Jul. 2016. The club had paid the city of Madrid EUR 595,000 for a parcel of land in the north of the city in 1998, in the context of a land swap agreement. The sale never took place and, in 2011, Madrid authorities, under a settlement agreement, refunded the club EUR 22.7 million, calculated to be the revised value of the land that couldn't be transferred anymore. The Commission determined the actual value of the land to be 4.3 million, arguing that Madrid's city Council had overpaid by approximately EUR 18.4 million and given the club an unfair advantage over other clubs.

criterion of 'advantage' pursuant to Article 107(1) TFEU and, hence, on perhaps the most controversial requirement of the notion of aid. In such a context, football clubs were considered in the same way as undertakings operating in other business environments, without therefore being recognized as having any specificity such as to justify a derogation or tempering of the rules and principles of State aid. So, the lesson that can be drawn, which is in line with the one mentioned above concerning the application of antitrust rules, is that the peculiarity of sporting discipline, its social and cultural value, do not affect at all (or affect very marginally) the assessment of the existence or non-existence of 'aid', according to the requirements provided for by Article 107(1) TFEU. There is certainly greater flexibility and room for manoeuvre when it comes to assessing the compatibility of aid, pursuant to Article 107(3) TFEU, but even in such case, on closer inspection, this is not specific to sport, given that justifications based on social, cultural and solidarity arguments, which in essence are capable of balancing the negative effects produced by a certain aid measure on competition, can be accepted also in different sectors, albeit in their own specific forms and with their own specific characteristics.

[C] Foreign Subsidy Regulation

From a comparative standpoint, it is worth taking into consideration the strand concerning the Foreign Subsidies Regulation, which came into force in July 2023,[101] with the express purpose of keeping a level playing field in the internal market, targeting subsidies and State aid granted from third countries to undertakings active in EU. The issue is of particular interest given that some football clubs operating in Europe are directly or indirectly controlled by non-EU government bodies or sovereign States.[102]

On the matter, two complaints relating to professional football clubs have been registered. In 2023 La Liga, the Spanish top-tier football league, presented formal complaints against Paris Saint Germain on the grounds of specific allegations of a breach of the FSR, occurring by means of distortive subsidies being awarded to the French team by 'the State of Qatar, which has allowed it to improve its competitive

101. Regulation (EU) 2022/2560 of the European Parliament and of the Council of 14 Dec. 2022 on foreign subsidies distorting the internal market, OJ L 330, 23.12.2022. The objective of the FSR is to close a longstanding regulatory gap by addressing the impact of subsidies coming from countries other than EU and EFTA Member States, whenever they are considered to distort the internal market. Such framework allows the Commission to intervene with a renovated set of powers, i.e., investigative and executive in nature, taking action against businesses which have received financial assistance outside of the scope of EU State aid law and with potential to distort internal competition.

102. That is the case of some of the most relevant and well-known football clubs in Europe: Paris Saint Germain (owned by Qatar Sports Investments (QSI) – itself owned by the Qatar Investment Authority (QIA), the sovereign wealth fund of Qatar) and Manchester City (ultimately owned by Sheikh Mansour, a member of the Abu Dhabi royal family and Vice President of the United Arab Emirates).

position, thus generating significant distortions in several national and EU markets'.[103] La Liga called upon the European Commission to apply the FSR to '*eliminate market distortions*' affecting European football. Under a softer spotlight, also in 2023, second-division Belgian club Royal Excelsior Virton publicly complained against SK Lommel,[104] another second-division Belgian club, having at object the alleged foreign origin of an investment of EUR 16.8 million which SKL had used to obtain its professional licence from the Belgian Football Federation.[105]

Being the European Commission's powers under the Foreign Subsidies Regulation somehow wide – and the case law in its early phase – the actual effects of this very recent implementation of EU laws are yet fully to be discovered. While the FSR certainly fills an (unjustified) gap, the possible application of the FSR raises new questions on the extent to which such new rules and limitations will be applied and is further evidence of the tendency to think of sport as any other business, on the assumption that every unbalance can be remedied on the basis of economic and financial considerations and relegating d the 'field', where competition actually takes place, to a secondary and to some extent 'incidental' role.[106]

[D] Training Aid

Finally, we should refer briefly to the issue of training aid, meaning financial support which is used for the training and education of young sportspeople, not constituting State aid.

In one of its earliest decisions, the Commission stated that financial support to the existing vocational training centres of French professional sports clubs, including football clubs, fell outside the scope of State aid law.[107] These were subsidies granted by local entities (*collectivités territoriales*) to every sports club and association, professional and non-professional alike. Such subsidies may be commercial (similar to sponsorship contributions) or cooperative, with purposes of a general and social interest (referred to as *missions d'intérêt général*).

Local departments may grant public subsidies to any sporting clubs or associations having youth training centres that meet certain organizational criteria laid down

103. The public complaint has been published on La Liga website, at https://www.laliga.com/en-GB/news/laliga-files-complaint-against-psg-with-european-commission.
104. SK Lommel has the same owners as the Premier League's club Manchester City FC, whose control is referrable to entities from the United Arab Emirates and China.
105. The public complaint has been published on the club's website, at https://www.revirton.be/subventions-etrangeres-certains-clubs.
106. On closer inspection, this is precisely the specificity of sport. The possibility of 'nullifying' differences on the playing field, where all 'economic' considerations magically vanish. After all, history is full of stories of 'small' clubs that prevailed thanks to organization and careful management of resources. Take, to mention just two examples, Leicester's astonishing premier league victory in 2016 or Atalanta's UEFA Europa League victory in 2024.
107. Commission Decision (EU) of 25 Apr. 2001 on State Aid N 118/00 France – *Subventions publiques aux clubs sportifs professionnels*, OJ C 333 28.11.2001.

by the governmental bodies, with up to an annual amount of EUR 2.3 million for each beneficiary in a single season.[108]

Such contributions are intended to encourage the development of young athletes in terms of both their sports and educational activities. The sports eligible for such subsidies are football, basketball, rugby and volleyball.

Under its Decision No. 118/00, the Commission found that such a system did not constitute State aid to professional sports clubs, because the measures were similar to schooling and initial training within the meaning set out in Regulation (EC) No. 68/2001 on the application of Articles 107 and 108 of the Treaty to training aid.

It should be noted that any subsidies so awarded could be used in meeting any operating and capital expenses incurred in connection with training centre activities. The operating costs and capital expenditure for a training centre may include, but are not limited to, compensation to employed staff and the costs of constructing and modernizing sports centres.

One may wonder if the new approach the Commission has recently taken on State aid to professional football clubs, discussed above, will be likely to affect the Commission's assessment of this kind of aid. While such measures may individually be exempted within the meaning of Article 107(3),[109] it can be argued that such subsidies have enabled some of the most important French professional football clubs (who enjoy economic benefits from their local authorities, as local clubs for more minor sports) to gain a competitive advantage over other European clubs.[110]

It should be added that in the *Olympique Lyonnais* case,[111] the ECJ found that the rules of the Treaty did not preclude a scheme which guaranteed compensation to the club which provided the training if, at the end of the training period, a young player signed a professional contract with a club in another Member State.[112] On the one hand, the public subsidies described above encourage French professional clubs to expand training for young players, contributing to the number and quality of the individuals trained in such centres. On the other, in *Olympique Lyonnais*, the ECJ confirmed the lawfulness of payments by third parties intended to compensate the clubs for expenses incurred in providing such training. In order to avoid the risk of overcompensation, the effects of such measures in combination (which are potentially cumulative) will require careful evaluation based on the European rules, given also the

108. This limit was imposed in Decree No. 2001/828 of 4 Sep. 2001 and transposed into Art. R113-1 of the *Code du Sport*. Law No. 2012-158 of 1 Feb. 2012 – Art. 10, amended the relevant provisions of the *Code du Sport*, and provided that the upper limit of the subsidies would be set out in a Decree by the French Council of State.
109. The new Block Exemption Regulation provides that the Regulation does not apply to aid which exceeds a threshold, for training aid, of EUR 2.2 million per training project.
110. *See* in this regard, the observations of A. Santa Maria in the previous edition of this book.
111. Case C-325/08, *Olympique Lyonnais SASP, supra*.
112. It must be noted that the case concerned the interpretation of the rules on the freedom of movement and not State aid law.

Commission's newly aggressive approach to questions of State aid to professional football clubs in particular.[113]

113. In this respect, it is interesting to note that in its judgment in *Olympique Lyonnais SASP, supra* the ECJ places weight upon the requirement that the measure be *proportional*. In other words, only compensation for *training costs actually incurred* may be considered justified under the European rules. Similarly, in its Decision No. 118/00 giving 'green light' to training aid, the Commission alluded to the risk of overcompensation and cross-subsidization ('spillover') in favour of the economic activities of professional clubs, requesting that the French authorities closely monitor the subsidies' allocation.

CHAPTER 17
Transport

Filippo Ghersini[*] & *Martino Basilisco*

§17.01 PRELIMINARY REMARKS

Transport, moving goods and persons from one place to the other, has always – throughout history – been quintessential to any economic system; this holds particularly true in a globalized world, where goods are often produced far away from their end market and where people have connections with the farthest corners of the globe.

A series of factors have – historically – resulted in governments playing a major role in the development and in the management of the transport sector: politically, the necessity of ensuring to citizens the ability to move from one place to the other and the strategic importance of transport networks; from an economic perspective, the possibility to transfer goods and people as instrumental to growth and development and the heavy financial burden of building a transport infrastructure.

The relevance of the transport sector, also as an enabler and facilitator to other business areas, has been apparent in recent years as transport networks and routes have been affected by disruptions – firstly during the COVID-19 pandemic, then as a result of the closure of a vital transit point as the Suez Canal, and then obviously due to the consequences of the Russian aggression of Ukraine.

This relevance has been reflected in the approach of Governments to the sector, which has alternatively been providing for direct intervention, or – more recently – seeking to discipline the transport sector and the relationship between its players through regulatory instruments. At the inception of the process of European unification, transport systems – be it by rail, air, or waterway – in virtually all Member States were owned and operated by State entities. Over the years, things gradually changed,

* His contribution to this book is in an entirely personal capacity: the views expressed therein are entirely his own and do not reflect the views of the Ministry of Foreign Affairs and International Cooperation or of the Italian Government.

and free competition started gaining a foothold in the transport sector: markets were gradually liberalized – often at the urge of European regulators,[1] and former public operators were privatized as private undertakings ventured into the arena.

At the same time, the inherently cross-border character of transports has made them a topic in European legal scholarship and practice. A significant part of this debate arises from the recurrent temptation of States to promote nationally oriented policies with regard to the provision of transportation services – policies which are often liable for conflicting with the European regulation on state aid.

Finally, the most recent developments in EU policy have naturally affected the transport sector: the consequences of the COVID-19 pandemic, in particular on the aviation sector, but to the extensive public investment programs that were subsequently launched at the EU and national levels, as well as to green transition policies – also involving State aid rules – especially in a sector with such a significant environmental footprint as transport.

First, during the COVID-19 outbreak, the transport sector was among those directly affected by the measures implemented by States to contrast the pandemic, such as travel freezes or limits on the capacity of means of transport. In this sense, the Commission acknowledged the possibility of invoking Article 107(2)(b) TFEU as a legal basis for the granting of aid to compensate undertakings for the damage suffered as a direct effect of restrictive measures.[2] In addition, extensive aid measures to remedy the damage resulting from the more general negative economic consequences caused by the COVID-19 outbreak, also in the transport sector, were put in place under the Temporary Framework, in view of the different legal basis of Article 107(3)(b) TFEU.[3]

Second, as Europe and its Member States worked to recover from the pandemic, the transport sector was involved in the investment policies launched in the framework of NextGenerationEU and of Member States' Recovery and Resilience Plans. In this context, in order to facilitate the notification process by Member States of investments qualifying as aid, the Commission published templates dedicated to each sector.[4] These include:

(i) electric recharging stations and hydrogen stations for road vehicles;
(ii) incentives for the acquisition of zero- and low-emission road vehicles;

1. The term *liberalization* – and its enforcement by the Commission – is held to refer primarily to a joint reading of the provisions of *Art. 3* TFEU – which states that the 'Union shall have exclusive competence in [...] the establishing of the competition rules necessary for the functioning of the internal market' – and of Art. 106 TFEU, which entrusts the Commission with a specific surveillance duty 'in the case of public undertakings and undertakings to which Member States grant special or exclusive rights'. A landmark decision on the enforcement of liberalization by European authorities has been, *inter alia*, the Commission Decision 94/114/EC of 21 Dec. 1993, *Refusal to grant access to facilities in the port of Rødby*, published in OJ L 55 of 26 Feb. 1994.
2. Communication from the Commission, *Temporary Framework for State aid measures to support the economy in the current COVID-19 outbreak*, 2020/C 91 I/01, C/2020/1863, OJ C 91I, 20.3.2020, pp. 1-9, para. 15.
3. For a more extensive discussion on the Temporary Framework and the different legal basis used, *see* Ch. 2.
4. Commission, *Recovery and resilience facility (RRF) guiding templates*, updated on 4.4.2023. https://competition-policy.ec.europa.eu/state-aid/legislation/rrf-guiding-templates_en.

(iii) other low-emission transport modes – rail and inland waterway (rail infrastructure, transhipment terminals, rail maintenance workshops, acquisition/retrofitting of rail rolling stock and acquisition/retrofitting of inland waterway fleets) and short-sea shipping (aid for the launching of short-sea shipping services).

Finally, but not less importantly, the Commission published in 2022 the new Guidelines on State aid for climate, environmental protection and energy,[5] as part of a wide-ranging program of reforms in favour of the green transition initiated within the EU, with the aim of providing more detail on the process of assessing the compatibility of environmental aid. This instrument also applies to aid for green mobility, specifying the conditions for compatibility of aid for certain investments to reduce or avoid emissions in the road, rail, waterborne, and maritime transport sectors.

In particular, the Guidelines do not apply to aid for investments in light-duty and heavy-duty road vehicles using gas (i.e., LNG, CNG, and biogas), and in the relevant gas refuelling infrastructure, except for LNG infrastructure exclusively for the refuelling of heavy-duty road vehicles, but apply to aid for the acquisition and leasing of clean vehicles (used for air, road, rail, inland waterway, and maritime transport) and clean mobile service equipment and for the retrofitting of vehicles and mobile service equipment, as well as to aid for the deployment of recharging or refuelling infrastructure for clean vehicles.

In addition, several Important Projects of Common European Interest ('IPCEI') approved by the Commission in recent years have as their object the development of new technology, such as batteries,[6] hydrogen,[7] and infrastructures for the transport sector.[8]

This chapter will attempt to provide an outline of the relationship between State aid policy in the EU and the transport sector, also in light of these recent new developments. On account of their different characters, the widely accepted subdivision of transport into inland transport, air transport, and maritime transport will be

5. Communication from the Commission – *Guidelines on State aid for climate, environmental protection and energy*, 2022, C/2022/481, OJ C 80, 18.2.2022, pp. 1-89.
6. Commission, press release, *State aid: Commission approves €3.2 billion public support by seven Member States for a pan-European research and innovation project in all segments of the battery value chain* (9 Dec. 2019); Commission, press release, *State aid: Commission approves €2.9 billion public support by twelve Member States for a second pan-European research and innovation project along the entire battery value chain* (26 Jan. 2021).
7. Commission, press release, *State Aid: Commission approves up to €5.4 billion of public support by fifteen Member States for an Important Project of Common European Interest in the hydrogen technology value chain* (15 Jul. 2022); Commission, press release, *State Aid: Commission approves up to €5.2 billion of public support by thirteen Member States for the second Important Project of Common European Interest in the hydrogen value chain* (21 Sep. 2022); Commission, press release, *Commission approves up to €6.9 billion of State aid by seven Member States for the third Important Project of Common European Interest in the hydrogen value chain* (15 Feb. 2024); Commission, press release, *Commission approves up to €1.4 billion of State aid by seven Member States for the fourth Important Project of Common European Interest in the hydrogen value chain* (28 May 2024).
8. Commission, press release, *State aid: Commission approves Danish public financing of Fehmarn Belt fixed rail-road link* (20 Mar. 2020).

maintained.[9] In particular, *inland transport* is held to include rail transport, road transport and transport on inland waterways – in accordance with Article 100(1) TFEU. A separate section will be devoted to intermodal transport, i.e., the transport that takes place employing different means.

§17.02 INLAND TRANSPORT

Inland transport is – unlike its air and maritime counterparts – subject to specific provisions on State aid, set forth in Articles 93 and 96 TFEU.[10,11] The provisions above apply alongside the general rules on State aid contained in Articles 107 and 108 TFEU, without constituting a substitution to or an exemption from them.[12]

In order to facilitate the application of the above-mentioned Treaties provisions in cases where distortion to competition is limited to a minimum, Council Regulation (EU) 2022/2586 ('Transport Enabling Regulation') enables the Commission to declare by means of regulations that aid for the coordination of transport or reimbursement for the discharge of certain obligations inherent in the concept of public service as referred to in Article 93 of the Treaty is compatible with the internal market, without the need of a formal notification to the Commission.[13]

Specific provisions have also been provided by Commission Regulation (EU) 2023/1315,[14] which amended the GBER by introducing, *inter alia*, detailed rules on exemptions for investment aid for recharging or refuelling infrastructure with electricity or hydrogen for vehicles, mobile terminal equipment or mobile ground handling

9. The term 'maritime transport' does not in this context encompass shipborne transport on inland waterways.
10. Article 93 states that: 'Aids shall be compatible with the Treaties if they meet the needs of coordination of transport or if they represent reimbursement for the discharge of certain obligations inherent in the concept of a public service.'
11. Article 96 states that: '1. The imposition by a Member State, in respect of transport operations carried out within the Union, of rates and conditions involving any element of support or protection in the interest of one or more particular undertakings or industries shall be prohibited, unless authorised by the Commission. 2. The Commission shall, acting on its own initiative or on application by a Member State, examine the rates and conditions referred to in paragraph 1, taking account in particular of the requirements of an appropriate regional economic policy, the needs of underdeveloped areas and the problems of areas seriously affected by political circumstances on the one hand, and of the effects of such rates and conditions on competition between the different modes of transport on the other. After consulting each Member State concerned, the Commission shall take the necessary decisions 3. The prohibition provided for in paragraph 1 shall not apply to tariffs fixed to meet competition'.
12. *See* Joined Cases C-209/84, C-210/84, C-211/84, C-212/84 and 213/84, *Ministère public v. Lucas Asjes and Others* [1986] ECR 1425 (paras 41-42).
13. State aid representing reimbursement for the discharge of public service obligations in relation to public passenger transport services (including public passenger transport by inland waterways and national sea waters) is not covered by Transport Enabling Regulation, as it already falls within the scope of Regulation (EC) No. 1370/2007.
14. Commission Regulation (EU) 2023/1315 of 23 Jun. 2023 amending Regulation (EU) No. 651/2014 declaring certain categories of aid compatible with the internal market in application of Arts 107 and 108 of the Treaty and Regulation (EU) 2022/2473 declaring certain categories of aid to undertakings active in the production, processing and marketing of fishery and aquaculture products compatible with the internal market in application of Arts 107 and 108 of the Treaty.

equipment (excluding recharging and refuelling infrastructure in ports), as well as investment aid for the acquisition of clean vehicles (powered at least partially by electricity or by hydrogen) or zero-emission vehicles and for the retrofitting of vehicles for road, railway, inland waterway and maritime transport.[15]

[A] Road Transport

Road transport is less resource-intensive and offers less space for economies of scale, as compared to other forms of transport. Accordingly, the sector has always been largely populated by private undertakings, from larger companies to a myriad of individual owner-operators – this holds true, in general, both for freight and for passengers.[16] These characteristics have influenced the way States intervene (and resort to aid) in this field, and arguably contribute to explaining that no specific regulation or guidance applicable to it has been approved to date.

The Commission has however recently launched the preliminary process, starting from a call for evidence that took place between March and April 2024, aimed at formulating a proposal for a new Transport Block Exemption Regulation ('TBER').[17] The TBER is to apply to least distortive forms of aid, facilitating a transition towards more sustainable land transport and it will exempt Member States from notification.

Roads are normally open to everyone, (i.e., to the generality of potential users) and, accordingly, are not as a rule seen as a part of an economic activity: it follows that they normally fall outside of the area of application of State aid rules.[18]

A partial exception to this is provided by toll roads, which are typically seen as an economic activity falling within this area of application.[19] Frequently, the case is that of motorways whose management is outsourced by the State to private undertakings. Cases where the construction and operation of the road are tendered out together are not, on the other hand, normally considered within the scope of the State aid regime. This leads in turn to the broader question of the applicability of State aid provisions to public (project) financing of infrastructure. An interesting case on this has recently

15. *See* Arts 36a and 36b of Regulation (EU) No. 651/2014.
16. Freight transport on roads has, in particular, been liberalized in the 1990s: cross-border transit in 1993 (Regulation EEC/881/92 on access to the market in the carriage of goods by road within the Community to or from the territory of a Member State or passing across the territory of one or more Member States, published in [1992] OJ L95/1), and domestic transport in 1998 (Regulation EEC/3118/93 laying down the conditions under which non-resident carriers may operate national road haulage services within a Member State, published in [1993] OJ L279/1). Both regulations have been amalgamated into Regulation EC/1072/2009 on common rules for access to the international road haulage market, published in [2009] OJ L300/72.
17. Commission, Annex to the Communication from the Commission, *Approval of the content of a draft for a Commission Regulation declaring certain categories of aid in the rail, inland waterways and multimodal transport sector compatible with the internal market in application of Articles 93, 107 and 108 of the Treaty*, Brussels, 18.6.2024, C(2024) 3946 final.
18. *See, inter alia*, Commission Decision of 9 Jun. 2010 in Case N 640/2008, *Transport infrastructure in Saxony*.
19. *See* Commission Decisions in Case N 134/2007, *Greece – Thessaloniki Submerged Tunnel*, and in Case N 151/2007 – *Poland – Construction and Operation of the A1 Motorway – Gdansk to Torun section*.

been decided by the Court of Justice:[20] the Court has, *inter alia*, looked into whether compensation granted by the State to the concession holder for alleged losses of revenue could amount to State aid – the Commission had argued that the compensation granted in the case at hand was excessive and in fact concealed a transfer of State resources. This possibility had also been investigated by the Court in the earlier *Aiscat* case.[21]

A different issue is posed by roads that are restricted to specific users or classes of users. Preferential or discriminatory access to these roads (or sections thereof) could be seen as constituting a form of State aid. In a pre-Brexit case, the Court has held that the ban on private hire vehicles (essentially a form of on-call taxi) running on bus lanes – something that livery taxis (i.e., black cabs) are able to do – does not constitute State aid granted to the latter.[22]

State aid to road transport may, in some instances, be deemed to be instrumental to general interest purposes. This can take place in connection with environmental objectives, as vehicular traffic and the resulting pollution have long been on governmental agendas at various levels as an issue to tackle. As much as the general orientation of EU policies – and of domestic policies alike – is to encourage a shift away from road transport, measures directed at decreasing its environmental impact have been cleared by the Commission as compatible with State aid.

This has become particularly relevant in the wake of the 'Green transition', as more and more Member States have sought to encourage a switch to more sustainable forms of transport – particularly, electric (or hybrid) vehicles – often through transfer of State resources (perhaps in keeping with a more general trend) and engendering a number of industrial, political, and legal consequences. Measures undertaken by States to this end straddle between the transport sector per se and the more purely industrial sector, and have also fallen within the catchment areas of specific aid regimes: examples include the 2022 Guidelines on State aid climate, environmental protection, and energy (CEEAG, dealt with elsewhere in this book),[23] which have been used to consider aid measures relating to charging stations for electric vehicles;[24] and the RDI

20. Case C-933/19, *Autostrada Wielkopolska S.A. v. European Commission and Republic of Poland*, 11.11.2021, ECLI:EU:C:2021:905.
21. *See* to this effect case T-182/10, *Aiscat v. Commission*, 15.1.2013, ECLI:EU:T:2013:9, paras 102 et seq.
22. Case C-518/13, *The Queen on application of Eventech Ltd v. Parking Adjudicator*, 14.1.2015, ECLI:EU:C:2015:9. The decision is a follow up to the previous England and Wales High Court case *Eventech Ltd (R on the application of) v. Parking Adjudicator* [2012] EWHC 1903 (Admin). Livery taxis (so-called black cabs) operating in London are able to run on bus lanes, thereby arguably saving time and providing a more competitive service to users; PHVs, their competitors on the on-call market, are on the other hand not permitted to do so. The Court does however not go into particular detail in motivating its decision on the point of selectivity, and accordingly the appeal judgment, which is currently pending, may witness a potential change of orientation in the decision.
23. *See* Ch. 15.
24. Cf., for instance, the EUR 1.8 billion German scheme for 'high power charging infastructures' for electric vehicles (the so-called Deutschlandnetz), approved by the Commission in 2022: *see* Commission decision of 14 Dec. 2022 in Case no. SA.104749, *Aid scheme for high power charging infrastructure in Germany*.

Framework, which has been employed to approve development of batteries for electric vehicles.[25]

[B] Rail Transport

Rail transport is particularly State aid intensive, so to speak: the construction and operation of railways are financially burdensome, and rail lines often rely – to different degrees – on public investment and funding to survive. Prior to the wake of liberalization of the 1990s, rail networks were mostly owned and operated by public entities across Member States: even today, the vestiges of former State railways and of large, national operators endure throughout Europe.

Railways are widely considered, in economic terms, a natural monopoly;[26] in broader competition law terms, this implies that they are perhaps the foremost example of the essential facility doctrine.[27] It follows that EU regulations mandate that rail infrastructure be open to all users in a fair and non-discriminatory manner, and that access be charged at rates in accordance with applicable provisions.[28] In State aid terms, the implication of this regime is that the construction of rail infrastructure by Member State governments does not amount to State aid as it is not an economic activity.[29] This is however not necessarily the case as circumstances vary, such as when the infrastructure is built by private undertakings,[30] or when it is not strictly a rail infrastructure.[31]

The rail transport sector was liberalized in a process that had begun as early as 1991,[32] which was completed in 2007,[33] and fully operational effective as of 1 January

25. The reference is to the 41.5 billion French scheme for the ProLogium project: *see* the 2023 Commission Decision of 3 Aug. 2023 in Case no. SA.106740, *Aid to ProLogium for the project 'Prometheus'*.
26. It is generally not economically sensible for a potential entrant into the market to build its own competing railroad infrastructure.
27. This principle was firstly tackled by the ECJ in Joined Cases C-6/73 and C-7/73, *Istituto Chemioterapico Italiano S.p.A. and Commercial Solvents Corp. v. Commission*, 6.3.1974, ECLI: EU:C:1974:18, and then affirmed in the landmark *Bronner* judgment; Case C-7/97, *Oscar Bronner GmbH & Co. KG v. Mediaprint Zeitungs – un Zeitschriftenverlag GmbH & Co. KG*, 26 Nov. 1998, ECLI:EU:C:1998:569.
28. Directive 2012/34/EU of the European Parliament and of the Council of 21 Nov. 2012 establishing a single European railway area (recast), OJ L 343, 14.12.2012, pp. 32-77.
29. *See* the Rail Guidelines at para. 4.
30. Commission Decision of 7 Jun. 2006 in case N 478/2004, *State guarantee for capital borrowings by Coràs Iompair Eirann (CIÉ) for infrastructure investment.*
31. Such as connections to other type of transport facilities. *See* Decision of the Commission of 20 Dec. 2011 in Case SA.33434, *Chantier multimodal sur le Grand Port maritime du Havre.*
32. Council Directive 91/440/EEC of 29 Jul. 1991 on the development of the Community's railways, OJ L 237, 24.8.1991, pp. 25-28.
33. Full liberalization was brought about by the so-called *Third Railway Package*, composed of four pieces of legislation: (i) Directive 2007/58/EC of the European Parliament and of the Council of 23 Oct. 2007 amending Council Directive 91/440/EEC on the development of the Community's railways and Directive 2001/14/EC on the allocation of railway infrastructure capacity and the levying of charges for the use of railway infrastructure; (ii) Directive 2007/59/EC of the European Parliament and of the Council of 23 Oct. 2007 on the certification of train drivers operating locomotives and trains on the railway system in the Community; (iii) Regulation (EC)

2010, and in 2012, a single European railway area was formally established, by means of Directive 2012/34/EU. Rail transport is governed, in addition to the norms of general application,[34] by specific provisions in the Treaty,[35] as well as by Regulation 1370/2007 –[36] which was amended in 2016 to address the opening of the market for domestic rail transport of passengers.[37] With the so-called Fourth Railway Package, the much-anticipated Regulation 2016/2337 has finally replaced the ageing Regulation 1192/69.[38] More recently, in 2023, the Commission has sought to facilitate rail interoperability across Member States, in the perspective of improving the competitiveness of rail transport, publishing, *inter alia*, the Technical Specifications for Interoperability.[39]

Passenger and freight rail transport are to an extent regulated separately, as passenger rail lines are often the object of some form of public service obligation.[40] The extent of measures granted for the execution of public service obligations is assessed by employing the *Altmark* test:[41] if the test has a positive outcome, the aid measure will not need to undergo the compatibility test pursuant to Regulation 1370/2007.[42] This latter Regulation does, on the other hand, set forth requirements – inspired by transparency and competitiveness principles – as concerns the procedures to be followed to award public services contracts,[43] and as concerns the content of these public services contracts.[44]

The Rail Guidelines mandate two specific cases of restructuring and rescue aid to the rail sector – the Rescue and Restructuring Guidelines apply residually to other cases:

1370/2007 of the European Parliament and of the Council of 23 Oct. 2007 on public passenger transport services by rail and by road and repealing Council Regulations (EEC) Nos 1191/69 and 1107/70; and (iv) Regulation (EC) 1371/2007 of the European Parliament and of the Council of 23 Oct. 2007 on rail passengers' rights and obligations.

34. Set forth in Arts 106, 107, and 108 TFEU.
35. Articles 93 and 96 TFEU, which in fact apply to inland transport in general.
36. Regulation (EC) 1370/2007 of the European Parliament and of the Council of 23 Oct. 2007 on public passenger transport services by rail and by road and repealing Council Regulations (EEC) Nos 1191/69 and 1107/70.
37. Regulation (EU) 2016/2338 of the European Parliament and of the Council of 14 Dec. 2016 amending Regulation (EC) No. 1370/2007 concerning the opening of the market for domestic passenger transport services by rail.
38. Regulation (EU) 2016/2337 of the European Parliament and of the Council of 14 Dec. 2016 repealing Regulation (EEC) No. 1192/69 of the Council of 26 Jun. 1969 on common rules for the normalization of the accounts of railway undertakings.
39. Document L:2023:222:TOC, published in Official Journal of the European Union, L 222, 8 Sep. 2023.
40. With the exclusion of certain fringe rail services, such as historic or tourist routes. *See* Art. 1 of Regulation 1370/2007.
41. Case C-280/00, *Altmark Trans GmbH and Regierungspräsidium Magdeburg v. Nahverkehrsgesellschaft Altmark GmbH, and Oberbundesanwalt beim Bundesverwaltungsgericht*, 24.7.2003, ECLI:EU:C:2003:415.
42. Directives 2004/17/EC and 2004/18/EC are not applicable to rail transport, pursuant to Art. 5 of Regulation 1370/2007.
43. Article 5, Regulation 1370/2007.
44. Article 4, Regulation 1370/2007.

(i) *Debt Cancellation.* Railway undertakings frequently find themselves in situations of heavy indebtedness. To address this issue, the EU directs Member States to establish mechanisms to reduce such indebtedness to levels '*which do not impede sound financial management*'.[45]

(ii) *Restructuring of the rail freight sector.* The Commission is bent on encouraging rail freight transit; this notwithstanding, in many Member States, freight rail operations take place at a financial loss. To overcome this problem, the Rail Guidelines provide for a specific exception allowing public funds to be employed to restructure freight divisions of rail enterprises,[46] with the eventual aim of allowing them to be financially viable and to compete on the market – it is required that freight divisions be legally separated from other railway operations.

Public financing of the upgrade and update of rolling stock is generally seen with favour by the Commission,[47] insofar as it allows for greater environmental sustainability,[48] or for better use of rail infrastructure, or else it contributes to regional development.[49]

Rail Guidelines are currently undergoing a review process by the Commission, which is expected to publish soon a new version, along with the TBER. The main purpose of the review is to take into account the main regulatory and market developments, such as the liberalization of the rail markets, as well as to ensure coordination with the objectives of the EU Green Deal and the Sustainable and Smart Mobility Strategy.

Among the main issues identified by the Commission with respect to the Rail Guidelines, there are: need to allow the market entry and expansion of new market players, as well as to ensure the modernization of fleets and the standardization and interoperability of the networks; the risk of cross-subsidization between commercial activities and public service obligations due to the limited transparency of financial flows within vertically integrated rail companies; the high level of indebtedness of railway undertakings, which impedes the application of the Rescue and Restructuring

45. *See* Art. 9 of Directive 2012/34/EU, establishing a single European railway area, published in [2012] OJ L 343/32. Then again, the criteria to assess this aid are, in general, those set out in the Rescue and Restructuring Guidelines.
46. Decision of the Commission of 11 Sep. 2009 in Case SA.31250, *BDZ*. *See also* Decision of the Commission of 28 Nov. 2007 in Case NN 47/2007, *Metronet rescue aid.*
47. Rolling stock means the vehicles – carriages and locomotives – that compose trains and that, in general, run on railways.
48. *See* Arts 18(2) and 19 of the GBER. The percentage of permissible aid grows in inverse proportion with the size of the undertaking involved: 35% for larger enterprises, 45% for medium enterprises, and 55% for smaller enterprises.
49. This is subject to certain conditions and, notably, only applies to initial investment for suburban or regional passenger services. It can also apply to replacement stock for outermost regions or in case the existing stock is particularly old (more than fifteen years). *See* paras 34, 35, and 36 of the Rail Guidelines. As for cases, *see* Decision of the Commission of 11 Sep. 2009 in Case SA.31250, *BDZ*, and Decision of the Commission of 22 Jan. 2014 in Case SA.37673, *Renewal of rolling stock for PKP IC to serve the interregional line Warszawa – Szczecin.*

Guidelines; the limited scope of the Block Exemption Regulation 1370/2007, especially in the freight segment.

Cable cars and similar infrastructure have a degree of commonality with rail transport.[50] On the other hand, however, their construction and operation are significantly more likely to result in restrictions of competition under Article 107(1), as the infrastructure is inherently prone to be managed by a sole operator and to target specific classes of users. Cable cars are, on the other hand, often unlikely to result in distortions to trade between Member States, as their market is often restricted to a geographically limited range of users.[51] In some cases, however, their construction may result in benefits to general interest.[52] As a side note, potential cable car operations fulfilling public service obligations would not fall under Regulation 1370/2007.[53]

[C] Inland Waterways

Inland waterways represent an important means of transportation in certain European regions and have recently been seen favourably by transport policies at the EU and national levels as a sustainable alternative to road transport. Accordingly, aid schemes to this sector have often been cleared on environmental grounds.[54] All the same, their role remains quantitatively limited as compared to other forms of transport: this, combined with the fact that riverine transport is often considered in the wider context of intermodality, has resulted in few State aid cases involving inland waterways being considered by the Commission.

§17.03 AIR TRANSPORT

[A] Historical Evolution and Applicable Provisions

In the last decades, the airline landscape, previously populated by state-owned national carriers, has undergone dramatic changes: the Commission had, in 1984, published its first guidelines on civil aviation, advocating liberalization in the sector.

The 1990s were a decade of declining revenues for flag carriers, as a number of privately owned companies were able to offer unprecedentedly low prices to passengers, quickly gaining large market shares. The first reaction of many Member States

50. Such as lifts ferrying skiers uphill.
51. Commission decision of 27 Feb. 2002, in Case N 376/2001, *Aid schemes for cableways.*
52. Commission Decision of 28 Jun. 2012 in Case SA.34056, *UK – Cable Car for London.*
53. With reference to public service obligations, the ECJ recently held that the competent authorities are required to compensate undertakings providing a public transport service for the net financial effect, positive or negative, on cost incurred and revenues generated in complying with the obligation for those undertakings, established through a general rule. *See* case C-614/20, *Lux Express Estonia*, 8.9.2022, ECLI:EU:C:2022:641.
54. *See* Commission Decisions: of 20 May 2008 in Case N 358/2007, *Czech Republic – Scheme for inland waterway transport*; of 2 Jul. 2008 in Case N 651/2007, *France – Scheme to boost inland waterway transport*; of 23 May 2011 in Case N 264/2010, *State aid scheme for the modernization of inland waterway freight transport.*

was to go to the rescue of their former national champions. In 1994, the Commission published a second, more comprehensive set of guidelines,[55] wherein a series of ancillary aviation-related services were granted exclusive rights.[56] What the 1994 Guidelines did not cover was the investment by States in airport infrastructures: at that time, infrastructure development was held to be a general measure of economic policy not falling under the scope of State aid provisions.[57]

Later on, however, both case law and policy orientations changed,[58] and in 2005, the Commission supplemented the 1994 Guidelines with additional ones which expressly extended the applicability of State aid rules to financing airport infrastructure, as well as to start-up aid granted to airlines serving smaller airports.[59] European airports are widely considered to have benefitted from route liberalization and airport privatization. A partial exception to this is constituted by the fulfilment of public service obligation which is, with respect to air services, disciplined by Article 106(2) TFEU and by Regulation 1008/2008.[60]

In 2014 – at the end of a consultation procedure with institutions and stakeholders – new Guidelines were published on State aid to airports and airlines.[61] The main areas of intervention of the Guidelines are:

(i) the test to determine whether aid has been granted under normal market conditions (so-called *MEO test*) has been updated specifying the need for internal documents – namely, a business plan – showing that a profitability analysis was in fact carried out *ex ante* with respect to the granting of public financing;[62]

(ii) investment in airport infrastructure; the level of maximum permissible aid is gauged on airport size, thereby allowing for the granting of greater aid to smaller airports;[63]

(iii) operating aid to regional airports[64] is to be phased out following a transitional period of up to ten years and providing for a differentiated and more comprehensive exception regime the smaller the airport is;[65]

---

55. *Commission Guidelines on the Application of Arts 92 and 93 and of the EC Treaty and Art. 61 of the EEA agreement to State aids in the aviation sector*, published in [1994] OJ C 350/5.
56. *Ibid.*, at para. 10.
57. The reference is, *inter alia*, to Decision of 14 Jun. 1998, NN 109/1998, *Manchester Airport*, and to Decision of 30 Mar. 1999, N 638/1998, *Subsidy to Aerelba*.
58. The landmark judgment on the point is the Case C-82/01 P, *Aéroports de Paris v. Commission*, 24.10.2002, ECLI:EU:C:2002:617.
59. *Guidelines on financing of airports and start-up aid to airlines departing from regional airports*, [2005] OJ C3 12/1 of 9 Dec. 2005.
60. Regulation (EC) No. 1008/2008 of the European Parliament and of the Council of 24 Sep. 2008 on common rules for the operation of air services in the Community (Recast).
61. *Guidelines on State aid to airports and airlines*, published in OJ [2014] C 99 of 4 Apr. 2014.
62. Article 3.4 of the new Guidelines.
63. *See, inter alia,* Annex 1 to the new Guidelines.
64. Pursuant to Art. 2.2, point (26), of the new Guidelines, a regional airport is an airport 'with annual passenger traffic volume of up to 3 million'.
65. *See* to this effect Art. 5.1.1 of the new Guidelines, and in particular para. 118 therein.

(iv) application of the SGEI regime to the air transport sector:[66] confirming the relationship between provisions on SGEI and on air transport, the new Guidelines provide for an almost-safe harbour for airports with less than 200,000 passengers per annum, de facto exempting them from prior notification on many instances;[67]

(v) newly operating routes – to which a certain extent of aid is allowed for a limited time – have been redefined reflecting market developments;[68] and

(vi) transparency and monitoring obligations unto Member States with respect to aid measures are increased, mandating for an annual report to be published.[69]

The Guidelines provided for a transitional period of ten years, starting on 4 April 2014, during which large airports (i.e., those with average annual traffic of more than 3 million passengers) may receive operating aid. By the end of the transitional period in 2024, all airports should have reached full coverage of their operating costs; past the deadline date, operating aid to airports should no longer have benefitted from the exemption provided by the Guidelines – with the exception of operating aid granted in accordance with applicable horizontal state aid rules, such as GBER and SGEI rules, as outlined below.

Applicability of the regime of the Guidelines on State aid to airports and airlines has however been extended (only with reference to aid scheme for airports with a capacity of up to 700,000 passengers per year), first in 2018,[70] until the end of the transitional period (until 3 April 2024), and then in 2023,[71] until 3 April 2027.

In order to have a more comprehensive view of it, it may prove useful to draw a distinction between the two branches of the aviation sector: ground and air services, i.e., airports and airlines.

[B] Airports

Air and maritime transport are addressed by no specific provision in the TFEU – unlike what is the case for inland transport[72] – with the exception of Article 100(2).[73] It follows that the applicable regulatory framework is governed by acts of the Commission.

66. On the SGEI (services of general interest) regime *see supra* Ch. 1.
67. *See* Art. 4.2 of the new Guidelines, in particular at para. 75. For airports located on islands, the threshold is raised from 200,000 to 300,000 passengers per annum.
68. Article 5.2 of the new Guidelines.
69. Article 8 of the new Guidelines.
70. Communication from the Commission concerning the prolongation of the specific regime for operating aid for airports with up to 700,000 passengers per annum provided for in the Guidelines on State aid to airports and airlines, C/2018/8411, OJ C 456, 18.12.2018, pp. 27-28.
71. Communication from the Commission extending the transitional period provided for in the Guidelines on State aid to airports and airlines concerning regional airports, 2023/C 244/01, C/2023/4494, GU C 244 del 11.7.2023, pp. 1-3.
72. *See supra* §17.02.
73. Article 100(2) TFEU states that: 'the European Parliament and the Council, acting in accordance with the ordinary legislative procedure, may lay down appropriate provisions for sea and air transport'.

Not all airport activities fall within the area of applicability of State aid rules.[74] Applying the economic activity criterion to this particular sector, as interpreted in the *Aéroports de Paris* case law,[75] it follows that activities that are economic in nature – airport management proper as well as the provision of airport and ground services to airlines – may be the addressee of unlawful State aid. Conversely, airport activities that fulfil necessities not economic in nature – such as air traffic control or law enforcement – have been deemed outside State aid rules.[76]

Handling, implying an overlapping of different players, has often proved a contentious issue, as in the *SEA Handling* case.[77] A 1996 Directive gradually opened this market up,[78] but a 2011 Commission proposal directed at further opening was withdrawn in 2014.

Public funding of airport managers does not amount to unlawful State aid in cases where 'a private operator, having regard to the foreseeability of obtaining a return and leaving aside all social, regional policy and sectoral considerations, would have granted the same funding'.[79] As described above, under the new Guidelines this evaluation is to take place considering a business plan to the end of assessing *ex ante* profitability.[80]

The same line of reasoning is followed, *mutatis mutandis*, with respect to assessing the relevance in terms of State aid of financing to airport infrastructure. The construction of facilities by governmental entities does not per se constitute State aid, but it may do so if it is '*inextricably linked*' to an economic activity – as held by the Court in a comparatively recent case which is nonetheless rapidly gaining landmark

74. For the purposes of this Chapter, the term 'airport' refers to the entity or group thereof performing the economic activity of providing airport services to airlines (i.e., the handling of aircraft from landing though take-off, of passengers as well as of freight) so as to enable airlines to provide air transport services – *see* Directive 2009/12/EC, at recital 1.
75. Case C-82/01 P, *Aéroports de Paris, supra.*
76. Case C-364/92, *SAT Fluggesellschaft v. Eurocontrol*, 19.1.1994, ECLI:EU:C:1994:7; Joined Cases T-443/08 and T-455/08, *Freistaat Sachsen and Land Sachsen-Anhalt and Mitteldeutsche Flughafen AG and Flughafen Leipzig-Halle GmbH v. Commission* [2011] ECR II-1311, upheld in appeal in case C-288/11 P, *Mitteldeutsche Flughafen AG and Flughafen Leipzig-Halle GmbH v. European Commission*, 19.12.2012, ECLI:EU:C:2012:821.
77. The case involves alleged State aid granted to the company providing baggage handling services in Milan's airports. *See* Commission Decision in Case C14/2010 – the last Chapter is the letter to Italy published on 20 Jan. 2015, while an array of cases are pending before the Court on the matter: *see, inter alia,* Case T-456/13, *SEA Handling v. Commission* 25.3.2015, ECLI: EU:T:2015:185; T-167/13, *Comune di Milano v. Commission* 13.12.2018, ECLI:EU:T:2018:940; T-673/14, *Italy v. Commission*; T-674/14, *SEA v. Commission;* T-688/14, *Airport Handling v. Commission* ECLI:EU:T:2015:588.
78. Council Directive 96/67/EC of 15 Oct. 1996 on access to the groundhandling market at Community airports.
79. The wording is taken from the Press release of the Commission, Memo 14/121, *State aid: Commission adopts new guidelines on state aid to airports and airlines (Aviation Guidelines)*, released on 20 Feb. 2014. The German airport tariff system, whereby the management of each airport sends its tariff schedule to the respective regional airport authority for approval, was considered by the Court as non-selective and therefore not constituting State aid. *See* Case C-524/14 P, *Commission v. Hansestadt Lubeck*, 21.12.2016, ECLI:EU:C:2016:971.
80. This assessment is often referred to as the 'MEO test', *See* Commission Decision of 19 Nov. 2013 in Case C 25/2007, *Finland – Tampere Pirkkala airport and Ryanair*, published in OJ L 309/13, at p. 27.

status.[81] According to case law, economic advantage is evaluated by comparing State investment in the project with the expected future revenue of the corresponding infrastructure, deducting State expenditure which is related to the performance of State duties, such as policing or healthcare.[82]

Once it has been established – through the tests described above – that a certain measure does constitute State aid, it needs to be evaluated if this aid is compatible with competition on the internal market.[83] This evaluation is carried out by the Commission upon notification, in failure whereof aid may not considered compatible. The criteria to assess whether this is the case or not can be summarized as follows:[84]

(i) *Contribution to a well-defined objective of common interest.* Such objectives can be the increase in the mobility of European citizens, the decrease in airport congestion, or the facilitation of development,[85] especially for remote areas.[86]

(ii) *Need for State intervention.* In an application of the economic concept of market failure, State intervention is deemed to be necessary when the market alone would be unable to bring about the same improvement. As anticipated above, in the case of airports this is evaluated progressively in comparison with the number of passengers: the more travellers per annum an airport has, the more it is assumed that it will be able to cover its capital costs without State aid.[87]

(iii) *Appropriateness of State aid as a policy instrument.* According to the principle of proportionality,[88] State aid must be the least distortive policy instrument available in the case at stake to attain the intended objective.

(iv) *Existence of incentive effect.* It needs to be verified if the investment project would have been economically sensible without any aid.

81. Case C-288/11 P, *Mitteldeutsche Flughafen and Flughafen Leipzig-Halle v. Commission, supra.* This orientation has been confirmed in subsequent decisions of the Court – such as in Case T-347/09, *Germany v. Commission*, 12.9.2013, ECLI:EU:T:2013:418. On the point *see also* a decision of the Commission setting forth certain operational boundaries to the *Leipzig-Halle* judgment: Decision SA.36346 of 27 Mar. 2014 *Germany – GRW land development scheme for industrial and commercial use*, published in OJ C/141/2014.
82. *See* Commission Decision of 25 Feb. 2009, C 9523, *Deutschland Flughafen Kassel – Calden.*
83. *See* Art. 61(3)(c) EEA Agreement.
84. *Inter alia*, in light of §5.1 of the Guidelines.
85. Accordingly, areas which are already served by an existing airport are unlikely to be viewed favourably by the Commission. *See* para. 85 of the new Guidelines.
86. *See, ex multis*, a decision not to raise objections by the Commission on an airport located in an overseas territory of France: *Projet de développmenet de l' aéroport de La Réunion*, published in JOCE C/44/2015.
87. In particular, the Guidelines identify tiers defined by specific thresholds: under 200,000 passengers per annum, where airports are assumed unable to cover their capital costs to a large extent; between 200,000 and 1 million passengers, where it is envisioned that airports *may not* be able to cover such costs to a large extent; between 1 and 3 million passenger, where airports should be able to cover their costs to a *larger* extent; between 3 and 5 million passengers, where save it for specific circumstances airports should be able to cover their costs; and finally above 5 million passengers, where the circumstances preventing cost coverage should be *exceptional. See* para. 89 of the Guidelines.
88. Article 5 TEU.

(v) *Proportionality of the aid amount.* Unlike point (iii) above, this criterion refers to the percentage of aid as compared to the total investment; as with the need for State intervention, this is calculated with respect to the number of passengers, with smaller airports admitting a greater share of State contribution.[89] Expense is allowed to different extents for different cost items.[90]

(vi) *Avoidance of negative effects on competition and trade.* For instance, the allocation of capacity resulting from the outcome of the investment should take place according to objective, transparent and non-discriminatory criteria.

Specific provisions have also been introduced in the GBER by Commission Regulation (EU) 2017/1084 of 14 June 2017,[91] regarding aid for regional airport infrastructure.[92] Notably, investment aid to regional airports with average annual passenger traffic of up to three million passengers is exempted from notification (except for airports located in the vicinity of an existing airport), provided that the other conditions are met: *inter alia*, aid intensity thresholds are respected and aid amount does not exceed the difference between the eligible costs and the operating profit of the investment. Simplified criteria are established for very small airports of up to 200,000 passengers per annum.

[C] Airlines

A recurring character of the debate on airlines – both from a political and an economic perspective – is the perceived importance for State governments to preserve flag carriers, either by retaining some form of control over them or – if control has been relinquished – by granting operating aid.[93] This has resulted in airlines often being involved in State aid proceedings by the Commission.

89. Here the tiers exemplified by the Commission are under 1 million passengers (permissible aid up to 75%); between 1 and 3 million passengers (up to 50%), and above 3 million passengers (up to 25%). *See* para. 101 of the new Guidelines.
90. Expenses such as non-aeronautical activities or ground handling services are not eligible for receiving compatible State aid.
91. Commission Regulation (EU) 2017/1084 of 14 Jun. 2017 amending Regulation (EU) No. 651/2014 as regards aid for port and airport infrastructure, notification thresholds for aid for culture and heritage conservation and for aid for sport and multifunctional recreational infrastructures, and regional operating aid schemes for outermost regions and amending Regulation (EU) No. 702/2014 as regards the calculation of eligible costs.
92. Article 56a GBER.
93. The case of the Italian flag carrier, Alitalia, is a paramount example to this effect, with Italian government officials in many instances declaring that the company were to 'remain Italian'. The phenomenon is nonetheless not unique to Italy; *see* to this effect – in Ireland, this time around – Case T-473/12, *Aer Lingus v. Commission*, 5.2.2015, ECLI:EU:T:2015:78. In this ruling the Court – while overturning the quantification of the recovery decision – has upheld the merits of the impugned Commission decision which had deemed as unlawful aid the application of a lower tax rate to flights in airports located within a 300 km range of Dublin. *See* Decision 2013/199/EU, *Ireland – Air travel tax*, published in [2013] OJ L119/30.

While on short-haul routes the strife has been between legacy carriers and new, low-cost, Europe-based competitors,[94] on longer-haul connections national airlines were able to retain much of their market space, but European operators had to confront growing competition from non-EU countries – who also thanks to important logistic and regulatory advantages (and, often, subsidies) have been able to offer competitive fares and services to passengers. In order to ensure that all carriers are granted the same rights and same opportunities to access air-transport-related services, in 2019, Regulation (EU) 2019/712 was enacted,[95] establishing mechanisms aiming at maintaining fair competition and high connectivity throughout the EU: in particular, the Commission is empowered to launch investigations and adopt repressive measures if a practice that distorts competition has caused injury or poses a clear threat of injury to an EU air carrier.

State aid to airlines can be considered admissible in two cases: social aid, and start-up aid to new air routes. This is without prejudice to other potential non-sector-specific reasons for compatibility.[96] Social aid can be considered compatible if *all* of the following conditions are met: (i) the aid is to be beneficial to final consumers; (ii) the aid is either to be directed only to specific categories of passengers[97] or to particularly remote regions;[98] and (iii) the aid is granted in a non-discriminatory way, i.e., to whichever airline may be operating that particular service.

State aid to airlines can be considered as compatible with the internal market if it is connected to the launching of a new route to the end of enhancing the connectivity of a region.[99] The criteria – the same set out above with respect to airports – have been adapted in detail by the Commission with reference to start-up aid granted to airlines.

94. In this context, 'domestic' is meant to refer to all intra-EU connections, regardless of whether they cross the borders of Member States.
95. Regulation (EU) 2019/712 of the European Parliament and of the Council of 17.4.2019 on safeguarding competition in air transport, and repealing Regulation (EC) No. 868/2004.
96. Such as rescue and restructuring aid, or aid granted to respond to particular contingencies – such as the 9/11 attacks, or geopolitical tensions affecting a particular region. To the former effect *see*, lastly, the decision whereby the Commission has declared compatible State aid granted to Polish flag carrier LOT. *See* Commission Decision of 9 Dec. 2014 in case SA.35900, published in JOCE L/25/2015. To the latter effect *see* Commission decision of 27 Jun. 2012 in Case SA.32523 – *Cyprus – Air carriers registered in Cyprus*.
97. Such as disadvantaged categories (the elderly, the disabled) or categories with particular mobility needs (students, military and government personnel). *See*, for instance, Commission decision N 169/2006 of 16 May 2006 – *UK – Air services in the Highlands and Islands of Scotland*, published in OJ C 272, at p. 10.
98. In this case the aid can be directed to the generality of the population of these remote areas – which are smaller islands, sparsely populated regions, or outlying territories. *See*, for instance, Commission decision N 426/2010 of 5 Jan. 2011 – *France – Air services between La Réunion and Metropolitan France*, published in OJ C 71, at p. 5, or Commission Decision of 29 Jun. 2011 in case SA.32888 – *Germany – Exemption from air transport tax as regards flights of people domiciled on islands and other cases*. Earlier on *see* Commission Decision N 399/1998 of 3 Sep. 1999, *Italy – Air links in favour of the residents of the minor islands of Sicily, Linosa, Lampedusa and Pantelleria*.
99. This principle was first set out in a 2004 Commission decision (Decision 2004/393/EC *Belgium – Charleroi airport and Ryanair*, published in [2004] OJ L137/1), then confirmed in the 2005 Guidelines, and lastly incorporated in the 2014 Guidelines.

The case of airlines is no exception as far as the notification obligation goes. In particular:

(i) *Contribution to a well-defined objective of common interest.* These are held by the Commission to amount to either increasing the mobility of European citizens or the connectivity of the regions involved or to facilitate development of remote regions.[100]
(ii) *Need for State intervention.* Then again, compatibility is assessed progressively in comparison with the number of passengers: the more travellers per annum the route has, the less it is held to warrant recourse to State aid.[101] Routes connecting remote regions constitute an exception in that they can be held compatible regardless of the number of passengers.
(iii) *Appropriateness of State aid as a policy instrument.* Also in this case, this analysis is carried out taking into account an *ex ante* business plan,[102] in failure whereof the airline is to commit itself to operate the route for at least as long as the time it receives State aid.
(iv) *Existence of incentive effect.* The route should not have been launched should aid not have been *granted.*
(v) *Proportionality of the aid amount.* Eligible costs are airport charges and they can be borne through State resources up to 50% of their amount.[103]
(vi) *Avoidance of negative effects on competition and trade.* If the service is likely to harm an existing transport service between the same two regions, it may not be considered compatible.

A particular case is that of aid having as its object relationships between airports and air carriers. This can take place when an airport, having at its disposal State resources, provides some form of aid using these resources to an airline. Also in this circumstance, the MEO test is employed to assess whether the dealings have occurred under normal market conditions – either comparing applicable conditions with a benchmark from the market or carrying out an *ex ante* profitability analysis.[104] Aid will need to be granted on a non-discriminatory basis (excluding measures targeting a very specific category of airlines).[105]

---

100. The assessment is carried out taking into account also different forms of transport – namely, high-speed railways. *See* paras 139 et seq. of the Guidelines.
101. In particular, the Guidelines identify tiers defined by specific thresholds: the general cut-off limit for compatibility is 3 million passengers per annum. *See* paras 141 et seq. of the Guidelines.
102. As a rule, the route should be able to become profitable in three years' time.
103. *See* para. 150 of the Guidelines.
104. On the boundaries of this case *see* Commission Decision of 27 Jan. 2011, in C 12/2008, *Slovakia – Agreement between Bratislava Airport and Ryanair*, published in [2011] OJ L 27, at p. 24, of the *Tampere Pirkkala* case, *supra*. Recently the Commission has decided to initiate formal investigation proceedings in a case of aid granted by the Belgian State to airlines operating in a certain airport via that airport's managing company: *see* Letter of 13 Jan. 2015, *Subside en faveur de certaines compagnies aériennes opérant à l ' aéroport de Bruxelles*, published in JOCE C/24/2015.
105. Also in this case the reference case is to the Joined Cases T-443/08 and T-455/08, *Freistaat Sachsen and Others v. Commission, supra.*

Aid to airlines has taken a crucial role during the COVID-19 crisis, as many Member States adopted measures aimed at supporting the aviation sector, approved by the Commission under the Covid State Aid Temporary Framework. These measures have sprouted a vast number of cases before EU Courts,[106] filed by competitors, in some cases ending with the annulment of the Commission's decision.[107]

§17.04 MARITIME TRANSPORT

[A] General Overview

The current EU policy on State aid in the maritime transport sector – both with respect to passengers and to goods – is governed by the 2004 Maritime Guidelines,[108] which

106. Since 2021, EU Courts have ruled in favor of the Commission: *see* for instance case T-259/20, *Ryanair DAC v. Commission*, 17.2.2021, ECLI:EU:T:2021:92; T-238/20, *Ryanair DAC v. Commission*, 17.2.2021, ECLI:EU:T:2021:91, T-378/20 *Ryanair DAC v. Commission* ('Danish case'), 14.4.2021, ECLI:EU:T:2021:194; T-379/20, *Ryanair v. Commission* ('Swedish case'), 14.4.2021, ECLI:EU:T:2021:195; T-388/20 *Ryanair DAC v. Commission* ('Finnair I'), 14.4.2021, ECLI:EU:T:2021:196; T-657/20 *Ryanair v. Commission* ('Finnair II'), 22.6.2022, ECLI:EU:T:2022:390; T-628/20, *Ryanair v. Commission* ('Spanish case'), 19.5.2021, ECLI:EU:T:2021:285; T-677/20, *Ryanair DAC and Laudamotion v. Commission* ('Austrian case'), 14.7.2021, ECLI:EU:T:2021:465; T-111/21, *Ryanair v. Commission* ('Croatian case'), 9.11.2022, ECLI:EU:T:2022:699; T-142/21, *Wizz Air Hungary v. Commission*, 29.3.2023; ECLI:EU:T:2023:164.

107. First, in the judgment T-665/20, *Ryanair DAC v. Commission ('Condor I')*, 9.6.2021, ECLI:EU:T:2021:344, the General Court annulled the Commission's decision due to the fact that the insolvency costs of Condor – which had already been granted restructuring aid, approved by Commission Decision C(2019) 7429 final of 14 Oct. 2019 on State aid SA.55394 (2019/N) – were included in the State aid scheme granted under the Covid Temporary Framework. The Commission soon after reapproved the decision, but it was again annulled in case T-28/22, *Ryanair DAC v. Commission* ('Condor II'), 8.5.2024, ECLI:EU:T:2024:301, based on the fact that the Commission should not have approved the restructuring aid without initiating a formal investigation procedure, as it should have questioned whether the aid at issue satisfied the requirement of adequate burden sharing.

Second, in case T-146/22, *Ryanair v. Commission*, 7.2.2024, ECLI:EU:T:2024:68 (*'KLM case'*), the General Court held that the Commission had erred in its assessment of the measures granted to the Dutch flag carrier, since it had not taken into account the aid already granted to the AirFrance. In fact, the two companies are part of the same group and controlled by the same holding company, which not only holds the majority of the capital, but also exercises effective control over both, thanks to governance veto rights as well as organic, functional and economic links. In addition, insufficient safeguards were in place to avoid cross-subsidization between the two branches of the group.

Third, in joint cases, T-34/21 e T-87/21, *Ryanair v. Commission* ('*Lufthansa case*'), 10.5.2023, ECLI:EU:T:2023:248, the General Court annulled the Commission's decisions concerning the German recapitalization of Lufthansa, amounting to EUR 6 billion, in the context of the Covid Temporary Framework, due to the fact that it did not require a mechanism incentivizing Lufthansa to buy back Germany's shareholding as quickly as possible, that it did not acknowledged Lufthansa significant market power at certain airports, and that the structural commitments imposed were not sufficient to ensure effective competition on the market.

108. *Community guidelines on State aid to maritime transport*, published in [2004] OJ C13/3 (the 'Maritime Guidelines').

substitute earlier guidelines published in 1989 and then in 1997.[109] In 2012, the Commission had opened consultations in view of a revamping of these Guidelines, but the shipping industry was virtually unanimous in taking a conservative approach, vocally recommending retaining the older provisions: the Commission received the advice, as in 2013 it formally communicated that the Maritime Guidelines would remain unchanged.[110]

Appreciating certain characteristics of EU State aid policy in the maritime transport sector might require a degree of understanding of the global shipping environment. In particular, and summarizing as much as possible, the last decades have witnessed significant change in the field of flagging (i.e., registering) of vessels: flying the flag of a certain country implies abiding with the regulations (on safety, employment, etc.) that are applicable in that jurisdiction. The consequence has been a flight from more regulation-intensive jurisdictions to jurisdictions with a more accommodating legislative scenario (so-called flags of convenience).[111]

Many jurisdictions have tried to prevent this trend by restricting domestic freight to vessels registered in their own naval registers. This did not happen in the EU, resulting in the number of ships registered in EU Member States plummeting between the mid-1980s and the late 1990s.[112] Certain niches of the shipping sector were granted a delay in the liberalization process; namely, this was the case of cabotage with outlying islands: in the Mediterranean, this exemption expired in 1999.[113]

This explains why the Commission's Guidelines put a heavy focus on developing the competitiveness of European fleets. It is in this perspective, and mindful of what the global shipping sector looks like, that under the Maritime Guidelines State aid to the shipping sector is, in general, admissible. The Guidelines extend their applicability, in addition to the transport of freight and passengers proper, to a number of seaborne economic activities, such as towage and salvage;[114] dredging;[115] utility-laying;[116]

---

109. Respectively the *Financial and fiscal measures concerning shipping operations with ships registered in the Community*, SEC(89) 921; and the *Community guidelines on State aid to maritime transport*, published in [1997] OJ C205/5.
110. Press release of the Commission of 2 Oct. 2013. The ECSA – European Community Shipowners' Association was only one of many stakeholders who welcomed this communication (*see* statement of Chairman Juan Riva published on the ECSA website). The Maritime Guidelines have been updated in 2017 only in relation to formal features, such as references to national maritime registries: *see* Communication from the Commission – Updating the Annex to Commission Communication C(2004) 43 – Community guidelines on State aid to maritime transport, C/2017/2328, OJ C 120, 13.4.2017, pp. 10-11.
111. It is estimated by the *Shipping Statistics Yearbook* that in 2013 over 60% of seagoing merchant vessels were flying flags of convenience – over 30% those of Panama and Liberia alone.
112. The EU did take a series of ancillary measures aimed at tackling the issue of flags of convenience, such as imposing inspections on health and safety reasons to vessels calling on European ports.
113. *See* Joined Cases C-15/98 and C-105/99, *Italian Republic and Sardegna Lines v. Commission*, [2000] ECR I-8855.
114. As long as at least 50% of the operational time of the tug is spent on maritime transport. *See* para. 3.1 of the Maritime Guidelines, and Case C-251/04, *Commission v. Greece*, 11.1.2007, ECLI:EU:C:2007:5. Towage within port waters or piloting is however not eligible, *see* Commission Decision 2010/213/EU *Poland* [2010] OJ L90/15.
115. That is the activity of excavating materials (usually, gravel or sand) from the seabed. Then again, as long as at least 50% of the operational time of the tug is spent on maritime transport.

marine research and exploration;[117] and ancillary activities, both offshore and on-shore.[118]

[B] Cases of Aid

Having established that State aid to the shipping industry enjoys a certain degree of acceptance, it may prove useful – for the sake of clarity – to break down the various grounds, circumstances, and modalities under which this aid is granted. In particular:

(i) *Tonnage tax* is a fiscal model that has been gaining acceptance throughout the EU to levy taxes on shipping companies in lieu of ordinary corporation taxes – generally calculated on the basis of revenue. In the context of the fiscal competition between Member States, shipping operators are encouraged to move to more fiscally efficient jurisdiction – the assumption being that tonnage tax is more advantageous than ordinary corporate taxes.[119] To countervail this tendency, Member States have – one after the other – adopted their own tonnage tax statutes.[120] From a common market perspective, tonnage tax can amount to State aid: the Commission has evaluated such schemes in many Member States – including Cyprus and Estonia –[121] clearing them as compatible.[122]

(ii) *Seafarer schemes.* Although tonnage tax is often seen as the most effective measure to help the European shipping industry, it can lead to an increase in tonnage but not necessarily in seafarer employment (in other terms, economic operators can fly EU flags on their vessels without necessarily employing domestic seafarers).[123] Notoriously, labour costs in Europe are often significantly higher than elsewhere: to help offset this differential, certain cost voices (namely income tax and social security contributions) can be reduced for seafarers employed onboard ships flying the flag of an EU (or EEA) Member State. Seafarer schemes have been held to fall within EU State aid rules and to contribute to the competitiveness of the EU

116. This applies both to cable and to pipeline laying activities.
117. *See* Commission Decision 2010/368/EC, *Germany*, in OJ C317/10.
118. The reference is, respectively, to onboard activities generally provided as a convenience to seagoing passengers (restaurants, retail outlets), and to activities instrumental to the provision of the transport service proper, such as unloading/loading of goods or container leasing.
119. This is paramount example of jurisdiction shopping and of its consequences in fiscal terms.
120. The countries who heralded this system were Greece, already in the 1950s, and the Netherlands in the mid-1990s. Other countries who have followed suit have generally chosen the one model or the other.
121. The reference is to Commission decisions respectively in Cases SA.51809 and SA.53469.
122. The reference is to schemes adopted in Belgium, Cyprus, Denmark, Finland, France, Germany, Ireland, Italy, Lithuania, the Netherlands, Poland, Slovenia, and Spain. The Commission has recently returned on the French case, *see* Decision of 4 Feb. 2015 in Case SA.14551. Rumours on the possibility of a harmonized tonnage tax system, that were circulating in recent years, seem for now to have been superseded.
123. 'Employment effects in different economic theories'. International Transport Forum (2019). 'Maritime Subsidies: Do They Provide Value for Money?' International Transport Forum Policy Papers, No. 70, OECD Publishing, Paris.

shipping industry in cases involving member States such as Cyprus, Denmark, Estonia, Poland, and Sweden.[124]

(iii) *Training aid.* Still, in terms of human resources, a critical part of the training that personnel working in the shipping industry receive takes place onboard. State aid discipline has reflected this relevance by allowing training, under certain conditions,[125] to be financed entirely with public funds under the 2014 GBER.[126] Training can be approved outside of the GBER framework, e.g., when it serves a public interest - such as environmental protection or safety - and when provided on a non-discriminatory basis.[127]

(iv) *Aid to undertakings in difficulty.* Aid to rescue shipping companies is admissible under the conditions of the Rescue and Restructuring Guidelines,[128] but, in the Commission's view, should not be used to disguise State financing - *inter alia*, through the means of public service compensation - of companies.[129]

(v) *Environmental aid.* Environmental impact plays an important role in determining compatibility - and lack thereof - of State aid in the transport sector: shipping is no exception. Aid aimed at renewing fleets introducing newer and less pollutant vessels can be deemed admissible, under the conditions set out in the applicable regulations on shipbuilding.[130] The concept of 'environmental impact' should be interpreted broadly here, referring both to an actual decrease in pollutants released in the environment[131] and to potential risks to the environment posed by safety conditions whereby goods - i.e., hazardous ones - are transported.[132]

---

124. The reference is to Commission decisions respectively in Cases SA.51809, SA.52069, SA.53469, SA.46380, SA.46740.
125. Individuals undergoing training should not belong to the crew and the vessels where the training takes place should be flying a European flag.
126. *See* Art. 31(5) of the GBER (Regulation (EU) No. 651/2014 of 17 Jun. 2014 declaring certain categories of aid compatible with the internal market in application of Arts 107 and 108 of the Treaty, published in OJ (2014) L 187/1); *see also* recital 53 therein.
127. *See*, for instance, Commission Decision of 27 Oct. 2014 in case SA.39112, *Germany – Guidelines for financial contributions for seafarer training*. *See also* the related Decision of 16 Oct. 2004 in Case N376/2004.
128. As lastly revised on 9 Jul. 2014, *see Communication from the Commission – Guidelines on State aid for rescuing and restructuring non-financial undertakings in difficulty*, published in OJ (2014) C249/1.
129. *See*, for instance, Commission Decision of 22 Jan. 2014 in Cases SA.32014, 32015 and 32016, *State aid to Tirrenia companies and their acquirers*, whereby aid was deemed incompatible and recovery was ordered, it having been found that the Italian State and its regional articulations had not complied with the conditions required by the Restructuring Guidelines. It should be noted that this decision was taken in light of an earlier version of the Rescue and Restructuring Guidelines.
130. *Framework on State aid to Shipbuilding*, published in [2011] OJ C364/9. Shipbuilding will not be treated in this Chapter.
131. Such as exhaust emissions. *See*, for instance, Commission Decision of 7 Dec. 2011 in Case SA.32118, *Investment aid to vessels*, and of 25 Apr. 2012 in Case SA.33382, *Viking Line*.
132. The landmark example to this effect is that of oil carriers, whose incidents have over the last decades caused several environmental disasters.

(vi) *Public service obligations.* The provision of public services in the maritime sector is disciplined by Article 106(2) TFEU as supplemented by Regulation 3577/92.[133] Several cases have looked into whether public service compensation was in line with State aid rules, particularly for what concerns the connection of island communities to mainland Europe.

(vii) *Particular shipping initiatives.* EU authorities have deemed certain initiatives related to shipping to deserve a particular exemption from State aid rules as instrumental to the pursuit of public policy objectives. Examples to this effect are the *Motorways of the Sea* and *TEN-T* projects, whose respective aims are to encourage short-sea shipping and to create transport corridors.[134,135]

(viii) *Privileged access to port infrastructure*: even if port infrastructure was not developed in order to benefit a particular undertaking nor awarded to it, it is possible that the conditions under which the infrastructure is made available to that undertaking for commercial use may involve a grant of State aid to it.[136]

[C] Port Infrastructure

The European regulatory landscape lacks, to date, comprehensive legislation on public financing of seaports, notwithstanding the economic relevance of the industry.[137] The Commission has, however, picked out 329 seaports defined 'key' which have been

133. Regulation (EEC) 3577/92 applying the principle of freedom to provide services to maritime transport within Member States (maritime cabotage), published in [1992] OJ L 364/7.
134. The *Motorways of the Sea* project was introduced with Decision No. 884/2004/EC of the European Parliament and of the Council of 29 Apr. 2004 amending Decision No. 1692/96/EC on Community guidelines for the development of the Trans-European transport network. *See also* the 2010 *White paper on Transport policy*.
135. The *TEN-T* project was at first introduced in 1995 with Council Regulation (EC) No. 2236/95 of 18 Sep. 1995 laying down general rules for the granting of Community financial aid in the field of Trans-European networks, last revised by Regulation (EC) No. 680/2007 of the European Parliament and of the Council of 20 Jun. 2007 laying down general rules for the granting of Community financial aid in the field of the Trans-European transport and energy networks (published in OJ L 162 of 22 Jun. 2007). Decision 661/2010/EU on Union guidelines for the development of the Trans-European transport network (published in OJ L 204/1), which had brought about certain changes, was late repealed with Regulation (EU) No. 1315/2013 of the European Parliament and of the Council of 11 Dec. 2013 on Union guidelines for the development of the Trans-European transport network and repealing Decision No. 661/2010/EU. *See also* the Transport Council Conclusions of 3 Dec. 2014 on infrastructure and the Trans-European Network.
136. *See* case T-108/16, *Naviera Armas SA*, 15.3.2018, ECLI:EU:T:2018:145.
137. EU Courts have specified that the provision of access to port infrastructure against a remuneration could itself be considered as an economic activity, regardless of the fact that such remuneration is set by law instead of by the concerned entity on a commercial basis. In addition, the qualification of the entity as 'undertaking' cannot be excluded by the fact that the concerned entity operates on the basis of a legal monopoly or that the concerned activity is performed on a non-profit basis, if the entity competes with other undertakings operating on a profit basis. *See* case T-696/17 *Havendendrijf Antwerpen NV v. Commission*, 20.9.2019, ECLI:EU:T:2019:652.

targeted for improvement of port operations,[138] *inter alia*, providing for what EU authorities call a '*an effective and fair application of the State aid rules in ports*'.[139]

Compatibility of State aid in favour of port infrastructure is evaluated pursuant to either Article 93[140] or – more frequently – to Article 107(3) TFEU. No specific guidelines on compatibility exist to date. Recent decisions have confirmed a trend of support towards public financing of port improvement: aid measures were variously approved in favour of ports of diverse size and importance: *inter alia*, for the building of an additional pier and for the improvement of a smaller cruise ship port in Greece;[141] for the enlargement of a fishing harbour and marina in Italy;[142] for the improvement of a cruise terminal in the United Kingdom;[143] and for the emergency reinforcement of soil underlying a port in Latvia.[144]

On the other hand, the Commission has been active in creating a more level playing field for ports, declaring the incompatibility of aid granted as tax exemptions for seaports and inland ports in several Member States.[145]

Specific GBER provisions for aid to maritime and inland ports have been introduced by Commission Regulation (EU) 2017/1084.[146] Therefore, notification is not due if the following conditions are met: (i) aid intensity does not exceed the relevant thresholds, depending on the size of the investment project; (ii) aid amount does not exceed the difference between the eligible costs and the operating profit of the investment. Simplified rules are established for very small aid amounts. In addition, any concession or other entrustment to a third party to construct, upgrade, operate or rent-aided port infrastructure should be assigned through a competitive, transparent, non-discriminatory and unconditional process.

---

138. The 329 seaports have been selected out of roughly 1,200 in the whole EU.
139. The reference is to the *Proposal for a Regulation of the European Parliament and of the Council establishing a framework on market access to port services and financial transparency of ports*, COM(2013) 296; *see also* the *Communication from the Commission – Ports: an engine for growth*, COM(2013) 295. The wording in the quote is taken from the press release of the Commission.
140. Commission decision of 5 Jun. 2013 in Case SA.35193, *Termini Imerese Port.*
141. *See* Commission decision of 19 Jun. 2013 in case SA.35738, *Aid for the upgrading of Katakolo port*, and Commission decision of 25 Jun. 2014 in case SA.38048, *Upgrading of the Port of Patras (5th pier)*. Katakolo is a smaller cruise ship port located in a village with a few hundred inhabitants, whereas the port of Patras is one of the main seafaring hubs in Greece.
142. Commission decision of 18 Dec. 2013 in case SA.36621, *Port of Capo d'Orlando*.
143. Commission decision of 11 Mar. 2014 in Case SA.35270, *Liverpool City Council Cruise Liner Terminal.*
144. Commission decision of 7 Aug. 2014 in Case SA.32771, *Investment aid to the Ventspils Free Port Authority – soil stabilization.*
145. *See* Commission decision concerning aid measure SA.25338 of 21 Jan. 2016, C(2016) 167 final; Commission decision on aid measure SA.38393 (2017/C) 5174 final; Commission decision on aid measure SA.38398 (2017/C) 5176 final.
146. Commission Regulation (EU) 2017/1084 of 14 Jun. 2017, introducing Art. 56b and 56c GBER.

§17.05 INTERMODALITY

Broadly speaking, 'intermodal' or 'multimodal' transport is transport which is carried out through a combination of more than one means of transport (e.g., rail and air).[147] The Commission defines it as 'a characteristic of a transport system whereby at least two different modes are used in an integrated manner in order to complete a door-to-door transport sequence', and sees it as conducive to a global approach which would enable the available transport capacity to be used more rationally – *inter alia*, pursuing public policy goals such as environmental protection.[148]

EU institutions had already tackled the concept of combined transport in the 1970s,[149] to later return on the point in 1992;[150] a few years later, the concept of 'intermodality' proper was defined,[151] and provisions on its financing were introduced.[152] As of today, there exists no specific provision on the relationship between State aid and intermodal transport.

In general, the Commission has taken a favourable view of aid aimed at increasing the degree of intermodality in transport, particularly in the perspective of a shift away from road transport in favour of other, more sustainable forms of transport, such as rail or waterways.[153]

In June 2024, the Commission launched a public consultation on its draft rules for land and multimodal transport, as well as on its new proposal for the Transport Block Exemption Regulation (TBER).[154] The draft Land and Multimodal Transport Guidelines ('LMT Guidelines') are intended to regulate land transport that does not fall within the block exemption, replacing the ageing Railway Guidelines and taking a more holistic way to the sector encompassing different means of transport. The stated goal of the

147. For the purposes of this chapter, 'intermodal' and 'multimodal' are used interchangeably.
148. *See* the *Roadmap to a Single European Transport Area – Towards a competitive and resource efficient transport system*, COM (2011) 144.
149. *See* Regulation (EEC) No. 1107/70 of the Council of 4 Jun. 1970 on the granting of aids for transport by rail, road and inland waterway.
150. Council Directive 92/106/EEC of 7 Dec. 1992 on the establishment of common rules for certain types of combined transport of goods between Member States, published in OJ [1992] L368.
151. Commission communication of 29 May 1997 on intermodality and the intermodal carriage of goods within the European Union: a systems logic for the carriage of goods; strategies and activities intended to promote efficiency, services and sustainable development [COM(97) 243 final].
152. Council Regulation (EC) No. 2196/98 of 1 Oct. 1998 concerning the granting of Community financial assistance for actions of an innovative nature to promote combined transport, published in OJ [1998] L277. This act was followed in 2003 by the so-called *Marco Polo Programme*, introduced with Regulation (EC) No. 1382/2003 of the European Parliament and of the Council of 22 Jul. 2003 on the granting of Community financial assistance to improve the environmental performance of the freight transport system, published in OJ [2003] L196.
153. This is seen as reducive of road congestion, air pollution and of the likelihood of accidents. *See*, for instance, Decision of the Commission of 20 Mar. 2013 in Case SA.35575, *Plain d'aide au report modal vers le transport par voies navigables*, where encouraging inland waterways usage at the expense of road traffic was seen as justifying State aid.
154. Commission, Annex to the Communication from the Commission, *Approval of the content of a draft for a Commission Regulation declaring certain categories of aid in the rail, inland waterways and multimodal transport sector compatible with the internal market in application of Articles 93, 107 and 108 of the Treaty, supra*.

Commission is that the LMT Guidelines and the TBER should, together, form 'an up-to-date and comprehensive rulebook for the granting of State aid in the sustainable land transport sector'.[155] Interested parties can submit their comments through September 2024, in view of an envisioned adoption in late 2025.[156]

155. Commission press release dated 18 Jun. 2024, available at: https://ec.europa.eu/commission/presscorner/detail/en/ip_24_3346.
156. *Ibid.*

Bibliography

Alain Ronzano, *Exoneration: The Court of Justice of the European Union annuls the decision of the General Court as the European Commission denounced the recuperation of unlawful aid in the form of exemption from the municipal tax on buildings, because of the lack of proof of the absolute impossibility of recovery (Scuola Elementare Marie Montessori / Commission), 6 November 2018*, Concurrences 1 (2019).

Alan Bates, *State Aids*, in *European Union Law of Competition* (2013).

Alberto Santa Maria, *European Economic Law* (2019).

Alberto Santa Maria, *L'odierno diritto internazionale dell'economia* (2021).

Alberto Santa Maria, *Lo sport professionistico e la concorrenza*, Giurisprudenza Commerciale, 945 (2004).

Alessandro De Stefano, *Le controversie sul recupero degli aiuti illegali e incompatibili dinanzi al giudice tributario prima della riforma della legge n. 234/2012*, in *Dizionario sistematico del diritto della concorrenza* (Pace ed., 2013).

Alessandro Zenca, *Il ruolo dei sistemi di garanzia dei depositi nel nuovo quadro regolamentare e il loro inquadramento nella normativa degli aiuti di Stato*, 24 Concorrenza e Mercato, (2017).

Alexander H. Türk, *Judicial Review in EU Law* (2011).

Alexander Rust, Claire Micheau, *State Aid and Tax Law* (2013).

Alice Pisapia, *Aiuti di stato: profili sostanziali e rimedi giurisdizionali* (2013).

Ana Vlahek, Matija Damjan, *European Commission's Banking Communication Question of Validity in the Slovenian Banking Bail-in Puzzle Annotation of the Judgment of the Court (Grand Chamber) of 19 July 2016 C-526/14 Tadej Kotnik and Others v Državni zbor Republike Slovenije*, 15 European State Aid Law Quarterly, 3, 458-467 (2016).

Andrea Andolina, *Crisis of res judicata and new techniques for dispute resolution: (selfstanding anticipatory) provisional measures on the merits*, in *I quaderni europei*, 5 et seq., (February 2009).

Andrea Biondi, Elisabetta Righini, *An Evolutionary Theory of EU State Aid Control*, in *The Oxford Handbook of European Law* (Anthony Arnull, Damian Chalmers eds, 2015).

Andrea Biondi, *Preserving the Playing Field: Subsidies Regulation in the TCA, The Law and Politics of Brexit*, 4, 218 (Federico Fabbrini ed., 2024).

Andrea Caligiuri, *Modelli costituzionali a confronto: la specificità della tutela dei diritti fondamentali nel processo di adattamento al diritto dell'Unione europea*, in *Giustizia amministrativa e diritto comunitario* (Caligiuri, Caranta, ed., 1992).

Andrea Caligiuri, Nicola Napoletano, Giuseppe Cataldi, *La tutela dei diritti umani in Europea: tra sovranità nazionale e ordinamenti sovranazionali* (2010).

Andrea Penta, *L'azione revocatoria fallimentare nell'Amministrazione straordinaria delle grandi imprese alla luce della recente sentenza n. 172 del 21 aprile 2006 della Corte costituzionale*, Dir. fall., 2, 834 (2006).

Andrea Pezza, *Which Role for Deposit Guarantee Schemes in the Financial Crisis? An Analysis of the Italian Situation*, 24 Concorrenza e Mercato (2017).

Andrea Vignini, *State Aid and Deposit Guarantee Schemes, The CJEU Decision on Tercas and the Role of DGSs in Banking Crises*, Legal Papers, Quaderni di Ricerca Giuridica della Consulenza Legale, Bank of Italy (2019).

Andreas Bartosch, *Procedural Rights Denied for Too Long: Is Legal Conservativism Finally Heading for its Götterdämmerung?*, in European State Aid Law Quarterly 579 (2011).

Andreas Bartosch, *The Procedural Regulation in State Aid Matters – A Case for Profound Reform*, in European State Aid Law Quarterly 474 (2007).

Andreas Haak & Barbara Thiemann. *Fostering Tech Sovereignty with a Level Playing Field on State Aid and Foreign Subsidies*, 21 European State Aid Law Quarterly 1, 20-30 (2022).

Andreas Reindl & Isabelle Van Damme, *The EU Foreign Subsidies Regulation* 60 (2024).

Andreas Stephan, *Will the New UK Subsidy Control Regime Help Level Up the Economy?*, 87 MLR 172 (2024).

Angelo Bertolotti, *Non ha fine il tormentato rapporto della legge Prodi con le norme comunitarie*, Dir. comm. (2001).

Ania Foszczynski, Agnieszka Stobiecka-Kuik, *Agriculture*, in *EU Competition Law*, 4 (Mederer, Pesaresi, Van Hoof eds, 2008).

Anke Meskens, *Mind the (Regulatory) Gap: The Commission's Legislative Proposal on Levelling the Playing Field in Public Procurement for Foreign Subsidies*, 17 European Procurement & Public Private Partnership Law Review, 2, 94-106 (2022).

Annalaura Giannelli, *La pregiudiziale amministrativa rinasce dalle proprie ceneri: la mancata impugnazione dell'atto illegittimo recide il nesso di causalità tra provvedimento illegittimo e lesion*, Foro it., III, 31 (2012).

Annalisa Negrelli, *Il primato del diritto comunitario e il giudicato nazionale; un confronto che si poteva evitare o risolvere altrimenti*, Riv. it. dir. pubbl. com., 1217 (2008).

Anselmo Barone, Massimo Fabiani, *La difficile convivenza della revocatoria fallimentare con l'amministrazione straordinaria*, in *Foro it.*, I, 1302 (2001).

Antonio Afonso, *Recovery of fiscal State aid*, in *State aid and tax law* (Alexander Rust & Claire Micheau eds 2013).

Antonio Tizzano, *La tutela dei privati nei confronti degli Stati membri dell'Unione europea*, Foro it., IV, 21 (1995).

Antonios Bouchagiar, *When Do Funds Become State Resources*, 1 EStAL 19 (2020).

Arancha Gonzales Laya, *The EU Foreign Subsidies Regulation*, 1 (Andreas Reindl & Isabelle Van Damme eds, 2024).

Armando Lamberti, *Il giudice nazionale e le decisioni della Commissione Europea. Gli atti di accertamento*, in *Aiuti di Stato fiscali e giurisdizioni nazionali: problemi attuali* (Andrea Mondini & Adriano Di Pietro eds, 2015).

Augusto Fantozzi, *Problemi di adeguamento dell'ordinamento fiscale nazionale alle sentenze della Corte Europea di Giustizia e alle decisioni della Commissione CE*, Atti del Convegno Aiuti di Stato nel diritto comunitario e misure fiscali, in *Rass. Trib.*, 2003, 2266.

Bart Creve, Locus Standi *Requirements for Annulment Actions by Competitors: the Resurfacing 'Unique Position Test' Ought to Be Discarded*, 13, European State Aid Law Quarterly II, 233 (2014).

Barthelemy, *La politique communautaire en matière d'aides dans le secteur agricole*, in *Rev. droit rur.*, 201 (1988).

Beatrice Zuffi, *Le sezioni unite ammettono la sola sospensione discrezionale del processo sulla causa dipendente allorché la causa pregiudiziale sia stata decisa con sentenza di primo grado impugnata*, Corriere giur., 1322 (2012).

Bruno Nascimbene, *Una disapplicazione 'condizionata' della legge Prodi?*, Corr. giur., 98 (2005).

Carlo Eugenio Baldi, *La disciplina degli aiuti di Stato* (2018).

Carmen Radu, Liviu Radu, *From the Next Generation EU to the National Recovery and Resilience Plan*, 14 Romanian Review of Social Sciences, 50, 64, 1 (2023).

Carmine Punzi, *Le procedure di amministrazione straordinaria nel sistema delle procedure concorsuali*, Dir. fall., I, 268 (2005).

Cavalaglio, *Requiem per la Prodi: ... e adesso?*, Fallimento, 1168 (2001).

Cesare Glendi, *Processo tributario e recupero di aiuti di Stato*, in Corr. Trib., 1670 (2008).

Cesare Glendi, *Recupero di aiuti di stato nella legislazione anti-crisi*, Corr. Trib., 997 (2009).

Chiara Fontana, *Gli aiuti di stato di natura fiscale* (2012).

Christian Califano, *Ordinamento tributario e ordinamento comunitario. Profili costituzionali*, 6 (2002).

Christopher Yukins, *State Aid, Protectionism and Public Procurement: An Uneasy New World Order*, 22(2) European State Aid Law Quarterly, 181-187 (2023)

Ciara Barbu-O'Connor, Andrea Biondi, *State Aid & National Enforcement: United Kingdom* in *State Aid & National Enforcement* (Derenne ed., 2024).

Cinthia Pinotti, *Gli aiuti di stato alle imprese nel diritto comunitario della concorrenza* (2000).

Claudio Biscaretti di Ruffia, *Gli aiuti di Stato a favore delle imprese agricole*, in *Scritti in onore di Anna Marzanati*, 27 *et seq*. (2018).

Claudio Biscaretti di Ruffia, *Introduzione alle regole di concorrenza dell'Unione europea per le imprese del settore agricolo*, in *Scritti in onore di Giuseppe Tesauro*, II, *Diritto e politiche dell'Unione europea* (2014).

Claudio Consolo, *Il percorso della Corte di giustizia, la sentenza Olimpiclub e gli eventuali limiti di diritto europeo all'efficacia esterna ultrannuale del giudicato tributario (davvero ridimensionato in funzione antielusiva Iva del divieto comunitario di abusi della libertà negoziale?)*, Riv. dir. trib., 1143 (2010).

Claudio Consolo, *La sentenza Lucchini della Corte di giustizia: quale possibile adattamento degli ordinamenti processuali interni e in specie del nostro?*, Riv. dir. proc., 224 (2008).

Claudio Sacchetto, *Il diritto comunitario e l'ordinamento tributario italiano*, Dir. Prat. Trib. Int., 13 (2001).

Claudio Sacchetto, *Principi di diritto tributario europeo e internazionale* (2011).

Clemente Ciampolillo, *Incompatibilità e recupero*, in *Aiuti di Stato in materia fiscale* (Salvini ed., 2007).

Conor Quigley, Anthony Collins, *EC State Aid Law and Policy* (2003).

Cristina Romariz, *Revisiting Material Selectivity in EU State Aid Law – Or 'The Ghost of Yet-To-Come'*, 39 European State Aid Law Quarterly (2014).

Cristina Schepisi, *Aiuti di Stato e giudici nazionali nella Bozza di nuova Comunicazione della Commissione: alcune riflessioni a prima lettura*, Eurojus, 2 (2021).

Cristina Schepisi, *Aiuti di Stato e tutela giurisdizionale* (2012).

Cristoforo Osti, *Alitalia: la dolorosa storia. I puntata*, Merc. Conc. Reg., 317 (2008).

Daniele Grespan, *EU Competition Law*, in 1, *Procedure Antitrust – Merger – State Aid* (Tosato Bellodi ed., 2014).

David du Parc Braham, Maria Marsden, *The UK's Subsidy Control Regime Subsidy Advice Unit Referrals – Tips and Best Practice*, 4 European State Aid Law Quarterly (2023).

Davide Diverio, *Gli aiuti di Stato al trasporto aereo e alle banche* (2010).

Davide Maresca, *Dell'investitore privato al debitore privato: l'evoluzione del modello di operatore economico in materia di aiuti di Stato*, Eurojus.it, 2, 228 et seq (2022).

Diane Fromage, Günter Herzig, Paul Weismann, *The way forward in the EMU: inflation, public debt and reforms for the next generation (Part III)*, EU Law Live: Weekend Edition, 141 special issue Madrid: EU Law Live, 2023 (2023).

Diane Wood, *State Aid Management in the United States*, 1 EStAL 40 (2013).

Dimitrios Skiadas, *Trade-Offs in Auditing the EU Recovery and Resilience Facility: Flexibility vs Compliance – A Greek Case Study*, Eucrim – The European Criminal Law Associations' Forum (2024).

Eddy De Smijter, *There's a New Kid in Town: The Foreign Subsidies Regulation*, 13(8) Journal of European Competition Law & Practice 529 (2022).

Editorial Comment, *The EU's Integrated Policy Approach Towards Competitiveness: The Interplay Between State Aid Control and Industrial Policies*, 61 Common Market Law Review 1-12 (2024).

Edoardo Gambaro, Francesco Mazzocchi, *Cases C-521/06 P,* Athinaiki Techniki v. Commission, *Judgment of the Court of Justice (Fourth Chamber) of 17 July 2008, [2008] ECR I-5829; Case C-322/09 P,* NDSHT v. Commission*; Case C-362/09 P,* Athinaiki Techniki v. Commission, *Judgment of the Court of Justice (Third Chamber) of 18 December 2010*, 48 Common Market Law Review 2083-2105 (2011).

Edoardo Gambaro, Francesco Mazzocchi, *Private Parties and State Aid Procedures: A Critical Analysis of the Changes Brought by Regulation 734/2013*, 53(2) Common Market Law Review 385-417 (2016).

Edoardo Gambaro, *Locus Standi of Natural and Legal Persons Before the European Courts in State Aid Cases*, in *Litigation and Arbitration in EU Competition*, 201 (Marquis & Cisotta eds, 2015).

Edoardo Gambaro, Massimiliano Pizzonia, *Il controllo delle sovvenzioni/aiuti nei rapporti fra il Regno Unito e l'Unione Europea*, Diritto del Commercio Internazionale, 269 (2021).

Edoardo Staunovo Polacco, *'La Legge Prodi' dopo la decisione della Commissione* CE 16 *maggio* 2000 *e gli altri provvedimenti degli organi comunitari*, Fallimento, 464 (2001).

Edoardo Staunovo Polacco, *Art. 6. Azioni revocatorie*, in *La legge Marzano. Commentario* (Castagnola, Sacchi eds, 2006).

Eduardo Gianfrancesco, *Incroci pericolosi: CEDU, Carta dei diritti fondamentali e Costituzione italiana tra Corte costituzionale, Corte di Giustizia e Corte di Strasburgo*, in *Corti nazionali e corti europee dopo il Trattato di Lisbona* (Pedrazza Gorlero ed., 2010).

Elena D'Alessandro, *Le sezioni unite e la tesi di Liebman sui rapporti tra art. 295 e 337 c.p.c.: much ado about nothing?*, Giur. it., 2601 (2012).

Emanuele Fazio, *Adapting Competition Law to the Digital Transition: Two Challenges*, Eu. Forum, 7, 981 (2022).

Enrico Allorio, *Diritto processuale tributario* (1969).

Enrico Altieri, *Prime impressioni sulla giurisdizione del giudice amministrativo in materia di aiuti di stato,* Riv. Dir. Trib., 197 (2013).

Enrico Scoditti, *Giudicato nazionale e diritto comunitario*, Corr. giur., 1221 (2007).

Enrico Tullio Liebman, *Manuale di diritto processuale civile*, VI, (Colesanti, Merlin, Ricci, eds, 2002).

Erik Meij, *Standing in Direct Actions in the EU Courts After Lisbon*, in *Fundamental Rights and Principles: Liber Amicorum Pieter van Dijk* (Van Roosmalen et al. eds, 2013).

Fabio Gencarelli, *La nouvelle politique communautaire en matière d'aides d'Etat en agriculture*, Rev. du droit de l'Union eur., (2008).

Fabio Gencarelli, *La politica agricola comune nella giurisprudenza comunitaria*, (2000).

Fabrizio Amatucci, *Il ruolo del giudice nazionale in materia di aiuti fiscali*, in *Rass. Trib.*, 1282 (2008).

Fabrizio Criscuoli, *Amicus curiae*, Enc. giur. Treccani, 2 (1988).

Ferdinando Albisinni, *La definizione di attività agricola nella nuova PAC, tra incentivazione e centralizzazione regolatoria, Riv. it. dir. pubbl. com.* 967 (2014).

Filip Krenek, Eddy De Smijter. *From a White Paper to a Proposal for a Regulation on Foreign Subsidies: Filling a Regulatory Gap in Protecting the EU Internal Market*, 129-148 (2022).

Francesco Corti, Alessandro Liscai, Tomas Ruiz, *The Recovery and Resilience Facility: Boosting Investment in Social Infrastructure in Europe?*, 15 Italian Labour Law e-Journal 15, 30, 1S (2022).

Francesco Macario, *Compatibilità costituzionale delle azioni revocatorie promosse nel corso del piano di ristrutturazione dell'impresa in crisi e sistema della responsabilità patrimoniale: cronaca di una frattura annunciata?*, Banca, borsa, 2, 440 (2006).

Francesco Maria Salerno, Federico Macchi, *Il* private enforcement *in materia di aiuti di Stato in Europa*, Eurojus, 3 (2021).

Francesco Paolo Luiso, *Diritto processuale civile* 1 (2014).

Francesco Tesauro, *Manuale del processo tributario* (2013).

Francesco Tesauro, *Manuale del processo tributario* (2020).

Francesco Tesauro, *Processo tributario e aiuti di stato*, Corr. Trib., 3665 (2007).

Francesco Tesauro, *Processo tributario e diritto comunitario*, in *La giurisdizione tributaria nell'ordinamento giurisdizionale* (Massimo Basilavecchia, Giuliano Tabet eds, 2009).

Franco Gallo, *L'inosservanza delle norme comunitarie sugli aiuti di Stato e sue conseguenze nell'ordinamento fiscale interno*, Atti del Convegno Aiuti di Stato nel diritto comunitario e misure fiscali, in Rass.Trib., 2281 (2003).

Friedrich Erlbacher, *Artt. 175-179*, in *Single Common Market Organisation* (Mögele-Erlbacher eds., 2011).

Gaetano Caputi, *La selettività in generale*, in *Agevolazioni fiscali e aiuti di stato*, (Ingrosso, Tesauro eds., 2009).

Gaetano Maria Giovanni Reale, *The National State Aid Register – Italy's Experience*, 23(1) European State Aid Law Quarterly 15-21 (2024).

Geoffrey Mamdani, Simone Ritzek-Seidl, *Rescue and Restructuring*, in *EU Competition Law*, IV, 2, 745 et seq. (Pesaresi, van de Casteele, Flynn, Siaterli eds, 2016).

Giancarlo Olmi, *Politique agricole commune, Commentaire Mégret* (1991).

Giangiacomo D'Angelo, *Giudicato tributario (esterno) e diritto comunitario: un equilibrio difficile*, Riv. dir. trib., 285 (2009).

Gianluca Belotti, *Gli aiuti di Stato nel diritto comunitario della concorrenza – della tutela dei terzi*, in *Dir. com. sc. int.*, 469 (1995).

Gianluca Contaldi, *La nozione di aiuto di Stato*, Eurojus, 3,107 et seq. (2019).

Gianni Lo Schiavo, *Burden Sharing Arrangements vs. Shareholders and Creditors: Kotnik, Dowling and the Current State Aid Policy in the Banking Sector*, 19(3) European Business Organization Law Review 581-613 (2018).

Gianpaolo Provaggi, *La Suprema corte sancisce l'efficacia immediata e diretta delle decisioni della commissione europea nell'ordinamento interno*, Rivista di giurisprudenza tributaria, 451 (2003).

Ginevra Bruzione, Miriam Cassella, *The Interplay of State Aid Control, Bank Supervision and Resolution: Rethinking the European Framework*, 24 Concorrenza e Mercato (2017).

Giorgio Giuseppe Poli, *Il giudizio di costituzionalità dell'art. 6 della 'legge Marzano': la Corte riconosce la legittimità delle revocatorie fallimentari nelle procedure di 'risanamento oggettivo*, Corr. giur., 1232 (2006).

Giorgio Meo, *L'amministrazione straordinaria delle grandi imprese in crisi*, in *Trattato di diritto fallimentare - Volume IV - Le altre procedure concorsuali* (Gabrielli, Luiso, Vassalli eds, 2014).

Giorgio Tarzia, *Amministrazione straordinaria delle grandi imprese in stato di insolvenza*, Dir. e pratica del fall., 3, 45 (2006).

Giorgio Tarzia, *Disapplicazione della legge Prodi per contrasto con la disciplina comunitaria*, Fallimento, 517 (2000).

Giorgio Tarzia, *Il regime transitorio della nuova legge sull'amministrazione straordinaria al vaglio della Corte di Giustizia CE*, Fallimento, 450 (2002).

Giovanni Amoroso, *Diritto comunitario vs. giudicato interno. La sentenza Lucchini a un triennio dalla sua emanazione*, in *Rass. dir. pubbl. eur.*, 187 (2011).

Giovanni Luchena & Biancamaria Raganelli, *Concorrenza e aiuti di Stato in Europa* (2022).

Giovanni Marino, *The Wane of the Res Judicata in the Italian Enforcement Proceedings*, I quaderni europei (2009).

Giovanni Raiti, *Le pronunce Olimpiclub ed Asturcom Telecomunicaciones: verso un ridimensionamento della paventata «crisi del giudicato civile nazionale» nella giurisprudenza della Corte di giustizia*, Riv. dir. proc., 670 (2010).

Giovanni Raiti, *The Crisis of Civil* Res Iudicata *in the EC Legal System*, I quaderni europei (2009).

Girolamo Strozzi, Roberto Mastroianni, *Diritto dell'Unione europea, Parte istituzionale* (2013).

Giulia Sonderegger, *A Critical Analysis of Rescue and Restructuring Aid*, ESALQ 264 (2019).

Giuseppe Chiovenda, *Istituzioni di diritto processuale civile* (1934).

Giuseppe Graziano, *La selettività e gli aiuti regionali*, in *Aiuti di Stato in materia fiscale*, (Salvini ed., 2007).

Giuseppe Pizzonia, *Agevolazioni fiscali per le cooperative, aiuti di stato, ruolo dei giudici nazionali*, Riv. Dir. Fin. Sc. Fin., II, 37 (2012).

Grazia Vitale, *The General Court's Ruling in Tercas: Between Imputability of the Aid to the State and Use of State Resources*, 4 European Papers, 2019, 3, 895-905 (2020).

Hanns Peter Nehl, *2013 Reform of EU State Aid Procedures: How to Exacerbate the Imbalance Between Efficiency and Individual Protection*, 13, European State Aid Law Quarterly II, 235 (2014).

Hanns Peter Nehl, *Judicial Protection of Complainants in EC State Aid Law: A Silent Revolution?*, 8, European State Aid Law Quarterly III, 401 (2009).

Hans Friederiszick, Lars-Hendrik Röller, Vincent Verouden, *European State Aid Control: An Economic Framework*, in *Handbook of Antitrust Economics* (Buccirossi ed., 2008).

Henrik Peytz, Thomas Mygind, *Direct Actions in State Aid Cases: Tightropes and Legal Protection?*, 2 European State Aid Quarterly 331 (2010).

Herve Guyomard et al., *How the Green Architecture of the 2023-2027 Common Agricultural Policy Could Have Greener*, 52 Ambio, 1327 et seq. (2023).

Holger Bielesz, Ulrich Soltész, *Judicial Review of State Aid Decisions – Recent Developments*, 25, European Competition Law Review III (2004).

Hugo López López, *General Thought on Selectivity and Consequences of a Broad Concept of State Aid in Tax Matters,* 9, European State Aid Law Quarterly IV (2010).

Ilaria Benedetti, Giulio Guarini and Tiziana Lauretti, *Digitalization in Europe: A Potential Driver of Energy Efficiency for the twin Transition Policy Strategy*, 89 Socio-Economic Planning Sciences (2023)

Irene Mecatti, *The Role of Deposit Guarantee Schemes in Preventing and Managing Banking Crises: Governance and Least Cost Principle*, 17(6) European Company and Financial Law Review 657 (2020).

Ivo Van Bael, Jean-Francois Bellis, *Competition Law of the European Community* (2021).

Jakub Kociubiński, *The New Normal? The European Union's Temporary Frameworks for State Aid*, 14 Wroc. Review Law, Adm. Econ. (2024).

Jan Blockx, Pierfranco Marriolo, *The Foreign Subsidies Regulation: Calling Foul While Upping the Ante?*, 28 European Foreign Affairs Review, Special Issue, 67-70 and 73 (2023).

Jan Winter, *The Rights of Complainants in State Aid Cases: Judicial Review of Commission Decisions Adopted under Article 88 (ex 93) EC*, 36 Common Market Law Review 521 (1999).

Jean Paul Keppenne, *Guide des aides d'État en droit communautaire* (1999).

Jean Paul Keppenne, *State Aid Litigation Before the Community Courts*, in *L. EC Competition Procedure* (Ortiz Blanco ed., 2006).

Jhon Milligan, Luke Sales, *Appeal Against Alitalia State Aid Decision by Ryanair Dismissed*, European State Aid Law Quarterly (2014).

Juan Jorge Piernas López, *The Transformation of EU State Aid Law ... and Its Discontents*, 60 Common Mark. Law Review 1623-1654 (2003).

Julio Baquero Cruz, Fernando Castillo de la Torre, *A Note on PreussenElektra*, 26 ELRev, 489, (2001).

Jürgen Kuling et al., *Third-Country State Aid Regulation: The European Debate on Foreign Subsidies: Necessity and Possibilities of a Reform*, 149–161 (2021).

Justyna Smela Wolski, *Legal Basis of the Proposal for Regulation on Foreign Subsidies*, 22 EStALII, 153-172 (2022).

Katrine Lillerud, *The National Transparency Registers in Action*, 18(3) European State Aid Law Quarterly 239-248 (2019).

Kelyn Bacon, *European Union Law of State Aid* (2013).

Kevin O'Higgins, *Overview of the Jurisprudence in State Aid Cases: Substance and Procedure: An Update*, 10, European State Aid Law Quarterly IV, 601 (2011).

Küllike Jürimäe, *Standing in State Aid Cases: What's the State of Play?*, 9, European State Aid Law Quarterly II, 303 (2010).

Lamanna, *Incompatibilità tra il 'regime di aiuti di Stato' introdotto dall'ex 'legge Prodi' e la normativa comunitaria: disapplicazione ed effetti conseguenti*, in *Fallimento*, 2003, 647.

Leigh Hancher, *Long-term Contracts and State Aid: A New Application of the EU State Aid Regime or a Special Case?*, in *Competition, Contracts and Electricity Markets: A New Perspective* (Glachant et al. eds, 2011).

Leigh Hancher, *State Aid Recovery: A New Public Order?*, European State Aid Law Quarterly, 1 (2013).

Leigh Hancher; Tom Ottervanger; Piet Jan Slot, *EU State Aids* (2012).

Lena Hornkohl, *Protecting the Internal Market from Subsidisation with the EU State Aid Regime and the Foreign Subsidies Regulation: Two Sides of the Same Coin?*, 3 Journal of European Competition Law & Practice 14, 137-151 (Gianni De Stefano e Paolo Ibanez Colombo eds, 2023).

Leo Flynn, *Remedies in the European Courts*, in *The Law of State Aid in the EU* (Biondi et al. eds., 2004).

Leonardo Bellodi, Daniele Grespan, *La procedura in materia di aiuti*, in *Il nuovo diritto europeo della concorrenza* (Tosato, Bellodi eds, 2004).

Lino Guglielmucci, *Lezioni di diritto fallimentare* (2004).

Lorenza Mola, *The Securitisation of International Economic Law and 'Global Security': An Analysis of the EU Law Approach Through the Prism of the Common Commercial Policy*, 12(1) Cambridge International Law Journal 105-128 (2023).

Lorenzo Bianchi, *Gli incerti confini dell'onere della prova nella procedura di recupero degli aiuti di Stato illegittimi*, Giur. Trib., 907 (2009).

Lorenzo Bianchi, *La politica agricola comune (PAC)* (2007).

Lorenzo Del Federico, *I principi di equivalenza ed effettività nelle procedure di recupero degli aiuti di Stato fiscali*, in *Agevolazioni fiscali e aiuti di Stato* (Ingrosso, Tesauro, eds., 2009).

Lorenzo Del Federico, *Tutela del contribuente ed integrazione giuridica europea* (2010).

Lorenzo Federico Pace, *Dizionario sistematico del diritto della concorrenza* (2013).

Lorenzo Federico Pace, *Recupero aiuti di stato e tutela cautelare*, Riv. dir. trib., 867 (2008).

Lowri Evans, *Delivering the State Aid Reform*, Concurrences, 4 (2006).

Luca Jeantet, *'Legge Prodi': aiuto di Stato integrale ed effettivo ovvero parziale? Il dibattito prosegue*, Giur. comm., 359 (2003).

Luciano Panzani, *Parità di trattamento tra creditori e tutela della concorrenza*, Fallimento, 761 (2006).

Luciano Vasques, *Limiti al diritto d'accesso e tutela delle parti nei procedimenti antitrust italiani e comunitari*, Foro it., IV, 159 (1997).

Luigi Costato, *La legge Prodi e la Corte di giustizia*, Studium iuris, 156 (2001).

Luigi Costato, Luigi Russo, *Corso di diritto agrario italiano e dell'Unione europea* (2023).

Luigi Daniele, *Private enforcement in materia di aiuti di Stato e ruolo dei giudici nazionali: la nuova Comunicazione della Commissione europea*, in *La 'modernizzazione' della disciplina sugli aiuti di Stato. Il nuovo approccio della Commissione europea e i recenti sviluppi in materia di public e private enforcement* (Schepisi ed., 2011).

Łukasz Stępkowski, *Judgment of the Court of Justice in C-526/14 Tadej Kotnik and Others v. Državni zbor Republike Slovenije and Permissibility of Granting State Aid to Financial Institutions*, 6(2) Polish Review of International and European Law 89-105 (2018).

Manlio Ingrosso, *La pronuncia pregiudiziale della corte di giustizia sulle agevolazioni fiscali alle cooperative italiane*, Rass. trib., 529 (2012).

Manuel Aalbers, Paul C. Adriaanse, *Recovery of Unlawful Aid in EU State Aids*, London, 1089-1116 (2021)

Marco Greggi, *Regime fiscale delle ristrutturazioni bancarie e aiuti di Stato: il caso BNP Paribas-BNL sotto la lente del Tribunale UE*, Rass. Trib., 1082 (2011).

Maria Cristina Vanz, *Azione di stato e petizione d'eredità: rapporto di pregiudizialità e sospensione necessaria del processo tra antichi dubbi e nuovi principi*, Famiglia e dir., 450 (2013).

Marianne Dony, Francois Renards, Catherine Smits, *Aides d'Etat* (2005).

Mario Barcellona, *Amministrazione straordinaria e aiuti di Stato: sulla compatibilità della disciplina transitoria dell'art. 106, d.lgs. n. 270/1999 con gli artt. 87 e 88 del Trattato* CE, in *Europa e diritto privato*, 1 (2002).

Marta Cartabia, *Considerazioni sulla posizione del giudice comune di fronte a casi di 'doppia pregiudizialità'*, Foro it., 1997, V, 222.

Marta Simoncini, *Different Shades of Legal Standing and the Right to Judicial Protection of Private Parties in the Banking Union: Trasta Komercbanka*, 57, Common Market Law Review, 6, 1867-1886 (2020).

Massimo Basilavecchia, *La giurisdizione* 75 et seq., in *Il giudizio tributario* (Consolo, Melis, Perrino eds, 2022).

Massimo Cataldo, *Amministrazione straordinaria delle grandi imprese in stato di insolvenza e disciplina della concorrenza nella Comunità europea*, Fallimento, 790 (2006).

Massimo Fabiani, *Dai pomodori ai latticini, ovvero dalla regola all'eccezione: un testo unico per l'amministrazione straordinaria e la gestione dei gruppi transnazionali*, Foro it., I, 1567 (2004).

Massimo Merola, Alessandro Cogoni, *Foreign subsidies and financial contributions: much fine-tuning ahead*, 8(1) Competition Law & Policy Debate 1-3 (2023).

Massimo Merola, *Rimedi per violazione delle norme sugli aiuti di Stato: misure repressive o di ripristino* (2018).

Massimo Merola, *The Forces Shaping State Aid Control in the EU*, in *What Shapes the Law? Reflections on the History, Law, Politics and Economics of International and European Subsidy Disciplines* (Luca Rubini, James Hawkins eds, 2016).

Massimo Montanari, *Art. 47-bis Sospensione di atti volti al recupero di aiuti di Stato e definizione delle relative controversie*, in *Commentario breve alle leggi del Processo tributario* (Claudio Consolo, Cesare Glendi eds., 2023).

Matteo Rescigno, *Le leggi Parmalat al vaglio della Corte Costituzionale*, Corr. Giur., 1237 (2006).

Maurizio Orlandi, *Art. 42*, in *Trattati dell'Unione europea*, (Tizzano ed, 2014).

Maurizio Orlandi, *La disciplina degli aiuti di Stato*, in *Il diritto privato dell'Unione europea*, 2 (Tizzano ed., 2006).

Maurizio Orlandi, *Le discriminazioni fiscali e gli aiuti di Stato nel diritto dell'Unione Europea* (2018).

Maurizio Pedrazza Gorlero, *Alla ricerca della 'forma condizionante'. Introduzione ai rapporti fra Corti costituzionali nazionali e Corti europee dopo il Trattato di Lisbona*, in *Corti nazionali e corti europee dopo il Trattato di Lisbona* (Pedrazza Gorlero ed., 2010).

Max Lienemeyer, Clemens Kerle, Helena Malikova, *The New State Aid Banking Communication: The Beginning of the Bail-in Era Will Ensure a Level Playing Field of Enhanced Burden-Sharing*, 13, European State Aid Law Quarterly II, 289 (2014).

Michael Erhart, *State Aid in the Field of Agriculture*, in *The EC State Aid Regime: Distortive Effects of State Aid on Competition and Trade* (Sanchez, Rydelski eds, 2006).

Nemeckova, *Agriculture and Forestry*, in *EU Competition Law*, 4, 2, 1199 et seq. (Pesaresi, Van de Casteele, Flynn, Siaterli eds, 2016).

Nerina Boschiero, *Commentario alla legge 31 maggio 1995, n. 218*, in *Le nuove leggi civili commentate*, 1041 (Bariatti ed., 1996).

Oliver Geiss, Tatiana Siakka, *Redrawing the Market Economy Operator Test: EU State Aid Law Post Frucona*, 39, ECLR VII, (2018).

Ornella Porchia, *Il procedimento di controllo degli aiuti pubblici alle imprese tra ordinamento comunitario e ordinamento interno* (2001).

Ornella Porchia, *L'esecuzione degli obblighi comunitari da parte delle autorità nazionali: il caso della legge Prodi, Contratto e Impresa/Europa*, 745 (2002).

Paolo Diman, *I 'crediti di gestione' al settore agricolo al vaglio della Corte di giustizia*, Dir. pubbl. comp. ed eur., 486 (2003).

Pasquale Russo, *Art. 42*, in *Commentario breve ai Trattati dell'Unione europea* (Pocar, Baruffi eds, 2014).

Pasquale Russo, *Le agevolazioni e le esenzioni fiscali alla luce de principî comunitarî in materia di aiuti di Stato*, among documentation for the conference, *'L'applicazione del diritto comunitario nella giurisprudenza della Sezione Tributaria della Corte di Cassazione'*, Rass. Trib., 330 (2003).

Pastor Merchante, *On the Rules of Standing to Challenge State Aid Decisions Adopted at the End of the Preliminary Phase*, 11, European State Aid Law Quarterly III, 601 (2012).

Patrizia De Cesari, *Amministrazione straordinaria, Aiuti di Stato – Revocatoria: la Cassazione torna a distinguere tra fase conservativa e liquidatoria*, Fallimento, 1168 (2006).

Patrizia De Cesari, *Diritto internazionale privato dell'Unione europea* (2011).

Peter L. Vesterdorf, Mogens Uhd Nielsen, *State Aid Law of the European Union* (2008).

Péter Staviczky, *Analysis of the State Aid-Related Proposals in the Letta Report*, 23(3) European State Aid Law Quarterly 258, 267 (2024).

Phedon Nicolaides, *Application of Article 107(2)(b) TFEU to Covid-19 Measures: State Aid to Make Good the Damage Occurred by an Exceptional occurrence*, 11(5-6), JECLAP 238-243 (2020).

Phedon Nicolaides, *Demystifying the Balancing of the Positive and Negative Effects of State Aid*, 23 EStAL 2 (2024).

Phedon Nicolaides, *In Search of Economically Rational Environmental State Aid: The Case of Exception from Environmental Taxes*, 10 European Competition Journal 1 (2014).

Phedon Nicolaides, Ioana Eleonora Rusu, *The Concept of Selectivity: An Ever Wider Scope*, 11, European State Aid Law Quarterly IV, 791 (2012).

Phedon Nicolaides, Mihalis Kekalekis, Maria Kleis, *State Aid Policy in the European Community* (2008).

Phedon Nicolaides, *Shedding Light into the 'Black Box' of State Aid: The Impact of Hinkley Point C on the Assessment of the Compatibility of State Aid*, 20 EStAL 4 (2020).

Philipp Werner, Martina Maier, *Procedure in Crisis? Overview and Assessment of the Commission's State Aid Procedure*, 8, EStAL II, 177 (2009).

Philipp Werner, Vincent Verouden, *EU State Aid Control: Law and Economics* (2016).

Pierpaolo Rossi Maccanico, *Aiuti di stato: divieti a maglie larghe specialmente in materia fiscale*, Fiscalità internazionale, 3, 244 (2010).

Pierpaolo Rossi, *Procedura in tema di aiuti*, in *Disciplina della concorrenza nella UE* (Frignani, Bariatti eds., 2012).

Pierpaolo Rossi, *Riflessi fiscali dell'applicazione a livello nazionale delle norme comuntarie sugli aiuti di stato*, Fiscalità internazionale, 210 (2009).

Pierre De Gioia-Carabellese, *Compatibilità della legge fallimentare con la disciplina comunitaria*, Fallimento, 694 (2001).

Piet Jan Slot, *Rescue and Restructuring Aid*, in *EU State Aid* 1013 (Hancher, Ottervanger, Slot eds, 2016).

Pieter VerLoren van Theemat, Berend Reuder, *European Competition Law – A Case Commentary* (2014).

Pietro Boria, *Diritto tributario europeo* (2010).

Pietro Missanelli, Martino Basilisco, *L'accordo commerciale tra UE e Regno Unito nel sistema WTO. Gli eventuali conflitti in tema di enforcement*, Diritto del Commercio Internazionale, 737 (2021).

Pietro Virga, *Diritto amministrativo – Attività e prestazioni*, IV (1990).

Preslava Dilkova, *The New Procedural Regulation in State Aid – Whether 'Modernisation' Is in the Right Direction?'*, 35, European Competition Law Review, II, 88 (2014).

Rene Barents, *Directory of EC Case Law on State Aids* (2008).

Riccardo Luzzatto, *La diretta applicabilità nel diritto comunitario*, Milan, 1983.

Richard Whish, David Bailey, *Competition Law* (2024).

Roberto Adam, Antonio Tizzano, *Manuale di diritto dell'Unione europea* (2017).

Rosanna De Nictolis, *Codice del processo amministrativo Commentato, Commento all'Art. 133* (2017)

Sanchez Rydelski, *The EC State Aid Regime – Distortive Effects of State Aid on Competition and Trade* (2007).

Sara Gobbato, *Fate Presto: Italy Starts Discussions on the National Recovery and Resilience Plan*, 19(4) European State Aid Law Quarterly 528 (2020).

Sara Poli, Elaine Fahey, *The Strengthening of European Technological Sovereignty and Its Legal Bases in the Treaties*, 2, Eurojus, 147 (2022).

Sekulić-Kovačević-Jovičić, *The EU State Aid Regime in Agriculture – Legal Aspect, Economics of Agriculture*, 1, 239 (2024).

Sergio Fiorentino, Daniela Gottuso, *La riforma della l. 234/2012 con riferimento agli aiuti di Stato*, in *Dizionario sistematico del diritto della concorrenza* (Pace ed., 2013).

Sergio Maria Carbone Carbone, *Il Regolamento (CE) 1346/2000 relativo alle procedure di insolvenza*, in *Diritto processuale civile e commerciale comunitario* (Carbone, Frigo, Fumagalli eds. 2004).

Sergio Maria Carbone Carbone, *La conoscenza del diritto straniero e il giudice italiano*, Dir. comm. internaz., 193 (2009).

Sergio Menchini, *Le sezioni unite sui rapporti tra gli art. 295, 297 e 337, 2° comma, c.p.c.: una decisione che non convince*, Riv. dir. proc., 683 (2013).

Silvia Cipollina, *I confini giuridici nel tempo presente* (2003).

Silvia Rainone, *From Deregulatory Pressure to Laissez Faire: The (Moderate) Social Implications of the EU Recovery Strategy*, 15 Italian Labour Law e-Journal, 1S, 31 (2022).

Sir Jeremy Lever, *EU State Aid Law – Not a Pretty Sight*, 12 EStAL I, 6 (2013).

Stefania Bariatti, *Filling in the Gaps of EC Conflicts of Law Instruments: The Case of Jurisdiction over Actions Related to Insolvency Proceedings*, in *Nuovi strumenti del diritto internazionale privato* (Venturini, Bariatti eds, 2009).

Stefania Gianoncelli, *Sulla compatibilità con il divieto di aiuti di Stato del regime agevolato delle società cooperative di produzione e lavoro*, Riv. Dir. Fin. Sc. Fin., II (2011).

Stefano Recchioni, *Pregiudizialità processuale e dipendenza sostanziale nella cognizione ordinaria* (1999).

Stephan Balthasar, *Locus Standi Rules for Challenges to Regulatory Acts by Private Applicants: The New Article 263(4) TFEU*, 35, European Law Review IV 542 (2010).

Tesauro, *Manuale di diritto dell'Unione europea* (De Pasquale, Ferraro eds, 2023).

Thibaut Kleiner, *Preferential Loans in Favour of Agricultural Undertakings: Admissibility, Legal Basis, Legitimate Expectations,* European State Aid Law Quarterly 423 (2006).

Thomas Jaeger, *The Inquisition Retakes Brussels (Via the New Procedural Regulation), European State Aid Law Quarterly* 441 (2013).

Thomas Verellen, Alexandra Hofer, *The Unilateral Turn in EU Trade and Investment Policy*, 28 European Foreign Affairs Review, Special Issue, 1-14 (2023).

Tilman Santarius, *Digitalization and Sustainability: A Call for a Digital Green Deal*, 147, Environmental Science & Policy, 11-14 (2023).

Tim Maxian Rusche, Claire Micheau, Henri Piffaut, Koen Van de Casteele, *State Aid*, in *The EU Law of Competition* (Faull & Nikpay eds, 2014).

Ulrich Soltész, Christian von Köckritz, *The 'Temporary Framework': The Commission's Response to the Crisis in the Real Economy*, 31, European Competition Law Review, 106-115 (2010).

Ulrich Soltész, *Foreign Subsidies Control: A Bureaucratic Monster?*, 22(2) European State Aid Law Quarterly 175-180 (2023).

Vanda Markovicova, *Artt. 180-182a*, in *Single Common Market Organisation* (Mögele-Erlbacher eds, 2011).

Victor Crochet, Vineet Hegde, *China's 'Going Global' Policy: Transnational Production Subsidies Under the WTO SCM Agreement*, 23 Journal of International Economic Law 841-863 (2020).

Vittorio Di Bucci, *Gli atti di recupero di aiuti illegali e il contenzioso davanti ai giudici nazionali*, in *Aiuti di Stato fiscali e giurisdizioni nazionali: problemi attuali* (Pietro, Mondini eds., 2015).

Wolfang Weiß, *Ex Officio Third Country Subsidies' Review: Similarities and Differences to State Aid Procedure*, 2 EStAl 136 (2022).

Wolfgang Mederer, Nicola Pesaresi & Marc Van Hoof, *EU Competition Law – State Aid (Volume IV)* (2008).

Wolfgang Weiß, *The Regulation on Foreign Subsidies Distorting the Internal Market A Path to a Level Playing Field?* (2024).

Zora Kovacic et al., *The Twin Green and Digital Transition: High-Level Policy or Science Fiction?*, 7, Environment and Planning E: Nature and Space, 6, 1 (2024).

Table of Cases

Cases of the Court of Justice

Case C-167/19, *European Commission v. Freistaat Bayern* 10.3.2022, ECLI:EU:C:2022:176, 131, 134

Case C-614/20, *Lux Express Estonia*, 8.09.2022, ECLI:EU:C:2022:641, 502

Case C-702/20 and C-17/21, *'DOBELES HES' SIA*, 12.01.2023, ECLI:EU:C:2023:1, 29, 76

Case C-320/21 P, *Ryanair v. Commission*, 23.09.2023, ECLI:EU:C:2023:712, 84, 124

Case C-321/21 P, *Ryanair v. Commission* 28.9.2023, ECLI:EU:C:2023:713, 124

Case C-210/21 P, *Ryanair DAC/Commission*, 23.11.2023, ECLI:EU:C:2023:908, 48, 130

Case C-590/14 P, *DEI and Commissionv Aloumininon tis Ellados*, 26.12.2016, ECLI:EU:C:2016:797, 25, 120, 150

Case C-558/22, *ARERA/Fallimento Esperia SpA*, 7.03.2024, ECLI:EU:C:2024:209, 61, 62

Case C-516/22 *Commission v. UK*, 14.03.2024, ECLI:EU:C:2024:231, 387

Case C-17/03, *Vereniging voor Energie, Milieu en Water (VEMW) v. Directeur van the Dienst uitvoering en toezicht energie*, 7.06.2005, ECLI:EU:C:2005:362, 171

Case C-45/86, *Commission v. Council* (*'Tariff preferences'*), 26.03.1987, ECLI:EU:C:1987:163, 233

Case C-7/04 P(R), *Commission v. Akzo Nobel Chemicals Ltd and Akcros Chemicals Ltd.*, 27.09.2004, ECLI:EU:C:2004:566, 268

Case C-372/97, *Italy v. Commission* (the '*Alzetta* appeal'), 29.04.2004, ECLI:EU:C:2004:240, para. 39, 251

Case C-626/22, *ILVA S.p.A. et al*, 25.6.2024, ECLI:EU:C:2024:542, 347

Case C-256/97, *Déménagements-Manutention Transport SA (DTM)*, 29.6.1999, ECLI:EU:C:1999:332, 56, 59, 324

Case C-2/08, *Amministrazione dell'Economia e delle Finanze and Agenzia delle entrate v. Fallimento Olimpiclub Srl.*, 3.09.2009, ECLI:EU:C:2009:506, 299

Case C-1/09, *Centre d'exportation du livre français - Ministre de la Culture et de la Communication v. Société internationale de diffusion et d'édition CELF and Ministre de la Culture et de la Communication v. SIDE*, 11.3.2010, ECLI:EU:C:2010:136, 176

Case C-650/22, *FIFA v. BZ*, 04.10.2024, ECLI:EU:C:2024:824, 473

Case C-200/97, *Ecotrade v. Altiforni and Ferriere di Servola*, 1.12.1998, ECLI:EU:C:1998:579, 37, 329

Case C-357/14 P, *Electrabel and Dunamenti Erőmű v. Commission*, 1.10.15, ECLI:EU:C:2015:642, 165

Case C-434/19 and C-435/19, *Poste Italiane and Riscossione*, 3.03.2021, EU:C:2021:162, 28, 29

Case C-224/12 P *Commission v. Netherlands and ING*, 3.04,2014, ECLI:EU:C:2014:213, 49

Case C-42/17, *Criminal proceedings against M.A.S. and M.B.*, 5.12.2017, ECLI:EU:C:2017:936, 206

Case C-687/17 P, *Aanbestedingskalender and Others/Commission*, 7.11.2019, ECLI:EU:C:2019:932, 43

Case C-188/92, *Textilwerke Deggendorf GmbG (TWD) v. Germany*, 09.03.1994, ECLI:EU:C:1994:90, 249, 296

Case C-5/86, *Commission v. Belgium*, 9.4.91987, ECLI:EU:C:1987:198, 186

Cases of the General Court

Index

A

B

C

R

S

T

U

INTERNATIONAL COMPETITION LAW SERIES

1. Ignacio De Leon, *Latin American Competition Law and Policy: A Policy in Search of Identity*, 2001 (ISBN 90-411-1542-0).
2. Wim Dejonghe & Wouter Van de Voorde (eds), *M & A in Belgium*, 2001 (ISBN 90-411-1594-3).
3. Yang-Ching Chao, Gee San, Changfa Lo & Jiming Ho (eds), *International and Comparative Competition Law and Policies*, 2001 (ISBN 90-411-1643-5).
4. Martin Mendelsohn & Stephen Rose, *Guide to the EC Block Exemption for Vertical Agreements*, 2002 (ISBN 90-411-9813-X).
5. Clifford A. Jones & Mitsuo Matsushita (eds), *Competition Policy in the Global Trading System: Perspectives from the EU, Japan and the USA*, 2002 (ISBN 90-411-1758-X).
6. Christian Koenig, Andreas Bartosch, Jens-Daniel Braun & Marion Romes (eds), *EC Competition and Telecommunications Law*, Second Edition, 2009 (ISBN 978-90-411-2564-4).
7. Jürgen Basedow (ed.), *Limits and Control of Competition with a View to International Harmonization*, 2002 (ISBN 90-411-1967-1).
8. Maureen Brunt, Economic Essays on Australian and New Zealand Competition Law, 2003 (ISBN 90-411-1991-4).
9. Ky P. Ewing, Jr., *Competition Rules for the 21st Century: Principles from America's Experience*, Second Edition, 2006 (ISBN 90-411-2477-2).
10. Joseph Wilson, *Globalization and the Limits of National Merger Control Laws*, 2003 (ISBN 90-411-1996-5).
11. Peter Verloop & Valérie Landes (eds), *Merger Control in Europe: EU, Member States and Accession States*, Fourth Edition, 2003 (ISBN 90-411-2056-4).
12. Themistoklis K. Giannakopoulos, *Safeguarding Companies' Rights in Competition and Anti-dumping/Anti-subsidies Proceedings*, Second Edition, 2011 (ISBN 978-90-411-3404-2).
13. Marjorie Holmes & Lesley Davey (eds), *A Practical Guide to National Competition Rules across Europe*, Second Edition, 2007 (ISBN 978-90- 411-2607-8).
14. Sigrid Stroux, *US and EU Oligopoly Control*, 2004 (ISBN 90-411-2296-6).
15. Tzong-Leh Hwang and Chiyuan Chen (eds), *The Future Development of Competition Framework*, 2004 (ISBN 90-411-2305-9).

16. Phedon Nicolaides, Mihalis Kekelekis and Maria Kleis, *State Aid Policy in the European Community: Principles and Practice,* Second Edition, 2008 (ISBN 978-90-411-2754-9).
17. Doris Hildebrand, *Economic Analyses of Vertical Agreements: A Self- Assessment*, 2005 (ISBN 90-411-2328-8).
18. Frauke Henning-Bodewig, *Unfair Competition Law: European Union and Member States*, 2005 (ISBN 90-411-2329-6).
19. Duarte Brito & Margarida Catalão-Lopes, *Mergers and Acquisitions: The Industrial Organization Perspective,* 2006 (ISBN 90-411-2451-9).
20. Nikos Th. Nikolinakos, *EU Competition Law and Regulation in the Converging Telecommunications, Media and IT Sectors*, 2006 (ISBN 90-411- 2469-1).
21. Mihalis Kekelekis, *The EC Merger Control Regulation: Rights of Defence. A Critical Analysis of DG COMP Practice and Community Courts' Jurisprudence,* 2006 (ISBN 90-411-2553-1).
22. Mark R. Joelson, *An International Antitrust Primer: A Guide to the Operation of United States, European Union and Other Key Competition Laws in the Global Economy*, Third Edition, 2006 (ISBN 90-411-2468-3).
23. Themistoklis K. Giannakopoulos, *A Concise Guide to the EU Anti-dumping/ Anti-subsidies Procedures*, 2006 (ISBN 90-411-2464-0).
24. George Cumming, Brad Spitz & Ruth Janal, *Civil Procedure Used for Enforcement of EC Competition Law by the English, French and German Civil Courts*, 2007 (ISBN 978-90-411-2471-5).
25. Jürgen Basedow (ed.), *Private Enforcement of EC Competition Law,* 2007 (ISBN 978-90-411-2613-9).
26. Jung Wook Cho, *Innovation and Competition in the Digital Network Economy: A Legal and Economic Assessment on Multi-tying Practices and Network Effects*, 2007 (ISBN 978-90-411-2574-3).
27. Akira Inoue, *Japanese Antitrust Law Manual: Law, Cases and Interpretation of the Japanese Antimonopoly Act*, 2007 (ISBN 978-90-411-2627-6).
28. René Barents, *Directory of EC Case Law on Competition,* 2007 (ISBN 978-90-411-2656-6).
29. Paul F. Nemitz (ed.), *The Effective Application of EU State Aid Procedures: The Role of National Law and Practice*, 2007 (ISBN 978-90-411-2657-3).
30. Jurian Langer, *Tying and Bundling as a Leveraging Concern under EC Competition Law*, 2007 (ISBN 978-90-411-2575-0).
31. Abel M. Mateus & Teresa Moreira (eds), *Competition Law and Economics – Advances in Competition Policy and Antitrust Enforcement*, 2007 (ISBN 978-90-411-2632-0).
32. Alberto Santa Maria, *Competition and State Aid: An Analysis of the EC Practice*, 2007 (ISBN 978-90-411-2617-7).
33. Barry J. Rodger (ed.), *Article 234 and Competition Law: An Analysis,* 2007 (ISBN 978-90-411-2605-4).

34. Alla Pozdnakova, *Liner Shipping and EU Competition Law,* 2008 (ISBN 978-90-411-2717-4).
35. Milena Stoyanova, *Competition Problems in Liberalized Telecommunications: Regulatory Solutions to Promote Effective Competition*, 2008 (ISBN 978-90-411-2736-5).
36. *EC State Aid Law/Le Droit des Aides d'Etat dans la CE. Liber Amicorum Francisco Santaolalla Gadea*, 2008 (ISBN 978-90-411-2774-7).
37. Cees Dekker, *Directory of EU Case Law on State Aids,* Fifth Edition, 2024 (ISBN 978-94-035-3708-5).
38. Ignacio De Leon, *An Institutional Assessment of Antitrust Policy: The Latin American Experience*, 2009 (ISBN 978-90-411-2478-4).
39. Doris Hildebrand, *The Role of Economic Analysis in EU Competition Law: The European School*, Fourth Edition, 2016 (ISBN 978-90-411-6245-8).
40. Eugène Buttigieg, *Competition Law: Safeguarding the Consumer Interest. A Comparative Analysis of US Antitrust Law and EC Competition Law*, 2009 (ISBN 978-90-411-3119-5).
41. Ioannis Lianos & Ioannis Kokkoris (eds), *The Reform of EC Competition Law: New Challenges,* 2010 (ISBN 978-90-411-2692-4).
42. George Cumming & Mirjam Freudenthal, *Civil Procedure in EU Competition Cases before the English and Dutch Courts*, 2010 (ISBN 978-90-411-3192-8).
43. A.E. Rodriguez & Ashok Menon, *The Limits of Competition Policy: The Shortcomings of Antitrust in Developing and Reforming Economies*, 2010 (ISBN 978-90-411-3177-5).
44. Mika Oinonen, *Does EU Merger Control Discriminate against Small Market Companies? Diagnosing the Argument with Conclusions*, 2010 (ISBN 978-90-411-3261-1).
45. Eirik Østerud, *Identifying Exclusionary Abuses by Dominant Undertakings under EU Competition Law: The Spectrum of Tests*, 2010 (ISBN 978-90-411-3271-0).
46. Marco Botta, *Merger Control Regimes in Emerging Economies: A Case Study on Brazil and Argentina*, 2011 (ISBN 978-90-411-3402-8).
47. Jürgen Basedow & Wolfgang Wurmnest (eds), *Structure and Effects in EU Competition Law: Studies on Exclusionary Conduct and State Aid*, 2011 (ISBN 978-90-411-3174-4).
48. George Cumming (ed.), *Merger Decisions and the Rules of Procedure of the European Community Courts*, 2012 (ISBN 978-90-411-3671-8).
49. Eduardo Molan Gaban & Juliana Oliveira Domingues (eds), *Antitrust Law in Brazil: Fighting Cartels,* 2012 (ISBN 978-90-411-3670-1).
50. Giandonato Caggiano, Gabriella Muscolo & Marina Tavassi (eds), *Competition Law and Intellectual Property: A European Perspective,* 2012 (ISBN 978-90-411-3447-9).
51. Ben Van Rompuy, *Economic Efficiency: The Sole Concern of Modern Antitrust Policy? Non-efficiency Considerations under Article 101 TFEU*, 2012 (ISBN 978-90-411-3870-5).

52. Liyang Hou, *Competition Law and Regulation of the EU Electronic Communications Sector: A Comparative Legal Approach*, 2012 (ISBN 978-90-411-4047-0).
53. Barry Rodger, *Landmark Cases in Competition Law: Around the World in Fourteen Stories*, 2012 (ISBN 978-90-411-3843-9).
54. Andreas Scordamaglia-Tousis, *EU Cartel Enforcement: Reconciling Effective Public Enforcement with Fundamental Rights*, 2013 (ISBN 978-90-411-4758-5).
55. Bernardo Cortese (ed.), *EU Competition Law: Between Public and Private Enforcement*, 2014 (ISBN 978-90-411-4677-9).
56. Barry Rodger (ed.), *Competition Law: Comparative Private Enforcement and Collective Redress across the EU*, 2014 (ISBN 978-90-411-4559-8).
57. Nada Ina Pauer, *The Single Economic Entity Doctrine and Corporate Group Responsibility in European Antitrust Law*, 2014 (ISBN 978-90-411-5262-6).
58. Urška Petrovčič, *Competition Law and Standard Essential Patents: A Transatlantic Perspective*, 2014 (ISBN 978-90-411-4960-2).
59. David Telyas, *The Interface between Competition Law, Patents and Technical Standards*, 2014 (ISBN 978-90-411-5418-7).
60. Katerina Maniadaki, *EU Competition Law, Regulation and the Internet: The Case of Net Neutrality*, 2014 (ISBN 978-90-411-4140-8).
61. Horacio Vedia Jerez, *Competition Law Enforcement and Compliance across the World: A Comparative Review*, 2015 (ISBN 978-90-411-5815-4).
62. Kadir Baş, *The Substantive Appraisal of Joint Ventures under the EU Merger Control Regime*, 2015 (ISBN 978-90-411-5816-1).
63. Alberto Santa Maria, *Competition and State Aid: An Analysis of the EU Practice*, Third Edition, 2025 (ISBN 978-94-035-2768-0).
64. Lúcio Tomé Feteira, *The Interplay between European and National Competition Law after Regulation 1/2003: "United (Should) We Stand?"*, 2016 (ISBN 978-90-411-5663-1).
65. Giovanni Pitruzzella & Gabriella Muscolo (eds), *Competition and Patent Law in the Pharmaceutical Sector: An International Perspective*, 2016 (ISBN 978-90-411-5927-4).
66. Małgorzata Cyndecka, *The Market Economy Investor Test in EU State Aid Law: Applicability and Application*, 2016 (ISBN 978-90-411-6102-4).
67. Damiano Canapa, *Trademarks and Brands in Merger Control: An Analysis of the European and Swiss Legal Orders*, 2016 (ISBN 978-90-411-6717-0).
68. Inge Graef, *EU Competition Law, Data Protection and Online Platforms: Data as Essential Facility*, 2016 (ISBN 978-90-411-8324-8).
69. Anders Jessen, *Exclusionary Abuse after the* Post Danmark I *Case: The Role of the Effects-Based Approach under Article 102 TFEU*, 2017 (ISBN 978-90-411-8996-7).
70. Baskaran Balasingham, *The EU Leniency Policy: Reconciling Effectiveness and Fairness*, 2017 (ISBN 978-90-411-8479-5).
71. Eugene Stuart & Iana Roginska-Green, *Sixty Years of EU State Aid Law and Policy: Analysis and Assessment*, 2018 (ISBN 978-90-411-8869-4).

72. Anna Renata Pisarkiewicz, *Margin Squeeze in the Electronic Communications Sector: Critical Analysis of the Decisional Practice and Case Law*, 2018 (ISBN 978-90-411-6246-5).
73. Ploykaew Porananond, *Competition Law in the ASEAN Countries: Regional Law and National Systems*, 2018 (ISBN 978-90-411-9102-1).
74. Corinne Ruechardt, *EU State Aid Control of Infrastructure Funding*, 2018 (ISBN 978-90-411-9099-4).
75. Amalia Athanasiadou, *Patent Settlements in the Pharmaceutical Industry under US Antitrust and EU Competition Law*, 2018 (ISBN 978-94-035-0113-0).
76. Miroslava Marinova, *Fidelity Rebates in Competition Law: Application of the 'As Efficient Competitor' Test*, 2018 (ISBN 978-94-035-0570-1).
77. Gabriella Muscolo & Marina Tavassi, *The Interplay Between Competition Law and Intellectual Property: An International Perspective*, 2019 (ISBN 978-90-411-8687-4).
78. Fevzi Toksoy, Bahadir Balki & Hanna Stakheyeva, *Merger Control in the EU and Turkey: A Comparative Guide*, Second Edition, 2022 (ISBN 978-94-035-4303-1).
79. Paulo Burnier da Silveira & William Evan Kovacic (eds), *Global Competition Enforcement: New Players, New Challenges*, 2019 (ISBN 978-94-035-0283-0).
80. Giovanna Massarotto, *Antitrust Settlements: How a Simple Agreement Can Drive the Economy*, 2019 (ISBN 978-94-035-1133-7).
81. Marc Veenbrink, *Criminal Law Principles and the Enforcement of EU and National Competition Law: A Silent Takeover?*, 2020 (ISBN 978-94-035-1434-5).
82. Ferdinand Wollenschläger, Wolfgang Wurmnest & Thomas M.J. Möllers (eds), *Private Enforcement of European Competition and State Aid Law: Current Challenges and the Way Forward*, 2020 (ISBN 978-94-035-0281-6).
83. Jorge Marcos Ramos, *Firm Dominance in EU Competition Law: The Competitive Process and the Origins of Market Power*, 2020 (ISBN 978-94-035-2030-8).
84. Ingrid Margrethe Halvorsen Barlund, *Leniency in EU Competition Law*, 2020 (ISBN 978-94-035-1722-3).
85. Jan Blockx, Mens Rea *in EU Antitrust Law: When Intentions Matter*, 2020 (ISBN 978-94-035-2353-8).
86. Maria Wasastjerna, *Competition, Data and Privacy in the Digital Economy: Towards a Privacy Dimension in Competition Policy?*, 2020 (ISBN 978-94-035-2220-3).
87. Maria Fernanda Caporale Madi, *Regulating Vertical Agreements: A Comparative Law and Economics Review of the EU and Brazil*, 2020 (ISBN 978-94-035-2650-8).
88. Martin Gassler, *Information Exchange Between Competitors in EU Competition Law*, 2021 (ISBN 978-94-035-3183-0).

89. Andrea Biondi, Gabriella Muscolo & Renato Nazzini (eds), *After the Damages Directive: Policy and Practice in the EU Member States and the United Kingdom*, 2022 (ISBN 978-94-035-1302-7).
90. Angelika S. Murer, *Blocking Patents in European Competition Law: The Implications of the Concept of Abuse*, 2022 (ISBN 978-94-035-3814-3).
91. Barry Rodger and Or Brook, Maciej Bernatt, Francisco Marcos & Annalies Outhuijse, *Judicial Review of Competition Law Enforcement in the EU Member States and the UK*, 2024 (ISBN 978-94-035-0238-0).